Sri Lanka

Brett Atkinson
Stuart Butler, Ethan Gelber, Michael Kohn

LEGEND

Primary Road
Secondary Road
Tertiary Road
Unsealed Road
Non Operational Railways

0 — 50 km
0 — 30 mi

ELEVATION

2100m
1500m
900m
450m
0

UPPUVELI BEACH (p263)
Smile at the sight of kilometres of uncluttered sand at splendid Uppuveli beach

SIGIRIYA (p217)
This mysterious rock fort has stunning frescoes, fascinating archaeological ruins and spectacular views from its summit

JAFFNA (p274)
The island's Hindu-Tamil centre: battle-scarred by civil conflict, but bustling, colourful and hopeful

ANURADHAPURA (p231)
The ancient capital is jam-packed with relics, including enormous dagobas, crumbling temples and finely carved Buddhas

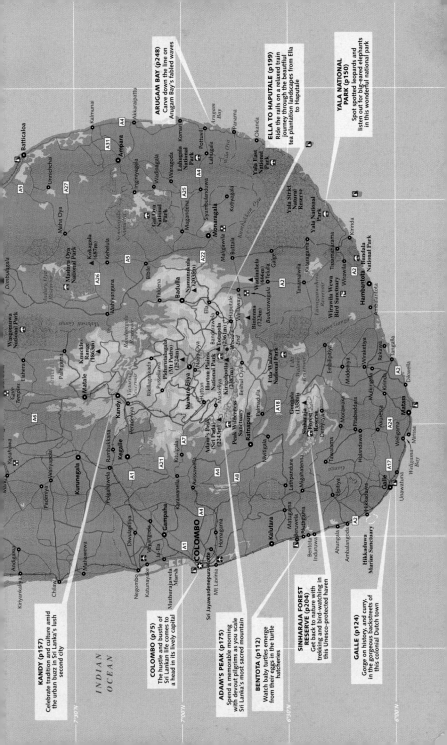

KANDY (p157)
Celebrate tradition and culture amid the urban buzz in Sri Lanka's lush second city

COLOMBO (p75)
The hustle and bustle of Sri Lankan life comes to a head in its lively capital

ADAM'S PEAK (p175)
Spend a memorable morning with devout pilgrims as you scale Sri Lanka's most sacred mountain

BENTOTA (p112)
Watch baby turtles emerge from their eggs in the turtle hatcheries

SINHARAJA FOREST RESERVE (p204)
Get back to nature with trekking and bird-watching in this Unesco-protected haven

GALLE (p124)
Gorge on history and curry, in the gorgeous backstreets of this colonial Dutch town

ARUGAM BAY (p248)
Carve down the line on Arugam Bay's fabled waves

ELLA TO HAPUTALE (p199)
Ride the rails on a relaxed train journey through the beautiful tea plantation landscapes from Ella to Haputale

YALA NATIONAL PARK (p150)
Spot spotted leopards and listen out for big-eared elephants in this wonderful national park

On the Road

BRETT ATKINSON
Coordinating Author

The early bird catches the worm or, in this case, unimpeded views from World's End (p187). At 7.30am my pre-dawn departure from Haputale (p190) was now making perfect sense. Below me were seemingly random scatterings of tiny settlements, and before me the land stretched out nonstop to Sri Lanka's south coast.

ETHAN GELBER The picture almost didn't happen. After a Woodlands Network (p194) cooking class, I can barely restrain myself. For two hours we've been chopping vegies, grinding coconuts, squeezing the pulp for milk, tasting and talking about herbs and spices. Mesmerising torture. I'm ravenous. And delighted. My first 'real' rice and curry.

MICHAEL KOHN On the road to Polonnaruwa (p221) I spotted an elephant outside a cafe. The proprietor gave him a pineapple, which the elephant devoured in one gulp. He said that the elephant was a 'regular customer' and came by almost daily for some attention and fruity snacks.

STUART BUTLER I like lizards, snakes and reptiles, so when my driver told me he'd show me some little lizards the last thing I expected was half a dozen tyrannosaurus wannabes chasing me around until I hand-fed them a fishy dinner!

For full author biographies see p326.

Traveller Highlights

With a kaleidoscope of attractions, Sri Lanka has been luring visitors since time immemorial. Marco Polo waxed lyrical about his travels here, but he wasn't the first to do so, and he won't be the last. We asked travellers, authors and Lonely Planet staff to recommend their favourite experiences, impressions and locations in Sri Lanka.

DALLAS STRIBLEY

1

WHILING AWAY THE DAY, BEACHSIDE

Walking through Hikkaduwa town (p117) or along the beach is a social occasion as Hikkaduwans are friendly and fun to be around. The 'Mambo Boys' are always up for a chat, a laugh or a game of ping pong. Or you can meander through the local art galleries (meet the artists as they work) and souvenir shops, which are filled with handicrafts. A must-buy: Sri Lankan masks.

Fionarhy, Traveller

DALLAS STRI

② THE HILL COUNTRY

Lush landscapes (p155) create a walker's paradise despite the lack of any useful signs. Tramp through tea plantations, pass women in bright saris with big baskets and bigger smiles, and stumble into villages for directions as the resident cow gets vocal.

Nick Boulos, Traveller, UK

ANDERS BLOMQV

③ ANURADHAPURA

We had some of our best experiences around Anuradhapura (p231). What we liked most about this place was Sri Maha Bodhi (p232) and all of its surrounding religious activity. It was a moving experience to see so many people praying at once. In an interesting contrast, it was funny to see all the monkeys outside the temple. We must have arrived at their lunch hour because there were thousands of them, all sitting around, eating bananas together.

Gal Livni, Traveller

HOT! HOT! HOT!

Ever had curry so fiery that not only is your mouth burning, but also your stomach, lips, eyes, ears and breath? Welcome to Sri Lanka, where even the mangoes and pineapples are served from little road-side stalls with curry on them! You haven't had hot food until you've experienced Sri Lankan cuisine.

Bigdreamer, Traveller

4

RICHARD NEBESKY

GALLE FACE HOTEL

Where the word 'sunsetting' was invented... You sit, they serve, you watch... How could life be any better? Best place (p92) to get away from the crazy pace of the city. Top-notch margaritas, too!

Edithka, Traveller

5

DALLAS STRIBLEY

6

RAY TIPPER

BUNDALA NATIONAL PARK

Bird-watching in Bundala National Park (p146) – the evening light was perfect, great flocks of water fowl were everywhere and a herd of elephants came crashing out of the undergrowth right on cue.

Stuart Butler, Lonely Planet Author, France

TRAVELLING BY TRAIN

There's no way I was going to get a seat on the slow train to Ella (p195), but with a prime standing-room only spot looking out at a rolling carpet of tea, that was fine by me. Outside, the colourful silk saris of Tamil tea pickers stood out in the sea of green, and inside, smiles expressed a shy welcome.

Brett Atkinson, Lonely Planet Author, New Zealand

7

ANTONY GIBLIN

ANDERS BLOM

8

SIGIRIYA

A 5th-century rock-top fortress, Sigiriya (Lion Mountain; p217) was accessible only by climbing into the mouth of a massive crouched lion carved into the rock. All that's left of the big cat are the paws, but the summit still boasts superb views.

Gregory McElwain, Traveller, USA

GREG

9

BENTOTA TURTLES

Holding a tiny newborn turtle in the palm of my hand in one of the turtle hatcheries around Bentota (see boxed text, p116) was an amazing experience.

Stuart Butler, Lonely Planet Author, France

AROUND KANDY

10

Walking Kandy's temple loop (p171) was a great way to see Sri Lanka's Hill Country. Dark forest, silent roads, rice paddies, friendly villages. Stone steps leading to 14th-century Buddhist art. The shopkeeper inviting us to join his family on the verandah, the monk asking us in for tea, children shouting enthusiastic greetings and knowledgeable adults pausing from their work to chat.

Miriam Vaswani, Traveller

LINDSAY HEBBERD / CORBIS

11

THE EAST

Having the entire east coast (p245) to myself, I felt like an explorer as I clambered up to ancient Buddhist statues lost in the jungle that hadn't seen a tourist for months.

Stuart Butler, Lonely Planet Author, France

RICHARD I'AN

12 MOPED TO UNAWATUNA

I hopped on the back of my boy's moped and we sped down the coast to Unawatuna (p132), stopping off in Galle (p124) for some city supplies. Unawatuna is stunning…took my breath away. They have worked so hard to get it back up and running and all they need is people. Truly lovely. Just lovely.

Niklondon23, Traveller

YADIO LEVY / AI

13 GLASS-BOTTOM BOAT RIDE

A ride in a glass-bottom boat lets you observe the natural behaviour of the creatures around: the fish, the sea turtles, the Sri Lankans swimming fully dressed and the tourists in comparatively immodest bathing suits.

Anusha Rasalingam, Traveller, USA

ADAM'S PEAK

Climbing Adam's Peak (p175) was my most magical experience in Sri Lanka. Among lights glowing in the darkness and the smell of ginger, I relished pilgrims' chants and encouraging cheerful smiles. Reaching the freezing top of the sacred mountain was a most fulfilling sensation.

Emmanuelle Chirouze, Traveller

14

GREG ELMS

15

FRESH FRUIT

I loved all the many different kinds of fresh fruit that were available everywhere. At home you can't get fruit like that, and every morning I could have a giant fruit salad and fresh juices throughout the day.

Heather Blanchard, Traveller

DALLAS STRIBLEY

16 **MIRISSA BEACH**

On the southern coast, this beach (p138) will give you a taste of paradise. Wake to a beautiful sunrise and then watch the sun cross directly overhead throughout the day, finally ending with a breathtaking and memorable sunset. Lined with coconut trees, the beach's buildings are hidden from the shore. You'll feel like you're in a desert paradise.

Karen Burrows, Traveller, New Zealand

ANDERS BLOMQVIST

RICHARD I'ANSON

17 DAMBULLA ROCK

A place of worship for many Buddhists, the Dambulla rock (p215) bears a temple at the foot of the hill as well as one at the top. The temple at the summit has some truly great paintings dating from the 19th century, a contrast from the modern-day painting at the new temple below.

Nilma Ekanayake, Traveller, Sri Lanka

MARK DAF

18 SURFING THE DREAM AT LAZY LEFTS

Wow! Easy paddle out to the left-hand reef point break at Midigama (p136). Surf's up at sunrise and sunset and it's one hell of a chilled session! Maximum six surfers. Cows on the beach… What more could you want? Oh, and super-friendly locals with big smiles!

Petitchatel, Traveller

Contents

Regional Map Contents

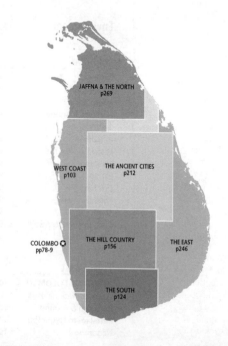

JAFFNA & THE NORTH
p269

WEST COAST
p103

THE ANCIENT CITIES
p212

COLOMBO
pp78-9

THE HILL COUNTRY
p156

THE EAST
p246

THE SOUTH
p124

Destination Sri Lanka

When the noted writer Sir Arthur C Clarke made his home in Sri Lanka in 1956, he claimed the island jewel of the Indian Ocean was the best place in the world from which to view the universe. The author of *2001: A Space Odyssey* passed away in 2008, but no doubt the futurist would have logged on to Google Earth to gaze back at his island home from an online universe. And concealed in the sky-high imagery of this teardrop-shaped nation, he would have recognised an amazing diversity for somewhere so compact.

Fringing the coasts is an array of gently arcing golden-sand beaches, now making a comeback after the devastation wreaked by the 2004 Boxing Day tsunami. Zoom closer to spy the giant tanks (artificial reservoirs) built by the first Sinhalese rulers around the ancient cities of Anuradhapura and Pollonaruwa. In the Hill Country, a layer of cotton wool clouds obscures the view, mirroring the misty mornings travellers often experience in this area of waterfalls and verdant tea plantations.

To the northwest, a gossamer-thin land bridge *almost* connects fragile Sri Lanka to the modern juggernaut that is India. Two and a half decades of civil war reinforces this bridge to Tamil Nadu is as much cultural as geographic.

The traditional conflict between the Sri Lankan military and the Liberation Tigers of Tamil Eelam (LTTE) ended in May 2009. International pressure is now on President Mahinda Rajapaksa's government to craft a durable political solution. Significant issues of ethnic and economic exclusion remain for Sri Lanka's Tamil population, and it's inconceivable that the path ahead will be free of tension and violence. Key questions remain. Will the rights of Sri Lanka's Tamil minority be taken up by less-radical advocates than the LTTE? And will the LTTE just fade away, or regroup and carry on its struggle in a less-structured, but potentially more threatening, manner? The world should also expect bitter recriminations from both sides as the cloud of propaganda that masked the final months of the conflict finally clears.

But it's wrong to imply travelling in Sri Lanka is challenging or dangerous. Irrespective of their cultural background, Sinhalese, Tamil and Muslim locals will welcome you with pride. Pride in their criminally underrated cuisine, pride in their national parks and wildlife, and – especially – pride in their national cricket team. Whether you're a humble three-wheeler jockey or a British-trained lawyer or doctor, the sport that frequently stops the nation is always worthy of discussion. How will the boys do in the upcoming series against New Zealand? Will the country be ready to host the World Cup in 2011? And have you seen how much that opening batsman from Kandy is earning in the new Indian Premier League?

From the days of Arab traders in the 7th century AD, Sri Lanka has always been buffeted by the ebb and flow of international commerce. In a new century, the debate is now about expatriate workers returning home jobless from the Gulf States, or the roller coaster price of tea. And in a country dependent on fuel imports, whatever happened to the government's idea of converting all of Sri Lankan's three million three-wheelers from petrol to gas?

Faced with funding a war and weathering a global financial crisis, Sri Lanka's proud population has been doing it tough for a few years. But equipped with a stellar combination of scenery, culture and history, a growing focus on sustainable tourism and (hopefully) a more settled society, Sri Lanka is firmly back on the radar for curious travellers seeking unique experiences.

FAST FACTS

Population: 21.1 million

Life expectancy: female 77%, male 73%

Adult literacy: female 90%, male 95%

Number of universities: 11

Year women received the right to vote: 1931

Number of three-wheelers: 3 million

Cost of a new three-wheeler: US$3500

Number of waterfalls: 103

Highest waterfall: Bambarakanda Falls (240m)

GDP per capita: US$4400

Getting Started

Compared with travelling in nearby India, Pakistan or Bangladesh, getting around Sri Lanka is enjoyably straightforward, but a little planning will go a long way towards making your trip more fulfilling, hassle-free and fun.

In the south and west of Sri Lanka and in the central Hill Country, you'll find a good range of accommodation from simple guest houses to heritage boutique hotels. In the recently war-ravaged north and east, options may be more limited. Public transport by bus or train is uniformly cheap, and even the cost of a car and driver is affordable compared with other destinations.

Sri Lanka's last 25 years have been beset by war and natural disaster. Hopefully the country can now look forward to a more settled future. Irrespective of what tomorrow brings to the Indian Ocean's fabled isle, you can be sure of a warm response from a well-educated, curious and welcoming population.

WHEN TO GO

Climatically speaking, the driest (and best) seasons in Sri Lanka are from December to March for the west coast, the south coast and the Hill Country, and from April to September for the ancient cities region and the east coast.

December through March are also the months when most foreign tourists visit, the majority of them escaping the European winter. During the Christmas to New Year holiday season, in particular, accommodation anywhere on the island can be tight due to the huge influx of foreign visitors.

July/August is the time of the Kandy Esala Perahera, the 10-day festival honouring the sacred tooth relic of the Buddha, and also the time for the Kataragama festival. In both towns accommodation during the festivals is very difficult to come by, and rates usually double or treble. Be sure to book rooms well in advance. Accommodation is also tight in Nuwara Eliya in mid-April, when many expatriate Sri Lankans return home to celebrate the Sinhalese New Year. Buses and trains are even more crowded at this time, crammed with local Sri Lankans returning to their hometowns for the New

---

DON'T LEAVE HOME WITHOUT...

- Bringing along a windbreaker, parka or jumper for cool nights in the Hill Country.
- Packing a travel umbrella.
- Checking with a Sri Lankan embassy or consulate to see whether you need a visa (p301).
- Confirming what medicines or inoculations you need (p312).
- Checking government travel advisories for the current security situation (see boxed text, p293). If you're heading into the North or East, consider registering your travel plans online with your government.
- Serious insect repellent to deal with the serious mosquitoes (p314) you'll probably encounter.
- Building up your chilli tolerance at your local South Asian restaurant of choice.
- Learning just a little about cricket, Sri Lanka's national sport (p53).
- Sunscreen – it can be expensive and hard to find in Sri Lanka.
- Leaving room in your luggage for the cheap-as-chips branded clothing you can pick up for a song at Colombo's House of Fashion (p98) or Nuwara Eliya's market (p183).

FOREIGNER PRICING

You will find Sri Lankans trying to overcharge tourists for anything from a bus fare to a gemstone necklace. In a country recovering from civil war and with a fragile economy that's at the mercy of the turbulence of global trade, it's not really that surprising. Most hotels have one price for foreigners and another for Sri Lankans and expat residents; often the difference will be as much as 70%.

Expect to pay significantly higher foreigners' entry fees, up to 10 or 20 times higher than those paid by locals, at some government-operated attractions. This is especially true of 'Must See' sights like the Pinnewalla Elephant Orphanage or the Ancient Cities, both of which have recorded an increase in admission fees of up to 400% in recent years. It's therefore not surprising that a few ordinary Sri Lankans occasionally try and secure a few extra rupees along the way.

It's not all-encompassing behaviour, though, and you're just as likely to be treated with respect and get the local price when you stop for a roadside king coconut or a few snacks at a local bakery.

At the time of writing annual inflation in Sri Lanka was running at around 10%. Economic commentators were expecting this level of inflation to be maintained for the next few years.

Year holiday season. For more information on the Sri Lankan New Year, see boxed text, p295.

Sri Lanka's climate means that it is always the 'right' beach season somewhere on the coast. The weather doesn't follow strict rules, though – it often seems to be raining where it should be sunny, and sunny where it should be raining. Rainfall tends to be emphatic – streets can become flooded in what seems like only minutes. Chances are the weather will soon clear up and sunny skies will make a speedy return. An exception is the Hill Country, an area that can be covered in a stubborn grey mist for days at a time. On the other hand, you could get lucky there at any time of the year and enjoy crystalline blue skies.

See Climate Charts (p292) for more information.

Out-of-season travel definitely has its advantages. Accommodation owners and transport providers are more likely to be open to negotiation, international airfares are often lower and you'll probably get a warmer welcome from the locals. It certainly doesn't rain *all* the time during the low season, but make sure that you pack a compact umbrella just to cover all bases.

The civil conflict between the Liberation Tigers of Tamil Eelam (LTTE) and the Sri Lankan military ended as a traditionally fought war in May 2009. Most of the LTTE's leadership were reported killed, and the unknown for the months and years ahead is whether or not a seriously weakened LTTE reverts to an increase in suicide attacks and bombings in the rest of the country. In Sri Lanka, be prudent when attending large gatherings, including protests and festivals.

Bombings of public transport have traditionally been of local buses, so if you stick to the air-conditioned and intercity buses, the situation will be significantly more secure. It's also worth noting that although the civil war caused 70,000 deaths from 1983 to 2008, that figure included no foreigners.

COSTS & MONEY

Sri Lanka is more expensive than India, but costs are still very reasonable. Simple double rooms with bathroom, mosquito net and fan cost about Rs 1000 to 1750, while an international-class hotel room may run to Rs 25,000 or more. Most top-end hotels quote room rates in US dollars, or increasingly euros, but US dollars, euros or rupees are all accepted.

HOW MUCH?

Air-con bus Colombo–Anuradhapura Rs 350

2nd-class train Ella–Haputale Rs 50

Lunch packet Rs 125

Cultural Triangle round ticket Rs 5400

Midrange guest house double room (Kandy) Rs 2200

The cost of accommodation in the touristy areas drops considerably out of season. Expect to pay triple the usual accommodation price in Kandy during the Kandy Esala Perahera and in Nuwara Eliya during the April New Year season. Because of the lack of tourism infrastructure following long years of war, room rates are also much higher than the norm in Jaffna.

Local food is reasonably priced, though it's about three times more expensive in guest houses than in local restaurants. Dinner costs around Rs 400 to 550 at a guest house, and as little as Rs 150 at a local restaurant. Dinner at the country's better restaurants costs around Rs 2500 per person.

At national parks, entry fees plus (often mandatory) 4WD hire and other extras add up to something between Rs 4000 and 7000.

Public transport is cheap. Hiring a car (or van) and driver for a day is around Rs 5500 to 6600.

TRAVELLING RESPONSIBLY

At the time of writing Sri Lanka was emerging from 25 years of civil war, and the global financial crisis was decreasing the income of many communities. Now, more than ever, is a good opportunity to take advantage of Sri Lanka's growing focus on sustainable tourism and responsible travel. For information on travelling sustainably within Sri Lanka, see the following websites.

TRAVELLING IN COMMUNITY STYLE *Ethan Gelber*

In this new age of green schemes, community-based tourism (CBT) in Sri Lanka has emerged as an important ethical travel trend. It encompasses initiatives collectively owned and operated by – and/or benefiting – marginalised villages. With the gulf between haves and have-nots gaping ever wider, redistributing a little wealth to people otherwise disengaged from mainstream tourism isn't a bad thing. Especially since CBT meets different, nonmainstream travel criteria championed by responsible travellers.

Until 2006 CBT activity in Sri Lanka was definitely on the rise, albeit somewhat hidden from view. By early 2009, however, due to the political upheaval, many initiatives had suffered terribly or had been suspended. When conditions improve, most will welcome you more enthusiastically than ever.

Use the following information and sources to help requite the awesome generosity of the people whose land you are exploring. You will be giving directly to those who need it most. Other worthy projects are detailed on *LOCALternative Sri Lanka – a responsible travel map* (see p297).

At One with Nature

Communities are rooted in place. Now some of them are focused on caring for the natural beauty around them, not just exploiting it.

Emace (www.bolgodalakesrilanka.com) Leads a community charge to rehabilitate and protect Bolgoda Lake. See p70.

IFS-Popham Arboretum (www.sacredcat.org/rukrakaganno/projects.php) Near Dambulla, Sri Lanka's only dry-zone arboretum is managed (with a visitors facility) by the Ruk Rakaganno (Guardians of Trees) charity.

Ittapana Mangrove Cultural Centre (☎ 034-492 3624) Inland from Aluthgama, trained by nonprofit environmental consultants (www.eecssrilanka.com), village entrepreneurs staff a mangrove forest visitors centre.

Nagenahiru (☎ 091-225 6621; nagenahiru@mail.ewisl.net) Boat tours, local eats and crafts sales are part of fishing-community projects around Madu Ganga Estuary (p70), spearheaded by Nagenahiru.

Rainforest Rescue International (www.earthresoration.org) Projects include guided forest, plant nursery and spice 'safaris'. See p73.

Sri Lanka Wildlife Conservation Society (SLWCS; www.slwcs.org) Innovative wildlife conservation programs involve community and voluntourist participation. See below.

Responsible Tourism Partnership Sri Lanka (www.responsibletourismsrilanka.org) This umbrella organisation combines the membership of the Ministry of Tourism, community-based tourism projects and some of Sri Lanka's most influential travel companies. Download its excellent Travellers' Tips summary.

Sri Lanka Wildlife Conservation Society (SLWCS; www.slwcs.org) Recognised by the UN in 2008 for community-based projects that made a tangible impact on poverty, the SLWCS has opportunities for volunteering. See p302 for more information on volunteering in Sri Lanka.

Lakdasun (www.lakdasun.org) Visit the helpful forums on this website to get up-to-date information from knowledgeable Sri Lankan locals on how to 'Discover, explore and conserve the natural beauty of Sri Lanka'.

LOCALternative Sri Lanka (www.localternative.com) Information on an excellent map (see p297), which details 170 opportunities to practise responsible tourism in Sri Lanka. For our pick of the best, see boxed text, opposite.

Responsible Travel (www.responsible-travel.org) A no-nonsense website with common-sense advice on travelling with a conscience.

TRAVEL LITERATURE
Considering what a colourful and culturally rich destination Sri Lanka is, it's surprising that more writers haven't left a trail of ink or keyboard strokes chronicling their experiences in the country.

Make Yourself at Home
Ecolodges are unique, down-to-earth and increasingly upscale, and some are staffed and supplied by – but also subsidise – local communities. For the latter, try **Galapita** (www.galapita.com), **Samakanda** (www.samakanda.org), **Tree Tops Jungle Lodge** (www.treetopsjunglelodge.com) and **Ulpotha** (www.ulpotha.com).

It's taken time and host-family training, but homestays are finally attracting interest. Sinharaja's **Mederapitiya Homestays** (☎ 041-227 3821, 077 386 3243) and **Kudawa Homestays** (☎ 045-222 5643, 077 386 3243) have strong community anchors. For more details, see p206 and p206.

Two more unique projects built around community participation:

Mahausakande (www.mahausakande.org) Tropical forest regeneration, holistic and healthy living and community support wrapped up in one; see p210.

Ranpathwila Enterprise (☎ 011-493 8800; sleco@sltnet.lk) Spend a night in a simple facility, cared and cooked for by villagers united by an ecofriendly poverty-reduction program.

Building Bridges Between People
Arugam Bay and Pottuvil host CBT initiatives, like the **Community Eco-Guide Association** (cega arugambay@yahoo.com), **Arugam Bay Tourism Association** (p251), fishermen society–managed Sea Safaris and Pottuvil Lagoon Ecotours. For more information, see p250.

CBT work sometimes needs a local mentor. Here are several of Sri Lanka's most able:

Gami Seva Sevana (www.gamisevasevana.org) The simple integrated hostel's meals are examples of this organisation's commitment to social and environmental security through organic farming and human development.

Responsible Tourism Partnership Sri Lanka (www.responsibletourismsrilanka.org) This member-based organisation helps promote sustainable tourism in Sri Lanka; see opposite.

Sarvodaya (www.sarvodaya.org) The multiproject Community Tourism Initiative of this large national charity emphasises direct communication between visitor and host.

Sewalanka Foundation (www.sewalanka.org) A busy national charity driving the development of a country-wide CBT network. Volunteering is also possible; see p302.

Sri Lanka Ecotourism Foundation (www.ecotourismsrilanka.net) This pioneering ecotourism organisation continues to help pave the way for CBT projects.

Vinivida NGO Coalition (☎ 032-225 8806; vinividaorg@yahoo.com) Helps 50-plus Puttalam-area community-based organisations empower underprivileged people. Traditional crafts is one tack.

Woodlands Network (www.visitwoodlandsnetwork.org) The long-standing CBT leader in Uva Province. See p194.

TOP PICKS

SRI
Colombo LANKA
Maldives

BRILLIANT BEACHES

Sri Lanka's east, south and lower west coasts are lined with bays, coves and beaches. Here are our favourite sea-and-sand getaways. The 2004 tsunami destroyed many coastal buildings and devastated many beach landscapes. Hard-working efforts from local communities and foreign volunteers removed tonnes of debris to quickly restore beaches such as Arugam Bay and Unawatuna.

- Kalkudah Bay Beach (p258)
- Mirissa (p138)
- Nilaveli (p265)
- Induruwa (p112)
- Unawatuna (p132)
- Arugam Bay (p248)

HILL COUNTRY SCENERY

Sri Lanka's Hill Country covers a huge chunk of the island and almost all of it could be classed as 'scenic'. For truly dramatic views, however, these are our top picks. Just remember to pack a spare memory card and be ready for a waterfall around (almost) every corner.

- Adam's Peak (p175)
- Knuckles Range (p175)
- Ella (p195)
- Haputale (p190)
- Horton Plains National Park (p187)
- Kandy Lake (p159)

ECOFRIENDLY SLEEPS

Sri Lanka's emerging sustainable tourism ethos means there's an increasing number of ecologically switched-on accommodation options. Many also offer other activities, including yoga, Ayurvedic treatments and excellent organic food.

- Kandy Samadhicentre (p174)
- Selara River Eco Resort (p204)
- Mangrove Cabanas & Mangrove Chalets (p144)
- Ranweli Holiday Village (p110)
- Rafter's Retreat (p178)
- Jetwing Vil Uyana (p220)

WINNING WAYS WITH WILDLIFE

For such a small island, Sri Lanka offers a diverse number of ways to interact with the local fauna. Many projects have a strong conservation focus, so you can feel good and do good at the same time.

- Turtle conservation (see boxed text, p116)
- Elephant Transit Home (p203)
- Whale watching (see boxed text, p142)
- Leopards in Yala National Park (p150)
- Bird-watching in Sinharaja Forest Reserve (p204)
- Mangrove cruises in Pottuvil Lagoon (p248)

Running in the Family by Michael Ondaatje recounts a return to Sri Lanka in the 1970s after growing up here in the '40s and '50s, and captures many of the little oddities that make up life in Sri Lanka.

RL Brohier records his travels around Sri Lanka as a British surveyor in the first half of the 20th century in *Seeing Ceylon* and *Discovering Ceylon*.

Both books capture lots of intriguing historical titbits that are hard to find elsewhere (even if they're not 100% accurate, on occasion).

A Village in the Jungle by Leonard Woolf is a sombre account of local life in Hambantota. First published in 1913, it is in the same vein as George Orwell's *Burmese Days*.

Woolf in Ceylon by Christopher Ondaatje (older brother of Michael) is part travelogue and part history revisiting Sri Lanka through the writings of Leonard Woolf. It's packed with excellent photography.

An engaging, insightful story, *July*, by Karen Roberts, tells of two neighbours – one Sinhalese, one Tamil – growing up together.

Elmo Jayawardena picked up literary prizes with *Sam's Story*, the tale of an illiterate village boy working in Colombo. It's a simple, often light-hearted read that deftly deals with the wider problems of society.

Sindbad in Serendib by Richard Boyle is an eclectic series of essays about the legendary sailor's voyages around this fabled isle.

More recently Paul Theroux included Sri Lanka in *Ghost Train to the Eastern Star*, retracing his original railway journey chronicled in *The Great Railway Bazaar*. As part of his time in Sri Lanka for *Ghost Train to the Eastern Star*, Theroux writes about meeting Arthur C Clarke before the death of the *2001: A Space Odyssey* author in 2008.

Published in 2007, *A Year in Green Tea and Tuk-Tuks* by Rory Spowers recounts what happens when a BBC journalist moves his family to Sri Lanka to transform a tea estate into an organic farm. It's a colourful read, and available at bookshops in Colombo and Kandy. For more information on Spowers' Samakanda project, see boxed text, p18.

INTERNET RESOURCES

Art Sri Lanka (www.artsrilanka.org) A gateway to Sri Lankan high culture, this website covers art history, contemporary art and religious art from various traditions.

Colombo Page (www.colombopage.com) Handy news portal summarising Sri Lankan news.

Ground Views (www.groundviews.org) Excellent citizen journalism website that provides an essential balance to the skewed reporting elsewhere on the internet.

InfoLanka (www.infolanka.com) This excellent and wildly diverse website includes recipes, news, travel, nature and entertainment information. Be prepared to spend at least a couple of hours here.

Lanka Library (www.lankalibrary.com) Travel, archaeology, nature and current events.

LMD (www.lmd.lk) Online version of Sri Lanka's leading business magazine, the *Lanka Monthly Digest*. Also provides opinionated comment on Sri Lankan politics and society.

National Peace Council of Sri Lanka (www.peace-srilanka.org) This website's regular newsletters provide a neutral and conciliatory balance to the overtly Sinhalese and Tamil point of view most commonly available online.

Sri Lanka Tourist Board (www.srilankatourism.org) The official tourism website, with tonnes of information. It's a good starting point, and its monthly e-newsletter is worth subscribing to.

Travel Sri Lanka (www.travelsrilanka.com) The substantial array of information was gleaned from the smart regular print magazine of the same name.

Itineraries
CLASSIC ROUTES

CAPITAL, COAST & HILLS

Three to Four Weeks / Colombo to Kandy

Start in **Colombo** (p75), sampling some of Sri Lanka's finest cuisine and visiting the city's vibrant Buddhist temples. Then hug the coast south, stopping off in **Hikkaduwa** (p117) for cafe-hopping, sunbathing and surfing. Slow down even more in the languid streets of **Galle** (p124) and its 17th-century Dutch city-within-a-fort. Maybe splurge on a restored colonial villa and local art.

From Galle, head inland to **Horton Plains National Park** (p187) for an early-morning start to visit World's End. Squeeze in a side trip to the 240m-high **Bambarakanda Falls** (p189), Sri Lanka's tallest waterfall, and spend a night or two experiencing the cool climate and British colonial heritage of **Nuwara Eliya** (p180).

Continue north to Kandy, stopping off for tea tasting at **Labookellie Tea Factory** (p179) and, if you haven't had enough waterfall action, **Ramboda Falls** (p179). **Kandy** (p157), Sri Lanka's main cultural centre, offers its mild climate, colonial architecture, frequent festivals and sumptuous Buddhist temples.

From Kandy it's a relatively easy ride back to Colombo, or straight to the airport at Negombo.

This 547km route takes you through Sri Lanka's highlights in under a month. Lie on palm-fringed beaches, check out colonial architecture and stare at stunning Hill Country views. Just watch out for the traffic on the Colombo–Galle road.

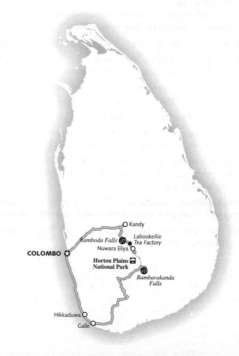

NEGOMBO & ANCIENT CITIES   Two to Three Weeks / Negombo to Mihintale

As the seaside city of **Negombo** (p105) is closer than Colombo to Bandaranaike International Airport, it's easy enough to kick off your trip here and skip the capital altogether. Whether or not you decide to spend a night or more in the historic city, Negombo is worth a stop to see the historic remains of the Dutch fort, charming Catholic churches, bustling fish markets and the rich marshlands of **Muthurajawela** (p110).

From Negombo, head northeast to North Central Province and into the Cultural Triangle, so-called because it contains three of the country's most significant historical sites; it's also a centre for handicrafts. Your first stop should be **Dambulla** (p214), a series of cave shrines painted with vivid Buddhist murals. From here it's a short jaunt to **Sigiriya** (p217), a 200m-tall rock outcrop that was once either a palace or a monastery (depending on whom you believe) and is truly one of the island's most amazing sights.

Further northeast the former royal capital of **Polonnaruwa** (p221) offers an inspiring collection of Buddhist sculptures and monastery ruins dating back nearly a thousand years. In the vicinity, **Minneriya National Park** (p228) is well worth a visit to view the largest herds of wild elephants in Sri Lanka, along with plenty of other wildlife.

Next head northwest to **Anuradhapura** (p231), an even older ex-royal capital with an extensive, well-preserved historical park containing the ruins of monasteries, palaces and dagobas (stupas). Stop off in **Mihintale** (p238), just 13km east of Anuradhapura, to view its small yet impressive collection of monastic ruins and dagobas, and the remains of an ancient Ayurvedic hospital.

This 347km trip through Sri Lanka's ancient cities region takes in centuries-old dagobas (stupas), monasteries, sculptures and palaces as it rolls across hilly green plains and farming valleys and meanders through arid, East Africa–like topography.

ROADS LESS TRAVELLED

TEA, TREKS & TEMPLES   Four Weeks / Kitulgala to Mirissa

Start in **Kitulgala** (p178), a gateway for rafting the Kelaniya Ganga, as well as for jungle hikes and bird-watching. Take the short hop to misty **Hatton**, **Dikoya** and **Maskeliya** (p177), three small towns in some of the most scenic parts of the Hill Country. Spend a few days tasting fragrant single-estate teas and bed down in luxurious ex-colonial tea planters' bungalows, or cosy guest houses in **Dalhousie** (p176), the traditional starting point for the pre-dawn ascent of Adam's Peak.

Head east to **Ella** (p195) for more hiking, wonderful views and guest houses renowned for having some of Sri Lanka's tastiest home-cooked food.

Travel southeast to **Monaragala** (p246), the jumping-off point for one of Sri Lanka's most atmospheric ancient Buddhist sites. **Maligawila** (p247) is home to an 11m-tall standing Buddha that's over a thousand years old.

Continue east to **Arugam Bay** (p248), with its easygoing surfers' vibe, excellent seafood and few travellers compared with the southern beaches. Don't miss a boat trip exploring the nearby Pottuvil Lagoon. After a few days on the beach, veer back inland via Monagala to **Wellawaya** (p202), and find time for a brief detour to Sri Lanka's tallest standing Buddha at **Buduruwagala** (p202).

Descend from Wellawaya to the coastal plains of **Kataragama** (p152), the terminus of the Pada Yatra, a pilgrimage that begins at the other end of the island. One of Sri Lanka's oldest and most venerated dagobas is in nearby **Tissamaharama** (p146), which is also a convenient entry point for forays into **Yala National Park** (p150). From 'Tissa', beach hop via **Hambantota** (p145) along the south coast to laid-back **Mirissa** (p138), a good base for going whale watching (see p142).

Expect hairpin curves and breathtaking views for much of this 474km outing; hike, taste a sample of Sri Lanka's tea, and view ancient Buddhist sites and some of Sri Lanka's quieter beaches.

TAILORED TRIPS

UNESCO WORLD HERITAGE SITES

Begin in sleepy **Galle** (p124), founded by the Portuguese in the 16th century and now one of Southeast Asia's best-preserved, fortified colonial cities. Detour inland to the **Sinharaja Forest Reserve** (p204), Sri Lanka's last major tropical rainforest. Continue north to **Kandy** (p157). The verdant, lakeside city served as the last capital of the Sinhala kings before British occupation. Kandy's Temple of the Sacred Tooth Relic is one of the world's most famous Buddhist pilgrimage sites. Find a good driver or negotiate Kandy's hectic bus station to begin a round trip to the Ancient Cities. The **Dambulla Cave Temples** (p214) have been a pilgrimage site for over 2000 years, with the five caves containing important Buddhist murals and statuary. At **Sigiriya** (p217) the remains of King Kassapa's palace (or possibly a monastery) grace the slopes and summit of a 370m granite outcrop. Don't miss the stunning frescoes as you ascend the sacred rock. At nearby **Polonnaruwa** (p221) the ruins of Sri Lanka's second royal capital include Buddhist and Brahmanic monuments, along with the impressive 12th-century city works created by King Parakramabahu I. Conclude your Unesco World Heritage ramblings by exploring the remains of monasteries, palaces and monuments at **Anuradhapura** (p231), Sri Lanka's most important royal capital.

MAKING A DIFFERENCE

Kick off in **Kosgoda** (see boxed text, p116) to release a baby turtle into the ocean, and also help out their hard-shelled relatives that have been injured by fishing nets. Continue to the **Sinharaja Forest Reserve** (p204) and the Sewalanka Foundation homestays in Mederapitiya or Deinyaya. After visiting the rainforest roll up your sleeves and help out on their tea and *kitul* palm plantations. At the **Elephant Transit Home** (p203) pay a pachyderm a visit to support the good work being done to rehabilitate injured and orphaned elephants back into the wild in the Uda Walawe National Park. Nearby is the low-key and ecofriendly **Selara River Eco Resort** (p204). At Bandarawela, visit **Woodlands Network** (p194) to learn the secrets of Sri Lankan cuisine with a cookery class at this Hill Country community tourism project. Nearby at **Rainforest Rescue International** (p302) you can volunteer on a forest estate and help develop the Uva Arboretum as an organic herb garden and ecotourism destination. Take a leisurely detour east to **Pottuvil** (p248) for a slow boat trip on Pottuvil lagoon and supplement the income of local fishermen and the regeneration of mangroves. After all your hard work, conclude at the **Kandy Samadhicentre** (p174). Treat yourself to a spiritual and physical makeover at this classy ecolodge that doubles as an Ayurvedic and yoga centre. The organic vegetarian food's got to be good for you, too.

History

PREHISTORY

Legend and history are deeply intertwined in the early accounts of Sri Lanka. Did the Buddha leave his footprint on Adam's Peak (Sri Pada) while visiting the island that lay halfway to paradise? Or was it Adam who left his footprint embedded in the rock while taking a last look at Eden? Was the chain of islands linking Sri Lanka to India the same chain that Rama crossed to rescue his wife Sita from the clutches of Rawana, king of Lanka, in the epic Ramayana?

Whatever the legends, the reality is that Sri Lanka's original inhabitants, the Veddahs (Wanniyala-aetto), were hunter-gatherers who subsisted on the island's natural bounty. Much about their origins is unclear. However, anthropologists generally believe that Sri Lanka's original inhabitants are descendants from the people of the late Stone Age and may have existed on the island since 16,000 BC. The first Sinhalese, originally from northern India, arrived in Sri Lanka around the 5th or 6th century BC. Traders and fisherfolk from South India who visited Sri Lanka from the 3rd century BC also made the island their permanent home. The intermingling of the new arrivals produced a harmonious multicultural society – a state that, unfortunately, did not continue in the centuries that followed.

> The early Sinhalese are credited with the invention of the pit valve, an ingenious irrigation device that contributed to their successful early settlement in Sri Lanka.

THE FIRST SINHALESE

A combination of luck, an emerging faith and good maritime skills contributed to the initial development of this teardrop-shaped island around the 4th century BC. With a contingent of 700 men, the North Indian prince Vijaya was banished on dilapidated ships from the subcontinent. Rather than death by drowning, destiny intervened, and legend has it they were blessed by the Buddha and made Sri Lankan landfall on the exact day that the Buddha attained enlightenment.

Vijaya and his fortunate crew settled around Anuradhapura (p231), forming the basis of the first Sinhalese kingdom that developed there in the 4th century BC. In the arid north, the early settlers used their significant engineering skills to construct water channels and reservoirs, known locally as tanks. Overcoming ongoing climatic challenges allowed these early settlements to prosper.

Buddhism arrived from India in the 3rd century BC, and today the mountain at Mihintale (p238) marks the spot where the conversion of King Devanampiya Tissa is said to have occurred. The earliest Buddhist emissaries also brought to Sri Lanka a cutting of the bodhi tree under which the Buddha attained enlightenment. It still survives in Anuradhapura, now garlanded with prayer flags and lights (p232), and is a popular pilgrimage site.

TIMELINE

Pre 6th century BC	6th–5th century BC	4th century BC
The island is inhabited by the Veddahs (Wanniyala-aetto), a group of hunter-gatherers who anthropologists believe were descendants of a late Stone Age society that existed on Sri Lanka since 16,000 BC.	Following the path of Indian mariners and traders, the ancestors of today's Sinhalese migrate from northern India to settle in Sri Lanka. The original settlers are thought to have come from Gujurat, Orissa and Bengal.	Vijaya, a shamed North Indian prince, is cast adrift, but makes landfall on Sri Lanka's west coast. His descendants settle around Anuradhapura amid northern Sri Lanka's arid plains and establish the first great Sinhalese kingdom.

WHAT'S IN A NAME?

Changing the country's name from Ceylon to Sri Lanka in 1972 caused considerable confusion for foreigners. However, for the Sinhalese it has always been known as Lanka and for the Tamils as Ilankai; the Ramayana, too, describes the abduction of Sita by the king of Lanka.

The Romans knew the island as Taprobane and Muslim traders talked of Serendib, meaning 'Island of Jewels' in Arabic. The word Serendib became the root of the word 'serendipity' – the art of making happy and unexpected discoveries. The Portuguese somehow twisted Sinhala-dvipa (Island of the Sinhalese) into Ceilão. In turn, the Dutch altered this to Ceylan and the British to Ceylon.

In 1972 'Lanka' was restored, with the addition of 'Sri', a respectful title.

Following the conversion of the king to Buddhism, strong ties were established between Sri Lankan royalty and Buddhist religious orders. Kings, grateful for monastic support, provided living quarters, tanks and produce to the monasteries. When the Buddhist monks protected the Sinhalese king Valagambahu from South Indian invaders, he expressed his gratitude by developing the huge cave-temple complex at Dambulla (p214) when he retook the throne. A symbiotic political economy between religion and state was established, an informal but powerful contract that is still vital in modern times.

Buddhism underwent a further major development when the original oral teachings were documented in writing. The early Sri Lankan monks developed the classical literature of the Theravada (doctrine of the elders) school of Buddhism (p42). Even today Buddhists of the Theravada school across Southeast Asia look to Sri Lanka for spiritual leadership.

The arrival of the tooth relic (of the Buddha) at Anuradhapura in AD 371 (see p159) further reinforced the position of Buddhism in Sinhalese society. Now the sacred relic resides in Kandy, and contemporary politicians see it as their duty to protect it.

Across seven centuries, Anuradhapura was defeated many times by waves of invaders from South India, but rebuilding was made possible through *rajakariya*, the system of free labour for the king. This free labour provided the resources to restore buildings, tanks and irrigation systems and to develop agriculture. The system was not banished from the island until 1832 when the British passed laws banning slavery.

Finally, in the 11th century AD, Anuradhapura was abandoned and a new capital was developed at Polonnaruwa (p221). It survived for more than two centuries and produced two more notable rulers. Parakramabahu I (r 1153–86), nephew of Vijayabahu I, was not content simply to expel the South Indian Tamil Chola empire from Sri Lanka, but carried the fight to South India and even made a raid on Myanmar. He also constructed many new tanks around the island, and lavished public money to make Polonnaruwa a

For a controversial account of Sigiriya, see former archaeologist Raja De Silva's *Sigiriya and its Significance*, which argues against earlier views about the site.

The bodhi tree in Anuradhapura has a 2000-year history of human care and custody, making it the world's oldest tree of this kind.

3rd century BC

The Indian emperor Ashoka sends his son and daughter to the island to spread the Buddha's teachings. The Anuradhapuran king Devanampiyatissa converts to Buddhism, establishing Sri Lanka's strong ties between government and religion.

2nd–1st century BC

The first South Indians arrive to make the island their permanent home. The Sinhalese king Valagambahu is forced to temporarily flee Anuradhapura by South Indian invaders, and shelters in the caves around Dambulla.

4th century AD

Buddhism is further intensified in Sri Lanka with the arrival in Anuradhapura of the sacred tooth relic of the Buddha. It quickly gains prominence as a symbol of both religion and sovereignty over the island.

great Asian capital. His predilection for war and massive public works schemes squandered resources and undoubtedly shortened Polonnaruwa's lifespan.

His benevolent successor, Nissanka Malla (r 1187–96), was the last king of Polonnaruwa to care for the wellbeing of his people. He was followed by a series of weak rulers, and with the decay of the irrigation system, disease spread and Polonnaruwa was abandoned. The lush jungle reclaimed the second Sinhalese capital in just a few decades.

Want to understand more about people's names in Sri Lanka? It's all revealed at http://asiarecipe .com/srinames.html.

After Polonnaruwa, Sinhalese power shifted to the southwest of the island, and between 1253 and 1400 there were another five different capitals. None were as great as Anuradhapura and Polonnaruwa.

TRADE & CONQUEST

At the heart of the Indian Ocean, Sri Lanka has been a trading hub even before Arab traders arrived in 7th-century AD with their new Islamic faith. Gems, cinnamon, ivory and elephants were the valued items of commerce. Early Muslim settlements took hold in Jaffna and Galle, but the arrival of a European power, focused as much on domination as trade, forced many Muslims inland to flee persecution.

When the Portuguese arrived in 1505, Sri Lanka had three main kingdoms: the Tamil kingdom of Jaffna, and Sinhalese kingdoms in Kandy and Kotte (near Colombo). Lorenço de Almeida, the son of the Portuguese Viceroy of India, established friendly relations with the Kotte kingdom and gained a Portuguese monopoly on the valuable spice trade.

Tamil-Portuguese relations were less cordial, and when colonial missionaries attempted to convert the locals to Catholicism, the Tamil king Sangily in Jaffna massacred the missionaries and their converts. Despite the resistance in Jaffna, Portugal eventually took over the entire west coast, but the Kandyan kingdom in the central highlands steadfastly resisted Portuguese domination.

The Portuguese brought along religious orders, including the Dominicans and Jesuits. Many coastal communities converted, but other resistance to Christianity was met with massacres and the destruction of local temples. Buddhists fled to Kandy, and the Hill Country city assumed its role as protector of the Buddhist faith, a sacred function further instilled by another three centuries of unsuccessful attempts at domination by other colonial powers.

In 1602 the Dutch arrived, just as keen as the Portuguese on dominating the lucrative traffic in Indian Ocean spices. In exchange for Sri Lankan autonomy, the Kandyan king, Rajasinha II, gave the Dutch a monopoly on the spice trade. Despite the deal, the Dutch also made repeated unsuccessful attempts to subjugate Kandy during their 140-year rule.

The Dutch were more business focused than the Portuguese, and canals were built along the west coast to transport cinnamon and other crops. Some

5th century AD	11th century AD	1505
After engineering the death of his father and expelling his older brother Mugalan, King Kasyapa constructs the spectacular rock fortress at Sigiriya. With the assistance of Indian mercenaries, Mugalan finally retakes the throne.	Weary of continued interference and conflict with South Indian neighbours, King Vijayabahu I moves the Sinhalese capital southeast to Polonnaruwa. During Polonnaruwa's decline across three centuries, Tamil kingdoms are established in Jaffna.	Following Polonnaruwa's decline, Sinhalese power moves south, and incursions by South Indians, Chinese and Malayans are rebuffed. The Portuguese arrive in 1505 and conquer the entire west coast. The Kandyan kingdom defeats their advances.

can be seen around Negombo today. The legal system of the Dutch era still forms part of Sri Lanka's legal canon.

The British initially viewed Sri Lanka in strategic terms, and considered the eastern harbour of Trincomalee as a counter to French influence in India. After the French took over the Netherlands in 1794, the pragmatic Dutch ceded Sri Lanka to the British for 'protection' in 1796. The British moved quickly, and by 1815 their influence expanded as far as Kandy. Three years later the first unified administration of the island by a European power was established.

The British conquest unsettled many Sinhalese, who considered that only the tooth relic custodians had the right to rule the land. Their apprehension was somewhat relieved when a senior monk removed the tooth relic from the Temple of the Sacred Tooth Relic (p159), thereby securing it (and the island's symbolic sovereignty) for the Sinhalese people.

Sinhalese angst further grew when British settlers began arriving in the 1830s, eager to grab a slice of the island's developing potential for agriculture. Coffee and rubber were largely replaced by tea from the 1870s, and the island's demographic mix was profoundly altered with an influx of Tamil labourers – so called 'Plantation Tamils' – from South India.

A strong British influence lingers in Sri Lanka, from elite private schools and well-tended cricket grounds and tea-estate bungalows, to the very British architecture of train stations, post offices and old-style red telephone boxes straight from a Yorkshire market town. English was demoted from being the official language after the pro-Sinhala imperatives of independence, but an increasingly globalised economy and the impact of the internet have again raised its profile and relevance.

Fourteen centuries after the initial arrival of Arab traders, international trade is once more a key determinant of Sri Lanka's place in the world.

NATIONALISM & INDEPENDENCE

The dawning of the 20th century was an important time for the grassroots Sri Lankan nationalist movement. Towards the end of the 19th century, Buddhist and Hindu campaigns were established with the dual aim of making the faiths more contemporary in the wake of European colonialism, and defending traditional Sri Lankan culture against the impact of Christian missionaries. The logical progression was for these groups to demand greater Sri Lankan participation in government, and by 1910 they had secured the minor concession of allowing a limited number of educated Sri Lankans to elect one lonely member to the Legislative Council.

During the turbulent days of WWI, nationalist forces gathered impetus as the traditional position of Britain as the world's most powerful and far-reaching empire was put under scrutiny. In 1915, after a Colombo protest

During the British administration, Major Thomas Rogers is reputed to have killed 1400 elephants.

1658	**1802**	**1815**
The first Dutch ships arrive in 1602. Following a treaty with the Kandyan kingdom, the Dutch establish a monopoly on the spice market and wrest control of coastal Sri Lanka from the Portuguese.	After taking over from the Dutch in 1796, Sri Lanka becomes a British colony. The island is initially viewed as a strategic bulwark against French expansion, but the island's commercial potential is soon recognised.	The British set their sights on ruling the entire island, and finally conquer the Kandyan kingdom in 1815. It's the first (and only) time all of Sri Lanka is ruled by a European power.

against Muslim business owners, the British reacted by jailing Buddhist activist leaders, including David Hewavitharane (also known as Anagarika Dharmapala or 'Protector of the Dharma'). Sinalhese anger at martial law was widespread, and by 1919 the nationalist mission was formalised as the Ceylon National Congress. Anagarika Dharmapala was forced to leave the country, and the mantle for further change was taken up by a variety of youth leagues, some Sinhala and some Tamil, but sharing a focus on eliminating inequalities. In 1927 Mahatma Gandhi visited Tamil youth activists in Jaffna, providing further momentum to the cause.

Further reform came in 1931 when the Donoughmore Constitution finally included the island's leaders in the parliamentary decision-making process. The move towards the constitution had begun three years earlier when the Donoughmore Commission toured Sri Lanka and interviewed islanders for four months. One of the recommendations was universal suffrage and Sri Lankan women were given the vote at the age of 21. At the same time British suffragettes were campaigning to have the voting age lowered from 28.

Under the 1931 constitution no one ethnic community could dominate the political process, and a series of checks and balances ensured all areas of the government were overseen by a committee drawn from all ethnic groups. Negotiation and compromise were elevated above mandate and coercion. However, both Sinhalese and Tamil political leaders failed to give much support to the country's pre-independence constitution, foreshadowing the problems that were to characterise the next eight decades.

Following India's independence in 1947, Ceylon (as Sri Lanka was then called) became fully independent on 4 February 1948. Despite featuring members from all of the island's ethnic groups, the ruling United National Party (UNP) really only represented the interests of an English-speaking elite. The UNP's decision to try and deny the 'Plantation Tamils' citizenship and repatriate them back to India was further indication of a still-rising tide of Sinhalese nationalism.

In 1956 this divide further increased when the Sri Lankan Freedom Party (SLFP) came to power with an agenda based around socialism and nationalism. One of the first tasks of the SLFP leader SWRD Bandaranaike was to make Sinhala the country's sole official language. It was a move designed to counter the remnants of the British colonial past, but it also served to aggravate Tamil-speaking communities in the North and the East. This decision marks a convenient beginning of Sri Lanka's Sinhalese-Tamil problems, but in reality issues had been simmering since the end of colonial rule.

In 1971 the anti-Tamil People's Liberation Party (Janatha Vimukthi Peramuna or JVP) attempted armed insurrection against the government. The uprising was crushed, but just a year later two pieces of government legislation were passed that found equal favour with the equally nationalistic SLFP and JVP.

Sir James Emerson Tennent's affable nature shines through in his honest and descriptive writing about 19th-century Sri Lanka, now serialised at www .lankaweb.com/news /features/ceylon.html.

1832	1843–59	1870s
Sweeping changes in property laws open the door to British settlers. English becomes the official language, state monopolies are abolished and capital flows in, funding the establishment of coffee plantations.	Unable to persuade the Sinhalese to labour on the plantations, the British import almost one million Tamil labourers from South India. Today the 'Plantation Tamils' form around 5% of the total population.	The coffee industry drives the development of roads, ports and railways, but leaf blight decimates the coffee industry, and plantations are converted to growing tea or rubber.

The renaming of Ceylon as Sri Lanka, and the promotion of Buddhism as the country's official religion both eased memories of colonial times, but both mandates also provided further separatist inspiration for the Hindu-worshipping Tamil minority in the North and the East.

THE ROOTS OF TAMIL OPPOSITION

During Polonnaruwa's decline the first Tamil kingdom established itself in Jaffna. Movements of people between India and Sri Lanka had been happening for centuries, but from the 5th and 6th centuries AD Hindu Tamil empires repeatedly threatened the Buddhist Sinhalese rulers.

With the decline of the Sinhalese northern capitals and the ensuing Sinhalese migration south, a wide jungle buffer zone separated the northern, mostly coastal Tamil settlements and the southern, interior Sinhalese settlements. For many centuries Jaffna was under the influence of South Indian kingdoms, and the jungle barrier called the Vanni kept the Sinhalese and Tamils largely apart. This changed with the arrival of the Portuguese, the Dutch and the British as they all ruled over Jaffna and the entire west coast. Colonial times saw more mixing of the two cultures and eventually substantial numbers of Tamil settlers from the North made their way south to Colombo. Sinhalese also headed to Jaffna. The influx of Tamil labourers to work on British plantations from 1843 to 1859 further changed the island's demographic mix, although these 'Plantation Tamils' were separated by geography, history and caste by the Jaffna Tamils.

The roots of Tamil-Sinhalese conflict date from British colonial times. British managers found Tamils to be agreeably capable at learning English and fulfilling the needs of the colonial administration. This apparent 'favouritism' saw Tamil candidates over-represented in universities and public service jobs, creating Sinhalese resentment and contributing to anti-Tamil sentiment in the 1950s (following independence in 1948).

Contemporary Sinhalese-Tamil difficulties date from the mid-1950s, when the economy slowed. Competition for wealth and work exacerbated existing Sinhalese-Tamil jealousies. The main political parties played on the Sinhalese fear that their religion, language and culture could all be swamped by Indians, thought to be the natural allies of the Tamils in Sri Lanka. The Tamils began to see themselves as a threatened minority, and pressed for a federal system of government with greater local autonomy in the North and the East, the main Tamil-populated areas.

Despite coming to power in 1956 with a manifesto promoting Sinhalese nationalism, SWRD Bandaranaike later began negotiating with Tamil leaders for a federation. This forward-thinking decision resulted in his assassination by a Buddhist monk in 1959. Despite this, Bandaranaike is still seen by many as a national hero who brought the government back to the common people.

William McGowan's *Only Man is Vile* is an incisive, unrelenting account of ethnic violence in Sri Lanka, penetrating deeply into its complexities.

Meanwhile, two pieces of legislation increased Tamil concern. The first piece, passed in 1970, cut Tamil numbers in universities. Tamils previously had won a relatively high proportion of university places. The second was the constitutional declaration that Buddhism had 'foremost place' in Sri Lanka and that it was the state's duty to 'protect and foster' Buddhism.

Unrest grew among northern Tamils, and a state of emergency was imposed on their home regions for several years from 1971. The police and army that enforced the state of emergency included few Tamils (partly because of the 'Sinhala only' law) and therefore came to be seen by the Tamils as an enemy force.

By Margaret Trawick, *Enemy Lines: Warfare, Childhood, and Play in Batticaloa* is a poignant memoir of living and working in eastern Sri Lanka and witnessing the recruitment of teenagers to the LTTE cause.

In the mid-1970s some young Tamils began fighting for an independent Tamil state called Eelam (Precious Land). They included Vellupillai Prabhakaran, one of the founders of the Liberation Tigers of Tamil Eelam (LTTE), often referred to as the Tamil Tigers.

Tamil was finally elevated to the status of 'national language' for official work, but only in Tamil-majority areas. Clashes between Tamils and security forces developed into a pattern of killings and counter reprisals, all too often with civilians in the crossfire.

The powder keg finally exploded in 1983, when an army patrol in the Jaffna region was ambushed and massacred by militant Tamils. It is reported that between 400 and 2000 Tamils were killed in Sinhalese reprisals and the largely Tamil Pettah district in Colombo was virtually levelled.

The government, the police and the army were either unable or unwilling to stop the violence. Tens of thousands of Tamils fled to safer, Tamil-majority areas, while others left the country altogether. Many Sinhalese moved south from Jaffna and other Tamil-dominated areas.

Not an easy read but an important one, *When Memory Dies* by A Sivanandan is a tale of the ethnic crisis and its impact on one family over three generations.

Revenge and counter-revenge attacks grew into atrocities and large-scale massacres. A 1985 government offer of limited Tamil authority was not sufficient to stop the conflict from escalating into a 25-year civil war that would eventually claim upwards of 70,000 lives.

PARALYSIS FOLLOWS ECONOMIC GROWTH

Elected in 1977, the new UNP prime minister, JR Jayawardene, made an all-out effort to lure back foreign investment. He attempted to emulate Singapore's successful 'open economy', and his policies yielded some successes. Unemployment was halved by 1983, Sri Lanka became self-sufficient in rice production in 1985, and expat Sri Lankans and tourists began bringing in foreign currency.

Jayawardene also introduced a new constitution – Sri Lanka's third – in 1978, which conferred greatest power on the new post of president, to which he was elected by parliament. In 1982 he was re-elected president in national polls (after amending his own constitution to bring the voting forward by two years) and then, in the same year, won a referendum to bypass the 1983 general election and leave the existing parliament in office until 1989. As usual there were allegations of electoral skulduggery.

1956	**1971**	**1970s**
The Sri Lankan Freedom party (SLFP) defeats the UNP on a socialist and nationalist platform. Protests, ethnic riots and conflict break out after a 'Sinhala only' language law is passed.	Incited by the People's Liberation Front (Janatha Vimukthi Peramuna or JVP), a Sinhalese Marxist insurrection explodes. The poorly organised movement, mainly of students and young men, is crushed leaving 25,000 dead.	Young Tamils begin fighting for an independent Tamil State called Eelam (Precious Land) in the north of Sri Lanka. The strongest and longest established group becomes the Liberation Tigers of Tamil Eelam (LTTE).

In 1987 government forces pushed the LTTE back into Jaffna. In an attempt to disarm the Tamil rebels and keep the peace in northern and eastern Sri Lanka, Jayawardene struck a deal with India for an Indian Peace Keeping Force (IPKF). A single provincial council would be elected to govern the region with substantial autonomy for a trial period.

It soon became clear the deal suited no one. The LTTE complied initially before the Indians tried to isolate it by promoting and arming other Tamil rebel groups. Opposition to the Indians also came from the Sinhalese, a revived JVP and sections of the sangha (community of Buddhist monks and nuns). This led to violent demonstrations.

The presence of the IPKF pushed the mood of young Sinhalese past boiling point. In 1987 the JVP launched its second revolution with political murders and strikes. With 16 years to study the failed 1971 revolt, the JVP, still led by Rohana Wijeweera, had prepared brilliantly. They were tightly organised, with recruits from students, monks, the unemployed, the police and the army.

By late 1988 the country was terrorised, the economy crippled and the government paralysed. The army struck back with a ruthless counter-insurgency campaign that still scars the country. Shadowy militias and army groups matched the JVP's underground warfare in brutality. They tracked down the JVP leadership one by one until Rohana Wijeweera was killed in November 1989. The rebellion subsided but tens of thousands had died in the three-year insurrection. Ironically a few years later new leadership brought the JVP into the political mainstream, and it now has seats in parliament and supports the current government and the president, Mahinda Rajapaksa.

Jayawardene was replaced as leader of the UNP by Ranasinghe Premadasa, the first leader from a common background. He promised to remove the Indian peacekeepers. When they withdrew in March 1990, they had lost more than 1000 lives in just three years. In June, however, the war between the LTTE and the Sri Lankan government escalated again. By the end of 1990 the LTTE held Jaffna and much of the North, although the East was largely back under government control.

In May 1991 Rajiv Gandhi was assassinated by an LTTE suicide bomber. A deadly new weapon had entered the sinister lexicon of warfare. It is assumed that Gandhi's assassination was in retaliation for his consent to Jayawardene's 1987 request for the IPKF. Soon after this, war between the LTTE and the Sinhalese intensified into a new decade.

ASSASSINATIONS & ELECTIONS

Although a high proportion of Tamils and Sinhalese longed for peace, extremists on both sides pressed on with war. President Premadasa was assassinated at a May Day rally in 1993. The LTTE was suspected, but never claimed responsibility.

The Sri Lanka Army is a major user of Israeli military technology, including the IAI Kifr fighter jet and the Gabriel anti-ship sea skimming missile.

At least one million land mines were laid during 1990s' Sri Lankan hostilities. Efforts to clear the mines have meant that thousands of displaced people have been resettled.

1983	**1987**	**1987–89**
Clashes between the Sri Lanka military and Tamil militants intensify, and the 1983 massacre of an army patrol near Jaffna ignites ethnic violence. Between 400 and 2000 Tamils were estimated killed by rampaging Sinhalese mobs.	Government forces push the LTTE back into Jaffna. An Indian Peace Keeping Force (IPKF) attempts to establish stability, but is also dragged into conflict with the LTTE.	The JVP return to launch a second Marxist insurrection, and attempt a Khmer Rouge–style peasants' rebellion in the countryside. When the uprising is finally crushed, up to 60,000 people have died.

Anil's Ghost by Booker Prize–winner Michael Ondaatje is a haunting novel about human rights amid the turmoil of late-20th-century Sri Lanka. The book has received much international commendation and some local condemnation.

The following year, the People's Alliance (PA), a coalition of the main opposition SLFP and smaller parties, won the parliamentary elections. Its leader, Chandrika Bandaranaike Kumaratunga, the daughter of former leader Sirimavo Bandaranaike, won the presidential election and appointed her mother prime minister.

Although the PA had promised to end the civil war, the conflict continued in earnest, and Kumaratunga was targeted by a suicide bomber just days before the December 1999 presidential election. She was injured, losing sight in her right eye, but won the election. Curiously enough, the economy was showing signs of life during this period. Garment exports grew, growth ticked along at 5% to 6% a year between 1995 and 2000, and the ongoing war partly solved unemployment in the rural south.

In the October 2000 parliamentary elections President Kumaratunga's PA won a narrow victory. Sirimavo Bandaranaike, the president's mother and three-time prime minister of Sri Lanka, died shortly after casting her vote.

In 2000 a Norwegian peace mission, led by Erik Solheim, brought the LTTE and the government to the negotiating table, but a ceasefire had to wait until after the elections of December 2001 – won by the UNP after the collapse of the short-lived PA government.

Ranil Wickremasinghe became prime minister. He and President Kumaratunga (both from different parties) circled each other warily. Under Wickremasinghe economic growth was strong at 6% per annum and peace talks appeared to progress. But in late 2003, while Wickremasinghe was in Washington meeting with George W Bush, Kumaratunga dissolved parliament (although it had a mandate to govern until 2007) and called for elections. By combining with the JVP, Kumaratunga formed a new party, the United People's Freedom Alliance, and in the subsequent elections defeated Wickremasinghe and his UNP.

John Richardson applies his lengthy experience in international resources and relationships to produce his huge tome *Paradise Poisoned*. Important and timely, it investigates terrorism in Sri Lanka, with recommendations that can be applied globally.

Peace talks stumbled. Time and talk passed, and the situation became ever more fraught. Accusations of bias and injustice were hurled from all sides. In October 2003 the US listed the LTTE as a Foreign Terrorist Organisation (FTO). Some believed this to be a positive move; others saw it as an action that would isolate the LTTE, thereby causing further strain and conflict. In early 2004 a split in LTTE ranks pitched a new dynamic into the mix. Among killings, insecurity, accusations and ambiguities, the Norwegians went home in September 2004. At that stage almost all of Sri Lanka, including most of the Jaffna peninsula, was controlled by the Sri Lankan government. The LTTE controlled a small area south of the peninsula and pockets in the East, but it still had claims on land in the Jaffna peninsula and in the northwest and northeast of the island.

Within three months one of the biggest natural disasters of the modern era impacted on Sri Lanka.

1994	1995–2001	2002
President Chandrika Kumaratunga comes to power pledging to end the war with the LTTE. Peace talks are opened, but hostilities continue. In 1999 Kumaratunga survives a suicide bomb three days before the presidential elections.	Hostilities between the Sri Lanka military and the LTTE intensify, and following more failed attempts at negotiation, the LTTE launches devastating bomb attacks, including the bombing of Kandy's Temple of the Sacred Tooth Relic in 1998.	After two years of negotiation, a Norwegian peace mission secures a ceasefire. Following 9/11, the US' 'War on Terror' classifies the LTTE as a Foreign Terrorist Organisation by 2003, handicapping financial support from Tamil expat communities.

AFTER THE TSUNAMI

An event beyond all predictions struck the island on 26 December 2004, affecting not only the peace process but also the entire social fabric of Sri Lanka. As people celebrated the monthly *poya* (full moon) festivities, the mighty waves of the Boxing Day tsunami cast their fury, killing 30,000 people and leaving many more injured, homeless and orphaned. Initially there was optimism that the nation would come together in the face of catastrophe, but this soon faded into arguments over aid distribution, reconstruction, and land tenure and ownership.

Meanwhile Kumaratunga, seeking to extend her presidential term, sought to have the constitution altered. Her plans were thwarted by a Supreme Court ruling, which directed that presidential elections occur in 2005. Among the numerous contenders, two candidates were the most likely victors – the then prime minister, Mahinda Rajapaksa, and the opposition leader, Ranil Wickremasinghe. With an LTTE boycott on voting, Rajapaksa, supported by the JVP and the Jathika Hela Urumaya (JHU or National Heritage Party; a party of Buddhist monks), won by a narrow margin. The LTTE's motives for the boycott were unclear, but their actions cost Wickremasinghe an expected 180,000 votes and the presidency and, perhaps, the country a better chance at peace. Cynical observers claimed that an escalation in the war was exactly what the LTTE wanted.

As President Rajapaksa pledged to replace the Norwegian peace negotiators with those from the UN and India; to renegotiate a ceasefire with the LTTE; to reject Tamil autonomy; and to refuse to share tsunami aid with the LTTE. Such policies did not auger well for future peace. Meanwhile LTTE leader Prabhakaran insisted on a political settlement during 2006, and threatened to 'intensify' action if this did not occur. Within days of coming to power, Rajapaksa reneged on his first undertaking and invited the Norwegians to continue their negotiations. But tensions were high and once again Sri Lanka was perched on a precipice. Killings, assaults, kidnappings and disappearances occurred on both sides, and commentators predicted the worst. As the first anniversary of the tsunami approached, world leaders, aid agencies and the global community pleaded with the government and the LTTE to stop the violence and return to peace talks. Both parties agreed, and in early 2006 the Norwegians were able to help negotiate a statement that included commitments to a ceasefire and to further talks.

ENDGAME?

Cracks were already showing in the Norwegian-brokered ceasefire when it was signed in February 2006, and by March the Sri Lankan Navy and the LTTE were again trading deadly salvos off the east coast near Trincomalee. Massive Sri Lankan Airforce airstrikes were delivered against the LTTE after an escalation in suicide and mine attacks, some targeting civilian

See http://news.bbc.co.uk/2/hi/south_asia/4125581.stm£ for a poignant, on-the-spot account by BBC journalist Roland Buerk of the impact of the 2004 tsunami on the Sri Lankan coastal town of Unawatuna.

Sri Lankan governments are elected for a six-year term, but it is not unusual for elections to be held early to satisfy political expediency.

In the most recent Sri Lankan elections (November 2005), support for either the United People's Freedom Alliance or the opposition United National Party (UNP) accounted for 98.72% of all votes cast.

2004	2005	2006
The Boxing Day tsunami devastates coastal Sri Lanka leaving 30,000 people dead. It's thought the disaster will help to unite the country, but optimism fades into wrangling between the government and the LTTE over aid distribution and reconstruction.	The 2005 presidential elections are won by the Sinhalese nationalist Mahinda Rajapaksa. Before the election Rajapaksa signs a deal with the Marxist JVP party, rejects Tamil autonomy outright and denies tsunami aid to the LTTE.	Norwegian-brokered peace talks recommence in February, but by midyear fighting between the Sri Lankan security forces and the LTTE is occurring again with ferocious regularity. By October peace talks in Geneva have failed again.

populations. More than 60 people died when a bus travelling from Anuradhapura struck a land mine. By August the fighting in the northeast was the most intense since the 2002 ceasefire, and peace talks in Geneva in October failed again. In June 2007 Sinhalese-Tamil tension further increased when police forced hundreds of Tamils from Colombo citing security concerns. A court ordered an end to the expulsions, but the actions set the scene for a period characterised by attacks and counter-reprisals from both sides. The optimistic days of negotiation and ceasefire seemed more distant than ever.

In January 2008 the Sri Lankan government officially pulled out of the ceasefire agreement, signalling a single-minded dedication to ending the 25-year-old civil conflict by military means. It was a dedication reinforced by its response to the LTTE offer of a unilateral ceasefire in support of the South Asian Association for Regional Cooperation (SAARC) in Colombo. The Sri Lankan response was emphatic. Defence Secretary Gotabhaya Rajapaksa (the younger brother of the president) dismissed the offer outright by claiming:

> The ceasefire announcement is a ploy by the LTTE when it is being militarily weakened…to strengthen it militarily under the guise of holding negotiations. There is no need for the government to enter into a ceasefire agreement with the LTTE.

A change in military strategy saw the Sri Lankan security forces fight fire with fire with an increase in guerrilla-style attacks. By July 2008 the important LTTE naval base of Vidattaltivu had been captured, and by August the Sri Lanka Army had entered the LTTE's final stronghold, the jungle area of the Vanni. The Sri Lankan government stated that the army was on track to capture the LTTE capital Kilinochchi by the end of 2008. Faced with a series of battleground defeats, the LTTE struck back with another suicide bomb in Anuradhapura, this time killing 27 people, including a former general in the Sri Lanka Army.

The government's prediction of the capture of Kilinochchi by the end of 2008 was only a few days out, and on 2 January 2009 Sri Lankan forces entered the town that had been the de facto capital of the unofficial Tamil Eelam state since 1990. On 8 January 2009 the LTTE abandoned the Jaffna peninsula and retreated for a final stand in the Vanni jungle. Amid growing claims of civilian casualties and humanitarian concerns for the 250,000 noncombatants hemmed in by the fighting, foreign governments and the UN called for an immediate ceasefire in February 2009. The Sri Lanka Army pushed on and on 6 February, just two days after Sri Lanka's independence day, the LTTE naval base at Chalai was captured, effectively cutting off fuel,

Sidebar notes:

Log on to YouTube to watch a BBC documentary on the development of the Sri Lankan civil war. Key words are Sri Lanka, Tamil Tigers and Evolution of the Ethnic War.

The *Battle Progress Map* on the website of the Ministry of Defence, Public Security, Law & Order graphically shows the escalating success of the Sri Lankan military across late 2008 and early 2009. See www.defence.lk/orbat/Default.asp.

2008	2008–09	February 2009
The Sri Lankan government pulls out of the 2002 ceasefire agreement, signalling a single-minded focus on a military solution. From 1983 to 2008, an estimated 70,000 people have died in the conflict.	A series of significant military victories escalates the Sri Lankan government's desire for a speedy resolution to the conflict. In January 2009 the military finally capture Kilinochchi, the administrative capital of the LTTE for 10 years.	Tens of thousands of Tamil civilians are trapped inside a rapidly diminishing war zone on Sri Lanka's northeast coast. International calls for a ceasefire to facilitate humanitarian aid are dismissed by the Sri Lankan government.

munitions and arms smuggled from other countries. Compared with just 12 months earlier, the LTTE had lost 99% of the territory it once controlled.

Across the following three months, the ongoing success of the Sri Lankan military restricted the LTTE to an increasingly narrow coastal strip on the country's northeast coast. While international concern grew for the welfare of the tens of thousands of Tamil civilians trapped by the fighting, the LTTE achieved a final defiant air strike into the heart of the Sri Lankan capital. Two light aircraft flown by the 'Black Air Tigers' conducted suicide missions into two Sri Lankan air force installations, killing two people and injuring 45.

In March 2009 the Sri Lankan government confirmed former LTTE military commander Karuna as the Minister of National Integration and Reconciliation, completing his transition since defecting from the LTTE in 2004. Amid claims that the Sri Lankan military was bombing Tamil civilians in supposedly 'safe areas', and counter claims that the LTTE was using Tamil civilians as human shields and stopping them from leaving the conflict zone, the United Nations High Commissioner for Human Rights Navi Pillay accused both sides of war crimes.

Amid intense humanitarian concerns for the plight of an estimated 50,000 Tamil civilians confined to a single stretch of beach, the LTTE offered the Sri Lankan government a unilateral ceasefire. Given the Sri Lankan military's objectives were so close to being fulfilled it was naturally dismissed as 'a joke' by the Sri Lankan Defence Secretary. Other efforts by Swedish, French and British diplomats to inspire a truce were also dismissed by a Sri Lankan government with ultimate battleground success in its sights after three decades. The reported April 2009 defection of two senior LTTE figures only increased their resolve for a decisive military solution.

The end came in May 2009 when the Sri Lankan military announced it had captured the last sliver of coastal land and had surrounded a few hundred last remaining LTTE fighters. The LTTE responded by announcing they had 'silenced their weapons' and that the 'battle had reached its bitter end'. Several senior LTTE figures were reported killed, including LTTE leader Vellupillai Prabhakaran. It is estimated up to 50,000 Tamil civilians escaped the fighting in the last 72 hours of the conflict.

Significant support for the battleground victory exists with the majority Sinhalese population, but the conditions of Tamil economic and ethnic exclusion that inspired the LTTE for so long still remain as challenges to be acknowledged and addressed. Amid United Nations' concerns that up to 7000 Tamil civilians were killed in the final five months of the war, international pressure grew to produce a political solution for the future of the Tamil community in Sri Lanka. What is certain is that the future may reveal the truth about the final days of the conflict, a truth potentially concealed by propaganda from both the Sri Lankan government and the LTTE.

Crucible of Conflict: Tamil and Muslim Society on the East Coast of Sri Lanka by Dennis McGilvary reinforces that future healing must recognise the country's cultural diversity.

April 2009	May 2009	May 2009
A unilateral declaration of a ceasefire by the LTTE is declared as 'a joke' by the Sri Lankan government. The LTTE is confined to a slim coastal strip of land, and is accused of holding Tamil citizens against their will as human shields.	Envoys from the EU call for a bilateral ceasefire as the UN estimates up to 50,000 Tamil civilians are still inside the war zone. The Sri Lankan government calls a halt to the use of heavy weaponry and aerial activity to limit further civilian casualties.	After almost 30 years, Asia's longest-running war ends in May when the LTTE concede defeat. Legitimate Tamil aspirations and grievances remain, but the future of the LTTE is uncertain.

The Culture

THE NATIONAL PSYCHE

Visitors to Sri Lanka notice first the gentleness of the land and people. Life is leisurely and time moves slowly and deliberately. Rivers make an unhurried journey to the coast where waves caress the sands. Inland, white-domed dagobas (stupas) pierce cobalt-blue skies and swathes of mist cling magnetically to rolling hills blanketed with tea plantations. Wattle-and-daub homes and large mansions settle easily within this natural environment. People wander with flowers to temples, and locals greet visitors with warmth and hospitality.

Sri Lanka's markets and bus stations are kinetic hubs of energy and movement, but the gentle sway of sarong, sari or skirt preserves a pace that's both slower and more refined. It's an essential and pragmatic response to the surrounding heat, dust and humidity.

Every so often, things are less gentle. Rivers swell, inundating the land and snatching lives. Tides rise, destroying everything in their path. Ethnic violence explodes and more lives are lost and shattered. Global economic problems force Sri Lankan workers to return home from overseas with a corresponding decline in income for their home villages. Poverty coexists with luxury as servants tend their masters as they have done for centuries. The modern exists beside the old as the young park their 4WDs near three-wheeler drivers, whose transport may be their only home.

But Sri Lankans continue to balance this chaos and duality and exude an alluring charm and a warm welcome. This island nation has welcomed visitors for millennia. Different faiths and ethnicities have mixed and married, yet fascinating distinctions still exist.

For the visitor, the overriding memory will be a nation of gentleness and hospitality.

Culture Shock! Sri Lanka by Robert Barlas and Nanda P Wanasundera gives travellers a confidence boost by offering a glimpse into the unknown and unfamiliar.

LIFESTYLE

Daily life for Sri Lankans depends very much on their position in society. Monks rise early to chant or meditate. Devotees make an early morning visit to the temple. Other Sri Lankans walk on Colombo's Galle Face Green or visit the gym. Tea pickers don their colourful clothes and hurry to the leaves. Servants prepare breakfast for the family. Stockbrokers and engineers are chauffeured to the office, farmers cultivate their land and stall holders arrange their *kadé* (street-side huts) with fruit and goodies.

For stunning images that evoke the splendour of Sri Lanka, its festivals, architecture, landscape and much more, see any of Dominic Sansoni's books.

Sri Lankan Life

Traditional Sri Lankan life was centred on the *gamma* (village), a highly organised hub of activity, where everyone fulfilled specific roles. Agriculture was the mainstay, with rice paddies dotting the landscape, buffalos wallowing in ponds and poultry pecking away under fruit trees. Some villages focused on particular products, such as pots or masks, and even today you might pass through 'Cane-furniture-gamma'.

Contemporary Sri Lanka is a fusion of old and new. Colombo's urban skyline has modern office blocks soaring above slowly crumbling colonial architecture. In the bustling market stalls of Pettah, pirated DVDs sit near live chickens as teens SMS their friends. Yet, in some isolated areas, homes lack running water and electricity. Many people still live the traditional village life, albeit with a TV, mobile phone and regular email contact with a brother working in Dubai or Saudi Arabia.

Around the Fort in 80 Lives is a wonderfully evocative photographic book by globetrotting photojournalist Juliet Coombe, now resident in Galle.

The belief that the geographic blessing of Sri Lanka's Indian Ocean location would transform the country into another Singapore has not eventuated. Modern buildings emerge, but their construction on marshland has the inevitable consequences of sewage blockages, flooding, and transport and pollution problems.

Employment

Villagers traditionally had a strong sense of duty to family, community, monarch and monk. The *rajakariya* (labour for the king) ethos ensured the achievement of massive projects such as temple building and tank construction. Vast tasks like harvesting crops were undertaken by all the community. Some people had agricultural or home duties, while others had more specific roles like astrologer or toddy tapper.

Graduates and teachers earn Rs 15,000 to 25,000 per month, higher than unskilled labourers and agricultural workers who earn around Rs 10,000 to 15,000 per month. In 2008 it was calculated that the monthly expenses for a family of five were around Rs 30,000. At the same time the minimum wage for a government employee was Rs 11,370. Despite an official unemployment rate of around 5%, many families rely on income from informal second or third jobs. Many Sri Lankans also travel offshore to work in construction, administration or as domestic servants, but the global financial crisis saw many workers return from the Gulf to their home villages. Many Sri Lankan garment factories serving Western retailers and consumers were also forced to downsize.

Around 22% of Sri Lankans live under the poverty line, although in areas like Nuwara Eliya and the north and east, this percentage rises to around 33%.

Society & Attitudes

Traditionally, marriages in Sri Lanka were arranged. Although young people may now choose their own partners, horoscopes, caste and parental approval are still important factors.

Homosexuality is illegal according to 1883 legislation passed by the British. The law is rarely enforced, but it pays to be discreet. Local members of the gay community report this legislation is sometimes used for harassment and bribery. Despite this tacit disapproval, the gay scene is becoming more confident, and Colombo now hosts an annual Gay Pride celebration (see p296).

Elderly are respected in Sri Lanka and usually remain an integral part of the extended family.

Although Buddhism discourages distinctions based on caste, a caste system still operates informally among Sinhalese. About 50% of Sinhalese belong to the highest caste, the Govigama, traditionally landowners, cultivators and the aristocracy.

Lower down the scale come the Karava (fisherfolk), Hakurus (makers of jaggery sweets), Berawaya (drummers), Paduvua (palanquin bearers), Radhu (washerfolk) and the Rodiya (beggars and itinerant entertainers). If you're reading newspaper advertisements for the Sinahlese marriage market, desirable 'qualities' for prospective partners is usually code for the 'right caste'.

For Hindus, caste is still more important. The Jaffna Tamils are mainly of the Vellala caste (landlords akin to the Govigama), and maximised their influence on land ownership last century. The Plantation Tamils, imported from southern India to work on the tea plantations, mainly come from lower castes.

Times are changing, however, and legislation and needs- and equality-based welfare programs are eroding traditional caste distinctions. Many younger people now undertake their lives ignoring caste and the disparities it may bring.

Across two decades the gender breakdown of Sri Lankans working overseas changed dramatically from 33% female and 67% male in 1987 to 53% female and 47% male in 2007. Most women work as domestic servants.

Each year approximately 1.6 million Sri Lankans work overseas (mainly in the Middle East), boosting the Sri Lankan economy by sending home US$1.5 billion, approximately 8% of Sri Lanka's GDP. The global financial crisis forced many to return to their home villages.

For gay information and contacts, visit www .utopia-asia.com/tipssri .htm.

Ritual & Ceremony

Traditionally, rites of passage, often celebrated with elaborate rituals, brought families and villagers together. These connections were sealed with beliefs that linked nature with the supernatural; the land, rivers, trees and sky were all seen as life givers and therefore land was tilled with respect and its produce was received with gratitude and ceremony. Every village had a protector deity (or several), usually associated with aspects of nature.

Tradition still has an important role at times of life transition. A newborn child may be named according to an auspicious time and letters, indicated by the astrologers. The child's first solid food is *kiri bath* (coconut-milk rice), the traditional food of ritual and celebration. It's common for children to receive a *pancha uda* (necklace of five weapons), containing small charms of a sword, bow, arrow, conch and trident – all symbols of protection.

A custom still practised by some families, especially in villages, is the daughter's coming-of-age. During her first period she is separated, usually in a room of her own. Female family members keep her company and feed her special foods. At a time determined by the astrologer, she is bathed and later celebrated with gifts of jewellery and clothes.

At weddings it is usual for mixed-faith couples to marry with customs from both religions. At Buddhist weddings, religious stanzas are chanted in Sinhala and Pali (a dialect of Sanskrit). The bride's little finger on her right hand is tied with thread to the little finger of the groom's left hand, the end of the thread is lit, and as it burns towards their hands, water is poured, extinguishing the flame and symbolising their union. The couple cut the *kiri bath*, sign the register and join the feast.

Hindu weddings take place in a temple around a fire that symbolises Brahman, the supreme being. Prayers are offered to Ganesh, sacred texts are recited and the end of the bride's sari is tied to the outer clothing of the groom. They circle the fire seven times, a symbol of commitment and union. After exchanging rings they are showered with rice and flowers.

The *nikaah* (Muslim marriage) is normally a simple affair. There is no religious ceremony, just an agreement by the couple. Celebrations and gift giving depend upon the orthodoxy of the couple – the greater the orthodoxy, the more humble the event.

At funerals mourners wear white, and white flags are strung along fences, providing a path to the place of cremation.

ECONOMY

Key drivers of Sri Lanka's economy include tourism, tea exports, garment and textile manufacturing, overseas aid, and remittances from overseas workers. Growth in GDP across recent years is around 5%, although most of Sri Lanka's traditional revenue sources underwent intense pressure during the global financial crisis.

At the time of writing Sri Lanka's monthly inflation rate was around 22%, putting intense pressure on the cost of transport and basic food items. Military spending by the government in the Sri Lankan civil war was estimated to be US$2 billion in 2008. In the 2008 budget, the Sri Lankan government allocated Rs 8536 per person for defence. In contrast, only Rs 2974 per person was allocated for health and Rs 2359 for education.

POPULATION

Unlike other countries, Sri Lankans have not made a marked exodus from country to city. Twenty-five percent of the population of 19.8 million lives in the city, many retaining close attachments to village life through family and continued land ownership.

Sri Lanka's population doubled from seven million to 14 million in the 30 years following the departure of the British in 1948. The annual growth rate has now slowed to less than 1%, about half the annual growth rate in neighbouring south Asian nations.

Since independence, Sri Lanka has had a creditable literacy and health record. Sinhala and Tamil are both national languages, with English defined as a 'link language'. Many Sri Lankans are bilingual, even trilingual.

Sinhalese

The Sinhalese constitute around 74% of the population, speak Sinhala and are predominantly Buddhist. Their forebears came from northern India in the 6th century BC.

Sinhalese sometimes divide themselves into 'low country' or 'high country' (ie Kandyan). The Kandyan Sinhalese are proud of the time when the Hill Country was the last bastion of Sinhalese rule. For Sinhalese Buddhists, Kandy is the island's spiritual hub.

Tamils

The Tamils constitute 18% of the population, are predominantly Hindu and speak Tamil. While religious and pilgrimage connections exist between Sri Lankan and Indian Tamils, they generally see themselves as discrete groups.

There are two distinct groups of Tamils in Sri Lanka, separated by geography, history and caste. The Jaffna Tamils are descendants of the South Indians who settled in northern Sri Lanka during the late centuries BC. Most still live in the North and along the northeast coast.

The other Tamils are the 'Plantation Tamils', brought by the British from India in the 19th century to work on tea plantations.

Muslims

About 9% of the population is Muslim – called Sri Lanka Moors – descendants of Arab or Indian traders from 1000 years ago. To escape persecution from the Portuguese, many moved into the Hill Country, and you'll still see predominantly Muslim towns like Hakgala near Nuwara Eliya.

Muslims have largely steered clear of the Sinhalese-Tamil troubles, though there has been some conflict in the East.

Veddahs

The Veddahs (Hunters), also called the Wanniyala-aetto (People of the Forest), are Sri Lanka's original inhabitants. Each wave of migration to Sri Lanka left the Veddahs with less forest on which to subsist. Today less than 2000 are said to exist, and only a diminishing number of people identify themselves as Veddah and retain a semblance of their old culture, encapsulating a hunter-gatherer lifestyle and close relationships to nature and their ancestors.

When the Dutch arrived in Sri Lanka there were Veddah communities as far north as Jaffna. Today there are two groups: Kele Weddo (jungle-dwelling Veddahs) and Can Weddo (village-dwelling Veddahs), living mainly in the area between Badulla, Batticaloa and Polonnaruwa.

Central to Veddah identity are their traditional hunting grounds in the Maduru Oya National Park. Sri Lankan law prohibits hunting and gathering in national parks and Veddahs have been arrested for such activities.

Deities and Demons by Nandadeva Wijesekera features vivid illustrations of past (sometimes enduring) Sri Lankan customs. To get through it you'll need to happily abandon all notions of syntax and feminism. Good luck.

For an interesting and humorous read see *The Postcolonial Identity of Sri Lankan English* by English scholar Manique Gunesekera.

To understand historical and contemporary Veddah life and customs, see www.vedda.org.

Other Ethnic Groups

The Burghers are Eurasian, primarily descendants of the Portuguese, Dutch and British. Even after independence, Burghers had a disproportionate influence over political and business life, but as growing Sinhalese nationalism reduced their role in Sri Lankan life, many Burghers emigrated to Australia and Canada. Look out for surnames like Fernando, de Silva and Perera.

RELIGION

Buddhism is the belief system of the Sinhalese and is followed by 70% of the population. It plays a significant role in the country, spiritually, culturally and politically, and Sri Lanka's literature, art and architecture are all strongly influenced by Buddhism. About 15% of the population, mainly Tamil, is Hindu. Muslims account for about 9% of the population, and Christians around 6%.

The different religions mix openly. Buddhists, Hindus, Muslims and Christians all visit the same pilgrimage sites – especially Adam's Peak and Kataragama – and a Catholic may also pay respect to the Hindu god. Think of it as spiritual insurance.

The Sri Lankan government, while seeing Buddhism as the island's foremost religion, initially established ministries representing each of the island's major faiths However, on election in 2005, President Rajapaksa combined these into a Ministry of Religious Affairs and Moral Upliftment. Concerned for its Buddhist heritage, the primarily Sinhalese government is opposed to proselytising by other religions, particularly Christianity. This has caused some tension as Christian groups endeavour to spread their faith.

Buddhism

Strictly speaking, Buddhism is not a religion but a philosophy and moral code espoused by the Buddha. Born Prince Siddhartha Gautama on the border of Nepal and India around 563 BC, the Buddha left his royal background and developed philosophies and disciplines for understanding and overcoming life's challenges.

In *Buddhism: Beliefs and Practices in Sri Lanka,* Lynn de Silva combines lucid writing, fascinating information and a scholarly (but never inaccessible) approach that casts light on much that can appear incomprehensible.

The Buddha taught that suffering is inescapable, and that everyone will experience suffering as long as they are attached to the sensual and material aspects of life. Freedom from suffering comes from developing a higher consciousness through meditation and by following a moral code. After many rebirths and many states of spiritual development, nirvana (enlightenment) is achieved, bringing freedom from the cycle of birth and death.

Central to the doctrine of rebirth is karma; each rebirth results from the actions one has committed, maybe in a previous life.

The conversion of the Sinhalese king to Buddhism in the 3rd century BC (p26) firmly implanted Buddhism in Sri Lanka. A strong relationship developed between Sri Lanka's kings and the Buddhist clergy.

Worldwide there are two major schools of Buddhism – Theravada and Mahayana. Theravada (*thera* means 'learned elder') scriptures are in Pali (the language of the Buddha's time), while Mahayana (Large Vehicle) scriptures are in Sanskrit. Theravada is regarded as more academic, and Mahayana as more universal.

Translating the Buddhist scriptures receives government support in Sri Lanka.

Mahayana Buddhism is practised in Sri Lanka, but the Theravada school is more widely adopted. Several factors have consolidated Buddhism (especially the Theravada stream) in Sri Lanka. Firstly, Sinhalese Buddhists attach vital meaning to the words of the Mahavamsa (Great Chronicle; one of their sacred texts), in which the Buddha designates them as the protectors of the Buddhist teachings. This commitment was fuelled by centuries of conflict between the Sinhalese (mainly

POYA DAYS

Poya days fall on each full moon. Devout Buddhists visit a temple, fast after noon, and abstain from entertainment and luxury. At their temple they make offerings, attend teachings and meditate. These days, which are public holidays in Sri Lanka, have been observed since ancient times. Each *poya* day is associated with a particular Buddhist ritual. For the specific dates of *poya* days from 2009 to 2012 see boxed text, p297.

Some notable days:

Durutu (January) Marks the first visit of the Buddha to the island.

Vesak (May) Celebrates the birth and enlightenment of the Buddha.

Poson (June) Commemorates Buddhism's arrival in Sri Lanka.

Esala (July/August) Sees the huge Kandy festival, which commemorates, among other things, Buddha's first sermon.

Unduwap (December) Celebrates the visit of Sangamitta, who brought the bodhi tree sapling to Anuradhapura.

Buddhist) and Tamils (mainly Hindu). For some Sinhalese, Mahayana Buddhism resembled Hinduism, and therefore defence of the Theravada stream was also crucial. Many Indian Buddhist sites were destroyed in the 10th century AD, further reinforcing the Sinhalese commitment to protect Buddhism.

Since the late 19th century an influential strand of 'militant' Buddhism has developed in Sri Lanka, centred on the belief that the Buddha charged the Sinhalese people with making the island a citadel of Buddhism in its purest form. It sees threats to Sinhalese Buddhist culture in Christianity and Hinduism. In recent years there have been attacks against Christian churches and communities. Sri Lankan Buddhism is historically intertwined with politics, and it was a Buddhist monk, dissatisfied with Prime Minister SWRD Bandaranaike's 'drift' from a Sinhala-Buddhist focus, who assassinated him in 1959.

Today some Buddhist monks strongly oppose compromise with the Tamils. Hard-line monks are also at the vanguard of Sinhalese nationalism, and in 2007 achieved a significant position of leverage in the Sri Lankan government through the Jathika Hela Urumaya (JHU or National Heritage Party). Conversely, many other monks are rightly dedicated to the spirit of Buddhism, and are committed to the welfare of devotees.

Besides regular festivals and other ways that Buddhism permeates people's daily lives, Buddhists gather at temples on *poya* (full moon) days to make *puja* (prayers and offerings) and to hear the ancient truths from the sangha (community of Buddhist monks and nuns).

Theravada Buddhism by Richard Gombrich details the context, history and practice of Buddhism in Sri Lanka.

Hinduism

Tamil kings and their followers from South India brought Hinduism to northern Sri Lanka. Today there are Hindu communities in Colombo, Kandy, the tea plantation areas, the North and the East.

Hinduism is a complex mix of beliefs and gods. All Hindus believe in Brahman. The myriad deities are manifestations of this formless being, through which believers can understand all facets of life. Key tenets include belief in ahimsa (nonviolence), samsara (the recurring cycle of births and deaths until one reaches a pure state), karma (the law of cause and effect) and dharma (teachings about laws for living).

Hindus believe that living a life according to dharma enhances the chance of being born into better circumstances. Rebirth can also take animal form, but it's only as a human that one may gain sufficient self-knowledge to escape the cycle of reincarnation and achieve moksha (liberation).

For more information on Hinduism, see www .bbc.co.uk/religion /religions/hinduism or www.hinduism today.com.

For ordinary Hindus, fulfilling one's ritual and social duties is the main aim of worldly life. The Hindu text Bhagavad Gita reinforces doing your duty is more important than asserting your individuality.

GODS & GODDESSES
The Hindu pantheon is prolific, and some estimates put the number of deities at 330 million. Here are the main celestial players; learn about the supporting cast at **Sanatansociety.org** (www.sanatansociety.org/hindu_gods_and _goddesses.htm).

Brahma & Saraswati
Brahma created the universe, and his consort, Saraswati, is the goddess of wisdom and music.

Vishnu & Lakshmi
Known as the preserver, Vishnu is lawful and devout. Vishnu's consort is Lakshmi, goddess of beauty and fortune.

Shiva & Parvati
The destroyer of ignorance and evil, Shiva has 1008 names and takes many forms. As Nataraja, lord of the *tandava* (dance), his graceful movements begin the creation of the cosmos.

Shiva's consort, Parvati, can be the universal mother or the ferocious and destructive Kali.

Islam
There are 1.8 million Sri Lankan Muslims, descendants of Arab traders who settled on the island from the 7th century.

Islam was founded in the 7th century in present-day Saudi Arabia by the Prophet Mohammed. Islam is monotheistic, and believes that everything has been created by Allah.

After Mohammed's death the movement split into two main branches – the Sunnis and the Shiites. Sunnis emphasise following and imitating the words and acts of the Prophet. They look to tradition and the majority views of the community. Shiites believe that only imams (exemplary leaders) can reveal the meaning of the Quran. Most of Sri Lanka's Muslims are Sunnis, although small communities of Shiites have migrated from India.

All Muslims believe in the five pillars of Islam: the shahada (declaration of faith: 'there is no God but Allah; Mohammed is his prophet'); prayer (ideally five times a day); the zakat (tax, usually a donation to charity); fasting during the month of Ramadan; and the haj (pilgrimage) to Mecca.

There is no overt support for fundamentalist or jihadi Muslim groups in Sri Lanka.

Christianity
Christianity in Sri Lanka potentially goes back to the Apostle Thomas in the 1st century AD, and it's certain that in the early centuries AD small numbers of Christians did establish settlements along the coast.

With the Portuguese in the 16th century, Christianity, specifically Roman Catholicism, arrived in force and many fishing families converted. Today Catholicism remains strong among western coastal communities. The Dutch brought Protestantism and the Dutch Reformed Church, mainly present in Colombo. Evidence of the British Christian denominations, such as Protestantism and Anglicanism, are the quaint stone churches that dot the Hill Country landscape.

In Hindu mythology elephants are seen as symbols of water, life and fortune. They also signify nobility and gentleness, the qualities achieved when one lives a good life. In Sri Lanka, only the elephant gets to parade with sacred Buddhist relics and Hindu statues.

In Pradeep Jeganathan's *At the Water's Edge* you get to feel Sri Lanka's raw edge. The writing in these seven short stories is raw, too, but it says much in few words.

In recent years groups of radical Sinhalese nationalist Buddhist monks have been implicated in attacks on Christian churches and communities (see p42).

WOMEN IN SRI LANKA

Sri Lanka became the first country in the world to have a female prime minister when Sirimavo Bandaranaike was elected to office in 1960. In 1994 her daughter Chandrika Bandaranaike Kumaratunga became president. This should be viewed more as a continuation of dynasty than an indicator of gender equality. Both mother and daughter only attained office following their husbands' assassination. Today only 5% of parliamentary members are women and their representation in local councils is under 2%; ratios unchanged since the 1930s.

Given the importance placed on education in Sri Lanka, girls have opportunities to move into most occupational areas. However, the actual opportunities depend greatly on their role in society. In general women are responsible for the home, and while professional woman may have domestic servants, poorer women may have to juggle running a household with working in a garment factory.

The Sri Lankan civil war also had catastrophic effects on women. A significant number of Sri Lankan households are now headed by women, and the **Coalition to Stop Child Soldiers** (www.child-soldiers.org) has reported that girls as young as 14 years were recruited by the Liberation Tigers of Tamil Eelam (LTTE) during the ethnic conflict.

Widowhood still remains a stigma. Other women avoid widows, fearful that they too may suffer the 'curse' of solo status. The practice of a man taking another wife is also not unheard of. This can have distressing effects on the first wife who, restricted by finance and the potential stigma, remains in an unhappy marriage. Improving opportunities for employment and financial independence are changing this situation slowly.

Sri Lanka's vibrant feminist movement acts as an umbrella organisation for several groups focusing on peace, missing relatives, racism, agricultural and factory workers, and refugees from ethnic conflict.

In most social situations women are demure and men do most of the talking. Women nod in the right places and laugh appropriately at unfunny jokes, even if they've heard them many times before. In this respect the gender roles in Sri Lanka are particularly conservative, and at odds with the depiction of independent Western women seen by Sri Lankan men in international media. Seemingly Sri Lanka's relative isolation during the civil war has also limited the capacity of certain elements of Sri Lankan male society to understand what is acceptable behaviour when dealing with female travellers.

See p302 for more on specific hassles and problems that women travellers may face.

ARTS

Dance

Sri Lanka has a rich dance heritage comprising three main schools: Kandyan dance, masked dance-drama and devil dance.

KANDYAN DANCE

This dance form flourished under the Kandyan kings and when Buddhist monks admitted it to temple courtyards, and it became an essential part of the Kandy Esala Perahera (see boxed text, p159).

Neloufer de Mel's *Women and the Nation's Narrative* probes Sri Lankan 20th-century history from a women's perspective. It's an important work that confronts conventional views about caste, colonialism, guerrilla warfare and morality.

At www.onlinewomenin politics.org/lk/lkorgs.htm you'll find links to various women's organisations. The Centre for Women's Research (www.cenwor.lk) has information on the estimated 900,000 Sri Lankan women working as domestic help in overseas countries.

MASKS FOR DANCE & FESTIVALS

There are three basic mask types: *kolam, sanni* and *raksha.*

The *kolam* mask – a form of disguise – is used in *kolam* masked dance-dramas. *Kolam* masks are generally only for dance, and not for sale to tourists.

The *sanni* mask is worn by dancers to impersonate and exorcise disease demons that range from blindness to outpourings of bile and phlegm. The grotesque ensemble is bookended by two cobras, and other cobras sprout from within the demon's head.

Raksha masks are used in processions and festivals. Of the 25 varieties, the *naga raksha* (cobra) masks feature protruding eyeballs and pointed teeth, and are topped with a coiffure of writhing cobras.

Most masks are made from a light wood called *kaduru,* which is smoke-dried before the mask is carved. The mask's base colour is yellow, trimmed with other colours, and glazed with resin powder and oil.

Watch masks being made in Ambalangoda and visit the museums detailing the mask-making process (p116).

Now considered Sri Lanka's national dance there are five types of Kandyan dance: *pantheru,* named after a tambourine-like instrument used to accompany dances after victory in war; *udekki,* involving the dancer singing and drumming; *naiyaki,* a graceful dance performed at the lighting of lamps before festivals; *ves,* the most sacred and most frequently seen dance, particularly in the Kandy *perahera* (procession); and *vannamas,* inspired by nature and deities.

Male Kandyan dancers wear a wide skirtlike garment. The dancer's bare chest is covered with necklaces of silver and ivory, with bangles of beaten silver on the arms and ankles. The dances combine great leaps and energetic back flips accompanied by the complex rhythms of the *geta bera,* a double-ended drum combining monkey and cow hides.

MASKED DANCE-DRAMA

There are four folk-drama dance forms: *kolam, sokari, nadagam* and *pasu.* Best known is the *kolam* (Tamil for costume or guise). *Kolam* has up to 53 characters, many with grotesque deformities, like bulging eyes and nostrils emanating tusks and cobras.

Performances, with singers and drummers, are traditionally held over several nights at Sri Lankan New Year (late April). After songs praising the Buddha, the master of ceremonies explains that *kolam* originated when a pregnant Indian Queen had cravings to see a masked dance-drama.

The best-known *kolam* plays are the *Sandakinduru Katava* and the *Gothayimbala Katava.* The *Sandakinduru Katava* is about a king who is out hunting and kills a man-bird creature who is later restored to life by the Buddha. In the *Gothayimbala Katava,* a demon falls in love with a married woman and is beheaded by her avenging husband. The demon regenerates itself over and over, until the husband is rescued by a forest deity. You're most likely to see *kolam* and devil dancing at Ambalangoda (p115).

DEVIL DANCE

Traditionally, devil dancing was performed to free a person from evil spirits or bad luck. There are many types of devil dance: *sanni yakku* exorcises the disease demon, *kohomba kankariya* ensures prosperity and the *bali* honours heavenly beings.

Three beings must be appeased: demons, deities and semidemons. Before the dance begins, palm-leaf shrines dedicated to each of the beings are built outside the victim's house. The beings must be tempted out into an arena. The dancers (all men) go through an astounding athletic routine, costumed in red headdresses hung with palm leaves and with white cloths wound tightly round their hips (which stays firm despite their gyrations). All the while, bare-chested drummers beat out a frantic rhythm on the *yak bera* (a double-ended, cylindrical drum). At the climax the dancers put on masks representing the demons, and the demon causing the distress is confronted by the chief exorcist. He exhorts, threatens and sometimes even bribes the demon to force it away.

Theatre

Theatre moved into the cities when a Parsi theatre company from Bombay (Mumbai) introduced *nurti* (new theatre) to Colombo audiences in the 19th century. *Nurti* was a blend of European and Indian theatrical conventions: stage scenery, painted backdrops and wings, an enclosed theatre, costumes, and music and song. It was to spawn a new profession – play writing – with writers drawing inspiration from Sanskrit drama and other sources, including Shakespeare.

The arrival of cinema almost killed off theatre. However, a breakthrough came in 1956 with *Maname* (King's Name), a play written by university professor Ediriweera Sarachchandra. It was staged in *nadagam,* a form of Sinhalese drama that developed from Catholic pageants. In *nadagam* the absence of masks and the inclusion of different musical forms enabled a greater audience connection with the plays. This combination of familiar folk tale and accessible staging made the play an instant hit and marked the beginning of a new era of experimentation and creativity. Sarachchandra is recognised as the father of modern Sri Lankan theatre, and his plays are still wildly popular.

Today Sri Lankan theatre is undertaking many innovative ventures on contemporary issues, particularly on the healing of trauma in the aftermath of conflict. Such projects are sponsored by the Alliance Française, the British Council and the Goethe Institut. It's worthwhile checking out what's on when you arrive in Colombo; for details, see p77. For listings on theatre venues in Colombo, see p97.

If you're in the Hill Country in May, look out for *Kamankoothu,* an ancient folk drama that depicts the story of Kama, the Hindu god of love (akin to Cupid). The performance lasts for several days, with whole villages taking part.

Literature

Sri Lanka has a rich literary tradition drawn from Sinhalese and Tamil cultures, with colonisation also having a marked influence.

Contemporary writing tends to deal with the trauma of war and with romance. A good place to start your discovery of contemporary Sri Lankan literature is at the annual Galle Literary Festival (p128).

SINHALESE LITERATURE

The first works of Sinhalese literature were composed by monks as they were the most educated and literate members of society. The earliest surviving texts date from the 10th century AD and focus on the study of Pali and Buddhism. In two major works, the Mahavamsa (Major Chronicle) and the Culavamsa (Minor Chronicle), the monks recorded Sinhalese history. Generally regarded as part history, part myth, the chronicles relate the arrival of Vijaya, Sri Lanka's first king, the lives of the royals and the coming of Buddhism.

Sri Lankan Theater in a Time of Terror: Political Satire in a Permitted Space by Ranjini Obeyesekere details the creative surge in Sri Lankan theatre during the time of the civil war in the 1980s.

Courageous, poetic and with a strong sense of place, Chandani Lokugé's novels *If the Moon Smiled* and *Turtle Nest* tackle the alarming and the elegant while evoking past and present Sri Lanka.

OLA & THE SINHALA SCRIPT

The elegant swirls and flourishes of the 58-letter Sinhala script developed partly due to the nature of the *ola* (the young leaves of the talipot palm), Sri Lanka's first writing material. Tough, with a distinct fibre, the leaves tend to be split by straight lines, but swirls don't cause damage.

Before they are used, the *ola* are boiled, dried, rolled and stretched. A steel-tipped stylus etches the writing, after which the leaf is buffed with a sticky blend of charcoal and *dummala* oil, made from fossilised resin from the paddy fields. Most of the resin is wiped off, emphasising the blackened letters. The resin also preserves the leaves, which can last as long as 500 years. The Sinhalese classics, the Pali canon, the Mahavamsa and numerous Jataka tales were engraved on *ola*.

You can sometimes see *ola* being inscribed by students outside the National Museum in Colombo.

The Thupavamsa (Chronicle of the Great Stupa) records the construction of the huge Ruvanvelisaya Dagoba (p232) in Anuradhapura. In the 13th century the works of Gurulugomi (who wrote in almost pure Sinhala) began a transition from Pali to Sinhala in Sri Lankan literature.

Poetry was an early literary form. The graffiti on the Sigiriya mirror wall (p219) is a fine example. The Jataka tales, stories of the Buddha's past lives, were also recorded in verse. Poems also explored the peace of the Buddha and the ravages of war.

From the mid-19th century the focus shifted from only religious subjects, and printing presses produced newspapers, periodicals and novels. Works by Buddhist writer and political activist Piyadasa Sirisena, as well as those by Martin Wickramasinghe and WA Silva, were very popular in the early part of the 20th century. Wickramasinghe's *Gamperaliya* (Overturning of the Village), which subsequently developed into a trilogy, received much critical praise for its exploration of Western influence on village life.

TAMIL LITERATURE

Tamil writing emanates from a strong literary tradition dating back over 2000 years. It shares its literary origins with Sanskrit, but while Sanskrit ceased to be a spoken language, Tamil continued and survived – still voiced and written much as it has been for many centuries. The first Tamil writing was poetry, possibly derived from songs. One of the most loved Tamil works, *The Kural*, was written by the poet Tiruvalur. While its writing is dated anywhere from 200 BC to AD 600, its 1330 couplets advocating compassion are as relevant today as when they were written.

See http://tamilelibrary
.org/teli/srilitt.html for
an indepth analysis of 50
years of Sri Lankan Tamil
literature.

The period from the late centuries BC to early centuries AD was a fruitful time for Tamil literature, with the Sangam – the academy of literature in Tamil Nadu (India) – nurturing a rapidly growing literary scene. Sri Lankan Tamils date their first poet, Eelattu Poothanthevanar, from the Sangam period. Two epics, *Silappadhikaram* and *Manimekhalai*, favourably compared with the Ramayana and Mahabharata, were produced by Tamil poets of the late Sangam period. The sciences, including astrology and medicine, were also favoured topics.

With such rich literary beginnings, Sri Lankan Tamil writing developed a strong sense of place and a robust awareness of the Tamils' social and political context. It has also been a significant influence within the Tamil diaspora. Through the colonial years, particularly the British period, Tamil writing explored and analysed the colonial experience. Tamil newspapers fostered greater debate and dissemination of information, vital in the pre-independence climate.

Post independence the literary debate mostly focused on politics. This vibrant literary movement was threatened in 1981 when the library in Jaffna was burnt down by a Sinhalese mob. Thousands of works, including ancient *ola* (the young leaves of the talipot palm) manuscripts, were lost. Local and global efforts re-established the library in March 2004. This attack, combined with the ongoing civil war, led to Resistance Literature – writing crafted to protect and promote Tamil language, literature and identity. For a poignant personal account, see boxed text, p278.

CONTEMPORARY LITERATURE

Much of Sri Lanka's more recent literature centres on romance and ethnic conflict. *Born to Labour* by CV Vellupillai describes the lives of tea-estate workers, while *Medusa's Hair* by Gannanath Obeyesekere is valuable for understanding Kataragama's fire-walking ceremony. For an entrée into the Burgher community, look at Carl Muller's *The Jam Fruit Tree*, for which he won the 1993 Gratiaen Prize. Jean Arasanayagam's poetry and short stories provide vivid and intimate accounts of the upheavals in Sri Lanka.

The country's best-known writer is Arthur C Clarke (1917–2008), the futurist and author of *2001: A Space Odyssey*. Clarke lived in Sri Lanka from the 1950s, and his book *The Foundations of Paradise*, set on the imaginary island of Taprobane, features places remarkably like Adam's Peak and Sigiriya.

Sri Lankan children know well the folk tales of Mahadenamutta, a village know-it-all who surrounds himself with blindly loyal sycophants. Mahadenamutta is the ideal character for satirical pieces about the exploits of contemporary politicians. The stories are regularly reproduced in newspapers and, with a bit of insight, can usually be regarded as more credible than some of the surrounding editorial.

Many Sri Lankan writers have migrated to other countries and written evocative and courageous works about their native land. Shyam Selvadurai explores relationships and societal expectations, particularly in regard to gay issues. His *Cinnamon Gardens* is a gutsy account of caste life in early-20th-century Sri Lanka, and *Funny Boy* is the story of a gay Tamil boy coming of age in Colombo in the years preceding the civil war.

Monkfish Moon, a book of nine short stories by Romesh Gunesekera, provides a diverse glimpse at Sri Lanka's ethnic conflict. Gunesekera was nominated for the Booker Prize in 1994 for his novel *Reef*, which also examines lives changed irrevocably by war.

The most well-known Sri Lankan expat writer is Michael Ondaatje, born in Colombo, but resident in Canada since 1962. Best known for the Nobel Prize–winning *The English Patient*, Ondaatje's Sri Lankan-themed books include *Running in the Family*, a comic and reflective memoir of his Colombo family in the 1940s, and *Anil's Ghost*, a stark and raw novel set against the background of the civil war in the 1980s and 1990s.

See the sidebar reviews and p19 for more titles.

Cinema

The first Sri Lankan-made film, *Kadavunu Poronduwa* (Broken Promise), was shown in Colombo in 1947, allowing audiences to hear Sinhala spoken on screen for the first time. Movies continued to be produced mostly in Indian studios though, until director Sirisena Wimalaweera opened a studio in Sri Lanka in 1951. Lester James Peries' first feature film, *Rekawa* (Line of Destiny), is considered the first truly Sinhalese film. It attempted to realistically portray Sri Lankan life and was the first film in Sri Lanka shot on location outside a studio.

Elephant dung is part of a curious concoction that is made into paper for stationery, artwork and books. The Millennium Elephant Foundation (p157) does a fine line in greeting cards. Don't worry – they're all odour free.

Following the success of the annual Galle Literary Festival, the inaugural Galle Film Festival was held in late October 2008. The annual event is a rare opportunity to view classic Sri Lankan films. See www.galle filmfestival.com.

Contemporary Sri Lankan directors tend to explore themes directly related to war. *Death on a Full Moon Day,* made in 2000 by Prasanna Vithanage, explores the story of a father who refuses to accept the death of his soldier son.

Indian director Deepa Mehta had to film *Water* (2005) in Sri Lanka after shooting in India was banned due to the film's volatile storyline involving a intercaste relationship. Filming recommenced in Sri Lanka following a four-year hiatus.

Today, despite some government support through the **National Film Corporation of Sri Lanka** (www.srilankafilmcorp.com), the local film industry struggles to compete with Bollywood movies, TV and the budget appeal of pirated Malaysian DVDs at knockdown prices. Most local cinemas only struggle to stay afloat by screening a diet of Bollywood epics and tawdry B-grade action flicks that usually go straight to DVD in Western markets.

Films shot on location in Sri Lanka include David Lean's *Bridge on the River Kwai* (1957) and Steven Speilberg's *Indiana Jones and the Temple of Doom* (1984).

With a wide variety of natural landscapes and an abundance of ancient and colonial architecture, the country may take off as a preferred location following the resolution of the civil war.

Music

For links to more information about contemporary Sri Lankan popstars, see the list at http://cityhits.blogspot.com/. It's also a good place to find out about electronica, hip-hop and dance gigs in Colombo.

Sri Lankan music has been influenced by Buddhism and Hinduism, the rhythms of the African slaves, the melodies of Europe and the energy of India.

Initially *baila*s (folk tunes with an African beat) were accompanied by guitar and the beat of drums or handclapping. Now electrified instruments strum the accompaniment. The most popular *baila* singers include Desmond de Silva – a legend in the 1970s and still going strong – and the more contemporary Shanaka and his Sri Lankan Vibes, who incorporate *baila*, hip-hop and pop.

One of Sri Lanka's best-known composers is Ananda Samarakone (1911–62), who wrote the Sri Lankan national anthem. Samarakone studied in India, where the work of the great poet and composer Tagore, who had transformed Indian writing and musical composition by refusing to work within their traditional forms, had a significant impact on him. Inspired, Samarakone introduced new musical and lyrical forms that involved great complexity.

Until the late 1990s Sri Lanka's popular music was mainly film music, Hindi pop and imitations of Western pop. The same influences linger, with most Sri Lankan pop now an amalgam of hip-hop, Hindi pop and soft Western pop.

Grammy Award–nominated hip-hop star and artist M.I.A. (Mathangi Arulpragasam) is of Tamil descent and was forced to leave northern Sri Lanka with her family as a refugee. Her father was an activist instrumental in establishing the Eelam Revolutionary Organisation of Students (EROS), a London-based collective in support of the LTTE.

Acts to watch out for include heavy metal from Stigmata, R&B from Bathiya and Santhush, Iraj and Samitha, and Centigradz, and hip-hop from wannabe rapper Ranidu. Delon is a Sri Lankan rapper based in the USA.

For more traditional sounds, visit the Kandy temple at dawn, where you'll hear the shrill conch shell as it announces morning *puja*. There, and throughout the island, you'll hear the animated rhythms of the Kandy drums, particularly at wedding celebrations.

For those with a classical bent, the **Sri Lankan Symphony Orchestra** (SOSL; ☎ 011-250 1209; www.symphonyorchestraofsrilanka.org) has occasional concerts in Colombo. See its website for details.

Architecture

Sri Lankan architecture is an expression of ancient and modern, aesthetic and functional. The simplest and most economical structure is the *cadjan* (coconut-frond matting) dwelling, made from timber frames covered with woven coconut fronds. No doubt they're similar to the structures favoured in ancient times by ordinary people. Particularly suited to Sri Lanka's climate, the *cadjan* dwellings' availability and low cost made them especially effective after the 2004 tsunami.

GEOFFREY BAWA – 'BRINGING POETRY TO PLACE'

The most famous of Sri Lanka's architects, Geoffrey Bawa (1919–2003) fused ancient and modern influences in his work. Architect Ranjith Dayaratne described it as 'bringing poetry to place'.

Using courtyards and pathways, Bawa developed pleasing connections between the interior and exterior of his structures. These connections frequently included contemplative spaces, as well as framed areas that enabled glimpses of spaces yet to be entered.

His designs were based within the environment. And he was not averse to the environment claiming his structures – at times he encouraged jungle growth along walls and roofs.

While Bawa created aesthetic beauty, he was also concerned with the functional aspects of architecture, opening and exposing structures to air and light while ensuring shelter and protection from harsh climatic elements.

His approach was important not only for its originality but also for its influence on architecture in Sri Lanka and abroad.

Bawa's work included the parliament house in Colombo and the Kandalama Hotel (p216) in Dambulla.

The historic building that houses Colombo's Gallery Cafe (p95) used to be Bawa's office and is now used as an exhibition space for art and photography.

BUDDHIST

One of the most striking features of Sri Lanka's architectural landscape is the dagoba – those smooth, limewashed bell-shaped structures that protrude above the treeline along the coast and dot the dry zone at Anuradhapura. The dagoba is actually a chamber for holding 'relics', the corporal remains or possessions of the Buddha or enlightened monks, along with other sacred material. In ancient times the *hataraes kotuwa*, a square structure above the lower bell shape, contained the relics, but later they were lodged in a granite piece (known as the mystic stone) just below the spire. You can see these stones at museums in Anuradhapura (p236) and Mihintale (p241).

Rising from the *hataraes kotuwa* is the furled ceremonial parasol called the *chatta*. The dagoba is very often surrounded by a *vahalakada* (platform), used by devotees to make a clockwise circuit; stairways to the *vahalakada* pass through gates situated at the cardinal points.

Dagobas are made of solid brick, which is then plastered and limewashed. Early dagobas were probably simple structures, but they became increasingly sophisticated. The Ruvanvelisaya and Mirisavatiya Dagobas, built in the 2nd century in Anuradhapura by King Dutugemunu, had their foundations established well below ground (stamped down by energetic elephants, the legend says). The Jetavanarama Dagoba (p235) in Anuradhapura, which dates from the 3rd century and is the focus of a gigantic reconstruction project, is nearly as high as Egypt's Great Pyramid of Khufu (Cheops). As it is mainly a repository for relics, the dagoba is not usually entered.

A uniquely Sinhalese architectural concept is the *vatadage* (circular relic house). Today you can see *vatadages* in Anuradhapura and Polonnaruwa, but perhaps the finest example is at Medirigiriya. The *vatadage* consists of a small central dagoba flanked by images of the Buddha and encircled by columns. It's thought that long ago these columns supported a wooden roof, but all traces of early wooden architecture have now disappeared.

Another Sinhalese style is the *gedige*, a hollow temple with thick walls topped by a trussed roof. Often the walls are so thick that stairways can be built into them. There are a number of *gediges* in Anuradhapura and Polonnaruwa and Nalanda (p214).

The Temple of the Sacred Tooth Relic (p159) is a magnificent example of Kandyan architecture. Surrounded by a large moat, long since dried up, from

To compare the Sri Lankan stupa with those in other Buddhist countries, see www.buddhamind.info/leftside/arty/build/styles.htm.

Gracing many temple courtyards, the bodhi tree (also known as *pipal*, or *Ficus religiosa*) is an important symbol of Sri Lanka. The Buddha achieved enlightenment under a bodhi tree – *bodhi* means 'enlightenment' – and a cutting from that sacred tree still grows at Anuradhapura (p232).

outside its most obvious feature is a *pathiruppuwa,* an octagonal structure from where the king traditionally delivered important public communications. Inside, the lower of the temple's two storeys contains an open pillared area that leads to several smaller shrines. The Audience Hall is a large impressive space with columns, edged with paintings and reliefs.

Geoffrey Bawa: The Complete Works by David Robson is a comprehensive book with stunning images. Detailing the life and work of the acclaimed architect, Robson cleverly demonstrates how Bawa's early life influenced his later work.

HINDU

In Sri Lanka, Hindu temples, known as *kovils,* are mostly dedicated to Shiva or Murugan. They consist of a prayer hall and shrine room, and there is a covered space that allows worshippers to take the ritual clockwise walk. The *sikhara,* a central dome- or pyramid-shaped edifice, towers above the shrine room. Walls and domes are often covered with ornate murals. Some temples have *gopurams* (gateway towers) that soar towards the heavens with brightly painted deities and saints.

EUROPEAN

The colonising Europeans also impacted on Sri Lanka's architecture. The Portuguese introduced high-pitched roofs and covered verandas. This style continued well after the Dutch defeated the Portuguese because, barred from administrative duties, they turned to the building trade to earn a living. The Dutch influence is characterised by fort ramparts and sturdy churches and administrative buildings. These robust features are often softened by ornamental edifices, small arches and delicate stained-glass windows. The historic Fort (p127) in Galle has wonderful examples of the Dutch style. The Dutch changed the Portuguese forts to suit their own architectural requirements, and the English continued the tradition. The English style is particularly apparent in the buildings in hill stations such as Nuwara Eliya. The addition of a pink post office and red post boxes are just other surreal touches.

Painting & Sculpture

Check out http://kooiiart .blogspot.com/, a regular and vey readable blog on the emerging Sri Lankan arts scene.

Images of the Buddha dominate the work of Sri Lankan sculptors. Limestone, which is plentiful, was used for early works (which means they haven't weathered well), but a variety of other materials has been used over the centuries, including jade, rock crystal, marble, emerald, pink quartz, ivory, coral and sometimes wood or metal. The Buddha is represented in three poses – sitting, standing or lying – with his hands arranged in various *mudras* (positions): *dhyana mudra,* the meditative pose, where hands rest lightly in the lap, with the right hand on the left hand; *abhaya mudra,* with right hand raised, conveying protection; and *vitarka mudra,* where the index finger touches the thumb, symbolising teaching.

The staircases at Sri Lanka's ancient temples and palaces reveal a wealth of finely sculpted detail, with the elaborately carved moonstones a notable feature. The bottom of either side of a staircase often has guardstones. A mythical beast, *makara* (a cross between a lion, a pig and an elephant), often stretches its form along the balustrade.

The first Galle Art Trail was held in conjunction with the inaugural Galle Film Festival in 2008. Works by local artists are displayed in Galle's heritage buildings and there are regular workshops and craft markets. See www.galearttrail.com.

Other notable examples of sculpture include the four *vahalkadas* (solid panels) at the Kantaka Chetiya (p239) at Mihintale.

Painting, like dance and music, was not encouraged by orthodox Buddhists, yet artists (influenced by Indian conventions) still produced works of art, including the shapely nymphs on the walls of Sigiriya (p219). However, most painting centred on sacred themes; the best examples are at Dambulla and Polonnaruwa.

Kolams (also called *rangoli*), the rice-flour designs that adorn thresholds in Tamil areas, have a purpose beyond decoration. The *kolams* are drawn by women at sunrise, and the rice flour is then devoured by

CULTURAL DOS & DON'TS

- You may see beggars in Sri Lanka, but not often and not many. More likely you'll be approached by people claiming to be collecting money for charity. The most well-organised of them usually have a clipboard and a badge with an official-looking logo. They are almost always con artists.
- Children may also ask for sweets, but if you respond you will encourage begging. It's best to donate to a reputable charity.
- Thousands of Sri Lankan children are sexually abused by locals as well as foreigners. If you suspect that such crimes are happening, follow the reporting procedures at the website for **End Child Prostitution & Trafficking** (ECPAT; www.ecpat.net).
- At temples, always remove shoes (and usually head coverings) and dress respectfully.
- Comply with 'No Photography' and 'No Flash' signs in temples and ancient sites as the use of a flash can irreparably damage frescoes and murals.
- Do not purchase products made of ivory, coral or turtle shells.
- Only seek the services of qualified Ayurvedic practitioners.
- Always use your right hand when giving or receiving.
- Kissing and hugging in public is not appropriate behaviour.
- Ask your guest house to boil water for you and recycle your water bottle.
- Avoid plastic bags. They're everywhere in Sri Lanka and badly damage the environment.
- For information on responsible hiking, see boxed text, p72.
- For information on responsible diving and snorkelling, see boxed text, p290.

small creatures, symbolising a reverence for all life, even the most small and insignificant.

Sri Lanka is rapidly developing a vibrant contemporary art scene. Locally woven and dyed fabrics are fashioned into striking garments, while numerous new art galleries, mainly in Colombo, exhibit work that is uniquely Sri Lankan: strong and evocative, and expressing traditional themes in modern styles. The **Sapumal Foundation** (Map pp84-5; 2/34 Barnes Pl, Col 7; admission free; 10am-1pm Thu-Sat) exhibits contemporary Sri Lankan art, while **Gallery Cafe** (Map pp84-5; ☎ 258 2162; 2 Alfred House Rd, Col 3; 11am-11pm) has exhibitions of painting and photography. For more art galleries in Colombo, see p89.

For a taste of some of Sri Lanka's stunning textiles and design, visit **Barefoot** (Map pp84-5; ☎ 258 0114; www.barefootceylon.com; 704 Galle Rd, Col 3). See p97 for details of other shops selling Sri Lankan crafts.

For more-detailed information on Sri Lankan art, visit www.artsrilanka .org. It's an absolute labour of love with online images of many Sri Lankan paintings.

Pottery

The art of crafting pots, often made of red terracotta with symbolic designs, encompasses beauty, utility and unique style. The pottery industry has recently received a boost with increased government funding.

SPORT

It's a cliché, but true – cricket is another religion in Sri Lanka. Sri Lankans may play field hockey, netball, soccer, tennis and rugby, but cricket outruns them all. Cricketers are current-day deities. Innings, wickets and scores are mantras throughout the nation, and cricket pitches (including on road sides and in forest clearings) are temples. As you travel around the country, you'll see every second billboard (literally) featuring a Sri Lankan

To see if Sri Lanka is keeping up its ranking on world cricket – number 6 at the time of writing – see www.cricinfo .com/db/NATIONAL/SL/.

Cricket newbies often struggle with the nuances of the sport. To understand the difference between gully and a googly, and square leg and leg before wicket, check out the tongue-in-cheek but informative guide at news.bbc .co.uk/sportacademy /bsp/hi/cricket/rules /html/default.stm.

cricketing hero extolling the virtues of everything from life insurance and mobile phones to biscuits and Coca Cola.

Sri Lanka does well in the shorter one-day and 20–20 forms of the sport, and won the Cricket World Cup in 1996 and were runners-up to Australia in 2007. The 2011 Cricket World Cup is being cohosted by Sri Lanka, India and Bangladesh. Pakistan was originally another host country, but this was changed after a terrorist attack on the Sri Lankan cricket team in Lahore in March 2009.

It's easy to see a big match – the main venue is the Premadasa Stadium in Kettarama, Colombo. Other venues include the Sinhalese Sports Club (SSC) in Cinnamon Gardens, Colombo, and ovals at Moratuwa, Borella (Sara Stadium), Kandy, Dambulla and Galle. See **Sri Lanka Cricket** (www.sri lankacricket.lk) for more information.

One entirely sedentary sport enjoyed by many Sri Lankans is betting on British horse and dog racing. Throughout Sri Lanka you'll see flashing neon signs announcing betting shops or 'Turf Accountants'.

Racing in Sri Lanka is frowned upon by the Buddhist establishment, so you'll see people in these hole-in-the-wall betting shops avidly studying the day's races in Aintree, Ascot and Hackney. Race commentaries are beamed from Britain, starting at about 6pm.

Local horse racing is restricted to occasional meetings at the racecourse in Nuwara Eliya (p183). The main event of the year is the Governor's Cup meeting held during Sri Lankan New Year in April.

MEDIA

Listen to Sri Lankan news online with live stream- ing at www.slbs.lk. For a younger perspective you can visit www.yesmu sicfm.com or www .tnlrocks.com.

The media in Sri Lanka comes in Sinhala-, Tamil- and English-language forms, and is both state and privately owned. After failed peace nego- tiations began in 2002, the government approved a radio licence for the formerly clandestine Tamil radio station 'Voice of the Tigers'. However, at the time of writing, the 'Voice of the Tigers' was limited to an online broadcast; see **Voice of Tigers** (www.pulikalinkural.com). Following the victory of the Sri Lankan government in the civil war, its future was uncertain.

State-controlled media generally tows the government line, especially regarding coverage of the Sri Lankan civil war. The ongoing ethnic conflict was characterised by wildly differing claims and counter-claims of battle- field success by the government and the LTTE, a situation exacerbated by the fact that journalists were banned from entering combat situations.

Lasantha Wickrama- tunga's final prophetic editorial for the Sunday Leader was completed before he died and published just a few days after his assassination. It's a poignant admission that he knew his days were numbered, and the withering column pulls no punches in pointing the finger of blame for his death. See www .thesundayleader .lk/20090111/editorial -.htm.

Despite this enforced insulation from the dangers of war, Sri Lanka is still regarded as one of the most hazardous countries in the world for journalists. **Free Media Sri Lanka** (www.freemediasrilanka.org), a lobby and advocacy group dedicated to protecting media freedoms and the safety of journalists in Sri Lanka, reported that 25 journalists were either killed or abducted in Sri Lanka across 2007 and 2008. Sri Lanka was ranked 165th out of 173 countries in the Reporters Without Borders 2008 press freedom index, the lowest ranking of any democratic country.

Other independent groups, including Amnesty International and Human Rights, also reported that the targeting of journalists escalated in recent years, especially in the months leading to the battlefield victories of gov- ernment forces in early 2009.

In January 2009 gunmen armed with grenades attacked the offices of Sisara TV, Sri Lanka's main private TV station, days after the state-owned *Daily News* criticised its reporting of the civil war. The following day Lasantha Wickramatunga, editor of the privately owned *Sunday Leader,* was gunned down and killed during Colombo's morning rush hour. Under Wickramatunga's editorship, the *Sunday Leader* was known for opposition to the government's focus on a solely military solution to the civil war, and for stories alleging corruption and self-interest among the country's rich and powerful. At the time of writing Lasantha Wickramatunga's murder was acting as a catalyst for demands for greater press freedom in Sri Lanka.

The internet is growing as an independent media space for Sri Lankans to debate and comment on their society, although access to the overseas-based **TamilNet** (www.tamilnet.com), a pro-LTTE website, is banned. The worst of racist anti-Tamil rhetoric is on display at the similarly dubbed spoof website, **Tamilnet.TV** (www.tamilnet.tv). A more balanced conversation on Sri Lankan society is available at **Groundviews** (www.groundviews.org).

Sri Lankans can choose from 10 daily newspapers, 10 radio stations and 10 TV channels. For quick links to the media visit www.abyznewslinks .com/srila.htm.

Food & Drink

Sri Lanka boasts a unique and exciting cuisine, shaped by the island's bounty and the influence of traders, immigrants and colonisers. In a world awash with more well-known cuisines, like Indian, Thai and Vietnamese, Sri Lankan cuisine is little known outside of the island's arcing coastline.

The distinctiveness of the island's cuisine comes from the freshness of its herbs and spices and the methods used to grind, pound, roast, temper and combine. Roasting the spices a little more, or a little less, delivers a very different outcome. The oil that distributes the flavours may be vegetable, sesame or, for a richer taste, coconut. Varieties of rice offer unique textures, fragrances and flavours. Curries may be prepared within delicious sauces, or they may be 'dry'.

Regional differences in cuisine are more about availability of ingredients than ethnicity. In the North the palmyra tree reigns, and its roots, flowers, fruits and seeds produce dishes ranging from curries to syrups, sweets, cakes and snacks. In the South rice is considered indispensable; fish and jackfruit are popular, too. In the fertile Hill Country there are vegetables and mutton, but fewer fish and spices.

In all parts of the country, the influence of outsiders is never far from the menu. Muslim restaurants serve up perfect flat breads and samosas introduced by Arab traders. Celebratory cakes often have a Dutch or Portuguese touch, and deliciously sweet desserts concocted from jaggery (brown sweet made from the *kitul* palm), coconut milk, cloves and cardamom are redolent of Malay traders from the spice islands further east.

> Sri Lankan cuisine shows influences from Arab traders, Malay navigators, Portuguese, Dutch and British colonists, and South Indian neighbours. Once you try it, you may wonder why you haven't heard more about it before.

STAPLES & SPECIALITIES

Rice is the main staple of Sri Lankan cuisine, and it is usually served at every meal – plain, spiced, in meat juices, with curd (buffalo-milk yoghurt) or tamarind, or with milk. Different varieties are cooked with subtle spices.

Rice flour is the basis of two popular dishes: hoppers (also called *ah-ppa* or *appam*), which are bowl-shaped pancakes, and dosas *(thosai)*. These paper-thin pancakes are usually served stuffed with spiced vegetables.

Popular breakfasts include hoppers, bread dipped in curry, and *pittu,* a mixture of rice flour and coconut steamed in a bamboo mould. *Kola kanda* (porridge of rice, coconut, green vegetables and herbs) is very nutritious. At lunch or dinner try some short eats (p59), or dine on a banquet of rice and curry.

> The word 'hopper' is an English adaptation of the Tamil word *appa* (rice cakes).

Rice & Curry

Sri Lankan rice and curry comprises small spiced dishes made from vegetables, meat or fish, and served with chutneys and *sambol,* a condiment made from ingredients pounded with chilli.

Most curries include chilli, turmeric, cinnamon, cardamom, coriander, *rampe* (pandanus leaves), curry leaves, mustard, tamarind and coconut milk. Dried fish is also frequently used to season dishes.

Sri Lankan food is slow to prepare, but hot to consume. Having endured centuries of Western complaints about spicy food, Sri Lankans have tempered it for Western palates, but if you like it hot, they'll readily oblige. If it's still not hot enough, just add some *pol sambol,* a chilli and coconut condiment.

If you don't like it hot, just remember the lighter the colour, the more subtle the heat. But if your mouth explodes, just reach for rice, yoghurt or cucumber. It's good to know also that alcohol dissolves chilli oil.

Because Sri Lankan food takes time to prepare, order early in the day and leave the cooks to work their magic.

> Cinnamon is native to Sri Lanka, and was imported to China and Egypt by Arab traders as early as 2000 BC. More than 80% of the world's cinnamon is still grown in Sri Lanka.

Fish & Seafood

Excellent fish and prawns are widespread, and in many coastal towns you'll find crab and lobster. Seer, a tuna-type fish, is a favourite. A southern speciality is the popular *ambulthiyal* (sour fish curry), made with *goraka,* a sour fruit. A simple, grilled fish is usually a less challenging alternative than the fiery flavours of Sri Lankan cuisine.

Sri Lanka exports over 11 million metric tonnes per year of seafood; almost 400 tonnes of that is crab and lobster.

Other Specialities

Hoppers are bowl-shaped pancakes that are skilfully fried over a high flame and sometimes served with an egg or banana in the middle. String hoppers are tangles of steamed noodles, often used instead of rice as a curry dip. At breakfast you might be offered string hoppers rolled up with grated coconut and sweet syrup from the *kitul* palm. Locals refer to them as 'pancakes', a slight misnomer, but still an essential accompaniment with your first coffee of the day.

Chilli lovers will thrive on 'devilled' dishes, where meat is infused with chilli. On your way from Colombo to Kandy, stop to buy a big bag of devilled cashews at Cadjugama (p156).

Lamprais is made from rice, meat and vegetables, all slowly baked in a banana leaf; open the leaf to release the aroma and tempt the senses. The name comes from the Dutch word *lomprijst,* and the dish dates back to the first Dutch settlers in the 17th century.

Desserts & Sweets

Sweets were traditionally eaten at the beginning of the meal, but this is rare now. *Wattalappam* (*vattalappam* in Tamil), a coconut-milk and egg pudding with jaggery and cardamom, is a favourite dessert, while curd with *kitul* (syrup from the *kitul* palm; also called treacle) is good at any time. Hardened *kitul* is jaggery, a candy and all-purpose sweetener. See p63 for other desserts and sweets.

Other Sri Lankan dishes dating from colonial times include Breudher (Dutch Christmas cake) and Bolo Fiado (Portuguese-style layer cake).

Fruit

Sri Lanka's largely tropical climate supports many fruit, including avocados, mangoes, melons, pineapples and guavas. At breakfast don't forget to add a squeeze of lime to your morning papaya.

The wooden-shelled woodapple is used for refreshing drinks, dessert toppings and jam. British writer Anthony Burgess reckoned the spiky-skinned durian tasted 'like eating sweet raspberry blancmange in the lavatory' – definitely an acquired taste, but worth trying by adventurous foodies. Rambutan is so prized that growers guard their trees to outwit poachers.

In season from July to September, mangosteen tastes like strawberries and grapes combined. The jackfruit, with its orange-yellow segments, is the world's biggest fruit. It tastes good fresh, or cooked up in a curry where it assumes the consistency of chicken.

Guava is a favourite food of the fruit-eating flying foxes you'll see soaring en masse away from the Peradeniya Botanic Gardens at dusk. They're the same species you'll also see unfortunately electrocuted on power lines. Ouch.

DRINKS
Nonalcoholic Drinks

In Sri Lanka's heat it's always wise to carry water. Bottled water is available everywhere, but an environmentally responsible alternative is to refill your bottle. Guest houses will boil water for you the night before.

Most Sri Lankans drink tea with spoonfuls of sugar. If you don't have a sweet tooth, be very assertive about lowering the dose.

Sri Lankans don't drink much coffee, and the local stuff can be rough and ready. It will quench your morning caffeine cravings, but outside of Colombo you'll only find a few places serving a decent espresso.

Lime juice is excellent. Have it with soda water, but ask for the salt or sugar to be separate. If not, you could be in for another serious sugar hit. Indian restaurants and sweet shops are a good spot for a *lassi* (yoghurt drink seasoned with sugar or salt). Another favourite drink is *faluda*, a syrup-and-milk drink containing soft shards of jelly. An old school and very British alternative is ginger beer – look out for the Elephant or Lion brands.

A refreshing, natural option is *thambili* (king coconut), on sale at roadside stalls everywhere for around Rs 20.

Alcoholic Drinks

Local (Lion Lager and Three Coins) and imported (Carlsberg, Heineken and Corona) beers are available. Both local brews are refreshing, if innocuous, lagers. Lion also sells a very good stout, with a whopping 8% alcohol content. The cosy bar at the Grand Hotel (p187) usually stocks it. Avoid the syrupy sweet local wines.

Other local alcoholic beverages include toddy, a drink made from the sap of palm trees. It has a sharp taste, a bit like cider. There are three types of toddy: toddy made from coconut palms, toddy from *kitul* palms and toddy from palmyras. Toddy dens are on village outskirts, where men can drink without disturbing others. It's usually a pretty tawdry scene. Fermented and refined toddy becomes arrack. Kalutara (p110), 40km south of Colombo, is the toddy and arrack capital. The best mixer for arrack is the local ginger ale.

Note that alcohol isn't sold on *poya* (full moon) holidays.

CELEBRATIONS

As a symbol of life and fertility, rice is the food for festivities. The Buddha is said to have derived energy from *kiri bath* (coconut-milk rice). *Kiri bath* is a baby's first solid food, and is also the food newlywed couples feed each other.

Dumplings are popular for celebrations, and in northern Sri Lanka the revelry includes gently dropping *kolukattai* (dumplings with edges pressed

Sri Lanka is the third-largest producer of tea in the world – 300,000 tonnes per year. For more interesting facts on Sri Lanka's tea, visit www.pureceylontea.com/srilankatea.htm.

The health benefits of drinking tea are considerable. Organic green tea has more than six times the level of antioxidants than spinach and cauliflower. Pretty good news if you're not a big fan of vegetables.

ESSENTIAL EATING & DRINKING HIGHLIGHTS

- Listening expectantly to the rhythmic chop-chop-chopping of the *kotthu rotti* (doughy pancake chopped and fried with meat and vegetables) maker. At the Kandy Muslim Hotel (p166) it adds a percussive soundtrack to the compelling buzz of commerce and three-wheelers outside.
- Kicking back with a gin and tonic in the bar at the Hill Club (p186) in Nuwara Eliya, before diving into the old-school colonial excesses of the formal set-course dinner. Make sure you linger to experience one of Sri Lanka's best billiard rooms.
- Melting into the sunset on Galle Face Green (p87) in Colombo with a few prawn *vadai* (deep-fried snacks made from lentil flour and spices) – don't forget the tangy chilli sauce – before retiring across the road to the Veranda bar at the Galle Face Hotel (p96).
- Taking a roadside break and recharging with a fresh *thambili* (king coconut). For just Rs 20 you'll get a super refreshing drink. Don't forget to scoop out the delicately sweet coconut flesh after you're finished.
- Deciding which curry to sample first as you're surrounded by the table full of options of a freshly prepared personal banquet at your family-run guest house in Ella (p198). Maybe the organic sweet-and-sour eggplant, or the surprisingly subtle garlic curry. Decisions, decisions.
- Buying fresh seafood from a fisherman on the south coast (p123), and then getting it cooked to perfection at your favourite end-of-the-day, sand-between-your-toes restaurant.

to resemble teeth) on a toddler's head while the family make wishes for the infant to develop healthy teeth. Sweet dumplings, *mothagam,* are offered to Ganesh in prayer.

Hindus celebrate the harvest at Thai Pongal in January. *Pongal* (milk boiled with rice and jaggery) is offered to the sun god in thanksgiving. The rice is then eaten in celebration of the harvest and its life-sustaining qualities.

Ramadan ends with the breaking of the fast and the Eid-ul-Fitr festival. Muslims eat dates in memory of the Prophet Mohammed, and then *congee* (rice cooked with spices, coconut milk and meat). On Eid-ul-Fitr, Muslims share food with family, friends and neighbours.

Aurudu (Sri Lankan New Year) is another time for celebration. After the sacred activities, feasting begins with *kiri bath* followed by *kaung* (oil cake), a Sri Lankan favourite. Food is always shared at New Year, stressing harmony among family, friends and neighbours.

> Don't expect a Guinness-style experience from Lion Breweries' Stout. Like the stouts brewed in the warmer climes of India, Jamaica and Australia, it's a tad sweeter than Dublin's finest. Expect coffee and chocolate flavours that go surprisingly well with Sri Lankan desserts.

WHERE TO EAT & DRINK

The best places to eat in Sri Lanka are usually private homes. Sri Lanka has never had a traditional dining-out culture, but tourism is slowly changing this, and in Colombo and traveller destinations, you'll find restaurants, cafes and bars.

Family-run guest houses are the best alternative to eating at someone's home. Most places tend to subdue the traditional fiery heat of Sri Lankan cuisine, so speak up if you want a spicy real-deal authenticity to your meal. One of the finest places to eat home-cooked food in a guest-house setting is Ella (p198). Most guest houses have their own vegie gardens and the average rice and curry meal showcases up to eight dishes. If you're keen, let them know by midafternoon so that they can prepare your meal from scratch.

In the larger upmarket hotels, traditional-style banquets are very popular, but you may end up sharing your meal alongside tour groups.

> Toddy tappers can tap up to 100 trees per day, and each tree may yield from 550L to 800L per year.

Outside of guest houses and resort hotels, Sri Lanka has plenty of places to eat. Simple restaurants – confusingly called 'hotels' – cater to locals with a simple menu of rice and curry. Often there's a lunchtime mini buffet on offer; at around Rs 150 it's a good-value way to fill up. Bakeries also serve short eats (see below), a favourite with busy workers and families.

More substantial restaurants often have a Chinese or Indian focus, and combine a lunchtime buffet with a more expensive á la carte menu later at night. If you're really watching your rupees, make lunch your main meal of the day.

Restaurants usually open between 7am and 10pm. Except in Colombo, most places close early – around 9pm is not uncommon – so it's best to check if you're planning to eat late. The type of food offered may vary during the day, with specific breakfast options and short eats available at opening, a fixed-price buffet at lunch and perhaps an à la carte menu in the evening. Fixed-price rice and curry lunch buffets are a good choice for thrifty travellers.

Most sit-down restaurants add 15% tax to the bill, and many also add a 10% service charge. However, the people waiting on you earn minuscule salaries and tips are usually appreciated.

> Vinodini de Silva's *Cultural Rhapsody, Ceremonial Food and Rituals of Sri Lanka* celebrates the cuisine customs of Sri Lanka across cultures, religions and regions. It's available online at www.vijithayapa.com or at the Vijitha Yapa bookshops in Colombo and Kandy.

Quick Eats

Short eats are meat-stuffed rolls, meat-and-vegetable patties (called cutlets), pastries and *vadai* (deep-fried snacks made from lentil flour and spices).

A plate of short eats is placed on your table, and you're only charged for what you eat. Most bakeries run on a 'two batches a day' system, with piping hot baked goodies coming out of the wood-fired ovens around 7.30am and 2pm daily.

See http://lanka
reviewed.blogspot
.com/for entertaining and
opinionated reviews of
eateries in Colombo and
around Sri Lanka.

Streetside huts (called *kadé* or boutiques by the Sinhalese, and *unavakam* by Tamils) sell *kotthu rotti,* a doughy pancake that is chopped and fried with fillings ranging from chilli and onion to vegetables, bacon and egg. You'll soon become attuned to the evening chop-chop sounds of the *kotthu rotti* maker. Along with the nasal whine of a three-wheeler, it's one of the sounds that will define your trip to Sri Lanka.

Also available from the *kadé* and bakeries are lunch packets. These self-contained food parcels are sold all over the country between 11am and 2pm. Inside you'll usually find rice, curry (generally chicken, fish or beef, though if you're vegetarian, you'll get an egg), curried vegetables and *sambol.* Expect to pay around Rs 100 to 125.

Drinking

If you fancy a beer, most traveller-friendly pubs are open from around 5pm to midnight. Beer is usually only served in larger restaurants and only from around 5.30pm. A few places serve beer at lunchtime, but this is strictly limited to around 11.30am to 2pm. Local men crowd 'wine shops' drinking arrack, toddy and warm beer. Save your rupees for another place, another night, when the beer and the ambience will be more chilled.

VEGETARIANS & VEGANS

Many Sri Lankan prepara-
tions are among the
world's hottest in terms
of chilli content. Good
luck, and remember to
keep a cold bottle of Lion
Lager handy.

Vegetarian food is widely available, and you'll find vegetable curries made from banana (ash plantain), banana flower, breadfruit, jackfruit, mangoes, potatoes, beans and pumpkins. Many short eats, including *rotti* (a doughy pancake) and samosas, are also available as vegetarian options. An accompaniment of *mallung* (spiced green leaves, lightly stir-fried) is common, as is *parripu* curry (*paruppa kari* in Tamil), a pulse curry. Some dishes contain dried Maldive fish, so you may wish to check this if fish is not part of your diet.

EATING WITH KIDS

Sri Lankans love children and children are welcome almost anywhere. They may thrive on the local food, but if not, Sri Lankan hospitality means

---

DIY GUIDE TO SRI LANKAN FOOD

Now that you know your *kitul* (syrup from the *kitul* palm) from your *kolukattai* (dumplings with edges pressed to resemble teeth), it's time to have your own crack at whipping up Sri Lankan cuisine in the kitchen. Unlike nearby India and Thailand, Sri Lanka doesn't have a big network of cookery courses, but there are a few low-key places that can impart the tasty knowledge you're seeking. Once you get home, continue to expand your culinary education online.

- Travellers are welcome to join the skilled kitchen crew at the **Rawana Holiday Resort** (p198) in Ella. Just let them know you're interested the day before. The cost is Rs 440, which also pays for the rice and curry banquet you're helping to prepare. The friendly owners will email you the recipes so that you can try them at home. Cookery classes (Rs 1500) are also available at the **Ella Holiday Inn** (p197) across the road.

- At the **Woodlands Network** (p194) in Bandarawela, you can help pick the organic vegies in the garden across the lane before you start cooking.

- Down in Unawatuna you'll visit the Galle market for provisions before a cookery course with Karuna at **Sonjas Health Good Restaurant** (p133).

- Check out **SriLankaFood.Net** (www.srilankafood.net) for tasty recipes from Aussie Sri Lankan Saronjini.

- More recipes are available online at **Malini's Kitchen** (www.infolanka.com/recipes), **Asia Food** (www.asiafood.org) and **Chandra'ge Sri Lankan Recipes** (www.chandrage.com).

DOS & DON'TS

- Always use your right hand to give and to receive.
- It's acceptable to use or to ask for cutlery. However, if eating with your hand, always use your right hand.
- It's acceptable to drink holding a glass in your left hand.
- Always wash your hands before you eat, for the sake of courtesy as well as hygiene.
- If you're invited home for a meal, remove your shoes before entering the house (although some people no longer follow this custom).

---

that people will go to any length to please children. Most places have a few Western-style dishes and there are the usual pizza and burger options in Colombo and Kandy.

To ease your children into Sri Lankan food, try a breakfast of *pittu*. The coconut-rice combination will be kind to their palates and the round shape may entice them. Also try hoppers (either the pancake or the string variety).

Cashew nut curry is another possibility, and curd and treacle makes an excellent dessert. A *bonda* (deep-fried ball made from lentil flour and spices) also makes a good snack. The profusion of fresh and exciting varieties of fruit should mean that even the fussiest of kids find something they like.

For more information on travelling with children, see p291.

> If a curry is too spicy for younger diners, try dousing the heat of the meat with the addition of a little milk.

HABITS & CUSTOMS

Eating Sri Lankan style is one of travel's greatest pleasures. Take your pick from a variety of locations and occasions. Start the day with a breakfast hopper at an open-air *kadé*. Squatting beside a fire, the hopper maker will gently flip the pancakes on the griddle. After he skilfully slices a tiny, sweet banana hanging near his head, you can wash down the light, crunchy fruit-filled hopper with a pot of hot, sweet tea. Not a bad way to start the day really.

By midafternoon you can look forward to another rice and curry mini banquet. Social events usually begin with light eats and lots of conversation. The main food comes later (often much later), when rice and myriad small curries are set out before you with the aromas from each plate creating a delicious combination.

> European custom often entails a leisurely end to the dining experience. Not so in Sri Lanka, where everyone leaves immediately once they've finished eating.

To fully enjoy the texture of the food, try eating with your fingers, Sri Lankan style. Just note the following etiquette. Once everyone is served, use the fingertips of your right hand to eat the food on your plate. Separate a little rice and gradually add some curry to form a mouthful-sized wad of food. Lift the wad and place it all in your mouth. Don't let the food pass the middle knuckles on your fingers and try not to drop any on the way to your mouth. With a bit of practice you'll be fine after a few attempts. Remove meat from bones with your fingers before you lift mouthful-sized quantities to your mouth. In the more upmarket establishments you will receive a finger bowl, but otherwise just visit the washroom once you're finished.

> Many Sri Lankans value the *gotukola* (pennywort) plant for its medicinal properties; it has been used to treat AIDS, restore memory loss and promote intelligence.

In traditional homes men and visitors may eat first, while the women will eat later. It's normal to take a small gift (chocolates, biscuits or arrack) if you're invited home for a meal. Don't be concerned if it's put aside, as gifts are not usually opened in front of the giver. And if you're out to talk business, it's customary to talk first, then eat.

EAT YOUR WORDS

Getting the food you want in Sri Lanka isn't so hard, as many people speak English. But if you'd like to try the local lingo, here are a few phrases, listed in Sinhala first, then in Tamil. For guidance on pronunciation take a look at p319. Just remember that language and culture are of vital importance to many Sri Lankans, so try to speak Sinhala to Sinhalese and Tamil to Tamils.

The beautifully produced *Sri Lankan Flavours* by talented chef Channa Dassanayaka offers recipes and personal stories of Sinhalese people and food.

May we see the menu?
menoo eka balanna puluvandha? — *unavu pattiyalai paarppomaa?*

What's the local speciality?
mehe visheshayen hadhana dhe monavaadha? — *ingu kidaikkak koodiya visheida unavu enna?*

Could you recommend something?
monavadha hondha kiyala obata kiyanna puluvandha? — *neengal ethaiyum shifaarsu seivingala?*

What dishes are available today, please?
kahmata monarada thiyennay? — *sappida enna irukkiradu?*

I'd like to order rice and curry, please.
bahth denna — *sorum kariyum tharungal*

I'm vegetarian.
mama elavalu vitharai kanne — *naan shaiva unavu shaappidupavan*

I don't eat meat.
mama mas kanne naha — *naan iraichchi shappiduvathillai*

I don't eat chicken, fish or ham.
mama kukul mas, maalu, ho ham kanne naha — *naan koli, meen, pandri iraichchi shaapiduvathillai*

I'm allergic to (peanuts).
mata (ratakaju) apathyayi — *(nilak kadalai) enakku alejee*

No ice in my drink, please.
karunaakarala maghe beema ekata ais dhamanna epaa — *enadu paanaththil ais poda vendaam*

That was delicious!
eka harima rasai! — *adhu nalla rushi!*

Please bring a/the...
... karunaakarala gennah — *... konda varungal*
bill		
bila	*bill*	
fork		
gaarappuvak	*mul karandi*	
glass of water		
vathura veedhuruvak	*thanni oru glass*	
knife		
pihiyak	*kaththi*	
plate		
pingaanak	*oru plate*	

Food Glossary

Food items are shown with the Sinhala name first, then the Tamil name, followed by a definition. Some foods only have a Tamil name, while others are the same in both languages.

RICE & BREADS

ah-ppa	*appam*	hopper (bowl-shaped pancake)
doon thel bath	*nei choru*	ghee rice with green peas
kiri bath	*paat choru*	coconut-milk rice
kotthu rotti	*kotthu rotti*	*rotti* chopped and fried with meat and vegetables

maalu paan	*maalu paan*	bread rolls stuffed with fish
masala dosa	*masala dosa*	*dosa* stuffed with spiced vegetables
pittu	*puttu*	rice flour and coconut steamed in a bamboo mould
rotti	*rotti*	doughy pancake
—	*thayir saatham*	curd (buffalo-milk yoghurt) rice
thosai	*dosa*	paper-thin rice- and lentil-flour pancake

VEGETABLE & FRUIT DISHES

ala thel dala	*urulakkilangu poriyal*	fried spicy potatoes
alukehelkan uyala	*vaalaikkal kari*	green banana curry
kangkung	*pashali keerai kari*	spinach with chilli
kiri kos	*palaakkai kari*	young jackfruit curry
—	*marakari*	mixed vegetables in a mild creamy sauce
murungah kari	*murungakkaai kari*	drumstick (fruit of the *kelor* tree) curry
nelum ala uyala	*thaamarai kilangu kari*	lotus roots in curry
parripu kari	*paruppa kari*	thick curry made from pulses
pathola kari	*pidalanggaai kari*	snake-gourd curry
umbah uyala	*maanggaai kari*	mango curry

MEAT

elu mus kari	*aattiraichi kari*	mutton curry
kukul mas hodhi	*kodzhi kari*	chicken curry
lamprais	*lamprais*	meat and vegetables baked with rice in a banana leaf
ooru mas miris badun	*pandri iraichi kari*	devilled pork

FISH

dhallo uyala	*kanawa meen kari*	cuttlefish black curry
kakuluwo uyala	*nandu kari*	crab curry
dhallo badhun	*kanavaai potiyal*	fried squid
—	*kool*	a dish akin to soup, combining many ingredients
malu hodhi	*meen kari*	fish curry

Sri Lanka is a growing force in the development of organic farming, with organic tea, cashew nuts and spices all being produced in increasing volumes.

SIDE DISHES & ACCOMPANIMENTS

—	*kekkairikkal thayir pachadi*	cucumber and yoghurt
lunu miris	*maashi sambol*	onion and fish *sambol*
mallung	*sundal*	spiced green leaves, lightly stir-fried
pol sambol	*thengaapu sambol*	coconut *sambol*
sambol	*sambol*	chilli condiment
seeni sambol	*seeni sambol*	sweet onion *sambol*
—	*semparathappu-thayir pachadi*	hibiscus flower and yoghurt

SWEETS

ali gyata pera	*butter fruit dessert*	avocado dessert
kiri aluwa	*alva*	sweetmeat made from rice flour, treacle and sometimes cashews
kiri dodol	*dhodhal*	coconut-milk, cashew and jaggery sweets
—	*laddu*	balls of flour sweetened with jaggery and deep-fried
—	*payasam*	sago cooked in coconut milk and jaggery (may contain nuts)

	rasavalli kilangu pudding	yam pudding
thala guli	ellu pahu	sesame sweet balls
wattalappam	vattalappam	coconut milk, egg, cardamom and jaggery pudding

SNACKS

bhoodhi	bonda	deep-fried ball made from lentil flour and spices
godambah	rolles	meat and vegetables wrapped in pastry
mas patis	iraichi patis	deep-fried beef pasties
polos cutlets	pinchu pilaakkai cutlets	jackfruit cutlets
vaddai	vadai	deep-fried doughnut-shaped snack of spiced lentil flour

GENERAL

co-ppuwa	glass	glass
han-duh	karandi	spoon
kiri	paal	milk
koh-pi	kahpee	coffee
lunu	uppu	salt
palathuru	paadham	fruit
seeni	seeree	sugar
thay	te-neer/plan-tea	tea
vathura	than-neer	water
vendhuwa	kooppai	bowl

Environment

THE LAND

Looking a lot like a plump pear, the island country of Sri Lanka dangles into the Indian Ocean off the southern end of India. At roughly 66,000 sq km it's slightly smaller than Ireland, but sustains 4.5 times as many people. That's nearly 21 million souls in a space stretching 433km from north to south and only 244km at its widest point – like the entire population of Australia taking up residence in Tasmania.

Thrust up out of the encircling coastal plains, the southern centre of the island – the core of the pear – is dominated by mountains and tea-plantation-covered hills. The highest point is broad-backed Mt Pidurutalagala (Mt Pedro; 2524m), rising above the Hill Country capital city of Nuwara Eliya. However, the pyramid profile of 2243m-high Adam's Peak (Sri Pada) is better known and far more spectacular.

Hundreds of waterways channel abundant rain from the south-central wet-zone uplands – haven of the country's surviving rainforests – down through terraced farms, orchards and gardens to the paddy-rich plains below. The Mahaweli Ganga, Sri Lanka's longest river, has its source close to Adam's Peak and runs 335km to Koddiyar Bay, the deep-sea harbour of Trincomalee. It's mostly off-limits as either nature preserve or for use in major hydroelectric and irrigation schemes.

North-central Sri Lanka is home to high, rolling hills, including some fantastically dramatic landscapes like the area around the Knuckles Range. These hills give way to plains that extend to the northern tip of the island. This region, portions of the southeast and most of the east comprise the dry zone.

Sri Lanka's coastline consists of hundreds of mangrove-fringed lagoons and marshes – some now protected wetlands – interspersed with fine white-sand beaches, the most picturesque of which are on the southwest, south and east coasts. A group of low, flat islands lies off the Jaffna peninsula in the north.

WILDLIFE

Animals

For a landmass of its size, Sri Lanka boasts an incredible diversity of *animalia*: 92 mammal species, 242 butterflies, 435 birds, 107 fish, 98 snakes and more. Given the fragility of the environment in which they live (see p72), it should come as no surprise that quite a few are vulnerable (see p68). What *is* a surprise is the somewhat limited protection they are afforded. Sadly, the loss of animal biodiversity in Sri Lanka seems inevitable, largely a function of how little the local population knows or can be expected to do about it.

Nevertheless, with very little effort, any visitor to Sri Lanka who escapes the clutch of its cities would be very unlucky not to run across some of its fauna, which is most at ease in the wild (see National Parks & Reserves, p69).

This section offers just an overview of some of your most common animal species. For a more thorough and learned look, check out *A Photographic Guide to Mammals of Sri Lanka* by Gehan de Silva Wijeyeratne, the well-known Sri Lankan naturalist who has also published extensively on the country's birds and butterflies, among other things.

MAMMALS

Sri Lanka's mammals include some of the most easily observable of the country's animal species, as well as some of the most invisible. Hard to spot are the solitary and mostly nocturnal leopard, Sri Lanka's top predator; the

The Mahaweli Ganga drains 16% of the island's fresh water and is the primary source for all irrigation in the dry zone.

The Nature of Sri Lanka, with stunning photographs by L Nadaraja, is a collection of essays about Sri Lanka by eminent writers and conservationists.

'Dedicated to images of Sri Lanka,' www .lakdasun.com provides excellent insight into discovering Sri Lanka's nature and wildlife.

THE PACHYDERM PREDICAMENT

Elephants occupy a special place in Sri Lankan culture. In ancient times they were Crown property and killing one was a terrible offence. Legend has it that elephants stamped down the foundations of the dagobas (stupas) at Anuradhapura, and elephant iconography is common in Sri Lankan art. Even today elephants are held in great affection. Of those in captivity, the Maligawa tusker, who carries the sacred tooth relic for the Kandy Esala Perahera, is perhaps the most venerated of all. In the wild, one of Sri Lanka's most incredible wildlife events is 'the Gathering' in Minneriya National Park (p228).

Despite being held in high regard, Sri Lanka's elephant population has declined significantly. Their plight has become a powerful flashpoint in the ongoing debate about human-animal conflict.

Dwindling Numbers

At the end of the 18th century an estimated 10,000 to 20,000 elephants lived unfettered across Sri Lanka. By the mid-20th century small herds of the decimated population (perhaps as few as 1000) were clustered in the low-country dry zone. Natural selection had little to do with that cull: under the British big-game hunting delivered a mighty blow to elephant life expectancy. Today experts disagree about whether numbers are increasing or diminishing, but the population is believed to be between 3000 and 4000 in the wild, half of which live on protected land, plus about 300 domesticated animals.

Human-Elephant Conflict – An Intractable Problem

Farmers in elephant country face an ever-present threat from animals that may eat or trample their crops, destroy their buildings and even take their lives. During the cultivation season, farmers maintain round-the-clock vigils for up to three months to scare off unwelcome raiders. For farmers on the breadline, close encounters with wild elephants are a luxury they can't afford.

Meanwhile, elephants, who need about 5 sq km of land each to support their 200kg-per-day appetites, no longer seem to have sufficient stock of food staples in the small wildlife safety zones where they are protected. Hunger (and perhaps curiosity) is driving them to seek fodder in other areas – manmade ones abutting their secure habitats. The resulting conflict pits elephants against farmers – both just trying to secure their own survival.

scavenging golden jackal; shaggy sloth bears; civets (catlike hunters related to weasels); mongooses; and the shy, armour-plated Indian pangolin, with overlapping scales made from modified hair.

Very audible but not always visible are troops of tree-bound cackling primates, like common langurs, also known as Hanuman or grey langurs; endemic purple-faced langurs; hairy bear monkeys; and toque macaques, notable for their distinctive 'dos – a thatch of middle-parted hair. The slow movements of the slender loris belie its ability to snatch its prey with a lightning-quick lunge.

At www.ecomaximus.co.uk find out how Eco Maximus' use of elephant dung to create hand-crafted paper is helping ease human-elephant conflict.

More often crossed, albeit at different times of the day, are the majestic Asian elephant (see boxed text, above); the omnivorous and tusked wild boar of Sri Lanka; and cervine creatures like the big, maned sambar and smaller white-spotted Axis deer. The bushy-tailed, five-striped palm squirrel is commonly seen scurrying around gardens and town parks. These are often also the locations of the large trees in which Indian flying foxes (large fruit-eating bats) camp by the hundreds.

REPTILES & FISH

Sri Lanka has many species of reptiles, including 98 snakes. Mugger crocodiles loll near bodies of water, which are also the natural habitat of the water monitor, a large (up to 3m in length) and colourful scavenging lizard with a particular fondness for eggs. The Indian cobra is the famous hooded snake associated with snake charmers. Highly venomous, it usually avoids confrontation.

The Solutions?

Many solutions have been tried, including arming farmers, providing them with noisemakers to scare elephants away, securing elephant corridors, relocating problem elephants, erecting electric fences to keep elephants in, and even setting up compensation funds for victims of elephant attacks. Nothing has proven entirely effective.

There are new ideas. One involves fencing *humans* in or, rather, elephants out of human areas. This approach has been proven very effective by the **Sri Lanka Wildlife Conservation Society** (SLWCS; www.slwcs.org), an award-winning wildlife conservation watchdog. Another is to give farmers alternative livelihood solutions and land practices that incorporate elephants. The collection and commercial use of elephant dung is one such possible enterprise.

A Worthy Opinion

Zoologist Andrew Kittle is a founding member and primary researcher of the Wilderness & Wildlife Conservation Trust in Sri Lanka.

'My take on the conflict is that Sri Lanka's predominant religious backgrounds – Buddhism and Hinduism – have had a very positive influence on wildlife conservation. There is an inherent conservation ethic that runs through both religions – overtly in Buddhism through the Buddha's teachings regarding *ahimsa* (respect for all living things) and more subtly in Hinduism (to me anyway) through the veneration of various animals – which has the effect of making respect for animals/wildlife reasonable and desirable.

There is no way that a Western country with its Judeo-Christian religious heritage could survive balancing a landmass of Sri Lanka's size, 20 million people and some 3000 elephants without having them all in zoos or fenced in protected areas. There are ample examples of large mammalian species going extinct or close to it due to human exploitation in these regions (bison in North America and Europe; large cats in Europe).

I think the conservation ethic that reigns here is exemplary. I work here with some degree of optimism that many species will be backed for conservation based not on economic or social principles, but on their own merit.'

Some 54 species of fish are found in Sri Lanka's waterways and marshlands, including prized aquarium varieties like the red scissor-tail barb and the ornate paradise fish. The British introduced several species of fish, including trout, which is still common around Horton Plains National Park (p187). There are myriad colourful tropical marine fish.

Sri Lanka has five species of marine turtle, all endangered or critically endangered: the leatherback, the olive ridley, the loggerhead, the hawksbill and the green. Though protected, they face significant threats from poachers and environmental hazards, but also benefit from conservation and egg-hatchery projects.

Various sources calculate the yearly average number of elephant deaths at 150 to 200. By contrast, humans (who outnumber elephants 5430 to one) lose 50 to 70 lives to elephants each year.

BIRDS

A tropical climate, long isolation from the Asian mainland and a diversity of habitats have helped endow Sri Lanka with an astonishing abundance of birdlife. There are more than 400 species, 26 of which are unique to Sri Lanka; others are found only in Sri Lanka and adjacent South India. Of the estimated 198 migrant species, most of which are in residence from August to April, the waders (sandpipers, plovers etc) are the long-distance champions, making the journey from their breeding grounds in the Arctic tundra.

Reference books on Sri Lanka's birds include *A Selection of the Birds of Sri Lanka,* by John and Judy Banks, a slim, well-illustrated tome that's perfect for amateur bird-watchers, and *A Field Guide to the Birds of Sri Lanka,* by John Harrison, a pricier hardback with colour illustrations that's one of the best field guides available.

The call of the black house crow is one of the first and most common bird sounds you'll hear in Sri Lanka.

TIPS FOR BIRD-WATCHERS

- Visit a variety of habitats – rainforest, urban parks and bodies of water in the dry zone – to see the full diversity of birdlife in Sri Lanka.

- February to March is the best time for bird-watching. You miss the monsoons and the migrant birds are still visiting.

- Waterbirds are active for most of the day.

- Although morning is always the best time to go bird-watching, in the evening you will see noisy flocks of birds preparing to roost.

- A pair of binoculars is an invaluable tool to help with identification. Small models can be bought cheaply duty-free and don't weigh much.

- Consider taking a tour with a specialist if you're keen to see the endemic species and achieve a healthy bird-watching tally, particularly if time is short (for operators, see p288).

- For a complete list of important bird areas in Sri Lanka, visit www.ibasrilanka.net.

Birders may also wish to contact the **Field Ornithology Group of Sri Lanka** (☎ 011-534 2609; www.ibasrilanka.net/demo), the national affiliate of Birdlife International. Based at the University of Colombo, it conducts a bird lecture on the last Saturday of every month.

Everything you ever wanted to know about sea turtles, including when and where to see them lay eggs, can be found at www.tcpsri lanka.org, the website of the Turtle Conservation Project of Sri Lanka.

ENDANGERED SPECIES

At the time of research the International Union for Conservation of Nature's Red List of Threatened Species counted 30 species in Sri Lanka as critically endangered and a further 34 as endangered. They include the Asian elephant (see boxed text, p66), purple-faced langur, red slender loris and toque macaque. All five of Sri Lanka's marine turtle species are threatened, as are the estuarine crocodile and the mild-mannered dugong, all of which are killed for their meat. Also under threat are several species of birds, fish and insects.

Plants

The southwestern wet zone is home to the country's surviving tropical rainforest, characterised by dense undergrowth and a tall canopy of hardwood trees, including ebony, teak and silkwood. Here the diversity and richness of plant life is very high. For example, although the wet zone accounts for only one-quarter of the island's surface area, it contains 88% of its flowering plants, almost a third of which are endemic.

The central hill zone has cloud forests and some rare highland areas populated by hardy grasslands and elfin (stunted) forests. The remainder of the island forms the arid dry zone, with a sparser cover of trees and shrubs, and grasslands that only erupt into bloom with the first rains.

What Tree Is That? by Sriyanie Miththapala and PA Miththapala contains handy sketches of common trees and shrubs in Sri Lanka, and includes English, Sinhala and botanical names.

The sacred bodhi tree was brought from India when Mahinda introduced the teachings of the Buddha to Sri Lanka in the 3rd century BC. Most Buddhist temples in Sri Lanka have a bodhi tree, but the most famous is the Sri Maha Bodhi (p232) of Anuradhapura, the oldest historically authenticated tree in the world. Also often found around Buddhist temples is the sal, sometimes called the cannonball tree for reasons that will be clear when you see its huge woody fruit. The sweet-scented flowers of the frangipani (or temple flower) tree are common temple denizens throughout the island and used as Buddhist offerings.

Other common trees are the banyan, bo or peepul, flame, rain, Ceylon Ironwood and neem, an assortment of names as colourful as their barks, leaves and especially flowers. There are traditional medicinal uses for almost all of them. In the Hill Country don't be surprised by the eucalypts planted to provide shade at tea estates.

Native fruit trees such as mangoes, tamarinds, wood apples and bananas grow in many private gardens, supplemented by introduced species like papayas and guavas. The jackfruit and its smaller relative, the *del* (breadfruit), will certainly catch your eye. The jackfruit tree produces the world's largest fruit; green and knobbly skinned, it weighs up to 30kg and hangs close to the trunk.

Greater botanical information can be gleaned from *The Illustrated Field Guide to the Flowers of Sri Lanka*, by Dr J de Vlas and J de Vlas-de Jong, a manual describing more than 1000 plant species.

The incorporation of one little piece of wood from the pihimbiya tree is said to bring good luck to the house.

NATIONAL PARKS & RESERVES

More than 2000 years ago enlightened royalty declared certain land areas off-limits to any human activity. The oldest of these, Mihintale (p238), was established by King Devanampiya Tissa in the 3rd century BC as the first wildlife sanctuary in the world. Almost every province in the ancient kingdom of Kandy had such *udawattakelle* (sanctuaries). All animals and plants in these reserves were left undisturbed.

Today's system of parks and reserves is mostly an amalgamation of traditionally protected areas, reserves established by the British and newly gazetted swaths set aside for things like elephant corridors. There are more than 100 of these areas under government guard, covering approximately 8% of the island. They are divided into three types: strict nature reserves (no visitors

---

CAPTIVE ELEPHANTS

By ideal Western standards, the conditions in which captive animals in Sri Lanka are kept are not as good as they could be. Whether an animal's lack of freedom is due to having been orphaned or injured and then reared by humans or purposefully captured and domesticated, the issue of 'proper' treatment is a nettlesome one.

The treatment of elephants at the government-run Pinnewala Elephant Orphanage (p157) has become particularly contentious. Both tourists and animal welfare groups have not had kind things to say about the health of the elephants, their living conditions, their treatment by mahouts and even the goals of the facility. (Created as a shelter for elephants, some say it is now a tourist showcase, more a moneymaking bonanza than an animal care centre.)

Pinnewala is often contrasted with the Born Free Foundation–supported Elephant Transit Home (ETH; p203). At ETH young orphaned elephants are nurtured until weaned and then released back into the wild. There's only limited contact with handlers and no interaction with visitors at all.

As with all things, however, there's a flip side. Pinnewala has been celebrated as one of the most successful captive-breeding projects in the world, in part because the resident elephants form their own groups and socialise freely in the shared open space. As for ETH, some conservationists have expressed concern about its ability to resist the pull of tourism, especially as it relies so heavily on private contributions to sustain operations.

Visitors to either facility should keep in mind a couple of things. First, Sri Lanka is actively addressing the bigger issues of the balance between animal conservation and human wellbeing (see boxed text, p66). This is a tedious process – a slow cultural shift – not helped by pressure from external parties that don't necessarily see the larger context. Success in mitigating human-elephant conflict would inevitably reduce reliance on operations like Pinnewala and ETH. Second, it is not tourists' indisputable right to see elephants, whether in the wild, at Pinnewala, at ETH or anywhere else. Their desire to do so – and the colour of their money – affects everything.

Travellers choosing to bypass both facilities may find greater reward working to bridge the human-elephant divide with organisations like the Millennium Elephant Foundation (p157) or the Sri Lanka Wildlife Conservation Society (p19).

allowed), national parks (visits under fixed conditions) and nature reserves (human habitation permitted). Sri Lanka also has two marine sanctuaries – the Bar Reef (west of Kalpitiya peninsula) and Hikkaduwa National Park (see p118).

All national parks come under the management of the **Department of Wildlife Conservation** (☎ 011-266 0380; www.dwlc.lk; 382 New Kandy Rd, Malambe), to whom enquiries and park lodging requests (circuit bungalows or camp sites) should be directed. Entry fees to all parks are paid directly at entrance gates, where transportation and guides (both required) can be arranged. The **Department of Forest Conservation** (☎ 011-286 6632; forlib@sltnet.lk; 82 Rajamalwatta, Battaramulla) also administers some areas, like Sinharaja and the Knuckles.

At the time of research, the proximity of Wilpattu National Park to the government-LTTE war zone had put it off-limits to visitors. Yala East was also shut, as was the park office of Gal Oya (although fishermen will still take visitors onto the tank). Yala, although open during the day, was not allowing bungalow stays.

Off the Beaten Track

A full 82% of Sri Lanka's land is controlled by the state in some form or another, and is therefore subject to a raft of legislation to combat destructive activity and protect sensitive areas like the scores of natural forests. The Major National Parks & Reserves box (opposite) only includes information about 11 of the 20 national parks and three other green spaces from among the 63 sanctuaries, long lists of forest reserves and countless wetlands both with and without official titles. Why not venture out to where most others don't?

Given the overcrowding at some of the better-known natural areas, new attention has been directed to other deserving national parks, such as Lunugamvehera as an alternative to Yala and Wasgomuwa instead of Gal Oya or Minneriya. The less-frequented British-era botanical gardens – Hakgala and Henaratgoda, in addition to Peradeniya (p171) – are equally far enough off the beaten track to be pleasantly free of hordes.

Sri Lanka is a signatory to the Ramsar Convention on Wetlands, which currently recognises three coastal zones: Bundala National Park (p146); the 915-hectare Madu Ganga Estuary near Balapitiya, 80km south of Colombo on the A2, site of one of the last pristine mangrove forests in Sri Lanka; and the Annaivilundawa Tanks Wildlife Sanctuary, just west of the A3 about 100km north of Colombo, a cluster of ancient, manmade, freshwater reservoirs that are now a safe haven for awesome wetland biodiversity.

The unique leopard project of the Wilderness & Wildlife Conservation Trust is described at www.wwct.org. It's intended as a baseline study for the future conservation of the Sri Lankan leopard.

The Department of Forestry & Environmental Science at the University of Sri Jayewardenepura maintains www.environmentlanka.com, a website with photos of Sri Lankan wildlife and essays on key environmental issues.

EARTH LUNG INITIATIVE

In October 2007 the Sri Lankan Minister of Tourism launched 'Towards a Carbon Clean Sri Lanka: A Tourism Earth Lung', thereby giving a green light (pun intended) to government-led environment-conscious collective action by Sri Lanka's tourism sector. The Tourism Earth Lung initiative 'seeks to influence and even lead efforts at stopping deforestation, ensuring reforestation, encouraging the use of alternative energy sources, and mitigating pollution at the source through local efforts', announced the driving force behind it, Renton de Alwis (see p73), then Chairman of the Sri Lankan Tourism Development Authority.

The initiative has been gaining real traction. Its lofty long-term goal of making Sri Lanka carbon neutral by the year 2018 may still be far out of reach, but it's certainly attracting more and more attention, both within Sri Lanka and beyond its borders. Visit www.earthlung.travel to learn more about it and some of the registered projects worth visiting or supporting.

MAJOR NATIONAL PARKS & RESERVES

Park	Area	Features	Best Time to Visit
Bundala National Park (p146)	6216 hectares	coastal lagoon, migratory birds, elephants	May-Sep
Gal Oya National Park	62,936 hectares	grasslands, evergreen forest, deer, Senanayake Samudra (tank), elephants, sloth bears, leopards, water buffaloes	Dec-Sep
Horton Plains National Park (p187)	3160 hectares	proposed Unesco World Heritage Site, montane forests, marshy grasslands, World's End precipice, sambars	Jan-Mar
Kaudulla National Park (p228)	6656 hectares	Kaudulla Tank, evergreen forest, scrub jungle, grassy plains, elephants, leopards, sambars, fishing cats, sloth bears	Aug-Dec
Knuckles Range (p175)	17,500 hectares	proposed Unesco World Heritage Site, traditional villages, hiking trails, caves, waterfalls, montane pygmy forest, evergreen forest, riverine forest, grasslands, scrub, paddy fields, 31 mammal species	Dec-May
Lunugamvehera National Park	23,498 hectares	grasslands, reservoir, elephants	May-Sep
Minneriya National Park (p228)	8889 hectares	Minneriya Tank, toque macaques, sambars, elephants, waterfowl	Jun-Sep
Sinharaja Forest Reserve (p204)	18,899 hectares	Unesco World Heritage Site, sambars, rainforest, leopards, purple-faced langurs, barking deer, 147 recorded bird species	Aug-Sep, Jan-Mar
Sri Pada Peak Wilderness Reserve (p175)	19,207 hectares	proposed Unesco World Heritage Site, Adam's Peak, hiking trails	Dec-May
Uda Walawe National Park (p203)	30,821 hectares	grassland, thorn scrub, elephants, spotted deer, water buffaloes, wild boar	May-Sep
Wasgomuwa National Park	39,322 hectares	evergreen forest, hilly ridges, grassy plains, elephants, leopards, sloth bears	Jun-Sep
Wilpattu National Park (p103)	131,693 hectares	dense jungle, scrub, saltgrass, elephants, leopards, sloth bears, deer, crocodiles	Jan-Mar
Yala East National Park (p253)	18,149 hectares	grassland, jungle, lagoons, mangrove swamp, waterfowl	Dec-Sep
Yala National Park (p150)	14,101 hectares	tropical thornforest, lagoons, elephants, sloth bears, leopards, water buffaloes, lesser flamingos	May-Sep

Also within easy reach of Colombo are the 37,400-hectare freshwater Bolgoda Lake, Sri Lanka's largest natural water basin starting 18km south of the city centre and the focus of a community-led conservation effort (see boxed text, p18), and Muthurajawela Marsh's Visitor Centre (p110).

For further listings of out-of-the-way green escapes, contact the government conservation departments or consult *LOCALternative Sri Lanka – a responsible travel map* (www.localternative.com; see p297).

RESPONSIBLE HIKING

Sri Lanka offers plenty of scope for hiking, particularly in the Hill Country. Note that under normal circumstances and other than in campgrounds and near bungalows, the only two national parks in which visitors are allowed to move about on foot (with or without an escort) are Horton Plains (p187) and Horagolla (a new 13-hectare park of wet-zone forest near Nittambuwa, 40km northeast of Colombo on the A1). Even then, you are exhorted to remain on marked trails. Please consider the following tips to help minimise your impact on the environment.

Rubbish

- Carry out *all* your rubbish. Don't overlook anything!
- Make an effort to carry out rubbish left by others. Lead by example.
- Never bury your rubbish. Digging disturbs the ground cover and encourages erosion. The rubbish may take years to decompose and be a threat to animals if uncovered.
- Minimise the waste you carry out by taking minimal packaging and no more food than you need. Take reusable containers or stuff sacks.
- On longer walks, don't rely on plastic water bottles. Instead, use purification methods with water found along the way.

Human Waste Disposal

- Contamination of water sources by human faeces can lead to the transmission of hepatitis, typhoid and intestinal parasites such as giardia and roundworms.
- Where there's no toilet, bury your waste. Dig a small hole 15cm deep and at least 100m from any watercourse. Consider carrying a lightweight trowel for this purpose. Cover the waste with soil and a rock. Carry out your toilet paper.

Going Local

- If you know you'll be passing through villages, buy provisions or eat locally rather than carry too much food. You'll bring important commerce and cross-cultural exchange.
- When passing through local communities, be respectful of local customs. Dress in a manner in keeping with expected values.

Wildlife

- If you come across an animal, keep a safe distance. Do not attempt to feed it.
- Do not pick, destroy or remove any plants or flowers.

Erosion

- Help keep erosion under control: stick to existing tracks. Avoid short cuts and, if a well-used track passes through a mud patch, walk through the mud; walking around the edge will increase the size of the patch.

ENVIRONMENTAL ISSUES

Conservation International has identified Sri Lanka (along with the Western Ghats of India) as one of the planet's 25 biodiversity hotspots. Being a hotspot is a two-edged sword. On the one hand it means the region is characterised by a very high level of 'plant endemism' (plants unique to the area). Sure enough, Sri Lanka tops the charts, with endemism in 23% of the flowering plants and 16% of the mammals. On the other hand, hotspots are targeted as habitats seriously at risk. One could hardly summarise the Sri Lankan situation more succinctly.

At the beginning of the 20th century about 70% of the island was covered by natural forest. By 1998 this had shrunk to about 29%. Worse, between 1990 and 2005 Sri Lanka had one of the highest recorded rates of primary forest destruction in the world: an 18% reduction in forest cover and 35% loss of old-growth tracts. *Chena* (shifting cultivation) is blamed for a good part of this deforestation, but irrigation schemes, clearance for cultivation and land 'development', armed conflict, temporary and new housing for refugees, and, most importantly, illegal logging have all been contributing factors.

Post-tsunami Coastal Regeneration

Although the 2004 tsunami had catastrophic consequences for human society, its effects on coastal and marine life were minimal. In a few cases the tsunami altered the lay of the land, but most of the flora and fauna habituated to seaside areas emerged perturbed but largely intact. Similarly, damage to coral reefs has been estimated at 5% or less. Rather, human disruptions such as coral harvesting to feed limekilns and, on the west coast between Chilaw and Puttalam, prawn farming have done (and continue to do) much more damage to coastal ecology than any disaster wrought by nature. Gem and sand mining have also degraded both land and water ecology since they influence the shape and flow of rivers.

If anything the tsunami highlighted the value of intact coastal vegetation – coral, sand dunes, mangroves, beach grass and plants – as barriers against natural seaborne threats. Accordingly, and in part in keeping with other major climate-change-prompted initiatives (see boxed text, p70), great attention has been turned to mangrove rehabilitation and tree planting along denuded coastal areas, as well as inland where deforestation has left gaping holes in the once continuous forest cover.

Organisations like **Rainforest Rescue International** (☎ 091-223 2585; www .earthrestoration.org; 37C Wekunugoda Rd, Galle), a driving force in nature- and village-based sustainable conservation and restoration of tropical forests, and the Responsible Tourism Partnership Sri Lanka (p19) have been active in these areas. Native plants destroyed by the tsunami have often been replaced by invasive species, already a growing problem throughout the country, but through networks of plant nurseries, the propagation, distribution and replanting of native stock has accelerated.

Supporting conservation and environmental awareness, the Green Movement of Sri Lanka is a consortium of 147 groups that are involved in natural resource management; check out its website at www .greensl.net.

THE FUTURE OF SRI LANKAN TOURISM

Renton de Alwis, former Chairman of the Sri Lankan Tourism Development Authority and instigator of the Tourism Earth Lung initiative (see boxed text, p70), reflects on Sri Lankan tourism:

'Sri Lanka is fortunate. We have retained 50% of our land area as a green cover, and about 29% as forest cover. Although the land area is small, it's still a huge plus. When you fly in from the east and traverse the country, all you see is green, except for a few patches of temples or villages on hillocks.

I believe that all Sri Lankans, especially those of us in tourism, should work towards becoming carbon neutral, or attempt in the least to be carbon clean. The Earth Lung initiative launched in October 2007 will provide an impetus and a platform for all our citizens to move in that direction.

I believe that it's not just about trading our carbon credit, but applying the principle of "trade before aid". We can tell the world: Come to destination Sri Lanka because it's green, because we're striving to be carbon clean. You don't have to feel "travel guilt" in visiting us. You can spend your money here, rather than buy our carbon credit. To me, carbon trading is equivalent to one acquiring merit and another buying it off to sin with it. The net effect on the globe, on Mother Earth, is still negative.

I believe that by adopting more environment-friendly lifestyles, Sri Lanka can be an example to the world of tourism. Our future lies in aiming at sustainable tourism, rather than going in for the mass market. We should stop counting heads. Sri Lanka should never be a destination for mass tourism. Larger volumes, if at all, should be limited to a few resort areas. The rest needs to be community-based experiential tourism.'

In 1991 Sri Lanka became one of the first countries in the world to impose a total ban on genetically modified foods.

What remains to be seen is how effective these regreening efforts are. In the present climate of conflict and economic stagnation, little new regeneration has been launched along coastal zones, although the government, in collaboration with major private players, has sweeping plans for the largely upscale redevelopment of tourism, especially in seaside areas – projects that many people, especially locals, don't always think are in keeping with the land's character or changes to the way people travel.

One final post-tsunami concern about which the jury is still out is over-exploitation of fish stock. What was once primarily a sustainable cottage industry was turned on its head by the overprovision of bigger and more powerful boats to the fishing community, whose original tools of trade were wiped out by the tsunami. There's little data, but the word from fishermen is that there aren't as many fish as there used to be.

Colombo

Colombo wears many hats. It is the administrative hub and political epicentre where traffic is frequently halted for official motorcades. It is the engine that drives the economy, sporting everything from bustling markets to gleaming skyscrapers. Most of all, it is a patchwork of peoples from around the island nation who come here to seek out their fortunes.

The legacies of colonial Colombo are still very much intact, right down to the rusting trains that chug through town, with locals dangling from carriages. Fort and Pettah, the oldest parts of the city, still brim with market activity and it's easy to get swept up by the crowds – or trampled by them if you're not careful.

Colombo has its cosmopolitan side, too, with wi-fi-equipped coffee shops, glitzy shopping malls, galleries and museums. The horrendous traffic around rush hour will give you a headache, but this is easily cured with a relaxing cocktail in one of the city's many fine restaurants. Colombo also offers the island's best nightlife if you're hankering for some urban buzz.

Colombo doesn't quite embody the paradisaical island image of Sri Lanka, but the main sites – a handful of temples and an excellent national museum – are easily visited in a day or two, making the city a good place to start or end a journey through Sri Lanka.

HIGHLIGHTS

- Buying up bagfuls of tea, clothing and handicrafts from the myriad shops and speciality stores such as **Barefoot** (p97) and **Paradise Road** (p98)

- Diving into the madness of **Pettah** (p83), where you can haggle for everything from jackfruit to gold necklaces

- Visiting Hindu **kovils** (p83) during the Thai Pongal festival or watching elephants and dancers parade during the Navam Perahera at **Gangaramaya Temple** (p89)

- Catching a live music act or dancing the night away in one of Colombo's **nightclubs** (p97)

- Walking through Sri Lanka's history in the remarkable **National Museum** (p87) in the heart of leafy Viharamahadevi Park

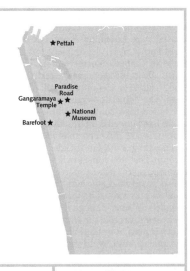

★ Pettah

Paradise Road
Gangaramaya ★ ★
Temple ★
Barefoot ★   ★ National Museum

■ TELEPHONE CODE: 011   ■ POPULATION: 2.2 MILLION   ■ AREA: 37 SQ KM

HISTORY

As far back as the 5th century, Colombo served as a sea port for trade between Asia and the West. During the 8th century Arab traders settled near the port, and in 1505 the Portuguese arrived. By the mid-17th century the Dutch had taken over, growing cinnamon in the area now known as Cinnamon Gardens, but it wasn't until the British arrived that the town became a city. In 1815 Colombo was proclaimed the capital of Ceylon.

During the 1870s the breakwaters were built and Fort was created by flooding surrounding wetlands. Colombo was peacefully handed over when Sri Lanka achieved independence in 1948. A new parliament was built in Sri Jayawardenepura-Kotte, an outer suburb of Colombo, in 1982.

Isolated Liberation Tigers of Tamil Eelam (LTTE) bomb attacks in Fort over the years caused Colombo's major businesses and institutions to disperse across the city. These days Colombo is spreading north and south along the coast as people migrate to the city to work.

ORIENTATION

Colombo is split into 15 postal-code areas, which are often used to identify the specific districts. Pettah, for example, is also referred to as Colombo 11 (or just Col 11), Slave Island is referred to as Col 2, and so on. See boxed text, p81, for a full listing of codes. From the visitor's point of view, Colombo is a long coastal strip extending about 12km south from Fort (Col 1). The spine of this strip is Galle Rd. Colombo's main train station, Fort, is actually in Pettah, as are the main bus stations – all 10 or 15 minutes' walk from Fort itself. The domestic airport is at Ratmalana Air Force Base, south of central Colombo, while Bandaranaike International Airport is at Katunayake, 30km north of the city.

Travelling south down Galle Face Centre Rd from Fort, you come to a large oceanfront lawn area called Galle Face Green. Inland from here is Slave Island, which isn't really an island at all as only two of its three sides are surrounded by water (though it really was used for keeping slaves in the Dutch colonial era). South is neighbouring Kollupitiya, followed by Bambalapitiya, Wellawatta, Dehiwala and finally the old beach resort of Mt Lavinia, which isn't officially part of Colombo but is definitely within its urban sprawl.

If you turn inland (east) from Kollupitiya you'll soon find yourself in Cinnamon Gardens, home of the national art gallery, the national museum, the university, Viharamahadevi Park, some of the most exclusive residential quarters and many embassies.

Finding addresses is complicated by the fact that street numbers start again each time you move into a new district. Thus there will be a '100 Galle Rd' in several different neighbourhoods.

Some Colombo streets have both an old English name and a post-independence Sinhala name. Ananda Coomaraswamy Mawatha is also known as Green Path, for example, while RA de Mel Mawatha is also still known as Duplication Rd.

Throughout Sri Lanka, Mw is an abbreviation for Mawatha, meaning 'Avenue'.

Maps

If you're going to be spending some time in Colombo, the 96-page *A–Z Street Guide* (Rs 400) extends as far south as Mt Lavinia and as far inland as Kelaniya, and also covers Galle, Kandy, Nuwara Eliya, Anuradhapura and Polonnaruwa. It also includes information on Colombo's suburban and inner-city buses. Free city maps without much detail are available in some hotels and the tourist information office; a slightly better map entitled 'City Map Collection' is sold in souvenir shops and bookstores for around Rs 150.

INFORMATION
Bookshops

Colombo has some excellent bookshops. Top-end hotels also often have bookshops where you'll find up-to-date foreign magazines and newspapers.

Buddhist Book Centre (Map pp84–5; ☎ 268 9786; 380 Bauddhaloka Mawatha, Col 7) Filled with books on Buddhism; about a third of the stock is in English.

Lake House Bookshop (Map pp84–5; ☎ 257 4418; Liberty Plaza, RA de Mel Mawatha, Col 3) Has an extensive range of books, along with foreign and local magazines and newspapers.

Vijitha Yapa Bookshop Crescat Boulevard (Map pp84–5; ☎ 551 0100; 89 Galle Rd, Col 3); Unity Plaza (Map p88; ☎ 259 6960; Galle Rd, Col 4) Stocks a comprehensive collection of foreign and local novels, magazines and pictorial tomes on Sri Lanka. The branch in Crescat Boulevard shopping centre is smaller.

Cultural Centres

Alliance Française (Map pp84-5; ☎ 269 4162; 11 Barnes Pl, Col 7) Hosts seminars, and shows films at 3pm on Tuesday and 6pm on Wednesday. Has a library.

American Information Resource Center (Map pp84-5; ☎ 233 2725; 44 Galle Rd, Col 3) Periodically hosts films and seminars, and offers a library and internet access (per day Rs 100).

British Council (Map pp84-5; ☎ 258 1171; 49 Alfred House Gardens, Col 3) Puts on regular free cultural events, including films (usually Friday and Saturday), exhibitions, concerts and lectures. There is a library as well.

Goethe Institut (Map pp84-5; ☎ 269 4562; 39 Gregory's Rd, Col 7) Screens German films and puts on music concerts, seminars and more.

Emergency

Accident Service (☎ 269 1111)
Fire & Rescue Service (☎ 242 2222)
Medi-Calls Ambulance (☎ 257 5475)
Police (☎ 243 3333)
Red Cross Ambulance (☎ 269 5434, 269 1095)
Tourist Police (Map pp84-5; ☎ 238 2209; 80 Galle Rd, Col 3; ☼ 24hr)

Internet Access

Internet cafes are surprisingly few in Colombo but there are enough to get you by. Most places charge around Rs 60 per hour.

Berty's Cyber Cafe (Map pp84-5; 380 Galle Rd, Col 3)
Bristol Cyber Cafe (Map pp80; 8/3/4 Bristol St, Col 1) Behind Air India in a yellow building.
Infotech Internet (Map p88; 46 Galle Rd, Col 6)
Mac Technologies & Cyber Cafe (Map pp84-5; Liberty Plaza, RA de Mel Mawatha, Col 3)

Colombo has several free wi-fi access spots, while others require the purchase of access codes. Free hotspots include the Gallery Cafe (p95), Barefoot Garden Cafe (p95), the Coffee Bean (p95), Bars Cafe (p94) and the Commons (p95). At Bandaranaike International Airport, there's free wi-fi at the Coffee Bean.

Left Luggage

Left-luggage services are available at the Fort train station's **cloakroom** (Map p80; per bag per day Rs 60; ☼ 4.30am-11.30pm). As you approach the station from Olcott Mawatha, it's on the extreme left of the building. Left-luggage facilities are also available at Bandaranaike International Airport (Rs 25 per bag per day).

Media

LT, distributed free at hotels, shops, bars and restaurants aiming for the expat market, carries listings of bars, clubs, restaurants, galleries and cultural events. *Travel Lanka,* distributed at similar venues to *LT* as well as at the tourist office, has information about concerts, plays and lectures held by cultural centres.

Hands on Colombo (www.handsoncolombo.com) serves the expat community with listings and reviews of everything from dentists to jewellers. The *Daily Mirror* is Colombo's English-language newspaper, available in bookshops, upmarket hotels and news-stands.

Medical Services

Avoid government hospitals, such as Colombo General, if you can. The following private hospitals have relatively high standards and English-speaking doctors.

Apollo Hospital Colombo (Map pp78-9; ☎ 453 0000; cnr Vijaya Kumaratunga Mawatha & Park Rd, Col 5) This is the largest private hospital in the country and has state-of-the-art facilities.

Asiri Central Hospital (Map pp84-5; ☎ 269 6412; 37 Horton Pl, Col 7) Modern hospital with lab services and central location.

Nawaloka Hospital (Map pp84-5; ☎ 254 4444; 23 Sri Saugathodaya Mawatha, Col 2)

Osu Sala (Map pp84-5; ☎ 269 4716; 255 Union Pl, Col 2; ☼ 24hr) A large pharmacy that's conveniently open round the clock.

Money

There are banks and ATMs all over the city, and several 24-hour bank branches in the arrivals hall at Bandaranaike International Airport.

There are several moneychangers in Fort; their offices are concentrated in and around Chatham St and Mudalige Mawatha (Map p80). Their cash-only rates are a little higher than you would get in a bank. You can change cash or travellers cheques at reduced rates in the main hotels.

Post

Sri Lanka Post (Map p80; DR Wijewardana Mawatha, Col 1; ☼ 7am-6pm, poste restante 7am-9pm, stamps & telephone 24hr) offers poste restante and can hold mail for two months – call ☎ 232 6203 to see if there's anything awaiting you. See p298 for postal rates.

COLOMBO

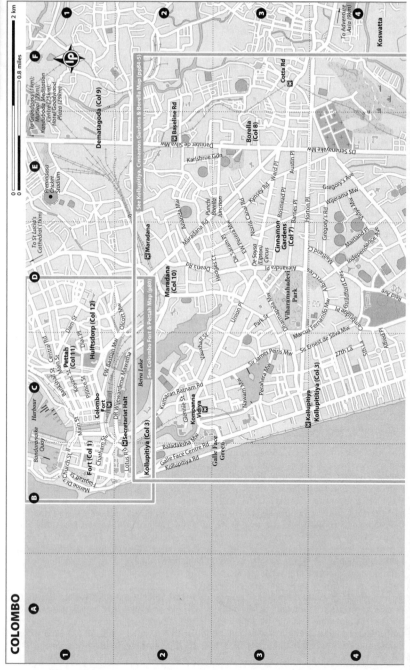

COLOMBO

0   0.8 miles
0   2 km

To Grandpass (1km);
Murewa (2km);
Kanduboda Meditation
Centre (22km);
Hotel/Goodwood
Plaza (290km)

Dematagoda (Col 9)

See Kollupitiya, Cinnamon Gardens & Borella Map (pp84–5)

Prenadasa
Cricket
Stadium

To St Luke's
Cathedral (1km)

Baseline Rd

Borella
(Col 8)

Danister de Silva Mw

DS Senanayake Mw

Karlshrue Gdn

Gregory's Ave

Wijerama Mw

Maradana Mw

Maradana
Rd

Punchi
Borella
Junction

Kynsey Rd   Ward Pl

Rosmead Pl   Barnes Pl   Austin Pl

Horton Pl

Maradana

Cinnamon
Gardens
(Col 7)

Gregory's Rd

Maitland Pl

Independence Ave

De Saram Pl

Elvie Perera Mw

North Canal

Dean's Rd

Alexandra
Pl

Viharamahadevi
Park

Albert Cres

Maitland Cr

Guildford Cres

Cambridge Pl

Reid Ave

Hedges Ct

De Soysa
(Lipton)
Circus

Manadana
(Col 10)

Ananda Mw

Harbour

Pettah
(Col 11)

Hulftsdorp (Col 12)

Olcott Mw

Dam St

Keyzer St

Prince St

Dias Pl

EW Bastian Mw

Dr Wijewardene Mawatha

Bankshall St
Central Rd

Main St

Bankshall St

Colombo
Fort

Union Pl

Park St

Marcus Fernando Mw

Sir Ernest de Silva Mw

Dharmapala Mw

27th La

Alfred Pl

Bandaranaike Quay

Fort (Col 1)

Secretariat Halt

Lotus Rd

Chatham St

Church St

Flagstaff St

Marine Dr

Beira Lake

See Colombo Fort & Pettah Map (p80)

Kumaran Ratnam Rd

Vauxhall St

Sir James Peiris Mw

Perahera Mw

Navam Mw

Kollupitiya (Col 3)

Glenvie St

Kompanna
Vidiya

Baladaksha Mw

Galle Face Centre Rd

Kollupitiya Rd

Galle Face
Green

Kollupitiya
(Col 3)

Kollupitiya Rd

Cotta Rd

Borella

Koswatta

To Adventure
Asia (9km)

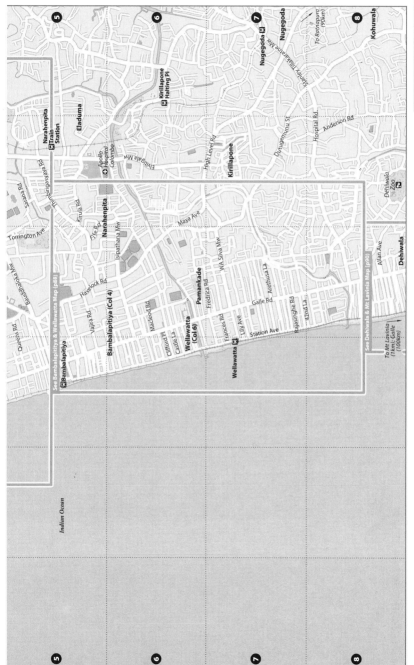

Narahenpita
Train
Station

Eladuma

Kirillapone
Halting Pl

Nugegoda

Nugegoda

To Rotnapura
(90km)

Kohuwala

Maradana Rd

Apollo
Hospital
Colombo

Kirula Rd

Narahenpita

Havelock Rd

Vajira Rd

Bambalapitiya (Col 4)

Bambalapitiya

MacLeod Rd

Clifford Pl

Castle La

Wellawatta
(Col 6)

Pamankade

Wellawatta

Fredrica Rd

Frances Rd

WA Silva Mw

Maya Ave

High Level Rd

Kirillapone

Elvitigala Mw

Durugenunu St

Hospital Rd.

Anderson Rd

Dehiwala
Zoo

Dehiwala

Allan Ave

Galle Rd

Lily Ave

Station Ave

Rajasinghe Rd

42nd La

Arethusa La

Torrington Ave

Baddegana Rd

Queen's Rd

Pld streets

Ispathana Mw

Thimbirigasyaya Rd

Narahenpita Rd

To Mt Lavinia
(1 km); Galle
(100km)

Indian Ocean

See Bambalapitiya & Wellawatta Map (p88)

See Dehiwala & Mt Lavinia Map (p90)

COLOMBO

COLOMBO FORT & PETTAH

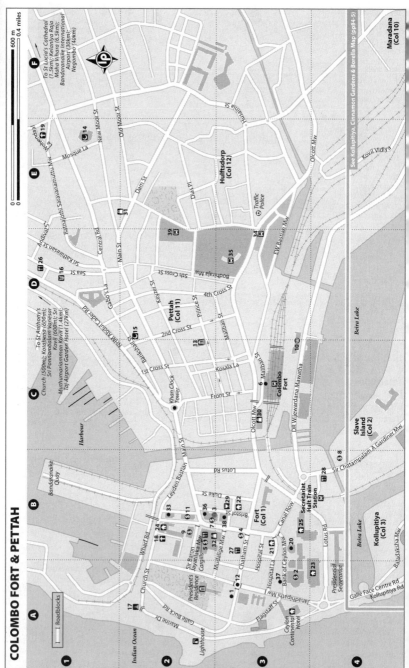

INFORMATION		
A Baur & Co Ltd	**1**	A3
Bank of Ceylon	**2**	A3
Bristol Cyber Cafe	**3**	B2
Commercial Bank (ATM)	**4**	B3
HSBC Bank	**5**	B2
JF Tours & Travels	**6**	C3
Moneychangers	**7**	B2
People's Bank	**8**	B4
Seylan Bank	**9**	B2
Sri Lanka Post	**10**	C3
Standard Chartered Grindlays Bank	**11**	B2

SIGHTS & ACTIVITIES		
Clock Tower	**12**	A3
Dutch Period Museum	**13**	C2
Grand Mosque	**14**	E1
Jami-Ul-Alfar Mosque	**15**	D2
New Kathiresan Kovil	**16**	D1
Old Kathiresan Kovil	(see 16)	
Sambodhi Chaitiya	**17**	A2
St Peter's Church	**18**	B2

Wolvendaal Church	**19**	E1
World Trade Center	**20**	B3

SLEEPING		
Colombo City Hotel	**21**	B3
Colombo YMCA	**22**	B3
Galadari Hotel	**23**	A4
Grand Oriental Hotel	**24**	B2
Hilton Colombo	**25**	B3

EATING		
Chettinad	**26**	D1
Curry Leaf	(see 25)	
Ginza Hohsen	(see 25)	
Harbour Room	(see 24)	
Pagoda Tea Room	**27**	B3
Seafish	**28**	B4

DRINKING		
Sri Lanka Ex-Servicemen's Institute	**29**	B3

ENTERTAINMENT		
Blue Leopard	(see 24)	

Tramps	(see 23)	

SHOPPING		
Bazaar	**30**	C3
City Cycle	**31**	E2
Millers	**32**	B2
Sri Lanka Gem & Jewellery Exchange	(see 20)	

TRANSPORT		
Air Canada	(see 20)	
American Airlines	**33**	B2
Asiana Airlines	(see 33)	
Bastian Mawatha Bus Station	**34**	D3
Central Bus Station	**35**	D3
Indian Airlines	**36**	B2
Kuwait Airways	**37**	A3
Malaysia Airlines	**38**	B3
Qatar Airways	(see 20)	
Saunders Pl Bus Station	**39**	D2
Sri Lankan Airlines	(see 20)	
Swiss Air	(see 1)	
United Airlines	(see 20)	

If you are sending home anything of particular value, you should consider using a courier service. Reliable couriers:

DHL Worldwide Express (Map pp84–5; ☎ 230 4304; Keells, 148 Vauxhall St, Col 2)

Mountain Hawk Express (Map pp84–5; ☎ 252 2222; 300 Galle Rd, Col 3) FedEx agent.

TNT Express (Ace Cargo; Map pp84–5; ☎ 230 8444; 315 Vauxhall St, Col 2)

Telephone & Fax

For international calls there are many relatively pricey private communication bureaus (which often have fax machines). A cheaper option is using the card-operated interna-

COLOMBO'S SUBURB CODES

Zone	Suburb
Colombo 1	Fort
Colombo 2	Slave Island
Colombo 3	Kollupitiya
Colombo 4	Bambalapitiya
Colombo 5	Havelock Town
Colombo 6	Wellawatta
Colombo 7	Cinnamon Gardens
Colombo 8	Borella
Colombo 9	Dematagoda
Colombo 10	Maradana
Colombo 11	Pettah
Colombo 12	Hulftsdorp
Colombo 13	Kotahena
Colombo 14	Grandpass
Colombo 15	Mutwal

tional direct dialling (IDD) telephones, of which there are many in Colombo.

Most internet centres in Colombo offer web-phone services, which cost about the same as regular internet access.

For domestic calls, **Sri Lanka Post** (Map p80; DR DR Wijewardana Mawatha, Col 1; 7am-6pm, telephone 24hr) sells Sri Lanka Telecom phonecards. Calls from its cardphones (which can be purchased in post offices only) are slighter cheaper than those from the private cardphones. However, it's probably more convenient to use one of the yellow Lanka Pay or Tritel cardphones.

If you are going to be making a lot of calls, it's easiest to buy a local SIM card for your mobile phone and purchase top-up cards as needed. See p300 for general information on phone services.

Tourist Information

Sri Lanka Tourist Board (SLTB; Map pp84–5; ☎ 243 7059; www.srilankatourism.org; 80 Galle Rd, Col 3; 9am-4.45pm Mon-Fri, 9am-12.30pm Sat) The country's national tourism office. The staff is friendly and can help book hotels among other services. It also maintains a 24-hour booth at the international airport (☎ 225 2411).

Travel Agencies

Colombo's plethora of travel agencies can help organise car hire, city tours or tours elsewhere in Sri Lanka. Following are some of the biggest operators, plus some recommended niche-market companies.

COLOMBO

COLOMBO IN...

One Day
For a healthy dose of south Asia at its most authentic, pay a morning visit to the markets of **Pettah** (opposite), sampling some fruit, popping into the small Hindu temples or browsing the jewellery shops on Sea St. While you're in the neighbourhood, learn about Sri Lanka's colonial history at the **Dutch Period Museum** (opposite) and enjoy this restored mansion's garden. On York St in nearby **Fort** (opposite) the rows of grand Victorian shop-houses offer a glimpse at British-era Colombo.

As an antidote to the hot and congested streets of Fort and Pettah, enjoy a peaceful lunch at the ultra-swanky **Gallery Cafe** (p95), followed by a browse through its adjacent **Paradise Road** (p98) shop, where you can pick out gifts for friends back home.

In the afternoon visit the eclectic Buddhist **Gangaramaya Temple** (p89) and take a stroll along the oceanfront with Sri Lankan families at **Galle Face Green** (p87) as the sun sets.

Two Days
Enjoy a high-society breakfast at the **Commons** (p95) or grab a *kotthu rotti* (doughy pancake chopped and fried with a variety of ingredients) at **Green Cabin** (p94) before tackling the excellent **National Museum** (p87) in pretty **Viharamahadevi Park** (p87).

Barefoot Garden Cafe (p95) is a good spot for lunch, as well as the perfect place to stock up on high-quality souvenirs for friends back home. An afternoon bus trip down Galle Rd lands you at **Mt Lavinia** (p89), Colombo's quiet beach getaway – bring along your swimwear for a refreshing dip in the sea. Let loose after dinner at **Tramps** (p97) or one of Colombo's other nightclubs.

A Baur & Co Ltd (Map p80; ☎ 244 8087; www.baurs .com; Baur's Bldg, 5 Upper Chatham St, Col 1) One of the few companies specialising in birdwatching tours. It's not possible to visit the office (it's in a security zone), so ring ahead for information.

Adventure Asia (off Map pp78-9; ☎ 586 8468, 277 3886, 0777 588360; www.ad-asia.com; 1112/7 Panipitiya, Talangama South, Battaramulla) A Western-run outfit specialising in white-water rafting, kayaking, hot-air ballooning and bicycling tours. Its office is about 9km east of the city. The company also has an adventure base, 34km east of the city, where an all-inclusive package (accommodation, meals, rock climbing and kayaking) costs US$50 per day.

Aitken Spence Travels (Map pp84-5; ☎ 230 8021; www.aitkenspencetravels.com; Vauxhall Bldg, 305 Vauxhall St, Col 2) One of the biggest tour operators; organises tour packages, hires out cars and drivers, and books hotels.

Jetwing Travels (Map pp84-5; ☎ 234 5700; www .jetwing.net; Jetwing House, 46/26 Nawam Mawatha, Col 2) Another big operator; has a large chain of upmarket hotels and organises tours within Sri Lanka and to the Maldives.

JF Tours & Travels (Map pp84-5; ☎ 258 7996; www .jftours.com; 189 Bauddhaloka Mawatha, Col 4) Specialises in steam-train tours (groups only) and booking train tickets in general. It also has an office at Colombo Fort train station.

Quickshaws (Map p88; ☎ 258 3133; www.quickshaws .com; 3 Kalinga Pl, Col 5) Organises standard tours but specialises in personalised tours with a car and driver. Also rents self-drive cars.

DANGERS & ANNOYANCES
Crime
While violence towards foreigners is uncommon, it helps to tell someone where you are going and when to expect you back.

Women in particular are urged to take care at night. Even couples should be very cautious about walking along lonely beach areas, such as those near Mt Lavinia, after dark.

Solo women should be careful when taking taxis and three-wheelers at night; if, as sometimes happens, your taxi turns up with two men inside, call another. Travellers should also avoid taking three-wheelers between the airport and Colombo at night; robberies are not unknown.

Watch out for pickpockets, especially on public transport, and keep your valuables locked up in your hotel room or with reception.

Ethnic Tension
In the past LTTE bombings were rare occurrences, and the future is still uncertain after the cessation of the civil war in 2009. The LTTE traditionally preferred military targets rather than civilians, so it's still best to give military installations a wide berth.

Scams & Touts

Colombo has its share of touts and con artists. Touts (sometimes disguised as officials) gather inside the airport's second arrivals hall waiting for jet-lagged visitors to emerge. You may be approached with claims that, for some reason or another (eg a bomb's just gone off somewhere), it's dangerous to travel any further unaccompanied. The pitch is that the tourists should, for their own safety, sign up for a tour on the spot. This can end up being a convenient scam if you do want to take a tour; however, if you want to travel independently double-check the current security situation with the Sri Lanka Tourist Board's information desk in the first arrivals hall.

You are likely to be approached at some stage by someone who, after striking up a conversation, asks for a donation for a school for the blind or some such cause – these people are invariably con artists. Galle Face Hotel, Cinnamon Grand Hotel and anywhere in between are favourite hunting grounds (because of the high concentration of top-end hotels).

In this area you will undoubtedly meet touts who will tell you about the 'once a year' elephant festival at Gangaramaya Temple. They will take you to the temple and charge you upwards of Rs 2000 for the service. Actually, there is an elephant at the temple every day and there is rarely a festival surrounding it. (But if it's the February *poya,* you can believe them as there really is an elephant festival at Gangaramaya!) A three-wheeler to the temple should cost no more than Rs 200.

As a rule of thumb, don't tell anyone it's your first day (or week) in the country. Touts love to prey on newbies and will try any trick in the book to hoodwink starry-eyed tourists. Even when coming into Colombo from the airport, have an idea where your hotel is so you can feign some in-country experience.

SIGHTS

Pettah, with its old temples and the Dutch Museum, has the highest concentration of sites in the city. Fort, with its colonial era buildings, is a sight unto itself. Colombo's 'must see' sight is the National Museum, located in Cinnamon Gardens.

Fort

During the European era Fort was indeed a fort, surrounded by the sea on two sides and a moat on the landward sides. Today it's a curious mix of brash modern structures, such as the World Trade Center, and venerable red-brick institutions from the Colonial-era, such as Cargills and Millers. The security presence is heavy here, curtailing vehicle access and some pedestrian access.

There's also a harbour (off-limits) and the large white dagoba (stupa) of **Sambodhi Chaitiya** (Map p80), perched about 20m off the ground on stilts – a landmark for sea travellers. A short walk east brings you to **St Peter's Church** (Map p80), which was converted from the Dutch governor's banquet hall and was first used as a church in 1804.

A good landmark in Fort is the **clock tower** (Map p80) at the junction of Chatham St and Janadhipathi Mawatha (once Queen St), which was originally a lighthouse.

Pettah & Kotahena

Immediately inland from Fort, the bustling bazaar of Pettah is one of the oldest districts in Colombo and one of the most ethnically mixed places in the country. You name it, and a boutique (street stall) will be selling it in Pettah. Each thoroughfare has its own speciality: Gabo's Lane and 5th Cross St specialise in Ayurvedic medicines, while jewellery stores line 2nd Cross St. The crowds in Pettah can reach Biblical proportions during the morning and late-afternoon rush hours as people go to and from work; try to time your visit for midday.

A 15-minute walk northeast of Pettah leads to the neighbourhood of Kotahena, home to several churches and Hindu temples.

DUTCH PERIOD MUSEUM

This unique **museum** (Map p80; ☎ 244 8466; 95 Prince St, Col 11; adult/child Rs 500/300; ☼ 9am-5pm Tue-Sat) was originally the 17th-century residence of the Dutch governor and has since been used as a Catholic seminary, a military hospital, a police station and a post office. The well-restored mansion contains a lovely garden courtyard. Exhibits include Dutch colonial furniture and other artefacts.

HINDU TEMPLES

Known as *kovil,* Hindu temples are numerous in Colombo, with a particularly high concentration in Pettah. All the following *kovils* are open from 6am to 6pm. On Sea St, the goldsmiths' street, **Old Kathiresan Kovil** (Map p80) and **New Kathiresan Kovil** (Map p80), both dedicated to the war god Murugan (Skanda),

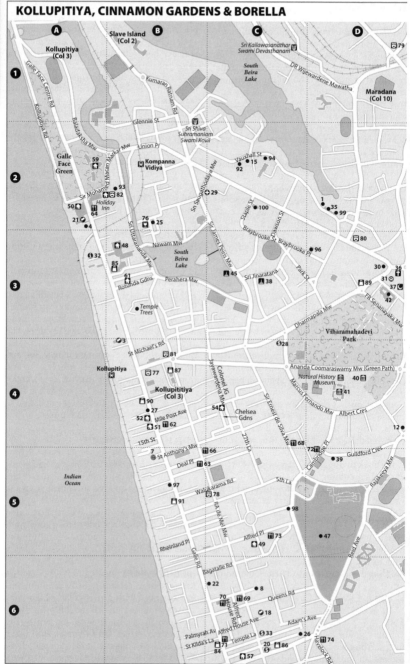

KOLLUPITIYA, CINNAMON GARDENS & BORELLA

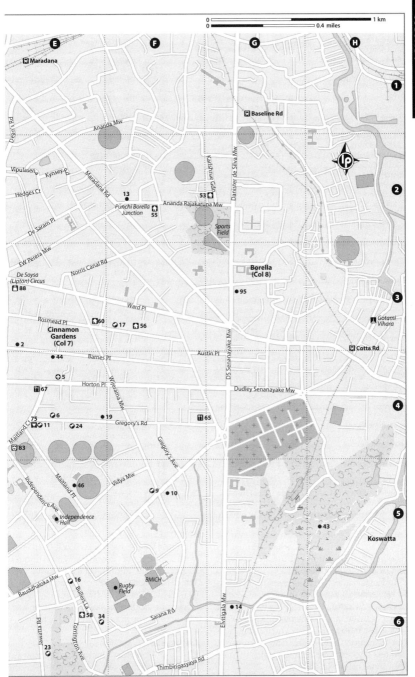

INFORMATION
Aitken Spence Travels **1** D2
Alliance Française **2** E3
American Embassy **3** B4
American Information
    Resource Center............................ **4** A2
Asiri Central Hospital **5** E4
Australian High
    Commission **6** E4
Berty's Cyber Cafe **7** B5
British Council **8** C6
British High
    Commission **9** F5
Buddhist Book Centre.......................**10** F5
Canadian Embassy.............................**11** E4
Central Cultural Fund........................**12** D4
Department of
    Archaeology ....(see 41)
Department of
    Immigration................................**13** F2
Department of Motor
    Traffic...**14** G6
DHL Worldwide
    Express...**15** C2
Dutch Embassy...................................**16** E6
French Embassy...................................**17** F3
German Embassy.................................**18** C6
Goethe Institut...................................**19** E4
HSBC Bank...**20** C6
Indian High
    Commission................................**21** A2
Indian Visa Office................................**22** C6
Italian Embassy...................................**23** E6
Japanese Embassy..............................**24** E4
Jetwing Travels...................................**25** B2
JF Tours & Travels...............................**26** C6
Lake House Bookshop.................(see 87)
Mac Technologies
    Cyber Cafe...............................(see 87)
Mountain Hawk
    Express...**27** B4
Nations Trust
    Bank/American
    Express...**28** C4
Nawaloka Hospital.............................**29** C2
Osu Sala...**30** D3
Post Office...**31** D3
Sri Lanka Tourist Board......................**32** A3
Standard Chartered
    Grindlays Bank............................**33** C6
Swedish Embassy...............................**34** E6
TNT Express...**35** D2

Tourist Police................................(see 32)
Vijitha Yapa Bookshook................(see 85)

SIGHTS & ACTIVITIES
Cinnamon Gardens
    Baptist Church.............................**36** D3
Colombo Club............................(see 59)
Dewata-Gaha Mosque **37** D3
Gangaramaya Temple.......................**38** C3
Lionel Wendt Centre.........................**39** D5
National Art Gallery...........................**40** D4
National Museum...............................**41** D4
Old Town Hall.....................................**42** D3
Royal Colombo Golf
    Club...**43** H5
Sapumal Foundation.........................**44** E4
Seema Malakaya
    Meditation Centre.......................**45** C3
Sri Lanka Cricket.................................**46** E5
University of Colombo.......................**47** D5

SLEEPING
Cinnamon Grand Hotel.....................**48** B3
Colombo House...................................**49** C5
Galle Face Hotel &
    Galle Face Regency.....................**50** A2
Hotel Renuka &
    Renuka City Hotel.......................**51** B4
Juliana Hotel.......................................**52** B4
Mrs Chitrangi de
    Fonseka's......................................**53** G2
Mrs Padmini
    Nanayakkara's..............................**54** C4
Mrs Swarna
    Jayaratne's...................................**55** F2
Parisare...**56** F3
Pearl City Hotel...................................**57** C6
Ranjit's Ambalama.............................**58** E6
Taj Samudra..**59** A2
Tintagel...**60** E3
YWCA National
    Headquarters...............................**61** B3

EATING
Amaravathi..**62** B4
Barefoot Garden Cafe.................(see 84)
Bars Cafe..**63** B5
Bavarian...**64** A2
Bayleaf...**65** F4
Chesa Swiss...**66** B5
Chutneys.....................................(see 48)
Coffee Bean...**67** E4

Commons..**68** C4
Crescat Boulevard.......................(see 85)
Cricket Club Cafe...............................**69** C6
Delifrance......................................(see 88)
Gallery Cafe...**70** C6
Green Cabin...**71** C6
Keells...(see 85)
Keells...(see 87)
Number 18...**72** D5
Paradise Road Cafe.....................(see 89)
Raffles...**73** C5
Sea Spray......................................(see 50)
Shanti Vihar...**74** D6

DRINKING
Clancy's Irish Pub...............................**75** E4
Galle Face Hotel...........................(see 50)
White Horse...**76** B2

ENTERTAINMENT
Bally's Casino......................................**77** B4
Bellagio Casino...................................**78** C5
Elphinstone Theatre..........................**79** D1
H2O...**80** D3
Liberty Cinema....................................**81** B4
Lionel Wendt Centre...................(see 39)
Zanziba...**82** B2
Zetter..**83** E4

SHOPPING
Barefoot...**84** C6
Crescat Boulevard..............................**85** B3
Lanka Hands..**86** C6
Liberty Plaza.......................................**87** B4
Mlesna Tea Centre.......................(see 85)
Odel Unlimited...................................**88** E3
Paradise Road.....................................**89** D3
Photo Technica............................(see 87)
Photo Technica...................................**90** B4
Photoflex...**91** B5

TRANSPORT
Air China..**92** C2
Automobile Association
    of Ceylon......................................**93** B2
Cathay Pacific.....................................**94** C2
Cycle Bazaar.......................................**95** G3
Emirates...**96** D3
Expo Aviation.....................................**97** B5
Royal Jordanian..................................**98** C5
Singapore Airlines..............................**99** D2
Thai Airways......................................**100** C2

are the starting point for the annual Hindu Vel festival held in July/August, when the huge *vel* (trident) chariot is dragged to various *kovils* on Galle Rd in Bambalapitiya.

In Kotahena, northeast of Pettah, you'll find **Sri Ponnambalam Vanesar Kovil** (off Map p80; Srimath Ramanathan Mawatha), which is built of South Indian granite, and **Sri Muthumariamman Kovil** (off Map p80; Kotahena St, Col 13). During the harvest festival of Thai Pongal (held in January), devotees flock to these temples, which become even more colourful and lively.

MOSQUES
The **Grand Mosque** (Map p80; New Moor St, Col 11) is the most important of Colombo's many mosques. In Pettah you'll also find the decorative 1909 **Jami-Ul-Alfar Mosque** (Map p80; cnr 2nd Cross & Bankshall Sts, Col 11), which has candy-striped red-and-white brickwork. Both mosques are closed to non-Muslims during prayer times and Fridays.

CHURCHES
The 1749 **Wolvendaal Church** (Map p80; Wolvendaal Lane, Col 11; 9am-3.30pm) is the most important

COLOMBO

Dutch building in Sri Lanka. When the church was built, this area was a wilderness beyond the city walls. The Europeans mistook the packs of roaming jackals for wolves, and the area became known as Wolf's Dale, or Wolvendaal in Dutch. The church is in the form of a Greek cross, with walls 1.5m thick, but the real treasure is its Dutch furniture. The Dutch governors had a special pew made with elegant carved ebony chairs, and the workmanship in the wooden pulpit, baptismal font and lectern is just as beautiful. The stone floor includes the elaborate tombstones of five Dutch governors.

The enormous, late-19th-century **St Lucia's Cathedral** (off Map p80; St Lucia's St, Kotahena; ☯ 5.30am-noon & 2-7pm) lies in the Catholic heart of the Kotahena district. The biggest church in Sri Lanka, it can hold up to 5000 worshippers. The interior is plain but the immense domed mass of the church is impressive.

One of the city's most interesting shrines is **St Anthony's Church** (off Map p80; St Anthony's Mawatha, Kotahena; ☯ 5-8.30am). Outside it looks like a typical Portuguese Catholic church, but inside the atmosphere is distinctly subcontinental. There are queues of devotees offering *puja* (offerings or prayers) to a dozen ornate statues; a statue of St Anthony said to be endowed with miraculous qualities is the centre of devotions. Mothers often bring pubescent daughters here to pray for protection from evil spirits that might take advantage of the girls' nascent sexuality. Photography is frowned upon.

Galle Face Green

Immediately south of Fort is Galle Face Green (Map pp84–5), a long stretch of lawn facing the sea. It was originally cleared by the Dutch to give the cannons of Fort a clear line of fire. Today its broad lawns are a popular rendezvous spot; on weekdays it's dotted with joggers, kite flyers and walkers, and on weekends (especially Sunday evenings) food vendors gather to feed the hordes.

The remaining structures of the 19th-century **Colombo Club** (Map pp84–5) face the green from the grounds of Taj Samudra hotel; the club's rooms are still used for functions. At opposite ends of the green are delightful old Galle Face Hotel and monolithic Ceylon Continental Hotel.

Cinnamon Gardens

About 5km south of Fort and 2km inland, Cinnamon Gardens is Colombo's ritziest address. A century ago it was covered in cinnamon plantations. Today it contains elegant tree-lined streets and the posh mansions of the wealthy and powerful, as well as the city's biggest park, several sports grounds and a cluster of museums and galleries.

The centrepiece of Cinnamon Gardens is the 50-acre **University of Colombo** (also called the University of Ceylon; Map pp84–5) campus, which originally opened as the Ceylon Medical School in 1870.

VIHARAMAHADEVI PARK

Colombo's biggest park, **Viharamahadevi Park** (Map pp84–5) was originally called Victoria Park but was renamed in the 1950s after the mother of King Dutugemunu (see p147). It's notable for its superb flowering trees, which bloom in March, April and early May. The broad Ananda Coomaraswamy Mawatha cuts across the middle of the park, while Colombo's white-domed **Old Town Hall** (also called White House; Map pp84–5) overlooks the park from the northeast. Working elephants sometimes spend the night in the park, happily chomping on palm branches. Northeast of the park, behind the Old Town Hall, is the bustling **DeSoysa (Lipton) Circus** (Map pp84–5). One corner of the roundabout is occupied by the upscale (and blissfully air-conditioned) Odel Unlimited shopping mall. Opposite is the **Cinnamon Gardens Baptist Church** (Map pp84–5), which dates to 1877. Located just south of the church is the **Dewata-Gaha Mosque** (Map pp84–5), a crumbling sun-bleached structure that bustles with people following the Friday afternoon prayers.

NATIONAL MUSEUM

Put Colombo's **National Museum** (Map pp84-5; ☎ 269 4767; Albert Cres, Col 7; adult/child Rs 500/300; ☯ 9am-5pm Sat-Thu) on your list of must-see sights. Within its hallowed halls you'll encounter all manner of art, carvings and statuary from Sri Lanka's ancient past, as well as swords, guns and other paraphernalia from the colonial period. There are fascinating 19th-century reproductions of English paintings of Sri Lanka, and an excellent collection of antique demon masks. Look out for the magnificent royal throne made for King Wimaladharma in 1693. The museum, built in 1877, is located on the south side of Viharamahadevi Park.

COLOMBO

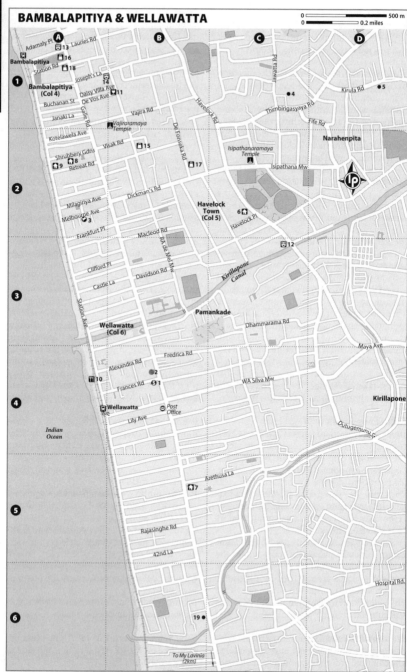

ART GALLERIES

Cinnamon Gardens is home to several worthwhile art galleries. If you've only time for one, visit the **National Art Gallery** (Map pp84-5; ☎ 269 3965; 106 Ananda Coomaraswamy Mawatha, Col 7; admission free; 🕑 9am-5pm, closed poya days), next to the National Museum. It has a permanent collection of portraits and landscapes, as well as some temporary exhibitions by Sri Lankan artists.

Just south of the National Museum, the stylish **Lionel Wendt Centre** (Map pp84-5; ☎ 269 3965; 18 Guildford Cres, Col 7; admission varies; 🕑 9am-1pm & 2-4pm Mon-Fri) has contemporary art and craft exhibitions, stages musical performances and has occasional sales of antiques and other items.

The **Sapumal Foundation** (Map pp84-5; ☎ 269 5731; 34/2 Barnes Pl, Col 7; admission free; 🕑 10am-1pm Thu-Sat) is located in what was once the home of artist Harry Pieris. Today this rambling tile-roofed bungalow is packed with some of the best examples of Sri Lankan art since the 1920s.

South Beira Lake & Around

South Beira Lake has been reduced in size over the years but remains a pretty centrepiece to the city. On its eastern side is the small but captivating **Seema Malakaya Meditation Centre** (Map pp84-5; 🕑 6am-6pm), designed by Geoffrey Bawa (see boxed text, p51) in 1985 and run by Gangaramaya Temple. The pavilions – one filled with Thai bronze Buddhas, the other centred on a bodhi tree and four Brahmanist images – are especially striking when illuminated at night.

A short walk east of the lake is the sprawling **Gangaramaya Temple** (Map pp84-5; ☎ 232 3038; Sri Jinaratana Rd, Col 2; 🕑 6am-6pm). Run by one of Sri Lanka's more politically adept monks, the temple complex has a library, a **museum** (donation Rs 100) and an extraordinarily eclectic array of bejewelled and gilded gifts presented by devotees and well-wishers over the years. Gangaramaya is the focus of the Navam Perahera (p91) on the February *poya* (full moon) day each year.

Dehiwala Zoo

By Western standards the conditions for the inhabitants of this **zoo** (Map pp78-9; ☎ 271 2751; Dehiwala; adult/child Rs 1000/500; 🕑 8.30am-6pm) are pretty dismal. Having said that, the place has steadily improved over the years. Still, most of the cages are too small and it's pretty depressing to see all the elephants chained up at the foot. The monkeys seem to have scored the best digs. The zoo is 10km south of Fort; you can get there on bus 118 from Dehiwala train station.

Kelaniya Raja Maha Vihara

This important Buddhist temple (off Map p80) is located 7km northeast of Fort, just off the Kandy Rd. Even if the thought of seeing yet another temple sends you reaching for the arrack, this one is worth the effort. The original temple was destroyed by Indian invaders, restored, destroyed again by the Portuguese, and restored again in the 18th and 19th centuries. The dagoba, which (unusually) is hollow, is the focus of the Duruthu Perahera in January each year. To reach the temple take bus 235 from in front of the traffic-police station, which is just northeast of the Bastian Mawatha bus station.

ACTIVITIES
Swimming

The only Colombo beach where you'd consider swimming is in Mt Lavinia, a somewhat faded resort area 11km south of Fort – and even that's borderline, with a severe

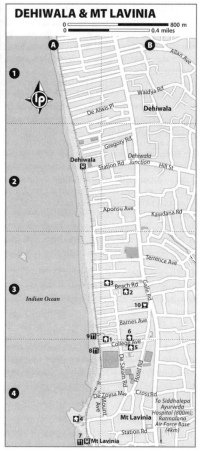

DEHIWALA & MT LAVINIA

SLEEPING
Berjaya Mount Royal Beach Hotel **1** B3
Blue Seas Guest House **2** B3
Haus Chandra **3** B3
Mount Lavinia Hotel **4** A4
Mrs Lyn Mendis' **5** B4
Tropic Inn **6** B3
EATING
Bu Ba **7** A4
Golden Mile **8** A4
Mughal Emperor **9** A3
DRINKING
Lion Pub **10** B3

a major centre for meditation instruction in the style of the late Mahasi Sayadaw. Accommodation and meals are offered free of charge, though donations are expected. Most meditators stay for an initial three-week training period, after which they can meditate on their own for as long as they like. White clothing (available on loan at no charge) must be worn. The Pugoda bus 224 passes the centre and can be caught from the Central Bus Station on Olcott MW.

Golf

Royal Colombo Golf Club (Map pp84–5; ☎ 269 5431; www.rcgcsl.com; Borella, Col 8; greens fee weekdays/weekend & holidays Rs 4000/5500, club hire Rs 200-1000, caddy Rs 550; ⏱ from 6am) has an 18-hole golf course at the Ridgeway Golf Links dating from 1879 – it was the third club in the British Empire to earn the 'royal' appellation. The links are in good condition. Call to reserve a tee time. Caddies are compulsory. Men must wear collars and decent shorts or trousers; for women, there's a one-word dress code: decency.

Ayurveda & Spas

Siddhalepa Ayurveda Hospital (off Map p90; ☎ 273 8622; Templers Rd) in Mount Lavinia is a full-service Ayurvedic health centre. **Taj Airport Garden Hotel** (off Map p80; ☎ 225 2950; www.tajhotels .com; 234-238 Colombo-Negombo Rd, Seeduwa), out near Bandaranaike International Airport, houses another Aryana Spa. Closer to the city centre, ayurvedic treatment is available at the Cinnamon Grand Hotel (p92).

Running

The Sri Lanka **Hash House Harriers** (www.colombo hash.com) get together twice a week for a leisurely jog around the city (and piss-up). Runs are at 5.15pm on Monday and 5.30pm on Wednesday. Check the website for starting points.

undertow at times and some foul waterways issuing into the ocean just to the north.

Visitors can use the pools at several top-end Colombo hotels for a fee. One of the nicest spots is the outdoor saltwater pool right by the seafront at Galle Face Hotel & Galle Face Regency (p92); it costs nonguests Rs 1000. A dip in the magnificently positioned pool at Mount Lavinia Hotel (p93) will cost Rs 600 and includes access to the hotel's private stretch of beach. Or head to Berjaya Mount Royal Beach Hotel (p93), which charges nonguests Rs 500.

Meditation

Kanduboda Meditation Centre (off Map pp78–9; ☎ 240 2306), 25km outside Colombo in Delgoda, is

FESTIVALS & EVENTS

The **Duruthu Perahera** is held at the Kelaniya Raja Maha Vihara (p89) on the January *poya*. The **Navam Perahera**, on the February *poya*, is led by 50 elephants; it starts from Gangaramaya Temple (p89) and is held around Viharamahadevi Park and South Beira Lake. During the **Vel** in July/August, the gilded chariot of Murugan (Skanda), the Hindu war god, is ceremonially hauled from the Kathiresan *kovil* (p83) to a *kovil* at Bambalapitiya.

See p294 for more information on nationwide festivals in Colombo.

SLEEPING

Colombo has accommodation to suit every taste. Most of the cheapies are family-run guest houses that are hidden down narrow lanes and unsigned. Despite their lack of promotion these guest houses are fairly easy to find provided you have the address. Midrange options are usually bland hotels catering to Indians or Maldivians. There are so many top-end options that you won't know where to start; their sheer number keeps prices competitive. Prices for top-end hotels can jump during the December holiday season, but budget and midrange places tend to have more stable room pricing.

Top-end hotels are found near Fort or Galle Face Green. Midrange places and guest houses are scattered across the city, but there are a few handy midrange places along Galle Rd. Mt Lavinia has some reasonably priced accommodation in quiet surrounds.

Fort & Pettah
BUDGET & MIDRANGE
Colombo YMCA (Map p80; ☎ 232 5252; 39 Bristol St, Col 1; dm/s Rs 200/250, s/d with fan Rs 400/500, r with fan & bathroom Rs 800) This old Y is seriously rundown and kind of depressing, but if you just want to find the cheapest bed in town this could be it. It offers 16-bed male-only dorms, and a few single and double rooms that are open to both men and women. There's a Rs 10 daily membership charge, as well as a Rs 100 key deposit.

Colombo City Hotel (Map p80; ☎ 534 1962; www .colombocityhotels.com; Level 3, 33 Canal Row, Col 1; r US$35; 🛜) Intimate and friendly, this boutique hotel has reasonable rates and a fine location in the historic Fort area. The 26 renovated rooms have TV. The sea views from the restaurant roof are outstanding. It's on a narrow alley opposite the World Trade Center.

TOP END
Grand Oriental Hotel (Map p80; ☎ 232 0391/2; goh@ sltnet.lk; 2 York St, Col 1; s/d/ste US$60/70/100) Opposite the harbour, this was Colombo's finest hotel 100 years ago, a place to see and be seen. Most rooms have been stripped of original features and renovated like a Spanish motel; the suites are pleasant but the standard rooms are boxy. There are superb views from the 4th-floor restaurant, Harbour Room (p94).

Galadari Hotel (Map p80; ☎ 254 4544; www .galadarihotel.lk; 64 Lotus Rd, Col 1; s/d US$83/95, ste from US$120; 🛇 🖵 🛋) This hotel is very popular with travellers from India, Malaysia and the Middle East. Although the decor is a bit tacky, the 446 rooms are comfortable and offer good views across the city. Restaurants include the Sheherezade Arabic Restaurant, and Stix (Chinese cuisine). The lobby-level nightclub, Gatsby's, is one of the city's busiest.

Hilton Colombo (Map p80; ☎ 249 2492; www .hilton.com; 2 Sir Chittampalam A Gardiner Mawatha, Col 2; r standard/executive US$147/236; 🛋) Among business travellers this place is known as the city's most efficient and most comfortable business hotel. With six restaurants (one of which is open round the clock), a pub, a 24-hour business centre, a fully equipped sports-and-fitness club and even a masseur at hand, you needn't even leave the hotel.

Kollupitiya
BUDGET
YWCA National Headquarters (Map pp84-5; ☎ 232 3498; natywca@sltnet.lk; 7 Rotunda Gardens, Col 3; dm Rs 550, d/tr/q Rs 2200/3300/4400; 🖵) This place has eight tidy, basic rooms that surround a leafy courtyard. It's a secure, homely refuge for female travellers; men can stay if they're with a female companion. There are women-only rooms with shared bathroom, while mixed rooms have private bathrooms. There's a cheap cafeteria (meals Rs 100 to 150), open from Monday to Saturday for breakfast, lunch and dinner.

MIDRANGE
Colombo House (Map pp84-5; ☎ 257 4900; www.colombo house.com; 26 Charles Pl, Col 3; s/d/tr Rs 2500/2900/3600, with air-con Rs 3000/3500/3750; 🛇) Lying on a quiet, leafy street not far from the University of Colombo, this ageing but attractive mansion has four large rooms.

COLOMBO

Mrs Padmini Nanayakkara's (Map pp84-5; ☎ 257 2095; 20 Chelsea Gardens, Col 3; s/d incl breakfast Rs 2000/3000) This place offers three small rooms in one of Colombo's classier neighbourhoods. It's a little cluttered with old books and antiques, but the house has some elegant furniture and a pretty little garden. Mrs Nanayakkara speaks fluent French.

Juliana Hotel (Map pp84-5; ☎ 533 4222; 316 Galle Rd, Col 3; r Rs 3500; ☒ 🖳) This midrange hotel is a little rough around the edges, but it remains a clean and functional option without breaking the bank. The facilities include a massage centre, internet cafe and Chinese restaurant. The location is very convenient for Colombo's main shopping areas.

Pearl City Hotel (Map pp84-5; ☎ 452 3800; www.pearlcityhotel.net; 17 Bauddhaloka Mawatha, Col 4; s/d Rs 3300/3850, deluxe Rs 3850/4400; ☒ 🛜) Standard rooms at the Pearl City are a little boxy and basic, but slightly better deluxe rooms are comfortable enough. It's a functional place with good aircon, a cafe and a central location.

Hotel Renuka & Renuka City Hotel (Map pp84-5; ☎ 257 3598; www.renukahotel.com; 328 Galle Rd, Col 3; s/d incl breakfast US$45/50; ☒ 🖳) Possibly the best-value midrange hotel in Colombo, the Renuka is split into the older Hotel Renuka and the newer Renuka City Hotel. Its 80 rooms are clean and well maintained and the staff is friendly. Added to this are two excellent, reasonably priced Sri Lankan restaurants. The complimentary all-you-can-eat breakfast is huge and a great way to start the day. The swimming pool is around 50m from the hotel, towards the sea.

TOP END

our pick **Galle Face Hotel & Galle Face Regency** (Map pp84-5; ☎ 254 1010-6; www.gallefacehotel.com; 2 Kollupitiya Rd, Col 3; hotel r US$86-120, Regency from US$115; ☒ 🖳) This 145-year-old *grande dame* of Colombo faces Galle Face Green to the north and the sea to the west. The sweeping stairways, high ceilings and grass courtyard buffeted by sea breezes look much the same as they did nearly 100 years ago. Just about everyone who visits Colombo shows up for a drink at the Veranda bar at some point, whether or not they stay at the hotel. While the northern wing still maintains an atmosphere of faded decadence, the southern wing has been renovated and caters to discerning tastes with a wine lounge, a state-of-the-art spa and a pricey fusion restaurant, 1864.

Taj Samudra (Map pp84-5; ☎ 244 6622; www.tajhotels.com; 25 Galle Face Centre Rd, Col 3; s/d with pool views US$85/95, with sea views US$95/105; ☒ 🖳 🐾) This is a vast edifice with elegant public areas and a well-tended 12-acre garden. The hotel has a 24-hour coffee shop (with an excellent Rs 800 buffet), a restaurant serving North Indian cuisine, another with Cantonese and Sichuan dishes, and a steak house.

Cinnamon Grand Hotel (Map pp84-5; ☎ 243 7437; www.cinnamonhotels.com; 77 Galle Rd, Col 3; s/d US$120/140; ☒ 🖳 🐾) This five-star hotel has a central location on Galle Rd and every available amenity. There's a fitness centre, a big outdoor swimming pool, several restaurants and a spacious lobby with a piano bar and confectionary. Attractive rooms are built around an enormous atrium. It's attached to the Crescat Boulevard plaza, which makes shopping easy.

Bambalapitiya, Havelock Town & Wellawatta

Mrs Marie Barbara Settupathy's (Map p88; ☎ 258 7964; jbs@slt.lk; 23/2 Shrubbery Gardens, Col 4; r incl breakfast from Rs 1700) The Settupathys offer five clean and tidy rooms. There's a sitting area with a TV and a minuscule pebble courtyard. To find the Settupathys' house, look for the church on the left as you come down Shrubbery Gardens. The guest house is at the end of the alley next to the church.

Hotel Sunshine (Map p88; ☎ 451 7676; sunshine.shrubbery@gmail.com; 5A Shrubbery Gardens, Col 4; r with/without air-con Rs 2500/1500; ☒) This small budget hotel rises steeply in between buildings. It has clean but plain rooms at reasonable rates, just a half-block from the sea.

Hotel Sapphire (Map p88; ☎ 238 3306; sapphire@slt.lk; 371 Galle Rd, Col 6; r standard US$45, s/d renovated US$58/64; ☒ 🖳 🐾) The two types of rooms here are the standard unrenovated rooms on the 2nd floor and the nicer refurbished rooms on the 3rd floor. If you plan on staying for a few days, they may throw in a free breakfast.

Havelock Place Bungalow (Map p88; ☎ 258 5191; www.bungalow.lk; 6-8 Havelock Pl, Col 5; r/ste US$110/150; ☒ 🖳 🐾) This handsome boutique hotel has seven rooms, refined decor, comfy lounge areas and a garden. The outdoor cafe here is also well worth a visit.

Cinnamon Gardens

Parisare (Map pp84-5; ☎ 269 4749; 97/1 Rosmead Pl, Col 7; s/d incl breakfast Rs 1000/1800) It's not the most luxurious guest house in town, but it's probably the most interesting. Parisare is a split-level home with few walls so that many of the common spaces are open-air. The original owners came from the countryside and asked the architect to make the place as nonurban as possible. The result is wonderful. Parisare is reasonably priced and very popular – book ahead.

Ranjit's Ambalama (Map pp84-5; ☎ 250 2403, 071 234 7400; www.ranjitsambalama.com; 53/19 Torrington Ave, Col 7; d with/without bathroom Rs 3800/2500; ⊠) This guest house is modern and airy, with a small leafy courtyard and a wealth of books on Buddhism. There are three homely rooms, two with attached bathrooms. All rooms have air-con, though you have to pay extra to use it (Rs 1250). Finding the house is a bit tricky. Coming down Torrington Ave from Bauddhaloka Mawatha, look for the mosque on the right, then take the first left at a small playground, and then the first right. It's the second house on the left.

Tintagel (Map pp84-5; ☎ 460 2122; www.tintagelcolombo.com; 65 Rosmead Pl, Col 7; s/d incl breakfast US$255/383; ⊠ 🖴 🛜 🛋) Set inside an old mansion, this ultrachic hotel amazes with its minimalist design, elegant contours and sharp colours. It is the brainchild of Shanth Fernando, the same designer who created Gallery Cafe (p95). Amenities include a fitness club and stunning ambience. Each room is unique and some include private splash pools. The service is impeccable.

Borella & Maradana
Mrs Swarna Jayaratne's (Map pp84-5; ☎ 269 5665, 0777 314977; indcom@sltnet.lk; 70 Ananda Rajakaruna Mawatha, Col 8; s/d Rs 1250/1600, with air-con Rs 1850/2200; ⊠) Mrs Jayaratne's guest house features two clean rooms with a shared bathroom. There's an attached guest sitting area with satellite TV, a balcony and a small patch of lawn. To get here catch bus 103 or 171 (Rs 7 from Fort train station) and get off at Punchi Borella Junction.

Mrs Chitrangi de Fonseka's (Map pp84-5; ☎ /fax 269 7919; 7 Karlshrue Gardens, Col 10; r US$40-60; ⊠) This is a modern home bubbling with eccentricity, including chintzy decor, lots of porcelain and an indoor fountain. The three spacious rooms have TV, air-con, and laptop and phone connections, and there's a fully equipped guest kitchen. Bus 103 or 171 from Fort will take you nearby; get off at Punchi Borella Junction.

Mt Lavinia
Blue Seas Guest House (Map p90; ☎ 271 6298; 9/6 De Saram Rd; s/d/tr incl breakfast Rs 1300/1725/2040) This large house down a quiet lane has 12 clean, simple and spacious rooms, some with balconies. There's a large sitting room decked out with colonial furniture, and a garden. Guests praise the staff members for their helpful attitude.

our pick **Mrs Lyn Mendis'** (Map p90; ☎ 273 2446; ranmal@bigfoot.com; 11 College Ave; d incl breakfast Rs 2500; ⊠) This friendly and easygoing guest house has a light-filled guest sitting area and a kitchen complete with stove and fridge. The breakfast is a veritable banquet and good value.

Tropic Inn (Map p90; ☎ 273 8653; www.tropicinn.com; 30 College Ave; s/d incl breakfast US$27/29; ⊠ 🖴) This multistorey hotel features 20 clean rooms in a simple, stylish building. There's an internal courtyard and many of the rooms have a balcony; all rooms have cable TV. The restaurant here has good-value light meals.

Haus Chandra (Map p90; ☎ 273 2755; hauschandra@wow.lk; 37 Beach Rd; s/d/ste/villa Rs 3500/5500/7500/13,800, all incl breakfast; ⊠ 🖴 🛋) Tucked along a quiet lane, this colonial-era residence turned hotel offers a variety of accommodation, from standard rooms to a charming villa that sleeps six. The two-person suite with antique furnishings, carpets and a fully equipped kitchen is a good option.

Berjaya Mount Royal Beach Hotel (Map p90; ☎ 273 9610-5; www.berjayaresorts.com; 36 College Ave; s/d US$60/65; ⊠ 🛋) This is a fading 1970s resort hotel where the rooms are dated but comfortable. In a nutshell, you're paying for its prime beach position.

Mount Lavinia Hotel (Map p90; ☎ 271 5221-7; www.mountlaviniahotel.com; 100 Hotel Rd; governor's wing s US$120-160, d US$140-180; ⊠ 🛋) Built in 1806 as the residence of the British governor, this magnificently marbled hotel overlooks the sea. About a third of the hotel – the part referred to as the 'governor's wing' – has colonial architecture; the remainder is modern. There's a private sandy beach and a beautifully positioned pool and terrace.

Airport
Hotel Goodwood Plaza (off Map p80; ☎ 225 2561; Canada Friendship Rd, Katunayake; s/d incl breakfast Rs 5000/6250) The basic motel-like rooms here are decent value, given the proximity to the airport. The hotel offers a shuttle (Rs 300) to and from the airport.

COLOMBO

EATING

Colombo unsurprisingly boasts the best selection of restaurants in Sri Lanka. In addition to good Sri Lankan food, you'll find North and South Indian, European, Malaysian, Japanese, Chinese and Korean cuisines.

For cheap, tasty food it's hard to beat a lunch packet. Sold between about 11am and 2pm on street corners and footpaths all over the city, the lunch packet contains rice and curry, usually made from vegetables, with fish or chicken as optional extras. It generally costs between Rs 100 and 125.

Fort & Pettah

Pagoda Tea Room (Map p80; ☎ 232 5252; 105 Chatham St, Col 1; mains Rs 75-150; ⏰ 9am-8pm) Hungry like the wolf? Duran Duran filmed its classic 1980s video for that very song in this venerable establishment. Although there's a variety of Sri Lankan, Malaysian, Chinese and Western dishes, the main focus is on inexpensive pastries.

Chettinad (Map p80; 293 Sea St, Col 11; rice & curry Rs 100; ⏰ noon-3pm & 6-11pm; �) Enjoy cheap South Indian and Sri Lankan food at this place in the heart of Pettah. The downstairs dining room is open to the street, and the menu is vegetarian only. Upstairs is air-con and offers both veg and nonveg meals; prices are about Rs 40 more than those downstairs. Bombay sweets are sold from a glass case in the lobby.

Harbour Room (Map p80; ☎ 232 0320; 2 York St, Col 1; mains Rs 350-600, buffets Rs 800; ⏰ 6-10am, 12.30-3pm & 6-10pm) Overlooking the city harbour from the 4th floor of Grand Oriental Hotel, this blandly decorated hotel dining room is worth visiting for its superb views. It has breakfast, lunch and dinner buffets, as well as an à la carte menu.

Seafish (Map p80; ☎ 232 6915; 15 Sir Chittampalam A Gardiner Mawatha, Col 1; mains Rs 700-1400; ⏰ noon-3pm & 6-11pm) At the end of an alley on the southern edge of Fort, the venerable Seafish serves seafood in a faded colonial-club setting.

Hilton Colombo has possibly the best array of upscale international restaurants in the city. **Curry Leaf** (Map p80; ☎ 249 2492; 2 Sir Chittampalam A Gardiner Mawatha, Col 1; buffet Rs 2000; ⏰ 7pm-midnight), tucked away in a lovely garden that recreates the atmosphere of a traditional village, serves excellent Sri Lankan food. It also has an arrack bar. **Ginza Hohsen** (Map p80; ☎ 249 2492; mains Rs 1000-1600) serves sushi and other Japanese fare (made with all-imported ingredients).

Kollupitiya

BUDGET

Green Cabin (Map pp84-5; ☎ 258 8811; 453 Galle Rd, Col 3; mains Rs 75-300; ⏰ 7.30am-8.45pm) This place is a bit of an institution in the local restaurant trade. It's well known for both its baked goods and its inexpensive Sri Lankan, Indian and Chinese dishes. The lunchtime buffet is excellent value – the mango curry, if it's on, is very good. For a snack try the vegetable pastries or the cardiac-arrest-inducing bacon-and-egg pies.

Amaravathi (Map pp84-5; ☎ 257 7418; 2 Mile Post Ave, Col 3; meals Rs 130-350; ⏰ noon-3pm & 6-11pm; ✖) Amaravathi offers some of the best South Indian cuisine in the capital for very reasonable prices. The menu includes three different vegetarian thalis ('all-you-can-eat' plates of rice, curries and accompaniments), plus a varied selection of veg and nonveg Madras- and Andhra-style dishes.

Crescat Boulevard (Map pp84-5; 89 Galle Rd, Col 3; mains Rs 135-250; ✖) A few steps from Cinnamon Grand Hotel, this shopping centre has a good food hall downstairs. You have a choice of Sri Lankan, Chinese, Malaysian or Indian cuisine – or burgers. Service is efficient, the surroundings are clean (with clean toilets nearby) and the prices are moderate.

Keells (Map pp84-5; Crescat Boulevard 89 Galle Rd, Col 3; Liberty Plaza RA de Mel Mawatha, Col 3) is a Western-style supermarket popular with expats.

MIDRANGE

Raffles (Map pp84-5; ☎ 255 2837; 35 Bagatale Rd, Col 3; mains Rs 200-500; ⏰ 10am-11pm; 🛜) This cosy restaurant includes several areas for a drink, and multiple dining rooms for a quiet dinner. Pastas, salads, soups, sandwiches and other light Western meals are available.

Bars Cafe (Map pp84-5; ☎ 478 6678; 24 Deal Pl, Col 3; mains Rs 400-600; ⏰ 11am-10pm; 🛜) Always reliable, Bars serves up tasty pastas, steaks, stir-frys, seafood, salads and excellent deserts. The atmosphere is smart and food comes up fast.

Bavarian (Map pp84-5; ☎ 242 1577; 11 Sir Mohamed Macan Markar Mawatha, Col 3; mains Rs 400-600; ⏰ noon-3pm & 6-11pm) Opposite Galle Face Hotel, this place does all things German. You may wish to visit during the happy hour (7pm to 8pm) to sample the draught German beer and wines.

Chutneys (Map pp84-5; ☎ 243 7437; Cinnamon Grand Hotel, 77 Galle Rd, Col 3; meals from Rs 500; ⏰ noon-3pm & 6-11pm) Decked out in black furnishings and pastel colour schemes, this chic-but-cheap restaurant offers some of the best South Indian fare in town. Try the signature dish, a 'cap dosa', one of 30 types of dosa (paper-thin rice- and lentil-flour pancakes) available. The dress code requires long pants. Despite the upscale atmosphere the prices make this place accessible to midrange budgets.

TOP END

Barefoot Garden Cafe (Map pp84-5; ☎ 258 9305; 704 Galle Rd, Col 3; sandwiches Rs 300-500, meals Rs 600-800; ☽ noon-3pm & 6-11pm) Located in the courtyard of the well-known Barefoot gallery (p97), this cafe serves sandwiches, snacks such as falafel in pita bread, and daily specials that usually include one Sri Lankan, one Thai, one Malay-Indonesian and several Western dishes. There's also a wine list.

Cricket Club Cafe (Map pp84-5; ☎ 250 1384; 34 Queens Rd, Col 3; meals Rs 600-900; ☽ 11am-11pm) This older-style bungalow with a garden and veranda is one of Colombo's most popular places to meet, drink and eat. It is packed with cricket memorabilia, needless to say. Options range from pasta to seafood to burgers with salad and chips. There's a good bar and an excellent selection of beers and wines.

Gallery Cafe (Map pp84-5; ☎ 258 2162; 2 Alfred House Rd, Col 3; mains from Rs 700; ☽ 11am-11pm; ☎) The historic building that houses Gallery Cafe used to be an office for Sri Lanka's most famous architect, Geoffrey Bawa (see boxed text, p51). The open-air cafe area looks over a pebbled courtyard, while the lounge bar is where Bawa's old office used to be – in fact, his desk is still there. The decor is stunning and the Sri Lankan–inspired dishes focus on fresh ingredients and bold, clean flavours. As a cheaper option, come for an afternoon coffee.

Chesa Swiss (Map pp84-5; ☎ 257 3433; 3 Deal Pl, Col 3; mains Rs 750-2200; ☽ 7-11pm) This classy restaurant serves delicious (and pricey) Swiss and French fare made from the freshest vegetables and meat imported from Australia. Lamb chops, duck breast, salmon fillet and beef tenderloin are a few of the menu items offered by European owners Catherine and Michael. A good selection of imported wines and beers is also available.

Sea Spray (Map pp84-5; ☎ 254 1010; 2 Kollupitiya Rd, Col 3; buffet lunch/dinner Rs 1100/1900; ☽ noon-3pm & 6-10pm) This quaint oceanside restaurant in Galle Face Hotel specialises in barbecued seafood; everything is fresh and tasty. The buffet is expensive, but you're also paying for the gorgeous seaside setting.

Wellawatta

Beach Wadiya (Map p88; ☎ 258 8568; 2 Station Ave, Col 6; mains from Rs 400; ☽ noon-3pm & 6-11pm) Renowned for its seafood, Beach Wadiya has attracted a popular following for decades, including an impressive list of celebrities: Princess Anne and Richard Branson, among others. Come early to pick a table inside the weather-beaten beach shack or outside in the sand, order a chilled Three Coins beer while a waiter fills you in on the day's catch, and receive your specially customised grilled or fried seafood platter. Reservations are recommended. Also, take care when entering the restaurant: you have to cross the railway tracks and there is no signal when trains approach.

Cinnamon Gardens

Paradise Road Cafe (Map pp84-5; ☎ 268 6043; 213 Dharmapala Mawatha, Col 7; light meals Rs 250-450) Part of the shop of the same name (p98), this cafe serves great coffee, milkshakes, cakes and light meals (such as quiche and spaghetti) in an airy veranda-style atmosphere upstairs. It's just southwest of De Soysa (Lipton) Circus.

Coffee Bean (Map pp84-5; ☎ 342 8788; 2 Maitland Cres, Col 7; coffee from Rs 150, sandwiches Rs 400; ☽ 6.30am-midnight; ☎) This US-based coffee outlet is wildly popular in Colombo and always attracts a young, hip crowd. Light meals are available.

Commons (Map pp84-5; ☎ 269 4435; 39A Sir Ernest de Silva Mawatha, Col 7; light meals Rs 400-500; ☽ 7.30am-midnight; ☎) This cafe has a strong following among Colombo's upwardly mobile. Customers lounge in soft seats arranged around low tables and feast on an array of Western dishes, including baked crab, burgers, pastas and wraps. The pancake and bacon breakfast is very good and the desserts are spot on.

Delifrance (Map pp84-5; Odel Unlimited, 5 Alexandra Pl, Col 7; coffee & lunch Rs 500; ☽ 10am-8pm) Filling sandwiches for shoppers on the go. It's on the ground floor of the very popular Odel Unlimited store.

Bayleaf (Map pp84-5; ☎ 269 5920; 79 Gregory's Rd, Col 7; mains Rs 650-1200; ☽ noon-3pm & 6-11pm) In a beautiful old mansion in one of Colombo's most exclusive streets, this place specialises in first-class pastries and baked goods, and has an à la carte menu with European fare. The management is friendly and engaging.

Number 18 (Map pp84–5; ☎ 269 4000; 18 Cambridge Pl, Col 7; mains from Rs 750; ✆ noon-3pm & 6.30-11pm) The menu here is a mix of Asian and Western dishes, with items such as Japanese tempura and pastas. For a local treat, try the Sri Lankan beef *smore* stew, which includes beef smoked for over seven hours. Film buffs will appreciate the cinematic theme.

Mt Lavinia

The beachfront here is lined with restaurants focusing on what most Mt Lavinia visitors expect: fresh seafood. Note that some restaurants have limited menus on weekdays because most local tourists come on the weekend.

Mughal Emperor (Map p90; ☎ 273 5809; 36 College Ave; mains from Rs 450; ✆ 11am-11pm) This North Indian restaurant is the newest place to make a splash on Mt Lavinia's beach. You can't miss its big yellow-and-red tent. The food is reasonably priced and high quality.

Bu Ba (Map p90; ☎ 273 2190; Mt Lavinia beach; mains from Rs 800; ✆ 8am-midnight) With candlelit tables right on the sandy beach, this seafood restaurant is a wonderful place for an evening meal. In the heat of the day you can retreat to the interior, little more than a grove of palm trees. Call ahead to find out what's on as weekend dance parties are sometimes held here. To find it, walk along the beach south of the Mount Lavinia Hotel.

Golden Mile (Map p90; ☎ 273 3997; 43/14 College Ave; mains Rs 1400-1600; ✆ 11am-midnight) Well-heeled visitors to Mt Lavinia often wash up at this open-air restaurant on the beach. The setting is romantic and you'll often get live music in the evenings. It specialises in Western-style seafood, with a variety of cooked prawns and a tasty seafood platter.

DRINKING

Galle Face Hotel (Map pp84–5; ☎ 254 1010-6; 2 Kollupitiya Rd, Col 3; ✆ 11am-midnight) Favourite gathering spots for a drink at this venerable institution include Veranda, a no-nonsense bar on the inside veranda, and the Checkerboard, a cluster of tables on the courtyard lawn facing the sea. Or go the whole hog and quaff imported wine while smoking Cuban cigars and nibbling French cheeses in the hotel's wine lounge.

Clancy's Irish Pub (Map pp84–5; ☎ 268 2945; 29 Maitland Cres, Col 7; ✆ 7am-3am Mon-Sat) Colombo's stab at Irishness offers pub grub and a variety of beers and ales, including Guinness. It's a popular spot, with regular quiz nights, live music on weekends and a few couches to sink into. All drinks are discounted 50% during the daily 6pm to 8pm happy hour. Long pants are required attire.

White Horse (Map pp84–5; ☎ 230 4922; 2 Nawam Mawatha, Col 2; ✆ 10am-2am) White Horse is a sparse, modern space with stainless-steel decor, and low couches and tables. On Friday nights the mixed crowd of locals and expats often spills out onto the street.

Bistro Latino (Map p88; ☎ 258 0063; 21 RA de Mel Mawatha, Col 4; ✆ 6.30pm-2am) This wine bar serves tapas (Rs 300 to 800) and plays recorded Latin jazz and salsa. The staff offers free salsa-dancing lessons.

Sri Lanka Ex-Servicemen's Institute (Map p80; 29 Bristol St, Col 1; ✆ 11am-11pm) If Billy Joel was from Sri Lanka, he would have started his career as the 'piano man' in this old bar for battle-hardened war heroes and salty-dog sailors. It serves Lion Lager at about the lowest prices you'll find outside a grocery store, but you're not paying for atmosphere. Solo women travellers are advised against drinking here.

Lion Pub (Map p90; Galle Rd, Mt Lavinia; ✆ 11am-11.30pm) Locals and tourists alike neck Lion Lager at this casual little bar that's not far from the beach. Look for the big lions at the gate.

ENTERTAINMENT

Colombo has a decent night-time scene but venues tend to be spread around the city and are poorly advertised, so you may need to hunt and peck around for the latest hip places. A night out may begin with dinner and live music, with some clubbing later on.

Casinos

Gaming is legal in Colombo, but only for foreign passport-holders. Most of the clientele are from Southeast and East Asia. Incentives to lure punters include free meals and drinks, plus free transport to and from the casino. Bets at most tables start at Rs 500. Most casinos are open 24 hours. Despite bearing identical names, those listed below have no relationship with the casinos in Las Vegas.

Bally's Casino (Map pp84–5; ☎ 257 3497; 14 Dharmapala Mawatha, Col 3) Near Liberty Plaza.

Bellagio Casino (Map pp84–5; ☎ 257 5271; 430 RA de Mel Mawatha, Col 3)

MGM Casino (Map p88; ☎ 259 1319; 772 Galle Rd, Col 4) Near Majestic City.

Cinemas

There are several mainstream cinemas that show Hollywood blockbusters, although often quite a while after they've been released elsewhere in the world. Tickets cost Rs 150 for adults and Rs 100 for children under 12. The foreign cultural centres show art-house films; see *LT, Travel Lanka* and the *Linc* for what's on.

Liberty Cinema (Map pp84–5; ☎ 501 3997; Dharmapala Mawatha, Col 3)

Majestic Cinema (Map p88; ☎ 258 1759; 4th fl, Majestic City, Galle Rd, Col 4)

Nightclubs

Most of Colombo's dance-oriented nightlife centres on the top hotels. All clubs have a cover charge of about Rs 500 to 600 (which usually includes one drink). Women usually get in free. The dress code is fashion-conscious but casual; entry is usually restricted to mixed couples and single women. Things get going at about 11pm and continue through to 6am. A lot of clubs in Colombo are fronts for prostitution and these are pretty obvious when you walk in the door. The places listed following (hopefully) aren't dealing in the sex trade.

Blue Leopard (Map p80; ☎ 232 0320; Grand Oriental Hotel, 2 York St, Col 1)

H2O (Map pp84–5; ☎ 258 6547; www.h2olanka.lk; 119 Union Place, Col 7) At the time of research this was the hottest club in the city. It has a glass dance floor and go-go girls, and sometimes hosts Western DJs.

Tramps (Map p80; ☎ 254 4544; Galadari Hotel, 64 Lotus Rd, Col 1)

Zanziba (Map pp84–5; ☎ 244 6589; 32B Huejay Court, 1/1 Sir Mohamed Macan Markar Mawatha, Col 3) An upmarket place with a handy location next to the Holiday Inn. Live bands sometimes play here.

Zetter (Map pp84–5; ☎ 268 2122; www.zetter.lk; 73/18 Maitland Cres, Col 7) This is a high-quality club and bar with a small but fun dance floor.

Live Music

Rhythm & Blues (Map p88; ☎ 536 3859; 19/1 Daisy Villa Ave, Col 4; admission weekday/weekend Rs 300/500; 6pm-4am Wed & Thur, 6pm-5am Fri & Sat, 6pm-2.30am Sun-Tue) This place has live rock, R&B and blues nightly. Despite the Daisy Villa Ave address, it's on RA de Mel Mawatha.

Barefoot Garden Cafe (Map pp84–5; ☎ 258 9305; 704 Galle Rd, Col 3; ☯ noon-3pm & 6-11pm) Hosts live jazz performances most Sunday afternoons; check its chalkboard for a schedule of events.

Clancy's Irish Pub (Map pp84–5; ☎ 268 2945; 29 Maitland Cres, Col 7; ☯ 7am-3am Mon-Sat)) Hosts live local bands most nights.

On the first Sunday of every month there are free jazz performances from noon to sunset at the rugby field (Map pp84–5), next to the Bandaranaike Memorial International Conference Hall (BMICH) in Colombo 7.

Sport

Sri Lanka Cricket (Map pp84–5; ☎ 267 9568; www.sri lankacricket.lk; 35 Maitland Pl, Col 7; ☯ ticket office 8.30am-5.30pm) The top sport in Sri Lanka is, without a doubt, cricket. You can buy tickets for major games from Sri Lanka Cricket, at the office next to Sinhalese Sports Club.

Theatre

Foreign cultural centres such as the British Council occasionally host live theatre performances. These are advertised in newspapers and magazines such as *LT*, as well as at cafes and hotels frequented by expats. The following are some other notable theatres in Colombo.

Elphinstone Theatre (Map pp84–5; ☎ 243 3635; Maradana Rd, Col 10) This finely restored 80-year-old theatre maintains a busy program that includes music, theatre and films.

Lionel Wendt Centre (Map pp84–5; ☎ 269 5794; 18 Guildford Cres, Col 7) Among other events, this gallery occasionally hosts live theatre.

Lumbini Theatre (Map p88; ☎ 250 3225; Havelock Rd, Col 5) This is the city's oldest theatre and one of the only places where you'll find modern Sinhala performances.

SHOPPING

If you missed out on buying Sri Lanka's plentiful handicrafts while travelling, don't worry – just about everything is available in Colombo. The better shops can easily arrange shipping.

Fabrics & Clothing

Sri Lanka has a thriving weaving industry that produces both hand- and machine-woven fabrics, and is a major garment manufacturer. All manner of clothing, ranging from beachwear to padded jackets, is sold in Colombo.

Barefoot (Map pp84–5; ☎ 258 0114; www.bare footceylon.com; 704 Galle Rd, Col 3) Designer Barbara Sansoni's beautifully laid-out shop, located in an old villa, is justly popular for its bright hand-loomed textiles, which are fashioned

COLOMBO

into bedspreads, cushions, serviettes and other household items (or sold by the metre). You'll also find textile-covered notebooks, lampshades and albums, and a large selection of stylish, simple clothing.

Odel Unlimited (Map pp84-5; ☎ 268 2712; www .odel.lk; 5 Alexandra Pl, Col 7) Head here to shop with the glamorous. You'll find everything from homewares to designer-label clothing and sportswear to banana soap.

House of Fashion (Map p88; ☎ 250 4639; cnr RA de Mel Mawatha & Visak Rd, Col 4) This three-storey surplus outlet for the nation's garment industry is the place to go for serious clothes shopping. Many items are hugely discounted.

Handicrafts & Collectables

Paradise Road (Map pp84-5; ☎ 268 6043; 213 Dharmapala Mawatha, Col 7) In addition to a variety of colonial and Sri Lankan antiques, you'll find a good selection of original homewares here. Paradise Road's Gallery Cafe (p95) carries a similar array of collectables. Both are excellent places to look for small gifts to take home.

Raux Brothers (Map p88; ☎ 533 9016; 7 De Fonseka Rd, Col 5) This 48-year-old antiques showroom, located in a large, beautiful colonial house, stocks an impressive range of furniture and artworks crafted from wood. There are genuine antiques and handcrafted new pieces. This is possibly the best antiques house in the city.

Lanka Hands (Map pp84-5; ☎ 451 2311; 135 Bauddhaloka Mawatha, Col 4) Here you'll find a good variety of local crafts, including jewellery, Sinhalese masks, brightly painted wooden toys and puzzles, cane furniture and basketry, drums and more. The prices are reasonable.

Gems & Jewellery

There are many gem dealers and jewellers along Galle Rd and RA de Mel Mawatha, and on Sea St in Pettah, where the shops can be on a tiny scale. The biggest outlets employ the most silver-tongued salespeople in the business.

Sri Lanka Gem & Jewellery Exchange (Map p80; ☎ 239 1132; www.slgemexchange.com; 4th & 5th fl, East Low Block, World Trade Center, Bank of Ceylon Mawatha, Col 1) This is your safest bet for price and authenticity. It contains 41 government-approved shops, plus a gem-testing laboratory.

Tea

Ceylon tea is sold in just about every place that sells foodstuffs, from minimarts to supermarkets. For the best quality and selection head to a **Mlesna Tea Centre** (Crescat Boulevard Map pp84-5; 89 Galle Rd, Col 3; Majestic City Map p88; Galle Rd, Col 4) or a Dilmah Tea Shop, located inside **Odel Unlimited** (Cinnamon Gardens Map pp84-5; 5 Alexandra Pl, Col 7; Majestic City Map p88; Galle Rd, Col 4). In these outlets you'll find a variety of teas packed in airtight canisters, ceramic containers and wooden or cardboard boxes, along with strainers, china and other tea-making paraphernalia.

Photographic Supplies & Repairs

Photoflex (Map pp84-5; ☎ 258 7824; 1st fl, 451/2 Galle Rd, Col 3)

Photo Technica (Kollupitiya Map pp84-5; ☎ 257 6271; 288 Galle Rd, Col 3; Liberty Plaza Map pp84-5; ☎ 257 7666; RA de Mel Mawatha, Col 3; Majestic City Map p88; ☎ 253 0766; Galle Rd, Col 4)

GETTING THERE & AWAY

Colombo is the international gateway to Sri Lanka, and it is also the centre of the island's bus and rail networks. You may find leaving Colombo by train is easier than by bus, though trains are usually less frequent and a little more expensive than buses. There's more order at the train stations than at the bus stations, and there's often less overcrowding once on board.

Air

Colombo's domestic airport is at Ratmalana Air Force Base, south of Mt Lavinia. There is no public transport to or from this airport, but AeroLanka runs its own shuttle bus. Because of the air force presence, security is heavy and you need to check in two hours before take-off.

Expo Aviation (Map pp84-5; ☎ 257 6941; info@expo avi.com; 464 Galle Rd, Col 3) and **AeroLanka** (Map p88; ☎ 250 5632; www.aerolanka.com; 500 Galle Rd, Col 6) operate flights between Colombo and Jaffna (one way Rs 10,000), while AeroLanka also flies to Trincomalee. At the time of writing, however, AeroLanka had temporarily suspended flights to Trinco.

Bandaranaike International Airport is at Katunayake, 30km north of the city and about 2km east of the Colombo–Negombo Rd. For information on international flights see p304.

The following airlines have offices in Colombo:

Air Canada (Map p80; ☎ 254 2875; counter@united holidays.lk; 06-02 East Tower, World Trade Center, Col 1)

Air China (Map pp84-5; ☎ 473 2485; www.air-china.com; 140A Vauxhall St, Col 2) Represented by Jetwing Air.

American Airlines (Map p80; ☎ 247 5323; www.aa.com; 9 York St, Col 1)

Asiana Airlines (Map p80; ☎ 243 0380; asiana.cmb@keells.com; 9 York St, Col 1)

Cathay Pacific (Map pp84-5; ☎ 233 4145; www.cathaypacific.com; 186 Vauxhall St, Col 2)

Emirates (Map pp84-5; ☎ 230 0200; Hemas House, 75 Braybrooke Pl, Col 2)

Indian Airlines (Map p80; ☎ 232 3136; skyindu@sltnet.lk; 4 Bristol St, Col 1)

Kuwait Airways (Map p80; ☎ 244 5531; www.kuwait-airways.com; Ceylinco House, 69 Janadhipathi Mawatha, Col 1)

Malaysia Airlines (Map p80; ☎ 234 2291; www.malaysiaairlines.com; 81 York St, Col 1)

Qatar Airways (Map p80; ☎ 577 0000; Level 3, East Tower, World Trade Center, Col 1)

Royal Jordanian (Map pp84-5; ☎ 230 1621; 40A Cumaratunge Munidasa Mawatha, Col 3)

Singapore Airlines (Map pp84-5; ☎ 230 0750; www.singaporeair.com; 315 Vauxhall St, Col 2)

Sri Lankan Airlines (Map p80; ☎ 019 733 5500, 019 733 5555; www.srilankan.aero; Level 3, East Tower, World Trade Center, Col 1)

Swiss Air (Map p80; ☎ 243 5403; Baurs Bldg, 5 Upper Chatham St, Col 1)

Thai Airways (Map pp84-5; ☎ 230 7100; JAIC Hilton, 200 Union Place, Col 2)

United Airlines (Map p80; ☎ 234 6024; 06-02 East Tower, World Trade Center, Col 1)

Bus

Colombo's bus stations are filthy, congested and disorganised. On the up side, there are plenty of buses going frequently in all directions, so once you've found your bus you needn't wait long for a departure. The city has three main bus terminals, all just east of Fort train station on the south edge of Pettah (Map p80). Long-distance buses leave from Bastian Mawatha station and Saunders Pl station; Central Bus Station on Olcott Mawatha is where many suburban buses start and stop. See boxed text, right, for details of selected services.

Train

The main train station, Colombo Fort (Map p80), is within walking distance of the city centre. Trains in transit often stop only for two or three minutes. See boxed text, p100, for details of services.

There's an **information office** (☎ 244 0048; ✆ 9am-5pm Mon-Fri, 9am-1pm Sat), which is in fact a branch office of JF Tours & Travels, at the front of Fort station. The helpful staff know everything about transport in and out of Colombo. Or you could try the information desk in the station. There is left-luggage storage at the station's **cloakroom** (per bag per day Rs 60; ✆ 4.30am-11.30pm).

GETTING AROUND
To/From the Airport

AeroLanka offers free shuttle services to the domestic airport at Ratmalana Air Force Base if you hold its tickets; otherwise you'll have to take a taxi.

Taxis and buses are the most convenient forms of transport to and from Bandaranaike International Airport. If you're arriving in the dead of the night, it's best to book a room

---

SELECTED BUS DESTINATIONS FROM COLOMBO

From Bastian Mawatha

Ambalangoda Regular/air-con Rs 90/180, two hours

Galle Regular/air-con Rs 104/230, three hours

Hikkaduwa Regular/air-con Rs 100/170, two to three hours

Kandy Regular/air-con Rs 124/250, 2½ to 3½ hours

Kataragama Regular/air-con Rs 195/410, 10 hours

Matara Regular/air-con Rs 159/300, four to five hours

Nuwara Eliya Air-con Rs 380, six hours

Tangalla Regular/semiluxe Rs 195/300, six hours

From Saunders Pl

Anuradhapura Regular/air-con Rs 224/350, five hours

Badulla Regular/air-con Rs 374/640, seven hours

Haputale Regular/air-con Rs 380/500, six hours

Kurunegala Regular/air-con Rs 99/200, four to five hours

Negombo Regular/air-con Rs 48/80, one to two hours

Ratnapura Regular/air-con Rs 106/215, three hours

Polonnaruwa Regular/air-con Rs 220/350, six hours

Trincomalee Regular/semiluxe Rs 265/380, eight hours

COLOMBO

MAIN TRAINS FROM FORT

Destination	Departure time	3rd-class fares (Rs)	2nd-class fares (Rs)	1st-class fares (Rs)	Duration (hr)
Anuradhapura	5.45am, 10.40am, 1.45pm	175	330	750	5
Anuradhapura (Intercity Express)	4.20pm	250	400	600	4
Anuradhapura (Night Mail)	9.30pm	175	330	750	5
Batticaloa (Intercity Express)	7.15pm	270	500	1000	9-10
Badulla via Kandy (Podi Menike)	5.55am	235	430	850	9
Badulla via Peradeniya Junction (Udarata Menike)	9.30am	235	430	850	9
Badulla (Night Mail)	8.15pm	235	430	850	9
Kandy via Peradeniya Junction	7am, 3.35pm	170	250	400	2½
Kandy via Rambukkana	10.30am, 12.40pm, 4.35pm, 5.40pm	115	210	—	3
Matara via Bentota, Hikkaduwa & Galle	6.50am, 8.35am, 10.30am, 2.05pm, 3.50pm, 4pm, 4.48pm	140	260	—	4
Negombo	4am, 5.10am, 5.41am, 7.30am, 9.35am, 11.30am, 1.10pm, 2.10pm, 4.30pm, 4.55pm, 5.15pm, 5.30pm, 6.05pm, 7pm, 8.20pm	45	—	—	2
Polonnaruwa	7.15pm	210	390	800	6-9
Trincomalee	8.45am, 8pm	235	440	850	8

and let the hotel or guest house know what time you'll be arriving. Staff *should* be able to organise a driver to pick you up from the airport, though it's easy enough to jump in a taxi.

Bus 187 to the airport (Rs 80) departs the Bastian Mawatha station every 15 minutes from 6am until 9pm. The buses are easy to find as there are men screaming out 'Airport! Airport!' whenever one is filling up. The bus stops 500m from the airport; waiting three-wheelers will take you the rest of the way for Rs 100.

From the airport, buses leave every 30 minutes between 4.30am and 11pm. As you exit the airport, walk to the right and flag down a three-wheeler, which will take you to the bus stand down the road. Taxi drivers will tell you there is no public transport.

It's possible, although not particularly convenient, to catch a commuter train to Colombo. The station is near the turn-off from the main road, about 500m from the terminal.

If you want a taxi, head to the Ceylon Tourist Board's **information desk** (☎ 225 2411; ☼ 24hr), in the first arrivals hall after you exit through customs, and find out the latest fixed rates. At the time of writing a one-way fare was Rs 2100 to Colombo (40 minutes to 1½ hours), Rs 1200 to Negombo (20 minutes) and Rs 4600 to Kandy (two to three hours). After you've exited the second arrivals hall that's full of hotel and hire-car agencies, you'll be pounced on by an army of taxi drivers – take your pick, as you'll know what you pay.

Avoid taking a three-wheeler between the airport and Colombo; it's a long, miserable journey and you'll be sucking in exhaust fumes all the way.

The airport itself is modern, clean and compact (with plenty of soft chairs if you need to crash for a few hours before a flight).

The departure terminal has the usual array of duty-free shops and facilities, as well as a branch of the Coffee Bean where you can access free wi-fi. Left-luggage facilities are available (Rs 25 per bag per day).

Public Transport
BUS

The *A–Z Street Guide* contains a detailed table and a map showing bus routes in Colombo. The Central Transport Board (CTB) and private bus companies operate parallel services. A timetable is not necessary – the buses can hardly be described as running to one. Buses going down Galle Rd from Fort or Pettah include 100, 101, 102 and 400, and can be picked up at the Central Bus Station. Fares vary from Rs 4 to 25, depending on distance.

Private semiluxury and luxury buses also ply Galle Rd, although they are far fewer in number than the regular buses. Sometimes they have a destination sign in English in the front window. Generally they have curtains and soft seats. The fare is about twice that for ordinary buses, but still a bargain.

TRAIN

You can use the train to get to the suburbs dotted along Galle Rd – Kollupitiya, Bambalapitiya, Wellawatta, Dehiwala and Mt Lavinia – and to avoid the smog, noise and hassle of bus travel. Timetables are clearly marked at the stations, though if you just turn up you shouldn't have to wait long. If you board the train at Fort train station, double-check that it stops at all stations or you may end up speeding to Galle. Train fares are fixed and are usually marginally lower than bus fares.

Taxi

Some taxis are metered, but often the driver won't use the meter – agree on the fare before setting off. A taxi from Fort train station to Galle Face Hotel (a little over 2km) should cost about Rs 200 (less if a meter is used). Getting to Mt Lavinia from Fort station should cost around Rs 1000.

A less fraught alternative is using one of Colombo's radio cab companies, which take anywhere from five to 20 minutes to arrive. All have air-con cars with meters and average Rs 50 per kilometre. Reliable companies include **Ace Cabs** (☎ 281 8818), **GNTC** (☎ 268 8688) and **Cool Kangaroo** (☎ 258 8588).

Three-wheeler

Everywhere you look you'll see a three-wheeler, often referred to as Bajaj after one of the Indian manufacturers. Darting through traffic in one of these might be called exhilarating by some and downright reckless by others.

As a rule of thumb you should pay no more than Rs 50 per kilometre, but agree on a fare before getting in. At times three-wheeler drivers will try their luck by asking for a ridiculous initial fare in the hope that you haven't got a clue. To this you can roll your eyes and bargain as best you can. From Fort, expect to pay Rs 300 to get to Cinnamon Gardens, Rs 500 to Bambalapitiya and Rs 800 to Mt Lavinia.

You'll generally get a better price hailing a three-wheeler on the street than using one that's waiting outside a hotel or sitting at a three-wheeler stand.

Keep in mind that it's often cheaper and less frustrating to take a metered taxi.

COLOMBO

West Coast

You don't have to be in Sri Lanka for long to realise that a good curry consists of a spicy melange of flavours and contrasts that, when mixed together, set your taste buds dancing for joy. Sri Lanka's west coast is a little like its cuisine: it consists of two or three utterly opposing tastes and numerous experiences that result in something so delightful it's hard to define. The rice, the essential of any curry, would have to be Colombo itself – there is masses of it and it seems to last forever. The far north could only be the coconut *sambol*; after all, this wild and little visited region seems to consist of almost nothing but coconut plantations and lagoons that sparkle in the sun. Just as dhal is a staple of any Sri Lankan meal, Negombo, the cheerful beach town crowned with church spires and encircled by bird-filled canals, is, thanks to its proximity to the airport, a staple of almost every visitor's Sri Lankan journey.

South of Colombo's rice bowl you get to a string of beach towns flavoured by the fruits of the sea. You could tuck into jackfruit curry or grilled seer fish in one of Bentota's chic boutique-hotel restaurants, but do make sure you avoid eating turtle-egg omelettes in Kosgoda, which is home to the fascinating turtle sanctuaries. Further south, in Ambalangoda, you can shop for Sri Lanka's famous devil masks and then celebrate by snacking on devilled prawns. Finally, you reach the backpacker haunt and laid-back beach party town of Hikkaduwa where nothing else but a banana pancake will do for dessert. Bon appétit!

HIGHLIGHTS

- Making your own tracks in the little visited **North** (opposite)
- Finding your feet after a long flight in charming, but ramshackle **Negombo** (p105)
- Feeling the stress levels drop under the palm trees of lovely **Bentota** (p112)
- Giving a baby turtle a helping hand in life near **Kosgoda** (see boxed text, p116)
- Learning the secrets behind the devil masks in **Ambalangoda** (p115)
- Raising a toast to the sunset after a hard day's diving and surfing in lively **Hikkaduwa** (p117)

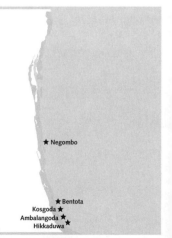

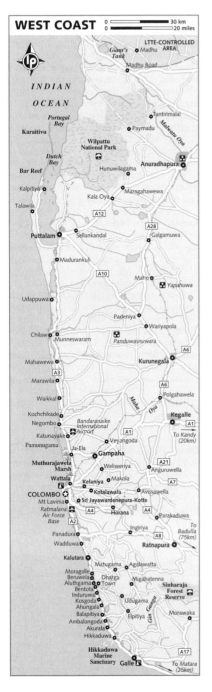

WEST COAST

Dangers & Annoyances

All along the west coast you have to watch out for dangerous currents, undertows and rip tides, particularly with the bigger seas during the wet season, which runs from April or May to October or November. The secret to safe swimming is actually to swim where the waves are biggest, or breaking most frequently, as calmer patches are normally plagued by deadly currents – it's these that drown people every year, not the waves. Watch where other people are swimming or ask reliable locals about when or where to go for a dip. In some places sea pollution is another deterrent – the further you are from town centres, especially Colombo, the better. At the time of research the far north of this area, around and including Wilpattu National Park, was closed due to fighting between the army and Liberation Tigers of Tamil Eelam (LTTE). This situation may have changed in the life of this book.

NORTH OF COLOMBO

Leaving Colombo most eyes look south, but for those with time on their hands and a sense of curiosity, or for those on the slow road towards Anuradhapura, then the northbound A3 heads out of Colombo, skirts some charming old Dutch canals, slides past some sandy beaches and gets utterly lost among a matted tangle of coconut groves. It all adds up to a wonderful sense of discovery. Much of this area remains completely unexplored by tourists and the chances of finding an untarnished beach is high – though of course tourist facilities are almost zero. The one place that does receive plenty of visitors is workaday Negombo, which, sitting close to the Bandaranaike International Airport, and with a wide range of places to stay and eat, makes for a perfect first or last taste of tropical Sri Lanka.

WILPATTU NATIONAL PARK

Due to security issues Wilpattu National Park was closed at the time of research, but there is every chance that it might well re-open during the lifetime of this book. If so you'll find dense pockets of jungle scrub interspersed with small clearings, and tanks that shrink in the dry season and swell in the monsoon. The park is home to up to 50 elephants and 50 or

---

THE 2004 TSUNAMI – AFTERMATH IN THE WEST

The tsunami caused significant damage to many places along the coast south of Colombo. However, the waters were fickle, and some beachside places were untouched while others were completely wiped out. Damage can still be seen away from the tourist developments around Beruwela, Bentota, Kosgoda and Ambalangoda. Between Ambalangoda and Hikkaduwa is where some of the most significant loss of life occurred. It was here that a train was trapped and hundreds of people lost their lives.

Initial efforts to enforce a buffer zone between the sea and developed areas have mostly been abandoned, though many beaches now sport highly unattractive protective berms.

---

more leopards, as well as spotted deer, sloth bears, wild pigs, crocodiles and more. At 1085 sq km, it is Sri Lanka's largest national park.

Getting There & Away

The turn-off to the park on the rough but paved Puttalam-Anuradhapura Rd (A12) is 26km northeast of Puttalam and 20km southwest of Anuradhapura. A further 8km of rough road leads to the park entrance and office at the barely discernable village of Hunuwilagama.

A bus from Puttalam to the junction for the park is Rs 70.

PUTTALAM & AROUND

☎ 032 / pop 42,000

With a pleasant setting on the edge of a lagoon, the old trading, pearling and fishing town of Puttalam is the kind of seriously go-slow place in which nobody understands the need for a watch. It used to be a handy base for trips into Wilpattu National Park, but with the park's closure almost nobody heads up this way nowadays.

The turn-off to the peninsula towns of Kalpitiya and Talawila is south of Puttalam, and leads past salt pans and a salt factory. The somewhat preserved Dutch fort on the peninsula road dates from 1670, but with the army occupying it you're unlikely to get a look inside. To the north of Kalpitiya a string of

islands guards Dutch Bay and Portugal Bay. However, security issues mean that you're unlikely to get far along this road at present.

At **Talawila** there's a Catholic shrine to St Anne. The church features satinwood pillars and is pleasantly situated on the seafront. Thousands of pilgrims come here in March and July, when major festivals honouring St Anne are held. The festivals include huge processions, healing services and a fair.

Accommodation in Puttalam is basic.

Senatilake Guest Inn (☎ 226 5403; 81A Kurunegala Rd; tw with/without air-con Rs 2200/1100; ❄) has 10 rooms, some of which are fan-only, and all of which are overpriced; the restaurant is good and the bus station is only some 300m away.

It feels like the country at the five-room **Dammika Holiday Resort** (☎ 226 5192; 51 Good Shed Rd; r with/without air-con Rs 1650/1100; ❄), a peaceful place 1km south of the town, where you'll find dark rooms that are so clean they smell of disinfectant. Meals in the pleasant dining rooms cost about Rs 250.

You can sit on the shady verandas of the **Rest House** (☎ /fax 226 5299; Beach Rd; r with/without air-con Rs 1650/1000; ❄) and watch cows graze on the grounds. The eight large rooms in this sleepy old place are gloomy, and those without air-con have filthy sheets and lots of flies to keep you company. By contrast the more expensive rooms are quite pleasant. The bar-restaurant is popular; the bus station is 500m away.

There are frequent buses to Colombo (regular/semiluxury/air-con Rs 116/195/230, three hours). You'll probably have to fight tooth and nail for a seat on a bus passing through from Colombo bound for Anuradhapura (Rs 100, two hours). You may also have to change at Kala Oya, on the boundary between Western Province and North Central Province.

There's infrequent train service to and from Colombo (2nd/3rd class Rs 230/130, 3½ hours). The station is 1km south of town.

PUTTALAM TO NEGOMBO

Although the A3 stays close to the coast, there are few ocean views from the road. Rather, when heading south to Negombo, you pass through an endless series of coconut plantations, which have their own rhythmic beauty.

The tiny village of **Udappuwa**, south of Puttalam, has a hectic morning fish market and an important Hindu temple with a large *gorpum* (this tower was covered in straw matting when we last visited, giving it the appearance of a giant haystack). A colourful festival is held here in August, when devotees test their strength by walking on red-hot coals. Nearby the village mosque and church glare at one another from opposite sides of the street. Tourists never venture down the ripped-out road leading to the village and there are no facilities at all. The beach is also filthy and no place for a swim. If you're not prepared to wait for one of the very rare buses from the junction, you'll either need to have your own transport or hitch – it will take time!

Twelve kilometres to the south of Udappuwa, **Chilaw** has a strong Roman Catholic flavour, and has elaborate statues to religious figures and local cardinals in the centre.

Munneswaram, 5km to the east of Chilaw, has a rather interesting Hindu temple that is an important centre of pilgrimage. There are three shrines at this complex; the central one is dedicated to Shiva. A major festival, also featuring fire walking, occurs here in August. Again few tourists come here, but that doesn't stop a possie of guides and touts attempting to wrangle some rupees out of you.

Buses are frequent all along the A3.

NEGOMBO
☎ 031 / pop 137,637

Negombo is a modest beach town located close to Bandaranaike International Airport. With a stash of decent hotels and restaurants to suit all pockets, a friendly local community, an interesting old quarter and a reasonable (though polluted) beach, Negombo is a much easier place to get your Sri Lankan feet from Colombo.

Culture vultures will find bustling Negombo town a historically interesting place that's strongly influenced by the Catholic Church. For the more natural-minded the narrow strip of land to the south of the lagoon, as well as the many different canals, make for good birdwatching.

The Dutch captured the town from the Portuguese in 1640, lost it, and then captured it again in 1644. The British then took it from them in 1796 without a struggle. Negombo was one of the most important sources of cinnamon during the Dutch era, and there are still reminders of the European days.

Orientation

The busy centre of Negombo town lies to the west of the bus and train stations. Most places to stay, however, line the main road that heads north from the town centre, running almost parallel to the beach. Closer to town, the road is called Lewis Pl; going 1km north of the centre, it becomes Porutota Rd. Called Ethukala, this neighbourhood has cafes, restaurants and tourist shops. As you go north the hotels become generally pricier and more luxurious. Along most of the road are footpaths that are good for relaxed strolling.

A breakwater divides the beach: to the north, hotels regularly clean the sand and it's all very neat; to the south, the beach is a bit more natural – it's not as clean and is often covered with various weeds.

Information

In the centre of town you'll find the **post office** (Map p106; Main St), a **Bank of Ceylon** (Map p106; Broadway) and a **Vijitha Yapa Bookshop** (Map p106; 135 Broadway), which has English-language novels, magazines, guidebooks and maps. There are numerous internet and telephone offices scattered along Lewis Pl and Porutota Rd, as well as near the bus and train stations. If this is your first stop in Sri Lanka, hotels can fix you up with guides and drivers for trips elsewhere in the country.

Sights

Close to the seafront near the lagoon are the ruins of the old **Dutch fort** (Map p106), which has a fine gateway inscribed with the date 1678. Also here is a green, called the Esplanade, where cricket matches are a big attraction. As the fort grounds are now occupied by the town's prison, the only way you'll get a peek inside is by stealing something; though you'd need to be very interested in old Dutch forts to go this far.

Several old Dutch buildings are still in use, including the **Lagoon Resthouse** (Map p106; Custom House Rd).

Each day, fishermen take their *oruvas* (outrigger canoes) and go out in search of the fish for which Negombo is well known. They're a fine sight as they sweep home into the lagoon after a fishing trip. Fish auctions on the beach and sales at the **fish market** (Map p106) near the fort are a slippery and very smelly sight, but one that's well worth forgoing some swimming-pool time for. The catch is not all

WEST COAST

WEST COAST

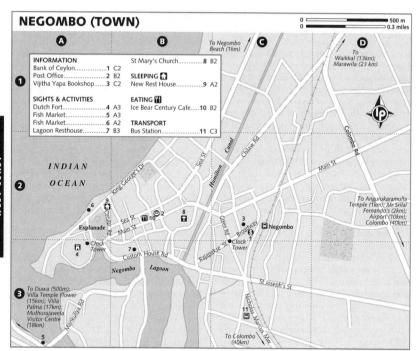

NEGOMBO (TOWN)

0 — 500 m
0 — 0.3 miles

INFORMATION
Bank of Ceylon.................1 C2
Post Office.....................2 B2
Vijitha Yapa Bookshop......3 C2

SIGHTS & ACTIVITIES
Dutch Fort......................4 A3
Fish Market.....................5 A3
Fish Market.....................6 A2
Lagoon Resthouse............7 B3

St Mary's Church..............8 B2

SLEEPING
New Rest House................9 A2

EATING
Ice Bear Century Cafe.....10 B2

TRANSPORT
Bus Station....................11 C3

INDIAN

OCEAN

To Negombo Beach (1km)

To Waikkal (13km); Marawila (23 km)

King George's Dr

Sea St

Hamilton Canal

Chilaw Rd

Main St

Colombo Rd

Esplanade

Circular Rd

Sea St

Main St

Clock Tower

Custom House Rd

Green Rd

Rajapakse St

Broadway

Negombo

Clock Tower

To Angurukaramulla Temple (1km); Mr Srilal Fernando's (2km); Airport (10km); Colombo (40km)

Negombo Lagoon

To Duwa (500m); Villa Temple Flower (15km); Villa Palma (17km); Muthurajawela Visitor Centre (18km)

Mankuliya Rd

St Joseph's St

Nicholas Marcus MW

To Colombo (40km)

from the open sea: Negombo is at the northern end of a lagoon that is renowned for its lobsters, crabs and prawns. Across the lagoon bridge there's a second **fish market** (Map p106). If you can stagger out of bed at 6am, it's a good place to watch the fishing boats return with their catches. If you're hanging around the markets, you won't have to wait long before you're invited to go out on an *oruva* or another kind of vessel; expect to pay around Rs 1000 per boat per hour. A **Fishers' Festival** is held here in late July.

Negombo is dotted with churches – so successfully were the locals converted to Catholicism that the town is sometimes known as 'Little Rome' (and another reason for the moniker is that many of the residents receive money from relatives working in Italy). The fading pink chamber of **St Mary's Church** (Map p106), in the town centre, has some thunderous religious ceiling paintings covering the nave. East of town the **Angurukaramulla Temple**, with its 6m-long reclining Buddha, is also worth seeing. The island of **Duwa**, joined to Negombo by the lagoon bridge, is famed for its Easter passion play.

The Dutch showed their love of **canals** here as nowhere else in Sri Lanka. Canals extend from Negombo all the way south to Colombo and north to Puttalam, a total distance of over 120km. You can hire a bicycle in Negombo from various hotels and ride the canal-side paths for some distance, enjoying the views and small villages along the way. The road over the lagoon bridge continues as a small coastal road between lagoon and ocean almost all the way to Colombo.

If you want to get close to the ocean waters but, hopefully at least on this polluted stretch, not in it too much, then **kitesurfing courses** using decent equipment and run by experienced surfers are available through the Pearl guest house (p108).

Sleeping

There are plenty of places along the beach in the budget and midrange categories. You can also find a couple of higher-priced places here and in Waikkal. Generally the closer the accommodation is to town, the rougher around the edges it is.

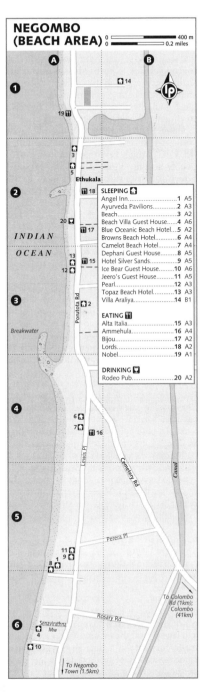

BUDGET

Beach Villa Guest House (Map p107; ☎ 222 2833; www .beachvillasrilanka.com; 3/2 Senavirathna Mawatha; tw from Rs 770; ☒) This backpacker classic has cheerfully gaudy decor, and is so close to the sea that you might want to consider snoozing in your swimwear. There's a cheap and pleasant cafe-restaurant and a wealth of travel advice. Cheaper rooms are fan-only.

Angel Inn (Map p107; ☎ 223 2558; 184/17 Lewis Pl; s/d without air-con Rs 800/1000, d with air-con Rs 1500) This new, three-room guest house might not have beach views, but in every other way it's truly excellent value with flawlessly clean and shiny rooms set around a small garden. Two rooms are fan-only and one has air-con.

Jeero's Guest House (Map p107; ☎ 223 4210; 239 Lewis Pl; r from Rs 1000, with air-con Rs 1800) With latticework window frames, comfortably worn-in furniture and breezy balconies, this is a well-priced and friendly option set around a pleasing garden just back from the beach.

New Rest House (Map p106; ☎ 222 2299; 14 Circular Rd; tw from Rs 1100) Back in 1958 Queen Elizabeth II made this very rundown government rest house her base while staying in Negombo. From what we can deduce the queen must be a cheapskate because she opted for the cheapest room. It's one of the few places to stay that's actually in Negombo town itself, but it's all fairly ropey nowadays. Still, if you've ever wanted to use the same toilet as the queen of England, this is the place to do it.

Dephani Guest House (Map p107; ☎ 223 8225; dephani@slt.lk; 189/15 Lewis Pl; s & d Rs 1300-1400) Prices are a little flexible at this personable little guest house, which has a shady garden full of sun-loungers and slightly gloomy, though spick and span, rooms. Cold-water showers only, and the mosquito nets are so full of holes that you'd better bring your own.

MIDRANGE

Hotel Silver Sands (Map p107; ☎ 222 2880; www.silver sands.go2lk.com; 229 Lewis Pl; r with/without air-con Rs 2750/1870; ☒) A beachfront option with neatly tiled rooms that have crazy tent-like mosquito nets and are decorated with bunches of plastic flowers. Fishy fans will love the rows of aquariums full of guppies, mollies and goodness knows what else.

our pick Ice Bear Guest House (Map p107; ☎ 223 3862; www.icebearhotel.com; 103/2 Lewis Pl; s/d from €16/22; ☒ 🛜) A gorgeous traditional villa with lots of colour and flair (or 'Swissness', as the sign says – to which you could also add 'and a little eccentricity'). This 'budget boutique' hotel has a variety of different types of rooms thrown about the beautiful dog- and duck-filled gardens. The rooms have flower-sprinkled beds, homely touches and hot water, though they could be kept a little cleaner. There is also a beachside cafe with tasty treats like homemade muesli, and classical music often wafts through the palms.

Topaz Beach Hotel (Map p107; ☎ 227 9265; topaz .beach.hotel@gmail.com; 21 Porutota Rd; s with/without air-con Rs 4000/3000, d Rs 4500/3500; 🖭 🖳) The chitter-chattering receptionist here will gleefully show you into one of their vivid and jolly rooms. The more expensive of these come with bunches of flowers and sea views, while in the cheaper rooms all you do away with are the flowers and the air-con units.

Pearl (Map p107; ☎ 492 7744; www.pearl-negombo .com; 13 Porutota Rd; s/d US$36/46; 🖭) This small, six-room beachfront pad might be discreet but it packs enough flair and comfort to gladden the heart of any weary traveller. The immaculate rooms are full of cheeky modern art and have DVD and CD players (with supplies). Room No 6, the only one with a double rather than twin beds, is easily the best.

our pick Villa Araliya (Map p107; ☎ 227 7650; villa.aralia@wow.lk; 154/10 Porutota Rd; s/d incl break-fast US$48/60; 🖭 🛜 🖳) This leading light in the Negombo hotel scene has a variety of modern rooms – some are all dashed up in multihued colours and others have ex-posed red-brick walls – but the uniting fac-tor between all the rooms is that they are supremely comfortable with big beds, high ceilings and bathrooms that you'll be happy to splash about in. It's on a quiet side-street that's a five-minute walk from the beach.

Camelot Beach Hotel (Map p107; ☎ 223 5884; camelothotel@slnet.lk; 345 Lewis Pl; s/d/tr US$51/56/63; 🖭 🖳) Unable to choose between a modern art gallery look, 1970s retro, horror-house hell, nouveau-riche tack or a Latin America birdwatchers paradise, this new hotel opted for a mish-mash of the lot. In fact the only style missing is medieval England – a shame considering the name. Surprisingly the re-sulting mix isn't at all unpleasant and the rooms are very comfortable. It has two pools: at the time of writing, one gross and green; the other lovely and blue!

TOP END

Blue Oceanic Beach Hotel (Map p107; ☎ 227 9000; www .jetwing.com; Porutota Rd; r from US$79; 🖭 🛜 🖳) A large and jolly package-tour hotel that's good value for couples. Rooms have tarted-up sofas, scar-ily big beds and, for the indecisive, both a shower and a bath in each room. As well as a good pool, there's a gym, various ayurvedic treatments and a decent restaurant.

Browns Beach Hotel (Map p107; ☎ 222 2031; www .aitkenspencehotels.com; 175 Lewis Pl; s/d/tr US$86/102/137; 🖭 🖳) Can you believe that back in the 1970s people actually thought that the mustard brown colour of this hotel was nice! Thank goodness those days are long gone. Depending on your point of view, this low-grade package-tour hotel is either delightfully retro or just plain dreadful. Either way it's overpriced.

Ayurveda Pavilions (Map p107; ☎ 227 6719; www .ayurvedapavilions.com; Porutota Rd; s/d villa incl breakfast from US$264/299; 🖭 🖳 🖳) Beautiful mud-wall villas with minimalist, yet luxurious, furnish-ings. The bathrooms are the real highlight and soaking in one of the steamy, flower petal–covered outdoor baths with someone special on a rainy afternoon is every bit as romantic as you hoped your holiday would be! There is a large range of treatments (available to nonguests from €15), which are included in the room price.

Beach (Map p107; ☎ 227 3500; www.jetwing.com; Porutota Rd; s & d US$307, tr US$430; 🖭 🖳 🖳) With its imposing gateways, echoey corridors and vaguely Pharaonic murals, this place feels like a temple – a temple to minimalist luxury that is. The rooms are close to perfect and the bathrooms, with walk-in showers and circular baths, actually are perfect. There's also a well-equipped spa and a pool that's lit up at night by flaming torches. There's even an in-house naturalist who will happily answer all of your birds-and-bees questions.

Eating & Drinking

There are lots of very so-so restaurants and cafes stringing the main road along the beach, with a few more exciting options in between.

Ammehula (Map p107; ☎ 487 3065; 286 Lewis Pl; meals Rs 200-400; 🕑 10am-10pm) The young own-ers of this cafe claim that the name means 'Go Away!' and the menu features a cartoon turtle cussing about how all the good fish come here. Besides seafood dishes there are sandwiches, salads and a long breakfast menu that includes Dutch pancakes. There's a small library of books for swapping.

Rodeo Pub (Map p107; ☎ 077 774 6474; 35 Porutota Rd; dishes Rs 300-700; ☷ 9am-midnight) Blathering, homesick expats and tourists who wish they'd never left, drown their sorrows at this wannabe European bar where graffiti's scrawled across the walls and bacon butties, pints of larger and cocktails with sexy names prop up the clientele. It's perfect, if you'd rather be in Benidorm.

Ice Bear Century Cafe (Map p106; ☎ 223 8097; 25 Main St; high tea Rs 390; ☷ 8am-6pm) In a lovingly restored peach-pink colonial-era town house, this new venture in the heart of Negombo offers a touch of refined class and all manner of Sri Lankan brews and mountains of homemade cakes and biscuits.

Bijou (Map p107; ☎ 531 9577; Porutota Rd; mains Rs 300-1000) You'll know this place is Swiss-owned when you see fondue (advance order, Rs 2000) and other Swiss and German specialities on the menu. It mixes up such heavy dishes with a wide range of seafood.

Alta Italia (Map p107; ☎ 227 9206; 36 Porutota Rd; meals Rs 400-600; ☷ lunch & dinner) For a casual beach resort this is a surprisingly formal Italian-run place with a long menu that includes fresh pasta, seafood grills and thin-based pizzas. Try the authentic risotto and finish with a *limoncello* or grappa. Or sample from the espresso machine, steaming behind the counter.

Nobel (Map p107; ☎ 227 4433; www.nobelcoffeehouse .com; 100/12 Porutota Rd; mains Rs 500) A trendy new restaurant with a young owner and a hip-hop sound-track. It has a good variety of Western dishes such as steaks (Rs 775) and lots of local vegie options.

ᴏᴜʀ ᴘɪᴄᴋ Lords (Map p107; ☎ 227 5655; 80B Porutota Rd; dishes Rs 850-1400; ☷ 10am-6pm) By far Negombo's most creative eating experience. Martin, the British owner of this half restaurant, half art gallery, brings a larger-than-life presence to the place and is a rare thing among expat restaurant owners in that he actually works on the floor and in the kitchen making sure that everything is just spot on. The food, which is so superbly prepared and presented that the thought of a free meal was enough to get the president himself to come and open the restaurant, is a hybrid of Western and Eastern flavours. The gallery displays excellent contemporary work by local artists.

Getting There & Away

Central Transport Board (CTB), private and intercity express buses run between Negombo and Saunders Pl, Colombo (regular/air-con Rs 48/80, one to two hours, every 20 minutes). Long queues form at the bus station on weekend evenings, when day trippers return to the capital. There are also trains to Colombo (2nd/3rd class Rs 80/45, two hours), but they're slower and rarer than the buses. You can get a taxi between Negombo and Colombo for about Rs 3000. Any hotel, guest house or travel agent will arrange a taxi for you.

For Kandy, ordinary buses run between 4.30am and 5.15pm every hour (Rs 112), or there are a couple of luxury buses that run in the mornings only (Rs 225). Whichever option you choose the journey takes around three or four hours.

Getting Around

Bus 270, for the Bandaranaike International Airport (Rs 14, 45 minutes), leaves every 15 minutes between about 5am and 9pm. It doesn't actually go all the way to the airport (for security reasons) but drops you very close by at Avariwatta, from which it's a walk that a snail could complete in a moment or two – and he's carrying his whole house! If you're not a snail, then a three-wheeler costs about Rs 400 from Negombo town or Rs 800 from Lewis Pl. A taxi costs around double this. The journey takes about 20 minutes and all hotels can arrange transport. Three-wheelers may not pick up passengers from the airport terminal, but you can catch one on the road outside the airport.

To get from the bus station to Lewis Pl or Porutota Rd, you can catch a Kochchikade-bound bus or splash out Rs 200 on a three-wheeler.

AROUND NEGOMBO
Waikkal & Marawila
☎ 031

The towns of Waikkal and Marawila lie about 3km inland of the coast on the A3. There are several mostly upmarket waterside hotels, which are self-contained and walled off from Sri Lanka. It's a very different scene from the bars and tourist shops at Negombo. On the plus side, the nearby beaches are long and golden, and the terrain is flat and palm covered.

On the coast near Waikkal, the **Ranweli Holiday Village** (☎ 227 7359; www.ranweli.com; s/d/tr US$84/92/110) is a showpiece ecofriendly hotel that has won dozens of prestigious international environmental awards. Away from recycling, tree planting and community development, you'll find that the gentle punt over the canal separating it from the mainland sets a romantic mood. The rooms are surprisingly plain and dull, but there's an unmistakable air of exclusivity to the place. All the vegetables served in the restaurant are organically grown in the local area. They organise an array of bird- and butterfly-spotting trips.

Most people reach Waikkal and Marawila by taxi or car and driver.

South of Negombo

The narrow belt of land between the gulf and lagoon south of Negombo is sometimes called **Pamunugama**, after its biggest settlement. It's a lovely strip of coconut palms, old Portuguese-style churches, cross-dotted cemeteries on dunes and pockets of tidy houses. There are some small hotels along here. Unfortunately though, the beach is steep, with a sheer reef drop-off that makes swimming little short of perilous no matter what the sea state.

This is also home to one of the best stretches of the old and straight-as-an-arrow **Dutch Canal** that runs along this entire length of coast. It's lined with small factories, fishing villages, mansions, nature areas and more. Hiring a bike in Negombo is an ideal way to tour this area.

Muthurajawela Marsh, which evocatively translates as 'Supreme Field of Pearls', is a little-known gem of a wetland at the southern end of Negombo's lagoon. The area had been a rich rice-growing basin before the Portuguese constructed a canal that ruined the fields with sea water. Over the centuries, Mother Nature turned Muthurajawela into Sri Lanka's biggest saline wetland, home to purple herons, cormorants and kingfishers. However, the marsh is under pressure from encroaching industrial development. The **Muthurajawela Visitor Centre** (☎ in Colombo 011-483 0150; Indigaslanda, Bopitiya, Pamunugama; ☼ 7am-4pm) is at the southern end of the road along Pamunugama, next to the Hamilton Canal. It has some moth-eaten displays and a 25-minute video on the wetland's fauna; but much more interestingly, it also runs boat trips. A two-hour **guided boat ride** (per person Rs 900) through the wetland is

highly recommended. The wetlands provide a home to some 75 bird species, as well as crocodiles, monkeys and even some very rarely seen otters. A percentage of the profits goes toward local conservation initiatives.

Very close to the Muthurajawela Visitor Centre is **Villa Palma** (www.villapalmasrilanka.com; Beach Rd, Pamunugama; r from Rs 3500; ⌘ ⌘), which has 18 large and simple rooms that are a bit musty and overpriced. It's popular with local wedding parties, which bring colour and life whereas the rooms don't.

SOUTH OF COLOMBO

Escaping the frenetic and sticky capital for the road south is a giant sigh of relief. Out go the congested streets and dark clouds of carbon monoxide and in come the sultry beaches of the Sri Lankan dream. Beginning with Wadduwa, there are beach towns big and small along the coast. Most independent travellers focus on surf-obsessed Hikkaduwa, but the Bentota area offers quieter, and maybe even more stunning beaches, as well as a bizarre twinning of package-holiday hotels and sumptuous boutique hideaways. Though this entire stretch of coast was heavily affected by the tsunami (see boxed text, p104), all the debris has long since been cleared away from in and around the big beach resorts.

KALUTARA & WADDUWA
☎ 034

The town of Kalutara was an important spice-trading centre controlled at various times by the Portuguese, Dutch and British. Today it has a reputation for fine basketware and the best mangosteens on the island. The fine beaches along here boast some good hotels.

Immediately south of the Kalu Ganga bridge on the main road is the massively, impressive **Gangatilaka Vihara**, which has a hollow dagoba (stupa) with an interesting painted interior depicting scenes from the life of the Buddha. Locals will insist that this is the only hollow dagoba in the world – though this is a hollow statement as there is at least one other in Yangon, Myanmar (Burma). By the road there's a small shrine and bodhi tree where drivers often stop to make offerings to ensure a safe journey.

Kalutara and Wadduwa, located 8km to the north of Kalutara, have a number of resorts, but there's little to halt travellers who are en route to the more laid-back beach spots further south. Some people use this area as a first or last stop in Sri Lanka, though it's still a good two congested hours through Colombo to the airport. Having said that, the beach here isn't bad considering its proximity to the capital. All of the following places are well off Galle Rd and on the beach.

Run by a gentle woman, **La Saman Villa** (☎ 222 1660; De Abrew Rd, Kalutara North; s/d incl breakfast Rs 2500/3000), an immaculate little guest house, has sparkling rooms with checked tile floors, big beds and hot-water showers – though unfortunately the downstairs rooms have said showers plonked directly above the toilets! Air-con is an additional Rs 500.

The huge **Tangerine Beach Hotel** (☎ 223 7295; www.tangerinehotels.com; De Abrew Rd, Waskaduwa, Kalutara North; s/d from US$82/89; 🖃 🖵 🖭) takes the best bits of both a fun holiday resort and a sincere and efficient business hotel and combines them into one happy bundle. From the disco flashy wall-hangings to the glossy pool complex, this is a very good-value hotel.

Blue Water (☎ 038-223 5067; www.bluewatersrilanka .com; Thalpitiya, Wadduwa; r US$238; 🖃 🖵 🖭) is an appropriate name because at this large and luxurious resort you virtually need a good ship and captain to navigate the immense and lush pool. Equally lush are the gardens, while the rooms follow the current fad for Asian minimalism. If the romance of it all makes you feel like tying the knot, then they'll even throw in an elephant or two to carry the lucky couple off into the sunset. Just to the north of this hotel, and standing in stark contrast, begins another world of wooden slum shacks strung along the roadside, outside of which stand entire families hopefully waving fish at passing motorists.

There are frequent buses to Kalutara and Wadduwa along the main coastal road.

BERUWELA & MORAGALLE
☎ 034

With easy access from Colombo and an offshore reef providing safe year-round swimming, Beruwela has, along with Bentota, been developed into one of Sri Lanka's chief package tour–resort zones. However, with its grubby beach, dirty surrounding town and poor-quality accommodation, it's quite hard to think of a worse spot for a beach holiday anywhere else on the west coast.

Moragalle is technically slightly north of Beruwela, but the towns have practically merged. Throughout this area there is a lot of tsunami damage; many hotels are closed for good. Large fishing boats washed far inland have now become part of the landscape.

The first recorded Muslim settlement on the island took place at Beruwela in 1024. The **Kechimalai Mosque**, on a headland north of the hotel strip, is said to be built on the site of the landing and is the focus for a major **Eid-ul-Fitr** festival at the end of Ramadan. It's part of a fascinating collection of mosques, churches and temples out by the fishing port and beach.

Sleeping
The tourist hotels are all very much aimed at the package groups that come to Sri Lanka to escape from the European winter and all are pretty poor value if booked independently.

Ypsylon Tourist Resort (☎ 227 6132; www.ypsylon -sri-lanka.de; Beruwela; s/d from €24/29; 🖭) The good news is that this German package-holiday hotel has the most attractive strip of beach in the area. The bad news is that the hotel itself is truly grim! When we last visited we got to say hi to a cockroach or two in one room, slipped on the water-logged floor of another and marvelled at the plastic sheeting covering the windows of most of the other rooms. The pool is tiny and not too clean, and the atmosphere depressing. The only reason to visit is for the dive school, where a four-day PADI Open Water course, with all equipment, costs €300.

Hotel Sumadai (☎ 227 6404; www.sumadai.com; 61 Maradana Rd, Beruwela; s/d incl half board €26/38; 🖃) Some of the rooms at this shabby package hotel have beach views, while others have lagoon views. It's popular with elderly German tourists who like to cover their backs in mud, wear strange hats on their heads and stroll around with nothing but a towel to protect their modesty. As such, unless this is your thing, it won't appeal very much. The management prefers to sell rooms by the week rather than by the day.

Taprospa (☎ 227 8400; www.taprospa.com; s/d US$75/80; 🖃 🖵 🖭) This is the best place in town, though that's not saying much. Modern art, consisting of pictures of voluptuous naked women being ravaged by horny devils, lines the reception area, but the rooms are drab enough to ensure that nobody feels like becoming a horny devil! It does have a sublime pool and beachside setting, though.

Getting There & Away

Aluthgama is the main transport hub serving Beruwela and Moragalle. See p115 for details. Local buses link all the towns along Galle Rd.

ALUTHGAMA, BENTOTA & INDURUWA
☎ 034

Protected from noisy Galle Rd by the sluggish sweep of the Bentota Ganga, the ribbon of golden sand that makes up Bentota beach is a glorious holiday sun-and-fun playground. While it's primarily dominated by big package hotels, it also has a number of smaller places catering to independent travellers. There are more such places in Aluthgama, a small town on the main road between Beruwela and Bentota.

Aluthgama has a raucous fish market, local shops and the main train station in the area. Induruwa doesn't really have a centre – it's spread out along the coast.

Orientation

Just south of the town centre of Aluthgama, the main road crosses the Bentota Ganga into Bentota, where there's the Bentota resort centre on the seaward side, with tourist facilities, shops and a few restaurants. From the bridge, the river turns north to flow parallel to the coast for a few hundred metres, divided from the sea only by a narrow spit of land that's home to some resorts (they're reachable by boat across the river). Induruwa is 5km south of Bentota.

Information

There are internet facilities in many of the more expensive hotels, and others are sprinkled throughout the towns. Just north of the river, the **Commercial Bank** (339 Galle Rd) has an international ATM. The Bentota resort centre has a post office. The **Cargills Food City** (☎ 227 1921; 331 Galle Rd, Aluthgama) sells a wide range of goods and has a pharmacy.

Sights

If it's a **beach** you want, then it's a beach you're going to get; the Bentota area is home to some of the best beaches in all the country. Yet there is something altogether odd about these magnificent stretches of sand – despite the huge number of hotels and the fact that most people come to Sri Lanka for the three S's of sun, sand and surf, the beaches around here are remarkably empty of people. Quite why this should be the case we're not sure, but if the sands of nearby Hikkaduwa are a bit too trodden for

your liking, then Bentota might be the place for you. Further watery fun is also available on the calm waters of the **Bentota Ganga**, though pollution can be an issue here.

Aluthgama has a bustling **market** every Monday, located across the train line, towards Dharga Town. A few kilometres inland on the south bank of the river is the **Galapota Temple**, which is said to date from the 12th century. To reach it, cross the bridge and take the side road to your left after 500m.

Fine beaches continue several kilometres south from Bentota. Induruwa has a small cluster of places to stay on a lovely, quiet length of beach, at the north end of which is the excellent **Turtle Research Project**, one of the turtle hatcheries in the area (see boxed text, p116).

Ten kilometres inland from Bentota is the **Brief Garden** (☎ 227 4462; admission Rs 350; ☻ 8am-5pm). A barely controlled riot of a *Jungle Book* garden, the grounds are a lovely place to get lost, while the house, which used to be the home of Bevis Bawa, brother of renowned architect Geoffrey Bawa, has an eclectic range of artwork on display – from homoerotic sculpture to a wonderful mural of Sri Lankan life in the style of Marc Chagall. The mural was created by Australian artist Donald Friend, who originally came for six days but stayed six years – definitely not the sort of house guest you want! Other, more short-term, guests included Vivien Leigh and Laurence Olivier, who stayed here during the filming of *Elephant Walk* in 1953. It's a good idea to plaster on some insect repellent as the gardens are a favourite of biting insects. To get here follow the road south from Aluthgama to Matagama Rd and turn inland to the Muslim village of Dharga Town. From here you will periodically see yellow signs saying 'Brief', but as everyone knows this place, it's easy enough to ask directions. There's no public transport.

Activities

The vast lagoon and river mouth make this an excellent area for water sports. Windsurfing, waterskiing, jet-skiing, deep-sea fishing and everything else watery are offered by local operators. **Sunshine Water Sports Center** (☎ 077 794 1857; River Ave, Aluthgama) and **Sun River Paradise Watersports** (☎ 077 623 7376; River Ave, Aluthgama) are independent operators that are both right on the riverfront. Besides renting out a wide range of equipment, they also run courses, which include windsurfing (Rs 10,000), waterskiing (Rs 2500) and surf/body-

SANJEEWA SENANAKE – TALKING TURTLES

Sanjeewa Senanake works as a volunteer at the Sea Turtle Project in Induwara (see boxed text, p116).

Sanjeewa, please tell us about the turtle project? I have been working at the turtle project since the tsunami and I do it just because I like the turtles and because our government does nothing for their conservation. Many of the other volunteers here are fisherman who come and work here in the day after they've finished at sea. We really try hard to get Sri Lankan school children and college students to come and see what we are doing here because in general Sri Lankans don't care about the environment, but if we can change the attitudes of the next generation…

What do local people think of the project? Some of the locals don't like these projects because they prefer to eat the eggs. If we find people eating turtle eggs, we inform the police. We pay people a little more than the market rate for any eggs they bring us, and before the babies are released back into the water they are tagged so they can be tracked.

What happened during the tsunami? When the tsunami came the manager grabbed his favourite two turtles and ran away from the waves with them, but one of the very rare albino turtles was lost and many others were lost or killed.

What can foreign visitors do to help? Apart from visiting the centre, donating money and buying some of the products we have in our shop here, they can spread the word about the work we do and also they can volunteer to work here.

board hire (Rs 700/200 per hour). If you're thinking of doing a surf course, then it's better to wait until you reach Hikkaduwa where the instructors are more likely to know how to surf themselves! There are also snorkelling tours, canoeing, deep-sea fishing and diving courses (from €65), where you can ogle the huge variety of fish (including large species such as barracuda), which seem unperturbed by the presence of divers.

Boat journeys along the Bentota Ganga are a peaceful, popular and bird-filled way to pass a late afternoon. Tours travel through the intricate coves and islands on the lower stretches of the river, which is home to more than a hundred bird species, plus a wide variety of amphibian and reptile species. Most trips last for three hours and charge Rs 3600 for a boat that holds up to four people. All hotels can point you to operators.

Sleeping

In among the package-holiday resort bubbles are a number of divine boutique hotels and guest houses, as well as one or two very rare budget offerings.

ALUTHGAMA

Hotel Hemadan (☎ 428 9019; www.hemadan.dk; River Ave; s/d from Rs 2200/2420; ⚡) A cosy Danish-owned guest house that has 10 large, clean rooms in an ageing building. There's a leafy courtyard and prime river-viewing opportunities. Better rooms have balconies and/or air-con. There are free boat shuttles across the river to the oceanside beach. It could be a little more welcoming.

German Lanka (☎ 558 2530; e.anamda@gmx.de; River Ave; s/d from Rs 2200/2500) If you speak German, or don't mind nobody else understanding a word you say, then this is a great-value, glowing-red guest house. Unlike its neighbours, the immaculate and sunny rooms are just right beside the river, leaving only just enough space to squeeze in a couple of shady trees and some tables and chairs on the outside terrace.

ourpick **Terrena Lodge** (☎ 428 9015; terrenalodge@ sltnet.lk; River Ave; s/d Rs 2300/2500) You'll struggle to wipe the smile off the face of the manager of this handsomely furnished, Austrian-owned place. Talking of smiles the friendly reception and five colourful rooms, which have flair, imagination and a touch of the old to them, will most likely put a smile on your face too. There is a pretty garden leading down to a riverside dining area and decent grub is available.

Anushka River Inn (☎ 227 5377; www.anushka-river -inn.com; River Ave; s/d/tr incl breakfast €25/30/40; ⚡) This German favourite is another top choice along this road. Its large rooms contain wooden beds, dressing tables and hot-water showers. The rooms without river views, with their shiny new feel, are actually the better deal as some of the others have a musty odour.

BENTOTA
Budget
Wasana Guest House (☎ 227 5206; tw Rs 1500) Behind the Southern Palm Villa, this century-old house has half-a-dozen very basic pink rooms, which on their own aren't up too much. However, the point of this place is that you're living with the host family, sharing meals and relaxing in the same gardens; in a tourist town like this, that's a rare treat indeed.

Midrange
Southern Palm Villa (☎ 227 0752; southernpalmvilla@ yahoo.com; s with/without air-con Rs 2500/1800, d Rs 3500/2000; ❄) Behind the city-sized Taj Exotica (and across the train tracks), this simple place has 15 clean rooms with colourful bedheads. It's not the newest building around, but it's kept tidy and the grounds are spacious. Some rooms have balconies from which you can hear – but not see – the surf. It's a short walk to the beach.

Wunderbar Hotel and Restaurant (☎ 227 5908; Galle Rd; s/d €45/50; ❄ ▨) In among the surrounding luxury is this solid, and much cheaper, midrange option that has spacious and well-thought-out rooms with a taste for vaguely erotic art. Some rooms have balconies with sea views, and the pool is more inviting than many others in town.

Amal Villa (☎ 227 0236; www.amal-villa.com; Galle Rd; s/d incl breakfast €35/65; ❄) Want the bad news first? This place is frequently full and is on the wrong side of the busy main road. And the good news? This charming and beautifully maintained German-run villa merges tropical oriental vibes with central European efficiency, which leaves it as a stand-out choice. The simple rooms, full of pure white lines and an old-fashioned flavour, have views inland over the rice paddies.

Top End
Club Villa (☎ 227 5312; www.club-villa.com; 138/15 Galle Rd; s/d incl half board US$198/220; ❄ ▢ ▨) Ever wondered what happened to the hippies who bummed across Asia in the 1960s and '70s? Well, while some dropped out of life completely, others went home and became investment bankers who now spend their dollars reminiscing in hotels like this Bawa-designed masterpiece. From the tie-dye pillows and cushions to the blissed out Buddha and Shiva statues, everything about this place reeks of hippy chic. Even the giant catfish that haunt

the numerous ponds seem to cruise about in a stoned state of permanent indolence.

Ayurveda Walauwa (☎ 227 5372; www.sribudhasa .com; 1-week package s/d from €875/1428; ❄ ▢ ▨) Just south of Club Villa, this long-standing and well-respected Ayurvedic centre is on the land side of Galle Rd. The 20 rooms are basic and would be overpriced on their own; fortunately the price includes all the treatments you can handle in a week, which makes it much more worthwhile. There's a lovely pool and a smoking area for those who want to destroy all the hard work they've put into the treatments.

ourpick Taruvillas Taprobana (☎ 428 7088; www.taruvillas.com; 146/4 Galle Rd; s/d from US$230/268; ❄ ▢ ▨) Step past the pearly gates and become a lotus-eater in the Garden of Eden at this exquisite boutique hotel – whatever way you look at it, this place is literally perfect. Drift around the luxuriant gardens peering at the tropical fish in the numerous ponds, dip a toe into the deep blue swimming pool, brush your hands gently over antiques collected from Sri Lanka, India and the Orient, and float like an angel into one of the sunflower yellow or seductive red, semi-open-plan rooms. But for goodness sake, whatever else you do, make sure you book in with someone special.

Saman Villas (☎ 227 5435; www.samanvilla.com; r from US$440; ❄ ▢ ▨) We would love to tell you just how incredible this place is, but the simple truth is that no words have yet been invented to describe the sheer opulence of this hotel complex. How opulent? Well, some of the rooms have private swimming pools – inside the bathroom! If you prefer your swimming more communal, there's also a heavenly infinity pool that merges into an ocean horizon and everywhere you go you will literally walk on flower petals. But the real clincher is the setting. Sited on the headland at the southern end of Bentota beach, the sea views are simply overwhelming.

INDURUWA
Long Beach (☎ 227 5773; Galle Rd; tw Rs 1400) The rooms might be basic but if you can't stretch to hotels with private pools, this place might just fit the bill. The rooms are located in the upstairs of a family house. There are green, shady gardens and, something that matches all the big-boy hotels, a gorgeous beach on the doorstep.

ourpick **Shunyata Villa** (☎ 227 1944; www.shunyata
-villa.net; Galle Rd; d from €80; ✷ 🖳 ⚏) This superb-
value five-room boutique hotel has wedding
day–white rooms scattered with large crystals
and filled with bright furnishings. The bathrooms in each are slightly different – some
have Jacuzzis, some have two baths and others
waterfalls for showers. It has a beautiful pool
and is right on a quiet bit of beach. The only
downside is that you might catch a little road
noise from some rooms. They also offer a
range of Ayurvedic treatments.

Eating

Almost all of the hotels and guest houses
have restaurants, and the seafood-heavy
meals that most serve are generally good. If
you want to escape the confines of your accommodation for a while, then the following
are recommended.

Chaplon Tea Centre (☎ 493 7293; Galle Rd, Bentota)
For a break from bronzing on the sands, come
to this tea centre. As well as buying some
of Sri Lanka's finest tea, you can also sit in
a wicker chair on the terrace and enjoy tea
and biscuits.

Amal Restaurant (☎ 227 0236; off Galle Rd, Bentota;
mains from Rs 350) Very close to the beach, this
restaurant sits on the opposite side of the road
to the hotel of the same name (opposite) and
serves fair seafood, steak, pastas and some
token curries. There are lovely sea views and,
should you wish to up the romantic ante, they
can arrange candle-lit beach dinners under
the stars. The set meals involve some truly
bizarre food combinations.

Of the hotel restaurants, almost all the top-
end package holiday resorts have restaurants
open to nonguests, though they are often
overpriced. Otherwise the **Wunderbar Hotel and
Restaurant** (☎ 227 5908; Galle Rd) has an enjoyable
1st-floor restaurant open to the sea breezes
and a decent selection of seafood and Western
dishes (Rs 400 to 600). Equally pleasant is the
riverside dining at the **Terrena Lodge** (☎ 428 9015;
River Ave), where grilled fish or steaks will set
you back between Rs 400 and Rs 700.

Getting There & Around

Beruwela and Bentota are both on the main
Colombo–Matara railway line, but Aluthgama,
the town sandwiched between them, is the station to go to as many trains do not make stops
at these smaller stations. Aluthgama has five or
six express trains daily to Colombo (2nd/3rd

class Rs 120/65, 1½ to two hours), and a similar
number to Hikkaduwa (2nd/3rd class Rs 70/40,
one hour), Galle (2nd/3rd class Rs 110/60, 1½
hours) and Matara (2nd/3rd class Rs 180/95, 2½
to three hours). There is also service to Kandy
(2nd/3rd class Rs 290/116, 1½ to two hours) at
3.40pm. Avoid the other, slower trains.

When you get off the train at the unusual
middle-platform station, you'll hear the usual
boring tales from the touts and fixers that the
hotel of your choice is 'closed', 'washed away'
or has 'magically turned into the Statue of
Liberty'. Just ignore them.

Aluthgama is also the best place to pick up
a bus, although there is no trouble getting *off*
any bus anywhere along the Galle Rd. There
is frequent service to both Colombo (regular/
air-con Rs 55/105, one to two hours depending on traffic) and Galle (regular/air-con Rs
75/150, 1½ hours).

Three-wheelers are available from
Aluthgama; fees range from Rs 50 for a local
trip to Rs 400 for the jaunt to Induruwa.

KOSGODA
☎ 091

The tsunami was hard on the coast around
Kosgoda, which is about 5km south of
Induruwa. Villages suffered, but the impact on
tourism was limited as this attractive stretch
of beach and coast had seen little development. The exception to this was the grave
damage suffered by the local turtle hatcheries,
the area's one big tourism draw (see the boxed
text, p116).

AMBALANGODA & AROUND
☎ 091

Ambalangoda is a sweaty and unattractive
town, which, not surprisingly, is completely
overshadowed by nearby Hikkaduwa as a
tourist destination. The main reason for visiting – and it's a good one – is to dig under
the surface of the Sri Lankan souvenir scene
and discover the magical meanings behind
the ubiquitous 'devil' masks. Genuine devil
dances, which drive out spirits causing illness, still occur irregularly in the hinterland
villages. Visitors are welcome, though you do
have to expect more curiosity and less English
from the villagers. The real catch is finding out
about one of these dances, but ask around and
count on good luck from the gods. In addition this is also the best place in the country
in which to buy these masks.

WEST COAST

HATCHING TURTLES

Five species of sea turtles lay eggs along the coasts of Sri Lanka. The green turtle is the most common, followed by the olive ridley and the hawksbill. The leatherback and loggerhead are both huge, reaching 2m or more in length. During what should be long lives (if they don't end up in a net, soup pot etc), female turtles make numerous visits to the beaches of the south coast to lay eggs in the sand of the very beach they themselves were born on. A few weeks later, hundreds of baby turtles make, as the many lurid nature specials will tell you, a perilous journey back to the water.

Most of the tiny turtles are quickly gobbled up by birds, fish, people and other critters with gullets. And many never hatch at all, since human egg-poachers work overtime to satisfy the demand for turtle omelettes. The turtle hatcheries on the coast aim to increase the odds for the turtles by paying locals for the eggs at a rate slightly above that, which they would fetch in the market (roughly Rs 8 to 9). The eggs are then incubated by the hatchery until they hatch. After a short stay in a tank (supposedly for protection against parasites), the babies are released under the cover of darkness to foil at least some of the birds.

The Kosgoda turtle hatcheries were all wiped out by the tsunami and many turtles were lost, but each has been rebuilt with the help of volunteers. While some naysayers in the scientific community question the benefits of the hatcheries, you have to say that even if only one extra baby turtle makes it to adulthood that's better than none. There's also no denying that turtles of any age are awfully cute and make for an entertaining visit. Three of the following hatcheries are in and around Kosgoda; the fourth is north of Kosgoda, near Induwara. They're sufficiently different enough from each other for you to easily take in all four. Visits rarely last more than about 20 minutes. Expect to see babies, as well as veterans who have been injured by nets and other calamities.

Kosgoda Turtle Centre (☎ 077 683 5427; admission Rs 200; ☷ 8am-6pm) Located behind a group of new homes built by a German woman for tsunami victims, this very basic place is hands-on and has some charming staff. There's an old albino turtle that has survived both man (nets) and nature (tsunami). Look for a sign on the west side of Galle Rd, 500m south of the 73km marker.

Kosgoda Turtle Conservation Project (☎ 226 4567; admission Rs 200; ☷ 8am-6pm) On the beach side of Galle Rd, just north of Kosgoda, this volunteer-run operation has been here for 18 years. It's a very simple affair.

Kosgoda Turtle Hatchery (☎ 225 8667; admission Rs 200; ☷ 7am-7pm) Turn down a small track at the 73km marker to find this operation, located in a quiet spot right on the beach. Arrive at 6.30pm and you can help release the day's hatchlings into the ocean.

Sea Turtle Project (☎ 227 1062; www.seaturtleszone.com; Induwara; admission Rs 200; ☷ 6am-6.30pm) This facility feels more commercial and established than the Kosgoda operations. For the very interested it's also possible to do voluntary work here for periods of between three weeks and six months. See website for more details.

This coast was hit hard by the tsunami. The proximity of Galle Rd, with its villages and the railway along the coast, meant that the waves caused enormous damage and loss of life. Evidence of the tragedy is continuous from the 88km to 94km markers.

Information

In Ambalangoda town, the **Commercial Bank** (Galle Rd) has an international ATM.

Sights & Activities

Ambalangoda is the centre of much of Sri Lanka's traditional culture. There are two mask shops (with free museums) on either side of the intersection of Galle Rd and Main St, 800m north of the train and bus stations.

Each is owned by a son of the famous mask-carver Ariyapala. The **Ariyapala Mask Museum** (☎ 225 8373; www.banduwijesooriyadanceacademy.org; cnr Galle Rd & Main St; ☷ 8.30am-5.30pm) is the better museum, with dioramas and explanations in English. It also sells the booklet *The Ambalangoda Mask Museum*, if you want to delve into the mysterious world of dance, legend and exorcism, and the psychology behind the masks. **Ariyapala Traditional Masks** (☎ 493 3319; 432 Galle Rd; ☷ 8am-7pm) is the other shop. The pieces on sale at both are rather expensive but utterly captivating.

MH Mettananda (☎ 225 8810; Galle Rd; ☷ 9am-5pm), who has a shop about 500m north of the stations, is one of the good mask carvers in Ambalangoda.

Dudley Silva (☎ 225 9411; 53 Elpitiya Rd; ◷ 9am-5.30pm) is a good place for batik – and the 140-year-old house is an attraction in itself. There's a signpost a little past MH Mettananda's shop as you head south towards the centre of town.

School of Dance (☎ 225 8948; www.banduwijesooriyadanceacademy.org; cnr Galle Rd & Main St) teaches the southern forms of dance such as *kolam* (masked dance-drama), Kandyan and Sabaragamu. It's located across the intersection from the Ariyapala Mask Museum, with which it's affiliated. The school is run by Bandu Wijesuriya, a descendant of a long line of famous mask carvers. Anyone can join the classes; there's a fee of Rs 500 per hour for foreigners who are normally given one-to-one tuition. Wijesuriya also teaches mask carving and painting, as well as traditional drumming and singing. Students can stay in hostel-style rooms for Rs 750 per night. There is talk of a theatre with regular dance shows being opened, but for the moment Rs 10,000 and two days notice will get you your own personalised dance show.

Sailatalarama Vihara lies 7km inland from Ambalangoda. This temple sits on a domed hill with broad views over spice plantations and lakes towards the ranges of the Province of Sabaragamuwa. The temple has a 35m-long sleeping Buddha statue, built by donations. Pilgrims approach the dagobas and *devale* (a complex designed for worshipping a Hindu or local Sri Lankan deity) via 208 steps, but there's also a road to the top. The statue is new and not the most outstanding example of its type and the compulsory 'donation' for foreigners (Rs 250) is a bit steep, but it's worth coming here for the rural scenery and the views. Also check out the photo on the wall of a German-based monk standing in front of a cow bowing down in gratitude to the monk for saving it from the slaughterhouse! A three-wheeler from Ambalangoda should cost about Rs 500 return, with waiting time.

Between Ambalangoda and Iduruwa the muddy **Madu Ganga** dances around the coastline forming a complicated network of lagoons and off-shoots. It's fantastic birding territory and in praise of this it's been made into a Ramsar site. Boat tours (Rs 2500 per boat, 1½ hours) are run by **Maduwa River Boats** (☎ 505 1317) from Balapitiya, a few kilometres north of Ambalangoda.

Sleeping & Eating

Compared with nearby towns, the accommodation scene in Ambalangoda is pretty dire and you may prefer to visit as part of a day trip. Most of the few options are north of the centre – note that Main St is one block west of Galle Rd, but the streets also intersect at the very north end of Main St, where Galle Rd veers west.

Sunny's Guesthouse (☎ 225 5846; Galle Rd; r Rs 1200) Around 3km south of town this friendly guest house has a handful of tidy, though uninspiring, rooms. A big plus in its favour is the free laundry and internet service. It's on the wrong side of the road from the scruffy beach. The waters from the tsunami actually rose high enough to reach the 1st-floor balcony – as the photos you'll no doubt be shown attest to.

Sumudu Guest House (☎ 225 8832; 418 Main St, Patabendimulla; s/d half board Rs 1200/1800; 🖳) Mr de Silva runs a truly fine family guest house situated near the intersection with Galle Rd. The century-old house is utterly enchanting with latticework window frames, up which explode a riot of tropical flowers. There's a shady communal terrace and the rooms, though not as fancy as the building itself, are still good value. Guests here are treated as one of the family and before you know it, they'll have the family photo album out for you to peruse. Air-con is an additional Rs 300.

Dream Beach Resort (☎ 225 8873; dbra@sltnet.lk; 509 Galle Rd; s/d Rs 3300/4400; 🖳) Close to a photogenic stretch of beach, the functional rooms are bland in the extreme (though better than you'd guess after a look at the exterior of the building). The restaurant doesn't win many fans.

Getting There & Away

Ambalangoda is on the main transport route between Colombo and Hikkaduwa, Galle and the South. Buses to and from Colombo (regular/air-con Rs 90/180, two to three hours) are common. Trains to Colombo (2nd/3rd class Rs 150/85, two hours) stop here less often. There are frequent buses to and from Hikkaduwa (Rs 20, 15 minutes) and beyond.

HIKKADUWA & AROUND
☎ 091

Down-at-heel Hikkaduwa is Sri Lanka's candy-floss and ice-cream beach resort par excellence. First 'discovered' by that much maligned group of people, the hippies, back

WEST COAST

in the 1970s Hikkaduwa has been a firm fixture on the tourist map ever since. This long exposure to international tourism has left it a little worse for wear. Uncontrolled and unplanned development has meant that the swaying palms of yesteryear have given way to an almost unbroken strip of cheap guest houses and restaurants that vie among themselves to be the closest to the lapping waves. This in turn has led to terrible beach erosion, and in parts the once famous sand has now been almost completely replaced with sand bags fighting a vain battle to retain what little beach remains. To make matters worse the appalling Colombo–Galle road, with its asphyxiating smog and crazy bus drivers, runs right through the middle of it all, which can make stepping outside of your guest house as deadly as a game of Russian roulette!

Bad as it sounds though there are glimmers of hope. Hikkaduwa still lives up to its reputation of providing cheap and cheerful fun in the sun. There's an increasing range of activities on offer and, with the town slowly waking up to its demise, an increasing number of higher-class places to stay and eat. Finally, and maybe most importantly, a new road, linking Colombo to Matara and Galle, is under construction some way inland and this promises to rid Hikkaduwa of another of its demons. None of that sounds enough? Then take solace in the fact that the sunsets remain as beautiful as ever.

Orientation

Services such as the train and bus stations, banks, post office and nontourist-oriented shops congregate in the northern end of Hikkaduwa proper, which was the original settlement. Further south is where the first tourist hotels, guest houses and restaurants opened up, but this area now seems overdeveloped and unappealing compared with Wewala and Narigama (around 2km south of the stations), where most independent travellers stay. These areas are more relaxed and spread out, and have better beaches than Hikkaduwa proper.

Information

There are numerous IDD telephone bureaus on Hikkaduwa's main street, many of them with internet facilities. From tourist libraries along Galle Rd (The Bookworm and the Sun

Beam Tourist Library were favourites of ours), you can borrow books written in numerous European languages. There's usually a small fee (Rs 100) per read, plus a deposit (say Rs 300), which is refunded on the safe return of the book.

Bank of Ceylon (Galle Rd) Near Commercial Bank; you can change money or travellers cheques here.

Commercial Bank (Galle Rd) Fittingly located in the commercial district, and has an international ATM.

Cyber Lounge Internet Cafe (Galle Rd; per hr Rs 180)

Main post office (Baddegama Rd)A five-minute walk inland from the bus station.

Net Flora Internet (Galle Rd; Rs 180 per hr; 🕘 7.30am-11pm)

Tharindu Pharmacy (☎ 545 1426; 238 Galle Rd) Has a basic selection of medicines.

Tourist Police Station (Galle Rd) It's so brand newthat they don't yet have a fixed phone line. Contact Sgt Wimal on ☎ 077 198 3218. It's at the eastern end of the tourist strip.

Sights & Activities

For many people a visit to Hikkaduwa begins and ends on the beach and you can't really fault them for that! However, not everything is perfect in paradise – uncontrolled development right on the foreshore has altered the natural process of sand replenishment and resulted in severe erosion, which has meant that in places the beach has virtually completely vanished and what remains is held in place by nothing but sandbags and faith. The widest belt of sand extends north and south from Narigama. Here you'll find a few simple lounge chairs that you can rent, or even use for free if they're part of a cafe. But don't expect a chaotic scene; there are a few vendors, but it's pretty relaxed.

The sands at Wewala are narrower and steeper, but this is where the best surf is.

CORAL SANCTUARY

Hikkaduwa's overexploited 'coral sanctuary' stretches out from the string of 'Coral' hotels at the north end of the strip to a group of rocks a couple of hundred metres offshore. You can swim out to the rocks from the Coral Gardens Hotel, where the reef runs straight out from the shore. The water over the reef is never more than 3m or 4m deep. Once upon a time this was a magnificent garden of fishy colours and flowering corals, but today the reef is sadly a shadow of its former self with much of the coral dying and the fish flip-

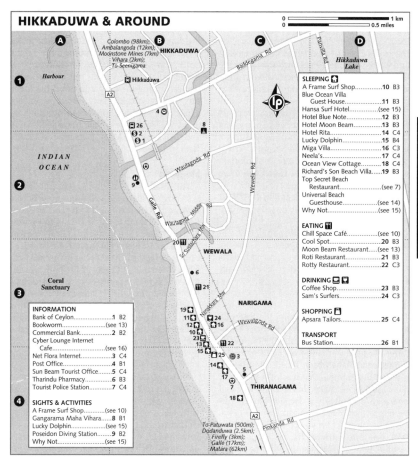

HIKKADUWA & AROUND

SLEEPING
A Frame Surf Shop..............10 B3
Blue Ocean Villa
 Guest House....................11 B3
Hansa Surf Hotel............(see 15)
Hotel Blue Note..................12 B3
Hotel Moon Beam..............13 B3
Hotel Rita..........................14 C4
Lucky Dolphin....................15 B4
Miga Villa..........................16 C3
Neela's..............................17 C4
Ocean View Cottage..........18 C4
Richard's Son Beach Villa.....19 B3
Top Secret Beach
 Restaurant....................(see 7)
Universal Beach
 Guesthouse..................(see 14)
Why Not..........................(see 15)

EATING
Chill Space Café................(see 10)
Cool Spot..........................20 B3
Moon Beam Restaurant......(see 13)
Roti Restaurant..................21 B3
Rotty Restaurant................22 C3

DRINKING
Coffee Shop......................23 B3
Sam's Surfers....................24 C3

SHOPPING
Apsara Tailors....................25 C4

TRANSPORT
Bus Station........................26 B1

INFORMATION
Bank of Ceylon....................1 B2
Bookworm......................(see 13)
Commercial Bank..................2 B2
Cyber Lounge Internet
 Cafe............................(see 16)
Net Flora Internet..................3 C4
Post Office............................4 B1
Sun Beam Tourist Office.......5 C4
Tharindu Pharmacy...............6 B3
Tourist Police Station............7 C4

SIGHTS & ACTIVITIES
A Frame Surf Shop............(see 10)
Gangarama Maha Vihara......8 B1
Lucky Dolphin..................(see 15)
Poseidon Diving Station........9 B2
Why Not..........................(see 15)

WEST COAST

ping away to more pristine spots. One of the big reasons for this demise has been coral bleaching, caused by oceanic and atmospheric conditions (quite probably man-made), which struck the reef in 1998, affecting about half the coral. The tsunami caused some further damage, but the real problem, as always, has been poor human management.

It's easy to see the coral. Dive shops and many hotels and guest houses rent out snorkelling gear for around Rs 300 a day, or less. Stay alert in the water so that you don't, say, get run over by a glass-bottomed boat (not a recommended vehicle for viewing the reef anyway, given the boats' running-into-coral proclivities).

SCUBA DIVING

The diving season runs from November to April. Professional Association of Diving Instructors (PADI) courses (open water from €165, advanced for €185), plus a selection of dives such as wreck dives, night dives and trips for those who just want to try out diving, are available from **Poseidon Diving Station** (☎ 227 7294; www.divingsrilanka.com; Galle Rd).

SURFING

The conditions for surfing are at their best from November to April. The Wewala and Narigama areas of the beach have a handful of tame reef breaks, as well as a beach break, all of which are perfect for beginner-to intermediate-level surfers. These waves, combined with its dreamy beaches and energetic nightlife, has made Hikkaduwa easily the most popular surf spot in Sri Lanka. The waves here tend to be fairly slow breaking and weak and, combined with the normally heavy crowds, experienced wave riders will probably find surfing Hikkaduwa a frustrating experience.

A Frame Surf Shop (☎ 545 8131; www.mambo.nu; 434 Galle Rd), located in A Frame Surf Shop guest house (opposite), repairs boards and has a selection of surfing gear. It rents out a variety of boards from Rs 600 per day. It also offers surfing tours throughout the island under the moniker 'Mambo Surf Tours'.

Many places to stay, such as **Why Not** (☎ 492 1261; Galle Rd), also rents out boards (Rs 200 per hour).

Kitesurfing is growing in popularity and **Lucky Dolphin** (☎ 227 5272; info@kiten.nl; 533 Galle Rd), a guest house in Narigama (opposite), rents out kitesurfing gear and offers lessons (four hours for US$50).

INLAND ATTRACTIONS

To take a break from the beach scene, just walk or cycle along any of the minor roads heading inland. They lead to a calmer, completely different, rural world. Just off Baddegama Rd is **Gangarama Maha Vihara**. This is an interesting Buddhist temple that has lots of popular educational paintings that are the work of one man over nearly a decade. The monks are happy to show you around. A further 2km along Baddegama Rd you come to **Hikkaduwa Lake**, home to monitor lizards and a lot of birdlife. Boat tours can sometimes be organised on the lake; ask around.

About 2km north of Hikkaduwa is the **Seenigama Vihara**, perched on its own island. It's one of only two temples in the country where victims of theft can seek retribution. People who have been robbed visit the temple and buy a specially prepared oil made with chilli and pepper. With the oil they light a lamp in their homes and recite a mantra. Sooner or later, maybe within weeks, the thief will be identified when they're struck down with misfortune, such as having a bicycle accident or being hit on the head by a falling coconut.

Have you ever wondered where that pretty little moonstone on your finger actually comes from? Head inland 7km to Mitiyagoda and you can descend (not literally) into the

mucky world of mining – 18th-century style! Moonstone has been mined in these sweltering forests forever and the **moonstone mines** (☻ 8am-5pm), little more than muddy rabbit holes, 6m or 7m long, are fascinating – as is the process of filtering out the precious stones, cutting them up and polishing them up ready for sale. Entrance is free, but expect a hardcore sales pitch in the on-site shop afterwards. To get there head towards Kahawa and turn inland to Mitiyagoda after which it's clearly signed.

Sleeping

Virtually all of Hikkaduwa's accommodation is strung out along Galle Rd, but none of it is anything to write home about. The best way to find something to suit is simply to wander down the road (or beach) and look at a variety of rooms. All budget accommodation prices can be bargained over. Prices given here are what you'd expect to pay in the high season; in low season, the same room may go for half the quoted price. Prices also vary according to which stretch of the strip you're on – down at the Narigama end, where the sands are wider, room rates tend to be higher. In the high season the best-value, smaller places fill up quickly; you may need to make a booking a few days ahead.

Most plots of land along the strip are quite narrow, which means that guest houses will only have a few pricey rooms with views of the water. In contrast, rooms closest to the road get a lot of noise, so be sure to get a room well away from the traffic. Many places are jammed right up against each other.

Finally, Hikkaduwa is not a place for those looking for a top-end resort. There's a collection of ageing resort-style hotels at the north end of the strip (all of which have 'Coral' in the name and none of which are worthy of inclusion here), but you'll have a more enjoyable experience at the guest houses to the south.

BUDGET

Unless otherwise noted, expect fans, mosquito nets, cold water and private bathrooms at these places.

Hansa Surf Hotel (☎ 222 3854; Galle Rd; r from Rs 500) This friendly dive has tatty, graffiti-covered rooms that are the cheapest in Hikkaduwa – and it shows!

Miga Villa (☎ 077 965 5973; Galle Rd; s/d Rs 600/800) This terracotta and lime-green colonial villa, set in gorgeous gardens, is an utterly wonderful oasis of pure eccentricity. Stuffed full of wooden statues and paintings of gods, animals and kings, and fluffed up with enormous bouquets of fake wedding-day flowers, it's virtually a museum in the making! It's normally used to host wedding parties and so can be noisy (though you'll probably end up being invited to dance along with everyone), but the basic, and none too clean, rooms are open to all-comers.

Richard's Son Beach Villa (☎ 227 7184; Galle Rd; r Rs 800) Unlike most places locally, this small single-storey guest house has a huge garden planted with coconut palms and other trees. There are hammocks hanging about, and an overall mellow vibe. The eight rooms are small but clean and about as cheap as things get. It's popular with returning guests for a good reason.

Why Not (☎ 492 1261; Galle Rd; r from Rs 1000) Well, why not indeed? This place is good value, and you can choose from bright and cheerful mellow-yellow downstairs rooms or a more impressive tree house–style raised cabana overlooking the surf (Rs 2500). There's a popular cafe with all your favourite creatures of the deep on the menu. Surfboards are available for rent.

Universal Beach Guest House (☎ 438 3040; 622 Galle Rd; s/d from Rs 1000/1200) A decent-enough place with small, clean, airy and comfortable rooms in a two-storey yellow block set back from the beach.

Hotel Rita (☎ 227 7496; www.ritas.net.ms; Galle Rd; r incl breakfast from Rs 1500; 🖳 🖳) Keeping passing travellers content for years, Rita's has tidy backrooms for those on a budget while midrange cruisers will find the fancier ocean-facing rooms, which are larger and have more attention to detail, to their pleasure. There's an in-house travel agency and a busy beachside restaurant.

MIDRANGE

Many places in the midrange category are not far removed from their budget guest-house roots. Room quality can vary wildly as a result of years of piecemeal additions.

Neela's (☎ 438 3166; 634 Galle Rd; r from Rs 2000) This pink palace is reaching for the stars – it's got so many floors. Its many rooms are excellent

value, with ocean-blue bathrooms and immaculately clean rooms. It has a friendly vibe and is an excellent choice.

Ocean View Cottage (☎ 227 7237; www.ocean viewcottage.net; Galle Rd; r from Rs 2000; 🖳 🖳 🖳) It's a little too big and modern to fit with most people's idea of a cottage, but with its vast and spotless rooms, you get a lot for your money. The pool is nice and there's a large grassy expanse leading down to the beach, but it's a long and lonely hike from anywhere else.

Lucky Dolphin (☎ 227 5272; info@kiten.nl; 533 Galle Rd; s/d Rs 2000/2500) With rooms that are as impeccably manicured as any Parisian poodle, this hotel represents real bang for your buck. Rooms come with four-posters, colourful windows, hot-water showers and a friendly management.

Top Secret Beach Restaurant (☎ 492 3268; www.srilanka-holiday.info; Galle Rd; s/d incl breakfast Rs 2000/2500) Right at the eastern end of the tourist strip, and on an appealing patch of beach, is this new and stylish guest house. It has driftwood furnishings and fancy bedspreads but only cold-water showers. Away from the rooms you'll discover an Arabian-style lounge area and a decent bar-restaurant that pins up a useful five-day surf forecast.

A Frame Surf Shop (☎ 545 8131; www.mambo .nu; 434 Galle Rd; s/d Rs 2500/3000; 🖳) A growing empire, this is also home to the popular Chill Space Café and a well-informed surf shop. The dozen rooms here are brushed up in funky colours and while only some have hot water, all have air-con. There's an Arabian-style lounge area on the 1st floor and incredible surf views from the 2nd.

Blue Ocean Villa (☎ 227 7566; blueocean@sltnet .lk; 420 Galle Rd; r incl breakfast Rs 3000; 🖳 🖳) Smart people rock up to this friendly place in the heart of all the action and score themselves a classy room that comes with wicker chairs, hot water and a rock-and-water world fantasy in the reception area. The only real downside we could come up with is that some of the rooms suffer from road noise.

Hotel Blue Note (☎ 438 3052; www.eureka.lk/blue note; 424 Galle Rd; r Rs 3100) Not as claustrophobic as some other places, the cabanas here, set around a little beachside garden, have blue and white beds, TVs and a slightly musty pong. It's aimed more at an older clientele than some of its party-going neighbours.

WEST COAST

Hotel Moon Beam (☎ 545 6800; hotelmoonbeam@ hotmail.com; 548/1 Galle Rd; s/d incl breakfast Rs 2200/3500; ✷) A smart midrange option with numerous spick-and-span rooms that are enlivened by pictures and wooden decorations. Piping-hot water gushes forth from the showers and some rooms have balconies with surf views. Bring your own mosquito net. The restaurant is highly recommended.

Eating & Drinking

Most of Hikkaduwa's best places to eat are connected to hotels and guest houses. Down on the sandy shores of Narigama, you can table-hop from one spot to the next through the night. Many places are good just for a drink and a few stay open past 11pm – but don't expect any raves here.

Rotty Restaurant (Galle Rd; rottis from Rs 70; ☺ 8am-1am) Start off with a cheese-and-bacon *rotti* (doughy pancake), wrap it up with a pineapple-and-banana *rotti*, and wash it all down with a mango juice at this simple and friendly place. It also does an excellent rice and curry for Rs 100.

Roti Restaurant (☎ 491 1540; 373 Galle Rd; meals Rs 80) Away from the beach and a whole world away from the beach restaurant scene, this hole in the wall right on the road sells over 60 kinds of *rotti*, ranging from garlic chicken to banana. There are also fresh shakes and lassis.

Coffee Shop (Galle Rd) Real Italian coffees, including hangover-busting espressos (Rs 150), give a pre-surf morning boost at this fashionable cafe.

Chill Space Café (☎ 545 8131; 434 Galle Rd; meals Rs 100-800) This almost comically surf, fashion-obsessed beachside cafe, which is situated in front of the A Frame Surf Shop (p121), features reasonable shakes, snacks, seafood and more, but basically you're paying for the atmosphere more than anything else. There are free beach chairs and occasional live music at night.

Cool Spot (327 Galle Rd; mains Rs 250-800) This family-run place has been serving up fresh seafood from a sky-blue vintage roadside house at the north end of the strip since 1972. There's a cool veranda where you can peruse the blackboard menu and delight in specialities, such as garlic prawns and the bulging seafood platter. It's someway north of the main independent tourist strip.

Moon Beam Restaurant (☎ 545 0657; 548/1 Galle Rd; mains Rs 300-500) This hotel (left) has easily the most attractive restaurant on the beach. It has a salty, open-air nautical decor, and tables where you can curl your toes in the sand. The seafood is truly excellent and it's also a good place for a sunset drink.

Sam's Surfers (Roger's Garage; 403 Galle Rd) A laid-back bar that shows recent movies every night at 7.30pm. It's very much a Brits-and-Aussies-abroad kind of place but is popular all the same.

Shopping

A good buy here is a pair of made-to-measure surfing board shorts (for men or women). Numerous tailors provide this service, but we were very impressed with the stitch work of **Apsara Tailors** (Galle Rd; men's shorts Rs 600, women's Rs 400; ☺ 10am-10pm). In reality, the opening hours are much more flexible than this.

Getting There & Away

BUS

There are frequent buses from Colombo (Rs 100, two to three hours). Buses also operate frequently to Galle (Rs 25, 30 minutes). Buses to Galle or beyond will drop you south of the bus station along the guest-house strip. When leaving Hikkaduwa you stand more chance of a seat if you start at the bus station.

TRAIN

The trains can get very crowded; avoid the really slow ones that stop everywhere. Check at the station for express departure times. Service on the coast line is fairly frequent; some destinations include Colombo (2nd/3rd class Rs 140/80, two to three hours), Galle (2nd/3rd class Rs 40/20, 30 minutes) and beyond to Matara.

Getting Around

A three-wheeler from the train or bus stations to Wewala or Narigama costs about Rs 120. Bicycle hire is easily available (Rs 150 to 200 a day), but it's hard to see how anybody could possibly enjoy cycling along crazy Galle Rd.

The South

Southern Sri Lanka overwhelms the senses. The landscape is one of utter beauty, the radiant green rice paddies and forests of swinging palm trees contrast starkly with beaches of ivory-coloured sand and an ocean of rich turquoise. The air is heavy with the scent of jasmine and cinnamon and the people drift past in clouds of bright colours. This beauty has been casting its spell on visitors for eternity, and when Marco Polo spoke so poetically of Sri Lanka it must surely have been this southern coast that filled his mind. For the visitor of today that same sense of romance and wonder remains. People here dance across fire on monsoon nights, idyllic sweeping bays cuddle up to a crumbling Dutch city with streets of art, fishermen float on stilts above the waves and at night turtles crawl up onto moonlit beaches.

No matter what you're after you'll find it here. Those who need to stretch their muscles can dive and snorkel across glowing coral reefs or learn to surf on gentle sandbars. The culturally inclined can soak up history in colonial forts and find works of Buddhist-inspired art in lonely caves. For the naturalist there are huge whales splashing through offshore swells, monkeys chattering through the trees and leopards moving like spirits in the night. And for everyone, no matter what their interests, there is the simple joy of knowing that dreams of paradise can come true.

HIGHLIGHTS

- Strolling the sculptured streets of whimsical **Galle** (p124)
- Slipping into the limpid, moonstone-coloured waters of **Unawatuna** (p132)
- Oohing, ahhing and staying forever on the perfect beaches of **Tangalla** (p142)
- Speeding through the tube at **Midigama** (p136)
- Spotting a spotty leopard and listening out for big-eared elephants in **Yala National Park** (p150)
- Walking on fire to make your peace with the gods at the spectacular **Kataragama festival** (p152)

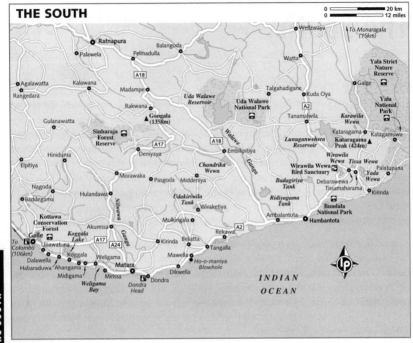

THE SOUTH

GALLE

☎ 091 / pop 90,270

Galle (pronounced gawl in English, and *gaar*-le in Sinhala) is a town of colour, texture and sensation totally unlike anywhere else in Sri Lanka. It is at once endlessly exotic, bursting with the scent of spices and salty winds, and yet also, with its wonderful collection of slowly decaying Dutch-colonial buildings, vaguely familiar, like a whimsical medieval European town unexpectedly deposited in the tropics. But above all else Galle is a city of trade and, increasingly, art. Today the Fort is crammed full of little boutique shops, cafes and hotels owned by local and foreign – a third of the houses are owned by foreigners – artists, writers, photographers, designers and poets.

Built by the Dutch, beginning in 1663, the 36-hectare Fort occupies most of the promontory that forms the older part of Galle and is an amazing collection of structures and culture dating back through the centuries. Just wandering the streets at random yields one architectural surprise after another. Its glories have been recognised by Unesco who have made the Fort a World Heritage Site.

A key part of the Fort's allure, however, is that it isn't just a pretty place. Rather, it remains a working community: there are administrative offices, courts, export companies, lots of regular folks populating the streets and a definite buzz of energy in the air.

Galle is easily reached as a day trip from Hikkaduwa and Unawatuna. But an increasing number of travellers are staying within the atmospheric walls of the Fort.

History

Although Anuradhapura and Polonnaruwa are much older than Galle, they are effectively abandoned cities – the modern towns are divorced from the ancient ruins. In contrast, both old and new Galle have remained vibrant.

Some historians believe Galle may have been the city of Tarshish – where King Solomon obtained gems and spices – though many more argue that a port in Spain seems a more likely candidate. Either way Galle only became prominent with the arrival of the Europeans. In 1505 a Portuguese fleet bound for the Maldives was blown off course and took shelter in the harbour. Apparently, on hearing a cock (*galo* in Portuguese) crowing, they gave the town its name. Another slightly less dubious story is that the name is derived from the Sinhala word *gala* (rock).

In 1589, during one of their periodic squabbles with the kingdom of Kandy, the Portuguese built a small fort, which they named Santa Cruz. Later they extended it with a series of bastions and walls, but the Dutch, who took Galle in 1640, destroyed most traces of the Portuguese presence.

After the construction of the Fort in the 17th century, Galle was the main port for Sri Lanka for more than 200 years, and was an important stop for boats and ships travelling between Europe and Asia. However, by the time Galle passed into British hands in 1796, commercial interest was turning to Colombo. The construction of breakwaters in Colombo's harbour in the late 19th century sealed Galle's status as a secondary harbour, though it still handles some shipping and yachts.

The tsunami hit Galle's new town badly and many people were killed around the bus station area. In contrast the solid walls of the Fort meant that damage was fairly limited in the old quarter.

For an interesting take on local history, buy a copy of *Galle: As Quiet As Asleep* by Norah Roberts, Galle's long-time librarian. Or, to learn more about the people of today's Galle, Juliet Coombe and Daisy Perry's book *Around the Fort in 80 Lives* should do nicely.

THE 2004 TSUNAMI – AFTERMATH IN THE SOUTH

The south coast was heavily affected by the tsunami. Much of Galle was damaged, although the walls of the Fort lived up to their name and protected the historic old town. The popular beach resort of Unawatuna was virtually wiped out, but was rebuilt quickly thanks to foreign generosity. Further east, Tangalla suffered heavily and many once-popular beach guest houses vanished. In the sparsely populated areas past hard-hit Hambantota, the waters changed the shape of the coast, although areas such as Yala National Park proved resilient to nature's forces.

Orientation

Sri Lanka's fourth-biggest town, Galle is 116km south of Colombo. The old town (the Fort) occupies most of the south-pointing promontory. Where the promontory meets the 'mainland' is the centre of the new town, with the bus and train stations, shops and banks. The two areas are divided by the grassy expanse of Galle International Cricket Stadium. Galle has a busy market area in the new town, on Main St.

The Fort's walls did a fine job of protecting the old town from the tsunami, while the newer commercial district was battered but rapidly recovered. However, residential areas near the water suffered heavily, scores of people died, and 'temporary' housing has become a permanent part of the future.

Information

Galle is a good source of supplies and other essentials for those heading east along the coast.

Places offering international direct-dialling services are common, and many phone places also offer internet access. There is no shortage of banks with international ATMs, both in the Fort and the new town.

Cargills Food City (☎ 223 3212; 3rd fl, 26 P&J City, Gamini Mawatha) This supermarket also has a pharmacy.

Commercial Bank (Church St) Has an international ATM.

Galle Library (Church St) Seems almost as old as the Fort. Has a small collection and students eager to try out their English.

Hatton National Bank (Wackwella St) Has an international ATM.

Lexcom (☎ 438 5521; 4th fl, 26 P&J City, Gamini Mawatha; per hr Rs 240) One of several internet cafes in the same building as Cargills Food City.

Main post office (Main St; per min Rs 4) Has a poste restante counter and an air-con internet centre. It's near the market.

Post office (Church St) A small branch office.

Sampath Bank (Wackwella St) Has an international ATM.

Sri Lankan Airlines (☎ 224 6942; 3rd fl, 16 Gamini Mawatha) You can book flights here; it also offers a full range of travel services.

Dangers & Annoyances

Galle has a small band of bamboozlers, fixers, flimflammers and other characters looking to pull a scam. A firm 'I have no interest in anything you have to offer' should do the trick – at least by the fourth repetition.

GALLE

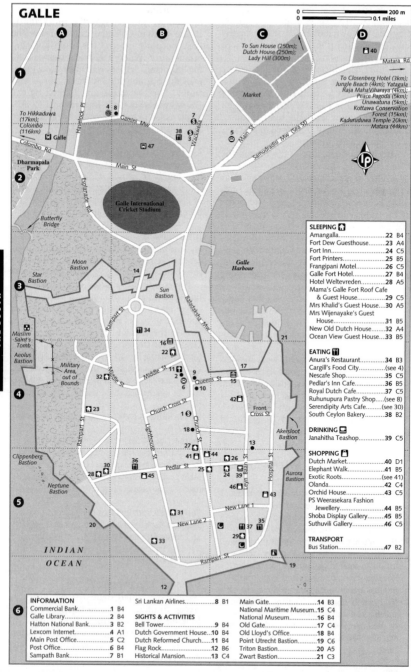

0 — 200 m
0 — 0.1 miles

To Sun House (250m);
Dutch House (250m);
Lady Hill (300m)

Market

To Closenberg Hotel (3km);
Jungle Beach (4km); Yatagala
Raja Maha Viharaya (4km);
Peace Pagoda (5km);
Unawatuna (5km);
Kottawa Conservation
Forest (15km);
Kaduruduwa Temple 20km;
Matara (44km)

Matara Rd

To Hikkaduwa
(17km);
Colombo
(116km)

Galle

Colombo Rd

Dharmapala
Park

Main St

Havelock Pl

Gamini Mw

Wackwella

Main St

Samudradid Mw (See St)

Galle International
Cricket Stadium

Butterfly
Bridge

Moon
Bastion

Galle
Harbour

Star
Bastion

Sun
Bastion

Esplanade Rd

Rampart St

Baladaksha Mw

Muslim
Saint's
Tomb

Aeolus
Bastion

Military
Area,
out of
Bounds

Middle St

Middle St

Queens St

Church Cross St

Lighthouse St

Rampart St

Church St

Front
Cross St

Akersloot
Bastion

Aurora
Bastion

Clippenberg
Bastion

Neptune
Bastion

Pedlar St

Leyn Baan St

Hospital St

New Lane 1

New Lane 2

Rampart St

INDIAN

OCEAN

THE SOUTH

SLEEPING 🏠

Amangalla	22 B4
Fort Dew Guesthouse	23 A4
Fort Inn	24 C5
Fort Printers	25 B5
Frangipani Motel	26 C5
Galle Fort Hotel	27 B4
Hotel Weltevreden	28 A5
Mama's Galle Fort Roof Cafe & Guest House	29 C5
Mrs Khalid's Guest House	30 A5
Mrs Wijenayake's Guest House	31 B5
New Old Dutch House	32 A4
Ocean View Guest House	33 B5

EATING 🍴

Anura's Restaurant	34 B3
Cargill's Food City	(see 4)
Nescafe Shop	35 C5
Pedlar's Inn Cafe	36 B5
Royal Dutch Cafe	37 C5
Ruhunupura Pastry Shop	(see 8)
Serendipity Arts Cafe	(see 30)
South Ceylon Bakery	38 B2

DRINKING 🍷

Janahitha Teashop	39 C5

SHOPPING 🛍

Dutch Market	40 D1
Elephant Walk	41 B5
Exotic Roots	(see 41)
Olanda	42 C4
Orchid House	43 C5
PS Weerasekara Fashion Jewellery	44 B5
Shoba Display Gallery	45 B5
Suthuvili Gallery	46 C5

TRANSPORT

Bus Station	47 B2

INFORMATION

Commercial Bank	1 B4
Galle Library	2 B4
Hatton National Bank	3 B2
Lexcom Internet	4 A1
Main Post Office	5 C2
Post Office	6 B4
Sampath Bank	7 B1
Sri Lankan Airlines	8 B1

SIGHTS & ACTIVITIES

Bell Tower	9 B4
Dutch Government House	10 B4
Dutch Reformed Church	11 B4
Flag Rock	12 B6
Historical Mansion	13 C4
Main Gate	14 B3
National Maritime Museum	15 C4
National Museum	16 B4
Old Gate	17 C4
Old Lloyd's Office	18 B4
Point Utrecht Bastion	19 C6
Triton Bastion	20 A5
Zwart Bastion	21 C3

Sights

The Fort area is home to about 400 houses, churches, mosques, temples and many old commercial and government buildings. To really experience it throw away all ideas of an itinerary and don't worry if you don't tick off every museum. Galle is an experience to savour, taste and touch rather than a list of prescribed sites, so wander those walls and streets at will, making your own discoveries as you go. And don't neglect the new town: there are all manner of interesting shops and markets along Main St and Matara Rd.

THE FORT WALLS

One of the most pleasant strolls you can take in town is the circuit of the Fort walls at dusk. As the daytime heat fades away, you can walk almost the complete circuit of the Fort along the top of the wall in an easy hour or two. You'll be in the company of lots of locals, shyly courting couples and plenty of kids diving into the protected waters.

The **Main Gate** in the northern stretch of the wall is a comparatively recent addition – it was built by the British in 1873 to handle the heavier flow of traffic into the old town. This part of the wall, the most heavily fortified because it faced the land, was originally built with a moat by the Portuguese, and was then substantially enlarged by the Dutch who split the wall in 1667 into separate Star, Moon and Sun Bastions.

Following the Fort wall clockwise you soon come to the **Old Gate**. The British coat of arms tops the entrance on the outer side. Inside, the letters VOC, standing for Verenigde Oostindische Compagnie (Dutch East India Company), are inscribed in the stone with the date 1669, flanked by two lions and topped by a cock. Just beyond the gate is the **Zwart Bastion** (Black Bastion), thought to be Portuguese built and the oldest of the Fort bastions.

The eastern section of the wall ends at the **Point Utrecht Bastion**, close to the powder magazine. The bastion is topped by an 18m-high lighthouse, which was built in 1938.

Flag Rock, at the end of the next stretch of wall, was once a Portuguese bastion. During the Dutch period approaching ships were signalled from the bastion, warning them of dangerous rocks – hence its name. Musket shots were fired from Pigeon Island, close to the rock, to further alert ships to the danger. On the **Triton Bastion** there used to be a windmill that drew up sea water, which was sprayed from carts to keep the dust down on the city streets. This part of the wall is a great place to be at sunset. There's a series of other bastions, as well as the tomb of a Muslim saint outside the wall, before you arrive back at your starting point.

INSIDE THE FORT

Most of the older buildings within the Fort date from the Dutch era. Many of the streets still bear their Dutch names, or are direct translations. The Dutch also built an intricate sewer system that was flushed out daily by the tide. With true Dutch efficiency, they then bred musk rats in the sewers, which were exported for their musk oil. There's a large Muslim community living and working inside the Fort, particularly at the southern end of the walled town. Many shops close for a couple of hours around noon on Friday for prayer time.

The **Dutch Reformed Church** (Groote Kerk, Great Church; cnr Church & Middle Sts; 🕑 9am-5pm), near the Amangalla Hotel, was originally built in 1640, but the present building dates from 1752 to 1755. Its floor is paved with gravestones from the old Dutch cemetery (the oldest dates from 1662); the friendly caretaker will tell you where remains are held in the walls and under the floor. The organ from 1760 still sits in the building and the impressive pulpit, made from calamander wood from Malaysia, is an interesting piece. Services are held each Sunday.

The ultra-posh hotel **Amangalla** (p129) was built in 1684 to house the Dutch governor and officers. As the New Oriental Hotel it was the lodging of choice for first-class P&O passengers travelling to and from Europe in the 19th century. Today it's the lodging of choice for first-class airline passengers.

Near the Dutch Reformed Church are a **bell tower** (built in 1901) and the old **Dutch Government House**. A slab over the doorway bears the date 1683 and Galle's ubiquitous cock symbol. Look for the **Old Lloyd's Office**, with its preserved ship arrival board, in the 19th-century commercial building just north of Galle Fort Hotel.

Entered via the Old Gate, the **National Maritime Museum** (admission Rs 300; 🕑 9am-5pm Sat-Wed) was closed for renovations at the time of research but will be open by the time you read this. Word is that it will be a very different creature from the fusty old dear of before.

The **National Museum** (Church St; admission Rs 45; ☟ 9am-5pm Wed-Sun) is housed in an old Dutch building near the Main Gate. The museum, with just a little more effort, would be superb; however, as it is, it has sad displays of traditional masks, information on the lace-making process, a few examples of the luxury items that once passed through the port, and religious items, including a relic casket.

If you think you've got a lot of clutter filling up the shelves at home, then just wait until you get a load of the **Historical Mansion** (31-39 Leyn Baan St; ☟ 9am-5.30pm Mon-Thu, Sat & Sun, 10am-noon & 2-5.30pm Fri), which is the private collection of one serious hoarding squirrel. Set in a well-restored Dutch house, it's not really a museum, as many of the exhibits have price tags. It's a junkyard of colonial artefacts, including collections of antique typewriters, VOC china, spectacles and jewellery. There's also a gem shop.

Activities

Hot-air ballooning is a romantic and wonderful way to see Galle and its surroundings from an entirely new angle. Contact **Adventure Asia International** (☎ 011-586 8468; www.ad-asia.com; per person from €170).

Tours

Author, photographer, historian, chef and just generally multitalented **Juliet Coombe** (☎ 077 683 8659) leads small group or individual tours of Galle, as well as child-friendly tours. She can normally be found at the Serendipity Arts Café (p130). Tours cost Rs 1500.

Festivals & Events

The **Galle Literary Festival** (www.galleliteraryfesti val.com) is an annual events held between 28 January and 1 February. Bringing together renowned Asian and Western writers, it's one of the best-regarded events of its type in Asia. A newer event that promises great things is the **Galle Film Festival** (www.gallefilmfestival .com). Showcasing the best of South Asian and Western fringe films, the festival takes place over the last few days of October and the first few of November (dates are not fixed). As if Galle wasn't enough of a work of art, the whole Fort area virtually becomes one giant artist's easel during the **Art Trail** (www.gallearttrail .com), which takes place at the same time as the film festival.

Sleeping

Galle has an ever-increasing number of truly amazing places to stay, but be warned: the European architecture comes with near European prices, so travellers of all budgets will need to splash out more cash here than in most other parts of the country.

FORT
Budget
Mrs Wijenayake's Guest House (Beach Haven; ☎ 223 4663; www.beachhaven-galle.com; 65 Lighthouse St; s & d Rs 800-1000; ☒) The wonderful Mrs Wijenayake has been playing host to grateful backpackers for ever and her knowledge of our needs shows in this superb guest house. Rooms range from the clean and simple with shared bathrooms to fancier air-con rooms. The family still talk of the extended stay by Lonely Planet cofounder Tony Wheeler in 1977.

Hotel Weltevreden (☎ 222 2650; piyasen2@sltnet .lk; 104 Pedlar St; s/d Rs 800/1000) A Heritage-Listed Dutch building, the Hotel Weltevreden has lovingly tended rooms painted in daring colours set around an equally well-loved courtyard garden. Plenty of friendly chit-chat with the elderly owner is included in the room price.

Mrs Khalid's Guest House (Huize Bruisen de Zee; ☎ 223 4907; sabrik@sltnet.lk; 102 Pedlar St; s/d from Rs 1000/1500) This tastefully restored Dutch house has spotless cool, white rooms, some of which have balconies with sea views. The communal areas are full of flowers, but the regime is strict – no alcohol, an evening curfew and pre-dinner prayers.

Midrange
our pick **Frangipani Motel** (☎ 222 2324; 32 Pedlar St; r from Rs 2000) Modern and kitsch in the most perfect of ways, this family-run guest house is the prize of Galle. The two downstairs rooms are neat and clean with hot-water bathrooms, while the larger rooms upstairs (Rs 3000) are airy and bright, with spicy ocean breezes billowing through the roof slats and a flower bedecked bed. There's a garden full of songbirds to eat and relax in, but for us, the best bit was the plastic indoor garden, complete with waterfalls and fish ponds. Highly recommended.

Fort Dew Guesthouse (☎ 222 4365; fortdew@yahoo .com; 31 Pedlar St; s/d Rs 2000/2500) Set close to the ancient city walls, next to a patch of parkland from which resonates the eternal thunk of ball on cricket bat, this guest house is a real find.

VILLAS IN PARADISE

If a fancy boutique hotel isn't exclusive enough for you, then the answer might lie in one of the string of extraordinarily lavish villas that have sprung up over the past couple of years along the south coast. The Fort area of Galle has a particular glut of such places, but make no mistake about it – when we say these are lavish, we really mean lavish. Fine modern art adorns the walls, heavenly swimming pools fill the courtyards and private cooks and butlers are on hand with a G&T at just the right moment. Needless to say, such a lifestyle doesn't come cheap and for most of these places you're looking at around US$500 a night, with three or four nights being a minimum stay. However, as they often comfortably sleep four or five, if you're travelling with friends then it can actually work out as an economical way to live like the other half – even if only for a while. For more see www.villasinsrilanka.com or www.lankarealestate.com.

It's whitewashed and simple, and contains absolutely everything you really need, including piping-hot showers.

Fort Inn (☎ 224 8094; rasikafortinn@yahoo.com; 31 Pedlar St; s with/without air-con Rs 2500/1500, d Rs 3000/2000; ☒) The ever-beaming owner of this three-room guest house will obligingly offer neatly attired rooms with hot showers and a perfect people-watching balcony. There's also a very enjoyable terrace cafe-restaurant with a Chinese-influenced menu that includes noodle soups (Rs 250 to 400).

New Old Dutch House (☎ 223 2987; www.newold dutchhouse.lk; 21 Middle St; r from US$30; ☒ ☐) All you really need to know is that this friendly place might well be the most immaculate and sparkly clean guest house in all of southern Sri Lanka. The spacious rooms have creaky, polished wooden floors and lovely soft beds. Breakfast can be enjoyed under the courtyards papaw trees listening to the ocean waves breaking on the rocks below the ramparts. The eight suite rooms are modern, all-white and come with satellite TV and fridge. Cheaper rooms share bathrooms and are fan-only.

Mama's Galle Fort Roof Café & Guest House (☎ 222 6415; mamasgallefort@yahoo.co.in; 76 Leyn Baan St; r from US$35; ☒) The two stylish and spacious rooms at Mama's, one of the rising stars of the Galle hotel scene, have a feeling of exclusivity to them, with comfortable beds in which sweet dreams are guaranteed, and showers that'll keep you singing for longer than is really necessary. The owners are delightful, the rooftop views superb, and the restaurant as good as you'll get for the price.

Ocean View Guest House (☎ 224 2717; www.ocean viewlk.biz; 80 Lighthouse St; r incl breakfast from US$35; ☒) The small and pleasingly old-fashioned rooms come in as many styles and flavours as there

are curries in Sri Lanka. The real clincher though is the beautiful rooftop garden, complete with luminous flowers, a bouncy lawn and one very happy tortoise. The guest house is entered from Rampart St.

Top End

The Fort is regaining some of the upmarket cachet it enjoyed during the colonial era.

Galle Fort Hotel (☎ 223 2870; www.galleforthotel.com; 28 Church St; r from US$202; ☒ ☐ ☒) Christopher Ong and Karl Steinberg have transformed a derelict 17th-century Dutch merchant's house into a fine boutique hotel. The 14 rooms are all different, with each room's design reflecting the part of the L-shaped structure it occupies. Some have two levels, others stretch across entire floors, and all are very comfortable. Linens are exquisite and there are antiques everywhere. What you won't find are distractions like TVs – rather, you can enjoy the large courtyard pool and the hospitality of the accommodating owners and staff. The restaurant serves excellent food and the bar is a stylish meeting place. The hotel also rents out several luxurious villas and has its own spa.

Fort Printers (☎ 224 7977; www.thefortprinters.com; 39 Pedlar St; ste from US$220; ☒ ☐ ☒) This 18th-century mansion was once used by printers, and you can still see the enormous wooden beams used to support the presses. Unlike most of Galle's boutique hotels they've done something a bit different here; rather than recreating the colonial highlife, they've filled the magnificent rooms and public spaces with colours and styles as brash as the modern art that coats the walls.

Amangalla (☎ 223 3388; www.amanresorts.com; cnr Middle & Church Sts; r from US$342; ☒ ☐ ☒) The Aman resorts group has converted a 17th-century town house into the ultimate in colonial decadence. The opening scene is one of massive, polished wooden floors and spiffily dressed staff, who lead you like royalty into giant rooms with beds that contain the biggest and fluffiest pillows we've ever seen, as well as bathrooms with beautiful free-standing tubs. Books about fine art and 18th century exploration line the numerous bookcases and outside you'll find a pool to die for. They also have private cottages, which start at around US$1500 a night – these are OK too. If this isn't in your budget, then you may at least want to hang out in the lobby for a drink.

OUT OF TOWN
Midrange
Lady Hill (☎ 224 4322; www.ladyhillsl.com; 29 Upper Dickson Rd; r from US$65; 🍴 💻 🐾) Morphing a 19th-century vicarage with a modern and really rather ugly block, this hotel has communal areas full of fish ponds and flowers and a lovely infinity pool, from which you can savour the succulent views of the city down below. The rooms themselves don't quite live up to expectation and differ little from a roadside motel.

Closenberg Hotel (☎ 222 4313; www.closenburg hotel.com; 11 Closenberg Rd; s/d incl breakfast from US$70/90; 🍴 💻) Built as a 19th-century P&O captain's residence in the heyday of British mercantile supremacy, this lovely bougainvillea-bedecked hotel, east of the centre, sits out on a promontory with views over Galle beach and the Fort. Four rooms in the original building are filled with antiques, and are a slowly decaying step back in time. The 16 rooms in the modern wing have been decorated in a manner sympathetic to the overall feel of the place, and are much more comfortable than those in the old wing.

Top End
Sun House (☎ 438 0275; www.thesunhouse.com; 18 Upper Dickson Rd; r from US$225; 🍴 💻 🐾) This gracious old villa, built in the 1860s by a Scottish spice merchant, has been renovated with superb taste. Located on the shady hill above the new town, the hotel has wonderful views towards the Fort. The spearmint-striped rooms are so perfect, you feel as if you've intruded into a photo shoot for one of those house decoration magazines. Our favourite was the red-and-white room with its mix of the old and new.

ourpick **Dutch House** (Doornberg; ☎ 438 0275; www .thesunhouse.com/doornberg.html; 23 Upper Dickson Rd; ste US$375; 🍴 💻 🐾) Cruise up to this 18th-century Dutch admiral's palace in your very own

1920s Rover, and live life like you're the star of a period drama. After a game of croquet on the lawn and a swim in the dreamy pool, retire to your room to write a novel or sketch a masterpiece on the artist's easel and then, if the high life gets tiring, take a break by clambering into the towering four-poster or by blowing bubbles of love in the bath. This place is seriously indulgent.

Eating & Drinking
Many of the places to stay in Galle have good places to eat, but nightlife remains very subdued.

FORT
Janahitha Teashop (cnr Pedlar & Leyn Baan Sts; 🕐 6am-7.30pm) A world away from all the posh restaurants and artsy cafes, this solidly locals-only teashop brews the best cuppa in the Fort.

Nescafe Shop (Rampart St; rotti from Rs 40 🕐 4.30am-6.30pm Mon-Fri, 10.30am-6.30pm Sat & Sun) There's no sign, but you can't really miss the *rotti*-slapping going on at this dark little cave of a cafe opposite the lighthouse. By far the cheapest place in the Fort to stuff your face.

Pedlar's Inn Cafe (☎ 077 314 1477; 92 Pedlar St; meals Rs 200-350; 🕐 8am-6pm Sat-Thu) A groovy little place in an old colonial house. Shakes, coffees and sandwiches can be enjoyed at long tables that are good for lounging. As well as a cafe, it doubles as a jewellery shop.

Royal Dutch Cafe (Leyn Baan St; meals from Rs 250; 🕐 Sat-Thu) Mixing cinnamon cake with biryani and ginger tea with a shop full of batiks, this is a chilled spot for a light lunch.

ourpick **Mama's Galle Fort Roof Café & Guest House** (☎ 222 6415; 76 Leyn Baan St; mains Rs 350) Eat under the twinkling star-lit sky with views of a spinning lighthouse at this guest house, which conjures up some of the most sensational curries in Galle – all at dirt-cheap prices. If the food really grabs you, ask about joining one of their cookery courses.

Serendipity Arts Cafe (☎ 077 952 5602; 100 Pedlar St; meals Rs 200-500) This photo-crammed hole-in-the-wall cafe has a fusion menu that includes Western sandwiches and Eastern curries, brilliant juices and shakes, bacon-and-egg hoppers and proper filter coffee. They claim that some of the recipes are generation's old family secrets – though we're assured that the ingredients aren't as old! It's an ideal place for lunch or breakfast. The cafe is owned and run by Juliet Coombe and her husband.

THE SOUTH

Anura's Restaurant (☎ 222 4354; 9 Lighthouse St; mains Rs 300-600) This tiny, bright-orange, hole-in-the-wall place serves fantastic light curries, various pastas and even what are reputed to be Galle's best pizzas. The paintings on the wall give it a trendy cafe-gallery feel.

Galle Fort Hotel (☎ 223 2870; 28 Church St; set menu US$45) The restaurant at this hotel (p129) serves superb, though very pricey, Asian fusion cuisine at tables set along the deep inner veranda. The dinner menu changes nightly. At other times there are baked goods, classic breakfast dishes, salads and sandwiches. The bar, overlooking Church St, feels like a colonial retreat, and is popular with the expat community.

NEW TOWN
Ruhunupura Pastry Shop (26 P&J City, Gamini Mawatha; ice cream Rs 50) Despite the name, this place specialises in ice cream. It's hot. Indulge.

South Ceylon Bakery (☎ 223 4500; 6 Gamini Mawatha; mains Rs 50-200) Opposite the bus station, this highly popular lunch spot, with its impossible-to-resist sweet and savoury short eats, and gut-bursting curries, is the most convenient place to eat in the new town.

Shopping
Galle's history makes it a natural spot for antique shopping, and you'll find several places inside the Fort.

Olanda (☎ 223 4398; 30 Leyn Baan St) A vast Aladdin's cave of antique furniture and general bric-a-brac are among the treasures you'll find here.

Elephant Walk (☎ 224 7977; 30 Church St) An arcade containing a collection of shops selling something that'll look just perfect on the wall or mantelpiece back home, as well as a small range of English-language books.

ourpick Shoba Display Gallery (☎ 222 4351; 67 Pedlar St) Beautiful lacework made right here in the shop – many of the finished products are used in the costumes of big-budget period dramas. The shop is the base for innovative charity Power of Hands Foundation (www .powerofhandsfoundation.com), which teaches local women dying crafts and ensures them a fair price for their work. Even if you're not buying, pop in to witness the process of making lace – amazing! If you're interested in a more hands-on approach, then (with advance notice) they'll teach you how to weave your own lacy wonder.

Suthuvili Gallery (Leyn Baart St) This small shop has simple displays of elaborate and beautiful polychromatic masks.

PS Weerasekara Fashion Jewellery (☎ 226 0329; Church St) Affordable and recommended jeweller that is several cuts above (ahem) the omnipresent gemstone vendors.

Orchid House (☎ 545 3344; 28A Hospital St) A new teashop with a side line in jewellery and the sweet smells of incense.

Exotic Roots (☎ 224 5454; 32 Church St) French artist Catherine creates beautifully colourful bowls and house decorations while her daughter mixes up the colours in striking paintings.

Look for the **Dutch Market** (Main St), selling Galle's freshest fruits and vegetables under a 300-year-old columned roof. There are other fresh food and spice markets along Main St, as well as a busy row of shops, many selling excellent merchandise at dirt-cheap prices. The entire area is worth a wander and a browse.

Getting There & Around
There are plenty of buses linking the towns along the coastal road. They leave from the bus station in the centre of Galle, opposite the cricket stadium. Major destinations include Colombo (regular/air-con Rs 104/230, three hours), Hikkaduwa (regular/air-con Rs 19/25, 30 minutes), Unawatuna (Rs 14, 10 minutes) and Matara (Rs 45, one hour).

There are express passenger trains to Colombo's Maradana station (2nd/3rd class Rs 180/100, three hours) from the town's vaguely art deco train station. Local trains serve Hikkaduwa (2nd/3rd class Rs 40/20, 30 minutes) and Matara (2nd/3rd class Rs 80/40, one to 1½ hours). There's a daily express to Kandy (2nd/3rd class Rs 320/175, 6½ hours).

A three-wheeler between Galle and anywhere in Unawatuna costs about Rs 300 to 400, depending on your negation skills.

AROUND GALLE
Huge and glistening, the **Peace Pagoda** was the gift of a Japanese Buddhist monk in 2005. It can be seen on a precipice at the east end of the bay. Take the first turn after the water ends as you drive east and follow a tree-lined track for about 1km. Along the way, you can visit isolated **Jungle Beach**, which can be reached down a steep path that begins by a huge tree (see Map p133).

The road heading north passes the **Kottawa Conservation Forest**, a 14-hectare wet evergreen forest about 15km northeast of Galle. There are walking tracks in the forest, but first get permission from the forest department office near the gate. Wear good walking shoes and trousers: the leeches are ferocious. Trees are identified with their botanical names, making this a good opportunity to get to know your Sri Lankan flora. In the small-sized park is a swimming spot fed by a waterfall.

About 10km east of Kottawa the 10m-high seated Buddha at **Kaduruduwa Temple** (donation Rs 100) rises above the surrounding paddy fields.

Just 4km inland from Unawatuna the **Yatagala Raja Maha Viharaya** (donation Rs 100) is a quiet rock temple with a 9m reclining Buddha. The mural-covered walls are painted in the typical style of the Kandyan period. Monks have been living here for at least 1500 years.

UNAWATUNA
☎ 091

Unawatuna is a place of dreams: a banana-shaped bend of boiling golden sand massaged by a gentle sea of moonstone blue. It's a place to dream of on drab Monday mornings at the office, a place to fantasise about when the chill claws of winter engulf you, a place where life always seems slow and easy, and where there's never a bill to be paid or a mortgage payment to be made. The Resplendent Isle does not get any more resplendent than Unawatuna.

In late 2004, however, this idyllic scene turned horrible. The tsunami caused major damage, washing away many guest houses and killing hundreds. Thanks to generous do-nations from foreigners who had vacationed here, as well as the efforts of teams of foreign volunteers who were drawn by Unawatuna's natural allures, reconstruction happened faster here than any other place in Sri Lanka.

Unfortunately, even paradise is plagued with greed, and the calamity was not turned into the opportunity to right some of the previous excesses of development. Business owners ignored plans for buildings to be set back from the water and rebuilt their places right on the sand. Some guest houses sit right on the high-tide mark and in fact, during big tides, they are now actually in the water. On some parts of the beach there is actually almost no beach at all left to play on; don't be surprised if within a few years some of the establishments have been washed away.

Orientation & Information

Unawatuna is mostly strung along small Wella Dewala Rd and its tributaries, which lead off the main Galle–Matara coast road. Formal names for these little tracks are not commonly used.

For most goods and services you'll have to make the short trip to Galle, as there are only a couple of rudimentary huts selling bottled water and crisps. Many places offer internet access, including **GG Happy Tours** (☎ 223 2838; gghappy@wow.lk; per hr Rs 200; 🕙 9am-10pm), which has also been recommended by a number of travellers for its tour and car-hire services.

Sights & Activities

Most people spend a lot of their time lying around the beach or slouching in cafes. To actually see something requires activity, but remember you're on holiday and activity is not good!

WATER SPORTS

Unawatuna doesn't have a lot in the way of surf thanks to a fringing reef, though there is a gentle right at the western end of the bay that a few locals ride.

You can hire snorkelling equipment from some of the beachfront places (or borrow it from guest houses) to explore the reefs a short distance from the west end of the beach.

There are several interesting wreck dives around Unawatuna, as well as reef and cave diving. The wreck dives include the *Lord Nelson,* a cargo ship that was wrecked about 10 years ago; it has a 15m-long cabin to ex-plore. The 33m-long *Rangoon* is one hour south of Unawatuna. The following places run diving courses and trips.

Sea Horse Scuba Diving Centre (☎ 228 3733) A well-regarded and long-standing outfit that rents out snor-kelling gear for Rs 800 per day. A Professional Association of Diving Instructors' (PADI) Open Water course costs €300.
Unawatuna Diving Centre (☎ 224 4693; www .unawatunadiving.com) Runs PADI courses from €300. Also rents out equipment and offers single dives.

WALKING

You can take some interesting walks over the rocks rising from the west end of the beach or up the hill behind Yaddehimulla Rd to catch views to the other side of the promontory. The rocky outcrop on the west end of the beach, **Rumassala**, is known for its protected medicinal herbs – legend has it that Hanuman dropped

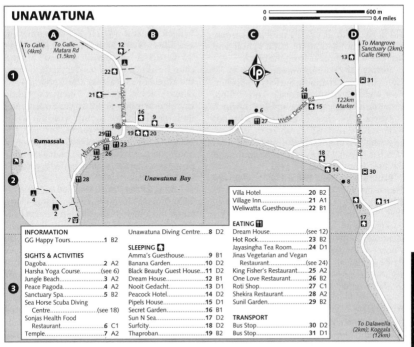

UNAWATUNA

0		600 m
0		0.4 miles

To Galle (4km)
To Galle–Matara Rd (1.5km)
To Mangrove Sanctuary (2km); Galle (5km)

Rumassala

Unawatuna Bay

122km Marker

To Dalawella (2km); Koggala (12km)

INFORMATION		
GG Happy Tours	1	B2

SIGHTS & ACTIVITIES		
Dagoba	2	A2
Harsha Yoga Course	(see 6)	
Jungle Beach	3	A2
Peace Pagoda	4	A2
Sanctuary Spa	5	B2
Sea Horse Scuba Diving Centre	(see 18)	
Sonjas Health Food Restaurant	6	C1
Temple	7	A2
Unawatuna Diving Centre	8	D2

SLEEPING		
Amma's Guesthouse	9	B1
Banana Garden	10	D2
Black Beauty Guest House	11	D2
Dream House	12	B1
Nooit Gedacht	13	D1
Peacock Hotel	14	D2
Pipels House	15	D1
Secret Garden	16	B1
Sun N Sea	17	D2
Surfcity	18	D2
Thaproban	19	B2
Villa Hotel	20	B2
Village Inn	21	A1
Weliwatta Guesthouse	22	B1

EATING		
Dream House	(see 12)	
Hot Rock	23	B2
Jayasingha Tea Room	24	D1
Jinas Vegetarian and Vegan Restaurant	(see 24)	
King Fisher's Restaurant	25	A2
One Love Restaurant	26	B2
Roti Shop	27	C1
Shekira Restaurant	28	A2
Sunil Garden	29	B2

TRANSPORT		
Bus Stop	30	D2
Bus Stop	31	D1

herbs carried from the Himalaya here. The **temple** right on the promontory is fenced off, but you can wander up to the **dagoba** (stupa) on top of the hill and on to the huge **Peace Pagoda** and isolated **Jungle Beach**; see p131 for more details. A slightly different kind of walk (Rs 250) can be found at the **Mangrove Sanctuary**; a disorganised work in progress, it one day might be a highly commendable local conservation effort protecting a swampy slab of snail, crab, bird and even monkey-filled mangrove forest a few minutes inland. Even though there is little infrastructure at the moment, it's well worth taking time out from the beach to pace the raised walkways through the tangled roots and trees. To get there look for the yellowing signs along the Galle–Matara road and then ask and ask.

Courses

Sonjas Health Food Restaurant (☎ 077 961 5310) runs highly recommended day-long cookery courses (Rs 3000) that tutor you in the finer points of Sri Lankan cuisine. The course is led by the lovely Karuna and a trip to Galle market is included in the price. Try to book at least a day in advance.

You can stretch and bend through a yoga course with **Harsha Yoga Course** (☎ 077 483 2451), which specialises in Ashtanga and Hatha yoga. Individual one-hour classes cost Rs 1000.

If a holiday means doing nothing more strenuous than being utterly pampered, the **Sanctuary Spa** (☎ 077 307 8583) should be music to your knotted muscles. A full treatment (male masseurs only) is around Rs 1600.

Sleeping

Unawatuna is packed with budget places to stay. Decent midrange places are becoming more common and there are even a few fairly luxurious options springing up.

BUDGET

Stay a few metres away from the beach for big savings. Unless noted, all of the following places are cold-water only.

Village Inn (☎ /fax 222 5375; r Rs 500-1000) An idyllic garden retreat that can't be beaten on price and quality. The owners are real charmers and the rooms with bathrooms, all of which have a balcony or veranda, are as clean as a whistle. There's also a dirt-cheap, but dirt-free restaurant.

Amma's Guesthouse (☎ 222 5332; r from Rs 700) The basic concrete cubicles inside this rambling old house, with its equally rambling garden, might not look too pretty, but it's cheap and just a few sandy paces from the beach.

Surfcity (☎ 224 6305; www.surfcity1.net; r from Rs 1000) The ever-expanding Surfcity emporium now includes an internet cafe, coffee shop, restaurant tour company and hotel, which has great-value clean rooms (three have hot water). Ravi, the owner, can arrange almost anything you might wish for, and the restaurant has unusual items such as hummus and flat bread on the menu.

Black Beauty Guest House (☎ 438 4978; www .black-beauty-sri-lanka.com; r with/without air-con Rs 3000/1500; 🖳 🖳) Located away from the beach, there is nothing remotely black about this guest house nor anything horsey, but there is plenty of beauty. The tranquil gardens provide a home to Spider-man, froggy mobiles and a flawless pool, and the bright-orange tower of a guest house has equally colourful rooms, though you pay a lot more for air-con.

MIDRANGE

Rooms can vary greatly in quality at these places, and some are more worthy of their rates than others.

Peacock Hotel (☎ 438 4998; www.peacockunawa tuna.com; r from Rs 2000) The number of bronzing backpackers lounging around here indicate that this is a popular choice – and with good reason. There's a huge variety of well-tended rooms (Rs 5000 for the king-of-the-castle choice) and all manner of traveller-related services. More expensive rooms have hot water.

Sun N Sea (☎ 228 3200; sunnsea.srilanka@yahoo.co.uk; s/d from Rs 2100/2500; 🖳) The stylish Sun N Sea has 10 rooms in a simple building right above the water. The views across the bay are superb. Furnishings are in easy-on-the-eye beiges, while the furniture is easy-on-the-backside rattan. The swanky downstairs rooms are much more expensive. A remnant of a door is displayed in the lobby – the former charismatic owner Muharam Perera (who has sadly since died) clung to it during the tsunami. There's also a decent restaurant.

Weliwatta Guesthouse (☎ 222 6642; weliwatta@ hotmail.com; r incl breakfast Rs 2500) This century-old buttercup-yellow villa has a couple of spacious and tidy rooms with hot-water bathrooms. You'll love relaxing in the luxuriant garden in a comfy chair with a cold drink and good book to hand. There's also a reasonable restaurant.

Nooit Gedacht (☎ 222 3449; www.sriayurveda .com; Galle-Matara Rd; r with/without air-con Rs 3000/2500; 🖳 🖳 🖳) A wonderful sense of blissful calm befalls anyone lucky enough to cross the threshold into this atmospheric 1735 Dutch colonial mansion. Today it's slightly tumbledown but perfectly enchanting and its large and clean rooms, with hot water and pint-sized living rooms, are just the ticket for those who crave Galle's colonial hotel experience but couldn't match the hefty price tags. There's a well-regarded Ayurvedic treatment centre.

Banana Garden (☎ 438 1089; r with/without air-con Rs 4000/2500; 🖳) If you're tall then it won't have taken you long to realise that Sri Lankan beds aren't built with you in mind. But good news! The Banana Garden loves tall people! As well as overstretched beds, most of the rooms have sumptuous views, and out front you'll find an equally tasty patch of sand that's perfect for catching the sunset.

Pipels House (☎ 222 6702; www.pipels.com; r Rs 3500, apt Rs 9000) This new place has vanilla-coloured white rooms with flashy photos on the walls and modern metal furnishings. The rooms all share a pretty mosaic-patterned bathroom, while the apartment has its own kitchenette, bathroom and living room. Whether you opt for a room or go the whole hog on the apartment, the asking price is a bit steep.

Thaproban (☎ 223 4588; www.thambapannileisure .com; r incl breakfast from US$45; 🖳 🖳) A perfect example of the current fashion for Asian minimalism, this is a great-value and very stylish place to stay that offers a five-star experience for a midrange price tag. Built largely of natural materials it's full of wood, with walls of either open stone or painted in shades of mango, and twinkling fountains. Some rooms have good sea views and there's a small spa. The restaurant is highly recommended.

our pick Dream House (☎ 438 1541; dreamhouse@ libero.it; s/d incl breakfast US$33/50) Set well back from the hustle of the beach, this is Unawatuna at its most chic. An exquisite Italian-owned house with four intimate and impeccable rooms that have been restored and decorated in a Rome-meets-the-tropics fusion. There's nothing overstated or brash about this place – it's just pure and simple class. There's also a stellar restaurant (opposite).

Villa Hotel (☎ 224 7253; www.villa-unawatuna.com; s/d incl breakfast US$45/50; ❄ 🖥) A lovely waterfront hotel built in a traditional but very tall style. The twirling wooden window slats have an Arabic feel and the interior of the rooms are attired in Indian art and ancient furnishings, while the bathroom is utterly modern. The highlight is the garden full of ornate 1920s English garden furniture.

Secret Garden (☎ 224 1857; www.secretgardenunawatuna.com; cottages from US$47, r from US$60) Creak open the door and, like the name suggests, step into a hidden botanical wonderland full of crazy tropical flowers and mischievous monkeys. This beautifully renovated 140-year-old house has a range of rooms that are colour coordinated with the flowers outside. If the beautiful rooms are a bit pricey, try one of the simple but good-value cottages outside. Various yoga and Ayurvedic courses are on offer.

Eating & Drinking

Almost all places to stay provide meals or have restaurants. The best way to choose from the many places on the beach may be to simply stroll around and see what looks good. Most places are good for a drink – see which ones are in favour when you're there. Just don't expect much past midnight. The places listed here offer something a bit different or have a little more character than the rest.

Roti Shop (rotti Rs 120-200) Dozens of sweet and savoury *rottis* rammed full of cheeses, fruits and more make for a quick and easy lunch.

Jayasingha Tea Room (meals Rs 150; ⊙ noon-3pm) Remind yourself of what Sri Lanka is supposed to taste like with one of the superb rice and curries up for grabs at the back of this grocery shop. Locals can't get enough of the food here, but foreign tourists are as rare as a mild chilli.

One Love Restaurant (meals Rs 250-400) This small and friendly place literally hangs above the water and the creaky wooden floorboards further enhance the sensation of being on a boat sailing across the seven seas. It's unusual in that its good range of curries allows you to eat like a local (a rarity in Unawatuna). Pumpkin curry is the house special.

King Fisher's Restaurant (meals Rs 300-400) If beach erosion hasn't swept it away by the time you read this (more likely than it sounds), then this tasty Thai restaurant will be a treat. The kitchen is housed inside an old shipping crate, but you eat on a wooden platform floating above the waves.

Sunil Garden (☎ 0777 472441; meals Rs 300-600) Sunil, the owner, sets a festive mood while cooking up seafood, pasta and more. On many nights he leads live music. This is *the* place for a beer, but if that's too racy for you, there is now a straight-out-of-the-city coffee and smoothie bar.

our pick Shekira Restaurant (meals Rs 300-600) With boats bobbing like ducks on the water just a few metres away, this romantic wooden fishermen's shack, with just a couple of candle-lit tables, is perfect for a cold sunset beer and an ultra-cheap fried fish dinner washed down with the owner's friendly banter.

Hot Rock (☎ 224 2685; meals Rs 350-450) A classic beachside seafood restaurant with delightful owners and such vivid colours, it looks like a Joseph and his amazing technicolour dream cafe.

Jinas Vegetarian and Vegan Restaurant (meals from Rs 500) This enjoyable garden restaurant offers a wide array of European vegetarian dishes, including vegie burgers, lasagne and the not very vegie-sounding peacock pie.

our pick Dream House (☎ 438 1541; mains Rs 500-600) Eat alfresco while being serenaded by classical music at this authentic and truly memorable Italian restaurant. Unusually for an Italian restaurant in Asia, the chef is actually of true-blue Latin stock, which ensures the tomatoes have been placed in just the right spot and the perfect amount of fresh basil has been added. Anywhere else in Unawatuna positively fades in comparison to here, but what's most surprising is the price – it's an undisputed bargain.

Getting There & Away

Coming by bus from Galle (Rs 14, 10 minutes) you can get off at the small road that leads into town, or get off at the next stop, where the ocean meets the main road, and walk in along the beach. A three-wheeler to or from Galle costs between Rs 300 and 400.

UNAWATUNA TO KOGGALA
☎ 091

Beyond Unawatuna the road runs close to the coast through Dalawella, Koggala and on to Ahangama and beyond. With numerous beautiful stretches of virtually deserted beaches and many picturesque coves, this is a perfect place to stick a pin in the map and find an empty stretch of fantastic sand to suit.

THE SOUTH

Along this part of the coast you will see stilt fishermen perching precariously like stalks above the waves at high tide. Each fisherman has a pole firmly embedded in the sea bottom, close to the shore, from which they perch on their poles and cast their lines. Stilt positions are passed down from father to son and are highly coveted.

Sights & Activities

Koggala Lake, next to the road, is alive with birdlife and dotted with islands, one of which features a Buddhist temple that attracts many visitors on *poya* (full moon) days and another that contains an interesting cinnamon plantain. Guided two-hour boat rides (Rs 3000; up to five people) are possible on the lake. To find the boatmen, look for the signs reading 'Bird Island' between Koggala and Ahangama.

There are several spice gardens around the lake, **Lagoon Herbal Garden** (☎ 077 201 8892; www .lagoonherbalgarden.com; ❤ 7am-7pm) is a good one to visit and will provide you with the chance to buy all manner of home remedies and to see how many of the plants are grown. It also offers cheap boat trips on the lagoon (Rs 1500).

Near the 113km marker, west of Koggala, is the **Martin Wickramasinghe Folk Art Museum** (admission Rs 200; ❤ 9am-5pm), which is set back from the road. It includes the house where this respected Sinhalese author was born. The exhibits are interesting and well displayed, with information in English and Sinhala. Among them is a good section on dance (including costumes and instruments), puppets, *kolam* (masked dance-drama) masks (including one of a very sunburnt British officer), kitchen utensils and carriages. The bookshop sells the author's works, many of which deal with local culture.

Just east of Koggala the **Kataluwa Purwarama temple** feels like the temple time forgot. Dating from the 13th century, it has some recently restored murals. A friendly monk will open the building and explain the murals. Some of the Jataka tales (stories from the Buddha's lives) painted here are 200 years old. The turn-off to the temple is at Kataluwa – you'll see the signs on the inland side of the road. Continue a couple of kilometres inland and ask for directions.

AHANGAMA & MIDIGAMA
☎ 091

The Ahangama and Midigama area are home to the most consistent, and possibly the best, surf in Sri Lanka. It's a very low-key area with

plenty of cheap, surfer-friendly accommodation and a scattering of pretty beaches (though the road often runs very close to the shore). The first spot is the consistent beach break at Kabalana Beach, which normally has something to ride even when it's tiny elsewhere. In Midigama itself, a spice pot–sized village built beside a curve of sand, there are a couple of reef breaks. Lazy Left is the aptly named wave that bends around the rocks and into the sandy bay – it's perfect for that first reef experience. A few hundred metres further down is Ram's Right, a hollow, shallow and unpredictable beast. It's not suitable for beginners.

Note that the water covers lots of rocks, coral and other hazards. Also, besides a few guest houses offering battered boards for rent (Rs 600 to 11000 per day), there are no places selling surf gear or offering repairs – you'll have to go to Hikkaduwa. If you are looking for **surf lessons**, Yannick, a Frenchman who has done much to help rebuild Midigama after the tsunami, runs a surf school in conjunction with the Subodinee Guesthouse (opposite). They charge €25 for a one-day course. They also have the best, and most expensive, range of boards for hire.

Sleeping & Eating
AHANGAMA

Many surfers stay in Ahangama and ride the waves in Midigama. The following are listed in the order you pass them coming from Unawatuna. There are no stand-alone tourist restaurants, but all the accommodation serves food.

7th Sky Idyll Hotel (☎ 077 721 7667; r from Rs 1700) Vibrant blue- and yellow-coloured beachfront guest house with fruity and tasty rooms and friendly management. It's popular with surfers wanting to ride Kabalana Beach.

Ahangama Easy Beach (☎ 228 2028; www.easybeach .info; s/d from €24/26; ❷ ▣ ☎) A Norwegian-run place that's popular with the new wave of surfers – connected permanently to their laptops and mobile phones. Mickey Dora would turn in his grave! The rooms though are excellent and immaculately clean with nicely tiled bathrooms and four-poster beds fit for a prince and princess. There are also air-con cabanas.

Villa Gaetano (☎ 228 3968; www.villagaetano.com; s/d incl half board Rs 2750/5500; ❷ ▣) Just after the 137km post, this place is right on the beach. The rooms are large and the four front rooms upstairs have balconies and great views. Some rooms have air-con and hot water. It's a bit overpriced.

RAMYADAVA GUNASEKARA – SURFING WITH RAM

Ramyadava (known to all and sundry as Ram) owns one of the long-standing surfer guest houses in Midigama.

'I think the first surfers arrived in Midigama in 1977. I was very young and had never seen surfers before. One day six Australian surfers arrived. I thought they were very strange and everyone in the village came down to watch them surf. My parents told me not to go near them because they were hippies and it might make problems if I touched them, because everyone thought that hippies were dirty! These surfers were the first foreigners to stay in Midigama, but after they left it was several years before more came.

Today people in the village know the surfers don't have germs and most people like them because they spend money here. They buy fruit from people, use the three-wheelers, eat at people's restaurants and so on. After the tsunami many of the surfers staying here gave money as well as books and clothing for the children. Some of them stayed on to help clean up and rebuild. Yannick, a French surfer, has done a lot for the village. He started a charity and obtained new boats for the fishermen and household utensils for everyone. But just after the tsunami a surfer was caught stealing people's stuff from the rubble. When he was caught he was beaten up by the other surfers and sent away. Before he did that I thought all foreigners were good people.'

Kabalana Beach Hotel (☎ 228 3294; www.kabalana .com; s/d from US$40/60; ❄ 🖳 🖳) At their best, the rooms here seem born of a local mother and a colonial father and include latticework window frames, four-poster beds and antique Indian furniture. However, despite no price difference, room quality varies a lot, and if you get a dud one, you'll feel cheated. There's a small pool and a painfully slow and bland restaurant.

MIDIGAMA

There are a couple of cheap guest houses at the prime surfing break (at the 139km marker), but not much else.

Subodinee Guesthouse (☎ 228 3383; r from Rs 650) Long ago when the first surfers showed up in Midigama, Jai and his wife Sumana had a small tea shop from which they served rice and curry to the strange newcomers. Today things have come a long way and they now have a huge range of rooms, which kick off as hot concrete cubes with shared bathrooms, and work their way up to impeccable individual bungalows (singles/doubles incl breakfast US$25/30) with hot water and all the trimmings. There's also a taxi service, surf school and board hire and, best of all, a highly recommended restaurant that with notice (an hour or two) can whip up a truly phenomenal rice and curry (Rs 350) – for our money it's one of the best on the island.

Rams Guesthouse (☎ 225 2639; r with/without bathroom Rs 500/400) The rooms at this eternally popular surfers hang-out are as basic as basic gets, but they are kept clean and have attached bathrooms. The upstairs rooms are slightly less dingy, though like all the rooms they suffer from road noise. Many surfers barely leave here for months on end, which gives it a friendly community vibe. The welcome is very warm and it's located right in front of what is probably the best wave on the island. See boxed text, above, for the owner's experiences with surfing.

Villa Samsara (☎ 225 1144; s/d incl half board €50/77) If you're a live-like-the-other-half surfer then the lovely Villa Samsara should float your board. Set in pleasant beachfront gardens, the four huge rooms recall by-gone days and are very well appointed. Ring in advance; it's not set up for casual visitors.

Getting There & Away

There are frequent buses along the southern coastal road connecting Ahangama and Midigama with other towns between Galle and Matara, and points beyond. The bus from Galle costs Rs 30 to Midigama. Many Colombo–Matara trains stop at Ahangama. Only a few local trains stop at Midigama.

WELIGAMA

☎ 041

Weligama (meaning 'Sandy Village'), about 30km east of Galle, is an interesting and lively blend of international beach resort and raucous Asian fishing town. You can spend a happy day wandering around, getting a feel for local life, dipping your toes in the ocean and marvelling at the denizens of the deep, who end their days being hacked up and sold from the roadside fish stalls.

THE SOUTH

Close to the shore – so close that you can walk out to it at low tide – is a tiny island known as Taprobane. It looks like an ideal artists or writers retreat, which indeed it once was: novelist Paul Bowles wrote *The Spider's House* here in the 1950s. Even better, the island was once owned by the French Count de Maunay-Talvande. If you really like it, why not stay here; though at over US$1000 a night, it's probably beyond the budget of many.

Sights & Activities

Scenic though the bay is, Weligama Beach is a bit shabby and not geared for sunbathers. It's primarily a fishing village, with **catamarans** lining the western end of the bay. You can organise a two-hour ride in one (about Rs 8000 per catamaran) through most of the guest houses. Though hardly the atypical tropical beach, Weligama is a very good place to learn to surf with soft, sandy beach waves that rarely exceed a metre. Both the Samaru Beach House (below) and the Weligama Bay View, next door, rent boards and provide lessons.

Snorkelling at Weligama is good, or you can scuba dive. **Bavarian Divers** (☎ 225 2708; www.cbg.de/bavarian-divers), close to the harbour at the western end of the beach, runs PADI courses (€295) as well as excursions such as wreck dives. It can also organise whale and dolphin diving and snorkelling trips.

Weligama is known for its **lacework**, and stalls are located on the main road along the coast.

Sleeping & Eating

Accommodation is spread out along the beach road, but compared with nearby Mirissa, most of it seems somewhat overpriced and poor value.

Dilkini Guesthouse (☎ 225 0281; r from Rs 650) On the edge of the village proper, this place has rooms that might be very ordinary, but there's a friendly welcome awaiting you and, in a town with unnaturally high room rates, these rock-bottom prices make this basic guest house the best value around. You wouldn't want to swim off the bit of beach it fronts.

Samaru Beach House (☎ 225 1417; samaru.beachhouse@tiscali.nl; 544 New Matara Rd; r from Rs 1300) Located at about the middle of the bay, this traveller-savvy eight-room place is right on the beach and has light and airy rooms that are sheltered from road noise. The better rooms have a veranda. Bikes and surfboards

may be rented and the owner can organise all manner of local tours and activities.

Barberyn Ayurveda Resort (☎ 225 2994; www.barberynresorts.com; s/d incl full board per week €560/770; 🍽 🖥 🏊) This fancy resort enclosed by forest, on the summit of a hill above the harbour, is Weligama's top offering. The rooms are elegant and pleasantly simple, and some have sea views. There is a minimum seven-night stay and the owners are only really interested in guests who also want to partake in their superb Ayurvedic facilities (€60 per person per day).

On the beachfront, close to the fish market, are a couple of happy little restaurants, including Ellen Food Café, with excellent fresh fish in exchange for some loose change.

Getting There & Away

There are frequent buses to Galle (Rs 31, one hour) and Matara (Rs 22, 30 minutes). Weligama is on the Colombo–Matara train line; destinations include Colombo (2nd/3rd class Rs 220/120, four hours), Galle (2nd/3rd class Rs 60/30, one hour) and Matara (2nd/3rd class Rs 30/15, 30 minutes).

MIRISSA
☎ 041

Crack open a coconut, slip into a hammock and rock gently in the breeze allowing the hours, days and even weeks to slip calmly by. Welcome to sleepy Mirissa, which is 4km southeast of Weligama, and a place so idyllic, only a fool would ever want to leave.

Mirissa is easily the least developed of the big south-coast beach resorts and is a good glimpse of what Unawatuna must have been like 15 years ago. For the moment most of the foreshore remains the domain of coconut trees and much of the tourist development remains hidden from view.

You'll need to go to Matara for most services, although there are internet and phone places, and small markets near the 149km marker.

Sights & Activities

Mirissa is designed for sitting and being, not for doing. Having said that, the water is deliciously clear and, around the reefs and rocks at either end, it's excellent for snorkelling. Surfers will find an inconsistent but fun right point at the western end of the bay. Many of the guest houses have snorkelling and surfing gear to rent.

If you do need to move, then there are some pleasant walks. One heads up a steep series of steps from the main road to the small **Kandavahari temple**, while the headland is a good spot to view Weligama Bay.

Sleeping & Eating

Meals are available at all of these places. Rooms only have cold water. Look for signs along the main road.

Katies Hideaway (☎ 077 747 2438; nalabank@yahoo .com; r Rs 500) Lovely Katies is hiding away down a dusty lane a couple of hundred metres back from the sea. It's a sunflower-yellow family home with two simple rooms with bathroom. If you choose to stay here, you'll very much be a part of the family.

our pick **Palm Villa** (☎ 225 0022; r Rs 600-1500) The French-speaking owner of this new guest house isn't an interior designer, but he probably should be. Each of the lovely rooms is uniquely decorated in a bright and modern fashion, and the bathrooms are a riot of mosaics. The more expensive rooms are set right on the beach and the garden is full of cock-a-doodling roosters and white bunny rabbits. Superb value.

our pick **Amarasinghe Guest House** (☎ 225 1204; r from Rs 700; 🖳) For those who want to be consumed by nature, this delightful place, adrift in a web of rural lanes five minutes back from the beach, is sublime. A range of agreeably ramshackle rooms (some with share bathrooms) and cottages lie scattered throughout gardens where the only disturbance will be the croaking of frogs and the chirping of birds. They grow all their own organically produced vegetables and spices, and the food receives rave reports.

Villa Seaview (☎ 578 4020; r from Rs 1000) Calling it a mere 'sea view' doesn't really do it justice. The views, over miles of forests, cliffs and idyllic beaches that barely see a footprint from day to day, are out of this world. And OK, the rooms are drab and basic, but that won't matter because you'll spend every waking second on your balcony relishing the 'Seaview'.

Dinus Resort (☎ 225 3616; www.srilankaholidays.blog spot.com; r Rs 1000-1500) One of the more salubrious beachside hang-outs, Dinus has large and cheap rooms with cool outdoor showers in one block and plusher rooms with bedspreads that are a coordinated flower, towel and bed sheet work of art. The restaurant is one of the tastier places to eat and it's right on the surf point. Boards, bikes and anything else you might require are available for hire.

Secret Ayurveda (☎ 077 329 4332; r Rs 1500) Secreted away at the end of a jungle lane, a few moments inland from the eastern end of the beach, is this family-run sanctuary of calm. The rooms are impressively clean and orderly, though the bathrooms are a little poky. As the name suggests, they also have a cheap but professional Ayurvedic centre, which has helped lower many a traveller's stress levels.

Getting There & Away

The bus fare from Weligama is Rs 9; a three-wheeler costs Rs 250. From Matara the bus fare is Rs 17. If you're heading to Colombo, it's better to catch a bus to Matara and change, as many buses will be full by the time they pass through Mirissa.

MATARA

☎ 041 / pop 76,254

Matara, 160km from Colombo, is a busy, sprawling commercial town that owes almost nothing to tourism. Ironically it's this very fact, and the opportunity it allows to see day-to-day Sri Lankan life unaffected by the hurly-burly of the nearby beach scenes, that make it worth visiting. The main attractions are its ramparts, a well-preserved Dutch fort and, most of all, its street life. If you really can't live without sand between your toes, then choose between people-watching and ice-cream munching on the main Matara Beach or snorkelling, surfing and lazing on the white sands of Polhena, 3km towards Colombo. Swimming in Nilwala Ganga (Nilwala River) is not recommended; crocodiles are active and hungry.

Orientation & Information

Matara is bisected by the Nilwala Ganga. Shops are located along Anagarika Dharmapala Mawatha, and Old Tangalla and New Tangalla Rds.

Cargills Food City (☎ 222 9815) Near Bandaranayaka Mawatha, this place has traveller supplies and a pharmacy.

Commercial Bank (Station Rd) Has an international ATM.

Crad Roks (171 Anagarika Dharmapala Mawatha; per hr Rs 50) Offers internet facilities, down a small side-lane off the main road.

Post office (New Tangalla Rd) Near the bus station.

Sampath Bank (Anagarika Dharmapala Mawatha) Has an international ATM.

Vijitha Yapa Bookshop (25A 1/1 Anagarika Dharmapala Mawatha) Good selection of novels, magazines, maps and guidebooks.

THE SOUTH

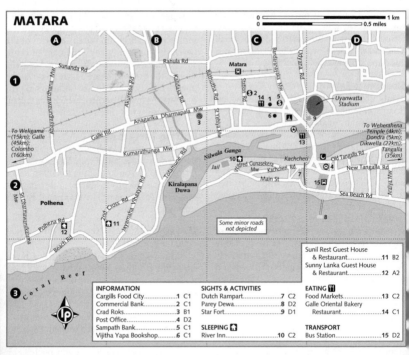

Sights

Seeing all Matara has to offer shouldn't take more than an hour or two. A pedestrian bridge near the bus station leads to a small island, **Parey Dewa** (Rock in Water), which is home to a tiny Buddhist temple with a very fancy modern bridge leading out to it. The beach on which it sits is a great place to go for an evening walk and have an ice cream with much of the rest of the town folk.

The smallish **Dutch rampart** occupies the promontory separating the Nilwala Ganga from the sea. Built in the 18th century to protect the VOC's kachcheri (administrative office), its structure is a little peculiar – it was originally meant to be a fort, but accountants, with their pesky cost-cutting exercises, dictated otherwise. Inside the rampart are quiet vestiges of old Matara. Wander the few streets and you'll see the odd colonial gem – though its real charm is that it is quieter than modern Matara.

The **Star Fort** (🕑 10am-5pm), about 350m from the main rampart gate, was built by the Dutch to compensate for deficiencies in the rampart. However, it's so small it could only have pro-

tected a handful of bureaucrats. The date of construction (1765) is embossed over the main gate, along with the VOC company insignia and the coat of arms of the governor of the day. Look for the two carved lions that guard the entrance gates. You can also spot the slots that once secured the drawbridge beams.

Sleeping

MATARA

Matara has several places to stay, but most are not very nice.

River Inn (☎ 222 2215; 96/1 Wilfred Gunasekera Mawatha; s/d from Rs 770/880) This tranquil family guest house has neat red-brick rooms and sparkling bathrooms. Some rooms have river views. It's next door to the town prison, which offers cheaper alternative accommodation.

POLHENA

Many travellers stay in Polhena, about 3km southwest of the centre. Most places serve meals and have cold water and fans. Note that the area is a warren of small tracks, so you may need to ask for directions. A three-wheeler from Matara costs Rs 250.

Sunny Lanka Guest House & Restaurant (☎ 222 3504; sunnyamare@yahoo.com; 93 Polhena Rd; r Rs 900) There's nothing special about this bog-standard guest house, but nothing to scream about either. It's certainly friendly.

Sunil Rest Guest House & Restaurant (☎ 222 1983; sunilrestpolhena@yahoo.com; 16/3A Second Cross Rd; s & d Rs 700-800; 🖵) An exceptionally friendly and helpful place, just back from the beach. The plain rooms are a real treat, and the food so good that even the French harp on about it! They can organise various excursions as well as diving trips. Note that they don't play the commission game, so many three-wheeler drivers will tell you it's closed down – it's not.

Eating

Just north of the bridge, on the main road, you'll see food markets and several fruit vendors with gorgeous displays of produce. Otherwise, dining choices are limited to some simple joints along the main road.

Galle Oriental Bakery Restaurant (41 Anagarika Dharmapala Mawatha; mains from Rs 80) The best central option is a classic old place with a wooden interior and display cases bulging with baked and savoury treats. The soups and curries are good.

Getting There & Away

BUS

The Matara bus station is a vast multilevel place. Look for tiny destination signs over the queuing pens. As Matara is a regional transport hub, services are frequent in all directions. Some of the major destinations:

Amapara Rs 270, eight hours
Colombo Regular/air-con Rs 159/300, four to five hours
Galle Rs 45, two hours
Ratnapura Rs 145, 4½ hours (morning only)
Tangalla Rs 96, 1½ to two hours

TRAIN

Matara's **train station** (☎ 222 2271) is the end of the coastal railway. Destinations include Galle (2nd/3rd class Rs 80/40, one to 1½ hours), Colombo (2nd/3rd class Rs 260/140, four hours), Vavuniya (for Anuradhapura; 2nd/3rd class Rs 520/280, 10 hours) and Kandy (2nd/3rd class Rs 410/225, seven hours).

MATARA TO TANGALLA

There are several other places of interest just off the road from Matara to Tangalla, including two superb examples of what one visitor labelled 'neo-Buddhist kitsch'.

Sights & Activities

WEHERAHENA TEMPLE

Just as you leave the outskirts of Matara, a turn inland will take you to this gaudy **temple** (admission by donation), where an artificial cave is decorated with about 200 comic book–like scenes from the Buddha's life. There's also a huge Buddha statue.

At the time of the late November or early December *poya*, a *perahera* (procession) of dancers and elephants is held at the temple to celebrate the anniversary of its founding.

DONDRA

About 5km southeast of Matara you come to the town of Dondra. Travel south from the main road for 1.2km and you'll reach the lighthouse at the southernmost point of Sri Lanka. There are good views from here, and there's a humdrum cafe nearby.

Buses from Matara will drop you in the centre of Dondra. From here you can three-wheel it or walk to the lighthouse.

WEWURUKANNALA VIHARA

If the Weherahena Temple is 'Marvel Comics meets Lord Buddha', then here it's Walt Disney who runs into him. At the town of Dikwella, 22km from Matara, a road turns inland towards Beliatta. About 1.5km along you come to a 50m-high seated Buddha figure – the largest in Sri Lanka.

The **temple** (admission Rs 100) is often thronging in worshippers. Before reaching the Buddha statue you must pass through a real hall of horrors full of life-sized models of demons and sinners. The punishments inflicted on these sinners include being dunked in boiling cauldrons, sawn in half and disembowelled. Finally there's the gigantic seated figure, which was constructed in the 1960s when kitsch was the name of the game.

Puja (literally 'respect'; offerings or prayers) is held every morning and evening.

You can reach the temple on any Matara–Tangalla bus that goes via Beliatta.

HO-O-MANIYA BLOWHOLE

About 6km northeast of Dikwella, near the 186km post, a road heads off for 1km to the (sometimes) spectacular Ho-o-maniya blowhole. During the southwest monsoon (June is the best time), high seas can force water 23m up through a natural chimney in

SEARCHING FOR MOBY DICK

In 2006 rumours started spreading through conservation circles of something big lurking in the waters off southern Sri Lanka. That thing was the blue whale, the biggest creature ever to inhabit planet Earth, and the word was that there was more than one of them. In fact, scientists have quickly come to the startling realisation that Sri Lanka may well be the best place in the world to see both this very rare gentle giant and its cousin the sperm whale. While whale-watching tours had long been popular off Trincomalee on the northeast coast, it was always understood that sightings were hit-and-miss up there. When experts realised that potentially large numbers of whales were migrating between the Bay of Bengal and the Arabian Sea, passing by the Sri Lankan coast very close to Dondra Head, they set out in search of them. They didn't have to look for long. Within 15 minutes of standing on Dondra Head and scanning the water with binoculars, they'd sighted the first blue whale. When they headed out to sea the sightings became even more spectacular, with up to five blue whales being seen within 8 sq km and an almost equally impressive tally of sperm whales, as well as numerous dolphins.

In the two years since then the first tentative whale-watching trips have been launched to great success, with whales being spotted almost every time. A number of operators have sprung up in all the south-coast beach resorts, but with the whole concept of whale watching being so new to this part of Sri Lanka and nobody completely sure how the whales will react to boatloads of gawping tourists, it pays to go with someone who really knows what they're doing. **Jetwing Eco Holidays** (☎ 011-238 1201; www.jetwingeco.com; 46/26 Navam Mawatha, Colombo) and **Sue Evans** (☎ 077 359 7731) don't just organise superb trips, but they were both in the team that first broke the news about the whales and have done the most to study and launch conservation efforts.

the rocks and then up to 18m in the air. At other times the blowhole is disappointing. There's an admission fee (Rs 50) and lots of people after your money.

Sleeping & Eating

This little-known stretch of coast features some gob-smackingly perfect beaches but much of the accommodation is very much top-end. Look for signs and watch the kilometre markers as you go; the following places are listed in the order you will reach them when travelling towards Tangalla.

Surya Garden (☎ 0777 147818; www.srilanka-vacanze .com; s/d incl breakfast Rs 3850/4400) Sri Lankan charm meats Italian flair at this personable little place, set 100m back from an idyllic beach. The three cabanas here could be described as imaginative and oh-so-very-chic mud huts. Don't worry though, there's nothing primitive about a stay here because the rooms are beautifully kitted out and feature amazing outdoor bathrooms. Not surprisingly, the menu features a lot of very tasty pastas. The turn-off is at the 189km marker.

Claughton Villa (☎ 011-250 9134; www.srilankayellow pages.com/claughton; d incl full board US$160; ❄ ☐ ☎) This beautiful colonial villa, with stunning views, sits on a knoll surrounded by rambling gardens that lead down to a heavenly pool

and a beach that's even better. The rooms go for the white and minimal look but it works well and there are big baths in each room. You can rent out the entire property. The turn-off is 500m east of the 184km marker.

Amanwella (☎ 047-224 1333; www.amanresorts .com; ste from US$829; ❄ ☐ ☎) Easily the most luxurious resort in Sri Lanka, as well as the most expensive. Each of the 30 suites has its own private plunge pool and is comfortable to such an extent that you may need to be prised out on check-out day. The modern design is dramatic; the open-air bathrooms are all natural stone. All of the units have ocean views, and some are right on the beach. Service is superb, and the food and beverages are as you'd expect. The resort entrance is near the 193km marker.

TANGALLA
☎ 047

Quickly, look up at the rain beating against the window and feel the chill in your bones. Now, close your eyes and dream of somewhere else. What do you see? Is it a gently bending beach of coconut-coloured sand washed by lazy azure waters? If it is, then what you're dreaming about has a name. It's called Tangalla and it's the perfect medicine for the wintertime blues.

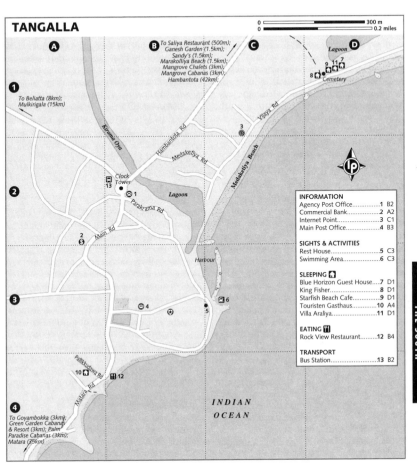

TANGALLA

To Saliya Restaurant (500m);
Ganesh Garden (1.5km);
Sandy's (1.5km);
Marakolliya Beach (1.5km);
Mangrove Chalets (3km);
Mangrove Cabanas (3km);
Hambantota (42km);

To Beliatta (8km);
Mulkirigala (15km)

Kirama Oya

Hambantota Rd

Medaketiya Rd

Vijaya Rd

Lagoon

Cemetery

Clock
Tower

Parakrama Rd

Lagoon

Medaketiya Beach

Main Rd

Harbour

Pallikkuduwa Rd

Matara Rd

To Goyambokka (3km);
Green Garden Cabanas
& Resort (3km); Palm
Paradise Cabanas (3km);
Matara (35km)

INDIAN
OCEAN

INFORMATION	
Agency Post Office............1	B2
Commercial Bank............2	A2
Internet Point............3	C1
Main Post Office............4	B3

SIGHTS & ACTIVITIES	
Rest House............5	C3
Swimming Area............6	C3

SLEEPING	
Blue Horizon Guest House....7	D1
King Fisher............8	D1
Starfish Beach Cafe............9	D1
Touristen Gasthaus............10	A4
Villa Araliya............11	D1

EATING	
Rock View Restaurant............12	B4

TRANSPORT	
Bus Station............13	B2

Information

The main post office is west of the Rest House and there is an agency post office opposite the main bus station. **Commercial Bank** (Main Rd) has an international ATM. For internet try **Internet Point** (Vijaya Rd, Medaketiya Beach; Rs 50 per hr; ☼ 8am-8pm).

Sights & Activities

There are some reminders of the colonial era on the knoll just south of the centre. The shady **Rest House** was once home to the Dutch administrators. It's one of the oldest rest houses in the country, and was originally built (as a plate on the front steps indicates) in 1774. As you round the head, note the many large boats now permanently stranded high

above the surf – this will give an idea of how far inland the tsunami came here.

Many locals swim off the cove by the harbour, but there are much nicer places to take to the sea. There are numerous lovely beaches in the area, with the pick being either the little coves around **Goyambokka** or **Marakolliya Beach**, a magnificently uncluttered string of sand without a footprint on it (though note that currents can be treacherous here and swimming isn't always safe).

A little further east of Marakolliya Beach is the equally blissful Rekawa Beach where, from April to September, green, hawksbill and occasionally even leatherback **turtles** struggle ashore at night to lay their eggs. A three-wheeler from Tangalla costs around

Rs 1000 and locals charge an 'entrance fee' of Rs 600 (refunded if you don't see any turtles). It's best to arrive well after dark and to be prepared for a long wait – bring a torch, but remember that the turtles are easily disturbed by artificial lighting, and don't use camera flashes. Once the eggs have been laid, the villagers gather up the eggs and remove them to a safer place, releasing the young back into the wild when they hatch two months later. The entrance fee goes towards the **Turtle Conservation Project** (www.tcpsrilanka.org).

Sleeping

There are several areas in and around Tangalla in which to stay.

GOYAMBOKKA

About 3km back towards Matara on the main road you'll come to a signposted turn-off at Goyambokka and a road lined with several guest houses. This is a quiet leafy area with a couple of sublime little coves that are generally almost deserted. Any bus travelling between Matara and Tangalla will drop you off at the turn-off. A three-wheeler from Tangalla bus station costs Rs 180.

Green Garden Cabanas & Resort (☎ 077 624 7628; s & d Rs 2000-3000) Set back from the beach, this guest house has well-kept cabanas with wooden floors and tidy bathrooms. There's also a more expensive stone cottage (additional Rs 500) that would seem more at home in a snowy mountain valley.

Palm Paradise Cabanas (☎ 224 0338; www.palm paradisecabanas.net; s/d incl half board €37.50/50; 💻) Set on a stunning sandy cove, the wooden cabanas are hidden behind a veil of trees and feel like something out of *Little Red Riding Hood*. The cabanas are ageing a bit, but being tucked up in your wooden hut listening to the waves is undeniably romantic. There is an in-house masseur.

TANGALLA

The following options are above the beach, just south of the centre.

Touristen Gasthaus (☎ 224 0370; sevenvilla@live .com; 19 Pallikkudawa Rd; r Rs 1500; 🐾) Slick and clean tiled rooms with air-con and hot water – a rare treat indeed in this price range. The owner is a calm and friendly man, and the only drawback we can come up with is that it's on the wrong side of the road from the sea.

MEDAKETIYA BEACH

This is the most popular area with budget travellers and a host of cheap and cheerful hotels and restaurants have sprung up to cater for them. Disappointingly the long sandy beach here, which extends eastward away from the town, can be quite dirty – as can the water.

King Fisher (☎ 224 2472; r from Rs 700) It might be a little too pretty in pink for our liking, but we can forgive this lapse in taste because the rooms are well-looked after and have big twin beds pushed together in a passionate embrace and encircled by a mosquito net. The price is hard to beat and the restaurant gets solid reviews.

Blue Horizon Guest House (☎ 224 0771; s/d incl breakfast from Rs 1000/1250; 💻) Rooms at this mustard-yellow multistorey joint might be small but they've got loads of love packed into them. Every inch is crammed full of chairs, pictures, tables and decorations – oh and even a bed. The owner is backpacker savvy and the attached restaurant is good.

Starfish Beach Cafe (☎ 060 248 5357; starfish tangalle@gmail.com; s/d from Rs 1000/1250) Run by a bunch of energetic young guys, this is a good option, with large and airy rooms that are as neat as a pin. The bathrooms have a deep-blue nautical look. The only downside is that the staff are a bit too keen to get you into the hotel, but those who take the lure will be rewarded.

Villa Araliya (☎ 224 2163; r Rs 1500) Wallowing at the back of the luxuriant gardens are two bungalows crammed with old-fashioned furniture, including lovely carved wardrobes. Those who aren't fans of large and inquisitive dogs may want to look elsewhere.

MARAKOLLIYA BEACH

Virtually a continuation of Medaketiya Beach, but much further out of town, the beach here is utterly breathtaking. Unfurling along the coast is a seemingly endless tract of soft sand backed by palms, tropical flowers and mangrove lagoons. At night, turtles lumber ashore to lay eggs; by day, a lucky tourist scours the sands for seashells.

Ganesh Garden (☎ 224 2529; www.ganeshgarden.com; tw Rs 1500) One of the first places to re-open after the tsunami and a magnet to budget-hungry travellers ever since. The simple rooms, which are arranged in two-storey blocks, are so clean that you won't want to put your backpack down for fear of dirtying the floor. The restaurant is something of a shrine to Bob Marley and the beach is just a stoned step away.

Sandy's (☎ 077 622 5009; d Rs 1500) Just two lurid orange rooms can be found at this friendly guest house with funky decorations, a few elephants (really!) and beds that extend out of the walls. The prices are very flexible.

our pick **Mangrove Cabanas** (☎ 077 790 6018; www.beachcabana.lk; cabana d €18) Sat slap-bang on a breathtaking stretch of near deserted beach, this superb place has several rustic but chic cabanas hidden under the trees. Inside the cabanas it's all light and joy, and with virtually everything made of twisted driftwood there's no such thing as a boring straight line. The attached bathrooms are spirited away below ground level and have showers big enough to hold a party in. The restaurant produces fresh food that is as stunning as the accommodation. One US dollar per guest goes towards local conservation efforts, which has led to the planting of several hundred trees and mangroves.

our pick **Mangrove Chalets** (☎ 077 790 6018; www .beachcabana.lk; d €28) If your idea of paradise is sitting on a deckchair on a scruffy beach, then you're going to hate this place – the big-sister establishment of Mangrove Cabanas. If, however, your idea of paradise involves drifting over a lagoon on a rope-pulled raft and arriving among a gentle riot of swinging palm trees on a sublime beach (with a natural pool perfect for kids) to find a couple of Mediterranean styled and highly romantic cottages in which nothing at all will disturb your silence and privacy, then this, almost perfect place, is for you.

Eating

Just about all guest houses serve food.

Rock View Restaurant (Matara Rd; meals Rs 200) This simple little wooden shack catches the breeze as well as the stunning sunsets from its cliff-top perch. Meals are as simple and delightful as the setting.

Saliya Restaurant (☎ 224 2726; Hambantota Rd; meals Rs 200-300; ☺ 7am-10.30pm) Sitting on wobbly stilts a short way east of the town centre, this eccentric wooden shack, stuffed full of old clocks and radios, has great seafood as well as rice and curry.

Of the hotel restaurants, the best are at the **Mangrove Cabanas** (☎ 077 790 6018; mains Rs 300-600).

Getting There & Away

Tangalla is serviced by bus. Following are some of the major destinations:

Colombo Regular/air-con Rs 195/300, six hours
Galle Rs 79, two hours
Hambantota Rs 49, one hour
Matara Rs 47, 1½ to two hours
Tissamaharama Rs 74, three hours

MULKIRIGALA

Dangling off a rocky crag, 16km northwest of Tangalla, and squirreled away among a green forest of coconut trees are the peaceful rock temples of **Mulkirigala** (admission Rs 100; ☺ 6am-6pm). Clamber in a sweat up the hundreds of steps and you'll find a series of cleft-like caves sheltering a number of large reclining Buddha statues, together with other, smaller, sitting and standing figures. Vying with these for your attention are some fantastical wall paintings depicting sinners pleasuring themselves with forbidden fruit on Earth and then paying for it with an afterlife of eternal torture – apparently it was worth it! Further on up, and perched on top of the rock, is a small dagoba with fine views over the surrounding country. There is a Buddhist school for young monks nearby.

Pali manuscripts found in the monastic library by a British official in 1826 were used for the first translation of the Mahavamsa (Great Chronicle), which unlocked Sri Lanka's early history for Europeans.

Mulkirigala can be reached by bus from Tangalla via either Beliatta or Wiraketiya (depending on the departures, it might be quicker to go via Wiraketiya than to wait for the Beliatta bus). A three-wheeler from Tangalla costs about Rs 1000 for a return trip.

HAMBANTOTA

☎ 047 / pop 11,134

Hambantota is a dusty little workaday fishing town, which offers few reasons to stop. Though having said that its utter dearth of tourists and immensely friendly population make it a good place to get an idea of what coastal Sri Lanka was like before the tourists. At least that's the case for the moment, but huge changes are currently afoot and in a few years' time Hambantota will be a very different place indeed. A massive new port and docks area are under construction just to the west of town and these will make Hambantota, one of the most important trade centres in the country. In addition to this an airport is also springing up with the purpose of both serving the port and allowing easy tourist access to the incredible beaches that litter this part of the country. Oh yes, the times are-a-changing for this particular backwater.

The **Hatton National Bank** (47 Wilmot St), about 200m up from the clock tower, has an international ATM. **Cargills Food City** (☎ 222 2267; Main Rd) has the usual travellers' supplies and a pharmacy.

Hambantota has a few touts angling to take travellers to Bundala or Yala National Parks. Ignore them as this is best arranged with your guest house in Tissamaharama.

Hambantota Rest House (☎ /fax 222 0299; r with/without air-con Rs 3600/2500; ﷯), nicely situated on the promontory overlooking the town and beach, is about 300m south of the bus station. The rooms in the historic wing are slightly palatial, definitely musty and certainly the pick of the bunch. The restaurant is the best eating choice locally.

A kilometre east of town on a pristine patch of beach, **Peacock Beach Hotel** (☎ 222 0377; info@ peacockbeachonline.com; s/d/tr US$63/66/73; ﷯ ﷯) isn't quite as impressive as its pompous and showy namesake. In fact, with its preference for drab browns and beiges, it's more akin to a peahen; but it is comfortable and the service is good.

The bus station is by the fish market in the town centre. Destinations include Tangalla (Rs 49, one hour) and Tissamaharama (Rs 35, one hour).

BUNDALA NATIONAL PARK

Much less visited than nearby Yala National Park (p150), **Bundala National Park** (adult/child US$10/5, plus per vehicle Rs 250, service charge per group US$8, plus VAT 12%) is a fantastic maze of waterways, lagoons and dunes that glitter like gold in the dying evening sun. This wonderland provides a home to thousands of colourful birds ranging from diminutive little bee-eaters to grotesque open-billed stalks. It is a wetland sanctuary of such importance that it has been recognised under the Ramsar Convention on Wetlands. It shelters some 150 species of birds within its 62-sq-km area, with many journeying from Siberia and the Rann of Kutch in India to winter here, arriving between August and April. It's also a winter home to the greater flamingo, and up to 2000 have been recorded here at one time. If you're a birder, you'll want to devote a lot of time to this park.

If you're a glamour puss after elephants, leopards and all the other big mammals, then you will be pleased to hear that Bundala National Park also has a small but very visible population of elephants (between 25 and 60 depending on the season), as well as civets, giant squirrels and lots of crocodiles. Between October and January, four of Sri Lanka's five species of marine turtles (olive ridley, green, leatherback and loggerhead) lay their eggs on the coast.

Bundala stretches nearly 20km along a coastal strip between Kirinda and Hambantota. Access (and jeep hire) is easiest from Tissamaharama and Kirinda, and jeep hire rates are the same as for Yala (for more on this see opposite). Unlike Yala, Bundala is open year-round, so allowing wildlife junkies to get a wet season fix. There's an excellent new visitors centre at the main gate.

TISSAMAHARAMA
☎ 047

In Tissamaharama (usually shortened to a less tongue-tying Tissa), eyes are automatically drawn upwards and outwards. Upwards to the tip of its huge, snowy-white dagoba and outwards, beyond the town's confines, to a wilderness crawling with creatures large and small. It's this wilderness that is most people's reason for visiting Tissa, and the town makes an ideal base for the nearby Yala and Bundala National Parks.

Orientation

If you're coming via Hambantota or Wellawaya, you'll pass the village of Deberawewa (look for the clock tower) about 2km before Tissa. Ignore the 'Tissamaharama' signs here and the accommodation touts who board buses and advise travellers to get off because 'this is Tissa'. Most places to stay are closer to the real Tissa, so go there.

Information

Nearly all the facilities are on Main Rd, where you'll find an agency post office. There's not much in the way of shopping, but there are some useful services. **Hatton National Bank** (Main Rd), **Commercial Bank** (Main Rd) and **Peoples Bank** (Main Rd) have international ATMs. Internet connections are slow, but **Sakura Communication** (☎ 223 9083; Main Rd; Rs 50 per hr; ☉ 7.30am-10pm) is a friendly place with internet access and phone calls.

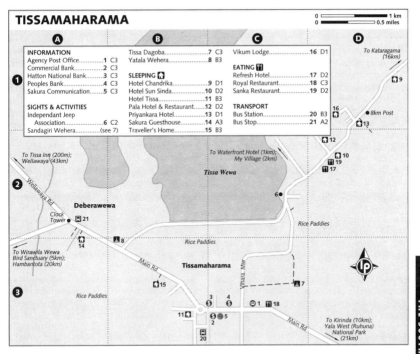

TISSAMAHARAMA

INFORMATION		
Agency Post Office............**1** C3		
Commercial Bank.............**2** C3		
Hatton National Bank........**3** C3		
Peoples Bank....................**4** C3		
Sakura Communication......**5** C3		
SIGHTS & ACTIVITIES		
Independant Jeep		
Association....................**6** C2		
Sandagiri Wehera............(see 7)		

Tissa Dagoba........................**7** C3		
Yatala Wehera......................**8** B3		
SLEEPING		
Hotel Chandrika.................**9** D1		
Hotel Sun Sinda................**10** D2		
Hotel Tissa.........................**11** B3		
Pala Hotel & Restaurant......**12** D2		
Priyankara Hotel................**13** D1		
Sakura Guesthouse.............**14** A3		
Traveller's Home................**15** B3		

Vikum Lodge.....................**16** D1		
EATING		
Refresh Hotel.....................**17** D2		
Royal Restaurant................**18** C3		
Sanka Restaurant...............**19** D2		
TRANSPORT		
Bus Station........................**20** B3		
Bus Stop............................**21** A2		

Map labels: To Kataragama (16km); To Tissa Inn (200m); Wellawaya (43km); Wellawaya Rd; Deberawewa; Clock Tower; To Wirawila Wewa Bird Sanctuary (5km); Hambantota (20km); Main Rd; Tissamaharama; Rice Paddies; Tissa Wewa; To Waterfront Hotel (1km); My Village (2km); 8km Post; Vihara Mw; To Kirinda (10km); Yala West (Ruhuna) National Park (21km)

THE SOUTH

Sights

The centrepiece of the town and its surrounds is the lovely **Tissa Wewa** (Tissa Tank), a huge man-made lake about 1.5km from the town centre. In the evening check out the huge flocks of egrets that descend onto the trees around the lake to roost. Pleasant boat trips are possible around the lake (Rs 500 per boat, per hour) from the Independent Jeep Association car park. Fight tooth and nail for a deal.

The large white restored **dagoba** between Tissa town centre and the *wewa* is believed to have been built by Kavantissa, a king of the kingdom of Ruhunu, which centred on Tissamaharama. The dagoba has a circumference of 165m and stands 55.8m high. It is thought to have held a sacred tooth relic and forehead bone relic. It's attractively lit up at night.

Next to the dagoba is a **statue** of Queen Viharamahadevi. According to legend, Viharamahadevi was sent to sea by her father, King Devanampiya Tissa, as penance after he killed a monk. Unharmed, the daughter landed at Kirinda, about 10km south of Tissa, and subsequently married Kavantissa. Their son, Dutugemunu, was the Sinhalese hero who liberated Anuradhapura from Indian invaders in the 2nd century BC.

Next to the Tissa–Deberawewa road is **Yatala Wehera**, built 2300 years ago by King Mahanaaga in thanks both for the birth of his son, Yatala Tissa, and for his safe escape from an assassination attempt in Anuradhapura. There's a small **museum** (admission free) next to the dagoba; its hours vary. The museum contains an extraordinary range of treasures dug up from around the dagoba, including an ornate, ancient bidet, which – as well as an elaborate filtration system that prevented any water pollution – had murals of ugly faces carved into it in order to stop the user thinking about sex!

Tours

Tissa is easily the easiest place from which to arrange tours of Yala National Park. The easiest thing to do is to arrange a safari through your accommodation, as this gives you a bit more certainty that the guide will do a good job. Alternatively, you can go to the gathering of safari touts in the Independent Jeep

Association car park on the edge of Tissa Wewa, but this can be a bit of a carnival-like experience. Despite the initial hassles, many of the guys who gather here are actually very knowledgeable about wildlife and genuinely concerned about making sure you have a good safari.

Most safari touts open negotiations at Rs 4500 per jeep for a half-day safari for up to four people (not including the raft of park fees), but they quickly drop to Rs 4000. This will get you the services of a guide, who should also double as a driver. There's no need to hire both a guide and a driver, as you'll need to hire an animal tracker once in Yala anyway. Check out the 4WD before you book a safari; obviously avoid rust buckets, but also look for some of the newer and grander models, which feature elevated, open seats that help with spotting animals. Good drivers provide binoculars.

Expect to leave your hotel about 5.30am so as to catch the animals at dawn and return around 10am. It's also possible to arrange dusk safaris and overnight trips on to the animal-filled lands surrounding the park.

Sleeping

The cheaper places to stay are in the town centre, but as there's no particular reason to be near the centre, and if you can afford them, you might want to consider one of the mid-range hotels around Tissa Wewa. Just about every place has a restaurant.

TOWN CENTRE

Traveller's Home (☎ 223 7958; travellershome@ sltnet.lk; tw with/without air-con Rs 1800/800; ✖ ☐) Surrounded by rice paddies, this traveller-aware guest house is just off Main Rd, about halfway between Tissa and Deberawewa. It's friendly, neat and good value. The seven varying rooms have features ranging from shared bathroom to posh air-conditioning. There are free bicycles for guests, and a safari display.

Hotel Tissa (☎ 223 7104; Main Rd; s with/without air-con Rs 1625/1125, d Rs 1875/1250) Taking a room in this freshly painted and appealing town house will allow you to become fully immersed in Sri Lankan family life, thanks to being virtually adopted by the family who run it. The simple rooms provide all that is needed in a room, and character is provided through the ample use of brass decorations.

TISSA WEWA

Most of Tissa's accommodation is near the Tissa Wewa, about 1.5km from the centre of Tissa. It's easy enough to get into town by bus (Rs 12) or by three-wheeler (Rs 90) from this area.

Pala Hotel & Restaurant (☎ 223 7648; Kataragama Rd; s/d Rs 1200/1500) Tightly tucked up a side street and squirreled away under some shady trees, this is a pleasant cheapie with several simple but perfectly polished, large rooms all with attached bathrooms, and paintings brightening up the walls. Air-con is an additional Rs 500.

our pick Vikum Lodge (☎ 223 7585; Kataragama Rd; tw with/without air-con Rs 1800/1200; ✖) Hidden down a squelchy and muddy side street in a blissfully peaceful location is this flowery gem of a guest house. The rooms, which are lovingly cared for and come with attached bathrooms, are only half the story. It's the luxuriant, botanical bonanza that surrounds them and the lovely family who own it that are the real stars of the show. The lodge has a small restaurant with Chinese and Sri Lankan dishes (Rs 200 to 300), but hurry if you want to be a part of this place, because it's up for sale (Rs 15 million and a slice of paradise is yours) and it might be very different in the future.

My Village (☎ 077 350 0090; myvillagesafari@yahoo .co.uk; Court Rd, Punchiakurugoda; s/d/tr US$20/30/35; ✖ ☐) Arriving at this lovely little guest house, hidden away behind unassuming plain walls, you won't be surprised to learn that this is the dream creation of a local designer. There are only three rooms, all of which are slightly different. Two have curly and bendy walls full of glass, and another, the honeymoon room, has suitably passionate red walls, passionate stag antlers on the wall and slightly less passionate twin beds! There is a stylish open-plan cafe and communal area where the free breakfast is served. Guests can use bicycles for free. A three-wheeler from town is Rs 150.

Waterfront Hotel (☎ 223 7287; Tissawewa Rd; s/d Rs 2500/4000; ✖ ☒) With a vaguely Balinese feel to it, this is a solid choice. The communal spaces are the highlight and feature aquariums and fish ponds in abundance, as well as a human pond in the form of a delightful swimming pool, while beyond that is an even bigger pond in the form of the lake. The rooms contain lots of carved stone furnishings, which contrast nicely with the soft white beds.

Hotel Sun Sinda (☎ 223 9078; Kataragama Rd; s/d incl breakfast Rs 3500/4000; ✳ ⬛) Greeted by small vases full of flower petals floating in water, and ponds so full of colourful tropical fish you may well be tempted to don snorkel and mask – if that doesn't appeal, there's an equally enticing pool. This is another decent option. The rooms are airy, comfortable and were clearly put together by an interior designer with a taste for the vaguely ethnic. The place is let down, however, by a stark and echoey restaurant, and a sterile atmosphere.

Hotel Chandrika (☎ 223 7143; Kataragama Rd; s/tw/tr without air-con Rs 3750/3830/4080, with air-con Rs 4050/4450/4750; ✳ ⬛) This slightly tacky hotel is very popular with tour groups and is a decent enough option with comfortable, though sterile, rooms set around a palm-lined courtyard and good pool. The staff are very attentive and friendly and the restaurant, which does a tasty curry (Rs 550), has a stunning collection of 1980s power ballads.

Priyankara Hotel (☎ 223 7206; www.priyanka rahotel.com; Kataragama Rd; s/d/tr incl breakfast Rs 5975/6975/7975; ✳ ⬛) It's hard to find fault with this superb hotel. Rooms, with high wooden ceilings, languidly rotating fans, hardwood furnishings and modern bathrooms, have lots of colonial style and views over the gorgeous pool, which in turn has views over the gorgeous rice fields and duck-filled ponds. The restaurant is equally classy, with Western and Asian dishes for between Rs 400 and Rs 600.

DEBERAWEWA

Sakura Guesthouse (☎ 223 7198; r from Rs 700) Highly basic rooms for an unbeatable price are found at this family affair. Your hosts' little daughters will be so fascinated by you that they'll trail you everywhere. It's a peaceful retreat where the beating of a beautiful butterfly's wings is the biggest disturbance. The family will pick you up (for free) from the bus station in Tissa or Deberawewa.

Tissa Inn (☎ 223 7233; www.tissainn.com; Wellaway Rd; s/d Rs 1150/1340; ✳) Fifteen hundred metres from the Deberawewa clock tower, this is a slightly rundown, in the most charming of manners, old hotel. It's worth checking out a few of the high-ceilinged rooms as quality varies, but at its best it's a spotless place of starched sheets and whirling fans.

Eating

Royal Restaurant (Main St; mains Rs 200-300) You get a right royal welcome here and a right royal feast, with cheap and tasty curries that will leave you stuffed and happy. Lot's of local families like to stop by for a big, noisy family lunch.

Sanka Restaurant (Kataragama Rd; mains Rs 200-300) A simple, open-sided restaurant with well-priced Chinese and Sri Lankan dishes and a tasty *nasi goreng* (fried rice).

Refresh Hotel (☎ 223 7357; Kataragama Rd; mains Rs 800-1000; ⏱ 11am-10pm) It seems that every tourist eats here and as one of the only restaurants in the neighbourhood that's hardly a surprise, but the food is tamed down to suit Western taste buds and is both bland in the extreme and highly overpriced.

Getting There & Away

Few buses go directly to the Hill Country, and if you can't get one you'll need to change at Wirawila junction (Rs 18, 30 minutes) and/or at Wellawaya (Rs 74). There are no buses to Yala National Park. Other major bus destinations from Tissa include Colombo (regular/air-con Rs 220/390, nine hours), Hambantota (Rs 35, one hour) and Kataragama (Rs 28, one hour).

AROUND TISSAMAHARAMA
Wirawila Wewa Bird Sanctuary

Between the northern and southern turn-offs to Tissa, the Hambantota–Wellawaya road runs on a causeway across the large Wirawila Wewa. This extensive sheet of water forms the Wirawila Wewa Bird Sanctuary. The best time for birdwatching is early morning.

Kirinda
☎ 047

Tiny Kirinda, 10km south of Tissa, is a place on the edge. On one side its sandy streets and ramshackle buildings give way to a series of magnificently bleak and empty beaches (heavy undertows and dumping waves make swimming here treacherous) that are perfect for long evening walks. In the other direction, tangled woodlands and sweeps of parched grasslands merge into wildlife-filled national parks. The village itself centres on a Buddhist shrine piled on top of some huge round rocks. Visible offshore are the wave-smashed Great Basses reefs with their lonely lighthouse. It's possible to hire boats to head out here for some incredible diving on calm days (around Rs 4000 for half a day) and diving equipment can normally be hired in town (Rs 2000 per day), but lessons aren't available. The diving here, though ranked by most people as the best in the country, is not for inexperienced divers – conditions are often rough and currents are strong. The window of opportunity for diving is also very narrow and basically confined to the period between mid-March and mid-April. For more on diving the Basses (and elsewhere), see www.divesrilanka.com. For boats and gear, speak to the owner of the Temple Flower Guesthouse (below).

Set on an old farm, **Suduweli** (☎ 072-263 1059; tw Rs 500, tw with bathroom from Rs 600, bungalows Rs 1500) is a heavenly spot a little way out of the village. Accommodation consists of basic but clean rooms in the main house, or a handful of comfortable and quiet Swiss Alpine–style cottages in the gardens. There's a small lake on the grounds that attracts rainbow-coloured flocks of birds, and there are croaking frogs and scurrying lizards everywhere. However, it's not all roses, as our reception wasn't as welcoming as we would have liked. You'd also better like mosquitoes because there are great clouds of the beasts.

Temple Flower Guesthouse (☎ 492 2499; templeflowerguest@yahoo.com; s/d Rs 1430/1650) is a delicious little guest house with a wonderful green colonial-style veranda shared between a couple of neatly attired rooms. Upstairs are further rooms, some with sunken walk-in showers and all with sea views. The food here is as delicious as the accommodation; there's real filter coffee and superb breakfasts and the owner is as friendly and helpful as can be. Jeep hire is Rs 4000 for half a day.

Elephant Reach (☎ 567 7544; www.elephantreach .com; s/d from US$85/95; ❄ 🖥 🏊) is a new top-end establishment on the edge of the village, and feels a lot like the kind of luxury lodge you'd expect to find on a Kenyan safari. The stylish communal areas are stuffed full of contorted wooden furniture and the rooms are equally well thought-out with huge showers, stone floors, hemp curtains and even TVs and DVD players in some rooms. Outside the lovely pool curls like a water snake around the gardens. The restaurant (mains Rs 500 to 800) receives mixed reports.

There is a bus from Tissa to Kirinda every half-hour or so (Rs 20).

YALA NATIONAL PARK

With trumpeting elephants, monkeys crashing through the trees, peacocks in their finest frocks and cunning leopards sliding like shadows through the undergrowth, Yala National Park (also known as Ruhunu) is *The Jungle Book* brought to glorious life. This vast region of dry woodland and open patches of grasslands is the big draw of this corner of Sri Lanka, and though it's far from Kenya, a safari here is well worth all the time, effort and cost.

Information

The entrance fees for **Yala National Park** (adult/child US$15/8, jeep & tracker Rs 250, service charge per group US$8, plus overall tax 12%; ☽ 6am-6.30pm 16 Oct-31 Aug) are payable at the main office, which is near the entrance, some 21km from Tissa. There are a few displays here of the pickled and stuffed variety. The road from Tissa is rough but passable, although a 4WD is necessary once in the park. Realistically the only way to visit the park is as part of a safari (see p147). Part of the entrance fee includes the services of an animal tracker – quality varies. Tips are both expected and usually earned; about Rs 200 each for the tracker and driver is average.

Sights

Yala combines a strict nature reserve with a national park, bringing the total protected area to 126,786 hectares of scrub, light forest, grassy plains and brackish lagoons. It's divided into five blocks, with the most visited being Block I (14,101 hectares), which, at the time of research, was the only one actually open to tourists. Also known as Yala West, this block was originally a reserve for hunters, but was given over to conservation in 1938.

With over 35 leopards, Yala West has one of the world's densest leopard populations and is renowned as one of the best places in which to see one of these stunning cats. *Panthera pardus kotiya,* the subspecies you may well see, is unique to Sri Lanka. The best time to spot leopards is February to June or July, when the water levels in the park are low. Elephants are also well-known inhabitants (the best time to spot them is also between February and July), and with luck you'll also get to see the shaggy-coated sloth bear or some of the fox-like jackals. Sambars, spotted deer, boars, crocodiles, buffaloes, mongooses and monkeys are here in their hundreds.

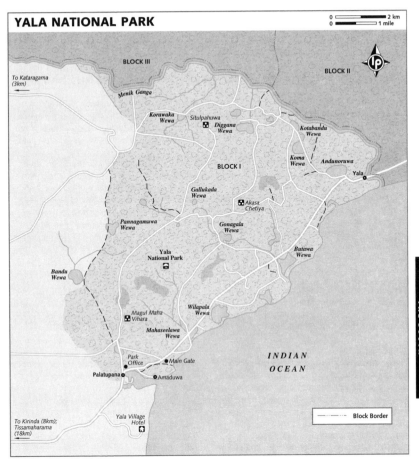

YALA NATIONAL PARK

BLOCK III

BLOCK II

To Kataragama
(3km)

Menik Ganga

Korawaka
Wewa

Situlpahuwa

Diggana
Wewa

Kotabandu
Wewa

Koma
Wewa

Andunoruwa

BLOCK I

Yala

Gallukada
Wewa

Akasa
Chetiya

Pannagamuwa
Wewa

Gonagala
Wewa

Yala
National Park

Butawa
Wewa

Bandu
Wewa

Wilapala
Wewa

Magul Maha
Vihara

Mahaseelawa
Wewa

INDIAN

OCEAN

Park
Office

Main Gate

Palatupana

Amaduwa

To Kirinda (8km);
Tissamaharama
(18km)

Yala Village
Hotel

Block Border

0   2 km
0   1 mile

THE SOUTH

Around 150 species of birds have been recorded at Yala, many of which are visitors escaping the northern winter. These birds include white-winged black terns, curlews and pintails. Locals include jungle fowl, hornbills, orioles and peacocks by the bucket load. The avian highlight, though, is the exceedingly rare black-necked stalk, of which there are only around ten individuals in the entire country.

Despite the large quantity of wildlife the light forest can make spotting animals quite hard; fortunately help is at hand in the form of small grassy clearings and lots of waterholes around which the wildlife congregates. The end of the dry season (March to April) is the best time to visit as during and shortly after the rains the animals disperse over a wide area.

As well as herds of elephants, Yala contains the remains of a once-thriving human community. A monastic settlement, **Situlpahuwa**, appears to have housed 12,000 inhabitants. Now restored, it's an important pilgrimage site. A 1st-century BC *vihara* (Buddhist complex), **Magul Maha Vihara**, and a 2nd-century BC chetiya (Buddhist shrine), **Akasa Chetiya**, point to a well-established community, believed to have been part of the ancient Ruhunu kingdom.

Note that Yala has recently been plagued with security issues, which has at times led to its closure. At the time of research it was once again open to tourists, but the security

THE LONG WALK TO KATARAGAMA

Forty-five days before the annual Kataragama festival starts on the Esala *poya* (full moon), a group of Kataragama devotees start walking the length of Sri Lanka for the Pada Yatra pilgrimage. Seeking spiritual development, the pilgrims believe they are walking in the steps of the god Kataragama (also known as Murugan) and the Veddahs, who made the first group pilgrimage on this route.

The route follows the east coast from the Jaffna peninsula, via Trincomalee and Batticaloa to Okanda, then through Yala National Park to Kataragama. It's an arduous trip, and the pilgrims rely on the hospitality of the communities and temples they pass for their food and lodging. During the many recent periods when the war has been raging, the risks to them were great and the walk has not always been completed.

Pilgrims arrive in time for the festival's feverish activity. Elephants parade, drummers drum. Vows are made and favours sought by devotees, who demonstrate their sincerity by performing extraordinary acts of penance and self-mortification on one particular night: some swing from hooks that pierce their skin; others roll half-naked over the hot sands near the temple. A few perform the act of walking on beds of red-hot cinders – treading the flowers, as it's called. The fire walkers fast, meditate and pray, bathe in Menik Ganga (Menik River) and then worship at Maha Devale before facing their ordeal. Then, fortified by their faith, they step out onto the glowing path while the audience cries out encouragement. The festival officially ends with a water-cutting ceremony (said to bring rain for the harvest) in Menik Ganga.

presence in the park remains high and you should check the situation before trekking out here. You can safely say that if the park is open to tourists, then visiting poses no risk.

Sleeping

Although most of the park was untouched by the tsunami, two resorts near the shore were demolished (with the loss of 49 lives – a memorial today stands on the beach beside the remains of one of the resorts). Today there is no accommodation within the park and nor is there likely to be in the near future.

Just outside of the entrance, **Yala Village Hotel** (☎ 047-223 9449; www.johnkeellshotels.com; s/d US$95/120; ✷ ✢) offers posh accommodation amid the sand dunes. Rooms are in individual bungalows, which come with satellite TV, fridge and elephant bedspreads. Talking of elephants, they often pass through the lodge grounds at night and their not-so-soft foot falls are likely to break into your dreams. The hotel has the first inklings of an environmental policy: some rooms run on solar power, some of the waste water is recycled, and there's a tree-planting scheme.

KATARAGAMA
☎ 047

Sheltered in the foothills, 15km northeast of Tissa, is Kataragama. A compelling mix of pomp and procession, religious piety and religious extravagance, this most holy of towns is a shot of oriental thrills at the end of an island-wide pilgrimage. Along with Adam's Peak (Sri Pada), this is the most important religious pilgrimage site in Sri Lanka and is a holy place for Buddhists, Muslims and Hindus alike. It is one of those wonderful places where the most outlandish of legends becomes solid fact and magic floats in clouds of incense. Many believe that King Dutugemunu built a shrine to Kataragama Deviyo (the resident god) here in the 2nd century BC and that the Buddhist Kirivehera dagoba dates back to the 1st century BC, but the site is thought to have been significant for even longer.

In July and August, the predominantly Hindu **Kataragama festival** draws thousands of devotees who make the pilgrimage over a two-week period (see The Long Walk to Kataragama, above). Apart from festival time, the town is busiest at weekends and on *poya* days. At these times it may be difficult to find accommodation, and the place will be buzzing; at other times it can feel like a ghost town. If you're staying in Tissamaharama you may just want to visit on a day trip.

Information

There's a **Bank of Ceylon** (Tissa Rd), which has an ATM, and a **post office** (Tissa Rd). Don't expect much help from the information office in the religious complex.

Sights

The sacred precinct is set on the other side of Menik Ganga, a chocolate-coloured (though not flavoured!) river in which pilgrims wash before continuing towards the shrines. The most important shrine is the **Maha Devale**, which contains the lance of the six-faced, 12-armed Hindu war god, Murugan (Skanda), who is seen as identical to the Kataragama Deviyo. Followers make offerings at daily *puja* at 4.30am, 10.30am and 6.30pm (no 4.30am offering on Saturday). Outside this shrine are two large boulders, against which pilgrims smash burning coconuts while muttering a prayer. The **Kirivehara** and **Sivam Kovil** shrines are dedicated to the Buddha and Ganesh (the remover of obstacles and champion of intellectual pursuits) respectively; there is also a **bodhi tree**.

Sitting beyond this temple complex is the **Kirivehara**, a large whitewashed Buddhist dagoba.

The Muslim area, close to the entrance, features the beautiful **ul-Khizr Mosque** with coloured tile work and wooden lintels, and tombs of two holy men.

Apart from the shrines, there are some other points of interest inside the temple complex. An **archaeological museum** (admission by donation; ⊙ 10.30am-12.30pm & 6.30-9pm) has a collection of Hindu and Buddhist religious items, as well as huge fibreglass models of statues from around Sri Lanka. A small **museum** has a display of Buddhist statues.

Sleeping & Eating

The accommodation in Kataragama is a sorry, and overpriced, lot and you'd do well to stay in Tissa and just make your visit a day trip.

Jacks Place Peace Hotel & Backpackers Hostel (☎ 072 408 8123; tw Rs 1000) Jack is a fictional character from space searching for world peace (good luck to him!) and he appears to have made this ramshackle and overpriced backpackers lodge his earthly base while on embarking on this impossible quest. His room, like all the others, is very simple, but contains a good, if slightly hippy, atmosphere. There are numerous philosophical statements on the walls, though these are somewhat tempered by the giant Pepsi poster… The hostel is 4km back along the Tissa road.

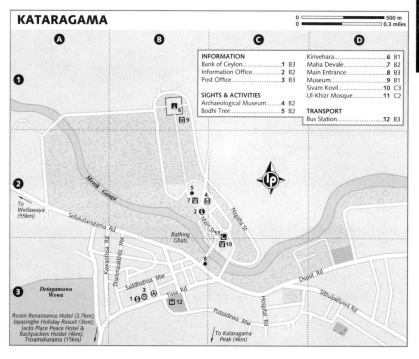

KATARAGAMA

INFORMATION		
Bank of Ceylon	1	B3
Information Office	2	B2
Post Office	3	B3

SIGHTS & ACTIVITIES		
Archaeological Museum	4	B2
Bodhi Tree	5	B2

Kirivehara	6	B1
Maha Devale	7	B2
Main Entrance	8	B3
Museum	9	B1
Sivam Kovil	10	C3
Ul-Khizr Mosque	11	C2

| TRANSPORT | | |
| Bus Station | 12 | B3 |

THE SOUTH

Jayasinghe Holiday Resort (☎ 223 5146; Tissa Rd; tw with/without air-con Rs 3000/2310; ✖ ⚼) This place, 3km from town, feels depressingly like an English seaside holiday camp in winter and has scruffy, overpriced rooms and a swimming pool that's popular with frogs.

Rosen Renaissance Hotel (☎ 223 6030-3; www .rosenhotelsrilanka.com; Tissa Rd; s/d Rs 5500/6000; ✖ ⚼) The smartest address in town, Rosen was designed for the businessmen who never came. The rooms, while pleasing enough, are very overpriced (though discounts come easily) and contain lots of marble and tack. The hotel's best asset is the pool, which has an un-derwater music system – ask them to play the *Jaws* theme tune! Go for the room-only deal because if you take the B&B option, you get charged an additional Rs 1400 for a breakfast that only costs Rs 700 if bought separately.

Getting There & Away

Following are some major bus destinations from Kataragama:

Colombo Regular/air-con Rs 195/410, 10 hours
Ella Rs 116, three hours
Kandy Rs 440, eight hours
Matara Rs 190, 3½ hours
Tissamaharama Rs 28, one hour

The Hill Country

The proud Sinhalese kingdom of Kandy resisted European domination for more than 300 years after the coastal regions first surrendered to the Portuguese in the 17th century, and even now the surrounding Hill Country region feels a world apart from the rest of Sri Lanka. The landscape is green and lush, with an emerald carpet of tea plantations, and with montane forest clinging improbably to serrated ranges bookended by waterfalls on almost every corner. The climatic norm is an everlasting, energising spring, with occasionally (much) cooler temperatures threatening to forever hijack your expectations of this 'tropical' country.

The Hill Country capital of Kandy remains the Sinhalese cultural and spiritual centre for all of Sri Lanka, and the bustling city is an interesting gateway to the rest of the region. It's a region that promises leisurely train rides through rolling tea plantations, poignant reminders of the days of British colonial rule, and some of Sri Lanka's finest opportunities for exploring the outdoors. In the south the verdant Sinharaja Forest Reserve is a compact slice of Sri Lanka's last remaining rainforest. Further north, the Horton Plains National Park provides a wide-open route to the dramatic escarpment of World's End. Around Ella and Haputale, fill your days with lazy day walks through surrounding tea estates before returning to some of Sri Lanka's best guest houses.

Before or after a few days on the beach, don't be too surprised if the Hill Country is another region in which the days also drift lazily by.

HIGHLIGHTS

- Experiencing the up-close-and-personal excitement of elephants, drummers and dancers at the **Kandy Esala Perahera** (p159)
- Getting away from Sri Lanka's energetic buzz by trekking in the rare montane forests of the **Knuckles Range** (p175)
- Joining devout pilgrims and following flickering torchlight to ascend the sacred heights of **Adam's Peak** (Sri Pada; p175)
- Rattling and rolling with Tamil tea pickers on a slowly, slowly train journey from **Haputale to Ella** (p190)
- Winding down with a few leisurely days in **Ella** (p195), combining excellent home-cooked food and spectacular walks
- Discovering your inner birdwatcher amid the tangled, overgrown perfection of the **Sinharaja Forest Reserve** (p204)
- Rising before dawn and being rewarded with an unimpeded view from the stunning heights of **World's End** (p187)

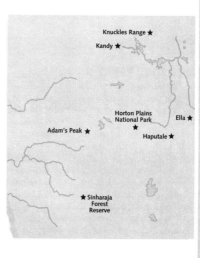

THE HILL COUNTRY

THE HILL COUNTRY

0 ——————— 20 km
0 ——————— 12 miles

COLOMBO TO KANDY

The **Henerathgoda Botanic Gardens** (☎ 033-222 2316) near Gampaha, off the Colombo–Kandy road about 30km northwest of Colombo, are where the first rubber trees planted in Asia were grown. Some original plantings dot the 37-acre gardens, together with 400 other plant varieties.

About 50km from Kandy is **Cadjugama**, famous for its cashew nuts. Brightly clad sellers beckon passing motorists with nuts they've harvested from the surrounding forest. A 1kg bag of still-warm chilli-infused cashews costs around Rs 900 – perfect for accompanying a couple of weeks of sundowner beers. At the 48km post is **Radawaduwa**, notable for woven cane items.

Kegalle, 77km from Colombo, is the nearest town to the **Pinnewala Elephant Orphanage** (opposite). Nearby is **Utuwankandu**, a rocky hill from where the 19th-century Robin Hood–style highwayman, Saradiel, preyed on travellers until the British executed him.

At **Kadugannawa**, just after the road and railway make their most scenic climbs – with views southwest to the large Bible Rock – is a tall pillar erected in memory of Captain Dawson, the English engineer who built the Colombo–Kandy road in 1826.

Cadjugama, Kegalle and Kadugannawa are on the A1, easily accessible by bus between Colombo and Kandy. Catch a train to Kadugannawa and the Henerathgoda Botanic Gardens at Gampaha.

Pinnewala Elephant Orphanage

This government-run **orphanage** (adult/child Rs 2000/1000, video camera Rs 500; ☺ 8.30am-6pm), near Kegalle, was created to protect abandoned or orphaned elephants. Now it's one of Sri Lanka's most popular attractions. Nowhere else, except at *peraheras* (processions), are you likely to see so many pachyderms at close quarters.

There are around 80 elephants of all ages. The creatures are largely well looked after, but the UK-based **Born Free Foundation** (www.bornfree .org.uk) has expressed concern over the amount of contact elephants have with the public and the fact that the facility has been used for breeding, contrary to its status as an orphanage. Check its website and make your own mind up. See boxed text Captive Elephants on p69 for more information.

The elephants are controlled by their *mahouts*, who ensure they feed at the right times and don't endanger anyone. Otherwise the elephants roam freely around the sanctuary area. The elephants are led to a nearby river for bathing daily from 10am to noon and from 2pm to 4pm. Meal times are 9.15am, 1.15pm and 5pm. The afternoon light is better for photographs, but there are also more visitors at that time. If it's been raining heavily, bathing in the river is sometimes cancelled as the waters are too high.

The orphanage is a few kilometres north of the Colombo–Kandy road. From Kandy take a private bus or Central Transport Board (CTB) bus 662 to Kegalle. Get off before Kegalle at Karandunpona Junction. From the junction, catch bus 681 going from Kegalle to Rambukkana and get off at Pinnewala. A three-wheeler from the junction to Pinnewala is around Rs 300. It's about an hour from Kandy to the junction, and 10 minutes from the junction to Pinnewala. Buses also link Colombo and Kegalle. A three-wheeler from Kandy to Pinnewala is around Rs 1500 one way.

Rambukkana station on the Colombo–Kandy railway is about 3km north of the orphanage. From Rambukkana get a bus going towards Kegalle. Trains leave Kandy at 6.35am (arriving at Rambukkana station at 8.11am) and 10.25am (arriving at 12.08pm).

Two kilometres from Pennewala, on the Karandupona–Kandy road, the **Millennium Elephant Foundation** (☎ 035-226 5377; www.millen niumelephantfoundation.org; admission Rs 600, elephant rides per 30min Rs 3000; ☺ 8am-5pm) is same-same, but slightly different, with 11 elephants rescued from situations as diverse as aggressive mahouts and retirement from working in temples. Volunteers are welcome at the Foundation – get ready to bathe the elephants in the river – and the facility also supports a mobile veterinary service. Volunteers are expected to stay at least three months (US$2525), but one-month assignments (US$1100) are also considered. Costs include all accommodation and food.

Most people visit Pinnewala as a day trip, but the nearby Tulip of Ceylon hotel (p174) makes a comfortable base for visiting Kandy. There are also a few OK guest houses at Pinnewala if it's too late to push on to Kandy from Colombo.

KANDY

☎ 081 / pop 112,000 / elev 500m

Some days Kandy's skies seem perpetually bruised, with stubborn mist clinging to the hills surrounding the city's beautiful centrepiece lake. Delicate Hill Country breezes impel the mist to gently part, revealing colourful houses and hotels amid Kandy's improbable forested halo. In the centre of town, three-wheelers careen around slippery corners, raising a soft spray that threatens the softer silk of the colourful saris worn by local women. Here's a city that looks good even when it's raining.

And when the rain subsides – and it does with frequency and alacrity – Kandy's cobalt blue skies reveal it as this island's other real 'city' after the brighter coastal lights of Colombo. Urban buzz is provided by busy spontaneous street markets and even busier bus stations and restaurants. History and culture are on tap, and 115km from the capital and at an altitude of 500m, Kandy offers a cooler and more relaxed climate.

Kandy served as the capital of the last Sinhalese kingdom, which fell to the British in 1815 after defying the Portuguese and Dutch for three centuries. It took the British another 16 tough years to finally build a road linking Kandy with Colombo. The locals still proudly see themselves as a little different – and perhaps a tad superior – to Sri Lankans from the island's lower reaches.

Kandy is renowned for the great Kandy Esala Perahera (p159), held over 10 days leading up to the Nikini *poya* (full moon) at the end of the month of Esala (July/August), but it has enough attractions to justify a visit at any time of year. Some of the Hill Country's nicest boutique hotels nestle in the hills surrounding Kandy, and the city is a good base for exploring the underrated terrain of the nearby Knuckles Range.

Orientation

The focus of Kandy is its lake, with the Temple of the Sacred Tooth Relic (Sri Dalada Maligawa) on its north side. The city centre is immediately north and west of the lake, with the clock tower a handy reference point. The train station, the market and the various bus stops are a short walk from the lake. The city spreads into the surrounding hills. Many places to stay look down on the town.

MAPS

The *A-Z Street Guide*, available at Vijitha Yapa bookshop, contains a detailed map. The tourist office has a more rudimentary offering.

Information

BOOKSHOPS

Buddhist Publication Society (☎ 223 7283; www.bps .lk; 54 Victoria Rd; ☿ 9am-4.30pm Mon-Fri, 9am-12.30pm Sat) The Buddhist Publication Society, on the lakeside 400m northeast of the Temple of the Tooth, is a non-profit charity that distributes the Buddha's teachings. Local scholars and monks occasionally give lectures, and there is a comprehensive library. See online for free information downloads. It's a good place to ask about meditation courses (p163).

Cultural Triangle Office (☿ 9am-12.30pm & 1.30-4pm) Opposite the tourist office, this has a selection of books for sale on the ancient cities. *Kandy*, by Dr Anuradha Seneviratna, is an informative guide to the city's heritage. Also available is *The Cultural Triangle*, published by Unesco and the Central Cultural Fund, which provides background information on the ancient sites.

Mark Bookshop (151/1 Dalada Vidiya) Books about Sri Lanka.

Vijitha Yapa (5 Kotugodelle Vidiya) Periodicals, newspapers (including foreign titles), maps, fiction and non-fiction.

CULTURAL CENTRES

Alliance Française (☎ 222 4432; allikandy@sltnet .lk; 642 Peradeniya Rd; ☿ 8.30am-6pm Mon-Sat) The Alliance hosts film nights (often with English-subtitled films), and has books and periodicals. Good coffee is available. Non-members can browse in the library.

British Council (☎ 223 4634; www.britishcouncil.org /srilanka; 88/3 Kotugodelle Vidiya; ☿ 9am-5pm Tue-Sat) British newspapers, CDs, videos and DVDs, and occassional film nights, exhibitions and plays. Non-members may read newspapers on presentation of a passport.

INTERNET ACCESS

Internet cafes charge around Rs 60 per hour. There is wi-fi available (Rs 100 per hour) at the Palm Garden Guest House (p165) and Sharon Inn (p165).

SkyNet (1st fl, 105 Kotugodelle Vidiya)

Visual Net (Haras Vidiya)

MEDICAL SERVICES

Lakeside Adventist Hospital (☎ 222 3466; lakeside@ slt.lk; 40 Sangaraja Mawatha) Has English-speaking staff.

MONEY

The following all have ATMs and exchange facilities.

Bank of Ceylon (Dalada Vidiya)

Commercial Bank (Kotugodelle Vidiya)

Hatton National Bank (Dalada Vidiya)

HSBC (Kotugodelle Vidiya)

POST & TELEPHONE

The main post office is opposite the train station. More-central post offices include one at the intersection of Kande Vidiya and DS Senanayake Vidiya. There are numerous private communications bureaus for IDD calling.

DHL (☎ 447 9684; 178 DS Senanayake Vidiya; ☿ 8.30am-5.30pm Mon-Fri; 8.30am-12.30pm Sat) Courier services – beside Pizza Hut.

TOURIST INFORMATION

Cultural Triangle Office (☿ 9am-12.30pm & 1.30-4pm) Located in a colonial building near the tourist office. Books are available for sale, a scratchy DVD on Kandy's history is shown, and you can buy Cultural Triangle round-trip tickets that cover many of the sites of the ancient cities. Within Kandy the round-trip ticket covers the four Hindu *devales* (complexes for worshipping deities) – for Kataragama, Natha, Pattini and Vishnu – two monasteries (Asgiriya and Malwatte) and the National Museum. It's also customary to make a donation (usually Rs 50 and upwards) at the *devales* and monasteries. The National Museum costs Rs 500 to enter without a Cultural Triangle ticket. For more information on these tickets, see p212.

Tourist Information Centre (☎ 222 2661; Palace Sq; ☿ 9am-1pm & 1.30-4.45pm Mon-Fri) In a pavilion near the Olde Empire Hotel.

Dangers & Annoyances

The back alleys of the town centre are worth avoiding after dark. Most habitués are local guys searching out gambling dens and late-night bars.

Touts mooch around the train station and the lake. You'll hear about guest houses that have mysteriously 'closed', 'been shut down' or are now 'infested with cockroaches'. All these transparent lies are good reasons to book ahead with a guest house; most will pick you up from the Kandy train station. Beware also of guys saying 'I work at your hotel' or 'I met you yesterday'. Just ask for more specific information – like, 'Which hotel?' and watch them drift away sheepishly.

While researching we also heard of solo women travellers being hassled around the lakeside at dusk and after dark. Get a three-wheeler back to your guest house to keep safe.

Sights
KANDY LAKE
Kandy Lake was created in 1807 by Sri Wickrama Rajasinha, the last ruler of the kingdom of Kandy. Several minor local chiefs protested because their people objected to labouring on the project. They were ruthlessly put to death on stakes in the lake bed. The central island was used as Sri Wickrama Rajasinha's personal harem. Later the British used it as an ammunition store and added the fortress-style parapet around the perimeter. On the south shore, in front of the Malwatte Maha Vihara, the circular enclosure is the monks' bathhouse.

A leisurely stroll around the lake, with a few stops on the lakeside seats, is a pleasant way to spend a few hours. Just note the warning (above) for solo women travellers.

TEMPLE OF THE SACRED TOOTH RELIC
Just north of the lake, this **temple** (Sri Dalada Maligawa; admission Rs 500, still/video camera Rs 150/300; ⏰ 5.30am-8pm, puja 5.30-7am, 9.30-11am & 6.30-8pm) houses Sri Lanka's most important Buddhist relic – a tooth of the Buddha. The temple was damaged when a bomb was detonated by the LTTE near the main entrance in 1998. The scars have been now repaired, but security remains high and there is significant screening of all visitors.

Freelance guides will offer their services for around Rs 400, and free audio guides are available at the ticket office. A newly installed elevator facilitates access for travellers with disabilities.

The tooth is said to have been snatched from the flames of the Buddha's funeral

KANDY ESALA PERAHERA
This *perahera* (procession) is held in Kandy to honour the sacred tooth enshrined in the Temple of the Sacred Tooth Relic. It runs for 10 days in the month of Esala (July/August), ending on the Nikini *poya* (full moon). Kandy's biggest night of the year comes after these 10 days of increasingly frenetic activity. A decline in elephant numbers has seen the scale of the festival diminish in recent years – in earlier times more than 100 elephants took part – but it is still one of Asia's most fascinating celebrations.

The first six nights are relatively low-key. On the seventh night, proceedings escalate as the route lengthens and the procession becomes more splendid (and accommodation prices increase accordingly).

The procession is actually a combination of five separate *peraheras*. Four come from the four Kandy *devales* (complexes for worshipping Hindu or Sri Lankan deities, who are also devotees and servants of the Buddha): Natha, Vishnu, Kataragama and Pattini. The fifth and most splendid *perahera* is from the Sri Dalada Maligawa itself.

The procession is led by thousands of Kandyan dancers and drummers beating drums, cracking whips and waving colourful banners. Then come long processions of up to 50 elephants. The Maligawa tusker is decorated from trunk to toe, and carries a huge canopy sheltering, on the final night, a replica of the sacred relic cask. A trail of pristine white linen is laid before the elephant.

The Kandy Esala Perahera is Sri Lanka's most magnificent annual spectacle. It's been celebrated annually for many centuries and is described by Robert Knox in his 1681 book *An Historical Relation of Ceylon*. There is also a smaller procession on the *poya* day in June, and special *peraheras* may be put on for important occasions.

It's essential to book roadside seats for the main *perahera* at least a week in advance. Prices range from Rs 5000 to 6500. Once the festival starts, seats about halfway back in the stands are more affordable.

THE HILL COUNTRY

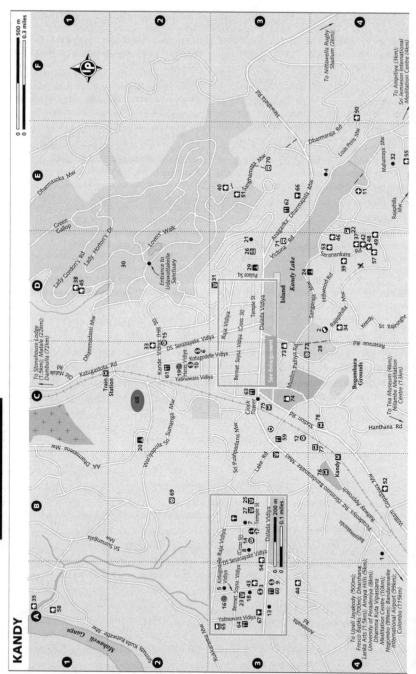

KANDY

THE HILL COUNTRY

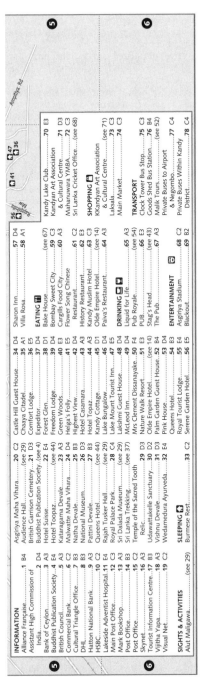

INFORMATION
Alliance Française................................1 B4
Assistant High Commission of
  India...2 D4
Bank of Ceylon....................................3 A3
Buddhist Publication Society......4 E4
British Council.....................................5 A3
Commercial Bank...............................6 C2
Cultural Triangle Office...................7 B3
DHL...8 B3
Hatton National Bank.......................9 A3
HSBC..10 C2
Lakeside Adventist Hospital.........11 E4
Main Post Office...............................12 C3
Mark Bookshop.................................13 A3
Post Office...............................(see 37)
Post Office..15 C2
Skynet..16 A3
Tourist Information Centre............17 B3
Vijitha Yapa..18 A3
Visual Net...19 C2

SIGHTS & ACTIVITIES
Alut Maligawa.........................(see 29)

Asgiriya Maha Vihara.....................20 C2
Audience Hall...........................(see 29)
British Garrison Cemetery..............21 D3
Buddhist Publication Society....(see 4)
Expeditor...22 E4
Hotel Suisse.............................(see 44)
Hotel Topaz.............................(see 44)
Kataragama Devale..........................23 A3
Malwatte Maha Vihara....................24 D4
Natha Devale....................................25 B3
National Museum.............................26 D3
Pattini Devale...................................27 D4
Queens Hotel...........................(see 44)
Rajah Tusker Hall..............................28 C4
Royal Palace Park......................(see 29)
Sri Dalada Museum................(see 29)
Sri Lanka Trekking....................(see 37)
Temple of the Sacred Tooth
  Relic..29 D3
Udawattakele Sanctuary................30 D2
Vishnu Devale...................................31 D3
Wedamedura Ayurveda..................32 E4

SLEEPING
Burmese Rest.....................................33 C2

Castle Hill Guest House...................34 D4
Chaaya Citadel..................................35 A1
Comfort Lodge..................................36 E5
Expeditor..37 D4
Forest Glen..38 D1
Freedom Lodge.................................39 D4
Green Woods.....................................40 E3
Helga's Folly.......................................41 E5
Highest View......................................42 D4
Hotel Casamara.................................43 A3
Kandy Cottage...................................44 A3
Lake Bungalow..................................45 D1
Lake Mount Tourist Inn..................46 D4
Lakshmi Guest House......................47 E5
McLeod Inn.......................................48 D4
Mrs Clement Dissanayake..............49 D4
Nature Walk Resort.........................50 E4
Olde Empire Hotel..................(see 14)
Palm Garden Guest House.............52 B4
Pink House...53 D4
Queens Hotel.....................................54 B3
Royal Tourist Lodge.........................55 E4
Serene Garden Hotel.......................56 E5

Sharon Inn..57 D4
Villa Rosa...58 A1

EATING
Bake House................................(see 67)
Bombay Sweet City..........................59 C3
Cargills Food City.............................60 A3
Flower Song Chinese
  Restaurant....................................61 C2
History Restaurant...........................62 E3
Kandy Muslim Hotel........................63 C3
Olde Empire Hotel..................(see 14)
Paiva's Restaurant............................64 A3

DRINKING
Liquid for Life...................................65 A3
Pub Royale..............................(see 54)
PUB..66 E3
Stag's Head...............................(see 43)
The Pub..67 A3

ENTERTAINMENT
Asgiriya Stadium...............................68 C2
Blackout..69 B2

Kandy Lake Club...............................70 E3
Kandyan Art Association
  & Cultural Centre...........................71 D3
Mahanuwara YMBA.........................72 C3
Sri Lanka Cricket Office.........(see 68)

SHOPPING
Kandyan Art Association
  & Cultural Centre..................(see 71)
Laksala...73 C3
Main Market......................................74 C3

TRANSPORT
Clock Tower Bus Stop......................75 C3
Goods Shed Bus Station..................76 B4
Malik Tours..............................(see 52)
Private Buses to Airport
  & Negombo....................................77 C4
Private Buses Within Kandy
  District...78 C4

pyre in 483 BC and was smuggled into Sri Lanka during the 4th century AD, hidden in the hair of a princess. At first it was taken to Anuradhapura, and moved through the country on the waves of Sri Lankan history, before ending up at Kandy. In 1283 it was carried back to India by an invading army but retrieved by King Parakramabahu III.

The tooth gradually grew in importance as a symbol of sovereignty, and it was believed that whoever had custody of the tooth relic had the right to rule the island. In the 16th century the Portuguese apparently seized the tooth, took it away and burnt it with devout Catholic fervour in Goa. Not so, say the Sinhalese. The Portuguese had actually stolen a replica tooth while the real incisor remained safe. There are still rumours that the real tooth is hidden somewhere secure, and the tooth kept here is only a replica.

The Temple of the Sacred Tooth Relic was constructed mainly under Kandyan kings from 1687 to 1707 and from 1747 to 1782, and the entire temple complex was part of the Kandyan royal palace. The imposing pink structure is surrounded by a moat. The octagonal tower in the moat was built by Sri Wickrama Rajasinha and used to house an important collection of *ola* (talipot-palm leaf) manuscripts. This section of the temple was heavily damaged in the 1998 bomb blast.

The main tooth shrine – a two-storey rectangular building known as the Vahahitina Maligawa – occupies the centre of a paved courtyard. The eye-catching gilded roof over the relic chamber was paid for by Japanese donors. The 1998 bomb exposed part of the front wall to reveal at least three layers of 18th- to 20th-century paintings depicting the *perahera* (see p159) and various Jataka tales (stories of the Buddha's previous lives).

Sri Lankan Buddhists believe they must complete at least one pilgrimage to the temple in their lifetime, as worshipping here improves one's karmic lot immeasurably.

The tooth shrine receives many worshippers and tourists, with fewer tourists in the morning. Wear clothes that cover your legs and your shoulders and remove your shoes.

During *pujas* (offerings or prayers), the heavily guarded room housing the tooth is open to devotees and tourists. However, you don't actually see the tooth. It's kept in a gold casket shaped like a dagoba (stupa), which contains a series of six dagoba caskets of diminishing size.

THE HILL COUNTRY

Most visitors can only view the dagoba casket from the doorway, which is 3m from the actual altar. Guards keep the queue moving so no one gets more than 15 seconds inside the shrine room. Thai and Japanese nationals – because of their country's generous temple donations – may be allowed into the tooth room upon advance request to the temple guardians.

Behind the shrine stands the three-storey **Alut Maligawa**, a newer and larger shrine hall displaying dozens of bronze sitting Buddhas donated by Thai devotees. The design resembles a Thai Buddhist shrine hall in tribute to the fact that Thai monks re-established Sri Lanka's ordination lineage during the reign of King Kirti Sri Rajasinha. The upper two floors of the Alut Maligawa contain the **Sri Dalada Museum** (admission included; 7.30am-6pm) with a stunning array of gilded gifts to the temple. Letters and diary entries from the British time reveal the colonisers' surprisingly respectful attitude to the tooth relic. More recent photographs reveal the damage caused by the truck bomb in 1998.

To the north inside the compound, and accessible only via the Temple of the Sacred Tooth Relic, is the 19th-century **Audience Hall**, an open-air pavilion with stone columns carved to look like wooden pillars. Adjacent in the **Rajah Tusker Hall** are the stuffed remains of Rajah, the Maligawa tusker who died in 1988 (see boxed text, p159).

NATIONAL MUSEUM

This **museum** (adult/child Rs 500/300, camera Rs 160; 9am-5pm Tue-Sat) once housed Kandyan royal concubines and now features royal regalia and reminders of pre-European Sinhalese life. On display is a copy of the 1815 agreement that handed over the Kandyan provinces to British rule. This document announces a major reason for the event.

> …the cruelties and oppressions of the Malabar ruler, in the arbitrary and unjust infliction of bodily tortures and pains of death without trial, and sometimes without accusation or the possibility of a crime, and in the general contempt and contravention of all civil rights, have become flagrant, enormous and intolerable.

Sri Wickrama Rajasinha was declared, 'by the habitual violation of the chief and most sacred duties of a sovereign', to be 'fallen and deposed from office of king' and 'dominion of the Kandyan provinces' was 'vested in…the British Empire'.

The tall-pillared audience hall hosted the convention of Kandyan chiefs that ceded the kingdom to Britain in 1815.

The National Museum, along with four *devales* and two monasteries – but not the Temple of the Sacred Tooth Relic itself – make up one of Sri Lanka's Cultural Triangle sites (p158).

BRITISH GARRISON CEMETERY

This **cemetery** (8am-5pm) is a short walk uphill behind the National Museum. There are 163 graves and around 500 burials. Some of the deaths were due to sunstroke, elephants or jungle fever. The Cargills of supermarket fame lie here. James McGlashan survived the battle of Waterloo but later succumbed to mosquitos. Donations are appreciated.

DEVALES

There are four Kandyan *devales* to the gods who are followers of Buddha and protect Sri Lanka. Three of the four *devales* are near the Temple of the Sacred Tooth Relic. The 14th-century **Natha Devale** is the oldest. It perches on a stone terrace with a fine *vahalkada* (solid panel of sculpture) gateway. Bodhi trees and dagobas stand in the *devale* grounds. Adjacent is the simple **Pattini Devale**, dedicated to the goddess of chastity. The **Vishnu Devale** on the other side of Raja Vidiya is reached by carved steps and features a drumming hall. The great Hindi god Vishnu is the guardian of Sri Lanka, demonstrating the intermingling of Hinduism and Buddhism.

Further away, the brightly painted tower gateway of the **Kataragama Devale** demands attention amid the bustle on Kotugodelle Vidiya. Murugan, the god of war, has six heads and 12 hands wielding weapons.

MONASTERIES

The principal *viharas* (Buddhist complexes) in Kandy have considerable importance – the high priests of the two best known, Malwatte and Asgiriya, are the most important in Sri Lanka. These temples are the headquarters of two of the main *nikayas* (orders of monks). The head monks also administer the Temple of the Sacred Tooth Relic. The **Malwatte Maha Vihara** is across the lake from the Temple of the Sacred Tooth Relic, while the **Asgiriya Maha**

Vihara is off Wariyapola Sri Sumanga Mawatha northwest of the town centre. It has a large reclining Buddha image.

UDAWATTAKELLE SANCTUARY
North of the lake this **forest** (adult/child under 12 Rs 600/300; 7am-5pm) has huge trees, good bird-watching and loads of cheeky monkeys. Be careful if you're visiting alone. Muggers are rare but not unknown; solo women should take extra care.

Enter by turning right after the post office on DS Senanayake Vidiya.

TEA MUSEUM
This **museum** (Map p170; 070 280 3204; www.purecey lontea.com; admission Rs 400; 8.15am-4.45pm Tue-Sun) occupies the 1925-vintage Hanthana Tea Factory, 4km south of Kandy on the Hanthana road. Abandoned for over a decade, it was refurbished by the Sri Lanka Tea Board and the Planters' Association of Sri Lanka. There are exhibits on tea pioneers James Taylor and Thomas Lipton (see boxed text, p190), and lots of vintage tea-processing paraphernalia. Knowledgeable guides can answer the trickiest of questions – trust us, we tried to stump them – and there's a free cuppa afterwards in the top floor tea room. Commandeer the telescope for great views while you're up there.

UNIVERSITY OF PERADENIYA
Ten years after the 1842 founding of the University of Ceylon in Colombo, the bulk of the university (Map p170) moved to Peradeniya, 8km south of Kandy. Today around 6600 students enjoy the leafy campus.

Activities
AYURVEDA
Wedamedura Ayurveda (447 9484; www.ayurvedawe damedura.com; 7 Mahamaya Mawatha; treatments Rs 1250-5000), southeast of the lake, is an Ayurvedic treatment facility with both male and female massage therapists. Residential packages (per week €600, including accommodation and food) are also available. It's a little dark and gloomy though, so if you're heading to Ella, visit the brighter Suwamadura (p196) instead.

Around Kandy, much nicer is the colourful ambience of the Ayurvedic treatment centre at **Amaya Hills** (Map p170; 223 3521; www.amayare sorts.com; Heerassagala; facial Rs 2500, oil massage & steam bath Rs 4000). Amaya Hills, which is also a resort (p174), is high in the hills on a winding road.

A three-wheeler from Kandy costs around Rs 1000 return. Make a day of it, have lunch and spend a few hours around the stunning pool.

GOLF
The **Victoria Golf & Country Resort** (off Map p170; 237 5570; www.srilankagolf.com; green fees US$35, club hire Rs 1000, caddy per round Rs 350) is 20km east of Kandy. Surrounded on three sides by the Victoria Reservoir and with the Knuckles Range as a backdrop, it's worth coming for lunch at the clubhouse and to savour the views. Claimed to be the best golf course in the sub-continent, it's a fairly challenging 18 holes.

MEDITATION
Visitors can learn or practise meditation and study Buddhism at several places in the Kandy area. Ask at the **Buddhist Publication Society** (p158) for details about courses. Many centres offer free courses, but a donation is appropriate and highly appreciated. See p173 for more information on nearby centres.

SWIMMING
A few hotels open their pools to nonguests. Most charge around Rs 300 per person.

South of Kandy lake, **Hotel Suisse** (30 Sangaraja Mawatha) has a pretty pool and garden, and the central **Queens Hotel** (Dalada Vidiya) conceals a quiet pool behind its stately facade.

In the hills, try the friendly **Hotel Topaz** (Anniewatte). A three-wheeler from town costs Rs 200.

TREKKING
Based at Expeditor guest house (p165), Sumone Bandara and Ravi Kandy at **Sri Lanka Trekking** (602 996 070; www.srilankatrekking.com) can arrange trekking around Kandy and camping and trekking expeditions to the rugged Knuckles Range (p175). Sumone and Ravi can also arrange mountain biking and rafting trips in other parts of the Hill Country.

WALKING
There are many walks around Kandy, including the **Royal Palace Park** (admission Rs 100; 8.30am-4.30pm), constructed by Sri Wickrama Rajasinha and overlooking the lake. Further up on Rajapihilla Mawatha are even better views over the lake, the town and the surrounding hills. For longer walks, there are paths branching out from Rajapihilla Mawatha. Ask at your guest house.

Sleeping

Kandy has many good guest houses, but a recent lack of tourists has seen a few less-salubrious places beginning to offer rooms by the hour to locals. At the time of writing, the following were all above board. Kandy's more comfortable hotels often occupy spectacular hilltop locations, and there's an increasing range of smaller, boutique-style accommodation within around 45 minutes' drive from Kandy (see p174). These places enjoy quiet locations and make a good base for day trips. You will need your own transport, though.

At the time of the Kandy Esala Perahera, room prices can treble or quadruple, and usually book out in advance. Booking far ahead may secure you a better deal.

The highest concentration of accommodation is along or just off Anagarika Dharmapala Mawatha; buses 654, 655 and 698 (or just ask for 'Sanghamitta Mawatha' at the clock tower bus stop) will get you there.

BUDGET

Burmese Rest (DS Senanayake Vidiya; s/d Rs 270/540) This former pilgrims' guest house, still the cheapest place to stay in Kandy, has six basic rooms downstairs with shared bathrooms – no running showers, just small plastic buckets. Upstairs are four larger rooms with shared toilet and shower facilities. The monks are friendly, and the courtyard is a slowly crumbling haven from busy central Kandy.

Pink House (☎ 077 764 8049; 15 Saranankara Rd; r with/without bathroom Rs 770/550) The Pink House is a throwback to the old days of overland travel. Tony Wheeler actually stayed here when he was researching the first Lonely Planet *Sri Lanka* guide. Almost thirty years on, you're still guaranteed an authentic family welcome – kids, dogs, everything – at this rambling old villa with simple rooms around a hidden courtyard.

Olde Empire Hotel (☎ 077 632 1867; www.oldeempirehotel.com; 21 Temple St; r Rs 530-1530) Just a short stroll from the Temple of the Sacred Tooth Relic, the Olde Empire has hushed colonial hallways leading to basic rooms, some with attached bathroom. There's a balcony overlooking the lake, and a cheap and popular restaurant downstairs. It attracts a few misguided Sri Lankan males though, and we've gotten occasional feedback of women travellers receiving unwanted attention.

Mrs Clement Dissanayake (☎ 222 5468; 18 First Lane; r Rs 800) This simple guest house elicited this response from a Lonely Planet traveller: 'In some ways I don't want this guest house in your book as I love having it all to myself'. That's what a friendly welcome and good food in a family home can inspire. First Lane runs off Dharmaraja Rd at the western end of the lake.

Lake Bungalow (☎ 222 2075; shiyan_d@ispkandyan.lk; 22/2B Sangaraja Mawatha; r Rs 880-1650) The decor is a throwback to the 1970s, with frilly touches like your Nana's house and a real homestay feel. With a full kitchen, this is a good option for self-caterers. You're perched above a pre-school, so expect the occasional chorus of 'The wheels on the bus go round and round...'

Lakshmi Guest House (☎ 222 2154; www.lakshmipg2.lkguide.com; 57/1/1 Saranankara Rd; r Rs 900-1980; ▢) One of the cluster of good guest houses up Saranankara Rd, Lakshmi is a slightly cheaper option from the owners of Palm Garden. That means you're guaranteed good food, very friendly service and a choice of 11 clean, if spartan rooms, some with shared bathroom.

Nature Walk Resort (☎ 077 771 7482; http://naturewalkhr.com; 9 Sanghamitta Mawatha; r with air-con Rs 2200, r with fan Rs 1100-1650; ⊠) Terracotta tiles and French doors lead to balconies with excellent forest views. The rooms are spacious and airy, and you can look forward to troops of monkeys in the morning and squadrons of bats at dusk.

Highest View (☎ 223 3778; www.highestview.com; 129/3 Saranankara Rd; r Rs 1300-2000) It's not quite the 'highest view' – that honour probably goes to the McLeod Inn – but the views are pretty good. Pastel-coloured rooms, quiet shared areas, and a spacious restaurant and bar add up to a good choice on winding Saranankara Rd.

Green Woods (☎ 223 2970; greenwoodkusum@sltnet.lk; 34A Sanghamitta Mawatha; r Rs 1320) Spend a few hours on the balcony of this welcoming spot, and you'll probably spy at least a few of the 45-plus bird species detailed in the guest book. Surrounded by gardens and forest, Green Woods is a relaxing escape from Kandy's bustle. Chico the dog will probably wake you up early to tick off a few more feathered species.

Forest Glen (☎ 222 2239; forestglensl@yahoo.com; 150/6 Lady Gordon's Dr, Sri Dalada Thapowana Mawatha; r Rs 1320-1650) Simple, very quiet rooms feature at this wonderfully secluded family guest house on a winding road on the edge of

Udawattakelle Sanctuary. It's popular with bird-watching types, and Kandy's bright lights are just a 10-minute walk away.

McLeod Inn (☎ 222 2832; mcleod@sltnet.lk; 65A Rajapihilla Mawatha; r with/without view Rs 1320/1650) This spot could easily charge loads more for the stupendous lake views. Instead they focus on a relaxed family atmosphere, spotless rooms and perhaps Kandy's best balcony for the essential end-of-the-day combination: a good book and a cold drink.

MIDRANGE

Expeditor (☎ 223 8316; www.expeditorkandy.com; 41 Saranankara Rd; r Rs 1540-1815) Lots of potted plants, balconies with views and the opportunity to share the living areas with the guest-house owners give Expeditor a cosy bed-and-breakfast feel. It's a good contact for trekking (p163).

Kandy Cottage (☎ 220 4742; www.kandycottage .com; 160 Lady Gordon Dr, Sri Dalada Thapowana Mawatha; r Rs 1540-2640; 🛜 🖳) Tucked away in a forested valley, the coolly whitewashed Kandy Cottage has three rooms with chunky wooden furniture, polished concrete floors and a bohemian, artists' vibe. And central Kandy is just a 10-minute stroll away.

Freedom Lodge (☎ 077 938 3171; freedomomega@ yahoo.com; 30 Saranankara Rd; r Rs 1650-2200; 🖳) Owned by a friendly family and surrounded by towering palm trees, Freedom Lodge has been one of Kandy's best guest houses for many years. That's what seven spotless rooms, excellent food and an authentic family atmosphere can achieve. The bathrooms are what you'd expect from somewhere much flasher. The owner offers Sri Lankan tours for US$60 per day.

Palm Garden Guest House (☎ 223 3903; www .palmgardenkandy.com; 8 Bogodawatte Rd, Suduhumpola; r Rs 1650-3025; 🛜 🖳) There are no lake views at this modern guest house up the road from the train station, but the rooms are spacious and spotless and the rooftop restaurant-bar is staffed by some of the nicest folk in town. Satellite TV will keep you in touch, and when you're ready to go exploring, rental cars and motorcycles, or cars with drivers, are on tap. Just be ready for the occasional train going past across the road. Palm Garden is a Rs 100 three-wheeler ride from the centre of town.

Sharon Inn (☎ 222 2416; www.hotelsharoninn .com; 59 Saranankara Rd; r Rs 1650-3300; 🛜) One of Kandy's longest established guest houses is still one of the best. Excellent views, art deco

styling, and nine scrupulously clean rooms decorated with Sri Lankan arts and crafts add up to a relaxing place to stay. The Sri Lankan-German owners can arrange cars and drivers, and the nightly buffet dinner at 7.30pm (Rs 825) is a tasty shortcut to understanding Sri Lankan Cuisine 101. Dinner is open to outside guests, so phone to make a booking.

Lake Mount Tourist Inn (☎ 223 3204; hirokow@ sltnet.lk; 195A Rajapihilla Mawatha; r with bathroom Rs 2500-3500, r without bathroom Rs 2000; 🔀) Down a quiet lane and with lake views, this guest house is run by a Sri Lankan-Japanese husband-and-wife team. Bring your diary up to date in the spacious lounge area before retiring to the spotless rooms. Air-con will set you back another Rs 1000.

Comfort Lodge (☎ 077 731 6626; www.hotel-comfort-kandy.com; 197 Rajapihilla Mawatha; r Rs 2200; 🖳) Whitewashed walls give this multilevelled six-room a vaguely Mediterranean ambience. The downstairs garden is spacious, and rooms have balconies.

Royal Tourist Lodge (☎ 077-349 9742; royalxx@slt .lk; 201 Rajapihilla Mawatha; r Rs 2200; 🖳) Cane furniture and garden patios combine to lift the three rooms at this comfortable spot into the very comfortable category. The owner's very friendly and it feels more like a welcoming bed and breakfast than a guest house.

Castle Hill Guest House (☎ 222 4376; ayoni@ sltnet.lk; 22 Rajapihilla Mawatha; r Rs 3300) Beautiful gardens, lake views and authentic 1930s architecture and decor feature at this four-bedroom villa. The rooms are almost overly spacious, and there's a lovely shared lounge of equally grand dimensions.

Hotel Casamara (☎ 222 4688; 12 Kotugodelle Vidiya; s/d/tr Rs 4500/4750/5000; 🔀 🖳) 'Luxury in the City' proclaims the brochure. That's stretching it a bit, but downtown Kandy's most business-oriented digs has comfy rooms with satellite TV, air-con and minibars. Upstairs, the rooftop 'Stag's Head' bar has Kandy's best views not involving a lake. Reception definitely brings an open mind to negotiation.

Serene Garden Hotel (☎ 222 7915; www.hotelserenegarden.com; 197 Rajapihilla Mawatha; s/d incl breakfast US$42/54; 🔀 🖳 🌊) This new hilltop place may look like an overdesigned apartment building, but the spacious rooms still have that crisp and clean 'just been built' ambience. This is the tropics though, so we'll see how long that lasts.

THE HILL COUNTRY

Queens Hotel (☎ 223 3026; www.queenshotel.lk; Dalada Vidiya; s/d/tr US$40/45/50; 🟦 🟦) Ambience and location are the key reasons for checking in here. While other Asian hotel landmarks like Hanoi's Metropole or Galle's New Oriental have been gussied up, the Queens Hotel hangs in there with an array of old-school rooms with charming floral decor, shiny polished floorboards, and a lobby that's big enough for a one-day cricket match. Travellers have reported that hot water's sometimes off the agenda, but this is still *the* place to be during the Kandy Esala Perahera. It's only a short walk from the Temple of the Sacred Tooth Relic and Royal Palace compound. Next door is the cosy Pub Royale.

Hotel Topaz (☎ 223 2326; topaz@eureka.lk; Anniewatte; r US$77; 🟦 🟦 🟦) On top of a hill overlooking the town, Topaz has 75 rooms, most with air-con. The decor is a little tired, but a friendly welcome, good views from the bar and a swimming pool tick the 'Worth Considering' box. The pool is open for nonguests (Rs 300), and a three-wheeler to/from town is Rs 200 each way.

TOP END

Chaaya Citadel (☎ 223 4365/6; www.chaayahotels.com; 124 Srimath Kuda Ratwatte Mawatha; s/d/tr US$88/100/125; 🟦 🟦) Designer chic rooms in chocolate tones and grey slate incorporate a riverside location with a breezy lobby and poolside bar at one of Kandy's nicest package-tour resorts. Come for lunch and use the pool (admission free with lunch) even if you're not staying here. It's 5km west of Kandy; a taxi costs around Rs 600.

Stonehouse Lodge (☎ 223 2769; www.stonehouse lodge.lk; 42 Nittawela Rd; r incl breakfast US$95-115) With a breezy, colonial style, lots of period furniture, and pristine black-and-white art deco bathrooms, the Stonehouse Lodge has the refined ambience of a members-only private club. It's just a short hop to central Kandy, but the spacious lawn and surrounding trees make it very private.

Villa Rosa (☎ 221 5556; www.villarosa-kandy.com; Asigiriya; s/d/tr/f US$100/140/230/250; 🟦 🟦) Dotted with antiques, and with stunning views over a secluded arc of the Mahaweli River, Villa Rosa is the kind of place you'd build if you moved to Sri Lanka. Spacious wooden-floored rooms in cool, neutral tones share the limelight with relaxing lounges and a what-do-I-read-next reading room. A separate pavilion houses yoga and meditation centres. Guests can use the pool at the nearby Chaaya Citadel (above).

Helga's Folly (☎ 223 4571; www.helgasfolly.com; 32 Frederick E de Silva Mawatha; r US$165-240, ste US$380; 🟦 🟦) Quick! Try and find a spare space on the walls. Interesting reminders of lives of the extremely well-lived decorate the interior of this quirky boutique hotel. That includes stags' heads, out-of-control candles and Gaudíesque one-off pieces of art. It's a deeply eccentric place that resonates with history; a roll call of celebs stayed here post WWII. Now the colourful Helga De Silva presides over the hotel, and each room is imbued with her individual touch. Don't expect a five-star stay, but look forward to an atmosphere that's unique and memorable. The restaurant is open to non-guests, but you'll need to book ahead.

Eating

Bombay Sweet City (21 Peradeniya Rd; sweets Rs 25-80) Fulfil your longing for sweet Indian snacks – especially if you've just flown in from India – at this hole-in-the-wall, eat-on-the-go kind of place. The cashew *barfi* (fudge-like sweet) is very moreish, and there's an orchard full of fresh fruit juices to battle Kandy's occasional three-wheeler haze.

our pick **Kandy Muslim Hotel** (Dalada Vidiya; mains Rs 25-100) No, it's not a hotel, but it is an always bustling eatery that offers Kandy's best samosas, authentically spiced curries and heaving plates of frisbee-sized, but gossamer-light, naan. It's a largely male domain, but women travellers will be treated with respect and offered a seat in the family section out the back. Don't miss the frantic theatre of the *kotthu rotti* (doughy pancake chopped and fried with meat and vegetables) guy out the front.

Bake House (☎ 223 4868; 36 Dalada Vidiya; mains Rs 80-150) Downstairs from The Pub (opposite), Bake House is versatility plus, with tasty baked goodies out the front and a more formal dining room concealed under the building's whitewashed colonial arches. At the time of writing, a makeover was being planned to up the 'colonial' spin of the architecture. Pop in just after 3pm, when the second bake of the day comes out and the short eats are still warm.

Olde Empire Hotel (☎ 222 4284; 21 Temple St; mains Rs 100-150) The modest dining hall at the Olde Empire (p164) is full of character and still serves delicious rice and curry and lunch packets. The flowers on the tables are delivered fresh every day apparently – always a good sign.

Paiva's Restaurant (37 Yatinuwara Vidiya; mains Rs 300-400) The Rs 175 lunchtime rice and curry is a handy intro to Sri Lankan cuisine, with three different rices and a multiplate array of curried accompaniments. In the evening choose between Chinese or North Indian à la carte menus. Both are good, and the friendly waiters will respect your request for 'spicy please?' Just as well the beer is cold, eh?

History Restaurant (☎ 220 2109; 27A Anagarika Dharmapala Mawatha; mains Rs 300-500; ☖ noon-11pm) With dishes from India, Italy, Thailand and Sri Lanka, this place could almost be called 'Geography'. The food's OK and there's a good selection of booze, but the real reason to go are the interesting B&W pics of old Kandy. And no, you're not required to take notes during the Kandyan history PowerPoint presentation that runs silently in the background. Monkeys look on from outside and already know all the answers.

Flower Song Chinese Restaurant (☎ 222 3628; 137 Kotugodella Vidiya; mains Rs 455-770; ☖ 11am-10.30pm Tue-Sun) This local family favourite is so popular that there was a security guard outside we when stopped by. That's what tasty and good-value Chinese standards can do for an eatery. And yes, you can get a beer, but only from 11am to 2pm and 5pm to 10pm.

Cargills Food City (Dalada Vidiya) For groceries and prepackaged meals. There's also a window for buying takeaway beer around the back.

Many people eat in their guest houses, which offer some of Kandy's tastiest food. Particularly good are **Sharon Inn** (☎ 222 2416; 59 Saranankara Rd; buffets Rs 660), whose buffet is at 7.30pm, and **Palm Garden Guest House** (☎ 223 3903; 8 Bogodawatte Rd, Suduhumpola; buffets Rs 825). Nonguests are welcome, but you need to book by mid-afternoon.

Drinking

In this sacred city, the legislation for pubs, bars and discos is very strict. The typical Kandyan goes to bed early, but there are a few places for an end-of-day gin and tonic. All the top hotels also have decent bars.

The Pub (☎ 232 4868; 36 Dalada Vidiya; ☖ 5pm-midnight) Does what it says on the tin, with Carlsberg and Lion Lager on tap, a few cocktails and the occasional Saturday night jazz gig. The Western food (think chips, pasta, club sandwiches) is uninspired and overpriced, but the twilight view from the balcony on to Kandy's noisy rush hour is an enlivening end to any day.

Pub Royale (Dalada Vidiya; ☖ 4pm-midnight) Beside Queens Hotel, this gloomy, dusty approximation of an English pub is a quiet escape from the diesel-infused intersection outside. The service is occasionally glacially slow, but the Three Coins beer is definitely Kandy's coldest; it froze in our glass when we last visited.

PUB (27A Anagarika Dharmapala Mawatha; ☖ 5pm-midnight) Look for the giant red neon sign above the Bamboo Garden Chinese restaurant and you've found this place with shared wooden tables and great lake views.

Stag's Head (☎ 222 4688; 12 Kotugodelle Vidiya; ☖ 5pm-midnight) On the top floor on the Hotel Casamara, this terrace bar offers views of Kandy's exuberant traffic coursing around the throngs below. It's more suitable for male travellers.

Liquid for Life (37 Yatinuwara Vidiya; juices 50-85; ☖ 7am-5pm) This brightly coloured spot for fresh fruit juice, with pineapple, mint, mango and more, is popular with kids on their way home from school. At least they're not getting hyper on fizzy drinks.

Entertainment
NIGHTCLUBS
Kandy's two nightclubs are in hotels. At both, entry for women is free, for mixed couples Rs 500, and there's usually no entry allowed for unaccompanied men from outside the hotel. Long trousers, covered shoes and a collared shirt are mandatory for the lads.

Blackout (☎ 447 9054; Swiss Residence Hotel, 23 Bahirawakanda) Located in the Swiss Residence Hotel, this is the only dance club within city limits. Nights of opening were changing at the time of writing, so call first. A three-wheeler should be around Rs 250 one way.

Le Garage (Map p170; ☎ 223 3521/2; Amaya Hills, Heerassagala; ☖ 9pm-3am Sat). Thirty minutes' drive southwest of town by three-wheeler (Rs 500), the Amaya Hills disco is open Saturday nights only.

KANDYAN DANCERS & DRUMMERS
See Kandyan dancers work through their athletic routines at three locales around Kandy.

Kandy Lake Club (Sanghamitta Mawatha; admission Rs 500) Located 300m up Sanghamitta Mawatha, this club starts its show at 7pm. The front seats are usually reserved for groups, so for good seats arrive at least 20 minutes early.

THE HILL COUNTRY

Kandyan Art Association & Cultural Centre
(Sangharaja Mawatha; admission Rs 500) There are shows
here at 5.30pm. The auditorium makes it easier to take photographs than at Kandy Lake
Club. It's on the northern lake shore. Arrive
early for a good look around the attached craft
showroom and workshops.

Mahanuwara YMBA (☎ 223 3444; 5 Rajapihilla
Mawatha; admission Rs 300) Southwest of the lake, the
YMBA guest house hosts shows at 5.30pm.

You can also hear Kandyan drummers
every day at the Temple of the Sacred Tooth
Relic (p159) and the other temples surrounding it – their drumming signals the start and
finish of the daily *puja*.

SPORT

The modest **Asgiriya Stadium**, north of the
town centre, hosts crowds of up to 10,000
cheering fans at international one-day
and test matches. The compact stadium
is reckoned to be one of the most attractive used for international cricket. Ticket
prices depend on the popularity of the two
teams. India versus Sri Lanka matches are
the most valued; seats in the grandstand
can cost up to Rs 3000, while standing
room in the public areas will cost Rs 200.
Tickets are also sold on the day, or you
can book grandstand seats up to a month
in advance through the **Sri Lanka Cricket office** (☎ 223 8533) at the stadium. The future
of Asgiriya Stadium is in doubt, however, and when India, Bangladesh and Sri
Lanka hold the 2011 Cricket World Cup,
games in Kandy will probably be played at
nearby Pallekele.

Rugby is played between May and
September at the Nittawella rugby grounds.

Shopping

The **Kandyan Art Association & Cultural Centre**
(Sangharaja Mawatha) has a good selection of
local lacquerwork, brassware and other craft
items in a colonial-era showroom covered in
a patina of age (see above). There are some
craftspeople working on the spot.

There's a government-run Laksala arts and
crafts shop to the west of the lake that has
lower prices than those of the Art Association
& Cultural Centre, but it has nothing on the
big Laksala in Colombo.

Central Kandy has shops selling antique
jewellery and silver belts, and you can buy
crafts in the colourful **main market** (Station Rd).

Kandy has a number of batik manufacturers. Check out the original designs at **Upali
Jayakody** (Peradeniya Rd) and **Fresco Batiks** (Peradeniya
Rd). You'll find antiques showrooms nearby,
including **Dharshana Lanka Arts** (923 Peradeniya Rd).

Getting There & Away

BUS

Kandy has one main bus station (the manic
Goods Shed) and a series of bus stops near
the clock tower. The Goods Shed bus station
has long-distance buses, while local buses,
such as those to Peradeniya, Ampitiya, Matale
and Kegalle, leave from near the clock tower.
However, some private intercity express buses
(to the airport, Negombo and Colombo, for
example) leave from Station Rd between the
clock tower and the train station. If you're
still confused, ask someone to point you the
right way.

Colombo

CTB buses run from the Goods Shed bus station every half-hour till 8.30pm (Rs 124, 3½
hours). There are also ordinary private buses
(Rs 140, three hours) and air-con intercity
express buses (Rs 250, 2½ to three hours).
Both services start at 5.15am and leave when
full throughout the day (on average every 45
minutes). The express and ordinary buses
leave from stand No 1.

International Airport & Negombo

Private intercity express buses to Bandaranaike
International Airport and Negombo leave from
the Station Rd bus stop. CTB buses leave from
the Goods Shed bus station. The first intercity
bus departs at about 6.30am and the last at
about 5.30pm. They tend to leave when full,
every 20 to 30 minutes. The fare for the three-
to 3½-hour journey is Rs 112 for the CTB bus
and Rs 225 for the air-con express bus.

Nuwara Eliya & Hatton

Private air-con buses (Rs 170) go to Nuwara
Eliya, and some go on to Hatton (or you can
change in Nuwara Eliya for Hatton). They
leave from the Goods Shed bus station every
half-hour between 5am and 5pm. Change at
Nuwara Eliya for Haputale and Ella.

Ratnapura

Ordinary buses (Rs 110) to Ratnapura leave
from the Goods Shed bus station every 45
minutes, from 5.30pm to 3.45am.

Anuradhapura

Buses leave from the Goods Shed bus station. Air-con intercity express buses (Rs 260) start at 4.30am and depart every half-hour until 6.30pm. The trip takes three hours. Ordinary buses (Rs 75) take about 30 minutes longer. You can also catch an air-con Anuradhapura-bound bus to Dambulla, but you must pay the full amount regardless of where you get down. The trip to Dambulla on an ordinary private bus costs Rs 150.

Polonnaruwa

Ordinary buses (Rs 150) leave the Goods Shed bus station roughly every 20 minutes from 4.30am until 6pm. The journey takes three hours, with a change of bus in Dambulla (included in the ticket price). Air-con buses (Rs 250) leave daily at 9.30am, 11.30am and 1pm.

Sigiriya

There's a CTB bus to Sigiriya from the Goods Shed bus station at 10.30am, which returns at 5.30pm (Rs 75). There are a couple of ordinary private buses per day for Rs 80. You can also take one of the more frequent Polonnaruwa-bound buses, then get off at the Sigiriya junction and take another bus the final 9km to Sigiriya.

TAXI

Many long-distance taxi drivers hang around the Temple of the Sacred Tooth Relic. Your guest house or hotel can organise taxi tours, but you may be able to get a cheaper deal if you organise it through these guys. Cars can generally be hired, with a driver and petrol, for approximately Rs 5500 per day. For a whole van, expect to pay around Rs 6500 per day.

Some guest houses advertise day trips to all three Cultural Triangle destinations (Sigiriya, Anuradhapura and Polonnaruwa), but this is an exhausting itinerary for both driver and passengers, and one that encourages manic driving. An overnight stay in Anuradhapura, Sigiriya or Polonnaruwa is a saner and safer option.

A taxi to Bandaranaike International Airport costs about Rs 4600, and to Colombo about Rs 5500.

TRAIN

For details of train services from Kandy, see the boxed table, below. Tickets can be bought and reserved up to 10 days in advance at Kandy's train station from counter 1 (open 5.30am to 5.30pm).

Seats are very popular in the 1st-class observation saloon on the Badulla-bound train, which originates in Colombo and after Kandy stops in Hatton (near Adam's Peak), Nanu Oya, Haputale and Ella. If you are unable to reserve a seat at the ticket window, enquire with the stationmaster, who can sometimes release further seating for tourists.

MAIN TRAINS FROM KANDY

Destination	Departure time	3rd-class fares (Rs)	2nd-class fares (Rs)	1st-class fares (Rs)	Duration (hr)
Badulla (Podi Menike)	8.20am, 10.45am	160	300	600	7½
Bandarawela (Podi Menike)	8.20am, 10.45am	135	250	475	6
Colombo (Intercity Express)	6.15am, 3pm, 6.33pm	170	250	400	2½
Colombo via Rambukkana	5am, 6.35am, 10.25am, 3pm, 4pm	115	210	—	3
Ella (Podi Menike)	8.20am, 11.45am	145	270	540	6½
Haputale (Podi Menike)	8.20am, 10.45am	125	210	550	5½
Hatton (Podi Menike)	8.24am, 11.10am	70	130	430	2½
Matale	5.05am, 7.04am, 10.20am, 2pm, 5.10pm, 6.40pm	30	—	—	1½
Matara via Bentota & Galle	5am	225	410	—	7
Nanu Oya (Intercity Express for Nuwara Eliya)	10.54am	—	380	650	
Nanu Oya (for Nuwara Eliya; Podi Menike)	8.40am, 10.45am	95	180	510	4

AROUND KANDY

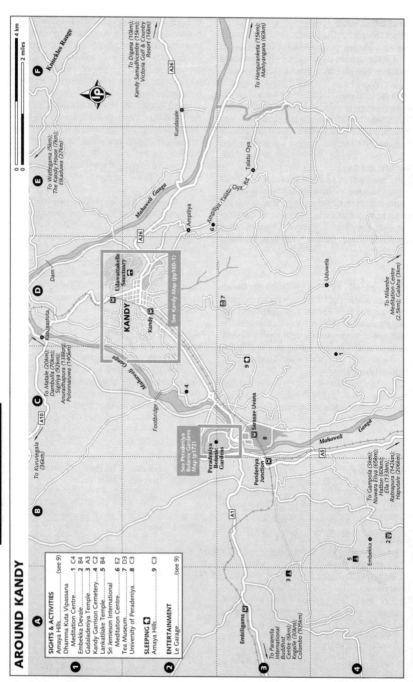

SIGHTS & ACTIVITIES
Amaya Hills...................................(see 9)
Dhamma Kuta Vipassana
  Meditation Centre......................**1** C4
Embekka Devale.............................**2** B4
Gadaladeniya Temple....................**3** A3
Kandy Garrison Cemetery.............**4** C2
Lankatilake Temple.......................**5** B4
Sri Jernieson International
  Meditation Centre......................**6** E2
Tea Museum..................................**7** D3
University of Peradeniya...............**8** C3

SLEEPING 🛏
Amaya Hills..................................**9** C3

ENTERTAINMENT 🎭
Le Garage....................................(see 9)

Getting Around

BUS
Buses to outlying parts of Kandy and nearby towns such as Peradeniya, Ampitiya, Matale and Kegalle leave from near the clock tower.

CAR & MOTORCYCLE
Hire cars and motorcycles for self-drive from **Malik Tours** (☎ 220 3513; www.palmgardenkandy.com; Palm Garden Guest House, 8 Bogodawatte Rd, Suduhumpola). Sedans are Rs 3300 per day with unlimited kilometres. A 250cc motorcycle costs Rs 2200 per day, discounted to Rs 2000 per day for five days or more. The price includes a helmet and insurance – but double-check with the company. Malik speaks French and can arrange cars with drivers for around Rs 6000 per day. Ask if Rajitha is available. Most other guest houses can arrange cars and drivers for a similar cost.

TAXI
With metered air-con taxis, **Radio Cabs** (☎ 223 3322) is a comfortable alternative to three-wheelers. You may have to wait some time for your cab, especially if it's raining and demand is heavy. With taxis (vans) that are not metered, settle on a price before you start your journey.

THREE-WHEELER
The standard cost for a three-wheeler from the train station to the southeast end of the lake is Rs 100 to 150. Drivers will ask foreign tourists for much more, but if you stick to your guns you'll get something approximating the local price.

AROUND KANDY
☎ 081
There are a few things worth seeing around Kandy that can be done as a morning or afternoon trip.

Sights & Activities

PERADENIYA BOTANIC GARDENS
The **gardens** (adult/child Rs 600/300; ☯ 7.30am-4.30pm) are 6km from Kandy. Before the British arrived these were royal pleasure gardens. Today they're the largest botanic gardens in Sri Lanka, covering 60 hectares and bounded on three sides by a loop of the Mahaweli Ganga.

There's a fine collection of orchids and a stately avenue of royal palms that was planted in 1950. A major attraction is the giant Javan fig tree on the great lawn. Covering 2500 sq

metres, it's like a giant, living geodesic dome as imagined by Escher or Hundertwasser. The graceful boughs are a preferred assignation for burgeoning Kandyan lovers. A few lingering crows add a slightly sinister touch.

Cannonball trees and cabbage palms punctuate a couple of the elegant avenues, and the avenue of double coconut palms (coco de mer) has massive fruit up to 20kg.

In the spice garden near the entrance, see nutmeg, cinnamon and cloves without a salesperson looking over your shoulder. Nearby, the snake creeper is also worth a look. Seek out the giant bamboo and Assam rubber trees, and also take a closer look at the memorial trees, an interesting grab bag of trees planted by the famous and slightly-less-famous. Consider the trees' different growth rates with the historical legacy of those who planted them.

An overpriced cafeteria (mains Rs 450 to 1000), about 500m north of the entrance, serves Western and Sri Lankan food on a roofed veranda. A better option is to stock up on picnic items. Just keep a close eye on the insistent posse of local dogs.

Bus 654 (Rs 8) from Kandy's clock tower bus stop goes to the gardens. A three-wheeler from Kandy is around Rs 700 return; a van is around Rs 1500. Many taxi drivers incorporate a visit to the gardens with the Pinnewala Elephant Orphanage or the Kandy temple loop.

KANDY GARRISON CEMETERY
This beautifully kept garden **cemetery** (Deveni Rajasinghe; ☯ 10am-noon & 1-6pm) was founded in 1817 for the internment of British-era colonists and is managed by the Commonwealth War Graves Commission. Although there are many 19th-century graves, most date from WWII. The most famous is that of Sir John D'Oyly, a colonial official who planned the bloodless British capture of Kandy in 1815 and then succumbed to cholera in 1824. This cemetery is 2km southwest of Kandy. Donations are accepted.

A TEMPLE LOOP FROM KANDY
Visiting temples around Kandy provides an insight into Sri Lankan culture and rural life. This loop takes in three 14th-century Hindu-Buddhist temples via the botanic gardens. There's a lot of walking involved, so you could narrow down your visit to one or two of the temples or take a three-wheeler trip to all three; expect to pay around Rs 3000 from Kandy. If

THE HILL COUNTRY

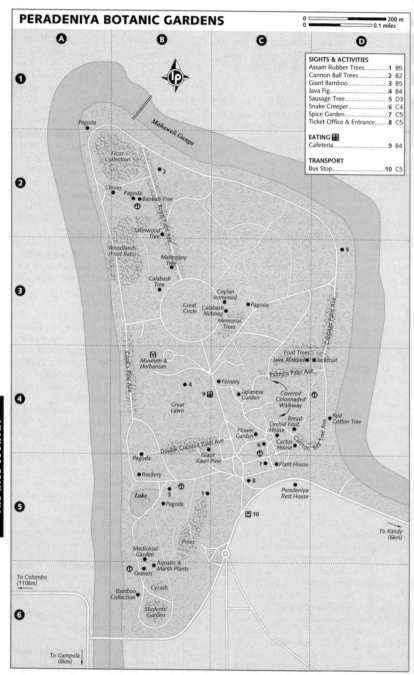

PERADENIYA BOTANIC GARDENS

0 ————————— 200 m
0 ————————— 0.1 miles

SIGHTS & ACTIVITIES
Assam Rubber Trees...........1	B5
Cannon Ball Trees.............2	B2
Giant Bamboo................3	B5
Java Fig....................4	B4
Sausage Tree................5	D3
Snake Creeper...............6	C4
Spice Garden................7	C5
Ticket Office & Entrance......8	C5

EATING 🍴
Cafeteria....................9	B4

TRANSPORT
Bus Stop...................10	C5

Mahaweli Ganga

Pagoda

Ficus Collection

2

Cloves
Pagoda
Baobab Tree

Satinwood Tree

Woodlands (Fruit Bats)

Mahogany Tree

Calabash Tree

Ceylon Ironwood

Great Circle

Calabash Nutmeg

Pagoda

Memorial Trees

Fruit Trees
Java Almond
Jackfruit

Palmyra Palm Ave

Museum & Herbarium

4

Fernery

9

Japanese Garden

Great Lawn

Covered Colonnaded Walkway

Red Cotton Tree

Bread Fruit

Orchid House

Cactus House

Flower Garden

6

Double Coconut Palm Ave

Pagoda

Giant Kauri Pine

7

Plant House

Rockery

8

Peradeniya Rest House

Lake

3

1

Pagoda

10

To Kandy (6km)

Medicinal Garden

Pines

Aquatic & Marsh Plants

Grasses

To Colombo (110km)

Cycads

Bamboo Collection

Students' Garden

To Gampola (8km)

THE HILL COUNTRY

PAINTING THE BUDDHA'S EYES

In making a Buddha image, craftspeople leave the *netra pinkama* (eye ritual) until last, and then only paint them in at an auspicious moment, painstakingly charted out by astrologers.

The act of creating the eyes consecrates the Buddha statue. For the *netra pinkama*, the painter, from the Sittaru subcaste of temple craftspeople and artists, is locked into the shrine with an assistant. Rather than looking directly at the face of the image, the painter adds the eyes using a mirror. When the eyes are finished, the painter is blindfolded and led outside to a place where his first gaze can be upon something that can be symbolically destroyed, such as a pool of water, which can be hit with a stick. There is quite a fear of dire consequences if there's a slip-up in the *netra pinkama*. In the 16th century Robert Knox explained the ritual this way: 'Before the eyes are made, it is not accounted a God, but a lump of ordinary metal...the eyes being formed, it is thenceforward a God.'

---

you're combining walking and public transport, you'll need to ask the way occasionally as the loop is not signposted.

First is the **Embekka Devale** (admission Rs 100). Catch the frequent bus 643 (to Vatadeniya via Embekka) from near the Kandy clock tower. The village of Embekka is about 7km beyond the botanic gardens (about an hour from Kandy). From the village it's a pleasant rural stroll of about 1km to the 14th-century temple. The finely carved wooden pillars are reputed to come from a royal audience hall in Kandy. Carvings include swans, eagles, wrestling men and dancing women. A local *perahera* is held every September.

From here to the **Lankatilake Temple** (admission Rs 100) is a 3km stroll beside rice paddies; you'll see the blue temple on the left. From Kandy you can go directly to the Lankatilake Temple on bus 666 or take a Kiribathkumbara or Pilimatalawa bus from the same stop as the Embekka buses. This Buddhist and Hindu temple features a Buddha image, Kandy-period paintings, rock-face inscriptions and stone elephant figures. A caretaker will unlock the shrine if it's not already open. A *perahera* takes place in August.

It's a further 3km walk to the **Gadaladeniya Temple** (admission Rs 100), or you can catch a bus from Kandy; bus 644, among others, will take you there. Built on a rocky outcrop and covered with small pools, the temple is reached by a series of steps cut into the rock. This Buddhist temple with a Hindu annexe is a similar age to the Lankatilake Temple and the Embekka Devale.

The main Colombo–Kandy road is less than 2km from Gadaladeniya Temple – you reach the road close to the 105km post. It's a pleasant stroll, and from the main road almost any bus will take you to the Peradeniya Botanic Gardens or on to Kandy.

MEDITATION

Nilambe Meditation Centre (☎ 077 781 1653; www.nilambe.org), close to Nilambe Bungalow Junction about 13km south of Kandy, can be reached by bus 633 (catch a Delthota bus via Galaha and get off at Office Junction); the trip takes about an hour. There are daily meditation classes and basic accommodation for 40 people. Stay for Rs 500 per day (including food). Blankets are supplied but you should bring a sleep sheet. There's no electricity, so bring a torch too. To reach Nilambe from Office Junction, you can walk a steep 3km through tea plantations or take a three-wheeler for Rs 250. A taxi from Kandy costs Rs 1250 one way.

Near Ampitiya, 4km southeast of Kandy, the **Sri Jemieson International Meditation Centre** (☎ 222 5057; Ampitiya Samadhi Mawatha) runs free five- and 10-day courses. Phone to find out when the next course starts. There are eight rooms for male students only; this is a monastery and temple. Women must stay off-campus but are welcome to meditate here during the day from 8am to 4.30pm. Catch a Talatu Oya bus from Kandy's clock tower bus stop. Look for the sign on the right-hand side about 3km along the Ampitiya–Talatu Oya road. It's a 1.2km walk to the centre.

Dhamma Kuta Vipassana Meditation Centre (☎ 238 5774; www.kuta.dhamma.org; Mowbray, Hindagala) offers free 10-day courses following the SN Goenka system of meditation. Booking ahead is mandatory. There's dorm accommodation for 90 students, with separate male and female quarters. Retreat schedules are posted at the Buddhist Publication Society in Kandy. Take a Mahakanda-bound bus from the clock tower bus stop in Kandy and get off at the last stop. It's a steep 2km walk; a three-wheeler costs Rs 250. A taxi from Kandy costs around Rs 800 to the bus stop.

The **Paramita International Buddhist Centre** (☎ 257 0732; www.paramitaibc.org), at the top of the Bolana Pass, 1km past Kadugannawa on the Colombo road, is another meditation centre. It runs one-week courses, with clean accommodation for men and women, lush gardens and a library.

Sleeping

If you want quiet days spent wandering along shaded tracks, with views of rolling hills, then stay just out of Kandy. Accommodation skews to midrange and top-end properties, but there are some lovely places worth splashing out for.

Kandy Samadhicentre (☎ 447 0925; www.the kandysamadhicentre.com; Kukul Oya Rd, Kandy; r Rs 3300-8800) Part boutique ecolodge and part Ayurvedic centre, this could be the most relaxing place to stay around Kandy. Thirteen pavilions dot a forested hillside, and each room is decorated with Asian textiles and four-poster beds. Simpler 'Mud House' rooms lack hot water but still share the same serene ambience. Food is both organic and vegetarian, and no alcohol is served. Reiki and shiatsu massage is also available. Transport to the lodge – 50 minutes east of Kandy – is Rs 2250 (arrange pick-up when making your booking).

Tulip of Ceylon (Map p156; ☎ 035-492 1951; www .tulipofceylon.com; Ilukgoda. Mawanella; s/d €27/30; ☐ ☑) Just a 20-minute drive from the Pinnewala Elephant Orphanage, the Tulip of Ceylon has 11 poolside rooms with stunning jungle and river views. The friendly local staff are all from the nearby village of Ilukgoda. Kandy is about 90 minutes away.

Amaya Hills (☎ 223 3521; www.amayaresorts.com; Heerassagala; r US$125; ☒ ☐ ☑) Hats off to the architects for making the most of Amaya Hills' perfect location. Perched in the hills, 20 minutes' drive southwest of Kandy, this hotel incorporates a stunning open lobby, a cliff-top swimming pool, and very comfortable rooms with lots of warm wooden tones and a Kandyan design motif. The well-equipped Ayurveda centre and Le Garage disco are both open to nonguests. It's a Rs 500 three-wheeler ride to Kandy, so you're better off having a driver.

The Kandy House (☎ 492 1394; www.thekandy house.com; Amunugama Walauwa; r US$250-380; ☐ ☑)

Almost two centuries ago, this beautiful courtyard villa housed the family of a local Kandyan chief. Now fully restored and decorated with colonial Dutch antiques, it sports eight guest rooms and suites. All rooms are named after local butterflies; the best suites have wonderfully private verandas. A garden infinity pool segues to emerald-green rice paddies. Note that rooms do not have air-conditioning.

EAST OF KANDY

Kandy is an important transport hub. Most travellers go west to Colombo, north to the ancient cities, or south to the rest of the Hill Country. It's also possible to go east to Mahiyangana and Badulla, and to Monaragala en route to Arugam Bay and Gal Oya National Park. Further northeast, Batticaloa can be reached by bus from Kandy.

The Buddha is said to have preached at Mahiyangana; a dagoba marks the spot. There are two roads to Mahiyangana. The A26 north road goes past the Victoria Golf Club and the Victoria Reservoir to Madugoda, before twisting downhill through 18 hairpin bends to the Mahaweli lowlands and the dry-zone plains. It's one of the country's hairiest bus rides. Going up you worry about overheating, and going down it's all about the brakes. Many vehicles didn't make it and now lie in the jungle beneath.

Drivers prefer the road along the southern shores of the Victoria and Randenigala Reservoirs, which is much faster and in better condition. This road closes at dusk, however, because wild elephants from the nature reserve are attracted to headlights. To travel from Kandy to the hills of Uva Province (including towns such as Ella and Haputale), it's quicker to take this road and then the route south to Badulla than to go via Nuwara Eliya.

Mahiyangana
☎ 055

Mahiyangana is a sprawling and sparsely settled town. The only highlight is the **Mahiyangana dagoba** where, according to legend, the Buddha preached on his first visit to Sri Lanka.

Tharuka Inn (☎ 225 7631; 89/1 Padiyathalawa Rd; s/d Rs 750/1150) About 1km from the bus station on the Ampara road, this is a multistorey building with slow country service. The clean, bland rooms (cold water only) will do for a night. A grape arbour and a mango tree struggle to add a bit of colour.

Sorabora Village Inn (☎ 225 7149; mdigital@bellmail.lk; r Rs 1500-3500; ▨) This 15-room hotel, restaurant and bar is a popular local option for wedding receptions on weekends, but during the week it's much quieter. Barcelona football fans will love the red-and-blue decor.

Sorabora Gedara Hotel (☎ 225 8307; www.soraboragedarahotel.com; s/d Rs US$22/28; ▨ ▣) The flashest digs in town come complete with a swimming pool. Treat yourself before another crowded bus journey, and douse today's bus dust in the adjoining bar.

Mahiyangana is a transport hub for the area, and there are regular buses to Badulla (CTB Rs 140), Polonnaruwa (private bus Rs 190), Ampara (CTB and private bus Rs 122), Monaragala (CTB Rs 85) and Kandy (private bus Rs 80, three hours). Travellers from Mahiyangana to Monaragala may need to change buses at Bibile.

Knuckles Range

So named because the range's peaks look like a closed fist, this 1500m-high **massif** (admission Rs 750) is home to pockets of rare montane forest. The area is good for hiking and has been nominated as a Unesco World Heritage Conservation Area.

Hotels in the Knuckles Range can organise guided hiking trips. In Kandy, see Sumone and Ravi at Sri Lanka Trekking (p163). A good source of information on the area is www.knucklesrange.org.

Green View (☎ 077 372 066; www.bluehaventours.com; Karagahinna; s/d Rs 990/1320) This seven-room hillside lodge has spectacular views of a forested mountain valley. It's showing its age a little, but Green View is a good spot for walking and nature tours. Book ahead and they'll pick you up from Kandy.

Rangala House (☎ 081-240 0294; www.rangalahouse.com; 92B Bobebila Rd, Makuldeniya, Teldeniya; s/d US$90/110; ▣) This former tea planter's bungalow ensconced on a steep forested hillside surrounded by spice trees contains three double rooms, each with attached bath, plus a large living and dining room with a fireplace. The big swimming pool is solar-heated, and after dark the 15m-long veranda – complete with barbecue – is an essential end-of-day rendezvous point. For US$270 you can rent the entire villa. Note that credit cards are not accepted.

Hunas Falls Hotel (☎ 081-247 6402; www.jetwing.com; Elkaduwa; s/d from US$109/117, ste from US$163; ▨ ▣ ▣) Perched on the edge of a working tea plantation and spice garden, this luxury hotel still makes room for an idiosyncratic six-hole golf course, a well-stocked fish pond and a tennis court. After an essential twilight massage, look forward to another stunning walk in the surrounding hills the following day.

A taxi from Kandy to Elkaduwa should cost Rs 1500. Alternatively, take a bus to Wattegama (from near the clock tower in Kandy), and then catch another to Elkaduwa.

ADAM'S PEAK (SRI PADA)

elev 2243m

Located in a beautiful area of the southern Hill Country, this lofty peak has sparked the imagination for centuries and been a focus for pilgrimage for over 1000 years. King Parakramabahu and King Nissanka Malla of Polonnaruwa provided *ambalamas* (resting places to shelter weary pilgrims) up the mountain.

It is variously known as Adam's Peak (the place where Adam first set foot on earth after being cast out of heaven), Sri Pada (Sacred Footprint, left by the Buddha as he headed towards paradise), or Samanalakande (Butterfly Mountain, where butterflies go to die). Some believe the huge 'footprint' crowning the peak to be that of St Thomas, the early apostle of India, or even of Lord Shiva.

The pilgrimage season begins on *poya* day in December and runs until **Vesak festival** in May; January and February are most busy. At other times the temple on the summit is unused, and between May and October, the peak is often obscured by clouds. During the pilgrimage season pilgrims and a few tourists make the climb up the countless steps to the top.

Walkers leave from the small settlement of Dalhousie (del-*house*), 33km by road southwest of Hatton, which is situated on the Colombo–Kandy–Nuwara Eliya railway and road. In season the route is illuminated by a sparkling ribbon of lights. Out of season you will need a torch. Many pilgrims prefer to make the longer, more tiring – but equally well-marked and lit – seven-hour climb from Ratnapura via the Carney Estate because of the greater merit thus gained.

As dawn illuminates the holy mountain, the diffuse morning light uncovers the Hill Country rising in the east and the land sloping to the coast to the west. Colombo, 65km away, is easily visible on a clear day.

Adam's Peak saves its breathtaking coup de grâce for just after dawn. The sun casts a perfect shadow of the peak onto the misty clouds down towards the coast. As the sun rises higher this eerie triangular shadow races back towards the peak, eventually disappearing into its base.

Information

There are no banking facilities in Dalhousie. The nearest ATMs are in Hatton. Access the internet at the **Slightly Chilled** (☎ 071 909 8710; www.slightlychilled.tv; per min Rs 3) guest house or **Punsisi Rest** (☎ 071 573 3450; per hr Rs 100).

For information on Adam's Peak visit www.sripada.org.

Activities

You can start the 7km climb from Dalhousie soon after dark – bring a good sleeping bag to keep you warm overnight at the top – or you can wait until about 2am to start. The climb is up steps most of the way (about 5200 of them), and with plenty of rest stops you'll reach the top in 2½ to four hours. A 2.30am start will easily get you there before dawn, which is around 6.30am. Start on a *poya* day, though, and the throng of pilgrims might add hours to your climb. We've heard of some travellers taking up to nine hours on a *poya* day.

From the car park the slope is gradual for the first half-hour, passing under an entrance arch and then by the Japan–Sri Lanka Friendship Dagoba. The pathway then gets steeper until it becomes a continuous flight of stairs. There are tea houses all the way to the top; some open through the night. A few are open out of season. The authorities have banned litter, alcohol, cigarettes, meat and recorded music, so the atmosphere remains reverential.

The summit can be cold, so it's not worth getting there too long before dawn and then sitting around shivering. Definitely bring warm clothes, including something extra for the top, and pack plenty of water. If you're in Dalhousie in the pilgrimage season, stalls at the market sell warm jackets and head-

gear. Otherwise stop in at the market at Nuwara Eliya (p183) for outdoor gear at bargain prices. Some pilgrims wait for the priests to make a morning offering before they descend, but the sun and heat rise quickly, so it pays not to linger.

Many people find the hardest part is coming down. The endless steps can shake the strongest knees, and if your shoes don't fit well, toe-jam also kicks in. Take a hat as the morning sun intensifies quickly. Remember to stretch your legs when you finish, otherwise you'll be walking strangely for a few days.

Between June and November, when the pathway isn't illuminated and there aren't many people around, travellers are urged to do the hike at least in pairs. Expect to pay around Rs 1000 for a guide.

Leeches may be about. A popular deterrent is an Ayurvedic balm produced by Siddhalepa Ayurveda Hospital. It costs only a few rupees and is available across Sri Lanka.

Sleeping & Eating

Dalhousie is the best place to start the climb, and it also has the area's best budget accommodation. Head to Dikoya (see opposite) for midrange and top-end options.

Out-of-pilgrimage-season buses may drop you off in Dalhousie's main square, but during the season buses stop near the beginning of the walk. In season there are a few tea shops, some of which stay open all night, where you can get an early breakfast or buy provisions for the climb.

Most guest houses are on the your left as you reach Dalhousie.

White House (☎ 077 791 2009; r Rs 440-550) About 100m beyond the River View Wathsala Inn (opposite), the White House has basic but clean rooms – those with hot water cost more – run by a single guy and his friendly dog. It's a laid-back place with nice gardens and a natural swimming hole in the nearby river. Guiding services are available for Rs 1000 per day.

Green House (☎ 060-222 3956; r Rs 440-880) Across the bridge at the start of the walking path, the Green House lives up to its name with a potted plant–filled garden and a breezy gazebo restaurant. The friendly Tamil family can arrange trekking guides, and after your knee-wrecking descent from Sri Pada will prepare a herbal bath (Rs 330) for an essential après-pilgrimage soak.

Punsisi Rest (☎ 071 573 3450; r Rs 880-1650; 🖳) A slightly prosaic location overlooking the village market, but with comfortable and spacious rooms up narrow staircases. Punsisi was in expansion mode when we visited, with a new view-friendly rooftop restaurant and a couple of cottages being completed. They'll pick you up for free from Hatton train station if you book ahead.

our pick **Slightly Chilled** (☎ 071 909 8710; www .slightlychilled.tv; r Rs 1100-2200; 🖳) Formerly called the Yellow House, Dalhousie's best option is now Slightly Chilled in name and very chilled in nature. Spacious and colourful rooms with polished wooden floors have great views of Sri Pada, and there's an airy restaurant. Mountain bikes can be hired, there's lots of information on other trails in the area and at night there are occasional big-screen movies. Slightly Chilled is on your left as you come into town, just before the White House.

River View Wathsala Inn (☎ 060-251 9606; www .adamspeaksrilanka.com; r Rs 1320-2750) Dalhousie's ritziest spot has 14 large rooms, some with shared bathrooms. Lots of balconies and nooks and crannies make it feel larger than it is, and it's easy to find a private space to take in the views. The restaurant is popular with tour groups, and the trailhead is a 10-minute walk away.

Getting There & Away

Reaching the base of Adam's Peak is quite simple, and if you're making a night ascent you've got all day to arrive. Buses run to Dalhousie from Kandy (from the Goods Shed bus station), Nuwara Eliya and Colombo in the pilgrimage season. Otherwise, you need first to get to Hatton or to Maskeliya, about 20km along the Hatton–Dalhousie road.

Throughout the year there are services to Hatton from Colombo, Kandy or Nuwara Eliya. There are also some direct buses from Nuwara Eliya and Colombo to Maskeliya.

There are buses from Hatton to Dalhousie via Maskeliya every 30 minutes in the pilgrimage season (CTB/private bus Rs 48/70, two hours). Otherwise, you have to take a bus from Hatton to Maskeliya (Rs 20, last departure about 7pm) and then another to Dalhousie (Rs 20, last departure about 8.30pm).

The *Podi Menike* and *Udarata Menike* trains from Colombo arrive in Hatton at 11.30am and 2.15pm, respectively. These trains continue to Nanu Oya (for Nuwara Eliya), as do the local trains that leave Hatton at 7.35am and 4.20pm. In the other direction (to Colombo) the *Podi Menike* passes through Haputale and Nanu Oya and reaches Hatton at 2.13pm; the *Udarata Menike* leaves Hatton at 10.55am. Mail train 46 leaves at 10.52pm.

A taxi from Hatton to Dalhousie should cost Rs 1400.

AROUND ADAM'S PEAK

Other than ascending the famous peak, travellers can arrange easier hikes through forests and connecting tea plantations in Dikoya, Hatton and Maskeliya, or go boating and fishing on the Castlereagh or Maussakelle Reservoirs. Local tea-estate bungalows can handle the arrangements.

A few local tea factories also offer tours and cuppings (tea tastings). The charming 19th-century Anglican church built on a promontory overlooking the Castlereagh Reservoir is worth a visit for its quaint stone architecture, atmospheric colonial cemetery, and sweeping views of the reservoir and adjoining tea plantations.

Hatton, the main train junction in the area, is a bustling tea-trading town with narrow, crowded streets and a good market.

Sleeping & Eating

At elevations of 1200m to 1400m, the area around Dikoya has the Hill Country's best selection of converted tea-estate bungalows. There are a couple of grimy local inns near the train station in Hatton and in Maskeliya, but these should be a last resort. With your own transport, it's possible to do Adam's Peak from Dikoya without overnighting in Dalhousie.

Castlereagh Family Cottages (☎ 051-222 3607; www.castlecottages.org; Norton Bridge Rd, Dikoya; cottages Rs 3300-6600) Further along the road to Hatton, look for the sign for this place just after a bridge. The nicely decorated cottages are in a lovely spot under eucalyptus trees on the edge of the Castlereagh Reservoir. The smaller cottage has a double bed and a room with two bunks. The bigger one has three double rooms, plus a kids' room. Both have kitchens and hot water.

Tea Trails (☎ 011-230 3888; www.teatrails.com; Dikoya; r €143, ste €176-215; 🎬 🖳) Tea Trails comprises a collection of four colonial-style

THE HILL COUNTRY

bungalows built for British tea-estate managers in the late 19th and early 20th centuries. Completely refurbished, the bungalows each have four to six large bedrooms, spacious dining and living areas, and verandas and gardens with views over Castlereagh Reservoir. Rates include Western and Sri Lankan meals prepared by a resident chef, along with complimentary wines and single-estate teas. Also on staff are an experienced guide who can lead hikes from bungalow to bungalow (or beyond), and a resident tea expert. If tea's not your tipple, have a single malt whisky or end-of-day gin and tonic around your bungalow's roaring fire. The Tea Trails bungalows are one of Sri Lanka's finest places to savour the luxury and leisure of the British colonial experience.

Getting There & Away

Castlereagh Family Cottages are along the main road between Hatton and Dikoya and can be reached by bus. Tea Trails can arrange pick-up for its guests in Colombo, Kandy or Hatton. A taxi from Hatton to any of these accommodations should cost around Rs 1200.

KITULGALA
☎ 036

Southwest of Kandy and north of Adam's Peak, Kitulgala's main claim to fame is that David Lean filmed his 1957 Oscar-winning epic *Bridge on the River Kwai* here. You can walk down a paved pathway to the site where the filming took place along the banks of the Kelaniya Ganga. The pathway is signposted on the main road, about 1km from Plantation Hotel in the direction of Adam's Peak. It is virtually impossible to head down the path without attracting an entourage of 'guides' who expect a few rupees for their troubles. If you know the film you'll recognise some of the places. Apparently the actual railways carriages used in the movie now lie at the bottom of the river, after being sunk in an explosive conclusion. You'll definitely have to bring your own scuba gear if you want a look.

Kitulgala's second claim to fame is **white-water rafting** along the Kelaniya Ganga. The typical trip takes in seven Class 2–3 rapids in 7km for US$30 per person, including transport and lunch. You'll be on the water for around two hours. Experienced rafters can opt for more-difficult Class 4–5 rapids

by special arrangement. Organise rafting through Rafter's Retreat (below) or Plantation Hotel (below).

The Kelaniya Ganga also has some good **swimming** spots; a popular hole is beside Plantation Hotel.

The area is famous for bird-watching, as well – 23 of Sri Lanka's 27 endemic bird species inhabit the surrounding forest. Channa Perera at Rafter's Retreat can arrange bird-watching outings.

A beautiful 85-year-old colonial bungalow serves as the hub for **⸢ourpick⸥ Rafter's Retreat** (☎ 228 7598; www.raftersretreat.com; r/cottages incl half board per person US$33/39), a rafting and bird-watching outfit that sprawls along the river-bank. The 10 eco-friendly riverside cottages are basic but very private, and three rooms near the old house are clean and spacious with unbelievably high ceilings. The breezy riverside restaurant is a great place for a few beers, and the food is excellent. Ask the jovial owner Channa to show you around his wonderful colonial house that was originally built by his grandfather. Imagine a friendlier version of the place from *The Addams Family* or *The Shining*. Caving and mountain-biking trips can also be arranged.

One corner of the dining room at **Kitulgala Rest House** (☎ 228 7233; www.ceylonhotels.lk; r with/ without air-con Rs 6300/5800; ⸢✗⸥ ⸢✉⸥) is a veritable shrine to the David Lean epic. Black-and-white stills punctuate a feature wall, and the hotel was actually used in the movie. The graceful colonial-style building is over 70 years old, and has 20 rooms with verandas facing the river. Satellite TV and minibars are more modern touches.

Further towards Adam's Peak than the Kitulgala Rest House, the eight stylish rooms at **Plantation Hotel** (☎ 228 7575; www.plantationgrou photels.com; Kalukohutenna; s/d Rs 6200/7395; ⸢✗⸥) are very comfortable; there's also a restaurant serving 'Western and Eastern' cuisine beside the river. Bird-watching and rafting trips can be arranged.

Plantation Resort (Royal River Resort; ☎ 228 7575; www.plantationgrouphotels.com Eduru Ella; s/d/tr Rs 8676/10200/10950; ⸢✗⸥ ⸢▢⸥ ⸢✦⸥) is a collection of open-air dining areas and plush guest rooms built alongside the rapids of the Ing Oya River. All rooms have fireplaces and river views. The restaurant is popular with day trippers and tour groups. The swimming pool is perched right beside the rushing river.

BM MARZOOKDEEN – BLUE FIELD TEA GARDENS

BM Marzookdeen is general manager at the Blue Field Tea Gardens near Ramboda Falls on the main road from Kandy to Nuwara Eliya.

The estate seems to go on forever. Just how big is Bluefields? It's actually quite small relative to other tea plantations in Sri Lanka, around 20 hectares maximum. It used to be about 80 hectares in earlier times.

Why is the Hill Country such a good place to grow tea? The legend is that Adam was sent here and God has given us an advantage. It's really a combination of the soil, the altitude and the climate.

How many people work on the Blue Field Estate? We've got around 350 workers in total, coming from around 160 families. Altogether, over 1000 people are supported by the work done on the estate.

What are some of the ways you support your workers? We've got a créche for childen up to 10 years of age, and then there is a government-sponsored school. Mothers get up to 12 weeks' paid parental leave.

How often are the tea bushes plucked? During the wet season bushes are plucked on average once a week, but in the dry season, this increases to once every five days. Our workers are contracted to pick at least 20kg of tea per day, and then they receive a bonus for picking a greater quantity.

What happens to the tea once it is processed in the tea factory? It's graded and then sent to the Colombo Tea Auctions. The auctions have been going since 1883, and more than 200 companies buy on behalf of businesses around the world. All the buying goes through just eight brokers. Around 95% of Sri Lankan tea goes through Colombo.

It's easy to stop at Kitulgala even if you are travelling by bus. If you're coming from Ratnapura, change at Avissawella, catch the bus to Hatton and get off at Kitulgala (Rs 54). When you're over Kitulgala, flag a bus on to Hatton from the main road (Rs 72).

KANDY TO NUWARA ELIYA

The road from Kandy to Nuwara Eliya climbs nearly 1400m as it winds through jade-green tea plantations and past crystalline reservoirs. The 80km of asphalt allow for plenty of stops at waterfalls and tea outlets.

At Pussellawa, 45km from Kandy, the 120-year-old **Pussellawa Rest House** (☎ 081-247 8397; www.ceylonhotels.lk; r with/without air-con US$55/50; ✪) has four reasonably well-maintained rooms in a colonial-style bungalow with fine views.

Kothmale Reservoir (also known as Puna Oya Reservoir) can be seen further up the road. It's part of the Mahaweli Development Project and blamed by some locals for climatic quirks in recent years. **Ramboda Falls** (108m), about 1.5km from the road, is a spectacular double waterfall.

Ramboda Falls Hotel (☎ 027-224 7275; www.ramboda fall.com; r from US$25) is 58km from Kandy and near Ramboda Falls and the Kothmale Reservoir; it's on your right as you travel from Kandy. There

are excellent views of the falls, especially from the three restaurants. Rooms are clean and spacious, but you'll need to be a fan of kitsch floral bedspreads. The alfresco beer garden is one of the nicest spots in Sri Lanka for a cold Lion Lager. To venture further, follow a narrow path to the falls. So just one beer, OK?

Maussawa Estate Eco Lanka Villa (☎ 051-223 3133; www.ecolanka.com; s/d incl full board €38/53) Combining ecotourism and an internationally recognised fair-trade garden, Eco Lanka Villa sits concealed on 50 acres of forest. Getting there from the main road joining Kandy and Nuwara Eliya is a rollicking adventure in itself. Once there, get busy trekking, bird-watching or bathing in the river. Afterwards relax in the main villa or the breezy garden restaurant. Everything is organic, vegetarian and very tasty. A percentage of profits is donated to the local village. Eco Lanka Villa is near the village of Pundaluoya, northwest of Nuwara Eliya. Advance reservations are essential.

On the A5, 5km before Nuwara Eliya, the **Labookellie Tea Factory** (☾ 8am-6.30pm) is a convenient factory to visit as it's right on the roadside. Buy well-priced quality teas and enjoy a free cuppa of tea with a slice of chocolate cake.

THE TEA HILLS

Tea came to Sri Lanka when extensive coffee plantations were decimated by disease in the 19th century. The first Sri Lankan tea was grown in 1867 at the Loolecondera Estate southeast of Kandy. The Hill Country combines warm climate, altitude and sloping terrain: a winning trifecta that's perfect for growing tea.

In 2008 Sri Lanka overtook Kenya as the second most important tea-producing nation, with an annual production of 330 million kg. Sri Lankan tea (branded internationally as 'Ceylon' tea) enjoys a premium positioning and its auction sale prices are more than 50% higher than main rival and market leader India. At the time of writing an increased emphasis on growing organic tea was helping Sri Lanka offset a major decline in prices during the global financial crisis. Despite this, wages for Tamil tea pickers remain very low – around US$3 per day at the time of writing (two-thirds the minimum wage for government employees) – and the hardworking pickers must pick a minimum of 20kg of leaves per day. Compulsory pension and funeral payments erode already low wages, and many Tamil families live in seriously substandard housing.

Tea bushes are pruned back to around 1m in height and squads of Tamil tea pluckers (all women) move through the rows of bushes picking the leaves and buds. These are then 'withered' (demoisturised by blowing air at a fixed temperature through them) either in the old-fashioned multistorey tea factories, where the leaves are spread out on hessian mats, or in modern mechanised troughs. The partly dried leaves are then crushed, starting a fermentation process. The art in tea production comes in knowing when to stop the fermentation, by 'firing' the tea to produce the final, brown-black leaf. Tea factories throughout the Hill Country provide tours to explain the process, usually using machinery and technology that are largely unchanged since the 19th century.

The many varieties of tea are graded by size (from cheap 'dust' through fannings and broken grades to 'leaf' tea) and by quality (with names such as flowery, pekoe or souchong). Tea is further categorised into low-grown, mid-grown or high-grown. The low-grown teas (under 600m) grow strongly and are high in 'body' but low in 'flavour'. The high-grown teas (over 1200m) grow more slowly and are renowned for their subtle flavour. Mid-grown tea is something between the two. Regular commercial teas are usually made by blending various types.

Approaching Nuwara Eliya, roadside stalls overflow with all sorts of vegies – a legacy of Samuel Baker, who arrived in 1846 and made Nuwara Eliya his summer retreat. The vegie-loving Baker introduced many different varieties, including quite a few you vowed not to eat once you reached adulthood. Watch out on the steep roadside approach to Nuwara Eliya for children selling flowers. If you're travelling with a loved one, you know what to do.

NUWARA ELIYA

☎ 052 / pop 25,966 / elev 1889m

Nuwara Eliya is often referred to as 'Little England'. The toytown ambience of Sri Lanka's main hill station makes it more like the TV show *Little Britain* – soothingly familiar, but with a disorienting surrealist edge. Three-wheelers whiz past red telephone boxes. Water buffalo daubed in iridescent dye for the Tamil festival of Thaipongal mingle outside a pink brick Victorian post office. A well-tended golf course morphs seamlessly into a rolling carpet of tea plantations. The dusty and bustling centre of town is a thoroughly Sri Lankan tangle, but scratch the surface a little to reveal colonial bungalows, well-tended hedgerows and pretty rose gardens.

In earlier times, Nuwara Eliya (meaning 'City of Light') was the favoured cool-climate escape for the hard-working and hard-drinking English and Scottish pioneers of Sri Lanka's tea industry. A rainy-day, misty-mountain ambience still blankets the town from November to February – don't come expecting tropical climes – but during April's spring release, the town is crowded with domestic holiday-makers enjoying horse racing and sports-car hill climbs and celebrating the Sri Lankan New Year. The cost of accommodation escalates wildly, and Nuwara Eliya becomes a busy, busy party town. For the rest of the year, the economy is based on tea, cool-climate vegetables, and even more tea. Treat yourself to a night at one of Nuwara Eliya's colonial hotels, play a round of golf

THE HILL COUNTRY

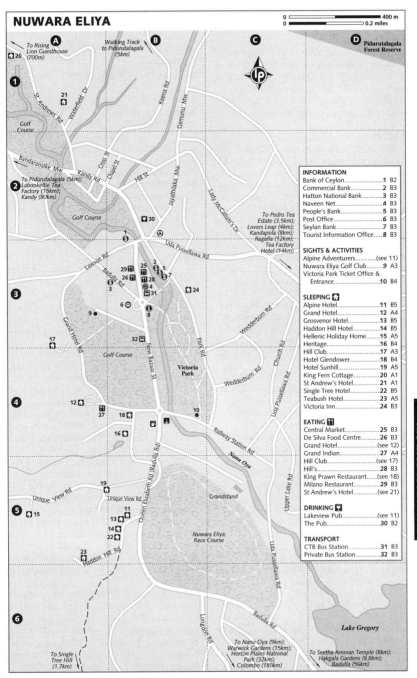

NUWARA ELIYA

0 — 400 m
0 — 0.2 miles

INFORMATION
Bank of Ceylon.....................**1** B2
Commercial Bank................**2** B3
Hatton National Bank..........**3** B3
Naveen Net.........................**4** B3
People's Bank......................**5** B3
Post Office..........................**6** B3
Seylan Bank........................**7** B3
Tourist Information Office.....**8** B3

SIGHTS & ACTIVITIES
Alpine Adventurers...........(see 11)
Nuwara Eliya Golf Club.......**9** A3
Victoria Park Ticket Office &
Entrance.........................**10** B4

SLEEPING 🛏
Alpine Hotel.......................**11** B5
Grand Hotel.......................**12** A4
Grosvenor Hotel.................**13** B5
Haddon Hill Hotel...............**14** B5
Hellenic Holiday Home........**15** A5
Heritage............................**16** B4
Hill Club............................**17** A3
Hotel Glendower................**18** B4
Hotel Sunhill......................**19** A5
King Fern Cottage...............**20** A1
St Andrew's Hotel...............**21** A1
Single Tree Hotel................**22** B5
Teabush Hotel....................**23** A5
Victoria Inn.......................**24** B3

EATING 🍴
Central Market...................**25** B3
De Silva Food Centre..........**26** B3
Grand Hotel......................(see 12)
Grand Indian.....................**27** A4
Hill Club...........................(see 17)
Hill's................................**28** B3
King Prawn Restaurant......(see 18)
Milano Restaurant.............**29** B3
St Andrew's Hotel.............(see 21)

DRINKING 🍷
Lakeview Pub....................(see 11)
The Pub............................**30** B2

TRANSPORT
CTB Bus Station.................**31** B3
Private Bus Station.............**32** B3

THE HILL COUNTRY

and a few frames of billiards, and escape into the town's curious combination of heritage and the here-and-now.

The town has an abundance of touts eager to get a commission for a guest house or hotel. They'll intercept you on arrival at Nanu Oya train station with fabricated reports of accommodation being closed, cockroach-infested or just plain crooked. Just ignore them.

History

Originally an uninhabited system of forests and meadows in the shadow of Pidurutalagala (aka Mt Pedro, 2524m), Nuwara Eliya became a singularly British creation, having been 'discovered' by colonial officer John Davy in 1819 and chosen as the site for a sanatorium a decade later.

Later the district became known as a spot where 'English' vegetables and fruits, such as lettuce and strawberries, could be successfully grown for consumption by the colonists. Coffee was one of the first crops grown here, but after the island's coffee plantations failed due to disease, the colonists switched to tea. The first tea leaves harvested in Sri Lanka were planted at Loolecondera Estate, in the mountains between Nuwara Eliya and Kandy. As tea experiments proved successful, the town quickly found itself becoming the Hill Country's 'tea capital', a title still proudly borne.

As elsewhere in the Hill Country, most of the labourers on the tea plantations were Tamils, brought from southern India by the British. Although the descendants of these 'plantation Tamils' (as they are called to distinguish them from Tamils in northern Sri Lanka) have usually stayed out of the ethnic strife endemic to Jaffna and the North, there have been occasional outbreaks of tension between the local Sinhalese and Tamils. The town was partially ransacked during 1983 riots.

At nearby Hagkala, there is a significant Muslim population, but internecine strife is not a problem.

Orientation

Most buses arrive and depart from the private bus station on New Bazaar St, although some CTB buses arrive on nearby Railway Station Rd. Over the road is Victoria Park. Further north along New Bazaar St is the central market and a collection of cheap eateries. Nearby is the Bank of Ceylon. Veer left into Kandy Rd, and you'll see the golf course on your left. Head south from the bus station along New Bazaar St to Queen Elizabeth Rd (also known as Badulla Rd). Many cheaper guest houses are clustered nearby.

Information

The following banks have ATMs and exchange facilities.

Bank of Ceylon (Lawson Rd)

Commercial Bank (Park Rd)

Hatton National Bank (Badulla Rd)

Naveen Net (17/1 New Bazaar St; per hr Rs 60; ☯ 8am-8pm) Internet, international phone calls, and CD photo downloads.

People's Bank (Park Rd)

Post office (Badulla Rd)

Seylan Bank (Park Rd)

Tourist Information Office (New Bazaar St; ☯ 9am-5pm) Maps, brochures and overpriced internet (Rs 120 per hour).

Sights

The lovely **Victoria Park** (adult/child Rs 60/30; ☯ dawn-dusk) at the centre of town comes alive with flowers around March to May, and August and September. It's also home to quite a number of Hill Country bird species, including the Kashmir flycatcher, Indian pitta and grey tit.

To see where your morning cuppa originates, head to the **Pedro Tea Estate** (admission Rs 75; ☯ 8.30am-12.30pm & 2-5pm), about 3.5km east of Nuwara Eliya on the way to Kandapola. Guided tours of the factory, originally built in 1885 and still packed with 19th-century engineering, run for a half-hour. Overlooking the plantations there's a pleasant tea house. A three-wheeler from Nuwara Eliya should cost Rs 700 to 800 return, including waiting time. The Single Tree Hotel (p184) runs trips for Rs 500 per person. Alternatively you could hop on a Ragalla-bound bus (bus 743) from the main bus station in Nuwara Eliya.

On the way out you'll pass Hawa Eliya, the former site of the Lion brewery, now relocated to Colombo. A side road takes you up to what's locally known as **Lovers Leap**. From here you get a good view of the countryside.

The **Hakgala Gardens** (adult/child Rs 300/200; ☯ 7.30am-5pm), 10km southeast of Nuwara Eliya (and about 200m lower), was originally a plantation of cinchona, the plant from which the antimalarial drug quinine is extracted. Later, the gardens were used for experiments in acclimatising temperate-zone plants to life in the tropics. The gardens were run by the same family for three generations until the 1940s. Today Hakgala sprawls across 27 hectares and is famed for its roses, ferns and medicinal plants.

Legend has it that Hanuman, the monkey god, was sent by Rama to the Himalayas to find a particular medicinal herb. He forgot which herb he was looking for and decided to bring a chunk of the Himalayas back in his jaw, hoping the herb was growing on it. The gardens grow on a rock called Hakgala, which means 'jaw-rock'.

The Hakgala Gardens are a short bus ride from Nuwara Eliya (take a Welimada-bound bus). On the way, near the 83km post, stop at the colourful Hindu **Seetha Amman Temple** at Sita Eliya. It's said to mark the spot where Sita was held captive by the demon king Rawana, and where she prayed daily for Rama to come and rescue her. On the rock face across the stream are circular depressions said to be the footprints of Rawana's elephant. Tamil wedding parties make it a point to stop here for *pujas*.

Activities

The Grand Hotel, St Andrew's Hotel, the Hill Club and Hotel Glendower all have snooker rooms. Nonguests can play for around Rs 250 per hour.

GOLF

Nuwara Eliya Golf Club (☎ 223 2835; negolf@slt.lk; 18 holes green fees weekdays/weekends & holidays Rs 3750/4250, 10 holes green fees weekdays/weekends & holidays Rs 2500/3250, caddie fee Rs 560), spreading north from Grand Hotel Rd, is beautifully kept and has a retinue of languid sleeping dogs guarding more than a few of the greens.

It didn't take the tea planters long to lay out land for drives and putts in their holiday town, and the club was founded in 1889. The club has been through tough times but survives to this day. Water hazards – in the form of rivers and streams – come into play on six holes. Temporary members pay Rs 100 per day. Hire golf clubs for Rs 1080 per day and golf shoes for Rs 168 per day. The club expects a certain dress code: for men, shirt with collar and pants or shorts (of a decent length), socks and shoes; and for women, 'decent' golf attire, which we assume means a skirt of a suitable length or pants. The club has a convivial wood-lined bar and a bad-minton hall and billiard room. Dinner in the dining room includes classic bland English cuisine, such as grilled lamb chops with mint sauce for around Rs 500.

CYCLING

Fat-tyre fans will find plenty of steep dirt trails radiating into the hills from the outskirts of town. Ask at the Single Tree Hotel or the Alpine Hotel about **mountain bike rental** (per day Rs 1000). A relatively challenging, but undeniably spectacular, 10km day trip is through the verdant blanket of tea plantations to the Labookellie Tea Factory (p179). There are a few hills to climb, but the reward of swooping downhill makes it worthwhile.

HORSE RACING

The Sri Lanka Turf Club sponsors horse racing at the 1875-vintage Nuwara Eliya Race Course. The most important event every year is the Governor's Cup race, held over the April Sinhala and Tamil New Year season. The races usually begin around 10.30am. At the time of writing, the grassy area inside the racetrack was being developed as a high-altitude sports centre. An international cricket arena is also planned. Nuwara Eliya's elevation of 1889m should make for some interesting matches.

HIKING

Sri Lanka's highest mountain, **Pidurutalagala** (2524m), rises behind the town. On top stands the island's main TV transmitter; the peak is out of bounds to the public. You can walk about 4km up as far as a concrete water tank; beyond is a high-security zone. Follow the path from Keena Rd, along a ravine through eucalyptus forest (the town's source of firewood) and into the rare, indigenous cloud forest.

An alternative walk is up **Single Tree Hill** (2100m), which takes about 90 minutes. Walk south on Queen Elizabeth Rd, go up Haddon Hill Rd as far as the communications tower and then take the left-hand path. Guest houses can supply you with a rudimentary map.

For longer hikes, ask at the Single Tree Hotel (p184). Guided walks in the surrounding hills cost around Rs 1500 to 2000. They can also arrange longer camping trips.

If you need clothing for cooler weather or trekking, head to the **market** on New Bazaar St for brand-name outdoor gear from Sri Lankan garment factories at bargain prices.

THE HILL COUNTRY

TENNIS

There are four clay tennis courts at the **Hill Club** (☎ 222 2653; www.hillclubsrilanka.net; per hr Rs 400). The fee includes balls and racquet hire. Try not to lob a ball into the Sri Lankan President's residence next door.

Tours

Most accommodation in town can arrange day trips by car or 4WD to Horton Plains National Park and World's End (p187). The standard price for up to five passengers is Rs 3000. One of the better 4WD tours is based at Single Tree Hotel (right). It takes about 1½ hours one way.

Single Tree can also arrange trips to the Pedro Tea Estate (Rs 500) and Labookellie (Rs 1000). For the ultimate waterfall experience, join its waterfall day trip (per van Rs 5500) that takes in 14 different cascades.

Alpine Adventurers at the Alpine Hotel (opposite) specialises in trekking, camping, mountaineering and rafting tours in the area.

Sleeping

Nuwara Eliya's budget hotels can be on the dreary side, so it's worth being a little choosy where you stay. There's a good range of colonial-style places, but you will pay more for a heritage ambience. Unlike other parts of Sri Lanka, there isn't a good range of backpacker-oriented guest houses. Two exceptions are the Single Tree Hotel and the excellent King Fern Cottage.

You'll need blankets to keep warm at night at almost any time of year. Another way of keeping warm is to get a fire lit in your room; expect to pay a whopping Rs 450 extra. Make sure the room has ventilation or an open window to avert carbon monoxide poisoning, which can be fatal.

During the 'season', around Sri Lankan New Year in April, rooms are three to five times their normal price. Prices also increase during long-weekend holidays and in August, when package tours descend from abroad.

BUDGET

our pick King Fern Cottage (☎ 077 358 6284; 203/1A St Andrews Dr; s/d Rs 1100/1320; ☺ Nov-May) Hands down Nuwara Eliya's funkiest place to stay, King Fern combines huge handmade beds, warm-as-toast bedspreads, and a laid-back ambience that sometimes sees the owner breaking out his drums for an after-dark, fireside session. It's all wrapped up in a rustic, timber pavilion beside a bubbling stream. Owner Nishantha is a qualified walking guide and will pick you up from Nanu Oya train station if you phone ahead.

Victoria Inn (☎ 222 2321; 15 Park Rd; r Rs 1100) Good-value rooms in a convenient location near Victoria Park. It's aligned with the Single Tree Hotel and the Alpine Hotel, so there's lots of walking and adventure-based activities on offer.

Haddon Hill Hotel (☎ 222 3500; 8B Haddon Hill Rd; s/d Rs 1200/1400) It's back to basics here with simple rooms and the opportunity to use the shared kitchen. For a 10% rate increase, upgrade to a room with a balcony overlooking the racecourse.

Single Tree Hotel (☎ 222 3009; singletreehtl@sltnet.lk; 178 Haddon Hill Rd; r Rs 1320-1650; ☐) Bright colours and loads of warm timber trim combine with satellite TV at one of Nuwara Eliya's most welcoming guest houses. The switched-on owners have a whole raft of suggestions for trekking, tours and transport.

MIDRANGE

Grosvenor Hotel (☎ 222 2307; 6 Haddon Hill Rd; s/d/tr Rs 1650/2200/3300) A century after service as the residence of the colonial governor, expansive hallways, spacious rooms and period furniture make the Grosvenor one of Nuwara Eliya's best-value colonial options. Thoroughly modern skylights illuminate the old library – a perfect spot to catch up on your travel diary.

Rising Lion Guesthouse (☎ 222 2083; www.hotel risinglion.net; 3 Sri Piyatissapura; r Rs 2200-2750) Perched atop St Andrews Rd, this place has superb misty-mountain vistas and an eclectic decor combining 1970s retro and Asian antiques (somehow it works). It's worth paying extra for a balcony with views and splashing out on a fire (Rs 400) to make things as cosy as possible. You'll soon forget you're in a tropical country.

Hotel Sunhill (☎ 222 2878; sunhill@itmin.com; 18 Unique View Rd; r from Rs 2500) Up a quaint hillside lane, the Sunhill is popular with visiting Sri Lankans. It's worth going for a more expensive deluxe room (Rs 3200) as the standard rooms are a tad pokey. Karaoke-phobics may want to avoid weekends.

Hellenic Holiday Home (☎ /fax 223 5872; 49/1 Unique View Rd; r Rs 2700-3500) This modern response to Nuwara Eliya's colonial overkill features huge picture windows perfect for enjoying the hilltop view, and spacious rooms arrayed around a labyrinth of stairs. A three-wheeler from the bus station costs Rs 150.

Alpine Hotel (☎ 222 3500; www.alpineecotravels.com; 4 Haddon Hill Rd; s/d/tr Rs 3600/4300/5000; 🦮 💻) The inn has 25 decent rooms and a large restaurant. Mountain bikes can be hired for Rs 1000 per day. The front desk can arrange hiking, trekking and bird-watching tours for guests. At the time of writing they were putting the finishing touches to their new Lakeview Pub (p186), with three levels perfect for end-of-day snooker, darts and imbibing.

Teabush Hotel (☎ 222 2345; www.teabushhotel.com; 29 Haddon Hill Rd; s Rs 3800-5000, d Rs 4200-5500, tr Rs 4600-6000; 💻) Lots of antique furniture peppers this 140-year-old tea planters' bungalow. The heritage charm of the shared, public areas is tempered by slightly more prosaic rooms, but the restaurant views are superb. The grassy rooftop lawn – yes, you read that right – is the perfect spot for sundowners. Hiking and bird-watching excursions can be arranged with the resident naturalist.

Hotel Glendower (☎ 222 2501; 5 Grand Hotel Rd; s/d/tr Rs 4500/4500/5200; 💻) This rambling colonial has period-style rooms, a pretty garden – complete with croquet set – and a cosy bar and restaurant. Our reception wasn't as welcoming as we would have liked, and some bedrooms are damp and dark; definitely have a look before you sign up. The attached King Prawn Restaurant (p186) does good Chinese.

Heritage (☎ 222 3053; heritage@slnet.lk; r US$45-55, ste US$80; 💻) Once a British governor's mansion, the Heritage has huge rooms – and even bigger suites – that are from the time when smart travellers journeyed with at least three steamer trunks. Teak furniture and a fine old bar make time travel to the 19th century very easy. It's a creaky old place though, so don't blame us if it inspires a few vivid dreams. High ceilings mean the rooms can get a tad chilly, so you may need a fire (Rs 400).

TOP END

Hill Club (☎ 222 2653; www.hillclubsrilanka.net; 29 Grand Hotel Rd; r US$52-130, ste US$150-180; 💻) Commanding its location with elegance and gravitas, the stone-clad Hill Club is the most profound evidence of Nuwara Eliya's colonial past. Up to 1970 it was reserved for British males, and one of its bars remained resolutely 'men only' until a few years ago. It's now open to Sri Lankans and women, and members retain reciprocal rights with London clubs. Temporary members (Rs 100 per day) are welcomed with open arms to ease the cash

flow. Tennis courts are available to guests and nonguests, and the lawns and gardens are immaculate. The suites are spacious and charming, but the regular rooms are small and have substandard furnishings given the price. (Head to the Grosvenor Hotel for better-value colonial accommodation.) Dinner at the Hill Club is a thoroughly retro and unique experience. See boxed text on p186.

Grand Hotel (☎ 222 2881; www.tangerinehotels.com; Grand Hotel Rd; s US$85-110, d US$100-140; 💻) Right by the golf course, this vast mock-Tudor edifice has immaculate lawns, a reading lounge and a wood-panelled billiards room. The deluxe rooms in the new wing are spacious and classy, but unfortunately the standard rooms don't attain the stellar standards of the lovely public areas.

St Andrew's Hotel (☎ 222 2445; www.jetwing hotels.com; 10 St Andrew's Dr; r US$100-140; 💻) North of town on a beautifully groomed rise overlooking the golf course, this was once a planters' club. There are terraced lawns with white cast-iron furniture, and five-course European dinners are served in the dining room beneath a pressed-copper roof. The difference between the less expensive and more expensive rooms is more substantial than the rates suggest. At nearby Ambewella, the hotel also runs Warwick Gardens (rooms US$156 to US$215), a beautifully restored planter's house with five bedrooms.

Eating & Drinking

For lunch there are plenty of good, cheap options in town, but for dinner you'll probably want to eat at your guest house or at one of the ritzier hotel eateries. Pubs open around 4pm but seldom stay serving after midnight.

De Silva Food Centre (90 New Bazaar St; mains Rs 180-250) This inexpensive eatery located along a busy main street serves Sri Lankan and Chinese fare. A few vegetarian *rotti* make a good lunchtime snack.

Milano Restaurant (94 New Bazaar St; mains Rs 180-380) This is a slightly classier version of De Silva Food Centre, with friendly service and a reliable menu of Sri Lankan, Western and Chinese dishes. Treat yourself to some sweet baked goodies and a coffee to set you up for the rest of the afternoon.

ourpick Grand Indian (Grand Hotel Rd; mains Rs 200-420; ⏱ 11am-11pm) In front of the Grand Hotel, the surroundings are a bit cafeteria-like, but the food and the service here are top-notch.

TRAVELLING THROUGH TIME AT THE HILL CLUB Brett Atkinson

Built in 1885 by a homesick British coffee baron as a refuge from the heat of the Sri Lankan coast, the Hill Club is a melancholy monument to the British Empire's glory days. In the library, the only sound is the lonely tick…tick…ticking of a grandfather clock. Churchill's *History of the Second World War* sits under paintings of the royal family.

The hottest ticket in town is dinner in the shabbily genteel dining room. The club's arcane dress code is prescribed at reception. 'Dress is informal except from 7.00pm onwards when Gentlemen shall wear Tie and Jacket and Ladies shall wear suitable attire befitting the attire of Gentlemen. Sri Lankan National Dress is of course permitted.'

Feeling confident that my dusty travelling gear won't make the grade as Sri Lankan National Dress, I venture into a wardrobe that time forgot and throw together a snappy ensemble worthy of old-school silver-service dining. The selection is at least a generation old: I team a wide-lapelled crimplene jacket with a tie that should really come with a volume knob. Give me some well-trimmed sideboards and a Ford Capri, and I'd be a doppelgänger for Bodie or Doyle from the 1970s Brit cop show *The Professionals*.

Dinner goes back even further than the decade that taste forgot. The typed menu promises (apparently canned) chicken and sweetcorn soup, beef Holstien (sic), or roast mutton (actually goat) with mint sauce. Lyonnaise potato and leeks *au gratin* add a defiant, not to say desperate, international flavour. Attentive waiters drift around, perhaps wondering why so many of them have been rostered on. Orange mousse for dessert provides a minor highlight before I demolish the waiters with a few frames in the billiard room. Outside, it's the 21st century, but at this stage of the night, I'm really not sure.

Try the *kadai* (dry curry cooked in a wok) chicken teamed with *kheema naan* (bread stuffed with meat). Unlike a few other places around town, there's normally an energetic buzz about the place. Make a night of it before or after brews and billiards at the bar at the Grand Hotel. From 3pm to 6pm the Grand Indian specialises in good-value samosas and tandoori sandwiches.

King Prawn Restaurant (Hotel Glendower, 5 Grand Hotel Rd; mains Rs 400-600; ☻ noon-2pm & 6-10pm) Chinese is the overriding culinary influence here, all delivered in a dining room transplanted from 1930s England. Thai flavours also linger in some of the dishes, and there's a good array of seafood on offer. You're a few miles inland here, so expect to pay a hefty premium. Service is rather stiff and formal, but very prompt.

St Andrew's Hotel (☎ 222 2445; 10 St Andrew's Dr; mains Rs 600-1100; ☻ noon-2.30pm & 6-10pm) There's a couple of restaurants at this venerable hotel. The Old Course Restaurant channels the culinary heritage of the British Empire, while the new Taste of Asia (open from 6pm) has lighter oriental flavours.

Hill Club (☎ 222 2653; 29 Grand Hotel Rd; set menu US$17, à la carte from US$7; ☻ 6-11pm) Dinner at Hill Club is an event in itself. The five-course set menu focuses on hearty meals like roast beef,

served, with all the trimmings, promptly at 8pm. The whole thing is carried off with faded colonial panache: gloved waiters, candles and linen tablecloths and serviettes. For the formal dining room, men must wear a tie and jacket – there are a few on hand, but they sometimes run out – or Sri Lankan national dress. Women must also be suitably attired in a dress or dress slacks. The dress code at the Hill Club's à la carte, casual restaurant is not so strict. If you're not staying the night here, you'll have to pay a Rs 100 temporary joining fee. The food doesn't live up to everyone's expectations, especially with such a relatively high price tag, but it's still a great experience (see boxed text, above). Come along an hour or so before dinner for a drink in the Hill Club's bars. It was only a few years ago that the 'Casual Bar' was resolutely enforced as 'men only'. In a new millennium all gender variations are now welcome.

The Pub (20 Kandy Rd; ☻ 4pm-late) The cheapest place to drink in town, but not recommended for solo female travellers.

Lakeview Pub (Alpine Hotel, 4 Haddon Hill Rd; ☻ 4pm-late) At the time of writing, the finishing touches were being added to this place at the Alpine Hotel. Lots of moody, dark timber, billiards, darts and a lake-view terrace promise to make it a popular spot.

Grand Hotel (Grand Hotel Rd; ☼ 5pm-late) Not the cheapest place to drink in town, but with a lovely period vibe enlivened by an open fire and vintage movie posters. The older waiters will most likely challenge you to a game of snooker in the adjoining billiard room. You'll be expected to pay for the privilege (Rs 500 per hour), but it is a quintessential Nuwara Eliya experience.

Self-caterers should head for the **central market** for fresh produce and to **Hill's** supermarket (New Bazaar St) for canned goods.

Getting There & Away

BUS
The trip from Kandy takes about four hours and costs Rs 170 in a private intercity express bus or van. It's a spectacular climb. Buses leave every 30 minutes to an hour. There are also buses to/from Colombo (intercity express Rs 380, six hours). There are direct CTB buses to Haputale (Rs 50, 2½ hours) a few times daily, or more frequent departures to Welimada (Rs 23, one hour), where you can change to a Haputale-bound bus (Rs 22). For Bandarawela there is a direct CTB bus (Rs 44, three hours) or you can change local buses at Welimada. For Matara on the south coast, one intercity express bus (Rs 260, seven to eight hours) departs around 7.30am.

TRAIN
Nuwara Eliya is served by the Nanu Oya train station, 9km along the road towards Hatton and Colombo. Buses meet the main trains (Rs 20 to Nuwara Eliya), so don't get sucked in by touts. Most Nuwara Eliya accommodation will pick you up – often for free – if you have already booked. A taxi from the station is around Rs 400.

The 8.56am *Podi Menike* from Colombo (via Kandy) reaches Nanu Oya at 12.24pm. The 9.45am *Udarata Menike* from Colombo (not via Kandy) reaches Nanu Oya at about 3.15pm. A new Intercity service launched in early 2009 leaves Kandy at 10.54am and arrives at Nanu Oya at 2.10pm. The all-seated service to/from Colombo costs 2nd/1st class Rs 380/650. Trips onwards to Badulla in 3rd/2nd class cost Rs 150/300.

Going west, the *Udarata Menike* to Colombo (not stopping in Kandy) leaves Nanu Oya at 9.57am; the *Podi Menike* leaves at 12.55pm, reaching Kandy (3rd/2nd/1st class Rs 95/180/510) at 4.35pm before continuing on to Colombo.

HORTON PLAINS NATIONAL PARK & WORLD'S END
The Horton Plains is a beautiful, silent, strange world with some excellent hikes in the shadows of Sri Lanka's second- and third-highest mountains, Kirigalpotta (2395m) and Totapola (2359m). The 'plains' themselves form an undulating plateau over 2000m high, covered by wild grasslands and interspersed with patches of thick forest, rocky outcrops, filigree waterfalls and misty lakes. The surprising diversity of the landscape is matched by the wide variety of wildlife. If you're lucky

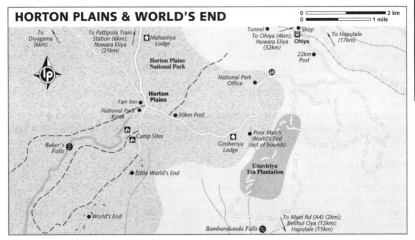

HORTON PLAINS & WORLD'S END

enough to have the paths to yourself – get there for a 7am start – it's a recharging escape from Sri Lanka's energetic bustle.

The plateau comes to a sudden end at World's End, a stunning escarpment that drops plunges 880m. Unfortunately the view from World's End is often obscured by mist, particularly during the rainy season from April to September. The early morning (between 6am and 10am) is the best time to visit, before the clouds roll in. That's when you'll spy toytown tea plantation villages in the valley below, and an unencumbered view south towards the coast. In the evening and early morning you'll need long trousers and a sweater, but the plains warm up quickly, so take a hat for sun protection. January to March have the clearest weather.

Information

Farr Inn, a local landmark, and the nearby national park office are reachable by road from Ohiya or Nuwara Eliya. It's a three-hour walk uphill from Ohiya train station. The new **national park office** (☎ 070 522042; adult/child US$20/9, car Rs 125r, service charge US$9; ☯ 6.30am-6.30pm) is around the 26km mark on the road from Ohiya to the start of the track. Farr Inn was a hunting lodge for high-ranking British colonial officials, but now incorporates a restaurant and visitors centre with displays on the flora, fauna and geology of the park. A small souvenir stand nearby has books on the park's flora and fauna.

Sights & Activities
WILDLIFE

As an important watershed and catchment for several year-round rivers and streams, the Horton Plains hosts a wide range of wildlife. The last few elephants departed the area in the first half of the 20th century, but there are still a few leopards, and sambar deer and wild boar are seen feeding in meadows at dawn and dusk. The shaggy bear monkey (or purple-faced langur) is sometimes seen in the forest on the Ohiya road, and occasionally in the woods around World's End (listen for a wheezy grunt). You may also come across the endemic toque macaque.

The area is very popular with birdwatchers. Endemic species include the yellow-eared bulbul, the fantailed warbler, the ashy-headed babbler, the Ceylon hill white-eye, the Ceylon blackbird, the Ceylon white-eyed arrenga, the dusky-blue flycatcher and the Ceylon blue magpie. Birds of prey include the mountain hawk eagle.

A tufty grass called *Crosypogon* covers the grasslands, while marshy areas are home to copious bog moss (sphagnum). The umbrella-shaped, white-blossomed keena *(Calophyllum)* stand as the main canopy over montane forest areas. The stunted trees and shrubs are draped in lichen and mosses. Another notable species is *Rhododendron zelanicum,* which has blood-red blossoms. The poignant purple-leafed *Strobilanthes* blossoms once after five years, and then dies.

WORLD'S END

This is the only national park in Sri Lanka where visitors are permitted to walk on their own (on designated trails only). The walk to World's End is 4km, but the trail loops back to Baker's Falls (2km) and continues back to the entrance (another 3.5km). The round trip is 9.5km and takes a leisurely three hours. Note that around 9am to 10am the mist usually comes down. All you can expect to see from World's End after this time is a swirling white wall. If you aim for a 5.30am departure from Nuwara Eliya or Haputale and get to World's End around 7am, you'll have a good chance of spectacular views.

Try to avoid doing this walk on Sundays and public holidays, when it can get crowded. And despite the signs, weekend groups of young Sri Lankan guys will do their utmost to make noise and inadvertently scare away the wildlife.

Guides at the national park office expect about Rs 750. There's no set fee for volunteer guides, but expect to donate a similar amount. Some guides are well informed on the area's flora and fauna, and solo women travellers may want to consider hiring one for safety's sake.

Wear strong and comfortable walking shoes, a hat and sunglasses. Bring sunscreen, and food and water, as the eatery at the Farr Inn is expensive. Ask your guest house to prepare a breakfast package for you, and reward yourself with an alfresco brekkie once you reach World's End. The weather can change very quickly on the plains – one minute it can be sunny and clear, the next chilly and misty. Bring a few extra layers of warm clothing. It is forbidden to leave the paths. There are toilets at Farr Inn.

There used to be a free alternative to World's End, dubbed Poor Man's World's End, but it has been fenced off and anyone caught in the area is fined Rs 10,000.

Tours

Hill Safari Eco-Lodge (below) in Ohiya can arrange guided hikes through the park. Guest houses in Nuwara Eliya and Haputale also operate trips to Horton Plains and World's End. Expect to pay around Rs 3000 per van.

Sleeping & Eating

There are two basic Department of Wildlife Conservation bungalows where you can stay: Giniheriya Lodge and Mahaeliya Lodge. The bungalows have 10 beds each, and the charge for foreigners is US$30 per day plus the US$20 park entry, US$2 per group for linen hire and a US$30 per group service charge. You must bring all of your own dry rations and kerosene. The lodges open up only when people are staying, and you must book ahead through the **Department of Wildlife Conservation** (☎ 011-256 0380; www.dwlc.lk; 382 New Kandy Rd, Malambe).

There are two camp sites (signposted near the start of the World's End track). These can also be booked through the Department of Wildlife Conservation. There is water at the sites but nothing else; bring everything you need. Because you are inside the national park you are obliged to pay the US$20 park entry fee and the camp-site fee (Rs 600 per day), plus a US$9 service charge per stay.

A more frugal alternative is to stay in nearby Ohiya. **Hill Safari Eco-Lodge** (☎ 071 277 2451; s/d incl half board Rs 1300/2600), about 1.5km from the Horton Plains junction down a very rough and winding road, has three family rooms with attached bathrooms and hot water. It's a former tea manager's bungalow on the Lower Bray tea estate. Hill Safari offers a seven-day trekking itinerary in the national park.

Opposite the Ohiya train station the first small **shop** (☎ 0777 404658; r Rs 880) you come to has two rudimentary rooms. Food is available at half the price of Farr Inn.

Getting There & Away

TAXI

A taxi from the Ohiya train station to/from Farr Inn (40 minutes one way) should cost about Rs 1600 return, including waiting time.

It takes about 1½ hours to get from Haputale to Farr Inn by road (Rs 3000 return). From Ohiya the road rises in twists and turns through forest before emerging on the open plains. Keep your eyes peeled for monkeys.

You can also drive to Farr Inn from Nuwara Eliya, a trip taking about 1½ hours one way (around Rs 3000 return by van).

There is a 4WD road that goes past the Bambarakanda Falls (the road signposted on the main road between Haputale and Belihul Oya) and emerges near Ohiya train station. It's pretty rough and usually impassable in wet weather.

TRAIN & FOOT

Given that the mist comes down at World's End at around 9am to 10am, you'll want to get there by at least 8am. You can walk to World's End, but it's a 30km round trip from Ohiya with some very steep ascents. Theoretically it would be possible to catch a night train to Ohiya and start the walk in the early hours, but as the trains are often delayed, you risk walking 15km up to World's End only to find the clouds have rolled in. It's better to arrive in Ohiya the day before if you really want to do the walk. The walk from Ohiya to Farr Inn is 11.2km, or 2½ to 3½ hours, along the road – you'll need a torch if you do it at night. Then you've got another 1½ hours to World's End. You'll need about two hours for the walk back down towards Ohiya. The trip up the main road has great views. A faster option is to catch a three-wheeler (Rs 1600) from Ohiya train station up to Farr Inn and the trailhead.

Keen walkers can also strike out for Farr Inn from Pattipola, the next train station north of Ohiya (a walk of about 10km along a 4WD track), or from Bambarakanda Falls, about four hours downhill from the plains (below). To make this a longer two-day hike, start from Haputale.

BELIHUL OYA
☎ 045

Belihul Oya is a pretty hillside region worth passing through on your way to or from the Hill Country – it's 35km from Haputale and 57km from Ratnapura. From here you can walk up to Horton Plains, a seriously strenuous undertaking.

About 11km towards Haputale, near Kalupahana, are the **Bambarakanda Falls**. Ask the bus driver to let you off at Kalupahana Juntion.

From the main road it's another Rs 350 by three-wheeler up a barely-there track.

At 240m, the Bambarakanda Falls are the highest in Sri Lanka. March and April are the best months for viewing the falls, but any visit after heavy rainfall should be worthwhile. At other times the water may be reduced to a disappointing trickle. From near the falls a challenging four-hour trail runs to Horton Plains.

A few hundred metres past the falls is the homey and rustic **Bambarakanda Holiday Resort** (☎ 057-567 0547; Bambarakanda Gardens, Kalupahana; s/d incl full board Rs 3850/7700). If you're really looking to get off the map for a few days, here's your chance. The rooms are basic and a bit dingy, but ideally you'll be out walking every day. The owners have a whole page of trail ideas, and the organic, vegetarian food comes from an adjacent garden. Don't be surprised if the friendly black-and-white dog shows you the way most mornings.

River Garden Resort (☎ 228 0222; www.srilankaecotourism.com; chalets per person US$48, camp sites per person incl full board US$27) has three chalets with spotless rooms set in a shady terraced garden above a stream. The 'ecolodge', 9km up the road, sleeps five (per person US$45). A camp site set in a shady area below the restaurant offers spacious two- to four-person tents with easy access to swimming in the river. River Garden Resort can arrange multiday adventure programs incorporating canoeing, trekking, mountain biking, rock climbing and caving.

Belihul Oya Rest House (☎ 228 7599; www.ceylonhotels.lk; Ratnapura-Haputale Rd; s/d/tr US$25/30/35, with air-con US$30/35/40; 🔀) has 14 clean but ageing rooms

and is perched beside a stream that rushes down from Horton Plains. A restaurant and lounge packed with comfy chairs sits near a natural rock pool. More expensive rooms with minibars are not worth the extra rupees.

HAPUTALE
☎ 057 / pop 4706 / elev 1580m

Perched at the southern edge of the Hill Country, the largely Tamil town of Haputale clings to a long, narrow mountain ridge with the land falling away steeply on both sides. The bowl-shaped Uva valley, surrounded by the Idalgashinna and Ohiya peaks, as well as the Horton Plains plateau, lies to the north and east of the ridge. On the other side, the foothills of the lower Uva descend all the way to the sea. On a clear day you can view the south coast from this ridge, and at night the Hambantota lighthouse pulses in the distance. On a not-so-clear day, great swathes of mist cling magnetically to the hillsides. Either way, it's a spectacular part of the country.

The town centre itself is a dusty ribbon of traffic, three-wheelers and small-scale commerce. Take a short walk, though, to be rewarded with extraordinary views. The railway hugs one side of the ridge in a minor victory for 19th-century engineering.

Haputale now mainly shows the influence of the Sinhalese and Tamil cultures, but the legacy of the British tea planters also lives on. Tea estates blanket the hillsides, punctuated by graceful planters' bungalows, all enveloped in a damp and heavy climate that must have made the British settlers feel right at home. The pretty Anglican church (St Andrew's) on

---

SIR THOMAS LIPTON – ONE VERY CANNY SCOTSMAN

His name now lives on in the hot-beverage aisle of your local supermarket, but Sir Thomas Lipton was a major success in business even before he became the biggest player in the global tea industry.

From 1870 to 1888 he grew his parents' single grocery shop in Glasgow to a nationwide chain of 300 stores. Recognising the potential of tea, he cannily bypassed the traditional wholesale markets of London, and went straight to the source by purchasing his own tea plantations in Sri Lanka. His network of 300 stores provided him with guaranteed distribution to sell tea at lower prices to an uptapped working-class market. It also inspired the winning advertising slogan, 'Direct from the tea gardens to the tea pot'.

Lipton's planet-spanning ambition wasn't only limited to trade. In 1909 he donated the Thomas Lipton Trophy for an international football competition 21 years before the first World Cup, and he was tireless in his (unsuccessful) attempts to win yachting's America's Cup. His well-publicised interest in the two sports ensured his brand became a household name on both sides of the Atlantic.

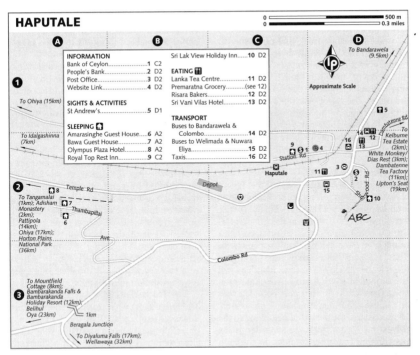

HAPUTALE

0 _____ 500 m
0 _____ 0.3 miles

INFORMATION		
Bank of Ceylon	1	C2
People's Bank	2	D2
Post Office	3	D2
Website Link	4	D2

SIGHTS & ACTIVITIES		
St Andrew's	5	D1

SLEEPING		
Amarasinghe Guest House	6	A2
Bawa Guest House	7	A2
Olympus Plaza Hotel	8	A2
Royal Top Rest Inn	9	C2

Sri Lak View Holiday Inn	10	D2

EATING		
Lanka Tea Centre	11	D2
Premaratna Grocery	(see 12)	
Risara Bakers	12	D2
Sri Vani Vilas Hotel	13	D2

TRANSPORT		
Buses to Bandarawela &		
Colombo	14	D2
Buses to Welimada & Nuwara		
Eliya	15	D2
Taxis	16	D2

Approximate Scale

To Bandarawela (9.5km)

To Ohiya (15km)

To Idalgashinna (7km)

To Tangamalai (1km); Adisham (2km); Pattipola (14km); Ohiya (17km); Horton Plains National Park (36km)

To Mountfield Cottage (8km); Bambarakanda Falls & Bambarakanda Holiday Resort (12km); Belihul Oya (23km)

Temple Rd

Thambapillai

Ave

Colombo Rd

Beragala Junction

To Diyaluma Falls (17km); Wellawaya (32km)

Depot

Haputale

Station Rd

Sherwood Rd

Dambatenne Rd

To Kelburne Tea Estate (2km); White Monkey/ Dias Rest (3km); Dambatenne Tea Factory (11km); Lipton's Seat (19km)

ABC

the Bandarawela road has a graveyard filled with poignant memories of earlier times.

Haputale has an array of good, cheap accommodation and makes a good base for visiting Horton Plains National Park, exploring other places in the area or just taking pleasant walks in cool mountain air. Guest houses arrange vans and 4WDs to Horton Plains for Rs 3000.

See www.haputale.de for more information.

Information

Haputale has a **Bank of Ceylon** (Station Rd) and **People's Bank** (Colombo Rd), both with exchange facilities and ATMs. The post office is in the centre of town. **Website Link** (No 3, UC Complex, Station Rd) has internet (per hour Rs 45), Skype and international calling, and CD photo burning.

Sights

DAMBATENNE TEA FACTORY

A few tea factories in this area are happy to have visitors. The most popular, **Dambatenne** (admission Rs 250; closed Sun), was built by Sir Thomas Lipton in 1890, one of the most famous

figures in tea history (see boxed text, opposite). A tour through the works is an education on the processes involved in the fermentation, rolling, drying, cutting, sieving and grading of tea. For further details about tea production, see The Tea Hills, p180.

Although it's 11km from Haputale, the popular factory is easily accessible. A bus for the estate workers goes from the bus station for Bandarawela to the factory and back again about every 25 minutes (Rs 15). A three-wheeler there and back costs about Rs 500.

DIYALUMA FALLS

Heading towards Wellawaya you'll pass the 171m-high Diyaluma Falls, Sri Lanka's third-highest waterfall, just 5km beyond the town of Koslanda. Cascading down an escarpment of the Koslanda Plateau, the stream is fairly small, but it quickly escalates after a downpour. By bus, take a Wellawaya service from Haputale and get off at Diyaluma (1¼ hours). The falls leap over a cliff face and fall in one clear drop to a pool below.

Climb up to some beautiful pools – ideal for swimming – and a series of minifalls at

THE HILL COUNTRY

the top of the main fall. Walk about 500m down the road from the bottom of the falls and take the estate track that turns sharply back up to the left. From there it's about 20 minutes' walk to a small rubber factory, where you strike off uphill to the left. The track is very indistinct, although there are some white arrows on the rocks. Ask the locals to make sure you're going the right way. At the top the path forks: the right branch (more distinct) leads to the pools above the main falls, the left fork to the top of the main falls.

ADISHAM MONASTERY

This Benedictine **monastery** (admission Rs 10; ⊗ 9am-12.30pm & 1.30-4.30pm Sat & Sun, poya days & school holidays) is about 3km west of Haputale. Follow Temple Rd along the ridge until you reach the sign at the Adisham turn-off. The elegant stone-block monastery once belonged to tea planter Sir Thomas Lester Villiers. To recreate his English lifestyle, he developed beautiful gardens and lawns amid the tropical surroundings and even had a Daimler car for transport, complete with an English chauffuer. Adisham is one of only 18 monasteries in the world belonging to the Sylvestrine Congregation, a suborder of the Benedictine fraternity founded in the 13th century. Inside, visitors are allowed to see the living room and library, and occasionally a couple more rooms.

There's a small shop selling produce from the monastery's lovely gardens and orchards. Buy some strawberry jam or wild guava jelly to enliven your next guest-house breakfast.

A taxi should cost Rs 500 return, including waiting time. Before you reach Adisham the road passes through **Tangamalai**, a bird sanctuary and nature reserve.

OTHER ATTRACTIONS

For more spectacular views – weather permitting – take the train to **Idalgashinna**, 8km west of Haputale. Walk back beside the train tracks enjoying a spectacular view with the terrain falling away on both sides.

Near the Dambatenne tea factory, the **Lipton's Seat** lookout rivals the views from World's End (and it's free). The Scottish tea baron Sir Thomas Lipton used to survey his burgeoning empire from here.

Take the signed narrow paved road from the tea factory and climb about 7km through lush tea plantations to the lookout. From the tea factory the ascent should take about

2½ hours. The earliest bus leaves Haputale at 6.30am. Look forward to the company of Tamil tea pickers going off to work as you walk uphill to Lipton's Seat.

Some visitors hike along the train lines from Haputale to **Pattipola** (14km, an all-day hike), the highest train station in Sri Lanka. From Pattipola you can continue via foot or taxi to Ohiya train station, and from there to the Horton Plains.

Sleeping & Eating

White Monkey/Dias Rest (☎ 568 1027; www.people freenet.de/diasrest; Thotulagala; s/d Rs 880/1100) Surrounded by a tea plantation and fruit trees 3km east of the train station, the White Monkey has a local atmosphere and two double rooms and a family cottage – all with superb views that rival that of World's End on a clear day. The owner is an experienced guide and can advise on interesting local treks whatever the weather. A three-wheeler from the train station is around Rs 250.

Royal Top Rest Inn (☎ 226 8178; 22 Station Rd; s/d Rs 880/1100) A short walk from the train station, this is a friendly place with pleasant views, a cheerfully gaudy living room and simple but clean rooms. There's a restaurant, a small outdoor area and a sunny shared balcony.

Amarasinghe Guest House (☎ 226 8175; www.amara singheguest.com; Thambapillai Ave; r Rs 990; ▢) With bright colours and Asian art, this is one of Haputale's longest-running guest houses. There are eight simple rooms – most with balconies – and a comfortable downstairs restaurant. The surrounding garden is a riot of tropical vegetation and colourful flowers. Mr Amarasinghe will pick you up from the train station at no charge. If you walk, follow the directions to Bawa Guest House (below) and then continue on to a further flight of steps, which will take you in the back way to Amarasinghe Guest House.

Bawa Guest House (☎ 071 808 0552; 32 Thambapillai Ave; r Rs 990) Housed in a spearmint-green villa, Bawa Guest House is now in its fourth decade of operation. After 30 years the friendly family has perfected their combination of homey, kitsch decor and a warm welcome. Mr Bawa is a bit of a gem buff and eagerly shares his wisdom. Pressure to buy is pleasingly low-key. If you're arriving at the Bawa Guest House by foot, follow Temple Rd until you see a yellow Bawa Guest House sign to the south, just off the side of the road. Go down the first flight of stairs and head along the path for about 250m.

Sri Lak View Holiday Inn (☎ 226 8125; www .srilakviewholidayinn.com; Sherwood Rd; r Rs 1100-1320; ▢) Haputale's best place to stay combines 16 spotless modern rooms with views that stretch a few hundred kilometres. If the weather's good, have an end-of-day beer on the grassy deck. Otherwise park yourself in the cosy restaurant. Multiple reader recommendations mean they must be doing something right.

Mountfield Cottage (☎ 072 421 3731; www.mount fieldcottage.com; Haldummulla; r Rs 2750-3850) Located on the Belihul Oya road, 9km from Haputale, this single-bungalow operation has grown to include new stand-alone cottages incorporating natural cliff faces in the interior walls. They might look like fibreglass, but a sly tap reveals 100% ages-old rock. Much more recent are the meals served in the attached seafood restaurant (Rs 400 to 600).

Olympus Plaza Hotel (☎ 226 8544; www.olympus plazahotel.com; Temple Rd; r Rs 3800/4800; ☎) This new multistorey place brings a snazzy, business-hotel feel to sleepy Haputale. That means you're guaranteed a billiard room, gym, karaoke and satellite TV. It's a tad overpriced, but reception is usually keen to negotiate if you're hanging out for a few away-from-home comforts. On weekends it's a popular wedding venue.

Kelburne Tea Estate (☎ 011-257 3382; www.kel burnemountainview.com; bungalows Rs 11,500-13,800) About 2km east of Haputale train station, Kelburne is a wonderful spot to relax for a few days. Add your name to the colourful global road sign – BYO compass – after a stay in one of three estate bungalows that totally define the word cosy. Brand new bathrooms contrast nicely with an array of supercomfy couches and loads of old *National Geographic* magazines to get you planning your next trip. There's one bungalow with two bedrooms and two bungalows with three bedrooms – a splurge-worthy bargain at Rs 11,500 for four people. Meals are also available from a resident cook. Forward bookings are essential.

You're best off eating in your guest house, but there are a number of OK places for short eats, dosas, *rottis*, and rice and curry, including the **Lanka Tea Centre** (Temple Rd), opposite the Welimada and Nuwara Eliya bus stand, and the **Sri Vani Vilas Hotel** (Dambatenne Rd), near the Bandarawela bus stand.

The best bakery in town is also nearby. Head to **Risara Bakers** for what just may be Sri Lanka's best samosas. Pop in there when you get back from World's End in the early afternoon. A fresh batch of still-warm baked goodies usually appears around 2pm. If you need self-catering for World's End, the **Premaratna grocery** is also tucked in around the bustling buses.

Getting There & Away

BUS

There are direct buses to Nuwara Eliya at 7am and 2pm (Rs 70, 3½ hours), but you can also go to Welimada (private bus Rs 38, two hours) and get an onward service. There are frequent buses to Bandarawela (Rs 20, one hour), as well as express buses to Colombo (Rs 500, six hours).

For the south coast change, at Wellawaya (Rs 70), 1½ hours down the hill from Haputale.

TRAIN

Haputale is on the Colombo–Badulla line, so you can travel directly by train to and from Kandy or Nanu Oya (for Nuwara Eliya). The train stops at Colombo (8½ to nine hours), Kandy (5½ hours), Nanu Oya (3rd/2nd class Rs 22/40, 1½ hours), Ohiya (40 minutes), Bandarawela (3rd/2nd class Rs 6/11, 30 minutes) and Badulla (3rd/2nd class Rs 24/44, two hours).

The daily train departures in the Badulla direction are at 5.07am, 11.25am, 2.09pm (on *Podi Menike*) and 5.34pm (on *Udarata Menike*). In the Colombo direction the trains depart at 7.47am (*Udarata Menike*), 10.48am (*Podi Menike)*, and 8.15pm (on the night mail) and 9.30pm. The *Udarata Menike* doesn't go via Kandy, but a slow train departs at 2.37pm.

BANDARAWELA

☎ 057 / pop 7188 / elev 1230m

Bandarawela, 10km north of Haputale but noticeably warmer, is a busy market town that makes a good base for exploring the surrounding area. Due to its agreeable climate, it's a popular area to retire to. Each Sunday morning the town has a lively market. Bandarawela has a fine old hotel dripping in colonial charm and the opportunity to cook Sri Lankan food with the excellent Woodlands Network. It's also a good transport hub if you're heading east or further into the Hill Country.

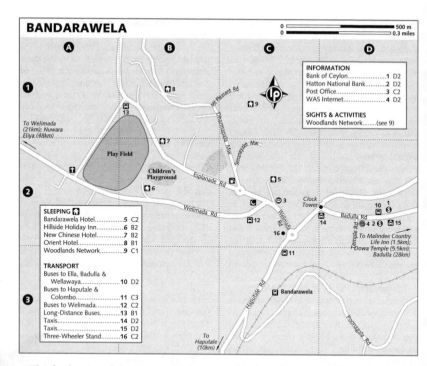

BANDARAWELA

INFORMATION
Bank of Ceylon......................1 D2
Hatton National Bank...........2 D2
Post Office............................3 C2
WAS Internet........................4 D2

SIGHTS & ACTIVITIES
Woodlands Network........(see 9)

To Welimada
(21km); Nuwara
Eliya (48km)

Play Field

Children's
Playground

Clock
Tower

To Malindee Country
Life Inn (1.5km);
Dowa Temple (5.5km);
Badulla (28km)

Bandarawela

To
Haputale
(10km)

SLEEPING
Bandarawela Hotel..............5 C2
Hillside Holiday Inn..............6 B2
New Chinese Hotel...............7 B2
Orient Hotel.........................8 B1
Woodlands Network............9 C1

TRANSPORT
Buses to Ella, Badulla &
Wellawaya.....................10 D2
Buses to Haputale &
Colombo.........................11 C3
Buses to Welimada.............12 C2
Long-Distance Buses...........13 B1
Taxis..................................14 D2
Taxis..................................15 D2
Three-Wheeler Stand..........16 C2

The focal point of the town is the busy junction just north of the train station. From here Haputale Rd goes southwest; Welimada Rd heads northwest then turns sharply left by a mosque; and Badulla Rd, with the main bus and taxi stops, heads downhill to the east.

Information

The post office is near the Bandarawela Hotel. For internet and international phone calls, head to **WAS Internet** (1st fl, Commercial Centre, cnr Temple Rd & Badulla Rd; per hr Rs 40; 7am-7pm).
Bank of Ceylon (Badulla Rd) ATM.
Hatton National Bank (Badulla Rd) ATM and cash advances on MasterCard and Visa.

Sights & Activities

DOWA TEMPLE

About 6km east of Bandarawela on the road to Badulla, the charming Dowa Temple is pleasantly situated close to a stream on the south side of the road. A beautiful 4m-high standing Buddha is cut into the rock face below the road. The walls of the adjacent cave shrine, cut from solid rock, are covered with excellent Sri Lankan–style Buddhist murals. The temple

is like a smaller version of Dambulla (p214), and, like the Royal Rock Temple at Dambulla, King Valagamba (Vattajamini Ahhya) also took refuge here in the 1st century BC during his 14-year exile from Anuradhapura. The temple is easy to miss if you're coming by bus, so ask the bus conductor to tell you when to alight. A three-wheeler or taxi from Bandarawela should cost Rs 600 to 700 return, including waiting time. A donation is expected at the temple.

WOODLANDS NETWORK

Founded by the late Dutch priest Harry Haas in 1992, **Woodlands Network** (222 3213; www.visitwoodlandsnetwork.org; 18 UCT, Dharmapla Mawath) is one of the most exemplary community tourism organisations in Sri Lanka. The centre offers alternative tourism services in the Hill Country, and can also advise on like-minded initiatives through the rest of Sri Lanka. Sri Lankan cooking lessons; meditation classes; and visits to temples, forest hermitages, tea plantations, farms and waterfalls can all be arranged. Woodlands also has a few rooms (opposite) and can also organise homestays for groups or individuals. Booking ahead is essential.

Sleeping & Eating

BUDGET

Woodlands Network (☎ 222 3213; www.visitwoodland snetwork.org; 18 UCT, Dharmapla Mawath; Rs 800) Simple rooms in a friendly homestay come with the great opportunity to learn all about Sri Lankan cooking. First you'll need to gather the organic vegies from Woodlands' garden just across the lane. Phone at least one day ahead.

Hillside Holiday Inn (☎ 222 2201; 34/10 Welimada Rd; s/d/tr Rs 1100/1650/2200) Just off Welimada Rd down a quiet lane, the Hillside combines a good restaurant – Chinese, Sri Lankan and Western food, you know the score – with clean rooms and views of the local cricket oval and a quaint English church.

Malindee Country Life Inn (☎ 222 3124; Badulla Rd, Bindunuwela; s/d/tr Rs 1100/1650/2200) Two kilometres east of town, this is a family-run inn with lots of marble and brass on display. The foyer–living room is an intriguing place to relax, and there's a pretty garden. A three-wheeler from town should cost Rs 250.

New Chinese Hotel (☎ 223 1767; 32 Esplanade Rd; r Rs 1320) Lacking character, but with clean rooms, two friendly big dogs, and a steady stream of big hits from the schoolkids playing cricket across the road. You've probably already figured out there's a Chinese restaurant downstairs.

MIDRANGE

Orient Hotel (☎ 222 2407; www.orienthotelsl.com; 12 Dharmapala Mawatha; s/d/tr US$40/44/47) The Orient's made a conscious effort to lift standards, with bright rooms decorated with colourful wall hangings, a billiard room and a sunny beer garden. The suite (US$62) is surprisingly flash, so if you want all mod cons for at least one night, here's your chance. Tour groups are occasionally seen lurking in the combined karaoke/lounge bar.

Bandarawela Hotel (☎ 222 2501; www.aitkenspence hotels.com; 14 Welimada Rd; s/d/tr US$50/58/79) Around 70 years ago, they wisely stopped updating the furniture at this venerable old tea planters' club. Now, in a new millennium, you can ease into relax-at-all-costs easy chairs, spacious rooms with high ceilings, and a cosy bar and billiard saloon. The tortoises in the garden look to be a similar age to the friendly old guy out the front who redefines the combination of a pith helmet, walk shorts, gloves and long socks as a contemporary fashion statement. The Bandarawela Hotel's elevated garden setting is a peaceful escape from the dusty city.

Getting There & Away

BUS

There are infrequent direct buses to Nuwara Eliya (Rs 75); you can also hop on a frequent bus to Welimada (Rs 60) and continue to Nuwara Eliya (Rs 40). There are regular buses to Haputale (Rs 23), Ella (Rs 25) and Badulla (Rs 50). Long-distance services include Colombo (Rs 245, six hours), Tissamaharama, Tangalla and Galle. Buses to Tissa, Tangalla and Galle leave from the long-distance station on Esplanade Rd. Change at Wellawaya for buses to Tissa or the south coast.

TRAIN

Bandarawela is on the Colombo–Badulla railway line. Trains to Colombo (via Haputale) leave at 7.14am (on *Udarata Menike*), 10.18am (on *Podi Menike*, via Kandy) and 7.41pm. A train runs to Kandy at 1.47pm. Trains to Badulla (via Ella) leave at 5.37am and 12.30pm.

Destinations include Kandy (3rd/2nd/1st class Rs 135/250/460), Badulla (3rd/2nd/1st class Rs 35/70/120), Nanu Oya (for Nuwara Eliya; 3rd/2nd/1st class Rs 55/100/200), Polonnaruwa (3rd/2nd/1st class Rs 285/530/960), Ella (3rd/2nd/1st class Rs 15/30/40), Colombo (3rd/2nd/1st class Rs 210/390/720) and Haputale (3rd/2nd/1st class Rs 15/30/40).

ELLA

☎ 057

Here's your chance to ease off the travel accelerator with a few leisurely days at some of the Hill Country's best-value guest houses. The views through Ella Gap are stunning, and on a clear night, you can even spy the subtle glow of the Great Basses lighthouse on Sri Lanka's south coast. Don't be too laid-back, though: definitely make time for easygoing walks through tea plantations to temples and waterfalls. After each day look forward to Sri Lanka's best home-cooked food and the minisplurge of an extended Ayurvedic treatment. Don't miss the incessant bliss of the *shiro dhara* (hot-oil head massage). You'll soon be ready to hit the road once more.

Information

There's a post office, and the **Bank of Ceylon** can change cash and travellers cheques. For an ATM or credit card advances, head to Badulla or Bandarawela. Internet access and

THE HILL COUNTRY

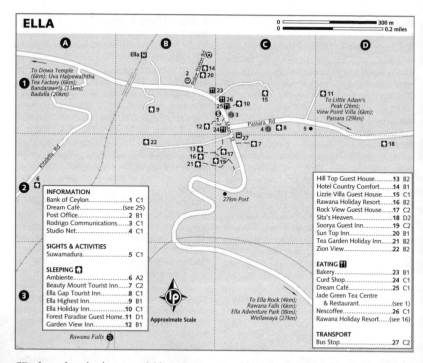

ELLA

0 — 300 m
0 — 0.2 miles

INFORMATION
Bank of Ceylon.....................1 C1
Dream Café.....................(see 25)
Post Office.........................2 B1
Rodrigo Communications......3 C1
Studio Net.........................4 C1

SIGHTS & ACTIVITIES
Suwamadura.....................5 C1

SLEEPING
Ambiente...........................6 A2
Beauty Mount Tourist Inn....7 C2
Ella Gap Tourist Inn............8 C1
Ella Highest Inn...................9 B1
Ella Holiday Inn.................10 C1
Forest Paradise Guest Home..11 D1
Garden View Inn................12 B1

Hill Top Guest House..........13 B2
Hotel Country Comfort.......14 B1
Lizzie Villa Guest House......15 C1
Rawana Holiday Resort........16 B2
Rock View Guest House.......17 C2
Sita's Heaven....................18 D2
Soorya Guest Inn................19 C2
Sun Top Inn......................20 B1
Tea Garden Holiday Inn......21 B2
Zion View.........................22 B2

EATING
Bakery.............................23 B1
Curd Shop.........................24 C1
Dream Café.......................25 C1
Jade Green Tea Centre
  & Restaurant................(see 1)
Nescoffee.........................26 C1
Rawana Holiday Resort......(see 16)

TRANSPORT
Bus Stop...........................27 C2

To Dowa Temple (6km); Uva Halpewaththa Tea Factory (6km); Bandarawela (11km); Badulla (20km)

Ella

Passara Rd

Kitalella Rd

Police Station Rd

To Little Adam's Peak (2km); View Point Villa (6km); Passara (29km)

27km Post

To Ella Rock (4km); Rawana Falls (6km); Ella Adventure Park (8km); Wellawaya (27km)

Approximate Scale

Rawana Falls

CD photo downloads are available at **Studio Net** (20 Passara Rd, per min Rs 3). If Studio Net's sole PC is being used, ask at **Dream Café** (per min Rs 5). **Rodrigo Communications** is a good source of travel information, especially the vagaries of local bus timetables. Nescoffee (p198) has a small selection of second-hand paperbacks.

Activities
HIKING

Ella is a great place for walking. Most accommodation can give you a hand-drawn map of local paths. Kick off with a stroll to what is locally dubbed **Little Adam's Peak**. Go down the Passara road until you get to the plant shop on your right, just past the 1km post. Follow the track to the left of garden shop; Little Adam's Peak is the biggest hill on your right. Take the second path that turns off to your right and follow it to the top of the hill. Part of this path passes through a tea estate. The approximately 4.5km round trip takes about 45 minutes each way. The final 20 minutes or so is uphill, but otherwise it's an easy walk. Get an early start from your guest house – around 7am – and you'll meet

Tamil families heading off to work in the tea plantations along the way. From atop Little Adam's Peak, waterfalls and a couple of tea factories shimmer from out of the mist that's often welded persistently to the surrounding hills.

Walking to **Ella Rock** is more demanding. Head along the train tracks (towards Bandarawela) for about 2.5km until you come to the metal bridge where you can see the small **Rawana Falls**. After passing the bridge, turn left towards the falls, cross a log bridge and follow the track up to Ella Rock, where you'll be rewarded with stunning views. The walk (approximately 9km in total) takes about two hours each way.

AYURVEDA
Suwamadura (☎ 567 3215; 25 Grand View, Passara Rd; 2hr full treatment Rs 3850; ☼ 9am-8pm) Spotless facility with trained staff offering a full range of treatment options, including massage, steam baths, herbal saunas, and the warm, soothing bliss of *shiro dhara*. The herbal sauna uses 50 different herbs, a few more than KFC's Colonel Sanders, and probably a whole lot better for you. Treat yourself after a long day's walking.

Sleeping

Touts might approach you on the train with tales that the hotel of your choice is too expensive, closed down or rat-infested. In fact, Ella has a high standard of accommodation, especially for guest houses, so they're most likely telling fibs.

BUDGET

Beauty Mount Tourist Inn (☎ 222 8760; s/d Rs 660/825) Clean and simple rooms cling to a forest-clad hill in the centre of Ella. The affable owner grows his own organic coffee, and the rice-and-curry dinners (Rs 250) are a veritable nine-course feast. Follow the path across the river and up the hill.

Garden View Inn (☎ 222 8792; s/d Rs 660/880) This inn has three simple rooms with bright, clean bathrooms in a family home. The owner has lots of information on walks in the area.

Soorya Guest Inn (☎ 222 8906; s/d Rs 660/880) Simple and central, with six rooms, a common balcony and a guest kitchen.

Lizzie Villa Guest House (☎ 222 8643; s Rs 660, d Rs 770-2200) You're trading off views for seclusion at this long-established place 200m off the main road. The rooms are simple but clean. Look forward to tasty food on the shady veranda with superfresh ingredients from the surrounding spice garden, vegie patch and orchard.

Hill Top Guest House (☎ 222 8780; s Rs 660-990, d Rs 770-1320; ⬚) Immaculate rooms, views of Ella Gap to die for and a welcoming family add up to one of Ella's best. The house is surrounded by verdant gardens, giving a sense of privacy. Good Sri Lankan meals are available.

Rawana Holiday Resort (☎ 222 8794; nalankumara@ yahoo.com; s Rs 660-1100, d Rs 880-1650) Perched high on a hillside overlooking Ella, this family-run guest house contains six balcony rooms with views, plus four less expensive interior rooms. Excellent food (p198) is served in the spacious open restaurant. Just watch out for the cheeky cat that occasionally ventures in from the Tea Garden Holiday Inn next door.

Rock View Guest House (☎ 222 8561; r Rs 880-1430) Oringally a Scottish tea planter's bungalow, Rock View combines spotless, freshly painted rooms with wooden floors and high ceilings, and new rooms with great Ella Gap views in an adjoining building. It's been in the same family for 50 years, and there are lots of poignant mementoes dotting the walls.

Forest Paradise Guest Home (☎ 222 8797; www.forest paradise.net; s/d Rs 880/990) Wake up to the sound of birds and the crisp aroma of pine trees at this friendly spot on a forest's edge. Rooms are clean and colourful, and the owner arranges trips into nearby Namunugala Hills (Rs 1500).

Sun Top Inn (☎ 222 8673; suntopinn@sltnet.lk; s/d/tr Rs 880/1100/1320; ⬚) Reader-recommended, and an easy downhill stroll from the train station, Sun Top is run by a friendly family. Bicycles are available for no charge, and there is a spacious and sunny shared lounge area.

Ella Highest Inn (☎ 567 6933; r Rs 1320) More like a cosy bed and breakfast than a guest house, the Highest Inn has a shared lounge with Asian art, a stereo and DVD player, and clean and comfortable rooms. It's surrounded by a tea plantation, so again, no views, just quiet seclusion.

Sita's Heaven (☎ 077 615 7030; jwimalasuriya@yahoo .com; r Rs 1320) Down a quiet forested lane five minutes' walk from central Ella, Sita's Heaven offers the best of both worlds, with privacy and great views. It's the kind of place where visitors end up staying longer than they planned.

MIDRANGE

Ella Gap Tourist Inn (☎ 222 8528; Passara Rd; r Rs 825-2750) Sleeping cats and dogs and shaded gardens give this place an easygoing atmosphere, perfect after a day's walking in the surrounding hills. Palm trees and planters chairs reinforce the languid tropical ambience. The older rooms inside the house are nicer than the smaller, newer rooms.

Tea Garden Holiday Inn (☎ 222 8860; d incl breakfast Rs 1650-2640) Friendly staff and a friendly cat feature at this hilltop spot with wraparound balconies and brightly coloured rooms. Get your sketch book out for the Ella Gap views, and then use a new page for the vista of Rawana Falls from the rear balcony.

Hotel Country Comfort (☎ 222 8500; www.hotel countrycomfort.lk; Police Station Rd; r Rs 1650-2750; ⬚) Down a quiet garden-trimmed lane near the train station, Country Comfort combines older – but darker – character-filled rooms in the original colonial building and spotless newer rooms with chunky wooden furniture, modern bathrooms and bay windows.

Ella Holiday Inn (☎ 222 8615; www.ellaholiday.com; d Rs 1650-3850, f Rs 6600; ⬚) Some of the spacious, colourful rooms have balconies at this friendly three-storey spot in the centre of town. The bathrooms are snazzy in black and white, and cookery classes are also available (Rs 1500). Ask for the quiet room with a superprivate balcony on the right-hand side of the hotel.

Zion View (☎ 072 785 5713; zionview@yahoo.com; r Rs 2200) This sparkling-new five-room place is both view-friendly and secluded, with incredible views through Ella Gap to the south coast. Owner Sena, who trained in Switzerland, knows what travellers want – supercomfy slat beds, hammocks and spotless wood-trimmed bathrooms. Zion View is uphill, off the main road opposite the bus stand.

Ambiente (☎ 222 8867; www.ambiente.lk; Kitalella Rd; s/d Rs 2300/3080, tr 3080-4180; 🖳) You get views of Ella's 'Big Three' – Little Adam's Peak, Rawana Waterfall and Ella Gap – at this motel-like place perched high on the edge of a working tea plantation. Rooms are comfortable and clean, but you are paying a premium for the stupendous views. Resident dogs Tim and Tina are your perfect canine walking guides. A three-wheeler from the train station should cost Rs 250. Don't even think about walking; it's very steep.

ourpick View Point Villa (☎ 077 357 3851; www .viewpoint-villa-ella.com; 8 Mile Post, Passara Rd; r Rs 3300; 🖳) Wonderfully isolated spot 6km from Ella on the Passara Rd, View Point's brightly coloured villas combine soaring wooden ceilings with the best bathrooms in the Hill Country. Food comes courtesy of the adjacent organic garden, and there are great hill and tea plantation views fom the breezy open verandas. A three-wheeler from Ella should cost around Rs 250. Motorcycles can be rented for Rs 1100 per day for off-the-beaten-path exploring.

Ella Adventure Park (☎ 077 352 352; www.wil dernesslanka.com; s/d/tr US$60/70/75, tree houses US$65) About 9km southeast of Ella on the Wellawaya road, this rustic place has log furniture, lots of natural stone and a quiet bush setting. Choose between tree houses and ecolodges. Accommodation is a bit expensive for the facilities, but you're paying for the pristine verdant ambience. There's an adventurous checklist of adrenalin-inducing activities to tick off, including canoeing (US$30), mountain biking (US$15), trekking (US$10) and a ropes course (US$25). Cool off afterwards in the natural swimming pool. Pick-ups from Ella train station are free; otherwise a three-wheeler is around Rs 600.

Eating & Drinking

Ella's guest houses are a great place to try excellent home-cooked food, perhaps some of the best eating you'll discover in all of Sri Lanka. All the guest houses and hotels serve meals; they ask for around four hours' advance notice. Especially good is the food at Rawana Holiday Resort – you can even join the friendly owner in the kitchen. Just let them know by midafternoon. In recent years, the sleepy village has even spawned a couple of places that stay open for a few beers later at night. If you've been walking in the surounding hills and tea plantations, you've probably earned a cooling end-of-the-day ale.

Curd (made with buffalo milk) and treacle (syrup from the *kitul* palm; sometimes misnamed 'honey') is a much-touted local speciality.

Curd Shop (Main St; meals Rs 150-250) Tiny hole-in-the-wall spot near the bus stand that's good for breakfast – around 15% cheaper than the guest houses – before or after an early-morning stroll to Little Adam's Peak. It's a good place to try curd and honey (Rs 90) or *kotthu rotti* (Rs 200). It's also handy for picking up sandwiches if you're going walking.

Nescoffee (Main St; meals Rs 200-400) This cool and compact roadside cafe/bar is an homage to Robert Nesta Marley and has nonstop reggae beats and Ella's coldest beer. You'll need it for the spicy devilled cashews. Breakfast is available from early in the day, and Nescoffee stays open 'till the last person leaves'. (Let your guest-house owner know if you're going to be late, because some places in Ella close their doors a tad early.)

Dream Café (Main St; mains Rs 300-500) Multiple reader recommendations fly the flag for this main-drag place with a cool, shady garden. It's a cosmopolitan wee spot with good espresso coffee, well-executed Western dishes like tortilla chicken wraps, and smoothies and salads for the healthy traveller. Don't be too pious, though: the beers are nice and cold. Internet (Rs 5 per minute) is also available.

ourpick Rawana Holiday Resort (☎ 222 8794; meals Rs 440) 'See you for rice and curry at 8 o'clock' certainly sells short one of the best eating experiences in Sri Lanka. Look forward to around eight different dishes, including sweet-and-sour eggplant, spicy potato curry, and Rawana's signature garlic curry, made with whole cloves of the 'stinking rose'. Wannabe vampires might want to eat elsewhere, but it's a must-visit for everyone else. The charming owner offers cookery classes in her kitchen and provides printouts of her surprising recipes. Everything is from her organic garden nearby. You'll need to book by midafternoon.

Also recommended:

Jade Green Tea Centre & Restaurant (Main St; meals Rs 200-400; 🕙 noon-10pm) Reader-recommended spot for good local food above the Bank of Ceylon.

Next door to Nescoffee is a busy bakery for good short eats. Get there around 8am and 4pm for when the food comes out of the wood-fired oven

Getting There & Away
BUS & TAXI
The road to Ella leaves the Bandarawela–Badulla road about 9km out of Bandarawela. Buses change schedule fairly often, so ask at Rodrigo Communications for an update.

Buses to Bandarawela cost Rs 25 and are fairly frequent. There are infrequent buses to Badulla, but you can get a bus to Bandarawela and change there for Badulla. To or from Kandy you must change at Badulla. Alternatively, you could go to Wellawaya, catch the intercity to Nuwara Eliya and then change again for Kandy.

Buses to Matara (CTB/intercity express Rs 145/270) stop at Ella around every hour from about 6.30am until about 2.30pm. The buses are likely to be quite full by the time they reach Ella, though the buses around noon are usually less busy. You can always catch a bus to Wellawaya (Rs 45) and change there for a service to the South or for Monaragala (for Arugam Bay). A bus heads to Galle every morning at 8am (Rs 330).

It costs Rs 700 to go by three-wheeler from Ella to Bandarawela.

TRAIN
Ella is an hour from Haputale and Badulla on the Colombo–Badulla line. The stretch from Haputale (through Bandarawela) has particularly lovely scenery. Roughly 10km north of Ella, at Demodara, the line performs a complete loop around a hillside and tunnels under itself at a level 30m lower.

Ella's train station is quaint, and the fares and timetables are well posted. You'll probably be met by a few touts spinning fictional tales; Ella's guest-house fraternity is perhaps the most competitive in all of Sri Lanka. Touts sometimes board the train a few stops before Ella.

The main trains to Colombo (3rd/2nd class, Rs 220/410) depart at 6.49am (*Udarata Menike*) and 9.49am (*Podi Menike*). These have a 1st-class observation car; seats inside the car

should be booked ahead (Rs 850). Another train to Colombo departs at 7.22pm. Trains depart to Kandy (3rd/2nd class, Rs 145/270) at 9.49am, 1.10pm and 7.22pm, and to Badulla at 6.08am, 1.13pm and 3.05pm. Costs include the following: Bandarawela (3rd/2nd class, Rs 15/30), Haputale (3rd/2nd class, Rs 25/50), Nanu Oya (for Nuwara Eliya; 3rd/2nd class, Rs 70/120), Hatton (3rd/2nd class, Rs 95/180) and Badulla (3rd/2nd class, Rs 25/40).

AROUND ELLA
You can visit the **Dowa Temple** from Ella; see p194.

The **Uva Halpewaththa Tea Factory** runs tours (Rs 150). Catch a bus to Bandarawela, get off at Kumbawela junction, and flag a bus going to Badulla. Get off just after the 27km post, near the Halpe Temple. From here you've got a 2km walk to the factory. A three-wheeler from Ella will charge Rs 400 return.

The 19m-high **Rawana Ella Falls** are about 6km down Ella Gap towards Wellawaya. During rainy months the water comes leaping down the mountainside in what is claimed to be the wildest-looking fall in Sri

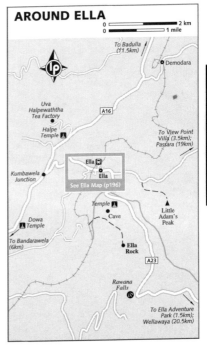

AROUND ELLA

0 2 km
0 1 mile

To Badulla
(11.5km)

Demodara

Uva
Halpewaththa
Tea Factory

A16

Halpe
Temple

To View Point
Villa (3.5km);
Passara (19km)

Ella

See Ella Map (p196)

Kumbawela
Junction

Temple

Cave

Little
Adam's
Peak

Dowa
Temple

To Bandarawela
(6km)

Ella
Rock

A23

Rawana
Falls

To Ella Adventure
Park (1.5km);
Wellawaya (20.5km)

THE HILL COUNTRY

Lanka, but during the dry season it may not flow at all. There are vendors selling food and trinkets, and the invariable array of 'guides' wanting to point out 'the waterfall' that's already blindingly obvious. Buses from Ella cost Rs 11, and a three-wheeler will cost Rs 100 return, including waiting time.

Further up the road and to your left as you approach Ella, a side road takes you to a little **temple** and a **cave** that is associated with the Ramayana story. You may visit the temple, which is part of a monastery, but remember to remove your shoes and hat, and to cover your legs and arms. The cave, located in a cleft in the mountain that rises to Ella Rock, is reputed to be where the king of Lanka held Sita captive. Boys will show you where the steep, overgrown and slippery track up to the cave starts.

BADULLA
☎ 055 / pop 42,572 / elev 680m

Badulla marks the southeast extremity of the Hill Country and is a transport gateway to the east coast. It is one of Sri Lanka's oldest towns, occupied briefly by the Portuguese, who torched it upon leaving. For the British it was an important social centre. But scratch the surface beyond the pretty gardens and clock tower, and any vestiges of a past including a racecourse and cricket club are lost in Badulla's typical Sri Lankan bustle. The railway through the Hill Country from Colombo terminates here. In British times, it was an important hub for transporting plantation products to Colombo.

Information
Bank of Ceylon (Bank Rd) has an ATM and exchange facilities. The **post office** (Post Office Rd) is opposite the market, a short stroll downhill from the bus station. Log on at **McAffee Internet** (7 Lower King St; per hr Rs 60).

Sights
PLACES OF WORSHIP
Most Sri Lankans visiting Badulla stop at either Muthiyagana Vihara or Kataragama Devale. **Muthiyagana Vihara** is a large Buddhist complex and includes a whitewashed dagoba

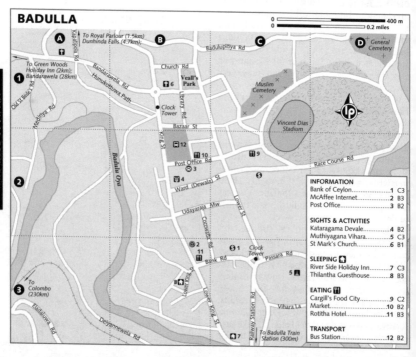

BADULLA

0	400 m
0	0.2 miles

INFORMATION
Bank of Ceylon...............................1 C3
McAffee Internet...........................2 B3
Post Office.......................................3 B2

SIGHTS & ACTIVITIES
Kataragama Devale......................4 B2
Muthiyagana Vihara......................5 C3
St Mark's Church............................6 B1

SLEEPING
River Side Holiday Inn..................7 C3
Thilantha Guesthouse.................8 B3

EATING
Cargill's Food City..........................9 C2
Market...10 B2
Rotitha Hotel................................11 B3

TRANSPORT
Bus Station....................................12 B2

in spacious grounds in the southeast of town. During festivals the resident elephant may be paraded around.

At **Kataragama Devale** the main objects of veneration are statues of the gods Kataragama, Saman and Vishnu. Uniquely, the *devale* was constructed in Kandyan style rather than South Indian Tamil style, with a long wooden shrine hall painted with murals depicting a *perahera*.

If you are a history buff, take a look through **St Mark's Church** and peruse the old headstones. Inside is a plaque commemorating the elephant hunter Major Rogers, who was killed by lightning. Legend has it that following a particularly severe thunderstorm in Haputale in 1845, Rogers stepped onto his veranda and proclaimed, 'It's all over now' to his wife. Ahh, not so fast, matey: one last bolt struck him dead.

Relatives of the 1500 elephants he killed in a four-year stint probably trumpeted in glee. Rogers' actual gravestone near Nuwara Eliya is now cracked in half, reputedly by another bolt of celestial energy.

DUNHINDA FALLS

Five kilometres north of Badulla are the 63m-high **Dunhinda Falls** (admission Rs 25). The best time to see them is June and July, but they're worth a visit at any time. It's a good spot for a picnic, but keep an eye out for light-fingered monkeys. Buses leave every 30 minutes from Badulla (Rs 30). From the bus stop the falls are about 1km along a clearly defined path. It's a bit of a scramble, so wear suitable shoes. You can see a lower waterfall on the walk, and there's a good observation spot at the end of the path. There are many snack places along the trail. Avoid public holidays and weekends, when the place can get packed. A three-wheeler from Badulla costs Rs 500 for the return trip.

Sleeping & Eating

In recent years, Badulla's cheaper guest houses have developed a reputation for being hire-by-the-hour kinds of places. You're better off paying a little bit more to ensure a good night's kip. A few cheaper places hover around the train station if you're really counting your rupees.

Green Woods Holiday Inn (☎ 223 1358; 301 Bandarawela Rd; s/d Rs 660/1320, bungalow Rs 3500; ❂)

Spearmint-green decor blends in with the surrounding forest at this place 3km out of town on the road to Bandarawela. Rooms have ceiling-to-floor windows and all have hot water. Ask for a quieter room away from the road, or for one of the more spacious forest bungalows. Decent Sri Lankan, Chinese and Western meals are available.

River Side Holiday Inn (☎ 222 2090; rahinn@sltnet .lk; 27 Lower King St; d/f Rs 1320/2200; ❂) Badulla's most efficiently run hotel is a modern affair with a variety of rooms. Standards vary, so have a squiz before saying yes. The rooftop bar/restaurant serves decent Sri Lankan and Chinese food, and is the only worthwhile spot in town for a cold beer. A word of caution though – Friday and Saturday nights feature the occasional tortured bout of karaoke.

Thilantha Guesthouse (☎ 060-256 4130; 28/4 Lower King St; r Rs 1650) Cosy rooms and a warm welcome in a location that's right under giant power pylons. At the weekends it's a popular spot for wedding receptions.

Royal Parlour (☎ 222 9695; 74 Mahiyangana Rd; s/d Rs 1925/2200; ❂) On the main road into town from Dunhinda Falls, the Royal Parlour has six modern rooms and a good restaurant. The TV in reception is continually tuned to live cricket. A three-wheeler from town is around Rs 50.

There are many local eateries along Lower St, near the intersection with Bazaar St. Self-caterers can buy groceries at **Cargills Food City** (Post Office Rd), and the colourful **market** opposite the post office has a surprisingly wide range of fruit and vegies.

If you're staying at the southern end of town, the **Rotitha Hotel** (☎ 071 421 3132; meals Rs 125-200) is a handy spot for breakfast before heading to the bus station. A few coconut *rotti*, string hoppers, *sambol* and coffee should be around Rs 125.

Getting There & Away
BUS

Buses run to Nuwara Eliya (CTB Rs 85) every 40 minutes until 4.30pm, to Bandarawela (private bus Rs 50) every 20 minutes from 6am until 4.50pm, and to Ella (private bus Rs 42) approximately every two hours until 5pm. There are also buses to Colombo (intercity express Rs 640) until 10pm, and to Kandy (CTB/intercity express Rs 170/315) until 2pm. For Monaragala (private bus Rs 115), buses leave every hour until 5.30pm.

THE HILL COUNTRY

TRAIN

The main daily services to Colombo (3rd/2nd/1st class Rs 235/430/850) depart Badulla at 5.55am *(Udarata Menike)*, 8.50am *(Podi Menike* via Kandy), 5.50pm (with sleeperettes) and 7.15pm (a slow train). Tickets to Kandy cost Rs 150/300/830 in 3rd/2nd/1st class.

WELLAWAYA

☎ 055

By Wellawaya you have left the Hill Country and descended to the dry plains that were once home to the ancient Sinhalese kingdom of Ruhunu. Wellawaya is simply a small crossroads town and, apart from the nearby Buduruwagala carvings, there's not much of interest in the area. Apart from a quick three-wheeler dash to the Buddha figures at Buduruwagala, you'll be focused on sorting out onward transportation. Roads run north through the spectacular Ella Gap to the Hill Country; south to Tissamaharama and the coast; east to the coast; and west to Colombo.

Information

Hatton National Bank and Bank of Ceylon – both with ATMs and exchange facilities – are near the bus station. Across the road from the bus station you'll find **CGM Internet** (per hr Rs 50).

Sights

About 5km south of Wellawaya, a side road branches west off the Tissa road to the rock-cut Buddha figures of **Buduruwagala** (admission Rs 200; ⏲ 9am-5pm). A small signpost points the way along a 4km road that crosses a series of delicate lakes. Keep an eye out for local birdlife, including many egrets and herons.

The name Buduruwagala is derived from the words for Buddha (Budu), images *(ruva)* and stone *(gala)*. The figures are thought to date from around the 10th century and belong to the Mahayana Buddhist school, which enjoyed a brief heyday in Sri Lanka during this time. The gigantic standing Buddha – at 15m, it is the tallest on the island – in the centre still bears traces of its original stuccoed robe, and a long streak of orange suggests it was once brightly painted.

The central of the three figures to the Buddha's right is thought to be the Mahayana Buddhist figure Avalokitesvara (the bodhisattva of compassion). To the left of this white-painted figure is a female figure thought to be

his consort, Tara. Local legend says the third figure represents Prince Sudhana.

The three figures on the Buddha's left-hand side appear, to an inexpert eye, to be of a rather different style. The crowned figure at the centre of the group is thought to be Maitreya, the future Buddha. To his left stands Vajrapani, who holds a *vajra* (an hourglass-shaped thunderbolt symbol) – an unusual example of the Tantric side of Buddhism in Sri Lanka. The figure to the left may be either Vishnu or Sahampath Brahma. Several of the figures hold up their right hands with two fingers bent down to the palm – a beckoning gesture. You may be joined by a guide, who will expect a tip. A three-wheeler from Wellawaya costs about Rs 450 return.

Back on the corner of the main road from Wellawaya, the new **Archeological Museum** (admission free; ⏲ 8.30am-5pm Wed-Mon) has stone and terracotta artefacts from nearby Buduruwagala.

Sleeping & Eating

Little Rose (☎ 567 8360; littlerose.inn@gmail.com; 101 Tissa Rd; s/d Rs 385/770) Just 500m from the bus station, this is your best option if you're staying overnight waiting for onward transport. In a quiet rural setting, the country home is surrounded by rice paddies and run by a welcoming family. Good, inexpensive meals are available. The shoebox-size single room shares a bathroom. A three-wheeler from the bus station costs about Rs 100.

There is a flurry of restaurants and snack stands across the road from the bus station.

Getting There & Away

Wellawaya is a common staging point between the Hill Country and the south and east coasts. You can usually find a connection here until midafternoon. Buses to Haputale (Rs 59) start running at around 5am, and the last bus leaves at about 5.30pm. There are regular buses to Monaragala (Rs 59, one hour), with the last bus leaving at about 6.30pm. Buses to Ella (Rs 45) run roughly every 30 minutes until 6pm. If you want to go to Kandy, catch a bus to Nuwara Eliya and change there. For Tissamaharama, change at Pannegamanuwa Junction. There are also buses to Tangalla (Rs 116, three hours) and Colombo (intercity express Rs 405, seven hours).

THE HILL COUNTRY

EMBILIPITIYA
☎ 047

Embilipitiya is a good base for tours to Uda Walawe National Park, as it's only 23km south of the park's ticket office. It's a busy, modern town built to service the surrounding irrigated paddy fields and sugar-cane plantations.

The bus station is in the centre of town, along with branches of Hatton National Bank, Seylan Bank, People's Bank, Commercial Bank and Sampath Bank. All have ATMs and exchange facilities and can arrange cash advances. There's an internet cafe opposite the central clock tower.

On the main road, 200m south of the bus station and opposite People's Bank, **Sarathchandra Tourist Guest House** (☎ 223 0044; r with/without air-con Rs 2500/1900; ❄) has clean rooms in a main building and separate cottages. There's also a restaurant and a billiards table. It's a friendly, well-run spot, and offers Uda Walawe tours for Rs 3000 per person (minimum of three people).

Around 1.5km south of the town centre and 600m south of Sarathchandra Tourist Guest House, **Centauria Tourist Hotel** (☎ 223 0514; ww.centauriatouristhotel.com; s/d/tr US$45/50/55; ❄ 🛋) combines a modern design with a languid, colonial ambience. The standard lakeside rooms are actually better value and more spacious than the deluxe rooms in the main building. If you're lucky you'll see water buffalo bathing in the lake. Rooms have (slightly noisy) air-con and a limited range of English-language satellite TV channels. There is a good restaurant (mains Rs 440 to 660), but weekend entertainment may include a couple of guys in straw hats playing mediocre versions of Boney M songs you're trying to forget. Uda Walawe 4WD tours cost Rs 3500 for up to six people. A three-wheeler to the hotel from the bus station costs Rs 200.

Buses leave regularly for most destinations from, or near, the bus station. There are CTB buses to Tangalla (Rs 49), Matara (Rs 76) and Ratnapura (Rs 138); the intercity buses cost about twice as much. Colombo intercity buses leave every 30 minutes (Rs 315).

UDA WALAWE NATIONAL PARK

With herds of elephants, wild buffalo, sambar deer and leopards, Uda Walawe is the Sri Lankan national park that best rivals the savannah reserves of Africa. The park's 30,821 hectares centre on the large Uda Walawe Reservoir, fed by the Walawe Ganga.

The entrance to the **park** (adult/child Rs 1850/975, service charge per group Rs 1000, vehicle charge per group Rs 420 ❄ 6am-6pm) is 12km from the Ratnapura–Hambantota road turn-off and 21km from Embilipitiya. Visitors buy tickets in a new building a further 2km on. Most people take a tour organised by their guest house or hotel, but a trip with one of the 4WDs waiting outside the gate should be around Rs 3000 for a half-day for up to eight people with driver. Last tickets are usually sold at 5pm.

Apart from stands of teak near the river, there's little forest in the park. The tall *pohon* grass, which grows in place of the forest, can make wildlife-watching difficult, except during dry months.

This is one of the best places in Sri Lanka to see elephants. There are about 500 in the park in herds of up to 50. There's an elephant-proof fence around the perimeter of the park, preventing elephants from getting out and cattle from getting in. The best time to observe elephant herds is from 6.30am to 10am and again from 4pm to 6.30pm.

Besides elephants, sambar deer and wild buffalo (their numbers boosted by domesticated buffaloes), there are also mongooses, bandicoots, foxes, water monitor lizards, crocodiles, sloth bears and the occasional leopard. There are 30 varieties of snakes and a wealth of birdlife; northern migrants join the residents between November and April.

Wildlife in Udu Walawe is under threat for several reasons, including illegal settlement and the associated grazing of cattle, as well as significant numbers of visitors in private vehicles. Another problem is poaching and the use of 'Hakka Patas', small explosive devices that are concealed in food and left on the banks of the Uda Walawe Reservoir, where wild boar graze. Though the explosives target wild boar, several elephants have been severely injured in recent years.

Helping to care for injured elephants from all over Sri Lanka is the nearby **Elephant Transit Home** (admission free; ❄ feedings 9am, noon, 3pm & 6pm), on the main road about 5km west of the park entrance. Supported by the **Born Free Foundation** (www.bornfree.org.uk), the complex is a halfway house for orphaned elephants. After rehabilitation, the elephants are released back into the wild, many into the Uda Walawe National Park. At the time of writing 64 elephants had been rehabilitated at the Elephant Transit Home and subsequently released. A boisterous group of around 30 juvenile and teenage pachyderms gets fed four times a day. Unlike the Pinnewala Elephant Orphanage, you can't get up close and personal with the elephants, but feeding time is still a lot of fun, and the good work being undertaken is undeniable. Most 4WD operators include a visit to the Elephant Transit Home in their trips. For more about Sri Lankan elephants, see boxed text, p66.

our pick **Selara River Eco Resort** (☎ 047-492 1340, 077 971 0184; Walawe Handiya; s/d/tr 1800/2500/3000) has six adobe and stone bungalows on a peaceful grassy expanse with a riverside location. Bathrooms are rustic designer-chic, with stone floors and natural waterfall-type showers. There's no air-con but still plenty of places to keep cool, including a two-storey tree house bar that's crammed with home-built wooden furniture. The attached restaurant does great things with lake fish, so it's worth plumping for the half-board option. A friendly monitor lizard (around 1m long) sometimes mooches around for a feed. Turn right from Embilipitiya Rd into Walawe Handiya, and go a further 5km before turning right at the Selera sign.

Walawa Safari Village (☎ 047-223 3201; kinjou@ dialogsl.net; RB Canal Rd; s/d incl full board Rs4500/9000, with air-con 5300/9800; 🌀) is 3km south of a small junction on the road from Embilipitiya to Uda Walawe and 10km from the park entrance. The clean and basic rooms are in a shaded garden setting, but it is overpriced. You're really paying for the location in proximity to the park. Trips to the park cost Rs 2000 per half day.

The park has four bungalows and three camp sites along the reservoir and the Walawa Ganga. You must prebook with the **Department of Wildlife Conservation** (☎ 011-256 0380; www.dwlc .lk). The bungalows each contain 10 beds; the charge is US$30 per person per day, plus the Rs 1850 park entry. Per group, there's also a US$2 charge for linen hire and a US$30 service charge. You must bring all of your own dry rations and kerosene. Camp sites cost US$8 per site per day, plus a US$6 service charge per trip. Students and children between six and 12 years of age pay half price (under six are free).

If you're staying at Embilipitiya and wish to organise a tour at the park, catch a bus to Tanamalwila (CTB/intercity express Rs 65/150) and ask to be dropped at the gate to the park.

SINHARAJA FOREST RESERVE

The last major undisturbed area of rainforest in Sri Lanka, this **forest reserve** (admission Rs 660, compulsory guide Rs 900) occupies a broad ridge at the heart of the island's wet zone. On most days the forest is shrouded by copious rain clouds that replenish its deep soils and balance water resources for much of southwestern Sri Lanka. Recognising its importance to the island's ecosystem, Unesco declared the Sinharaja Forest Reserve a World Heritage Site in 1989.

Sinharaja (Lion King) is bordered by rivers: the Koskulana Ganga in the north and the Gin Ganga in the south. An old foot track that goes past the Beverley Estate marks the eastern border, close to the highest peak in the forest, Hinipitigala (1171m). Towards the west the land decreases in elevation.

The reserve comprises 18,899 hectares of natural and modified forest, measuring about 21km east to west and 3.7km north to south. It was once a royal reserve, and some colonial records refer to it as Rajasinghe Forest. It may have been the last redoubt of the Sri Lankan lion.

In 1840 the forest became British crown land, and from that time some efforts were made toward its preservation. However, in 1971 loggers moved in and began selective logging. The logged native hardwoods were replaced with mahogany (which does not occur naturally here), logging roads and trails snaked into the forest and a wood-chip mill was built. Following intense lobbying by conservationists, the government called a halt to all logging in 1977. Machinery was dismantled and removed, the roads gradually grew over and Sinharaja was saved. Much of the rest of Sri Lanka's rainforest stands on mountain ridges within a 20km radius of the forest.

There are 22 villages around the forest, and locals are permitted to enter the area to tap palms to make jaggery (a hard brown sweet) and treacle, and to collect dead wood and leaves for fuel and construction. Medicinal plants are collected during specific seasons. Rattan collection is of more concern, as the demand for cane is high. Sinharaja attracts illegal gem miners, too, and abandoned open pits pose a danger to humans and animals and cause erosion. There is also some poaching of wild animals.

Information

Tickets are sold at the main Forest Department office at Kudawa and at Deodawa, 5km from Deniyaya on the Matara road.

There are several park access points, but the most relevant to travellers are those via Kudawa in the northwest and via Mederapitiya (reached from Deniyaya) in the southeast. At the time of writing the road via Mederapitiya was being upgraded, but the road via Kudawa was in serious need of repair and required 4WD access.

The drier months (August and September, and January to early April) are the best times to visit. Hinipitigala stands for most of the year under drizzles and downpours. Sinharaja receives between 3500mm and 5000mm of rain annually, with a minimum of 50mm in even the driest months. There's little seasonal variation in the temperature, which averages about 24°C inside the forest, with humidity at about 87%.

See www.sinharaja.4t.com for detailed information on the history, flora and fauna, and the challenges faced by the Sinharaja Forest Reserve.

In Deniyaya, the People's Bank has an ATM and exchange facilities. Internet access is available at iTechnology, 100m downhill from the police station.

Sights & Activities
WILDLIFE

Sinharaja has a wild profusion of flora. The canopy trees reach heights of up to 45m, with the next layer down topping 30m. Nearly all the subcanopy trees found here are rare or endangered. More than 65% of the 217 types of trees and woody climbers endemic to Sri Lanka's rainforest are found in Sinharaja.

The largest carnivore here is the leopard. Its presence can usually be gauged only by droppings and tracks, and it's seldom seen. Even rarer are rusty spotted cats and fishing cats. Sambar, barking deer and wild boar can be found on the forest floor. Groups of 10 to 14 purple-faced langurs are fairly common. There are three kinds of squirrels: the flame-striped jungle squirrel, the dusky-striped jungle squirrel and the western giant squirrel. Porcupines and pangolins waddle around the forest floor, mostly unseen. Civets and mongooses are nocturnal, though you may glimpse the occasional mongoose darting through the foliage during the day. Six species of bats have been recorded here.

Sinharaja has 45 species of reptiles, 21 of them endemic. Venomous snakes include the green pit viper (which inhabits trees), the hump-nosed viper and the krait, which lives on the forest floor. One of the most frequently found amphibians is the wrinkled frog, whose croaking is often heard at night.

There is a wealth of birdlife: 160 species have been recorded, with 18 of Sri Lanka's 20 endemic species seen here.

Sinharaja has leeches in abundance. In colonial times the British, Dutch and Portuguese armies rated leeches as their worst enemy when they tried to conquer the hinterland (which was then much more forested), and one British writer claimed leeches caused more casualties than all the other animals put together. These days you needn't suffer as much because all guides carry antileech preparations.

DENIYAYA & AROUND

Kotapola, 6km south of Deniyaya, has a superb early 17th-century **rock temple**. It's well worth the climb. The **Kiruwananaganga Falls**, some of the largest in Sri Lanka (60m high and up to 60m wide), are 5km east of Kotapola on the road towards Urubokka. The **Kolawenigama Temple**, 3km from Pallegama (which is 3km from Deniyaya), is of modest proportions but has a unique structure that resembles Kandy's Temple of the Sacred Tooth Relic. It was built by King Buwanekabahu VII in recognition of the protection given to the tooth relic by the villagers. The shrine has Kandyan-style frescoes.

Sleeping & Eating

It's more convenient to visit the reserve from Deniyaya if you don't have your own wheels, although Kudawa has better accommodation options.

DENIYAYA

Sinharaja Rest (☎ 041-227 3368; sinharaja_rest@yahoo .com; Temple Rd; r Rs 1100-1320) Brothers Palitha and Bandula Rathnayaka are both certified forest guides, so staying here makes it easy to maximise your time. The six rooms at their home are fairly basic, but there's good home cooking and a lovely private garden. Day trips to the Sinharaja Forest Reserve cost Rs 2200 per person, including transport, guiding and lunch, but excluding the Rs 660 entrance fee. Trips are also open to nonguests. If you give the brothers a week's notice, they can arrange overnight stays in forest bungalows.

Mederapitiya Homestays (☎ 041-227 3821, 077 386 3243; r Rs 1100, s/d incl full board Rs 2200/3300) Up a winding series of roads 9km from Deniyaya are these basic village homestays run in conjunction with the Sewalanka Foundation (www.sewalanka .org). Visitors are encouraged to take part in local activities, including small-scale tea production and *kitul* palm plantation work. Booking is essential. Ask for Pradeep Priyadarshana.

Deniyaya Rest House (☎ 041-227 3600; r Rs 1320) Like most former government rest houses in Sri Lanka, this place has the best location in town, with great views over the countryside. The large rooms are clean enough, and there's a bar and restaurant where you can tally up your leech bites over a stiff drink.

our pick **Rainforest Lodge** (☎ 077 706 8128; www .rainforestlodge-srilanka.de, in German; r Rs 2220-3300) Located in perfect isolation up a 300m path bisecting a tea plantation, Rainforest Lodge has sparkling and spacious rooms with high-quality bathrooms. Colonial-style furniture and French doors add a heritage touch. The views include a green trifecta of rainforest, rice paddies and tea gardens, and good food is served up by a welcoming local family.

KUDAWA

The Forest Department at Kudawa has some bungalows with fairly basic accommodation. Contact the **Forest Department HQ** (☎ 011-286 6633; forest@slt.lk; 82 Rajamalwatte Rd, Battaramulla), in Colombo, for information.

Kudawa Homestays (☎ 045-222 5643, 077 386 3243; r Rs 1100, s/d incl full board Rs 2200/3300) These basic village homestays are run in conjunction with the **Sewalanka Foundation** (www.sewalanka .org). Some of the homestay owners run bird-watching trips, and visitors are encouraged to take part in village life. Forward booking is essential. Ask for Saman Kumara.

Singraj Rest (☎ 045-225 5201; Koswatta; r Rs 1650) At Koswatta, 3km from Kalawana, this is a country hotel with seven rooms, a restaurant and a bar – the latter is just about the only entertainment in these parts. A three-wheeler here from Kalawana costs about Rs 350.

Blue Magpie (☎ 045-243 1872; 115 Pirivena Rd; s/d incl full board Rs 2200/4400) This lodge stands close to the park offices where the road ends. Rooms are basic but comfortable, and the river just outside is ideal for post-trekking dips. Sri Lankan meals here are excellent, and there's every chance you'll see scores of birds from the restaurant veranda.

Martin Wijesinghe's (☎ 045-568 1864; Forest View; r half/full board Rs 3410/5610) Right on the park's boundary near Kudawa, this is a basic but friendly place with five double rooms and a family room. It's about 4km from the ticket office down a very rough road. Martin used to work as a forest ranger and has a wealth of information, books and photographs about Sinharaja.

Rainforest Edge (☎ 045-225 5912; www.rainforest edge.com; Balwatukanda, Weddagala; s/d/tr US$150/212/287; 🖭) Managed by the same company that runs Boulder Garden, this rustic seven-room boutique lodge is in nearby Weddagala.

Boulder Garden (☎ 045-225 5812; www.bouldergar den.com; Sinharaja Rd, Koswatta; s/d/tr US$213/252/286, ste US$315-334; 🖭) This brilliantly designed ecoresort offers 10 rustic rooms – two of them in actual caves – built among boulders and streams. Meals are available in a beautiful garden restaurant. It's a little damp-smelling, but you are deep in the rainforest, after all. Activities on tap include kayaking, caving, bird-watching, abseiling and mountain biking.

Getting There & Away

BUS

From Ratnapura to Deniyaya (CTB Rs 140) there are buses roughly every hour from 6.45am until the afternoon. There are also several buses to and from Galle (CTB Rs 145), although you can always catch one of the more frequent buses to Akuressa (Rs 38 from Deniyaya) and change there.

There's an intercity express bus to and from Colombo (Rs 345, 5½ hours); if you want a CTB bus you're better off going to Akuressa or Pelmadulla and changing. For Ella and Nuwara Eliya, catch a bus to Pelmadulla and change there.

To reach Kalawana you can take a bus from Ratnapura (Rs 105 for an express). For Kudawa you can get a bus all the way from Colombo to Weddagala (4km before Kudawa, Rs 310), and then change in Weddagala to a Kudawa-bound bus.

Wherever you start, try to get moving as early as you can because the roads are often damaged by flooding.

CAR & MOTORCYCLE

If you have a car, the road through Hayes Tea Estate, north of Deniyaya en route to Madampe and Balangoda (for Belihul Oya, Haputale or Ratnapura), is very scenic.

SINHARAJA TO RATNAPURA

The A17 goes north from Deniyaya and passes through **Rakwana**. The view from above the town is a sweeping panorama across the plains of Uda Walawe National Park, with the escarpment of the Peak Wilderness Sanctuary to the north.

The best place to stay is the **Rakwana Rest House** (☎ 045-224 6299; r Rs 1650), a British-era bungalow with four pleasant rooms, a fine veranda, dining and drinks.

From Rakwana the road reaches a southern spur of the Hill (and tea) Country before hitting the important junction town of Pelmadulla, located between Ratnapura and Haputale.

There are around four buses per day between Rakwana and Ratnapura (Rs 65, two hours), and four between Rakwana and Deniyaya (Rs 82, 3½ hours).

RATNAPURA

☎ 045 / pop 48,230

Sitting among well-irrigated valleys between Adam's Peak and Sinharaja Forest Reserve, busy Ratnapura ('City of Gems' in Sanskrit) is a famous trading centre for the area's ancient wealth of gemstones. The region's wet and humid climate encourages the formation of riverbeds, which are the perfect environment for gemstones to develop.

Surrounding the town, the unappreciated rural scenery includes paddy fields cloaking the valley floors and hillside stands of rubber trees and tea bushes. Many villagers keep alive old Sinhalese traditions, such as leaving candles outside the front door at dusk to prevent evil spirits from entering.

Ratnapura was the traditional start of the toughest pilgrimages up to Adam's Peak. In clear weather it can be the best place for appreciating the full height of the sacred mountain, since the Hatton side from Dalhousie – now the preferred starting point – sits at a higher elevation.

The attractive road route from Ratnapura to Haputale skirts the southern edge of the Hill Country before ascending into the hills.

The bus station is around 200m northwest of Main St, which has banks with ATMs and exchange facilities. Check email at **Blue Line Net** (per hr Rs 50) on the northwest edge of the bus station.

Sights

The town's **National Museum** (☎ 222 2451; adult/child Rs 300/150; ⊙ 9am-4.30pm Tue-Sat) displays the fossilised remains of various animals (including rhinos and elephants) discovered in gem pits. Local culture and history are also well represented, with an interesting series of old black-and-white photographs.

There are several 'gem museums' that contain modest displays on gem lore, along with less-than-modest showrooms where you're encouraged to purchase 'local' gems at 'local' prices. A reputable place to purchase gems with relatively low sales pressure is **Ratnapura Gem Bureau, Museum & Laboratory** (☎ 222 2469; Pothgulvihara Mawatha, Getangama; admission free; ⊙ 9am-4pm). There's a good display of local minerals

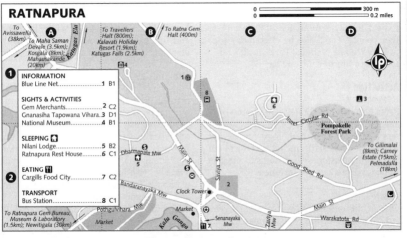

and gems, as well as information on mining and polishing. A return three-wheeler trip from the centre of town should cost about Rs 400, including waiting time.

The **Maha Saman Devale**, 4km west of the city, is an architectural treasure well worth visiting. Perched on a small hill, it has a handsome series of broad courtyards and multi-roofed, whitewashed pavilions in the Kandyan style. Originally built in the 13th century, the temple was destroyed by the Portuguese and then rebuilt during Dutch colonial times. The main sanctuary is dedicated to Saman, while side shrines honour the Buddha and Pattini. The major festival is a *perahera* on Esala *poya* (July/August); it's not as well known as the Kandy Esala Perahera, with which it coincides. You can take a three-wheeler from the town centre for about Rs 150.

The outskirts of town are dotted with **gem mines** and, although none cater specifically to tourists, most guest houses can arrange visits. Half-day trips are around Rs 2000.

You can also observe **gem merchants** selling their wares along Saviya St northeast of the clock tower. The biggest local gem market, however, convenes most mornings (*poya* days being an exception) in **Newitigala**, a 40-minute drive away (hiring a taxi for half a day should cost around Rs 2500). Both markets are usually over by 3pm.

There's a full-size replica of the Aukana Buddha at the **Gnanasiha Tapowana Vihara**, on top of a hill overlooking town; you can walk to it through Pompakelle Forest Park. There are some **caves** at Kosgala, about 8km from town.

You can also use Ratnapura as a base for a day trip to Sinharaja Forest Reserve. Expect to pay around Rs 6000 for up to four people. You'll also be offered day trips to Uda Walawe National Park, but it's really too long a journey for one day.

Activities

GEMOLOGY

Ratna Gem Halt (☎ 222 3745; www.ratnapura-online .com; 153/5 Outer Circular Rd; courses per day Rs 2000) offers a five-day basic gemology course that teaches students skills, including how to cut and polish gemstones. Excursions to the gem mines and markets are included.

HIKING

One of the oldest routes up Adam's Peak (p175) started at the Maha Saman Devale with the worship of Saman, the patron deity of the trek up the holy mountain. Peak-baggers and pilgrims today pick up the Gilimalai pilgrimage route from the road-head at Carney Estate, 15km, or one hour, away from Ratnapura by bus. It takes six to eight hours to reach the top of the peak, and five to seven hours to descend. Leeches are a particular menace on this trail.

Before the road was built, the village of **Gilimalai** ('Swallowed Mountain' – there's no view from here) was the first *ambalama* (rest hall) on the journey. The next stop was at **Pallebadole** (elevation 600m), a hill village with a dagoba and pilgrims' lodgings. Further uphill is **Nilihela**, a gorge; pilgrims tell a story of a woman named Nili who tried to save her child from falling over the edge, but fell herself. Pilgrims pause to call out her name, and the eerie echoes send out her answer, ever more faintly. The trail winds up to Diyabetma on the saddle of a ridge, and then up the steep final ascent to the footprint on the summit. See www.lakdasun.net for a detailed map and trail notes.

Much closer to town there are fewer arduous walks than to Adam's Peak. Three kilometres north of town are the 6m-high **Katugas Falls**, which are quite pleasant but are crowded on Sundays and public holidays. The lush **Pompakelle Forest Park**, behind Ratnapura Rest House, is laced with walking trails through this lush forest.

Sleeping & Eating

Ratna Gem Halt (☎ 222 3745; www.ratnapura-online .com; 153/5 Outer Circular Rd, r Rs 660-1650) This family-run, seven-room guest house north of town has family hospitality, good Sri Lankan food and fine views of emerald-green rice paddies. The cheapest rooms have no hot water and no views. It's run by a gem dealer who also runs gemology courses (left), and arranges half-day trips to the gem mines and markets (Rs 1200). A three-wheeler from the bus station is Rs 70.

Travellers Halt (☎ 222 3092; 30 Outer Circular Rd; no30_fernando@yahoo.com; s/d/tr Rs 1100/1320/1980; 🖪) Just over 1km out of town in the direction of Polhengoda Village, the family-owned Travellers Halt has nine rooms in a sprawling old house. The rooms are clean and pleasant, and management is keen to arrange tours. A three-wheeler from the bus station should cost Rs 100. Air-con is an additional Rs 1000.

GEMS

In Ratnapura, gems are still unearthed by ancient methods. Miners look for seams of *illama*, a gravel-bearing stratum likely to hold gemstones. It's usually found in the upper reaches of newly buried riverbeds; gems are heavier than gravel and aren't carried further downstream. From Colombo to Ratnapura you'll see gem-mining operations in paddy fields, but others dot the hills around Ratnapura.

Gem mining is a cooperative effort, requiring different people to dig the *illama*, wash the muddy gravel and search expertly through the pebbles. Profits are divided between all the members of the cooperative. Children are sometimes sent down the shafts, which can be either vertical or horizontal.

Types of Gems

In Ratnapura, people will soon discreetly offer you an unbelievable bargain. If you're not a gem buff, prepare to be ripped off. Synthetic stones are very hard to spot, even for experts.

A stone's value depends on several factors, including rarity, hardness and beauty. Gems are still cut and polished by hand, although modern methods are also coming into use. Some stones are cut and faceted (*en cabochon*); others are simply polished. Some of the more popular types of stone are listed here.

Corundrums includes sapphires and rubies, both second only to diamonds in hardness. The most valuable rubies are red, but these are not found in Sri Lanka in commercial quantities. You will see pink rubies, which are also correctly called pink sapphires. Rubies and sapphires are the same type of stone, with gradations of colour depending on the precise proportions of the chemicals in their make-up. Star rubies and star sapphires are Ratnapura specialties. The stones are comparatively dull, but a starburst appears when illuminated. Other sapphires are yellow, orange, white and, most valuably, blue. Sri Lanka has produced three of the world's largest blue sapphires, including the Star of India (displayed at the New York Museum of Natural History). Beware of pink or blue spinels being passed off as sapphires.

Cat's-eyes and alexandrite are the best-known gems in the chrysoberyl group. Cat's-eyes, with their catlike ray known as chatoyancy, vary from green through a honey colour to brown. Alexandrite is valued for its colour change under natural and artificial light. One rip-off to watch for is tourmalines, which are far less valuable, being sold as cat's-eyes.

The best-known stone in the beryl group, the emerald, is not found in Sri Lanka. Aquamarine is found here, and is reasonably priced since it is not as hard or lustrous as other stones.

The appearance of a zircon can approach that of a diamond, although it is a comparatively soft stone. Zircon comes in a variety of colours, from yellow through orange to brown and green.

Quartz varies from transparent to opaque, and is usually quite well priced. Colours vary from purple amethyst to brown smoky quartz, and yellow or orange citron.

The moonstone (feldspar) is Sri Lanka's special gem. Usually smooth and grey in colour, it is also found in a less common, subtle shade of blue.

Among the other precious stones, attractive spinels are fairly common and come in colours from transparent or opaque. Garnets are a poor man's ruby; light-brown garnets are often used in local rings. If you're offered topaz in Sri Lanka, it's most likely quartz.

Kalavati Holiday Resort (☎ 222 2465; fax 222 0020; Polhengoda Village; r with/without air-con Rs 3025/2200; ❄) Around 2.5km from the Ratnapura bus station, Kalavati has an extensive herb garden and is kitted out with antique furniture. Rooms are basic, but the gardens and quiet languid ambience are a good escape from Ratnapura's gem-fuelled hustle. There's an attached restaurant. A three-wheeler from the bus station costs about Rs 150.

Ratnapura Rest House (☎ 222 2299; keerhi.rrh@gmail.com; r with/without air-con Rs 3630/2420; ❄) Darting sparrows and a vintage Morris Minor car bring the colonial era alive at this classic old government rest house. The rooms are simple but clean, and the terrace restaurant is a perfect combination of slowly poured gin and tonics and languidly rotating ceiling fans. And because it's a government rest house, you just know it's got the best location in town.

THE HILL COUNTRY

Nilani Lodge (☎ 222 2170; hashani@sltnet.lk; 21 Dharmapala Mawatha; r Rs 2800, with air-con Rs 3300; ❄ ▣) This 1970s-era concrete hulk redeems itself with friendly staff, a newly refurbished restaurant (mains Rs 400 to 600) and excursions to the gem mines. It's a favourite haunt of overseas gem buyers.

Mahausakande (☎ 036-567 1421; www.mahausakande.org; Kiriella; s/d incl full board US$30/60) Nature conservation – it's part of a rainforest regeneration project – healthy and holistic eating, and nature walks are the attraction at this very worthy community tourism project 30 minutes from Ratnapura. Alcohol and tobacco aren't allowed, and you should try and give them two weeks' notice for bookings.

There are several eateries around Main St that serve reasonable rice and curry for low prices. There's also a Cargills Food City.

Getting There & Away

Any bus coming from Colombo (CTB/intercity express Rs 106/215, four hours) is likely to be jam-packed. For Hatton or Nuwara Eliya you'll have to catch a bus to Avissawella (Rs 32) and then change there. If you're going to Haputale, Ella and Badulla, you'll probably first have to catch a bus to Balangoda (Rs 42). The CTB bus to Embilipitiya (for Uda Walawe National Park) costs Rs 178. To get to Galle you must change at Matara (Rs 145, 4½ hours). There are also direct buses to Kandy (Rs 110, six hours).

THE HILL COUNTRY

The Ancient Cities

If crumbling temples, lost cities and sacred sites get your heart racing, it's time to peel yourself off the beach and head up-country. It was here on the hot central plains of Sri Lanka that ancient Sinhalese dynasties set up their capitals, built ambitious irrigation systems and supported massive artistic and architectural endeavours. Eventually these kingdoms fell, as kingdoms do, giving nature a chance to reclaim the land.

For more than a century, archaeologists have been slowly shedding the many layers of history from this overgrown landscape. The Rock Fort at Sigiriya, the bulging dagobas (stupas) of Polonnaruwa and the serene Buddhas scattered around Anuradhapura are but a few of the sites now considered national treasures. Recognising their historical and cultural value, Unesco has bequeathed protected status to some of the bigger sites.

The area covered in this chapter lies roughly between Kandy, Anuradhapura and Polonnaruwa, colloquially known as the 'Cultural Triangle'. Amateur archaeologists and anyone interested in Buddhist art will want to maximise their time in this area. Lay travellers should mix in some of the excellent national parks – there are great opportunities for spotting elephants, deer and other game.

You'll need a minimum of three days to hit the major attractions in this chapter, but plan on five or more days to take it all in at a leisurely pace. The roads up here are in good condition and there is accommodation to suit all tastes. The region can be explored as a loop trip, or you can hunker down in a central place such as Sigiriya and go on a series of day trips.

HIGHLIGHTS

- Admiring the fine artwork carved into the **Polonnaruwa Quadrangle** (p223) and other ancient buildings at this one-time Sinhalese capital

- Scaling the rock fortress at **Sigiriya** (p217), known for its epic views, outstanding art and mind-boggling ruins

- Cycling around the ruins of **Anuradhapura** (p231), where each twist and turn reveals ever grander temples and dagobas

- Go Buddha spotting in **Dambulla** (p215), where a series of rock caves contains some of Sri Lanka's most stunning paintings, temples and Buddhist images

- Spotting elephants and other wildlife in the lush **Minneriya National Park** (p228)

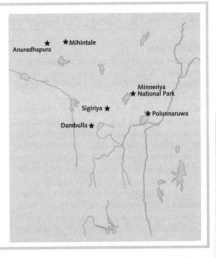

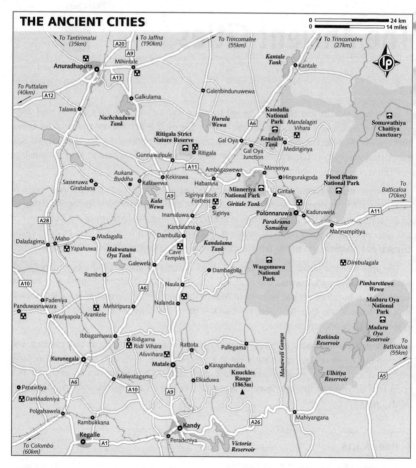

THE ANCIENT CITIES

Information

Foreign visitors must purchase tickets to visit the major Cultural Triangle sites as well as a few of the minor ones. You can buy either a 'round ticket' that covers most of the major sites, or individual tickets at the sites themselves. Currently a round ticket costs Rs 5400 (payable either in US dollars or in the rupee equivalent) and covers the following: Anuradhapura, Polonnaruwa, Sigiriya, Ritigala, Medirigiriya and Nalanda, plus a few sites in Kandy (but *not* the Temple of the Sacred Tooth Relic).

The round ticket is valid for three months from the date of purchase. In theory, you must finish using your ticket within three weeks of the first time you use it, but in practice no one checks the dates that closely. The ticket entitles you to one day's entry only – if you wish to spend a second day at any site, you pay the full day's fee. If paid for individually, the tickets cost US$25 each for Anuradhapura, Polonnaruwa and Sigiriya; US$10 for Medirigiriya; and US$5 for Ritigala and Nalanda. All foreign nationals and even foreigners with resident visas must pay the full amount. There are no student discounts on the round ticket, though sometimes you can get half-price tickets for individual sites if you sweet-talk the ticket seller. Children under 12 years are charged half-price, while those under six get in free.

Many Buddhist shrines within the Cultural Triangle area, including the Dambulla cave shrines, Sri Maha Bodhi and Mihintale, are run by the sangha (community of Buddhist monks and nuns) and charge separate entry fees, varying from Rs 100 to 1000.

Round tickets can be bought at the Anuradhapura, Polonnaruwa and Nalanda ticket offices. You can also buy them at the **Colombo Cultural Triangle office** (☎ 011-267 9921; 11 Independence Ave, Col 7; ⏱ 8.30am-4pm Mon-Fri) and the Cultural Triangle office in Kandy (p158).

Security is good in this region, although Anuradhapura, which contains a large military base, has seen bombings. In the past, Tamil rebels have preferred military targets, so just stay clear of these for safety's sake.

Getting Around

The towns and cities of the Cultural Triangle are well connected by public and private buses, and in some cases by train. Distances are not great and most roads are sealed, so getting around by public transport is relatively comfortable (although buses can be very crowded at certain times of day and during holiday periods). Departures between major towns and tourist sites are fairly frequent, so you needn't wait long for a ride.

On the other hand, many visitors hire a car and driver to visit the ancient cities. A sedan that can comfortably carry three passengers (four if you don't have much luggage) will cost around Rs 2500 to 2800 per day. For more than four people, a minivan is a better choice; these cost around Rs 3000 to 3500 per day (not including petrol).

MATALE
☎ 066 / pop 37,900

This midsize regional city at the heart of the island lies in a broad, fertile valley at an elevation of 300m. The road to Kandy, 24km south, ascends past paddy fields, areca palm plantations and pepper vines. Other regional specialities include vanilla, rubber, cinchona and cardamom. The area is also famous for *kohila* (a type of watercress) and small, mild chillies. The town's pleasant park includes a monument to the leaders of the 1848 Matale Rebellion – one of the less famous contributions to the Year of Revolutions!

Sights

Not far north of the bus stop for Kandy is an interesting Hindu temple, the **Sri Muthumariamman Thevasthanam** (admission Rs 200; ⏱ 8am-6pm). A priest will show you

the five enormous, colourful ceremonial chariots pulled along by people during an annual festival.

A drive east through **Knuckles Range**, east of Matale, presents some remarkable mountain views. The B38 heads uphill from the north end of town to a pass near Rattota, while other roads head southwest to the hill villages of Elkaduwa and Karagahandala before winding down to Kandy and the Victoria Reservoir. For more details about Knuckles Range, see p175.

ALUVIHARA

If the idea of a monastery built from a sheer rock wall sounds intriguing, make sure to pull off the road 3km north of Matale for a look at **Aluvihara** (admission Rs 100; ⏱ 7am-6pm). This unique series of monastic caves are picturesquely situated among rocks that have fallen from the mountains high above the valley. Legend has it that a giant used three of the rocks as a base for his cooking pot, and the name Aluvihara (Ash Monastery) refers to the ashes from the cooking fire.

The first cave you come to contains a 10m reclining Buddha and impressive lotus-pattern murals on the ceiling. Another is filled with cartoonlike murals of the realms of hell – if you're considering straying from the straight and narrow, you may think twice after seeing the statues of devils meting out an inventive range of punishments to sinners in the afterlife. One scene shows a sexual sinner with his skull cut open and his brains being ladled out by two demons.

Up a flight of rock steps is a cave dedicated to Buddhaghosa, the Indian scholar who is supposed to have spent several years here while working on the Tipitaka. Although histories affirm that Buddhaghosa lived in Anuradhapura in the 6th century AD, there's no clear evidence he stayed at Aluvihara. Nonetheless the cave walls are painted with scenes showing Buddhaghosa working on *ola* (palm-leaf) manuscripts.

Stairs continue to the summit of the rock bluff, where you'll find a dagoba and sweeping views of the surrounding valley.

The Tipitaka was first transcribed from oral and Sinhalese sources into Pali text by a council of monks held at Aluvihara in the 1st century BC. Two thousand years later, in 1848, the monks' library was destroyed by British troops putting down a revolt. The long process of replacing the *ola* manuscripts still occupies monks, scribes and craftspeople today. You can see their **workshop** (payment by donation); the donation includes having your name inscribed on a small length of *ola*. For information about *ola* manuscripts, see boxed text, p48 .

A three-wheeler from Matale to Aluvihara will cost about Rs 250 return, including waiting time, and a bus will cost Rs 7.

MATALE HERITAGE CENTRE
About 2km north of Matale, this **heritage centre** (☎ 222 2404; 33 Sir Richard Aluvihara Mawatha; admission free; ☉ 9am-5pm Mon-Sat) draws on the rich craft traditions of the area, producing quality batik, embroidery, carpentry and brasswork. It occupies a sprawling compound of bungalows, workshops and gardens. The centre's Aluvihare Kitchens does meals for groups of four or more if you book by phone a day ahead; it costs Rs 900 per person for a banquet with three kinds of rice and up to 25 different curries. A three-wheeler from Matale will cost about Rs 250 return, including waiting time.

There are many **spice gardens** and several **batik showrooms** along the road between Matale and Aluvihara. The various treats you can expect on a tour of the gardens include milkless cocoa tea sweetened with vanilla and banana, and various creams and potions claimed to make hair shine or cure flatulence. Prices at some spice-garden shops are high, so check in a market before you set out so that you can compare prices.

Sleeping & Eating
Rock House Hotel (☎ 222 3239; 17/16A Hulangamuwa Rd; r Rs 1650) If you're looking for peace and quiet, the Rock House is your place. It's set in a pretty garden, just to the south of the Matale Rest House (it is signposted on the main road). The seven rooms are a little bland and there is no air-con or hot water, but if you're not picky about such things it's a fine choice.

Matale Rest House (☎ 222 2299; Park Rd; s/d Rs 2200/3000, with air-con Rs 2700/3500; ❄) This slightly more upmarket choice in Matale is the old government-run guest house. It offers hot water and air-con to the weary traveller, though the rooms themselves have an institutional air about them. The rest house has a broad front lawn and a garden centring on a lovely bodhi tree that predates the hotel. Chinese and Sri Lankan meals at the restaurant cost around Rs 700.

A&C Restaurant (☎ 367 4501; 3/5 Sir Richard Aluvihara Mawatha; set menu Rs 700; ☉ 11am-4pm) The A&C is a real treat. The restaurant has been carved out of a local home, so dining here feels a bit like popping in to see the relatives. Tasty home-cooked Sri Lankan meals whipped up by the proprietors are varied and flavourful. To get here from Matale, take the same turn-off as the Matale Heritage Centre, but then take a sharp left rather than the road to the centre.

Getting There & Away
Bus 594 runs from Kandy to Matale (normal/intercity express Rs 30/65, 1½ hours) six times daily. Buses to Dambulla or Anuradhapura will drop you at Aluvihara (Rs 7) or the spice gardens. There are six trains daily on the pretty 28km spur line between Matale and Kandy (Rs 30, 1½ hours).

NALANDA
☎ 066
Nalanda is known for the venerable **Nalanda Gedige** (adult/child Rs 500/250), about 25km north of Matale and 20km before Dambulla. Built in the style of a South Indian Hindu temple, it consists of an entrance hall connected to a taller *shikara* (holy image sanctuary), with a courtyard for circumambulations. There is no sign of Hindu gods, however, and the temple is said to have been used by Buddhists. This is one of the earliest stone buildings constructed in Sri Lanka.

The temple's richly decorated stone-block walls, reassembled from ruins in 1975, are thought to have been fashioned during the 8th to 11th centuries. The plinth bears some Tantric carvings with sexual poses – the only such sculptures in Sri Lanka – but before you get excited, the carvings are weather-beaten and it's difficult to see much. Entry is included in the Cultural Triangle round ticket (see p212).

The site is beside a tank (artificial lake) 1km east of the main road – a sign marks the turn-off near the 49km post. Anuradhapura buses from Kandy or Matale will drop you at the turn-off.

DAMBULLA
☎ 066 / pop 68,200
Dambulla's famed Royal Rock Temple features in just about every tourist pamphlet produced in the country – you'll be familiar with its spectacular Buddha-filled interior long before you arrive in town. Despite its slightly commercial air, this remains an important holy

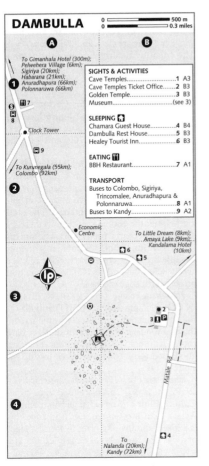

DAMBULLA

0 — 500 m
0 — 0.3 miles

To Gimanhala Hotel (300m);
Pelwehera Village (6km);
Sigiriya (20km);
Habarana (21km);
Anuradhapura (66km);
Polonnaruwa (66km)

SIGHTS & ACTIVITIES
Cave Temples.........................1 A3
Cave Temples Ticket Office.......2 B3
Golden Temple........................3 B3
Museum.............................(see 3)

SLEEPING
Chamara Guest House..............4 B4
Dambulla Rest House..............5 B3
Healey Tourist Inn.................6 B3

EATING
BBH Restaurant.......................7 A1

TRANSPORT
Buses to Colombo, Sigiriya,
Trincomalee, Anuradhapura &
Polonnaruwa.......................8 A1
Buses to Kandy.......................9 A2

Clock Tower

To Kurunegala (55km);
Colombo (92km)

Economic
Centre

To Little Dream (8km);
Amaya Lake (9km);
Kandalama Hotel
(10km)

Matale Rd

To
Nalanda (20km);
Kandy (72km)

place and should not be missed if you are anywhere nearby. You can visit it as a day trip on public transport from Kandy, or stop by on your way to or from Sigiriya. If you decide to stay the night, there is decent accommodation for all budgets. The Commercial Bank of Ceylon has a couple of ATMs here, accepting Visa and MasterCard.

Sights
CAVE TEMPLES
The beautiful **Royal Rock Temple** (adult/child Rs 1100/ free; 7am-7pm) sits 100m to 150m above the road in the southern part of Dambulla. The hike up to the temples begins along a vast, sloping rock face with steps in some places. The ticket office is at the gate near the mon-

strous Golden Temple, and your receipt is checked at the entrance at the base of the hill. Cultural Triangle tickets are not valid here. Photography is allowed inside the caves, but you're not allowed to photograph people. There are superb views over the surrounding countryside from the level of the caves; Sigiriya is clearly visible.

The caves' history as a place of worship is thought to date from around the 1st century BC, when King Valagamba (Vattajamini Ahhaya), driven out of Anuradhapura, took refuge here. When he regained his throne, he had the interior of the caves carved into magnificent rock temples. Further improvements were made by later kings, including King Nissanka Malla, who had the caves' interiors gilded, earning the place the name Ran Giri (Golden Rock).

There are five separate caves containing about 150 Buddha images. Most of the paintings in the temples date from the 19th century.

At the foot of the hill facing the highway stands the modern **Golden Temple**, a very kitschy structure completed in 2000 using Japanese donations. On top of the cube-shaped building sits a 30m-high Buddha image in the *dhammachakka mudra* (wheel-turning pose). Signs claim it's the largest Buddha in the world, but it's not even the largest in Sri Lanka. A **museum** (adult/child Rs 100/50; 7am-9pm) displays replicas of the cave paintings, imported Buddha images and little else, with only brief labels in Sinhala.

Cave I (Devaraja Viharaya)
The first cave, the Temple of the King of the Gods, has a 15m-long reclining Buddha. Ananda, the Buddha's loyal disciple, and other seated Buddhas are depicted nearby. A statue of Vishnu is held in a small shrine within the cave, but it's usually closed.

Cave II (Maharaja Viharaya)
The Temple of the Great King is arguably the most spectacular of the caves. It measures 52m from east to west and 23m from the entrance to the back wall; the highest point of the ceiling is 7m. This cave is named after the two statues of kings it contains. There is a painted wooden statue of Valagamba on the left as you enter, and another statue further inside of Nissanka Malla. The cave's main Buddha statue, which appears to have once been

THE ANCIENT CITIES

covered in gold leaf, is situated under a *makara torana* (archway decorated with dragons), with the right hand raised in *abhaya mudra* (pose conveying protection). Hindu deities are also represented. The vessel inside the cave collects water that constantly drips from the ceiling of the temple – even during droughts – which is used for sacred rituals.

Cave III (Maha Alut Viharaya)
This cave, the New Great Temple, was said to have been converted from a storeroom in the 18th century by King Kirti Sri Rajasinghe of Kandy, one of the last Kandyan monarchs. This cave, too, is filled with Buddha statues, including a beautiful reclining Buddha, and is separated from Cave II by only a masonry wall.

Cave IV (Pachima Viharaya)
The relatively small Western Cave is not the most westerly cave – that position belongs to Cave V. The central Buddha figure is seated under a *makara torana*, with its hands in *dhyana mudra* (a meditative pose in which the hands are cupped). The small dagoba in the centre was broken into by thieves who believed that it contained jewellery belonging to Queen Somawathie.

Cave V (Devana Alut Viharaya)
This newer cave was once used as a storehouse, but it's now called the Second New Temple. It features a reclining Buddha; Hindu deities, including Kataragama (Murugan) and Vishnu, are also present.

Sleeping & Eating
Healey Tourist Inn (☎ 228 4940; Matale Rd; s/d Rs 700/900) This place has the look and feel of an expanded family home. Rooms are a little boxy, but there are common areas in which you can put your feet up, so to speak. Its nothing luxurious, but the owners are friendly and helpful. The Healey is located near the post office and within walking distance of the caves and bus station.

ourpick Little Dream (☎ 072 289 3736; r Rs 800) Out in the middle of nowhere, the Little Dream is a great choice if you want to hook up with a local family and get to know life in rural Sri Lanka. It's close to the Kandalama Tank, a great place to escape the oppressive afternoon heat. Snoozing in the hammock is just as pleasurable. It's about 8km along the road to Amaya Lake (right); a three-wheeler will cost about Rs 350 from the clock tower.

Chamara Guest House (☎ 228 4488; Matale Rd; r Rs 1200-1500) Rooms at the Chamara are a little small, but they are clean and well maintained. The friendly management whips up some delicious Sri Lankan food.

Dambulla Rest House (☎ 228 4799; Matale Rd; s/d/tr Rs 2000/2500/3000; ✲) A one-storey affair of semimodern design, this Ceylon Hotels Corporation–operated rest house has four large, comfortable rooms, plus a reliable restaurant (meals Rs 500 to 700) and bar. The food here is pretty good.

ourpick Gimanhala Hotel (☎ 228 4864; gimanhala@sltnet.lk; 754 Anuradhapura Rd; s/d/tr Rs 3800/4100/4900; ✲ ☐ ☲) This excellent midrange choice offers nice accommodation and a convenient location by the main road. The staff are helpful, the rooms sparkle and there's a swimming pool in a pretty yard. The restaurant's daily lunch buffet is popular with tour groups. Breakfast costs another Rs 200. It's about 800m beyond the Colombo junction on the north edge of town.

Pelwehera Village (☎ 228 4281; s/d US$45/50; ✲) Three kilometres north of Dambulla (at Bullagala Junction) and just off the main road, this is a modern place with 10 spotless, bare rooms with hot water. The restaurant serves good food too – it's a nice place to stop for a bite to eat.

Amaya Lake (☎ 446 8100; www.amayaresorts.com; villas from US$114; ✲ ☲) This place used to be called Culture Club but has changed its name to Amaya Lake. Boy George references aside, this is a lovely and inviting place to spend a night or two. The huge, breezy complex has 106 stylish villas set in beautiful gardens. Facilities include tennis and badminton courts, a gorgeous pool, Ayurvedic spa and birdwatching trails. Adjacent to a traditional village are 11 'ecolodges', which were built with locally found natural materials and methods and have solar hot water. The Ayurvedic cuisine available at the in-house restaurants uses herbs and vegetables cultivated in the village. To get here from Dambulla, follow the Kandalama road for about 3km, then veer left and continue for another 6km or so.

Kandalama Hotel (☎ 228 4100; www.aitkenspencehotels.com; s/d/tr US$150/175/235; ✲ ☲) The Kandalama has a 'wow' factor that is rare in these parts. Designed by renowned architect Geoffrey Bawa (see boxed text, p51), the hotel emerges from the forest like a lost city, its walls and roofs covered in vines that allow it to blend into the natural environment. The hotel has won all sorts of awards for its environmentally friendly design and its superb cuisine. There is no shortage of activities on offer, including birdwatching walks and 4WD safaris, and as at Amaya Lake, there's a hotel-supported traditional village, Puranagama.

BBH Restaurant (Anuradhapura Rd; dishes Rs 70-250) This place does brisk business with the local crowd, thanks to its tasty Sri Lankan meals and snacks.

All of the accommodation listed has restaurants. Those with food worth recommending include **Dambulla Rest House** (☎ 222 2299; meals Rs 500-700), **Chamara Guest House** (meals Rs 300-500), **Pelwehera Village** (meals Rs 400-600) and **Gimanhala Hotel** (meals Rs 500-600).

Getting There & Away

Dambulla is 72km north of Kandy on the road to Anuradhapura. The Colombo–Trincomalee road meets this road 2km north of the cave temple and then splits off from it a couple of kilometres further north, leading to Sigiriya and Polonnaruwa. Because Dambulla is on so many major routes, plenty of buses pass through with varying frequency.

Buses frequently run to Polonnaruwa (Rs 85, 1½ hours, 66km), Anuradhapura (Rs 65, two hours, 68km), and Kandy (Rs 150, two hours). There are buses to Sigiriya (Rs 24, 40 minutes) roughly every 30 minutes; touts will tell you otherwise to get you into a three-wheeler. The bus takes four hours to get to Colombo (Rs 160).

You can flag buses plying this busy route to go between the two parts of Dambulla, or take a three-wheeler for Rs 50.

Habarana-bound buses will take you to the nearest train station at Habarana, 23km to the north, from which you can catch a Kandy-bound bus to get to Dambulla.

SIGIRIYA

☎ 066 / pop 1000

Sigiriya rock is many things to many people. For history buffs it has associations with both king and clergy. Art aficionados will appreciate the brilliant frescoes painted high up on its sheer walls. For casual tourists, Sigiriya is simply an awesome sight, with amazing views and impressive archaeological discoveries. Whatever attitude you bring to the rock, its unlikely you'll come away disappointed. The leafy village that has grown up near its base serves the comings and goings of tourists and pilgrims and is of relatively recent origin.

History

From a geologic point of view, Sigiriya is the hardened magma plug of an extinct volcano that long ago eroded away. Peppered with natural cave shelters and rock overhangs – supplemented over the centuries by numerous hand-hewn additions and modifications – the rock may have been inhabited in prehistoric times.

Popular myth says that the formation served royal and military functions during the reign of King Kassapa (AD 477–495), who allegedly built a garden and palace on the summit. According to this theory, King Kassapa sought out an unassailable new residence after overthrowing and murdering his own father, King Dhatusena of Anuradhapura.

A new theory, supported by archaeological evidence instead of local legend, suggests that Sigiriya was never a fortress or palace, but rather a long-standing Theravada and Mahayana Buddhist monastery built several centuries before the time of King Kassapa. Monks were using it as a mountain hermitage by the 3rd century BC, and there is abundant evidence to show it had become an important monastery by the 10th century AD. The ancient site's much-treasured frescoes of buxom women were not portraying ladies from Kassapa's court as was popularly believed. Instead, they were intended to represent Tara, an important Mahayana Buddhist goddess.

After the 14th century, the monastery complex was abandoned. British archaeologist HCP Bell discovered the ruins in 1898, which were further excavated by British explorer John Still in 1907.

Unesco declared Sigiriya a World Heritage Site in 1982.

Orientation & Information

The village, on the south side of the rock, is just a collection of grocery stores, guest houses and small restaurants. The **Centre for Eco-Cultural Studies** (CES; www.cessrilanka.org; Hotel Rd; ☒ 9am-5pm Mon-Fri) and **Sigiriya Ecocultural Tour Guide Association** (Setga; Hotel Rd; ☒ 8am-6pm) have an information desk with brochures on the region's fauna. These organisations run a range of wildlife and cultural expeditions, including tours of the Sigiriya rock. Note that both may close in the low season.

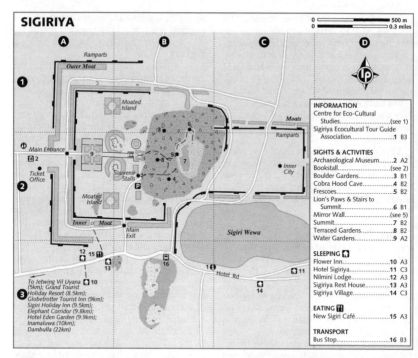

SIGIRIYA

Sights

Sigiriya is covered by the Cultural Triangle round ticket (p212); if you don't already have one of these, a single ticket costs US$25. Both single and round tickets are sold near the site entrance and at Sigiriya Rest House (p220).

Hopeful guides hang around the entrance to the site and will also approach you once you're inside. CES/Setga does a three- to four-hour tour of the royal complex for US$10 per person. On a relatively busy day you can eavesdrop on the commentaries given to tour groups, as long as you can find one in your language.

The site's **archaeological museum**, near the entrance, was under renovation at the time of research. A small **bookstall** (☉ 8am-4pm) is outside.

An early or late ascent of the rock avoids the main crowds and the fierce heat. Allow at least two hours for the return trip, and more on very busy days. Bring plenty of water and wear a hat as it's often too windy near the summit to carry an umbrella. The ascent involves a steep climb, so if you're not fit it may be tough. Beware of 'helpers' who latch on to visitors who look as if they're having difficulty.

The verifiable theory that the Sigiriya rock complex was always a Buddhist monastery has not caught on with the locals. Hence the terms traditionally used to describe the various features on the rock city assume it was once a royal palace.

ROYAL GARDENS

The landscaped gardens around Sigiriya consist of water gardens, boulder gardens and terraced gardens.

The usual approach to the rock is through the western (and most elaborate) gate. This takes you through beautiful symmetrical **water gardens**, which extend from the western foot of the rock; bathing pools, little islands with pavilions that were used as dry-season palaces, and trees frame the approach to the rock. The rock rises sheer and mysterious from the jungle. A series of steps leads up through the boulders at its base to the western face, and then ascends it steeply.

The **boulder gardens**, closer to the rock, feature rocks that once formed the bases of buildings. The steplike depressions in the sides of boulders were the foundations of brick walls and timber columns. The cistern and audience hall rocks are impressive.

The base of Sigiriya has been landscaped to produce the **terraced gardens**.

FRESCOES

Halfway up the rock, there's a modern spiral stairway leading up from the main route to a long, sheltered gallery in the sheer rock face.

In this niche is a series of paintings of buxom, wasp-waisted women, popularly believed to represent either *apsaras* (celestial nymphs) or King Kassapa's concubines. Modern theory suggests the female forms represent aspects of Tara – a bodhisattva and one of the most important figures in Tantric Buddhism. They are similar in style to the rock paintings at Ajanta in India, but have a specific character in their classical realist style. No one knows the exact dates of the impressive frescoes, though it's unlikely they date as far back as the 5th century (when King Kassapa reigned).

Protected from the sun in the sheltered gallery, the paintings remain in remarkably good condition, their colours still glowing. They're at their best in the late afternoon light. Flash photography is not allowed.

MIRROR WALL

Beyond the fresco gallery the path clings to the sheer side of the rock and is protected on the outside by a 3m-high wall.

This wall was coated with a smooth glaze upon which visitors of 1000 years ago felt impelled to note their impressions of the women in the gallery above – or so says local legend. The graffiti, inscribed between the 6th and 14th centuries, are of great interest to scholars because they show the development of the Sinhala language and script, and because they demonstrate an appreciation of art and beauty. You'll have to look hard beyond the modern mess to see the ancient messages.

One typical graffito reads, 'The ladies who wear golden chains on their breasts beckon me. As I have seen the resplendent ladies, heaven appears to me as not good.' Another reads, 'A deer-eyed young woman of the mountainside arouses anger in my mind. In her hand she had taken a string of pearls and in her looks she has assumed rivalry with us.'

LION'S PAWS

At the northern end of the rock the narrow pathway emerges on to the large platform from which the rock derives its later name – the Lion Rock, Sigiriya. HCP Bell, the British archaeologist responsible for an enormous amount of archaeology in Sri Lanka, found the two enormous lion paws when excavating here in 1898. At one time a gigantic brick lion sat at this end of the rock, and the final ascent to the top commenced with a stairway that led between the lion's paws and into its mouth. The lion symbolism serves as a reminder to devotees ascending the rock that Buddha was Sakya-Simha (Lion of the Sakya Clan) and that the truths he spoke of were as powerful as the sound of a lion's roar.

The 5th-century lion has since disappeared, apart from the first steps and the paws. Reaching the top means clambering up across a series of grooves cut into the rock; fortunately there is a handrail.

SUMMIT

The top of the rock covers 1.6 hectares. At one time it was covered with buildings, but only the foundations remain today. The design of this so-called palace, and the magnificent views it commands, suggests that Sigiriya was more a place of residence than a fortress. A 27m-by-21m pond hewn out of the rock looks for all the world like a modern swimming pool, although it may have been used merely for water storage.

Dr Raja de Silva, Sri Lanka's former archaeological commissioner, has pointed out that there is no archaeological evidence of a palacelike structure anywhere on the summit. In particular there is a complete absence of stone bases, post holes, visible foundations for cross walls or window sashes, and a lack of lavatory facilities. Instead what you see is an enclosed terrace lying next to the ruins of a dagoba, suggesting it was a spot reserved for meditation.

A smooth stone slab (the so-called king's throne, possibly another meditation spot) sits 30m away from the ruins of a dagoba. You can sit and gaze across the surrounding jungle as Kassapa – or the Buddhist monks – probably did over 1500 years ago.

COBRA HOOD CAVE

This rocky projection earned its name because the overhang resembles a fully opened cobra's hood. Generally you will pass by this cave after descending the rock on your way to the south gate and the car park. Below the drip ledge is an inscription from the 2nd century BC that indicates it belonged to Chief Naguli, who would have donated it to a monk. The plastered interior of the cave was once embellished with floral and animal paintings.

Sleeping

BUDGET

Nilmini Lodge (☎ 567 0469, 077 306 9536; nilmini_lodge@ yahoo.com; r with/without bathroom Rs 800/400, with air-con Rs 1500; 💻) Any place that chauffeurs its guests around in a 50-year-old Morris Minor is worth mentioning. Not only does Nilmini offer a cool taxi service, it also lends out push bikes at no cost. The guest house itself is pretty small and basic, but clean and comfortable enough for a short stay. It's close to the rock.

Flower Inn (☎ 567 2197, 568 9953; s/d Rs 800/1000) An obvious choice for travellers with a floral fetish, this is a small family home absolutely bursting with flowers, both plastic and genuine. The very nana decor is maintained by a friendly family that tries hard to please. Good Sri Lankan meals are hot, fresh and inexpensive. It's on the same side of the rock as the Sigiriya Rest House.

Sigiri Holiday Inn (☎ 077 598 5133; sholidayinn@yahoo. com; Sigiriya Rd; r with/without hot water Rs 1500/800) This is a compact and friendly place 500m from the Inamaluwa junction on Sigiriya Rd. With spotless bathrooms and an outdoor restaurant, it's a pleasant spot. Rooms downstairs are smaller and don't have hot water. Keep your windows closed as monkeys roam the area.

Globetrotter Tourist Inn (☎ 078 875 4350; rajag una8@sltnet.lk; Sigiriya Rd, Inamaluwa; r with/without air-con Rs 2000/1500; 🔀) The father-and-son team that runs Globetrotter will do their best to make you feel welcome. Their property includes five rooms in separate earthen cottages that are, suffice it to say, pretty basic.

MIDRANGE

Grand Tourist Holiday Resort (☎ 567 0136, 228 6166; Sigiriya Rd; r with/without air-con Rs 2300/1800; 🔀) This place has several cabins set around frog-filled ponds. It's not as grand as the name suggests – the rooms are actually pretty average – but the common dining area is nice enough and they have Ayurvedic massage. It's about 4km from Inamaluwa junction.

our pick Sigiriya Rest House (☎ 228 6299; www.cey lonhotels.lk; s/d incl breakfast US$30/35; 🔀 💻 🛜) This simple but tastefully designed rest house has lovely views of the rock and a peaceful atmos-

phere. The 14 rooms are clean and tastefully decorated in faux colonial. There's a large, airy restaurant with friendly service.

Hotel Eden Garden (☎ /fax 228 6635; www.edengar denlk.com; Sigiriya Rd, Inamaluwa; r with/without air-con Rs 3600/3000; 🔀 🛋) Despite the rather ungainly facade, this is a good spot: large, clean rooms, some with balconies, overlook a well-kept garden, and there's a pool (Rs 200 for nonguests). Hotel Eden Garden is 100m from the junction, at Inamaluwa.

Hotel Sigiriya (☎ 228 6821; inquiries.sigiriya@serendi bleisure.lk; Hotel Rd; s/d incl breakfast Rs 5000/5800; 🛋 🛋) Twitchers flock to this place, lured by its resident naturalist who leads birdwatching trips. The hotel has 76 rooms, and there are great views of the rock from the dining room and large pool area (Rs 250 for nonguests). It's about 1km past the Sigiriya Rest House.

TOP END

Sigiriya Village (☎ 223 6803; sigiriyavillage@sltnet.lk; r US$152; 🔀 🛋 🛋) This is one of the prettiest hotels in Sigiriya, thanks to its spectacular views of the rock that reflect off the shimmering swimming pool; nonguests can use the pool for Rs 200. This hotel also sets itself apart by growing its vegetables in a chemical-free garden for the restaurant, so you can be assured of freshness. Bikes are available to rent for Rs 250 per hour.

Jetwing Vil Uyana (☎ 011-234 5700; www.jetwing hotels.com; Kibissa; r from US$500; 🛋) For the jet-setter, Jetwing's luxurious safari resort is hard to beat. Enter the open-air lodge where you check in and enjoy a welcome drink while observing nature go about its business: crocodiles swim in the pond, monitor lizards dart through the grass and elephants come for an afternoon dip. The individual cottages, designed in a classy minimalist style, also have spectacular views of the lush property. If it gets too hot, take a dip in the private pool assigned to each cottage. The resort includes a fitness centre, and a resident naturalist is on hand to give walking tours. Breakfast/lunch/dinner cost US$15/16/20. You'll get a substantial discount if you book ahead through Jetwing in Colombo.

Elephant Corridor (☎ 228 6951; www.elephant corridor.com; Kibissa; ste from US$575; 🛋) Hidden away on 200 acres of unfenced grasslands between the Kandalama Hills and Pothana Lake, this boutique resort takes its name from the wild elephants that often wander through the area. Each of the 21 cavernous, high-ceilinged suites comes equipped with giant-screen TV, DVD player, binoculars, an artist's easel and pastels and a private plunge pool. Breakfast/lunch/dinner cost US$19/24/32. The turn-off is 4km from the Inamaluwa junction en route to Sigiriya, down a dirt track and just beyond the Grand Tourist Holiday Resort.

Eating

New Sigiri Cafe (dishes Rs 125-280) This shop does made-to-order meals, offering both Sri Lankan and Western food.

Guest houses offer meals of home-cooked rice and curry for around Rs 350. **Flower Inn** (☎ 567 2197, 568 9953), **Nilmini Lodge** (☎ 567 0469, 077 306 9536; nilmini_lodge@yahoo.com), **Globetrotter Tourist Inn** (☎ 078 875 4350; rajaguna8@sltnet.lk; Sigiriya Rd, Inamaluwa) and **Grand Holiday Tourist Resort** (☎ 567 0136, 228 6166; Sigiriya Rd) have especially good food.

Getting There & Away

Sigiriya is about 10km east of the main road between Dambulla and Habarana. The turn-off is at Inamaluwa. Buses run to Dambulla about every 30 minutes from around 7am (Rs 28, 40 minutes), but they are less frequent in the afternoon. The last bus to Dambulla leaves at around 7pm (but double-check this to confirm the time). Three-wheelers run from Dambulla to Sigiriya (Rs 700) and to Habarana (Rs25, 30 minutes, hourly departures).

POLONNARUWA

☎ 027 / pop 106,000

Polonnaruwa was a thriving commercial and religious centre 800 years ago. From here, kings ruled the central plains of Sri Lanka, free-marketeers haggled for rare goods and the pious prayed at any one of its numerous temples. The glories of that age may now be relegated to the history books, but enough archaeological remnants exist to give a pretty good idea of how the city looked in its heyday. The fact that it's conveniently close to several national parks also draws a number of visitors.

The monuments within the archaeological park are arranged in a reasonably compact garden setting. It is best to explore by bicycle, which you can rent from several places in town.

History

For three centuries Polonnaruwa was a royal capital of both the Chola and Sinhalese kingdoms. Although nearly 1000 years old, it's much younger than Anuradhapura and generally in better repair (though smaller in scale).

The South Indian Chola dynasty made its capital at Polonnaruwa after conquering Anuradhapura in the late 10th century: Polonnaruwa was a strategically better place to guard against any rebellion from the Ruhunu Sinhalese kingdom in the southeast. It also, apparently, had fewer mosquitoes! When the Sinhalese king Vijayabahu I drove the Cholas off the island in 1070, he kept Polonnaruwa as his capital.

Under King Parakramabahu I (r 1153–86), Polonnaruwa reached its zenith. The king erected huge buildings, planned beautiful parks and, as a crowning achievement, created a 2500-hectare tank, which was so large that it was named the Parakrama Samudra (Sea of Parakrama). The present lake incorporates three older tanks, so it may not be the actual tank he created.

Parakramabahu I was followed by Nissanka Malla (r 1187–96), who virtually bankrupted the kingdom through his attempts to match his predecessors' achievements. By the early 13th century, Polonnaruwa was beginning to prove as susceptible to Indian invasion as Anuradhapura was, and eventually it, too, was abandoned and the centre of Sinhalese power shifted to the western side of the island.

In 1982, Unesco added the ancient city of Polonnaruwa to its World Heritage list.

Orientation

Polonnaruwa has both an Old Town and, to its south, a sprawling New Town. The main areas of ruins start on the northern edge of the Old Town and spread north. Accommodation is mostly in and around the Old Town. The main bus and train stations are in Kaduruwela, a few kilometres east of the Old Town on Batticaloa Rd. However, buses from anywhere except the east go through the Old Town on their way in, so you can get off there.

The ruins can be conveniently divided into five groups: a small group near the Polonnaruwa Rest House on the banks of the tank; the royal palace group to the east of the Polonnaruwa Rest House; a very compact group a short distance north of the royal palace group, usually known as the quadrangle; a number of structures spread over a wide area further north, known as the northern group; and the small southern group, towards the New Town. There are also a few other scattered ruins.

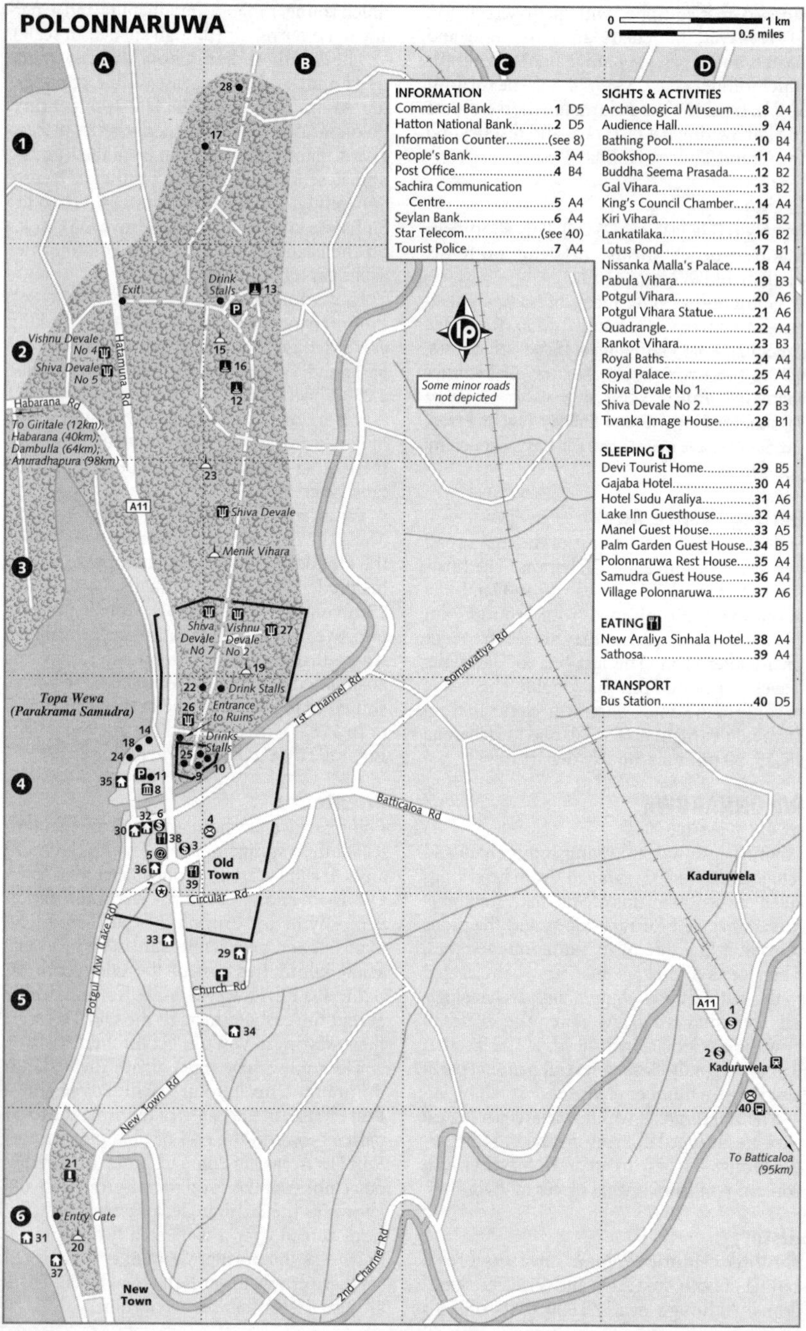

POLONNARUWA
0 1 km
0 0.5 miles
INFORMATION
Commercial Bank 1 D5
Hatton National Bank 2 D5
Information Counter (see 8)
People's Bank 3 A4
Post Office 4 B4
Sachira Communication Centre 5 A4
Seylan Bank 6 A4
Star Telecom (see 40)
Tourist Police 7 A4
SIGHTS & ACTIVITIES
Archaeological Museum 8 A4
Audience Hall 9 A4
Bathing Pool 10 B4
Bookshop 11 A4
Buddha Seema Prasada 12 B2
Gal Vihara 13 B2
King's Council Chamber 14 A4
Kiri Vihara 15 B2
Lankatilaka 16 B2
Lotus Pond 17 B1
Nissanka Malla's Palace 18 A4
Pabula Vihara 19 B3
Potgul Vihara 20 A6
Potgul Vihara Statue 21 A6
Quadrangle 22 A4
Rankot Vihara 23 B3
Royal Baths 24 A4
Royal Palace 25 A4
Shiva Devale No 1 26 A4
Shiva Devale No 2 27 B3
Tivanka Image House 28 B1
SLEEPING
Devi Tourist Home 29 B5
Gajaba Hotel 30 A4
Hotel Sudu Araliya 31 A6
Lake Inn Guesthouse 32 A4
Manel Guest House 33 A5
Palm Garden Guest House 34 B5
Polonnaruwa Rest House 35 A4
Samudra Guest House 36 A4
Village Polonnaruwa 37 A6
EATING
New Araliya Sinhala Hotel 38 A4
Sathosa 39 A4
TRANSPORT
Bus Station 40 D5
Some minor roads not depicted
Exit
Drink Stalls
Vishnu Devale No 4
Shiva Devale No 5
Hatamuna Rd
Habarana Rd
To Giritale (12km); Habarana (40km); Dambulla (64km); Anuradhapura (98km)
A11
Shiva Devale
Menik Vihara
Shiva Devale No 7
Vishnu Devale No 2
Drink Stalls
Entrance to Ruins
Drinks Stalls
Topa Wewa (Parakrama Samudra)
1st Channel Rd
Somawatiya Rd
Batticaloa Rd
Old Town
Circular Rd
Church Rd
Potgul Mw (Lake Rd)
New Town Rd
Entry Gate
New Town
2nd Channel Rd
Kaduruwela
To Batticaloa (95km)

Information

The Cultural Triangle round ticket (p212) is valid for Polonnaruwa. There's an **information counter** (☎ 222 4850; ⏰ 7.30am-6pm) at the museum, near the Polonnaruwa Rest House. You can get maps and brochures and buy tickets to the site; individual entry costs $US25/15 (adult/child). Near the museum entrance is a well-stocked bookshop. Officially the site closes at 6pm, but in practice you can stay till dark. Tickets are not checked at the Polonnaruwa Rest House group or at the southern group, but the other three groups are within a single big enclosure, which you have to enter from Habarana Rd, just north of the royal palace. Although the ticket technically allows you only one entrance, you can ask a ticket collector to sign and date your ticket so that you can enter again. This way you could visit the site in the morning, take a break over midday to avoid the heat and head back to the site in the late afternoon. Don't believe three-wheeler drivers who say you don't need a ticket if you travel with them.

There's a Seylan Bank near the channel. In Kaduruwela, there are several banks on Batticaloa Rd within 350m of the bus station on the new-town side. All of the following banks listed have ATMs.

Commercial Bank (Batticaloa Rd)

Hatton National Bank (Batticaloa Rd)

People's Bank (Batticaloa Rd; ⏰ 8.30am-3.30pm Mon-Fri)

Post office (Batticaloa Rd) In the centre of the Old Town.

Sachira Communication Centre (70B Habarana Rd; per hr Rs 60; ⏰ 7.30am-noon & 3-10pm) Internet access.

Seylan Bank (Habarana Rd)

Star Telecom (Kaduruwela; per hr Rs 60; ⏰ 9.30am-8pm) Internet access; in the bus station.

Tourist Police (☎ 23099; Batticaloa Rd) In the Old Town on the main traffic circle.

Sights

ARCHAEOLOGICAL MUSEUM

The **Archaeological Museum** (⏰ 9am-6pm) is first class. It's designed so that you walk from one end to the other, passing through a series of rooms, each dedicated to a particular theme: the citadel, the outer city, the monastery area and the periphery, and Hindu monuments. The latter room contains a wonderful selection of bronzes. Of particular interest are the scale models of buildings, including the *vatadage* (circular relic house), which show how they might have looked in their heyday

– if you follow the theory that they once had wooden roofs. To enter, you'll need a current round ticket or a one-day ticket. It's worth visiting before you head out to the site.

ROYAL PALACE GROUP

This group of buildings dates from the reign of Parakramabahu I. Parakramabahu's **Royal Palace** was a magnificent structure measuring 31m by 13m, and is said to have had seven storeys. The 3m-thick walls have holes to receive the floor beams for two higher floors; however, if there were another four levels, these must have been made of wood. The roof in this main hall, which had 50 rooms in all, was supported by 30 columns.

Parakramabahu's **Audience Hall** is notable for the frieze of elephants, each of which is in a different position. There are fine lions at the top of the steps.

In the southeast corner of the palace grounds, the **Bathing Pool** (Kumara Pokuna) has two of its crocodile-mouth spouts remaining.

QUADRANGLE

Only a short stroll north of the royal palace ruins, the area known as the quadrangle is literally that – a compact group of fascinating ruins in a raised-up area bounded by a wall. It's the most concentrated collection of buildings you'll find in the ancient cities. Besides the ruins described below, there's a **recumbent image house**, **chapter house**, **bodhisattva shrine** and **bodhi tree shrine**.

In the southeast of the quadrangle, the **vatadage** is typical of its kind. Its outermost terrace is 18m in diameter, and the second terrace has four entrances flanked by particularly fine guardstones. The moonstone at the northern entrance is reckoned to be the finest in Polonnaruwa, although not of the same standard as some at Anuradhapura. The four entrances lead to the central dagoba with its four Buddhas. The stone screen is thought to be a later addition, probably by Nissanka Malla.

At the southern end of the quadrangle, the **Thuparama Gedige** is the smallest *gedige* (hollow Buddhist temple with thick walls) in Polonnaruwa, but is also one of the best – and the only one with its roof intact. The building shows a strong Hindu influence and is thought to date from the reign of Parakramabahu I. There are several Buddha images in the inner chamber, but they're barely visible in the late afternoon light.

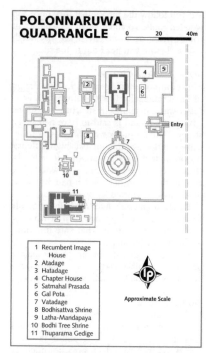

POLONNARUWA QUADRANGLE

0   20   40m

Entry

Approximate Scale

1 Recumbent Image House
2 Atadage
3 Hatadage
4 Chapter House
5 Satmahal Prasada
6 Gal Pota
7 Vatadage
8 Bodhisattva Shrine
9 Latha-Mandapaya
10 Bodhi Tree Shrine
11 Thuparama Gedige

On the north side of the **Gal Pota** (Stone Book) is a colossal stone representation of an *ola* book. It is nearly 9m long by 1.5m wide, and 40cm to 66cm thick. The inscription on it – the longest such stone inscription in Sri Lanka (and there are many!) – indicates that it was a Nissanka Malla publication. Much of it extols his virtues as a king, but it also includes the footnote that the slab, weighing 25 tonnes, was dragged from Mihintale, nearly 100km away.

Also erected by Nissanka Malla, the **Hatadage** is a tooth-relic chamber; it is said to have been built in 60 days.

The busy Nissanka Malla was also responsible for the **Latha-Mandapaya**. This unique structure consists of a latticed stone fence – a curious imitation of a wooden fence with posts and railings – surrounding a very small dagoba. The dagoba is encircled by stone pillars shaped like lotus stalks, topped by unopened buds. It is said that Nissanka Malla sat within this enclosure to listen to chanted Buddhist texts.

In the northeast corner stands the unusual ziggurat-style **Satmahal Prasada**, which consists

of six diminishing storeys (there used to be seven), shaped like a stepped pyramid.

A shrine for the tooth relic, the **Atadage** is the only surviving structure in Polonnaruwa dating from the reign of Vijayabahu I.

CLOSE TO THE QUADRANGLE

Along the road leading north from the quadrangle, a gravel road branches off to the right just before you reach the city wall. Most of the following structures are on this road, as are many others. Several buildings in this area are Shiva Devales (Hindu temples), relics from the south Indian invasion of the 10th century.

Just south of the quadrangle, the 13th-century Hindu temple **Shiva Devale No 1** displays the Indian influence that returned after Polonnaruwa's Sinhalese florescence. It is notable for the superb quality of its stonework, which fits together with unusual precision. The domed brick roof has collapsed, but when this building was being excavated a number of excellent bronzes, now in the Archaeological Museum (p223), were found.

Similar in style, **Shiva Devale No 2** is the oldest structure in Polonnaruwa and dates from the brief Chola period, when the Indian invaders established the city. Unlike so many buildings in the ancient cities, it was built entirely of stone, so the structure today is much as it was when built.

Pabula Vihara, also known as the Parakramabahu Vihara, is a typical dagoba from the period of Parakramabahu I. It is the third-largest dagoba in Polonnaruwa.

NORTHERN GROUP

You will need a bicycle or other transport to comfortably explore these spread-out ruins, all north of the city wall. They include the Gal Vihara, probably the most famous group of Buddha images in Sri Lanka, and the Alahana Pirivena monastic group. The Alahana Pirivena group consists of the Rankot Vihara, Lankatilaka, Kiri Vihara, Buddha Seema Prasada and the other structures around them. The name of the group means 'crematory college' – it stood in the royal cremation grounds established by Parakramabahu.

The 54m **Rankot Vihara** dagoba, the largest in Polonnaruwa and the fourth largest on the island, has been ascribed to the reign of King Nissanka Malla. Like the other major dagobas in Anuradhapura and Polonnaruwa, the dome consists of earth fill covered by a brick mantle and plaster. The construction clearly imitates the Anuradhapura style. Surgical instruments found in a nearby ruined 12th-century hospital are said to be similar to those used today.

Buddha Seema Prasada is the highest building in the Alahana Pirivena group, and it was the monastery abbot's convocation hall. This building features a fine *mandapaya* (raised platform with decorative pillars).

Built by Parakramabahu and later restored by Vijayabahu IV, the huge **Lankatilaka** *gedige* has 17m-high walls, although the roof has collapsed. The cathedral-like aisle leads to a huge standing headless Buddha. The outer walls of the *gedige*, decorated with bas-reliefs, show typical Polonnaruwa structures in their original state.

Construction of the dagoba **Kiri Vihara** is credited to Subhadra, King Parakramabahu's queen. Originally known as the Rupavati Chetiya, the present name means 'milk white' because when the overgrown jungle was cleared away after 700 years of neglect, the original lime plaster was found to be in perfect condition. It is still the best-preserved unrestored dagoba at Polonnaruwa.

Gal Vihara is a group of beautiful Buddha images that probably marks the high point of Sinhalese rock carving. They are part of Parakramabahu's northern monastery. The Gal Vihara consists of four separate images, all cut from one long slab of granite. At one time each was enshrined within a separate enclosure. You can clearly see the sockets cut into the rock behind the standing image, into which wooden beams would have been inserted.

The standing Buddha is 7m tall and is said to be the finest of the series. The unusual position of the arms and sorrowful facial expression led to the theory that it was an image of the Buddha's disciple Ananda, grieving for his master's departure for nirvana, since the reclining image is next to it. The fact that it had its own separate enclosure, along with the discovery of other images with the same arm position, has discredited this theory and it is now accepted that all the images are of the Buddha.

The reclining image of the Buddha entering parinirvana is 14m long. Notice the subtle depression in the pillow under the head and the wheel symbol on the pillow end. The other two images are both of the seated Buddha. The one in the small rock cavity is smaller and of inferior quality.

Unfortunately authorities have constructed a very unsightly metal roof structure over the Buddhas at Gal Vihara. This means that some portion of the each statue is always in shade and it's impossible to take a well-exposed photograph.

A track to the left from the northern stretch of road leads to unusual **Lotus Pond**, nearly 8m in diameter, which has five concentric, descending rings of eight petals each. The pool was probably used by monks.

The northern road ends at **Tivanka Image House**. *Tivanka* means 'thrice bent', and refers to the fact that the Buddha image within is in a three-curve position normally reserved for female statues. The building is notable for the carvings of energetic dwarfs cavorting around the outside, and for the fine frescoes within – the only Polonnaruwa murals to have survived. Some of these date from a later attempt by Parakramabahu III to restore Polonnaruwa, but others are much older.

SOUTHERN GROUP

The small southern group is close to the compound of top-end hotels. By bicycle it's a pleasant ride along the bund of the Topa Wewa (Topa Tank).

Also known as the library dagoba, the **Potgul Vihara** is an unusual structure. A thick-walled, hollow, dagoba-like building, it is thought to have been used to store sacred books. It's effectively a circular *gedige,* and four smaller solid dagobas arranged around this central dome form the popular Sinhalese quincunx arrangement of five objects in the shape of a rectangle (one at each corner and one in the middle).

Another interesting structure in the southern group is the **statue** at the northern end. Standing nearly 4m high, it's an unusually lifelike human representation, in contrast to the normally idealised or stylised Buddha figures. Exactly whom it represents is a subject of some debate. Some say that the object he is holding is a book and thus the statue is of Agastya, the Indian Vedic teacher. The more popular theory is that it is a yoke representing the 'yoke of kingship' and that the bearded, stately figure is Parakramabahu I. The irreverent joke is that the king is really holding a piece of papaya.

THE ANCIENT CITIES

REST HOUSE GROUP

Concentrated a few steps to the north of the Polonnaruwa Rest House are the ruins of the **Nissanka Malla's palace**, which aren't in anywhere near the same state of preservation as the royal palace group.

The **Royal Baths** are the ruins nearest to Polonnaruwa Rest House. Furthest north is the **King's Council Chamber**, where the king's throne, in the shape of a stone lion, once stood. It is now in Colombo's National Museum (p87). Inscribed into each column in the chamber is the name of the minister whose seat was once beside it. The mound nearby becomes an island when the waters of the tank are high; on it are the ruins of a small summer house used by the king.

Sleeping

BUDGET

Devi Tourist Home (☎ 222 3181; Lake View Watte; s/d/tr Rs 1500/650/800, r with hot water Rs 1800, with air-con Rs 1900; ✿) Among the cheapies, this one is probably the best in terms of service and cleanliness. It has five rooms arranged around a garden. The guest house is about 1km south of the Old Town centre and down Church Rd (there's a sign on the main road). The friendly owner is a member of Sri Lanka's small Malay population. Bicycles are available for Rs 200 per day.

Samudra Guest House (☎ 222 2817; Habarana Rd; r Rs 500-800) A rambling old house with a friendly owner, the Samudra offers pleasant service and basic rooms. For a little more privacy, have a look at the cabana at the bottom of the garden. The hosts can organise trips to Minneriya National Park (p228) and Kaudulla National Park (p228). Bicycles can be hired for Rs 150.

Manel Guest House (☎ 222 2481, 077 743 5358; New Town Rd; r Rs 700-900) In a quiet spot just outside the Old Town wall, friendly Manel's spacious rooms differ in price according to the bathroom standards. Very good meals are served under the veranda. The co-owner, Mr Bandula, trawls the town for backpackers in his rickshaw, so it's likely you'll meet him before reaching the place.

Lake Inn Guesthouse (☎ 077 690 6787; 1 1st Channel Rd; r with/without air-con r Rs 1800/900; ✿) Just off the main road in the Old Town and next to Seylan Bank, Lake Inn has four dim but passable rooms. Service is pretty lacklustre, so the only real reason to stay is the handy location.

Palm Garden Guest House (☎ 077 802 0405; New Town Rd; r with air-con/fan Rs 1500/1000; ✿) Located down a quiet back road this place offers respite for the weary backpacker. You can get meals here, rent a bike or just relax in the shade of a palm tree. It's affiliated with the Manel Guest House.

Gajaba Hotel (☎ 222 2394; Kuruppu Gardens, Lake Rd; s/d Rs 1000/1500, d/tr with air-con Rs 2000/2500; ✿) The Gajaba is a well-worn place (one of the oldest in town) and noise can be a problem; on the upside, it has a decent garden restaurant and a central location near the tank. Five rooms come with air-con and two with hot water. Good Sri Lankan food is available. You can hire bicycles for Rs 250 per day.

MIDRANGE & TOP END

Village Polonnaruwa (☎ 222 2405; fax 222 5100; Potgul Mawatha; s/d without air-con Rs 1500/2500, d with air-con Rs 3500; ✿ ▨ ▨) The bland 1970s motel-style is nothing to write home about, but on the bright side, it's clean, friendly and close to the lake. Nonguests may use the pool if they buy a drink or meal. There's also a tennis court and a spa. It's about 2km south of the Old Town.

Polonnaruwa Rest House (☎ 222 2299; http://cey lonhotels.lk; Potgul Mawatha; s/d Rs 3750/4150; ✿ ▨) Perched over Topa Wewa, this ageing rest house has some of the best views in town. Built in the early 1950s specifically for a visit by Queen Elizabeth II, the hotel has been a local landmark ever since. While renovation is long overdue, the place is decently maintained. If you book ahead you can even reserve the 'Queen's Room,' where Elizabeth put up her feet. It has a bar and a restaurant with a decent selection of food, but service can be slow and the portions disappointingly small.

Hotel Sudu Araliya (☎ 222 4849; www.hotelsudu araliya.com; Potgul Mawatha; s/d US$50/55; ✿ ▨ ▨) With a flashy lobby, well-tended grounds and an idyllic setting near the tank, Sudu Araliya would be the best place in town if it weren't for the bland rooms and old furnishings. However, it does have a top-notch Ayurvedic centre and a garden-themed bar. Bicycle hire and boat trips on the tank are available.

Eating

New Araliya Sinhala Hotel (Habarana Rd; mains Rs 150; ☻ 8am-9.30pm) This popular local eatery serves Sri Lankan meals for breakfast, lunch and dinner, including rice and curry and *kotthu rotti* (*rotti* chopped up and mixed with meat and vegetables).

Sathosa (24hr) This supermarket is opposite the People's Bank.

Guest houses and hotels are safe bets for good eating in Polonnaruwa, a town not exactly renowned for cuisine. Among the better hotel and guest house dining rooms are **Devi Tourist Home** (222 3181; Lake View Watte; meals Rs 300-600), **Gajaba Hotel** (222 2394; Kuruppu Gardens, Lake Rd; meals Rs 300-600), **Polonnaruwa Rest House** (222 2299; http://ceylonhotels.lk; Potgul Mawatha; meals Rs 500-900), **Manel Guest House** (222 2481, 077 743 5358; New Town Rd; meals Rs 150-300) and **Lake Inn Guest House** (222 3220; meals Rs 200-500).

Getting There & Away
BUS
Polonnaruwa's main bus station is actually in Kaduruwela, a few kilometres east of the Old Town on Batticaloa Rd. Buses to and from the west pass through the Old Town centre, but if you're leaving Polonnaruwa and want to make sure you get a seat, start off at Kaduruwela.

Central Transport Board (CTB) buses run regularly to Kandy (Rs 78, three hours). Aircon intercity buses to Kandy (Rs 150, four hours) run until 4pm via Dambulla and Habarana. If you want to get to Dambulla, catch this bus.

CTB buses for Anuradhapura (Rs 120, three hours) leave regularly from 5.15am to 4.15pm; there are no air-con buses. Or you can go to Habarana and pick up another bus there, but a lot of people do this and seats are rare.

There are regular CTB buses to Colombo (Rs 220, six hours) until 7.15pm. The intercity air-con buses (Rs 350) leave every 30 minutes during the day.

TRAIN
Polonnaruwa is on the Colombo–Batticaloa railway line and is about 30km southeast of Gal Oya, where the line splits from the Colombo–Trincomalee line. The train station is at Kaduruwela, near the bus station.

Trains to Colombo (1st/2nd/3rd class Rs 210/390/800, six to seven hours) depart at 8.13am, 8.40pm and 10.30pm. For Trincomalee there is a direct train at 3.15pm, or you can catch the 8.13am Colombo train and change at Gal Oya for a 12.30pm Trinco-bound train.

Getting Around
There are frequent buses (Rs 8) between the Old Town and Kaduruwela, where the bus and train stations are located. A three-wheeler costs Rs 100.

Bicycles are the ideal transport for getting around Polonnaruwa's monuments, which are surrounded by shady woodland. Bicycles with gears can be hired for about Rs 200 a day from a couple of places in the town's main street. Some guest houses also hire bicycles (usually gearless) from Rs 150 a day.

For around Rs 500, a car and driver or three-wheeler can be hired for about three hours, which is long enough to have a quick look around the ruins.

AROUND POLONNARUWA
Giritale
 027 / pop 14,300
Twelve kilometres northwest of Polonnaruwa on the Habarana road, Giritale is a sleepy village alongside the 7th-century Giritale Tank. It's a good base for visiting Polonnaruwa and Minneriya National Park, especially if you have your own transport.

A simple place near the tank, **Woodside Tour Inn** (224 6307; Polonnaruwa Rd; s/d Rs 1100/1500) has a pretty garden setting and a big mango tree. The 10 older rooms are bare but fine, and the five new rooms upstairs have balconies from which you can almost smell the mangoes.

Set along the roadside, **Hotel The Village** (077 900 7755; Polonnaruwa Rd; r with/without air-con Rs 2000/1400;) is a little ramshackle in appearance, but the rooms are tidy and the management is friendly. The rooms can get very hot so air-con is essential in the warm months.

The modern **Royal Lotus** (224 6316; www .theroyallotus.com; s US$55-84, d US$71-100;) sits high on a hillside, and every room has views of Giritale Tank below. Rooms are large and comfortable and the public areas are breezy and open, as befits the warm, dry climate. Breakfast is an additional Rs 100. Nonguests can use the pool for Rs 250.

Giritale Hotel (224 6311; s/d/tr incl breakfast US$75/80/100, luxury s/d/tr US$85/95/120;) has plain but good-value rooms and eight luxury rooms. The restaurant has great views of the Giritale Tank, even if the food is rather mediocre. Ayurvedic massage is available.

Several steps up from the Royal Lotus in the posh stakes, **Deer Park** (224 6272; www.col oursofangsana.com; r from Rs 9000;) has 77 tastefully designed cottages in single units, duplexes and four-unit blocks. All cottages have lovely garden sitting areas, while the most expensive have views of Giritale Tank. Also on the premises are two restaurants

THE ANCIENT CITIES

(Sri Lankan and international), a fitness centre, a squash court, a new spa with Ayurvedic, Thai and Balinese treatments, and the Mahout Adventure Club (an ecotourism agency). The resort offers a number of innovative excursions, including safari jeep rides (Rs 3800) and birdwatching trips (Rs 4500).

Mandalagiri Vihara

Near Medirigiriya, about 30km north of Polonnaruwa, is the Mandalagiri Vihara, a *vatadage* virtually identical to the one at Polonnaruwa. While the Polonnaruwa *vatadage* is crowded among many other structures, the Mandalagiri Vihara stands alone atop a low hill. The site is uncrowded, and the country back road out here makes for a pretty drive.

An earlier structure may have been built here around the 2nd century, but the one that stands today was constructed in the 7th century by Aggabodhi IV. A granite flight of steps leads up to the *vatadage*, which has concentric circles of 16, 20 and 32 pillars around the dagoba. Four large Buddhas face the four cardinal directions. This *vatadage* is noted for its fine stone screens. There was once a hospital next to the *vatadage* – look for the bath shaped like a coffin.

The site is included in the Cultural Triangle round ticket (p212); individual tickets cost US$8/4 (adult/child). It's rare, however, that anyone materialises to check your ticket. Tickets are not sold at the site, so buy one from the information counter at the museum in Polonnaruwa (p223) before you come.

Mandalagiri Vihara is best visited as a half-day trip from Giritale. There are no places to stay or eat, nor are there any worth mentioning in nearby Medirigiriya.

Without your own transport, getting to Medirigiriya is time-consuming. It's about 24km northeast of Minneriya village, which is on the Polonnaruwa–Habarana road. To reach Medirigiriya by bus, first catch a bus to Minneriya, change to a bus headed for Hingurakgoda (Rs 17, every 15 minutes) and then take a bus to Medirigiriya (Rs 20, every 20 minutes). The *vatadage* is 3km from the Medirigiriya bus stop. A three-wheeler from Medirigiriya to the Mandalagiri Vihara is about Rs 250 to Rs 300, including waiting time.

NATIONAL PARKS

The national parks around Polonnaruwa and Habarana offer excellent access to elephants and other animals without the crowds of Yala National Park. To visit either Minneriya or Kaudulla, you must be accompanied by a licensed guide and you must enter and leave by vehicle. Both parks are well served by tours. Prices cost around US$35 per person including entry fees and snacks for a four-hour trip from Habarana; more expensive trips usually have better food and drink or nicer vehicles. Costs are the same for Minneriya or Kaudulla. However, Habarana is closer to Kaudulla and Polonnaruwa is closer to Minneriya; the less time you spend travelling, the longer you have in your chosen park.

Minneriya National Park

Dominated by the ancient Minneriya Tank, this **national park** (adult/child US$15/8, service charge US$8, charge per vehicle Rs 125; ⏰ 6am-6pm) has plenty of scrub and light forest in its 8890 hectares to provide shelter for its toque macaques, sambar deer, leopards and elephants, to name a few. The dry season, from June to September, is the best time to visit. By then water in the tank has dried up, exposing grasses and shoots to grazing animals; elephants, which number up to 150, come to feed and bathe during what is known as 'the Gathering' (see boxed text, p66); and flocks of birds, such as little cormorants and painted storks, fish in the shallow waters.

The park entrance is on the Habarana–Polonnaruwa road. A visitor centre near the entrance sells tickets and has a variety of exhibits about the park's natural history.

Kaudulla National Park

This **park** (adult/child US$10/6, service charge US$8, charge per vehicle Rs 125) stands on the fringe of the ancient Kaudulla Tank. It established a 6656-hectare elephant corridor between Somawathiya Chaitiya National Park and Minneriya National Park. Just 6km off the Habarana–Trincomalee road at Gal Oya junction, it is already a popular safari tour from Polonnaruwa and Habarana because of the good chance of getting up close and personal with elephants. In October there are up to 250 elephants in the park, including herds of juvenile males. There are also leopards, fishing cats, sambar deer, endangered rusty spotted cats and sloth bears.

The best time to visit is from August to December. A catamaran is available for boat rides on the tank.

HABARANA

☎ 066

This small town serves as a regional crossroads as well as a base for eco-adventures. Outfitters here offer trips out to Minneriya and Kaudulla National Parks and elephant rides near the town. There is accommodation to suit all budgets and good transport links; Habarana has the nearest train station to Dambulla and Sigiriya.

Elephant rides around the tank can be arranged for a pricey US$20 to US$30 per person per hour. In the creek near town you can watch the mahouts scrubbing down their elephants; guides and most locals can point the way.

One of the more reliable outfitters for an organised national park trip (which is the only way you can visit the park) is **Elephant Voyage** (☎ 227 0106; Dambulla Rd), located near the Habarana Inn. They do jeep hire for Rs 2500 to Minneriya and Rs 3250 to Kaudulla.

Sleeping & Eating

Habarana Inn (☎ 227 0010; Dambulla Rd; s/d Rs 1500/2500) This basic place is the town's cheapest place to sleep. The seven rooms are clean and simply furnished. It's just past Cinnamon Lodge, on the Dambulla road. The restaurant serves Sri Lankan (rice and curry Rs 600), Western and Chinese dishes.

Habarana Rest House (☎ 227 0003; www.cey lonhotels.lk; r with/without air-con Rs 2500/1600; 🄌) This one-storey rest house, set in a pleasant garden, has four rooms fronted by a long shaded veranda. It's right on the crossroads where the buses congregate. Meals are available (curry and rice Rs 400).

Both of Habarana's neighbouring top-end resort hotels are part of the Keells group and offer similar services and facilities – pools, birdwatching walks, 4WD and elephant safaris, Ayurvedic treatments and views of the tank.

NIMAL PIETHISSA – THE MAKING OF A MAHOUT

Nimal Piethissa is a 28-year-old mahout (elephant handler) living in Habarana. Nimal worked as an apprentice for three years in Kandy before beginning work as a freelance mahout. We met up with him at the Habarana watering hole where mahouts take their elephants for a daily scrub.

Why did you choose this career? I always liked elephants as a boy and thought about doing this job from a young age. My parents agreed and allowed me to leave school so I could become a mahout apprentice. The money is OK, I make around Rs 7000 per month, plus it's lots of fun. On the downside, it's not a very prestigious job. Westerners like to romanticise this work, but in Sri Lanka it's considered a dirty job. When I tell the local girls it's an instant turn-off, no one really wants to marry a mahout.

What is the most difficult aspect of the job? These animals are pretty temperamental, so the most difficult part of the job is controlling their temper and dealing with them when they become angry. Usually food, sweet food and fruits, will calm them down. They especially like sugar cane, pineapples and bananas. If that doesn't work, we rub them and push specific pressure points with a *hindua* (pole). If they are not feeling well we can give them medicine, usually leaves from the *cohomba* tree work wonders.

How do you control them? Mostly with the *hindua*. People get frightened when we hit them with it but they are so big that it doesn't affect them much – like someone whacking you with a chopstick. We also have 26 words that we use to control them; for example, 'daha' is 'go' and 'ho' is 'stop'.

How much do they eat? Up to 300kg a day – grass mostly but also coconut husk and fruit. They also need to eat at night, so we usually need to wake up around 2am and then again at 5am. Elephants can travel long distances for food if they need to. Their sense of smell is one of the best among mammals – they can smell food up to 15km away.

Which elephants are the best to work with? It's considered an honour to work with king elephants. These are the elephants you usually see in the temples. A king elephant must have seven parts that touch the ground – four feet, the tail, the trunk and the penis.

How long can elephant live? Some live up to 70 years – if they have a good mahout to take care of them!

Village (☎ 227 0047; village@chayahotels.com; s/d incl breakfast US$84/118; ✉ 💻 🏊) This nice place offers spacious terraced rooms with verandas. The restaurant looks over the swimming pool, and there are also badminton and tennis. The lakefront setting makes for easy birdwatching before breakfast.

Cinnamon Lodge (☎ 227 0012; lodge@keells.com; s/d incl breakfast US$108/116; ✉ 💻 🏊) The 150 spacious rooms come in vaguely Portuguese colonial-style duplexes, and set in 11 hectares of lush landscaping. A nature trail leads to a tree-house platform for viewing birds and monkeys. It has a Thai restaurant and fitness centre.

Getting There & Away

Buses leave from the crossroads outside the Habarana Rest House. A direct intercity bus from Colombo departs hourly (Rs 190, five hours). From Habarana there are very frequent departures in all directions: you can pick up the air-con Trinco–Colombo bus, or buses travelling between Anuradhapura and Ampara, Batticaloa and Colombo, or Kandy (via Dambulla) and Trincomalee, but you're not guaranteed a seat. If you are embarking on a long-haul trip, it's best to start as early as possible.

The train station is 1km out of town on the Trincomalee road. There are trains leaving for Polonnaruwa (3rd/2nd class Rs 55/110) and Batticaloa (3rd/2nd class Rs 130/260) at 11.34am, and for Colombo (3rd/2nd class Rs 180/330) at 12.33am.

RITIGALA

Deep inside the Ritigala Strict Nature Reserve, off the Anuradhapura–Habarana road, are the partially restored **ruins** of an extensive monastic and cave complex. The ruins lie on a hill, which at 766m isn't exactly high, but is nevertheless a striking feature in the flat, dry landscape surrounding it. The 24-hectare site is isolated and almost deserted. The site is included in the Cultural Triangle round ticket (p212); otherwise, individual tickets cost Rs 1800/1000 (adult/child).

The true meaning of the name Ritigala remains unclear – *gala* means 'rock' in Sinhala, but *riti* may come from the Pali *arittha,* meaning 'safety'. Thus Ritigala probably a place of refuge, including for kings, as long ago as the 4th century BC.

Ritigala also has a place in mythology. It's claimed to be the spot from which Hanuman (the monkey god) leapt to India to tell Rama that he had discovered where Sita was being held by the king of Lanka. Mythology also offers an explanation for the abundance of healing herbs and plants found in Ritigala: it's said that Hanuman, on his way back to Lanka with healing Himalayan herbs for Rama's wounded brother, dropped some over Ritigala.

Monks found Ritigala's caves ideal for an ascetic existence, and more than 70 such caves have been discovered. Royals proved generous patrons, especially King Sena I, who in the 9th century made an endowment of a monastery to the *pamsukulika* (rag robes) monks.

Ritigala was abandoned following the Chola invasions in the 10th and 11th centuries, after which it lay deserted and largely forgotten until it was rediscovered by British surveyors in the 19th century. It was explored and mapped by HCP Bell in 1893.

Sights

Ritigala has none of the usual icons: no bodhi tree, no relic house and no Buddha images. The only embellishments are on the urinals at the forest monastery – it's been conjectured that by urinating on the fine stone carving the monks were demonstrating their contempt for worldly things.

Near the Archaeology Department bungalow are the remains of a *banda pokuna* (artificial pond), which apparently fills with water during the rainy season. From here it's a scramble along a forest path via a donations hall to a **ruined palace** and the **monastery hospital**, where you can still see the grinding stones and huge stone baths. A flagstone path leads upwards; a short detour takes you to what is often described as a stone fort – or, more accurately, a lookout.

The next group of ruins of note are the double-platform structures so characteristic of forest monasteries. Here you can see the **urinal stones**, although they almost certainly weren't always in this exact spot. Scholars think they were used for meditation, teaching and ceremony. Someone from the Archaeology Department bungalow will accompany you (and will expect a tip, say Rs 300) but may be reluctant to take you beyond this point – although the ruins extend right up to the top – because of wild animals and dense vegetation.

You'll need at least 1½ hours to see the site properly. Staff at the Archaeology Department bungalow sell tickets to the site and check all tickets, although there's no one present after about 4pm.

Getting There & Away

Ritigala is 14km northwest of Habarana and 42km southeast of Anuradhapura. If you're coming from Habarana, the turn-off is near the 14km post. It's a further 10km to get to the Archaeology Department bungalow (which is 3km past the turn-off at the Wildlife Department bungalow). Its best to take your own transport here, but note that the road may be impassable in the wet season (October to January). From Kekirawa, three buses (Rs 20, 30 minutes) per day come here, departing at 6am, 3pm and 5pm.

AUKANA

According to legend, the magnificent 12m-high standing **Aukana Buddha** (admission Rs 500) was sculpted during the reign of Dhatusena in the 5th century, though some sources date it to the 12th or 13th century. Aukana means 'sun-eating' and dawn, when the first rays light up the huge statue's finely carved features, is the best time to see it.

Note that although the statue is still narrowly joined at the back to the rock face it is cut from, the lotus plinth on which it stands is a separate piece. The Buddha's pose, *ashiva mudra*, signifies blessings, while the burst of fire above his head represents the power of total enlightenment.

It's easy to catch a bus to Kekirawa from Dambulla (Rs 28) or Anuradhapura (Rs 45). There are five or six buses a day between Kekirawa and Aukana (Rs 6, 15 minutes, five or six per day). Aukana is on the railway line from Colombo to Trincomalee and Polonnaruwa, and the station is just a short walk from the statue. Four trains a day stop here; only 2nd and 3rd class fares are available and services run to Colombo (Rs 250/400, four hours), Trincomalee (Rs 280/450, five hours) and Polonnaruwa (Rs 120/200, two hours). A van from Kekirawa will set you back about Rs 1500 for a Kekirawa–Aukana–Kalawewa (or back to Kekirawa) circuit; a three-wheeler costs about Rs 700. Departing from Habarana, a van to Aukana will cost you about Rs 2000 return.

ANURADHAPURA

☎ 025 / pop 56,600

While it's not quite as grandiose as Burma's Bagan or as mysterious as Cambodia's Angkor Wat, the ruins of Anuradhapura remain one of the South Asia's most electrifying sights. The sprawling complex contains a rich collection of archaeological and architectural wonders: enormous dagobas, soaring brick towers, ancient pools and crumbling temples, built during Anuradhapura's 1000 years of rule over Sri Lanka. Still today it's not completely dead; in fact, several of the sites remain in use as holy places and temples; this adds some life to the place, a sharp contrast to the fairly moribund ruins at Polonnaruwa.

Current-day Anuradhapura is a rather pleasant, planned city. Mature trees shade the main guest house areas, and the main street is orderly compared to the ugly concrete agglomerations seen in many other regional centres.

History

Anuradhapura first became a capital in 380 BC under Pandukabhaya, but it was under Devanampiya Tissa (r 247–207 BC) – during whose reign Buddhism reached Sri Lanka – that it first rose to great importance. Soon Anuradhapura became a great and glittering city, only to fall before a South Indian invasion – a fate that was to befall it repeatedly for more than 1000 years. But before long the Sinhalese hero Dutugemunu led an army from a refuge in the far south to recapture Anuradhapura. The 'Dutu' part of his name, incidentally, means 'undutiful' because his father, fearing for his son's safety, forbade him to attempt to recapture Anuradhapura. Dutugemunu disobeyed him, and later sent his father a woman's ornament to indicate what he thought of his courage.

Dutugemunu (r 161–137 BC) set in motion a vast building program that included some of the most impressive monuments in Anuradhapura today. Other important kings who followed him included Valagamba (r 109–103 BC), who lost his throne in another Indian invasion but later regained it, and Mahasena (r AD 276–303), the last 'great' king of Anuradhapura, who was the builder of the colossal Jetavanarama Dagoba. He also held the record for tank construction, building 16 of them in all, plus a major canal. Anuradhapura was to survive for another 500 years before finally being replaced by Polonnaruwa, but it was harassed by invasions from South India again and again – invasions made easier by the cleared lands and great roads that were a product of Anuradhapura's importance.

Orientation

The ancient city is northwest of the modern town of Anuradhapura. The main road from Kandy, Dambulla and Polonnaruwa enters the town on the northeastern side then travels south to the centre, which is a spread-out affair with two bus stations – the old bus station (intercity express buses leave from near this station) and the new bus station 2km further south. Buses heading for the new bus station usually call at the old one on the way through, and will also let you off anywhere else along the route.

There are also two train stations. If you're just arriving by train, the northern station is the one most convenient for places to stay and the ruins.

The ancient city is rather spread out. There is one important starting point for exploring it – the Sri Maha Bodhi (the sacred bodhi tree) and the cluster of buildings around it. There are plenty of cold-drink stalls scattered around the site, as well as plenty of people willing to act as a guide.

Information

An US$25/15 (adult/child) entry ticket or a round ticket for the Cultural Triangle (see p212) is required by foreigners visiting the northern areas of the ancient city. Both types of ticket can be bought at the **ticket office** (7am-7.30pm) near the Archaeological Museum (p236) on the west side of the city, and a **booth** (Trincomalee Rd; 7am-7.30pm) near Sri Maha Bodhi. Unfortunately your ticket, whether single or round, is valid for one day's visit only. This is a real shame considering the ancient city remains are easily worth two or more days of exploration.

You must pay an extra Rs 30 to visit the nearby Folk Museum (p236), and Rs 50 for the Isurumuniya Vihara (p236). Entry to the Sri Maha Bodhi compound area costs Rs 100, but if things aren't busy you may not be approached for the money.

Hotel Shalini (222 2425; 41/388 Harischandra Mawatha, per hour Rs 50) Has internet facilities for nonguests, as do a few other hotels and guest houses.

Netona (252 Main St; per hr Rs 50) Internet facilities.

People's Bank (Main St) Changes travellers cheques.

Post Office (Main St)

Seylan Bank (Main St) ATM.

Sights

Remember to remove your shoes and hat before approaching a dagoba or the sacred bodhi tree.

SRI MAHA BODHI

The **Sri Maha Bodhi**, the sacred bodhi tree, is central to Anuradhapura in both a spiritual and physical sense. The huge tree has grown from a cutting brought from Bodhgaya in India by the Princess Sangamitta, sister of Mahinda (who introduced the Buddha's teachings to Sri Lanka), so it has a connection to the geographical heart of the Sinhalese religion.

The sacred bodhi tree is the oldest historically authenticated tree in the world; it has been tended by an uninterrupted succession of guardians for over 2000 years, even during the periods of Indian occupation. There is not one but many bodhi trees here; the oldest and holiest stands on the top platform. The steps leading up to the tree's platform are very old, but the golden railing around it is quite modern. The railing and other structures around the trees are festooned with prayer flags. Thousands of devotees come to make offerings at weekends and particularly on *poya* (full-moon) days. April is a particularly busy month as pilgrims converge on the site for *snana puja* (offerings or prayers). You must remove your shoes and hat before entering this site.

BRAZEN PALACE

So called because it once had a bronze roof, the ruins of the **Brazen Palace** stand close to the bodhi tree. The remains of 1600 columns are all that is left of this huge palace, said to have had nine storeys and accommodation for 1000 monks and attendants.

It was originally built by Dutugemunu more than 2000 years ago, but through the ages was rebuilt many times, each time a little less grandiosely. The current stand of pillars (now fenced off) is all that remains from the last rebuild – that of Parakramabahu around the 12th century.

RUVANVELISAYA DAGOBA

Behind the Folk Museum, this fine white **dagoba** is guarded by a wall with a frieze of hundreds of elephants standing shoulder to shoulder. Apart from a few beside the western entrance, most are modern replacements for the originals from 140 BC.

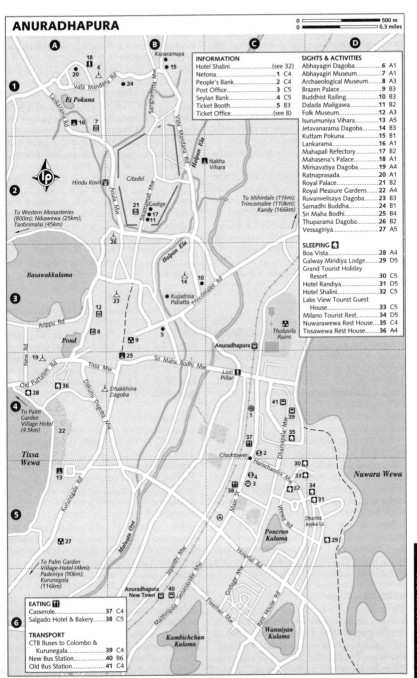

ANURADHAPURA

0 500 m
0 0.3 miles

INFORMATION

Hotel Shalini	(see 32)
Netona	1 C4
People's Bank	2 C4
Post Office	3 C5
Seylan Bank	4 C5
Ticket Booth	5 B3
Ticket Office	(see 8)

SIGHTS & ACTIVITIES

Abhayagiri Dagoba	6 A1
Abhayagiri Museum	7 A1
Archaeological Museum	8 A3
Brazen Palace	9 B3
Buddhist Railing	10 B3
Dalada Maligawa	11 B2
Folk Museum	12 A3
Isurumuniya Vihara	13 A5
Jetavanarama Dagoba	14 B3
Kuttam Pokuna	15 B1
Lankarama	16 A1
Mahapali Refectory	17 B2
Mahasena's Palace	18 A1
Mirisavatiya Dagoba	19 A4
Ratnaprasada	20 A1
Royal Palace	21 B2
Royal Pleasure Gardens	22 A4
Ruvanvelisaya Dagoba	23 B3
Samadhi Buddha	24 B1
Sri Maha Bodhi	25 B4
Thuparama Dagoba	26 B2
Vessagiriya	27 A5

SLEEPING

Boa Vista	28 A4
Galway Miridiya Lodge	29 D5
Grand Tourist Holiday Resort	30 C5
Hotel Randiya	31 D5
Hotel Shalini	32 D5
Lake View Tourist Guest House	33 C5
Milano Tourist Rest	34 D5
Nuwarawewa Rest House	35 C4
Tissawewa Rest House	36 A4

EATING

Casserole	37 C4
Salgado Hotel & Bakery	38 C5

TRANSPORT

CTB Buses to Colombo & Kurunegala	39 C4
New Bus Station	40 B6
Old Bus Station	41 C4

This dagoba is said to be King Dutugemunu's finest construction, but he didn't live to see its completion. However, as he lay on his deathbed, a false bamboo-and-cloth finish was placed around the the dagoba so that Dutugemunu's final sight could be of his 'completed' masterpiece. Today, after incurring much damage from invading Indian forces, it rises 55m, considerably less than its original height; nor is its form the same as the earlier 'bubble' shape. A limestone statue south of the great dagoba is popularly thought to be of Dutugemunu.

The land around the dagoba is rather like a pleasant green park, dotted with patches of ruins, the remains of ponds and pools, and collections of columns and pillars, all picturesquely leaning in different directions. Slightly southeast of the dagoba, you can see one of Anuradhapura's many monks' refectories. Keeping such a number of monks fed and happy was a full-time job for the lay followers.

THUPARAMA DAGOBA
In a beautiful woodland setting north of the Ruvanvelisaya Dagoba, the **Thuparama Dagoba** is the oldest dagoba in Sri Lanka – indeed, probably the oldest visible dagoba in the world. It was constructed by Devanampiya Tissa in the 3rd century BC and is said to contain the right collarbone of the Buddha. Its 'heap-of-paddy-rice' shape was restored in 1862 in a more conventional bell shape and to a height of 19m.

The surrounding *vatadage*'s slender, capital-topped pillars, perhaps the dagoba's most unique feature, enclose the structure in four concentric circles. Impressions on the dagoba pediments indicate the pillars originally numbered 176, of which 41 still stand. Although some Sri Lankan scholars believe these once supported a conical wooden roof, there is no archaeological evidence for this theory, nor does it follow any known antecedent in South India, whose dagobas were the prototypes for virtually all Sinhalese dagobas.

NORTHERN RUINS
There is quite a long stretch of road, which starts as Anula Mawatha, running north from the Thuparama Dagoba to the next clump of ruins. Coming back you can take an alternative route through the Royal Palace site and then visit the Jetavanarama Dagoba.

Abhayagiri Dagoba
The huge **Abhayagiri Dagoba** (confused by some books and maps with the Jetavanarama), created in the 1st or 2nd century BC, was the centrepiece of a monastery of 5000 monks. The name means 'Hill of Protection' or 'Fearless Hill' (though some local guides mistakenly claim 'Giri' was the name of a local Jain monk). The monastery was part of the 'School of the Secret Forest', a heretical sect that studied both Mahayana and Theravada Buddhism. Chinese traveller Faxian (also spelt Fa Hsien) visited in AD 412.

The dagoba was probably rebuilt several times to reach its peak 75m height. It has some interesting bas-reliefs, including one near the western stairway of an elephant pulling up a tree. A large slab with a Buddha footprint can be seen on the northern side, and the eastern and western steps have unusual moonstones made from concentric stone slabs.

Mahasena's Palace
This ruined **palace** northwest of the Abhayagiri is notable for having the finest carved moonstone in Sri Lanka. Photographers will be disappointed that the railing around it makes it almost impossible to achieve an unshadowed picture. This is a peaceful wooded area full of butterflies, and makes a good place to stop and cool off during a tour of the ruins.

Ratnaprasada
Follow the loop road a little further and you will find the finest guardstones in Anuradhapura. Dating from the 8th century, they depict a cobra king and demonstrate the final refinement of guardstone design. You can see examples of much earlier guardstone design at the Mirisavatiya Dagoba (opposite).

In the 8th century a new order of *tapovana* (ascetic) monks settled in the fringes of the city, among the lowest castes, the rubbish dumps and the burial places. These monasteries were large but unelaborate structures; ornamentation was saved for toilets, now displayed at the Archaeological Museum (p236). The monks of **Ratnaprasada** (Gem Palace) monastery gave sanctuary to people in trouble with the authorities, and this led to a major conflict with the king. When court officials at odds with the king took sanctuary in the Ratnaprasada, the king sent his supporters to capture and execute them. The monks, disgusted at this invasion of a sacred place, departed en masse. The general populace, equally disgusted, besieged the Ratnaprasada, captured and executed the king's supporters and forced the king to apologise to the departed monks in order to bring the monks back to the city and restore peace.

To the south of the Ratnaprasada is the **Lankarama**, a 1st-century-BC *vatadage*.

Samadhi Buddha

After your investigations of guardstones and moonstones, you can continue east from the Abhayagiri to this 4th-century **statue**, seated in the meditation pose and regarded as one of the finest Buddha statues in Sri Lanka. Pandit Nehru, a prominent leader in India's independence movement, is said to have maintained his composure while imprisoned by the British by regular contemplation of a photo of this statue.

Local authorities recently erected a modern metal roof over the statue, somewhat spoiling the artistic integrity of this masterpiece.

Kuttam Pokuna (Twin Ponds)

The swimming pool–like **Twin Ponds**, the finest bathing tanks in Anuradhapura, are east of Sanghamitta Mawatha. They were likely used by monks from the monastery attached to Abhayagiri Dagoba. Although they are referred to as twins, the southern pond, which is 28m in length, is smaller than the 40m-long northern pond. Water entered the larger pond through the mouth of a *makara* (mythical multispecies beast) and then flowed to the smaller pond through an underground pipe. Note the five-headed cobra figure close to the *makara* and the water-filter system at the northwestern end of the ponds.

Royal Palace

If you return south along Sanghamitta Mawatha, after about 1.5km you'll pass through the **Royal Palace** site. Built by Vijayabahu I in the 12th century after Anuradhapura's fall as the Sinhalese capital, the palace is indicative of the attempts made to retain at least a foothold in the old capital.

Close to it are a deep and ancient well and the **Mahapali refectory**, notable for its immense trough (nearly 3m long and 2m wide) that the lay followers filled with rice for the monks. In the Royal Palace area you can also find the **Dalada Maligawa**, a tooth-relic temple that may

have been the first Temple of the Tooth. The sacred Buddha's tooth originally came to Sri Lanka in AD 313.

JETAVANARAMA DAGOBA

The **Jetavanarama Dagoba's** massive dome rises from a clearing back towards the Sri Maha Bodhi. Built in the 3rd century by Mahasena, it may have originally stood over 100m high, but today is about 70m. This was a similar height to the Abhayagiri, with which it is sometimes confused. When it was built it was the third-tallest monument in the world, the first two being Egyptian pyramids. A British guidebook from the early 1900s calculated that there were enough bricks in the dagoba's brick core to make a 3m-high wall stretching from London to Edinburgh.

Behind it stand the ruins of a monastery that housed 3000 monks. One building has door jambs over 8m high still standing, with another 3m underground. At one time, massive doors opened to reveal a large Buddha image.

BUDDHIST RAILING

A little south of the Jetavanarama Dagoba, on the other side of the road, there is a stone **railing** built in imitation of a log wall. It encloses a site 42m by 34m, but the building within has long disappeared.

MIRISAVATIYA DAGOBA

Mirisavatiya Dagoba is one of three very interesting sites that can be visited in a stroll or ride along the banks of the Tissa Wewa. This huge dagoba, the first built by Dutugemunu after he captured the city, is across the road from the Tissawewa Rest House. The story goes that Dutugemunu went to bathe in the tank, leaving his ornate sceptre implanted in the bank. When he emerged he found his sceptre, which contained a relic of the Buddha, impossible to pull out. Taking this as an auspicious sign, he had the dagoba built. To its northeast was yet another monks' refectory, complete with the usual huge stone troughs into which the faithful poured boiled rice.

ROYAL PLEASURE GARDENS

If you start down the Tissa Wewa bund from the Mirisavatiya, you soon come to the extensive **royal pleasure gardens**. Known as the Park of the Goldfish, the gardens cover 14 hectares and contain two ponds skilfully

THE ANCIENT CITIES

designed to fit around the huge boulders in the park. The ponds have fine reliefs of elephants on their sides. It was here that Prince Saliya, the son of Dutugemunu, was said to have met a commoner, Asokamala, whom he married, thereby forsaking his right to the throne.

ISURUMUNIYA VIHARA

This **rock temple** (admission Rs 200), dating from the reign of Devanampiya Tissa (r 247–207 BC), has some very fine carvings. One or two of these (including one of elephants playfully splashing water) remain in their original place on the rock face beside a square pool fed from the Tissa Wewa, but most of them have been moved into a small museum within the temple. Best known of the sculptures is the 'lovers', which dates from around the 5th century AD and is built in the artistic style of the Indian Gupta dynasty of the 4th and 5th centuries.

South of the Isurumuniya Vihara are extensive remains of the **Vessagiriya** cave monastery complex, which dates from much the same time.

MUSEUMS

Anuradhapura's **Archaeological Museum** (admission with Cultural Triangle or Anuradhapura ticket free; ⊗ 8am-5pm Wed-Mon, closed public holidays) also houses a ticket office for the ancient city. It has a restored relic chamber, as found during the excavation of the Kantaka Chetiya dagoba at nearby Mihintale (p239), and a large-scale model of Thuparama Dagoba's *vatadage* as it might have been if a wooden roof (for which there is no physical or epigraphic evidence) had existed.

In the museum's grounds are the carved squatting plates from Anuradhapura's western monasteries, whose monks had forsaken the luxurious monasteries of their more worldly brothers. To show their contempt for the effete, luxury-loving monks, the monks of the western monasteries carved beautiful stone squat-style toilets, with their brother monks' monasteries represented on the bottom! Their urinals illustrated the god of wealth showering handfuls of coins down the hole.

A short distance north of the Archaeological Museum there's a **Folk Museum** (admission Rs 50; ⊗ 8.30am-5pm Sat-Wed, closed public holidays) with dusty exhibits of country life in Sri Lanka's North Central Province.

The Chinese-funded **Abhayagiri Museum** (admission free; ⊗ 10am-5pm), just south of the Abhayagiri Dagoba, commemorates the 5th-century visit of Chinese Buddhist monk Faxian to Anuradhapura. Faxian spent some time living at the Abhayagiri monastery translating Buddhist texts, which he later brought back to China. The museum, arguably the most interesting in Anuradhapura, contains a collection of squatting plates, jewellery, pottery and religious sculpture from the site. There is a bookshop selling Cultural Triangle publications.

TANKS

Anuradhapura has three great tanks. **Nuwara Wewa**, on the east side of the city, is the largest, covering about 1200 hectares. It was built around 20 BC and is well away from most of the old city. The 160-hectare **Tissa Wewa** is the southern tank in the old city. The oldest tank, probably dating from around the 4th century BC, is the 120-hectare **Basawakkulama** (the Tamil word for tank is *kulam*) to the north. Off to the northwest of the Basawakkulama are the ruins of the **western monasteries**, where the monks dressed in scraps of clothing taken from corpses and, it's claimed, lived only on rice.

Sleeping

Anuradhapura is well endowed with midrange accommodation choices, and there are a couple of good budget picks as well. The greatest concentrations of places to stay is found off Harischandra Mawatha near the Nuwara Wewa. If you're taking the train to Anuradhapura, be aware that touts begin boarding a few stations before arrival, and will try very hard to steer you away from places not paying them a commission.

BUDGET

Lake View Tourist Guest House (☎ 222 1593; 4C/4 Lake Rd; s/d Rs 800/900, with air-con Rs 1350/1500; ⊗) On a lane off Harischandra Mawatha, almost opposite the Grand Tourist Holiday Resort, this is a friendly place with 10 rooms, some with hot water; the ones in the front of the building looking out towards Mihintale are best. The owners are cheerful, and the Sri Lankan food is good. Bicycle hire is Rs 250.

ourpick Milano Tourist Rest (☎ 222 2364; www.milanotrest.com; 40/596 JR Jaya Mawatha; s/d Rs 1200/1500, with air-con Rs 1800/2200; ⊗ 🖳) One of the best deals in town, Milano is a comfortable and modern house with huge private rooms, comfy beds and satellite TV. The management is friendly, and even drivers rave about its comfortable guest quarters. Bikes are available for Rs 200.

MIDRANGE & TOP END

Boa Vista (☎ 223 5052; shanidacunha@live.com; 142 Old Puttalam Rd; s/d Rs 1500/2000, with air-con Rs 3000/4000; ❄ ▢) A welcoming Sri Lankan–Canadian couple run this guest house by the lake. The large building is well lit and roomy and has excellent views from the upper-floor rooms. Breakfast is available for an extra Rs 300 and there is bike hire. Boa Vista doesn't pay touts commissions, so many three-wheeler drivers will tell you the guest house is full or closed.

Hotel Shalini (☎ 222 2425; www.hotelshalini.com; 41/388 Harischandra Mawatha; r with/without air-con Rs 2300/1700; ❄ ▢) This place has a cute gingerbread-house-like annexe with a pleasant open-air restaurant, rooftop garden and internet cafe. Rooms can be a little boxy and those without windows should be avoided. You can rent bicycles for Rs 250 a day, or take a tour of Anuradhapura's ancient city for Rs 1500 (Rs 3000 for Mihintale and Anuradhapura combined). The friendly owners will pick you up (or drop you off) for free at the bus or train station if you make arrangements in advance.

Grand Tourist Holiday Resort (☎ 223 5173; thegranddami@yahoo.com; 4B/2 Lake Rd; r with/without air-con Rs 2700/2200; ❄ ▢) Though grandly titled, this is really a large house converted into a tourist bungalow with nine rooms. It's an old property with a nice porch that has views out to Nuwara Wewa. The rooms are large and have high ceilings; air-con is optional but well worth it as the old home can get suffocatingly hot at night.

Hotel Randiya (☎ 222 2868; www.hotelrandiya.com; 19A/394 Muditha Mawatha; s/d/tr Rs 3100/3600/4100; ❄ ▢) The 14-room Hotel Randiya looks good from the outside, with its *walawwa* (minor palace) bungalow-style architecture. Inside, rooms are a little small and have too much drapery. The price includes either a Western or a Sri Lankan breakfast.

our pick Tissawewa Rest House (☎ 222 2299; hotels@quickshaws.com; r with/without breakfast US$75/35; ❄) A Raj-era relic with a style all its own, the century-old Tissawewa is authentic right down to the shower railings and claw-foot bathtubs. Besides high-ceilinged lounge areas and verandas, it has 4.4 hectares of gardens with mahogany and teak trees. A big veranda looks out on gardens with lots of monkeys who have no qualms about stealing your afternoon tea. Bikes are available at a pricey Rs 750 per day. Even if you're not staying here, it's a good place to come for lunch (meals Rs 500) as a way to break up your tour of the ruins. Guests can use the swimming pool at the Nuwarawewa Rest House.

Galway Miridiya Lodge (☎ 222 2519; miridiya@sltnet.lk; Wasaladantha Mawatha; s/d US$43/46; ❄ ▢ ▣) This motel-style hotel has 1980s decor and tiny TVs. It's not a bad set-up – just about 25 years past its prime. Out back there is a pretty garden running down to the tank. Nonguests may use the pool for Rs 350. This place is popular with groups.

Nuwarawewa Rest House (☎ 222 3265; hotels@quickshaws.com; Dhamapala Mw; r US$47.50; ❄ ▢ ▣) Anuradhapura's other rest house lacks the history and charm of Tissawewa. Rooms are fairly bland, and the furnishings are due for some modernising. The rest house does have a decent lakeside location and a nice pool, but it's a little overpriced – you could try bargaining. Bikes are available for Rs 450 per day and nonguests can use the pool for Rs 500.

Palm Garden Village Hotel (☎ 222 3961; www.palmgardenvillage.com; Old Puttalam Rd, Pandulagama; r US$95, villas US$120; ❄ ▣) Accommodation at Anuradhapura's top hotel, 6km west of town, is in very spacious rooms in well-designed duplex units or separate villas. They're set in 38 hectares of gardens complete with tennis courts, an Ayurvedic centre, a fitness centre and a Catholic chapel – not to mention resident deer, peacocks and the occasional elephant. A three-wheeler from town costs Rs 350.

Eating

There's little in the way of eating places apart from the guest houses and hotels.

Salgado Hotel & Bakery (Main St; dishes Rs 100-130) This is an old-fashioned place serving Sri Lankan breakfasts, short eats and biscuits.

Casserole (279 Main St; mains Rs 70-250; ⊙ 7am-8.30pm) A busy, very clean air-con spot serving Sri Lankan, Chinese and Western meals. There's a supermarket downstairs. For a good dessert, try the *wattalappan* (egg, coconut milk, cardamon and jaggery pudding).

Getting There & Away

BUS

Anuradhapura has 'old' and 'new' bus stations – the old bus station is further north, closer to the train station. CTB buses to Colombo and Kurunegala leave from near the old bus station. Buses heading south start at the old bus station and stop by the new bus station, while buses heading north to Vavuniya and east to Trincomalee start from the new bus station. It is easier to get a good seat from the starting point.

There are departures to Trinco (Rs 150, 3½ hours) at 7.30am, 10.30am and 12.30pm; to Kandy (Rs 260, three hours), via Kekirawa and Dambulla, twice hourly between 5.30am and 6.30pm; and to Polonnaruwa (Rs 150, three hours) hourly from around 6.30am to 10pm. Buses to Kurunegala (Rs 125, two hours) leave every 30 minutes from about 6am; those to Colombo (regular/air-con bus Rs 224/350, five hours) leave every 30 minutes between 4.30am and 7pm. For Puttalam you may have to catch a bus to Kala Oya (private bus Rs 20, 30 minutes), and then another on to Puttalam (Rs 27, one hour). Buses to Kala Oya pass the road to Wilpattu National Park (p103); get off at Maragahawewa and change for Hunuwilagama).

TRAIN

Anuradhapura has two train stations: the main Anuradhapura station and the smaller Anuradhapura New Town station further south. Trains to Colombo (four to five hours) depart at 6.37am, 8.40am, 2.15pm and 11.40pm. First-class seats are available on the 6.37am intercity express and the 2.15pm and 11.40pm trains. Prices vary depending on the train; for the intercity express it's Rs 250/400/600 for 3rd/2nd/1st-class seating. For Matara (3rd/2nd Rs 280/520, 9½ hours) and Galle (3rd/2nd class Rs 250/460/860, 8½ hours), catch the *Rajarata Rajini* at 5am. You can also travel from Anuradhapura to Kandy by any train heading south, changing at Polgahawela (intercity express 3rd/2nd/1st class Rs 220/370/550).

Getting Around

The city is too spread out to investigate on foot. A three-hour taxi trip costs about Rs 900 and a three-wheeler about Rs 650. But a bicycle (Rs 200 to Rs 450 a day) is the nicest and most leisurely way to explore the ruins. Roadblocks around Sri Maha Bodhi also make a bicycle the best way to explore Anuradhapura. However, you can't take a bicycle everywhere: near the bodhi tree shrine you will have to park your bike and walk.

There's also a terrific bike track along the bund of Nuwara Wewa. Most guest houses in town rent bicycles.

Numerous buses run between the old and new bus stations via Main St.

MIHINTALE
☎ 025

This sleepy town and temple complex holds a special place in the annals of Sri Lankan lore. In 247 BC, King Devanampiya Tissa of Anuradhapura was hunting a stag on Mihintale Hill when he was approached by Mahinda, son of the great Indian Buddhist emperor, Ashoka. Mahinda tested the king's wisdom and, considering him to be a worthy disciple, promptly converted the king on the spot. Mihintale has since been associated with the earliest introduction of Buddhism to Sri Lanka.

Exploring Mihintale hill does involve quite a climb, so you would be wise to visit it early in the morning or late in the afternoon to avoid the midday heat. There are seven authorised guides who charge around Rs 350 for a ton of information over two hours or so. It pays off if you have a deep interest in Buddhism and the site's history. Mihintale is 13km east of Anuradhapura.

Each year a great festival, the **Poson Poya**, is held at Mihintale on the Poson full-moon night (usually in June).

Sights

HOSPITAL

A ruined **hospital** and the remains of a **quincunx** of buildings, laid out like the five dots on a die, flank the roadway before the base of the steps to the temple complex. The hospital consisted of a number of cells. A *bat oruwa* (large stone trough) sits among the ruins. The interior is carved in the shape of a human form, and the patient would climb into this to be immersed in healing oils. Inscriptions have revealed that the hospital had its specialists – there is reference to a *mandova*, a bone and muscle specialist, and to a *puhunda vedek*, a leech doctor.

STAIRWAY

In a series of flights, 1840 ancient granite slab steps lead majestically up the hillside. The first

MIHINTALE

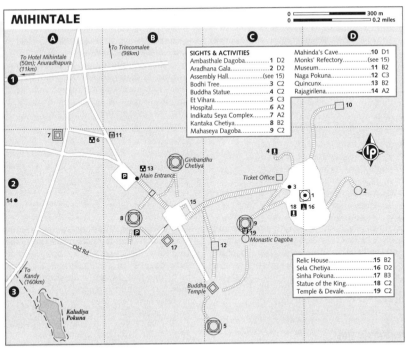

flight is the widest and shallowest. Higher up the steps are narrower and steeper. If you have a problem with stairs, Old Rd from the west avoids most of them.

KANTAKA CHETIYA

At the first landing a smaller flight of steps leads to this partly ruined **dagoba** off to the right. It's 12m high (originally it was higher than 30m) and 130m around at its base. A Brahmi inscription found nearby records donations for the dagoba. While exactly who built it is open to conjecture, Devanampiya Tissa (r 247–207 BC) had 68 cave monasteries built, and the dagoba would have been constructed near these. King Laji Tissa (r 59–50 BC) enlarged it. So the dagoba was built sometime in between, and is certainly one of the oldest at Mihintale. It is noteworthy for its friezes (see p240). Four stone flower altars stand at each of the cardinal points, and surrounding these are well-preserved sculptures of dwarfs, geese and other figures.

South of the Kantaka Chetiya, where a big boulder is cleft by a cave, if you look up you'll see what is thought to be the oldest inscription

in Sri Lanka, predating Pali in Sri Lanka. The inscription dedicates the mountain's shelters to meditation, now and for eternity. Through the cave, ledges on the cliff face acted as meditation retreats for the numerous monks once resident here. There are around 70 different sites for contemplation.

MONKS' REFECTORY & RELIC HOUSE

At the top of the next flight of steps, on the second landing, is the **monks' refectory** with huge stone troughs that the lay followers kept filled with rice for the monks.

Nearby, at a place identified as the monastery's **relic house**, are two inscribed stone slabs erected during the reign of King Mahinda IV (r 975–91). The inscriptions laid down the rules relating to the relic house and the conduct of those responsible for it. One inscription clearly states that nothing belonging to the relic house shall be lent or sold. Another confirms the amount of land to be given in exchange for a reliable supply of oil and wicks for lamps and flowers for offerings. Also known as the Mihintale tablets, these inscribed stones define the duties of the monastery's many

SCULPTURAL SYMBOLISM

The four *vahalkadas* (solid panels of sculpture) at the Kantaka Chetiya are among the oldest and best preserved in the country and are the only ones to be found at Mihintale.

Vahalkadas face each of the four cardinal directions and comprise a series of bands, each containing some sort of ornamentation. The upper part usually contained niches in which were placed sculptures of divine beings. At either end of each *vahalkada* is a pillar topped with the figure of an animal, such as an elephant or a lion. How or why these sculptural creations came into being is subject to speculation, but one theory is that they evolved from simple flower altars. Others suggest they were an adaptation from Hindu temple design.

The cardinal points in traditional sculptural work are represented by specific animals: an elephant on the east, a horse on the west, a lion on the north and a bull on the south. In addition to these beasts, sculptures also feature dwarfs (sometimes depicted with animal heads), geese (said to have the power to choose between good and evil), elephants (often shown as though supporting the full weight of the superstructure) and *naga* (serpents, said to possess magical powers). Floral designs, apart from the lotus, are said to be primarily ornamental.

servants: which servants gather firewood and cook, which servants cook but only on firewood gathered by others, and so on. There are also rules for monks: they should rise at dawn, clean their teeth, put on their robes, meditate and then go to have their breakfast (boiled rice) at the refectory, but only after reciting certain portions of the scriptures.

ASSEMBLY HALL

On the same level as the relic house, this **hall**, also known as the convocation hall, is where monks met to discuss matters of common interest. The most senior monk would have presided over the discussions, and the raised dais in the middle of the hall was apparently where this person sat. Sixty-four stone pillars once supported the roof. Conservation of this site began in 1948. The main path to the Ambasthale Dagoba leads from here.

SINHA POKUNA

Just below the monks' refectory on the second landing, and near the entrance if you are coming via the old road, is a small **pool** surmounted by a 2m-high rampant lion, reckoned to be one of the best pieces of animal carving in the country. Anyone placing one hand on each paw would be right in line for the stream of water from the lion's mouth. There are some fine friezes around this pool.

AMBASTHALE DAGOBA

The final steep stairway, lined with frangipani trees, leads to the place where Mahinda and the king met. The **Ambasthale Dagoba** (admission Rs 250) is built over the spot where Mahinda stood. Nearby stands a **statue of the king** in the place where he stood. On the opposite side of the dagoba from the statue is a cloister and behind that, a large, white sitting **Buddha statue**. Stone pillars surround the dagoba and may once have been used to hold offerings (or if you believe the local theory, to support a wooden roof). You must remove your shoes and hat, and umbrellas aren't allowed.

The name Ambasthale means 'Mango Tree' and refers to a riddle that Mahinda used to test the king's intelligence (opposite).

Nearby is the **Sela Chetiya**, which has a stone rendering of the Buddha's footprint. It's surrounded by a railing festooned with prayer flags left by pilgrims, who have also scattered coins here.

MAHASEYA DAGOBA

A stone pathway to the southwest of the Ambasthale Dagoba leads up to a higher **dagoba** (arguably the largest at Mihintale), thought to have been built to house relics of Mahinda. The **bodhi tree** to the left of the base of the steps is said to be one of the oldest surviving ones. From here there is a view over the lakes and trees to Anuradhapura, a horizon studded with the domes and spikes of all the massive dagobas. A small **temple** at the foot of the dagoba has a reclining Buddha and Technicolor modern frescoes – donations are requested. A room at the side is a **devale** (a complex designed for worshipping a Hindu or local Sri Lankan deity) with statues of major gods – Ganesh, Vishnu, Murugan (Skanda) and Saman.

MAHINDA'S CAVE

There is a path leading northeast from the Ambasthale Dagoba down to a **cave** where there is a large flat stone. This is said to be where Mahinda lived and the stone is claimed to be where he rested. The track to the cave is hard on tender bare feet.

ARADHANA GALA

To the east of Ambasthale Dagoba is a steep path over sun-heated rock leading up to a point with great views. A railing goes up most of the way. Aradhana Gala means 'Meditation Rock'.

NAGA POKUNA

Halfway back down the steep flight of steps from the Ambasthale Dagoba, a path leads to the left, around the side of the hill topped by the Mahaseya Dagoba. Here you'll find the **Naga Pokuna** (Snake Pool), so called because of a five-headed cobra carved in low relief on the rock face of the pool. Its tail is said to reach down to the bottom of the pool. If you continue on from here, you eventually loop back to the second landing.

ET VIHARA

At an even higher elevation (309m) than the Mahaseya Dagoba are the remains of a dagoba called **Et Vihara** (literally, 'Elephant Monastery'). The origin of the name is open to conjecture, but it may have been named after the monastery nearby. The Mihintale tablets mention Et Vihara and its image house.

MUSEUM

There is a small **museum** (admission free; ☻ 9am-5pm Wed-Mon, closed public holidays) on the road leading to the stairs. Each room is dedicated to particular finds, including bronze figurines, fragments of frescoes and remnants of stone tubs from the hospital. The collection includes a replica of the interior of an 8th-century dagoba and a 9th-century gold-plated *ola* manuscript. Pottery fragments from China and Persia are also on display.

INDIKATU SEYA COMPLEX

Back on the road leading to Old Rd and outside the site proper are the remains of a monastery enclosed in the ruins of a stone wall. Inside are two dagobas, the larger known as **Indikatu Seya** (Dagoba of the Needle). Evidence suggests that this monastery was active in fostering Mahayana Buddhism. The main dagoba's structure differs from others in Mihintale; for example, it's built on a square platform.

Nearby is a hill that's been dubbed **Rajagirilena** (Royal Cave Hill) after the caves found here with Brahmi inscriptions in them. One of the caves bears the name of Devanampiya Tissa. A flight of steps leads up to the caves.

KALUDIYA POKUNA

Further south along the same road is the **Kaludiya Pokuna** (Dark Water Pool). This artificial pool was carefully constructed to look realistic, and features a rock-carved bathhouse and the ruins of a small monastery.

Sleeping & Eating

Hotel Mihintale (☎ 226 6599; ceylonhotels.lk; s/d with air-con incl breakfast US$40/55; 🕍 🖵) Run by the Ceylon Hotels Corporation, this is on the main road near the turn-off to the site. There are 10 mostly large and clean rooms, and the staff are friendly. The setting is pleasant. The pavilion cafe at the front is a good place to pause for a cool drink and a toilet stop.

Getting There & Away

It's a fairly short bus ride (Rs 28) from Anuradhapura's new bus station to Mihintale. A return taxi, with two hours to climb the stairs, costs about Rs 900; a three-wheeler is about Rs 700. It takes less than an hour to cycle here.

MAHINDA'S RIDDLE

Before Mahinda initiated King Devanampiya Tissa into Buddhism, he needed to gauge the king's intelligence. He decided to test the king with a riddle. Pointing to a tree he asked him the name of the tree. 'This tree is called a mango,' replied the king. 'Is there yet another mango beside this?' asked Mahinda. 'There are many mango trees,' responded the king. 'And are there yet other trees besides this mango and the other mangoes?' asked Mahinda. 'There are many trees, but those are trees which are not mangoes,' said the king. 'And are there, besides the other mangoes and those trees which are not mangoes, yet other trees?' asked Mahinda. 'There is this mango tree,' said the king, who as a result passed the test.

YAPAHUWA

Although it's only roughly half the height of Sigiriya and receives far fewer tourists, this **rock fortress** (admission Rs 500; 8am-6pm) rising 100m from the surrounding plain is quite impressive in its own right. The granite outcropping of Yapahuwa (pronounced yaa-pow-a), also known as Fire Rock, was used in the early 13th century as a defensible refuge against the invading South Indian armies. Between 1272 and 1284, King Bhuvanekabahu I used the rock as his capital and kept Sri Lanka's sacred Buddha tooth relic here. Indian invaders from the Pandavan dynasty captured Yapahuwa in 1284 and carried the tooth relic to South India, only for it to be recovered in 1288 by King Parakramabahu I.

Yapahuwa's steep ornamental staircase, which led up to the ledge holding the tooth temple, is one of its finest features. One of the lions near the top of the staircase appears on the Rs 10 note. The porches on the stairway had very fine pierced-stone windows, one of which is now in the museum in Colombo; the other is in the museum on-site.

The **museum** is to the right of the site entrance. On display are stone sculptures of Vishnu and Kali, fragments of pottery and the carved stone screen, but labels are in Sinhala. Behind the museum is something more fascinating – a **cave temple** that contains some 13th-century frescoes and images of the Buddha made from wood and bronze. The temple is usually locked, but a monk will open it for you if you ask, although you are expected to make a donation. Photography is not allowed.

Yapahuwa is 4km from Maho railway junction, where the Trincomalee line splits from the Colombo–Anuradhapura line, and about 5km from the Anuradhapura–Kurunegala road. It's possible to take a three-wheeler from the Anuradhapura–Kurunegala road to the site, although occasional buses do travel to here from Maho. A three-wheeler from Maho costs Rs 300 one way. A three-wheeler from the main road and back would cost about Rs 700 with waiting time. Most trains going to and from Colombo stop at Maho.

PADENIYA

About 85km south of Anuradhapura and 25km northwest of Kurunegala, where the Puttalam and Anuradhapura roads branch off, is the Kandyan-style **Padeniya Raja Mahavihara** (donations appreciated), which is worth popping into if you're passing by. It's a pretty, medieval temple with 28 carved pillars and a stunning elaborate door (said to be the largest in Sri Lanka) to the main shrine. There is also a clay-image house and a library, as well as a preaching hall with an unusual carved wooden pulpit.

PANDUWASNUWARA

About 17km southwest of Padeniya on the road between Wariyapola and Chilaw are the 12th-century remains of the temporary capital of Parakramabahu I. It's nothing on the scale of Anuradhapura or Polonnaruwa, but it's worth stopping in if you're heading past. The sprawling site, covering some 20 hectares, hasn't been fully excavated. The turn-off to the site is at Panduwasnuwara village, where there is a small **museum** (donation expected). Most of the museum labels are in Sinhala.

Near the entrance to the site is a moat, the massive citadel wall and the remains of a palace. Further on are image houses, dagobas and living quarters for monks. Follow the road past the school and veer left; you will shortly come to a restored tooth temple with a bodhi tree and, beyond that, the remains of a round palace (apparently once multistoreyed) enclosed in a circular moat.

There are many stories about who lived in this palace and why it was built. Legend has it that it kept the king's daughter away from men who would desire her; it had been prophesised that if she bore a son, he'd eventually claim the throne. Another story is that it was built to house the king's wives and, intriguingly, that there was once a secret tunnel that led from the king's palace and under the moat to the queens' palace. However attractive these stories are, historians have not been able to conclude why the palace was built.

Buses run between Kurunegala (via Wariyapola) and Chilaw on a regular basis, and it is possible to be dropped off at Panduwasnuwara village and to walk the remaining 1km. However, it's far more practical to come with your own transport.

RIDI VIHARA

Literally the 'Silver Temple', **Ridi Vihara** (donation Rs 100) is so named because it was here that silver ore was discovered in the 2nd century BC. Although not on the beaten track, it's well worth a visit to see its wonderful frescoes and the unusual Dutch (Delft) tiles in the main cave.

The main attraction here is the golden statue in the main cave, called the **Pahala Vihara** (Lower Temple). Also within the Pahala Vihara is a 9m recumbent Buddha that rests on a platform decorated with a series of blue-and-white tiles, which were a gift from the Dutch consul. The tiles depict scenes from the Bible, including Adam and Eve being banished from the Garden of Eden and the transfiguration of Christ.

The nearby **Uda Vihara** (Upper Temple) was built by King Kirthi Sri Rajasinghe. The entrance has a Kandyan-period moonstone. It's interesting to try to pick out some of the clever visual tricks used by the fresco artists; in one case, what appears to be an elephant at a distance reveals itself on closer inspection to be a formation of nine maidens. Hindu deities and images of the Buddha are represented in the caves.

Outside the temple complex you can see an abandoned dagoba at the top of a smooth rocky outcrop. On the way up, to your right, is an ancient inscription in the stone, said to have been etched on King Dutugemunu's behalf. An easy 10-minute walk starts to the

right of this abandoned dagoba (as you are walking up to it). Head past a modern pavilion to an abandoned bungalow; nearby, on the top of the cliff, is a slab from which you get the most magnificent views.

Ridi Vihara is situated east of the Kurunegala–Dambulla road. If you are coming by car from Kurunegala, the turn-off to Ridigama village is on your right just past Ibbagamuwa village. The temple is about 2km from Ridigama via Temple Junction. Buses run between Kurunegala and Ridigama village (Rs 28, approximately every 45 minutes). From the village you can take a three-wheeler to the temple (approximately Rs 500 return, including waiting time).

KURUNEGALA
☎ 037 / pop 29,000
Kurunegala is a busy market town and transport hub between Colombo and Anuradhapura, and Kandy and Puttalam. The town itself is not particularly interesting, but the region around Kurunegala is rich in archaeological sites and temples.

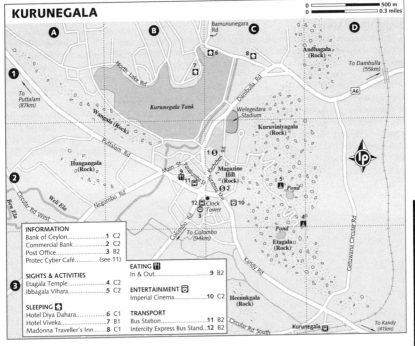

KURUNEGALA

0 ___ 500 m
0 ___ 0.3 miles

INFORMATION		
Bank of Ceylon	1	C2
Commercial Bank	2	C2
Post Office	3	B2
Protec Cyber Café	(see 11)	

SIGHTS & ACTIVITIES		
Etagala Temple	4	C2
Ibbagala Vihara	5	C2

SLEEPING		
Hotel Diya Dahara	6	C1
Hotel Viveka	7	B1
Madonna Traveller's Inn	8	C1

EATING		
In & Out	9	B2

ENTERTAINMENT		
Imperial Cinema	10	C2

TRANSPORT		
Bus Station	11	B2
Intercity Express Bus Stand	12	B2

The large, smooth rocky outcrops that loom over the low-rise buildings are a striking feature of this city. Named for the animals they appear to resemble (Tortoise Rock, Lion Rock etc), the outcrops are, unsurprisingly, endowed with mythological status; it's said that they were formed when animals that were endangering the free supply of water to the town were turned into stone.

Information

Bank of Ceylon (Kachcheri Rd) Changes travellers cheques; it's 450m north of the post office.
Commercial Bank (Suratissa Mawatha) ATM.
Protec Cyber Café (Puttalam Rd) Internet access inside the bus station.
Post office (Colombo Rd)

Sights

There's a road going up **Etagala**, a large black boulder on the eastern side of the city. The views are extensive from here. On the way up you pass a small shrine, **Ibbagala Vihara**, and at the head of the road there is a **temple** named after the rock itself. The town also boasts the fine old **Imperial Cinema** (Kandy Rd; tickets adult/child Rs 150/100), which still pulls a crowd to dramas and romantic comedies today.

Sleeping & Eating

There are a few hotels around town, but the most pleasant are around the lake. A three-wheeler to these places should cost Rs 60 to 100 from the train station.

Madonna Traveller's Inn (☎ 222 3276; 44 North Lake Rd; r with/without air-con Rs 2500/1200; ❄) The rooms in this old house are a little dim, but the restaurant is busy and gets a good local crowd. The fan rooms are OK value, but you'll pay well over the odds to get the air-con switched on.

Hotel Diya Dahara (☎ 526 6662; diyadahara2004@yahoo .com; 7 North Lake Rd; s/d Rs 1700/2700; ❄) Situated on Kurunegala Lake, this place has a decent setting and nice garden. The rooms are a little shabby, but they do have air-con and TV. The grandiose building across the street is under the same management and has slightly larger rooms.

Hotel Viveka (☎ 222 2897; www.hotelviveka.com; 64 North Lake Rd; r with/without air-con Rs 2200/1800; ❄) This 150-year-old villa, kept up with lots of spit and polish, has an elegant veranda looking over the lake. The six rooms are spartan cubes with new bathrooms. Some interesting framed photos grace the main room, and the hotel has Kurunegala's most convivial bar and restaurant. Weddings are often held here on weekends.

In & Out (18 Puttalam Rd; light meals from Rs 100; ⏲ 7am-10pm) It's nothing fancy, but this bakery and cafe serves up a good array of Western and Sri Lankan dishes. Smoothies, omelettes and sandwiches are available. Their rice and curry for Rs 125 is a good lunch deal.

Getting There & Away

Intercity buses depart from a yard behind the clock tower. You may be dropped here when you arrive. Intercity express buses to Anuradhapura (CTB/express Rs 73/116, two hours) leave every 30 minutes between 6am and 5.30pm. There are CTB and express buses to Colombo (express Rs 200, four to five hours) and Kandy (express Rs 54, one hour). Local buses and buses to Negombo (Rs 130, 3½ hours) leave from the nearby bus station on Puttalam Rd.

The train station, 2km from the town centre, sees frequent visits from trains on the Northern Line. There are eight trains between Kurunegala and Colombo daily (2nd/1st class Rs 170/400, two to three hours) and four trains daily to Anuradhapura (2nd/1st class Rs 190/360, three hours).

The East

Tumbling out of the cool Hill Country, the world you enter is one of unexplored beaches stretching for mile after dazzling white mile and tropical lushness bursting with elephants and flamboyant peacocks strutting about like catwalk models. There are scattered jungle ruins haunted with the ghosts of days past, youthful villages built around perfect waves, and gaudy Hindu temples filled with bright blue gods and celestial beings. It's a place where anything can occur, where the sense of adventure is strong and genuine and, sadly, it's also a place in turmoil. A land of shell-shocked towns recovering from a dark period of war and a population that's anxious for a better tomorrow.

So few foreign travellers bother to visit the east coast that you're likely to find a very heartfelt welcome and a great generosity of spirit. But you'll need to tread gently. Ethnic conflicts remain unresolved – not just between Sinhalese and Tamils, but also between Tamils and Muslims, and between Tamil factions. For inquisitive travellers, learning about these complex interrelationships is part of the excitement. But sensitivity and tact are crucial.

Meanwhile, some roads remain closed, checkpoints are common and nobody knows for sure what tomorrow will bring, but for the first time in a generation there's hope that the bad old days of bloodshed are finally ending. So, before the rest of the world catches on, shouldn't you go tumbling over the edge of the hills and into a magical tropical wonderland?

HIGHLIGHTS

- Hanging ten on the endless rights of chilled-out **Arugam Bay** (p248)
- Waiting with baited breath for the **wild elephants** to come and pay their respects at Ampara's Peace Pagoda (p253)
- Being an explorer on the frontier of Sri Lankan tourism almost anywhere in the east
- Hearing the other side of the story and seeing the leftovers of war for what they really are on the battered streets of **Trincomalee** (p260) and **Batticaloa** (p255)
- Building sandcastles on the divine sands of **Uppuveli beach** (p263)

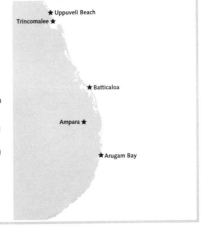

★ Uppuveli Beach
Trincomalee ★

★ Batticaloa

Ampara ★

★ Arugam Bay

MONARAGALA

☎ 055

If you're coming from the touristy Hill Country, then Monaragala – which nestles beneath Peacock Rock, a round-topped hunk of forest-covered mountain – will most likely be your first stop on the eastern shoreline of the country. With its frontier feel and warm welcome, it's a good first introduction. Conversely, if you're coming from the east and are heading for the hills, you'll find foliage-packed Monaragala a refreshingly cool introduction to the mist-shrouded highlands.

Information

The **Commercial Bank** (Bus Station Rd) and several other banks dotted along Wellawaya Rd all have ATMs. In the market area, **Samudura Communications** (☎ 227 6765; per hr Rs 50; ☯ 7.30am-8pm) has the cheapest internet connection for miles around.

Sights & Activities

An easy but beautiful hike starts near the bus station. Walk five minutes past a colourful little Hindu **Ganesh Temple**, where the priest will probably be as happy to see you as he would Lord Ganesh himself, to the ageing **rubber factory**, then veer left to a rock-paved footpath that climbs between attractive boulder fields through Monaragala's famous rubber plantations. A much more demanding hike is the six-hour round trip to the summit of the densely forested **Peacock Rock** (to make it appear more peacock-like, drink a couple of bottles of arrack before viewing…). There is no set trail up the mountain and you'll need a guide, which can be organised through most guest houses for around Rs 800 to 1000. From the summit you can check the surf at Arugam Bay on a clear day.

Sleeping & Eating

Sunshine Guesthouse (☎ 227 6313; Wellawaya Rd; s/tw Rs 1200/1650) The new sister hotel of the Victory retains its shiny, just-out-of-the-wrapper appearance and has small rooms that are neatly tiled and have nets and pint-sized bathrooms.

Queens Inn (☎ 227 7126; Obbegoda village; r Rs 1650) Six kilometres out of Monaragala in the direction of Pottuvil, in the blink-and-you'll-miss-it village of Obbegoda, is this charming little guest house run on the same sort of lines as

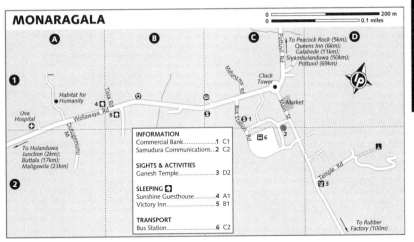

MONARAGALA

INFORMATION
Commercial Bank...................1 C1
Samudura Communications...2 C2

SIGHTS & ACTIVITIES
Ganesh Temple.....................3 D2

SLEEPING
Sunshine Guesthouse............4 A1
Victory Inn..........................5 B1

TRANSPORT
Bus Station.........................6 C2

a south European pension. Currently they have just three polished-up rooms with attached bathrooms, but more are on the way. There is a pleasant outdoor restaurant with a memorable chicken fried rice (Rs 275), and the owners are the most delightful couple you could hope to meet. If you call in advance they'll arrange a three-wheeler from town; otherwise one will cost Rs 250.

Victory Inn (☎ /fax 227 6100; 65 Wellawaya Rd; s Rs 1650, d with/without air-con Rs 3000/2450; ❄) The exterior looks like a 1970s architectural horror film, but the interior has rooms that are pleasantly old-fashioned and very comfortable. The restaurant has a decent lunch and dinner buffet for Rs 350 and is the most relaxing and formal place to eat in town.

For very cheap meals there are various fly-friendly dives around the bus station.

Getting There & Away

The most reliable buses to Pottuvil (for Arugam Bay) depart at 6am and 11.20am, with a later 2.20pm service if demand is sufficient. Alternatively, take a bus to Siyambulanduwa and change. To Ampara, buses leave roughly twice-hourly until 3.30pm (Rs 130) using two possible routes: via Siyambulanduwa (for Arugam Bay) or via Inginyagala. Colombo-bound intercity buses (Rs 260, seven hours) run at roughly 45-minute intervals until late, though there are gaps in the schedule. Services run very frequently to Wellawaya (Rs 59, 50 minutes) for the Hill Country, passing though Buttala; change in Buttala for Kataragama.

AROUND MONARAGALA
Yudaganawa (Udhagannawa)

A massive and ancient dagoba (stupa) lies quietly hidden in a forest clearing at Yudaganawa (compulsory 'donation' Rs 100) just 3km west of the little village of Buttala. Only the bottom third remains, but the setting is charming and your imagination can run riot with thoughts of how amazing it must have looked back in its day. Exactly how ancient it is is a little hard to tell due to the tradition of pilgrims adding new bricks to the now slowly regrowing dagoba! More interesting than the dagoba itself is the small building in front housing beautiful 300-year-old carved-wood Buddhas and some faded paintings (including one of Ganesh after a Weight Watchers course). It's 1.5km from Wellawaya Rd.

Just before reaching the main site you'll pass the moss-encrusted ruins of the much smaller 12th-century **Chulangani Vihara**, with a pudding-shaped dagoba and fragments of a decapitated 7th-century Buddha.

Maligawila & Dematal Vihara

Two inscrutable **ancient statues** (admission free; 🌙 dawn-dusk) stand in an appealingly shady forest glade at Maligawila (mali-ga-wila). The site is delightful and the surrounding village so diffuse that it's virtually invisible. Ferreted away among the trees lie the extensive 7th-century remnants of **Pathma Vihara** and its two lovely Buddha statues. Sitting atop five crumbling, moss-covered flights of stairs is the 10m-high **Maitreya Bodhisattva** (Avalokitesvara). It was

THE EAST

reconstituted between 1989 and 1991 from over 100 fragments unearthed in the 1950s. Sadly, it's shaded by a banal corrugated canopy.

A few minutes' walk in the opposite direction, and playing peek-a-boo with the clouds, is a magnificent 11m-tall **Buddha statue**, considered by some to be among the tallest freestanding ancient Buddha in existence. Carpeted in thick green moss and with its feet often adorned in flowers left by pilgrims, this is a very beautiful statue despite the recent addition of a scaffolding harness.

To get to Maligawila from Monaragala, take any bus heading toward Buttala and get out at the village of Kumbukkana; from there hop on one of the handful of daily buses to Maligawila (Rs 32). From Maligawila, buses to Buttala (Rs 45) leave several times a day, and from Buttala you can connect to the south coast or the highlands. The journey to Maligawila from Monaragala, past jungles and paddy fields, is as much a highlight as the ruins themselves and offers a great chance to glimpse rural Sri Lankan life. If you are heading towards Buttala it's possible to hop off the bus at **Dematal Vihara**, a gorgeous temple lost in a sea of picturesque paddy fields.

POTTUVIL

☎ 063

The scrappy Muslim-majority town of Pottuvil is the southernmost sizable town on the east coast. For most tourists it's simply the transport hub for reaching Arugam Bay, just 3km further south, where all the accommodation is located. However, Pottuvil does have some banks near the bus stand (no ATMs) and a decent market.

Hidden away in the backstreets are the ancient ruins of **Mudu Maha Vihara**. This lovely little site, partly submerged in the encroaching sand dunes, features a fine 3m-high standing Buddha statue whose eroded face stares jealously at two petite Bodhisattva figures. The **beach** just behind is wide, beautiful and undeveloped, though it's also unshaded, windy and not safe for swimming.

Aside from practical considerations, one very good reason for venturing to Pottuvil is for the delightful two-hour **mangrove tours** (www.arugambay.com/pages/eco.html; per 2-person boat Rs 3000 or negotiable Rs 2500 direct). Outrigger canoes take visitors punting across the lagoon where you can potter about among the mangroves searching for mighty big and toothy croco-

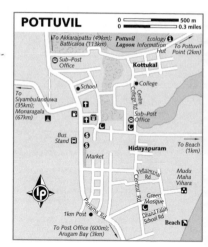

diles, monkeys making mischief in the trees and birds, birds, birds everywhere you look. It's best to go either early in the morning or last thing in the evening. Unfortunately, none of the boat conductors are likely to speak much Sinhala let alone English (they speak Tamil) and the 'guide' you paid for in Arugam Bay doesn't normally bother accompanying you on the boat. Though you can organise mangrove tours yourself for less, it's much easier to arrange everything through the Arugam Bay Hilton Guest House (p251).

Buses depart for Colombo (Rs 350, 10 hours) via Monaragala at 8.30am and 6pm. Otherwise take one of several daily departures to Monaragala (Rs 100, 1½ hours) and change.

To Batticaloa there's a bus at 11am (Rs 120).

Buses heading to Panama via Arugam Bay (Rs 25) nominally run at 9am, 1pm and 3.30pm, though in reality they actually leave only when full. As it's only Rs 200 to Arugam Bay by three-wheeler, it may not be worth the wait.

ARUGAM BAY

☎ 063

Lovely Arugam Bay, a moon-shaped curl of soft sand, is home to a famed point break that many regard as the best surf spot in the country. If you're not a surfer, there are plenty of other reasons to draw you all the way out here. The village, which is the only real traveller centre in the east, is packed with good-value guest houses and restaurants and has a mellow, swing-another-day-in-a-hammock kind of vibe that's totally removed from the brash west-coast beach resorts. In addition Arugam Bay makes a great base for all kind of wild adventures in the surrounding hinterland. These range from tracking elephants in the scrubby wilds of the nearby national parks, poking your nose into little-known Buddhist temples hidden in a tropical dreamscape, punting a boat through mangrove swamps and taking long walks along lonely beaches.

During the low season (November to April) things get very quiet and many places shut up shop altogether, though NGO types still come for weekend getaways and the sea is better for swimming.

Information

The nearest banks are in Pottuvil and the nearest post office is 500m southwest of the village, between Arugam Bay and Pasarichenai. Unreliable and expensive internet connections are available at the Arugam Bay Hilton (p251) and Stardust Beach Hotel (p251).

Dangers & Annoyances

Single women might receive unwanted attention on the beaches (considering wearing a T-shirt over your swimsuit on the beach fronting the village), and there have been cases of attempted sexual assault in secluded areas, particularly south behind the surf point. Use normal common sense. There is a tourist police post on the beach.

Activities

SURFING

The long right point break at the southern end of Arugam Bay is considered the best surf spot in Sri Lanka and offers consistent surf from April to September, with some good (and much quieter) days until November. Locals, as well as some travelling surfers, might try and tell you that Arugam Bay is a world-class spot, or even that it's one of the 10 best surf spots in the world; both these statements are slightly fanciful to say the least. However, it consistently produces long and fairly fat slow-breaking waves that are ideal for intermediate surfers. Surf averages 1m to 1.5m, with a few rare 2m days. On small days it can be very shallow and sectiony while at any size there can be lots of boils and bumps to deal with. In season it can get dangerously busy, and learners should stick to the gentle beach break further inside of the point.

There are many more breaks of similar quality, most of which need a decent-sized swell, including, to the north, Pottuvil Point (Rs 1000 return by three-wheeler), which is a slow right-hander ideal for learners, and, to the south, Crocodile Rock, Peanut Farm, Panama and Okanda, which is rumoured to be the best of the lot.

Places that rent out boards:

A-bay Surf Shop (bodyboards & surfboards per day Rs 500) This long-standing surf shop has the best selection of boards suitable for learners. In addition it offers a ding-repair service, wax, sunscreen and surf lessons.

Arugam Bay Hilton Guest House (surfboards per day Rs 600) As well as some not very learner-friendly boards, this guest house (p251) also offers decent overnight surf tours (Rs 7000 for two people).

Mambo's (bodyboards/surfboards per day Rs 600) A wide range of bashed-up boards, including some that are better suited to more experienced surfers, can be found at this excellent guest house (p251).

Surf & Sun (surfboards per day Rs 600) The surf-savvy owners of this guest house (p251) organise surfing excursions. The boards available for hire aren't ideal for learners.

THE 2004 TSUNAMI – AFTERMATH IN THE EAST

The East bore the brunt of the December 2004 tsunami, yet it seems to have received the least help in rebuilding. Certainly, there are still dozens of NGO workers racing about in huge 4WDs, and donations of fishing dinghies have been so generous that some villagers have reportedly gathered a small fleet. However, rehousing has been relatively slow and highly controversial, with a blanket exclusion zone preventing rebuilding within 200m of the sea: what use is a home far inland to a fisher who has no transport to reach the sea? In the lead-up to the November 2005 election, the 200m rule was softened or removed altogether in many places and now houses with a beach view are springing up again.

For years to come you're likely to see ruined beachside buildings, especially in hard-hit areas like Kalmunai. Much more has been done to rebuild Arugam Bay's sea-facing properties. Central Batticaloa and Trincomalee both survived fairly intact, but Nilaveli beach has only recently scrabbled back to life and Kalkudah beach remains virtually deserted.

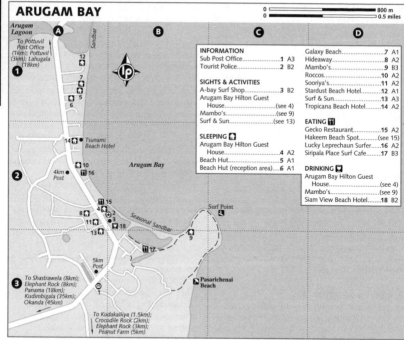

ARUGAM BAY

SWIMMING

Seas are OK for swimming during low season, but ask locals before plunging in at lesser-known beaches, where rips might be strong. The safest swimming is at the southern end of Arugam Bay, just where the beach starts to bend around towards the point. However, though it's very attractive, this is essentially a fishing beach and not ideal for lounging around on.

NATURE-WATCHING

Highly relaxing **mangrove tours** (Rs 3000 including transfers) on Pottuvil lagoon (p248) can be booked at the Arugam Bay Hilton Guest House (opposite). This grassroots initiative, which has been highly commended in recent international sustainable-travel awards, supplements the incomes of local fishers, and a percentage of profits is donated to an important mangrove replanting program.

The Hilton also offers two-hour **dolphin safaris** in the high season (May/June to September; Rs 6000 for up to four people). There's a good chance of seeing crocodiles and elephants around Crocodile Rock on Pasarichenai Beach, just south of Arugam Bay proper.

For **bird-watching**, the various nearby lagoons are marvellous for waterfowl and waders, while Brahminy kites regularly soar above the surf point. The choice twitching sites are Pottuvil lagoon and the various ponds and lagoons between Arugam Bay and Panama.

Sleeping

Note that many of the restaurants listed in the Eating section have rooms, and most of the guest houses below serve meals; the line between the two is blurred.

The term 'cabana' is applied to anything from ultrabasic plank or *cadjan* (coconut-frond matting) huts to rather luxurious full-facility concrete bungalows. Low-season discounts of 20% to 35% are common.

BUDGET

Many locals have erected a cabana or two or rent out cheap rooms to tourists.

Sooriya's (☎ 072 408 1211; r from Rs 300) Run by Ram, a saddhu lookalike (and live-alike), this hangout has extremely basic cubical rooms, each of which is named after a place of spiritual significance. In the words of the owner, it's aimed 'at long stayers here for months and months, not surfers and that lot'.

Tropicana Beach Hotel (☎ 077 127 264; d_asmin@ yahoo.com; tw with/without bath Rs 500/300) The banana and coconut shacks here might be simple, but they're shown more love than many of the more expensive places. One room has its own bathroom, and the rest share a single non-too-clean bathroom. The nice couple who run it will involve you in family life.

ourpick **Beach Hut** (☎ 224 8202; cabanas with/without bath Rs 1000/600) It's hard to beat this place for atmosphere, value, excellent food and thoroughly friendly management. It's also one of the more eccentric of the cheapies, with a handful of cabanas perched halfway up the palm trees like tree houses. Some even come with bathrooms, giving you a loo with a view! All have wooden windows that you open with an ingenious rope-and-pulley system that allows you to check the surf without getting out of bed. If you're a vertigo sufferer you'll be delighted to hear that they also have some more down-to-earth cabanas. There is a popular restaurant (mains Rs 400 to 500) with lots of famished-surfer favourites.

Arugam Bay Hilton Guest House (☎ /fax 224 8189; www.arugambay.lk; cabanas from Rs 1000; tw from Rs 1000, tr Rs 2000; 🖳) The colourful and cheerful rooms at this classic beachfront hang-out have been keeping surfers stoked for years. All the rooms have pleasing attached bathrooms and some have vague point-break views. One of the cabanas is so close to the beach that it's virtually swimming. The restaurant is one of the better bets in town, with meals for Rs 400 to 500. The owner, who runs the noteworthy Arugam Bay Tourism Association, organises a range of tours and activities in the area (opposite). Visa and MasterCard are accepted.

Surf & Sun (☎ 602 641 044; www.thesurfnsun.com; huts Rs 1200, cottages Rs 1500) Scattered across the lush, tropical gardens of this delightful place are a series of cottages with monster double beds, hammocks swinging lethargically in the breeze and some crazy trees growing out of the showers. The cheaper huts aren't quite as inviting. The restaurant (mains Rs 500 to 600) is a good one, with weekly barbecues in season and pizzas that aren't half bad.

MIDRANGE

Galaxy Beach (☎ 224 8415; www.galaxysrilanka.com; cabanas from Rs 1500) The clean and spacious tree-house cabanas are built like birds' nests high up in the palms. Drop out of your perch and down through a trapdoor to discover a private flower-filled outdoor garden bathroom. The ground-level cabanas are equally inspiring and have creaky wooden ladders leading up to roof terraces.

Roccos (☎ 077 664 2991; www.roccoshotel.com; d from Rs 1500) Eye-catching lamps made of recycled bottles draw you in at night, and the bright colours add excitement to what would otherwise be fairly plain rooms. The rooms closer to the sea are smaller but have ocean views.

ourpick **Hideaway** (☎ 224 8259; tissara@eureka.lk; d Rs 2200, cabanas/bungalows Rs 2750/4400) The Hideaway is truly a gorgeous place in which to hide away from the mean old world beyond its gates. Set at the back of some foliage-heavy gardens, the open-fronted colonial villa is draped in bougainvillea and surrounded by frolicking squirrels and geckos. The downstairs consists of a communal area full of easy chairs and sofas, as well as a TV and a stack of wildlife DVDs. There's also an excellent restaurant run by a jolly fellow whose only concern in life seems to be your culinary satisfaction. Upstairs are a handful of thoughtfully decorated rooms with wooden-slat windows; in the garden are several individual cabanas that have much more privacy, as well as terraces. There are also two superbly luxurious bungalows with air-con and sea views.

Stardust Beach Hotel (☎ 224 8191; www.arugambay .com; cabanas Rs 2300, d from Rs 5000; 🍴 🖳) The only real resort-style place in town, this Danish-run place sits on a rough and wild patch of beach at the southern end of the village and is very popular with NGO workers. The spotless rooms are swish, with lots of pleasing touches, comfortable furniture and blue-and-white-tiled bathrooms. The cabanas are so fancy-pants, it's hard to refer to them as mere cabanas. The attached restaurant is much more formal than anywhere else, but has unusual treats like salads and hummus. It's not the friendliest of places, though. A range of yoga courses (Rs 1200 for three one-hour classes) and massages (Rs 3000 for a one-hour full-body massage) are on offer.

Mambo's (☎ 091 545 8131; tw Rs 2500) First and foremost, this surfer favourite is right next to the main surf point, allowing you to virtually tumble out of bed and land, bleary-eyed, in the line-up. If that weren't enough of a plus, then the solid new bungalows and cabanas here are in excellent health – superclean and with funky paint jobs and driftwood and sea-shell decorations. Some have little terraces to relax on, and there are lots of trees creating cool, shady patches. The attractive bar-restaurant has good views of the waves and decent traveller-friendly meals (Rs 300 to 600).

Eating & Drinking

Other than the hotel restaurants mentioned above, there are few alternatives. The following offer better meals than beds.

Hakeem Beach Spot (snacks Rs 10-30; mains Rs 50-100; ☾ 5am-8pm Sat-Thu) This little locals' eating shack might be a bit too popular with flies to make you want to sit down for a meal, but the banana and coconut pancakes (Rs 10) make for a perfect presurf power snack.

Lucky Leprechaun Surfer (☎ 077 635 1965; mains Rs 200-300; ☾ 7.30am-10.30pm) High above the beach, with fantastic views and heavenly breezes, this is a great place to watch the waves while being served a wide range of fishy food. It's also a popular place for a sundowner.

Siripala Place Surf Cafe (mains Rs 300-400) Right next to the spot where the fish are first hauled out of the deep blue, the seafood here is as fresh and tasty as can be. Despite the name, it's refreshingly unsurfy.

Gecko Restaurant (mains from Rs 400) The English–Sri Lankan owners of this chilled restaurant serve an excellent and varied menu for those with the homesick blues. Most of the dishes are homemade in their entirety and include such treats as salads, some superb pasta dishes, burgers, full English breakfasts, muesli, ice cream and apple pie.

Mambo's (☎ 091 545 8131), the **Arugam Bay Hilton Guest House** (☎ /fax 224 8189; www.arugambay.lk) and **Siam View Beach Hotel** (☎ 077 320 0201; www.arugam .com) organise frequent beach and full-moon parties in season, and all are good spots for a drink on any night.

Getting There & Around

Almost all buses arrive and depart from nearby Pottuvil, where you'll need to hop into a three-wheeler to Arugam Bay (whole vehicle Rs 200, per person shared Rs 40). The only exception are the rare buses from Pottuvil to Panama (p248), which pass by Arugam Bay. Three-wheelers to the beach at Panama cost around Rs 1000 for a return trip with waiting time; to Peanut Farm it's around Rs 600. The Arugam Bay Hilton (p251) rents motorbikes for Rs 1000 per day.

SOUTH OF ARUGAM BAY
Arugam Bay to Panama

Kilometres of untouched sandy beaches stretch south of Arugam Bay. The roughly asphalted lane to Panama stays somewhat inland but intersects with lagoons where you can spot waterfowl, wading birds, wallowing water buffalo and even the odd elephant. It's a beautiful, savannah-like landscape, which stands in utter contrast to the lush greenery found elsewhere in the east.

Panama itself is a dusty, searing hot gathering of huts with an end-of-the-world atmosphere. The only sights in the village are an attractive white **dagoba** at the entry to the village and a wide but unshaded arc of sandy beach a kilometre east of town. Heavy seas, however, mean that swimming is usually unsafe (and surfers won't have any joy on these dumpy shore breaks). At the northern end of the beach, close to the jellyfish-processing plant (jellyfish caught here are sent to the Far East for use in cooking), is a fairly lame right point break that is good for novice surfers.

The road from Arugam Bay to Panama is low in places and may be under water in the wet season (beware of crocodiles). If it's not too bad, you can make the trip in a three-wheeler (return with waiting time Rs 1000) or wait for a rare bus.

At the time of research the road south of Panama, and all the attractions listed following, were closed due to fighting between LTTE and the army. With luck the situation may have improved by the time you pass by, but if it hasn't, don't underestimate the dangers of travelling beyond Panama. We spent several hours pleading to no avail with the police to allow us to continue on towards Okanda. The very next day we heard that a monk who had been allowed beyond that same checkpoint had been killed by LTTE fighters.

Panama to Okanda

The superb 4700-hectare site of **Kudimbigala Forest Hermitage** is a marvellous jumble of forgotten Sigiriya-style outcrops set in dense jungle. Over 200 shrines and hermits' lodgings are set in caves or sealed rocky overhangs here. While none is individually especially interesting, the atmosphere is fantastic and the dagoba-topped summit of the highest rock offers vast panoramas across the eccentric landscape and expansive forest canopy. There are glimpses of lagoon and sandbars towards the shore, and the far southwestern horizon is distantly serrated by the spiky Weliara Ridge.

Okanda

The Arugam–Okanda road ends at the entry gate for Yala East National Park. Immediately east of the gate is Okanda, a seasonal settlement for local fishers and home to the **Murugan Devale** (a *devale* is a complex designed for worshipping a Hindu or Sri Lankan deity). Though relatively small, the main temple has a very colourful *gopuram* (gateway tower), which survived the 2004 tsunami and is a major point on the Pada Yatra pilgrimage to Kataragama (see boxed text, p152). In trouble-free years, thousands of pilgrims gather here during the two weeks before the July *poya* (full moon) before attempting the last, and most dangerous, five-day leg of the 45-day trek from Jaffna.

The temple is of great spiritual importance as it marks the supposed point at which Murugan (Skanda) and his consort Valli arrived in Sri Lanka on stone boats.

Just five minutes' walk from the temple is a sweeping beige-white beach with an excellent right **point break** which, in peace time, is popular with surfers fleeing the crowds at Arugam Bay.

Yala East National Park & Kumana Reserve

Even in good times this 18,149-hectare **park** was much less frequently visited than its busy neighbour, Yala National Park. For the visitor, the result was a less 'zoolike' experience. However, with fewer staff to prevent poaching, the range and density of animals were also less.

The best-known feature is the 200-hectare **Kumana bird reserve**, an ornithologically rich mangrove swamp some 22km beyond Okanda. May to June is nesting season. The park also includes ruins, deer, elephants and (touted but rare) leopards. There have been sightings of Sri Lanka's very rare black-necked stork.

In the past, some agencies, including Colombo-based **Eco Team** (☎ 011-553 0833; www.srilankaecotourism.com; 20/43 Fairfields Gardens, Colombo) and Arugam Bay Hilton Guest House (p251), arranged camping trips within the park; should the security situation improve and the park reopen, these are likely to recommence.

AMPARA
☎ 063

Laid-back Ampara sits in the midst of succulent countryside dappled with paddy fields, lakes and palm groves. Though the town itself won't hold you, its disarmingly friendly people and a few low-key sights may have you lingering longer than you expected.

Orientation & Information

Ampara is very spread out. DS Senanayake Rd is the main commercial street. Several banks towards the clock tower have ATMs.

Commercial Bank (DS Senanayake Rd) Has an ATM and changes money.

Sabee Bookmart (☎ 492 1455; Regal Junction; per hr Rs 600; ⊙ 8am-6.30pm) The town's only internet point has a single, slow and very expensive connection.

Sights

West of the clock tower and bus station, DS Senanayake Rd leads towards Inginyagala, passing scenic Ampara Tank. After about 2km a short right turn brings you to the graceful **Japanese Peace Pagoda**. The pagoda itself is large rather than beautiful, and despite still being a spring chicken in pagoda years it's starting to look a little tatty. The incense-smoked **image room** next door, with its gaudy collection of Buddha statues, is far more interesting, and the friendly resident nun is liable to hand out sweets if you're well behaved!

A better reason than religious enlightenment for coming here is to get up close and personal with herds of passing **wild elephants**. Each evening, at around 5pm to 6pm, the elephants pass through a narrow passageway in the undergrowth right in front of the pagoda. The point is even marked 'Wild Elephant Crossing'. But this is no circus show. There is a palpable sense of awe among those who come to watch; after all, wild elephants kill people around Ampara every year (see the boxed text on p66). Birdwatchers will also find the pagoda platform a handy perch for spotting the hundreds of **waterbirds** that flit about the facing lake.

The central Buddhist **Mandala Mahavihara** (Kachcheri Rd) has a large pagoda. Its interior is somewhat tackily painted with Buddhist scenes and a cloud-dotted 'sky'. The **Sri Manika Pillaiyar** (Inginyagala Rd) gives Ganesh a lovely view across Ampara Tank; it's at the 24km post.

THE EAST

CENTRAL AMPARA

0 ——————— 500 m
0 ——————— 0.3 miles

INFORMATION	
Commercial Bank	1 B2
Sabee Bookmart	2 B2

SIGHTS & ACTIVITIES	
Mandala Mahavihara	3 B2

SLEEPING ⬆	
Ambhasewana Guest	4 B2
Ariyasiri Rest	5 B2
Chinese & Western Food	
Court	6 B2
Monty Guest House	7 B3

EATING 🍴	
Chinese & Western Food	
Court	(see 6)
Monty Guest House	(see 7)
New City Food Cabin	8 A2
Why Not Pastry Shop	9 A2

TRANSPORT	
Bus Station	10 A2

Sleeping

Ambhasewana Guest (☎ 222 3865; 51st Ave; r with/without air-con Rs 2000/750; 🌀) A friendly little guest house on a quiet side street not far from the town centre. The large and airy rooms with gently swaying fans are a bargain, but if you can't resist the urge of switching on the air-con units then be prepared to pay big time for the pleasure.

Ariyasiri Rest (☎ 077 450 2485; 3rd Ave; r from Rs 925) This place is visible from DS Senanayake Rd, but is entered through a squalid, narrow crack in the wall of the side street. The entry is enough to put off all but the hardiest customer. Yet if you dare to squeeze through the first building of demoralising, cramped dosshouse rooms, you'll find a surprisingly

pleasant second house in the rear garden. The four rooms here, off a communal upstairs dining area, are neat and clean. Some share sparkling bathrooms; others have private facilities but are mustier.

Monty Guest House (☎ 222 4859; C32 1st Ave; s with/without air-con Rs 3025/1925, d with/without air-con Rs 3300/2475; 🌀 🖳) Like a family of rabbits on heat this place keeps on multiplying in size – yet another huge new extension is likely to be completed by the time you show up. Unfortunately, it remains overpriced, and the cheaper rooms consist of flaking walls, ant-sized cold-water bathrooms, no nets and lots of noise. The air-con rooms, however, are palatial and have hot-water showers. It's an NGO favourite. Monty's is hidden away in a peaceful, green residential area that's a 10-minute stroll south of Commercial Bank.

our pick **Chinese & Western Food Court** (☎ 222 2215; terrelb@gmail.com; Gabada Rd; r Rs 4500; 🛜) The most unexpected thing in Ampara is this funky little hotel set above the restaurant of the same name. The modern rooms, all of which are fan-only, are splashed out in bright colours (the orange-and-green rooms are the coolest) and have trendy tables and chairs, hot-water showers, satellite TV and DVD players (with a stack of films), and shady balconies with deckchairs. Internet is available in all rooms, and the price includes breakfast.

Eating

Why Not Pastry Shop (☎ 222 3932; DS Senanayake St; pastries from Rs 60) A bright, clean and modern pastry and snack shop that is an ideal spot for a cold drink and some respite from the steamy streets.

New City Food Cabin (mains Rs 70-150; 🕒 7am-9pm) The cleanest and brightest of several budget eateries around the clock tower, this place rings with the deafening knife-work of the *kotthu rotti* (doughy pancake chopped and fried with meat and vegetables) maker each evening.

Chinese & Western Food Court (☎ 222 2215; Gabada Rd; mains Rs 300-650; 🕒 11.30am-3pm & 6-10.30pm) Set in a tropical garden, this is far and away Ampara's most alluring dining place. The wide range of well-prepared dishes includes stir-fried cuttlefish and excellent 'crumb chicken' – think Kentucky smeared with crushed garlic.

Monty Guest House (☎ 222 4859; meals Rs 500) You can feast on a wide range of local dishes, as well as passable pasta and burgers, on either the pleasantly cool outdoor terrace or the spacious indoor dining room. It's a good place to meet up with NGO workers and the odd passing tourist.

Getting There & Away
Direct buses to Kandy (Rs 191, five to six hours) leave six times a day from 4.30am, with the last at 7.15pm. You could also take the Colombo bus and jump off in Kandy, though you might be asked to pay the full fare to the capital. Buses to Colombo (Rs 332, 10 hours), which can be prebooked, leave at 6.15am, 8.30am, 4pm and 7pm.

For Arugam Bay you could minibus-hop via Akkaraipattu (Rs 40) and then Pottuvil. Or, more attractively, take any southbound bus to Siyambulanduwa (Rs 65) and change there. For Batticaloa, minibus-hop via Kalmunai (Rs 40) or take one of the direct buses (Rs 280) at 10.30am, 12pm and 2.30pm.

For the Hill Country there's a slow 6.45am service to Nuwara Eliya (Rs 264, nine hours).

AROUND AMPARA
Buddhangala
When approached through the secondary-growth scrub from Ampara or viewed across the paddies from the Ampara–Kalmunai road, **Buddhangala Rock Hermitage** (donation appropriate) looks to be little more than a slight bump on the horizon. Yet at around 150m tall, it's the highest point in the area: from the top there's a wide panorama of impressively wild views. Thanks to a very conscientious monk-guide and a useful explanatory pamphlet in English, the site's special spiritual relevance comes to life. The site is said to be 1800 years old, and when the old temple (whose remains you can see to the left of the main shrine) was excavated in 1964, a gold casket containing a tooth of the Buddha himself was discovered. This is now housed inside the dagoba. Within an ancient cave overhang there's a small but interesting case of museum-style treasures, including a human skeleton, which the monks use for meditation purposes.

The hermitage is 7km from Ampara; three-wheelers cost Rs 500 return.

Deegawapi
Deegawapi (Dighavapi Cetiya) is the one place in southeastern Sri Lanka that the Buddha supposedly visited in person – and three times at that – making the place of particular spiritual importance to Buddhists. It was built during the reign of King Saddartissa (137–119 BC) and patched up in the 2nd and 18th centuries AD before becoming lost in the jungle. Rediscovered in 1916, it has for decades been at the centre of disputes with the area's predominantly Muslim population, who fear the site could become a bridgehead for Sinhalese colonisation. Deegawapi's aged chief monk was killed in one such spat in 1952.

For many tourists the site isn't quite interesting enough to warrant the lengthy detour. While the vast central dagoba stub is massive, its ancient red bricks lack the appealing forest setting of similar Yudaganawa. Nonetheless there is the compensation of a small **archaeological museum** (admission free; ☽ 8.30am-3.30pm Wed-Mon), whose flexible opening hours are flexible, and numerous ancient flower altars and jumbled Buddha and elephant carvings are ranged around the dagoba's circumference.

BATTICALOA
☎ 065
Batticaloa, Batti for short, has no must-see sights. Nonetheless the vibe is right, and the steamy centre oozes an intangible charm, magnified by the palm-filtered sunlight glancing off the nearby lagoons. Around town, the beaches are gorgeous if utterly undeveloped. Even though Batticaloa has suffered from severe civil strife in the recent past, it feels a little less on edge than Trincomalee. The situation can change fast though, so check the latest beforehand.

Orientation
Central Old Batti is a bridge-linked island sheltered within a complex lagoon system. To the north is a double-pronged peninsula; the eastern prong (Koddamunai) shares the commercial centre and hosts the train station. Koddamunai itself is linked by a big bridge to a long, beach-edged southern peninsula (Kallady), down which New Batti extends for some 10km towards Kalmunai.

Information
Bank of Ceylon (Covington Rd) Has an ATM.
Commercial Bank (Bar Rd) Has an ATM.
Net2Phone Communication (☎ 490 0866; 259 Trino Rd; per hr Rs 40; ☽ 8am-9pm) Internet phone calls for Rs 4 per minute to most Western countries.
People's Bank (Covington Rd) Has an ATM.
Post office (Post Office Rd)
Wisdom Internet Cafe (☎ 222 7065; 70/1 Bar Rd; per hr Rs 40; ☽ 6.30am-8.30pm)

THE EAST

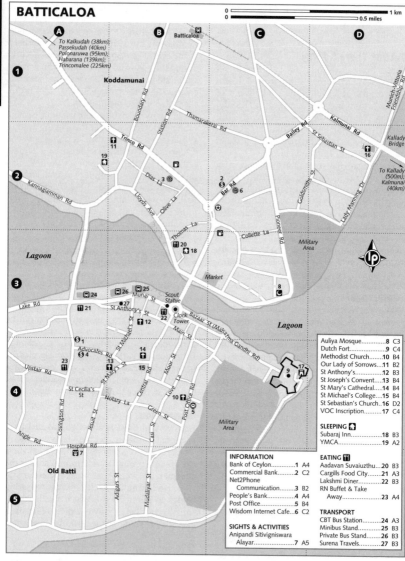

BATTICALOA

INFORMATION

Bank of Ceylon	1	A4
Commercial Bank	2	C2
Net2Phone Communication	3	B2
People's Bank	4	A4
Post Office	5	B4
Wisdom Internet Cafe	6	C2

SIGHTS & ACTIVITIES

Anipandi Sitivigniswara Alayar	7	A5
Auliya Mosque	8	C3
Dutch Fort	9	C4
Methodist Church	10	B4
Our Lady of Sorrows	11	B2
St Anthony's	12	B3
St Joseph's Convent	13	B4
St Mary's Cathedral	14	B4
St Michael's College	15	B4
St Sebastian's Church	16	D2
VOC Inscription	17	C4

SLEEPING

Subaraj Inn	18	B3
YMCA	19	A2

EATING

Aadavan Suvaiuzthu	20	B3
Cargills Food City	21	A3
Lakshmi Diner	22	B3
RN Buffet & Take Away	23	A4

TRANSPORT

CBT Bus Station	24	A3
Minibus Stand	25	B3
Private Bus Stand	26	B3
Surena Travels	27	B3

Sights & Activities
OLD BATTI

Wandering around Old Batti is particularly atmospheric late at night: cicadas call and water drips, but not a soul stirs on the eerily empty streets. Dim street lamps give lugubrious form to shadows around the various colonial edifices like the pompous sky-blue **St Joseph's Convent** (St Mary's St), **St Michael's College** (Central Rd), which is so drenched in vines and creepers that the brickwork is starting to be broken away, and the sturdy 1838 **Methodist Church** (Post Office Rd). Of the dozens of churches, the most eye-catching is the huge blue, eight-sided, unfinished **Our Lady of Sorrows** (Trinco Rd), the vaguely Mexican, earth-toned **St Anthony's** (St Anthony's St) and the

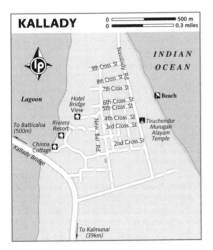

KALLADY

grand, turquoise **St Mary's Cathedral** (St Mary's St). St Mary's was rebuilt in 1994 following its partial destruction during fighting between local Tamils and Muslims. Beside Kallady Bridge is the fairly modern **St Sebastian's Church** (Kalmunai Rd), built in the shape of a whale.

Of the many Hindu temples, **Anipandi Sitivigniswara Alayar** (Hospital Rd) is visually the finest, with a magnificent *gopuram* that's decorated with a riotous festival of intertwined god figures.

The 6m-thick walls of Batti's **Dutch fort** (Bazaar St) surround the rambling kachcheri (administrative office). The fort itself contains government offices and isn't very interesting, but the stroll along the eastern fringe between the walls and the water is nice. By the eastern entrance gate you'll find a couple of old canons guarding the District Secretariat Office, while inside, on the 1st floor of the office opposite the entrance gate, is a stone slab engraved with a 1707 **VOC inscription**; it was recently removed from the fort walls and now balances precariously on a chair.

A great place to observe the fort is from across the water, beside the tiny **Auliya Mosque** (Lady Manning Dr), with its curious green minaret.

KALLADY

Kallady has an idyllic strip of beach, but the rubble of tsunami damage remains everywhere. Notice the colourful leaning tower of the **Tiruchendur Murugan Alayam temple** (Navalady Rd), which sits near the beach between Third and Fourth Cross Sts. Built in 1984 as a stop-

ping point on the Pada Yatra pilgrimage to Kataragama, its Murugan image is said to have opened its own eyes before the painter could do the job. The structure was slammed by the tsunami, leaving its small *gopuram* leaning at an alarming angle.

Sleeping

There's nowhere luxurious to stay in Batti. Many options are decidedly poor value by Sri Lankan standards; nevertheless, most are fully booked, so reservations are wise.

CENTRAL BATTI

YMCA (☎ 222 2495; Boundary Rd; tw with/without air-con Rs 1100/660, tr with/without air-con Rs 1430/880; 🕸) This is an excellent option that's only likely to get better with the completion of a new wing. Prices of these new rooms, which are modern and immaculate, weren't known at the time of research. The older rooms are also good value and have three beds per room.

Subaraj Inn (☎ 222 5983; subaraj_inn@yahoo.com; 6/1 Lloyds Ave; r from Rs 2280; 🕸 🖭) In *Only Man Is Vile*, William McGowan gets smuggled into Batti around 1987 to find Subaraj as the only hotel, its outside wall chipped and pocked with bullets fired by the 'peacekeeping' Indian army. Fortunately, things are better today, and this comfortable and slightly quirky hotel has charming, colonial-style rooms – though many do lack windows. The bar and restaurant areas are cosy and offer easy conversations. Popular with NGO workers, it's advisable to book ahead. Visa and MasterCard accepted.

KALLADY

Peaceful and close to the beach, these places are a Rs 120 three-wheeler ride from the town centre.

Hotel Bridge View (☎ 222 3723; 63/24 New Dutch Bar Rd; r with/without air-con Rs 2420/1100; 🕸) This quiet little garden hotel has modern, tiled rooms surrounded by greenery. The showers only spurt forth cold water, and the fan-only rooms are a little dingy. Any bridge views are imagined. The restaurant has decent staples, with curries ranging from Rs 120 to 400 and biryanis from Rs 250 to 350.

Chinna Cottage (☎ 222 5790; 21/9B New Dutch Bar Rd; r with/without air-con Rs 1980/1380; 🕸) The ice-blue rooms here have two pluses. First are the comfortable beds with nets and little terraces with views of the water. The second are the tacky posters of waterfalls and Alpine scenes that adorn the walls. Basic meals can be prepared on request. The owner doesn't speak English.

Riviera Resort (☎ 222 2165; www.riviera-online.com; New Dutch Bar Rd; tw with/without air-con from Rs 3500/1540; 🔀) Perched at the water's edge with views of Kallady Bridge and the lagoon, this peaceful spot, which is very popular with NGO workers, offers a wide range of neat and clean, if unsophisticated bungalows. The more expensive rooms have hot water and small terraces, but you pay a lot more for the privilege of air-con.

Eating & Drinking

Aadavan Suvaiuzthu (☎ 264 7219; 22 Lloyds Ave; cakes from Rs 30; 🕑 6am-8pm) Tickle those taste buds with something sweet at this pleasant snack bar and bakery decked out in bright colours.

Lakshmi Diner (23 Munai Rd; curries Rs 60; 🕑 5.30am-9pm) There's no English sign, but this place, facing a scout statue, is easy to spot. Flies and rubbish-laden floors are off-putting, but the eat-with-your-fingers vegetarian curries are cheap and excellent. There are several other very similar places close by.

RN Buffet & Take Away (☎ 222 2684; 42 Covington Rd; lunch buffets Rs 450; 🕑 11am-3.30pm) This superclean little eatery above a grocery shop offers a six-dish lunch buffet that's not excessively spiced. Unfortunately, military restrictions in the neighbourhood mean it's closed in the evenings. The restaurant also does a mean line in savoury pastries and cold drinks. It's run by a delightful English-speaking couple who get their inspiration from a Delia Smith recipe book!

The guest houses **Riviera Resort** (☎ 222 2165; New Dutch Bar Rd; mains Rs 400-500) and **Subaraj Inn** (☎ 222 5983; 6/1 Lloyds Ave; mains Rs 200-450) have places to eat that serve fair local, Chinese and occasional Western options. Both have decent little bars. You need to allow at least an hour's preparation time at the Riviera.

For self-caterers there's a branch of the excellent **Cargills Food City** (8am-10pm) on Munai Rd.

Getting There & Away
BUS
CTB buses, private buses and minibuses have adjacent bus stations on Munai St.

To prebook Colombo departures (Rs 500, 10 hours), drop by **Surena Travels** (☎ 222 6152; Munai St) and book your bum a place on its 6.30am departure.

For Polonnaruwa (Rs 150, two hours) there are four private buses at 10.30am, 12.30pm, 2.30pm and 4.30pm. There's a Badulla-bound CTB bus (Rs 200) at 5.30am, which goes via Maha Oya. For Arugam Bay or Ampara go via Kalmunai (Rs 50, 1½ hours). There are frequent buses and minibuses, and a direct CTB bus at 2pm, to Pottuvil (Rs 120, four hours).

At the time of research, due to fighting between the army and the LTTE, Trincomalee buses were generally travelling via Habarana rather than the shorter coastal route; there's a single private 'express service' leaving at 5.50am (Rs 250, nine hours) and a CTB one at 6am (Rs 250).

TRAIN
You'll need to book ahead for berths or sleepers on the 5.50pm and 8.15pm overnight trains to Colombo (Rs 270/500/1000 for 3rd/2nd/1st sleeper class) via Polonnaruwa and Valaichchenai. A day train departs for Colombo at 5.50am.

AROUND BATTICALOA
Kalkudah & Passekudah Beaches
☎ 065
Nuzzling either side of the palm-tipped Kalkudah headland, a little to the north of Batticaloa, are two breathtaking curves of sand. **Passekudah Beach**, the most northerly, is also the most visited and at weekends you might find two or three carloads of local beachgoers hanging out. At the southern end of the beach, gaudy little fishing boats add splashes of colour to the stunning pale sands. Head north along the beach, past the LTTE-destroyed hotels, and it'll be just you and the crabs making footprints. Swimming here is normally safe.

Kalkudah Bay Beach, just over the headland to the south, is the kind of fantasy beach that makes you want to chuck away your return air ticket and lounge forever under the palms. The easiest approach to this beach is now blocked by an army camp at the end of the Valaichchenai–Kalkudah road. To reach the sand, bypass the camp and use the partly rebuilt beach-access lane 800m further southwest.

SLEEPING & EATING

The road southwest from Kalkudah village was once lined with modest hotels. Now only rubble remains amid the palms – some Tiger induced, some tsunami made. Now there are only three basic guest houses, set back about 2km from the beaches on the Valaichchenai–Kalkudah road. Food is available by advance request.

The New Land Guesthouse (☎ 568 0440; tw Rs 500) With its shady terrace, large gardens and rooms that are pleasing to the eye, this is a good-value option.

New Pearl Inn (☎ 060-264 5420; s/d Rs 500/600) This inn has half-a-dozen basic green cells with nets, attached bathrooms and loads of friendly mosquitoes.

Simla Inn (☎ 077 603 1272; r Rs 1500) Victoria, the owner of Simla Inn, is legendary for her great curries and her incredible perseverance in adversity. Her Simla Inn was the only guest house to sit out the raging battles of the 1990s civil war. Then, having finally patched up all the bullet holes, the building got flattened by the 2004 tsunami. Unperturbed, Simla has risen again, 100m west of New Pearl and now offers two excellent and immaculately clean rooms with tiled bathrooms, though you'll need to bring your own mosquito net. Those on a supertight budget might be able to blag one of the ultrasimple driver rooms for Rs 500.

To get to the beaches you'll probably have to pass through the small market town of Valaichchenai, where you will find Stephens Snack Bar, close to the Mirovadai junction on the road to Batticaloa. A more loved and flower-filled tea shop you will rarely have the pleasure of coming across. For more on Mr Stephens, see boxed text, below.

TEA WITH MR STEPHENS

Sitting proudly inside his immaculate tea shop, the elderly Mr Stephens, dressed in a dapper white suit, is a gentleman in the truest sense of the word. I was lucky enough to bump into him while pausing for chai at his brand-new, beautifully decorated tea stand in Valaichchenai near Kalkudah beach. His excitement at finally meeting a real-life tourist after so many years was genuine and touching, but his tragic life story was heartbreaking.

'I used to work as an administrator and steward at one of the beach hotels in Kalkudah in the early 1980s, when tourism boomed. I had a certificate from one hotel. Back then there were many tourists here and many hotels. They were the good days. In the morning people had breakfast and then they stayed on the beach until 4pm. Then they would change for dinner and drink and eat until 9pm, after which they would dance to Bob Marley and Stevie Wonder until three in the morning. I used to dance, too, but only after a drink. Now I have not danced for 15 years.

Then the problems started [the war] and the tourists left. Everything closed and everybody left. For me it was very difficult. I had no money, so I became a fisherman and lived in a hut on the beach with my wife. We were happy. Then, one day, I had to go to Colombo for something. I left on the bus very early in the morning. It was 26 December 2004. I came back as soon as I heard, but I had lost everything. The tsunami destroyed my house, killed my wife and most of my friends were dead. I had nothing anymore. Not even my boat. For three years after that I wasn't able to work and I slept in the church. The government have given me nothing. I asked, but no, nothing. It's because I couldn't prove what I had before, because I was living in what they called a temporary house, but it was our home. Even the NGOs gave me nothing. This is common here in the East. Many people have received nothing. I am not angry about it, though. I talked to God and prayed that one day things would get better and then they did. Three months ago my friend lent me Rs 1000 and gave me this patch of land here. With the money I have built this snack bar and it's going well. I sleep here behind the table and many people come, especially for breakfast. I am saving some money, which I will use to buy a plastic cover to put on the roof when the rains start. Life is better now and maybe now the war is ending many tourists will start to come and it will be like the old days again.'

When finally I left his tea shop, Mr Stephens embraced me and, with tears in his eyes, thanked me again and again for coming. For me it was the most moving encounter I have ever had while travelling.

GETTING THERE & AWAY

Three daily buses from Batticaloa (at 6.30am, 10.30am and 3.30pm; Rs 35) run to Kalkudah, passing by all three guest houses. The last certain return to Batticaloa is 1.30pm, though if there is sufficient custom (far from certain), then a 4pm service might also run. Slow but much more frequent buses serve Valaichchenai (Rs 30, 1½ hours), which is 5km from the beaches. Get off in Valaichchenai's market area, where you can catch a three-wheeler for Kalkudah (Rs 150); the bus station is 1.5km closer to Kalkudah, but finding three-wheelers is harder there.

Buses on the Colombo–Polonnaruwa–Batti route might drop you off at the Valaichchenai junction on the A15.

Be aware that there is a different train station called Kalkudah: it's tiny and very isolated, 2km southwest of Kalkudah beach on the seldom used short-cut road from Kumburumoolai. Should you jump off a train here, turn left (north) and walk through the well-marked minefield towards the beach-access road.

TRINCOMALEE

☎ 026 / pop 57,000

After many rough years, fascinating Trincomalee (Trinco) is once again open to tourists. The town, which sits beside one of the finest natural harbours in the world, is old almost beyond reckoning and is possibly the site of historic Gokana in the Mahavamsa (Great Chronicle). Trinco's appeal, aside from

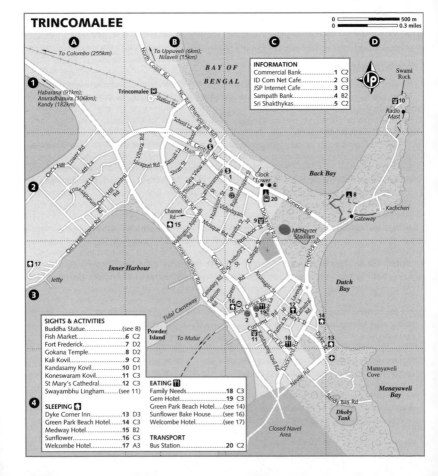

TRINCOMALEE

0 ——— 500 m
0 ——— 0.3 miles

INFORMATION	
Commercial Bank	1 C2
ID Com Net Cafe	2 C3
JSP Internet Cafe	3 C3
Sampath Bank	4 B2
Sri Shakthykas	5 C2

SIGHTS & ACTIVITIES	
Buddha Statue	(see 8)
Fish Market	6 C2
Fort Frederick	7 D2
Gokana Temple	8 D2
Kali Kovil	9 C3
Kandasamy Kovil	10 D1
Koneswaram Kovil	11 C3
St Mary's Cathedral	12 C3
Swayambhu Lingham	(see 11)

SLEEPING	
Dyke Corner Inn	13 D3
Green Park Beach Hotel	14 C3
Medway Hotel	15 B2
Sunflower	16 C3
Welcombe Hotel	17 A3

EATING	
Family Needs	18 C3
Gem Hotel	19 C3
Green Park Beach Hotel	(see 14)
Sunflower Bake House	(see 16)
Welcombe Hotel	(see 17)

TRANSPORT	
Bus Station	20 C2

WE'RE NOT IN KANSAS ANYMORE

Anyone venturing into this region should not forget that most of the east coast was a conflict zone until recently. At the risk of spelling out the blindingly obvious, don't snap unauthorised photographs of soldiers, checkpoints, military posts or potentially strategic sites like ports and bridges. Be aware that many locals will be too nervous to speak openly in public about politics. Patience and understanding pay off.

the nearby beaches of Uppuveli and Nilaveli (p263), is both the sense of being a pioneer in a town quite unused to tourists and the mix of peoples and cultures found on the streets.

That same diversity, however, has led to bloodshed many times in the recent past: although the city was safe at the time of research, keep your ear to the ground for the latest. If you've never visited a very recent ex-war zone, you'll find Trinco a shock – it feels like a Baghdad-on-Sea.

Orientation

Trinco's commercial heart is squeezed into a narrow isthmus that leads south to a large out-of-bounds peninsula occupied by the navy. Historic Trinco is a small thumb of rock jutting northeast, guarded by the remnant walls of Fort Frederick.

Information

Of the several banks along Central Rd, **Commercial Bank** (193 Central Rd) and **Sampath Bank** (262 Central Rd) have the most reliable ATMs.

Places offering internet access:

ID Com Net Cafe (325 Court Rd; per hr Rs 50; ⏰ 8am-8pm Mon-Sat) Also has very cheap internet phone calls, from Rs 5 per minute.

JSP Internet Cafe (380 Court Rd; per hr Rs 50; ⏰ 7am-8pm Mon-Sat, to 1pm Sun)

Sri Shakthykas (81A Rajavarothayam St; per hr Rs 50; ⏰ 7.30am-8.30pm Mon-Sat, 9am-8pm Sun)

Sights & Activities

Walking around the tangled streets of Trinco is a surreal experience. The place seems almost completely deserted. Shops are kept shuttered up and open only when a customer bangs on the door, and the streets, which are empty of traffic and civilians, are haunted by packs of stray dogs and groups of soldiers manning checkpoints at every corner. All in all it's hard not to think of this as an occupied city.

FORT FREDERICK AREA

Built by the Portuguese, **Fort Frederick** was rebuilt by the Dutch. Today, British insignias crown the tunnel-like gateway that pierces the fort's massively stout walls. Parts of the fortress are under military jurisdiction, and anyone entering will have to undergo a stringent security check. Despite this, a stroll up to the big new standing **Buddha statue** at the **Gokana Temple** and on up to **Swami Rock**, a 130m-high cliff nicknamed Lovers' Leap, and the revered **Koneswaram Kovil** is highly worthwhile. This temple houses the rescued *lingam* (Hindu phallic symbol) known as the **Swayambhu Lingam** (⏰ viewing 7am-11.30pm & 4-6pm), making it one of Sri Lanka's most spiritually important Hindu sites (see below).

OTHER RELIGIOUS SIGHTS

Kali Kovil (Dockyard Rd) has the most impressive, eye-catching *gopuram* of Trinco's many Hindu temples. Most others are outwardly rather plain, including the important **Kandasamy Kovil** (Kandasamy Kovil Rd), dedicated to

RAWANA & THE SWAYAMBHU LINGAM

The radio-mast hill opposite Swami Rock is considered to be the site of the mythical palace of the 10-headed demon king Rawana. He's the Hindu antihero of the Ramayana, infamous for kidnapping Rama's wife, Sita. Along with Sita, he supposedly carried to Lanka the Swayambhu Lingam, taken from a Tibetan mountaintop. This *lingam* (phallic symbol) became the object of enormous veneration. However, in 1624, the proselytising Catholic-Portuguese destroyed the surrounding cliff-top temple, tipping the whole structure, *lingam* and all, into the ocean. It was only retrieved in 1962 by a scuba-diving team that included writer Arthur C Clarke. Clarke described the discovery in *The Reefs of Taprobane*. For cameraman Mike Wilson, who first spotted the *lingam*, the experience proved so profound that he renounced his career and family to become Hindu Swami Siva Kalki (see http://kataragama.org/sivakalki.htm).

Murugan. However, at sunset *puja* (prayer or offerings) times, chanting and incense billow forth atmospherically from many more.

Of the churches the 1852 Catholic **St Mary's Cathedral** (St Mary's St) is particularly attractive, with a sky-blue neobaroque frontage and a tiled, towered rear.

BEACHES & WHALE-WATCHING

Trinco's most famous beaches are at Uppuveli and Nilaveli, but right in the centre, picturesque **Dutch Bay** is also attractive. Swimming is possible despite sometimes dangerous undertows. However, it's more a place for strolling, and ice-cream sellers cater to the evening *passeggiata*. Don't consider bathing in **Inner Harbour**, where the water is so polluted that at times fish die off en smelly masse. **Manayaweli Cove** is an appealing curl of fishing beach reached by strolling past **Dhoby Tank**, where local washers do their laundry.

In the past you used to be able to organise whale-watching trips from here, though at the time of research the navy had put a halt to such games (see opposite). It's worth asking if the rules have changed.

Further fishy interest is provided at the raucous daily **fish market** near the bus station. Early mornings are busiest.

Sleeping
BUDGET

For good reason many Western visitors don't stay in town at all, preferring the accommodation in Uppuveli (p264), just 6km north.

Dyke Corner Inn (☎ 222 0318; 210/1 Dyke St; r Rs 800) You can't top the location, right on the sands of Dutch Bay, but you can top everything else about the filthy communal rooms on offer here. Still, if you're the sort of twisted person who really loves getting down and dirty with a bed full of inquisitive cockroaches, then you might just have found your ticket here.

Sunflower (☎ 222 2963; 154 Post Office Rd; tw Rs 1000) A simple and satisfying place located above a bakery where occasional wafts of slow-baking cakes (and sometimes wafts of slow-baking rubbish in the streets outside) will drift into your sleep. It's well maintained, the owners are friendly and the showers mildly tepid.

MIDRANGE

Medway Hotel (☎ 222 7655; fax 222 2582; 250 Inner Harbour Rd; tw with/without air-con Rs 3000/2000; 🕸) The eight sizable rooms at this pleasant hotel are clean, though spartan, and have beds comfortable enough to stay snuggled up in for hours. The fragrant frangipani-and-hibiscus garden shades you from the views and smells of Inner Harbour bay.

Green Park Beach Hotel (☎ 222 2369; lathu@sltnet.lk; 312 Dyke Rd; s/d/tr Rs 2500/2750/3100; 🕸) One of the better-value places to stay, the suitably green Green Park has wonderful views over the Indian Ocean. It's been recently renovated and has spotless rooms and modern, tiled bathrooms. If the beach bores you, then kick back with a cocktail in hand beside the kids 'ball pool' hidden away under the stairs.

Welcombe Hotel (☎ 222 2373; welcombe@sltnet.lk; 66 Orr's Hill Lower Rd; s/d/tr US$45/45/60; 🕸 🕸) By far the most creative architectural statement in Trinco's hospitality industry, the upmarket Welcombe's semi-Japanese taste for modern angles and lines looks great. However, style doesn't always prove comfortable, and your bum will soon start complaining about the wooden-board armchairs. The beds are perfect for arguing couples – they're so big that if you sleep at opposite ends, one of you will be virtually in Colombo. In a previous incarnation this site was a secretive naval centre rumoured to have harboured a torture chamber. Sweet dreams!

Eating & Drinking

Basic eateries are dotted all over town, especially on NC Rd, Main St and in the busy block of Court St between Customs and Post Office Rds. However, few really deserve recommendation.

Sunflower Bake House (154 Post Office Rd; mains Rs 80; 🕒 6am-9pm) Below the hotel of the same name, this place has a range of sweet and sour pastries that make for a good breakfast and some dirt-cheap, but dirt-free, rice-and-curry lunches for Rs 80.

Gem Hotel (65 Post Office Rd; mains Rs 80-120) This jack-of-all-trades restaurant is one of the more popular lunch spots with locals. The buffet curries here won't cost more than Rs 120, no matter how many times you go back for a refill.

Family Needs (☎ 222 7314; 145A Dockyard Rd; mains Rs 150-300; 🕒 5-9.30pm) This shack-fronted rice-and-curry place, which you'd never look at twice, actually makes an epic fried rice and, if you give plenty of notice and if they have some cheese and, and, and, might just be able to conjure up a decent pizza.

Green Park Beach Hotel (☎ 222 2369; 312 Dyke Rd; mains Rs 250-400; 🕑 7-10am, noon-2pm & 6-10pm) With a relaxed atmosphere and vast menu of mainly north Indian dishes, this hotel restaurant is one of the nicer places to eat.

Welcombe Hotel (☎ 222 2373; 66 Orr's Hill Lower Rd; mains Rs 500-800) There's appealing alfresco dining at this hotel restaurant, which serves some original and mostly successful Western dishes, including lamb chop in wine and rosemary, and jumbo prawns in lemon-garlic butter.

Getting There & Away

BUS

Currently travelling by bus to and from Trincomalee involves passing endless, tedious military roadblocks where everybody has to pile off the bus and be subjected to a bag and body search (as does the bus itself). All this means that you end up virtually walking most of the way to your final destination! On entering the heavily guarded bus station, you and your belongings will also be subjected to a search. All buses depart from this bus station.

Private buses to Colombo (Rs 380, seven hours) leave Trinco hourly throughout the day, as well as a few at night – though with the current security situation, it's probably better to take a bus in daylight hours. You can use these to get off anywhere en route, including Habarana, Dambulla or Kurunegala.

For Anuradhapura there is a CTB bus at 12.30pm or a private bus at 7am. Both cost Rs 120. There are four private buses daily to Kandy (Rs 185, six hours) leaving at 6am, 10am, 1.35pm and 2.45pm. It's currently completely impossible to travel overland to Jaffna or in fact anywhere much further north of Nilaveli. It's also impossible to travel south to Batticaloa via the coast road. Instead you must make the long detour inland to Habarana. A CTB bus makes this arduous journey at 6am and a private one at 7am. For either of these the cost is Rs 230 and it takes an (optimistic) seven hours.

TRAIN

There are two trains daily between Trinco and Colombo Fort via Habarana. The useful overnight sleeper service leaves Trinco at 7pm (3rd/2nd/1st sleeper class Rs 235/440/850, nine hours). The daytime train trundles down the tracks at 7am. Note that, just as at the bus station, anybody entering the train station is subjected to a heavy body and baggage search. You must therefore arrive at the station with

plenty of time to spare as, not surprisingly, it takes the police a long time to search all the potential passengers and if you're not done by the time the train's ready to leave, tough!

AROUND TRINCOMALEE
☎ 026

Apart from Arugam Bay, the only east-coast beaches with any tourist infrastructure are north of Trinco at Nilaveli and Uppuveli. There's much more choice at Uppuveli (6km from Trinco), though even here the utter dearth of visitors means that it's fairly limited.

Uppuveli

So what if the journey was long and tough. You're here now, and one look at that beach, one moment spent digging your toes into its scrunchy sand, one instant to let a smile of unrestrained joy cross your face, and you'll be glad you came. This is the isle of serendipity at her glorious best.

INFORMATION

There are no banks. As yet the only internet is a dismally slow, exorbitantly expensive connection at **Hotel Club Oceanic** (per hr Rs 350). **St Joseph's Medical Service** (🕑 24hr) has an around-the-clock medical centre just south of Uppuveli's hotel area. Payment is mostly donation based.

SIGHTS

If the beach isn't holding your attention (an impossible feat), you can stroll up to the beautifully kept, yet immensely sad, **Commonwealth War Cemetery** (Nilaveli Rd; 🕑 dawn-dusk). This is the last resting place for over 600 servicemen who died at Trinco during WWII, most of them during a Japanese raid on 9 April 1942 that sank over a dozen vessels. The simplicity of the lines of graves and their often moving epitaphs bring a tear to the eye. Donations are appreciated.

Beachfront **Salli Muthumariamunam Kovil** is 4km by road from Uppuveli but only a short hop by boat; it's directly across Fishermen's Creek, masked from view by green-topped rocks.

ACTIVITIES

Uppuveli used to be the preferred starting point for a life on the ocean waves with dolphin- and whale-watching boat trips or snorkelling and diving excursions to Pigeon Island. Unfortunately you won't be doing anything more energetic now than a lazy swim and a spot of sunbathing because the navy has banned

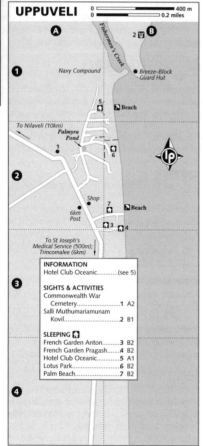

UPPUVELI

0 — 400 m
0 — 0.2 miles

Navy Compound

Fishermen's Creek

Breeze–Block Guard Hut

Beach

To Nilaveli (10km)

Palmyra Pond

Beach

Shop

6km Post

Beach

To St Joseph's Medical Service (500m); Trincomalee (6km)

INFORMATION
Hotel Club Oceanic............(see 5)

SIGHTS & ACTIVITIES
Commonwealth War
Cemetery.........................1 A2
Salli Muthumariamunam
Kovil...............................2 B1

SLEEPING
French Garden Anton..........3 B2
French Garden Pragash.......4 B2
Hotel Club Oceanic.............5 A1
Lotus Park.........................6 B2
Palm Beach.......................7 B2

diving, snorkelling and boat trips due to real security risks (LTTE suicide bombers using boats as torpedos and scuba divers sticking mines to the bottom of naval frigates – it's happened). With some effort it's sometimes possible to arrange such activities from Nilaveli (opposite).

SLEEPING

As things currently stand, you will probably be the only tourist around; any other foreigners are likely to be NGO workers. As the Sri Lankan government recently announced the expulsion of many NGOs, you might not even find any of them. Therefore don't be surprised to find the accommodation scene here in even more dire straits than present. Ferocious mosquitoes make a net essential.

Budget

French Garden Anton (☎ 078 979 1024; d Rs 500) Uppuveli's cheapest offers very basic pink cubes that get awfully hot and sweaty and certainly can't be described as clean. It's set a short way back from the beach. Some have mosquito nets. Meals available with advance notice.

French Garden Pragash (☎ 060 220 397; tw Rs 750) These unsophisticated boxlike rooms could do with a bit more care and affection, but there are pluses, including the charming old gentleman who runs it and the gorgeous beachside location. Simple rice-and-fish meals available on request (Rs300).

Palm Beach (☎ 222 1250; tw/tr Rs 1300/1500, with air-con 1750/2000; 🅧) At the time of research this place was temporarily closed because the owners were busy waltzing around Italy. There was nobody else available to show us around or give us the latest prices, but from what we could see it's certainly worth a look. Rates include breakfast.

Midrange

Lotus Park (☎ 222 5327; www.lotustrinco.com; s/d Rs 3000/3250; 🅧 🅡) Second only to Club Oceanic, this increasingly rundown place has large but boring rooms in the main block or much more exciting beach bungalows within splashing distance of the waves. The bungalows are the same price as the rooms and come with views you'll dream about on dreary winter mornings for years to come.

Hotel Club Oceanic (☎ 222 2307; www.john keellshotels.com; Sampaltive Post; s/d from Rs4000; tr from Rs4500; 🅧 🅡 🅡) Ignore the ugly exterior; once inside Uppuveli's only real resort, you'll discover airy and supremely comfortable ocean-blue rooms with piping-hot showers and satellite TV. It sits on a fine curve of beach and has a pool that, while good, is not quite as good as the sea. This is where almost every tourist in Uppuveli stays, yet rates still drop like a sinking submarine if you start to walk away.

EATING & DRINKING

The only restaurants are in hotels and guest houses.

Lotus Park (☎ 222 5327; mains Rs 350-500) Believe the menu and you'll think that the cooks here can whip up anything under the sun. Anything that's fish, curry or a bizarre Sri Lankan version of pasta, that is. Still, the beachfront dining is nice.

Hotel Club Oceanic (☎ 222 2307; buffets Rs 800-1000) The excellent dinner buffet at this top-end hotel is a favourite of NGO workers for miles around. If you know that quantity doesn't always equate to quality, then choose from the à la carte menu featuring reasonable Western and better Sri Lankan dishes. Drinks cost (a lot) extra.

GETTING THERE & AWAY
Irakkandy-bound minibuses from Trinco's bus terminal run roughly every half-hour, supplemented by occasional small CTB buses. All pass through Uppuveli (Rs 15, 20 minutes) and Nilaveli (Rs 40, 45 minutes). Three-wheelers from Uppuveli cost Rs 250 to Trinco and Rs 400 to Nilaveli.

Nilaveli
You get to Uppuveli Beach and think to yourself, 'Well that's that then. This is perfection. I need go no further'. But then someone mentions lyrical sounding Nilaveli just around the corner and all of a sudden your heads a-twitter, for here is a beach that maybe surpasses even Uppuveli in the died-and-gone-to-heaven stakes.

SIGHTS & ACTIVITIES
Nilaveli Beach
For years Nilaveli has been considered one of Sri Lanka's most perfect beaches. It certainly has that feeling of paradise-island remoteness, with plenty of bending palms swaying over the golden sand. Good it may be, but in reality things aren't quite as heavenly as they seem here. It's not far from the recent front line and soldiers are everywhere, which kind of spoils the happy holidays' mood. This is made plainly obvious in the numerous army checkpoints on the road into town and the massive military camp that sits right in the middle of the beach.

Pigeon Island
Floating in the great blue a short way offshore, **Pigeon Island**, with its powdery white sands and glittering coral gardens, tantalises with possibilities. However, though it used to be a very popular day-trip destination, today – thanks to a navy ban on boat trips, diving and snorkelling excursions and anything else that could be termed as fun in the sun – it has gone back to being the archetypical desert island. Having said that, for the really determined, it's possible to reach, but you must first arrange a naval escort through the Nilaveli Beach Hotel

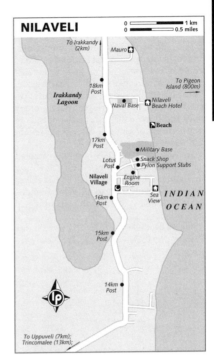

(p266). This will cost around Rs 2500 for half a day (give a day's notice). They'll normally pick you up in a small zodiac boat, but it doesn't hurt to request an aircraft carrier. The navy can also sometimes lend you snorkelling or even diving equipment for a negotiable fee, though don't expect any diving lessons. Single women may want to think twice about sitting in a bikini on a remote island with a load of sailors for company...

SLEEPING & EATING
With the temporary peace of a few years ago, there were high hopes for tourist developments along this spectacular stretch of coastline. In the previous edition of this book, we even forecast a splurge of hotel development taking place. Alas, we were wrong: the peace turned sour, almost no tourists at all visit Nilaveli now and many hotels have shut down again.

Most accommodation is at least a 400m walk east of the main road, starting from the approximate kilometre point noted. Guest houses and hotels can arrange food, but there are no alternative dining options.

Mauro (☎ 492 0633; s with/without air-con Rs 2530/1870, d with/without air-con Rs 2750/2090; 🏊 🔊) The rooms in this long two-storey building front a narrow, manicured garden that extends past a very tempting swimming pool to possibly the east coast's most attractive stretch of beach, facing Pigeon Island. The rooms, which are starting to show their age, could be cleaner, but the pretty vines and flowers that run up the outside of each make up for a lot. The curry-heavy restaurant serves meals for around Rs 500.

Sea View (☎ 071 418 2538; tw Rs 2000) Situated right on the beach, the two-storey Sea View has basic white rooms and stained bed sheets above an isolated dining room. While friendly, the lack of many alternatives is its only real plus.

Nilaveli Beach Hotel (☎ 222 6294; www.tangerine tours.com; s/d/tr US$40/45/50; 🏊 🔊 🖳) Newly re-built after the tsunami and offering superb value, the Nilaveli Beach Hotel is easily the best place to stay in the whole Trincomalee region. The stylish cottages, full of cool-to-the-touch stone floors, high-quality wooden furniture and elegant bed covers, are spread through lovely gardens that are a popular monkey playground. The excellent restaurant (mains Rs 600, set menus from Rs 750) specialises in pasta and, not surprisingly, seafood – lots of it and always good.

GETTING THERE & AWAY

Buses and minibuses to Irakkandy leave Trinco's bus terminal about every half-hour. All pass through Uppuveli (Rs 15) and Nilaveli (Rs 40).

A three-wheeler between Nilaveli and Trincomalee costs Rs 650.

Jaffna & the North

Towering, ornate Hindu temples, colourful saris draped effortlessly over women on bicycles, the sweet fragrance of fruit trees on a tropical breeze – the cultural contrasts between the North and the rest of Sri Lanka are immediately apparent. The differences run deep: from the language (the rapid-fire staccato of spoken Tamil, a real change from singsong Sinhala) to the cuisine (singularly spiced and, in the right season, complemented by mangoes that are the stuff of legend) and the low-lying palmyra-palm-spotted landscape. Even the light in the North has a distinctive quality, reflected as deep garden greens in Jaffna's quiet suburbs or softening the battle-scarred centre. Yet, you are still certainly in Sri Lanka – just an area much set apart.

For good reason, especially given the recent history, tourists are unusual here and get a rare welcome. The people of the peninsula, although much embattled, remain proud of their heritage and eager to share it. Meeting the industrious, highly educated locals is a memorable reward for those who do make the journey. Conversations sometimes fascinatingly underscore the gulf of misunderstanding between the Tamil heartland and the Sinhalese South.

The history of conflict in the North need not scare you off. However, in light of the recent military victory against the Liberation Tigers of Tamil Eelam (LTTE), who once ran the Vanni region virtually as a separate country, be prepared for army checkpoints, road closures, no-go zones and reduced services. Sensitivity, tact and open-mindedness will be key, but then they always should be.

Also be prepared for drenching rain during the northeastern monsoon (October to January) or tough dry heat the rest of the year. In sweaty August, Jaffna goes wild during the extraordinary Nallur festival.

HIGHLIGHTS

- Contemplating the many faces of **Jaffna** (p274) – leafy and green, brash and commercial, scarred by war

- Slipping into a trance during a mesmerising *puja* (offerings or prayers) at Jaffna's **Nallur Kandaswamy Kovil** (p276), the most important Hindu temple of the North

- Gliding across the shallow waters of the offshore islands, such as sacred **Nainativu** (p285) or desolate **Delft** (p285)

- If the roads reopen, discovering the **Vanni** (p272), the country so fiercely fought over during 25 years of war

History

When Arab traveller Ibn Batuta visited Ceylon in 1344, he reported that the powerful Hindu–Tamil kingdom of Jaffna extended south as far as Puttalam. Over several centuries territorial controls were extended and retracted, but even under colonial regimes Jaffna, like Kandy, remained highly autonomous. This lasted until the 19th century, when British bureaucrats decided it would be more convenient to administer the whole of Ceylon as a single unit.

GROWING CONFLICT

British managers found Tamils to be agreeably capable at learning English and fulfilling the needs of the colonial administration. This apparent 'favouritism' saw Tamil candidates overrepresented in universities and public service jobs, creating Sinhalese resentment and contributing to anti-Tamil sentiment in the 1950s (following independence in 1948). This eventually led to the infamous 1956 'Sinhala only' language policy (see p29).

Now it was the Tamils' turn to feel discriminated against. As passions on both sides rose, one of the defining moments came in 1981, when a Sinhalese mob burnt down Jaffna's library (see p278), sowing the seeds for civil war. Small-scale reprisals followed, but the world only took notice two years later, in 1983, when full-scale anti-Tamil massacres erupted in Colombo.

The horror of this 'Black July' prompted a groundswell of sympathy for Tamil armed resistance groups, and brought funding from fellow Tamils in southern India. The LTTE came to virtually control the North for a while.

During the rest of the 1980s and 1990s, several Sri Lankan governments gained and lost leverage over the LTTE, particularly in and around Jaffna, which changed hands several times and even saw the disastrous involvement of an Indian Peace Keeping Force (IPKF) from 1987 to 1990.

AN END IN SIGHT?

In 2002, following a Norway-brokered ceasefire agreement, a careful optimism reigned. In the North, refugees, internally displaced persons and long-absent émigrés began to return, bringing an economic boost to devastated Jaffna. Nongovernmental organisations (NGOs) startled tackling, among other things, an estimated two million landmines.

But large swaths of the Vanni – the mainland area of the North under LTTE control – remained too dangerous to farm, and the Sri Lanka Army's (SLA) nervously tentative hold on the Jaffna peninsula led to the creation of despised no-go High Security Zones (see p282).

The 2004 tsunami absolutely devastated the northeastern coast. Although there was limited cooperation between the government

---

STAYING SAFE

At the time of writing, the Sri Lankan government was claiming military victory against the Liberation Tigers of Tamil Eelam (LTTE), the endgame following a major offensive to regain control of the Vanni, the mainland area of the North previously under LTTE control.

Foreign governments, such as those of the United Kingdom and Australia, had issued stern travel warnings and classed the Vanni as a 'do not travel' zone. With all land routes across this theatre of war closed, it was still possible for independent travellers to fly to Jaffna, although movement in town and around the peninsula was somewhat restricted. This may change in the life of this book.

At the time of writing, isolated killings as well as arrests and disappearances continued with depressing regularity, and the root reasons for the civil unrest are far from solved. Violence has not been aimed at foreigners, but situations could turn dangerous instantly and dramatically.

Although NGOs made progress clearing landmines during the ceasefire, thousands remain, along with tonnes of unexploded ordnance. Walk only on roads or very well-trodden paths. Do not wander on deserted beaches.

With traditional hostilities now over, conditions for residents and travellers should change quickly for the better. Nevertheless, before considering a visit, research thoroughly and keep a careful eye on the news and fast-changing politics of the region. For two very different perspectives, try www.defence.lk and www.tamilnet.com.

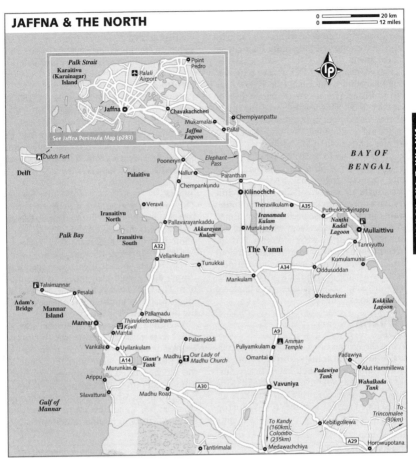

JAFFNA & THE NORTH

0 — 20 km
0 — 12 miles

and LTTE, bitter contests ensued over who was to control the millions of dollars of foreign aid that poured into Sri Lanka following the disaster.

The presidential election of November 2005 brought no new hope for lasting peace (see boxed text, p277). By mid-2006 the ceasefire agreement was in tatters. Major military operations by both sides resumed in the North and East, and a wave of disappearances and killings in 2006 and 2007 prompted human-rights groups and the international community to strongly criticise all belligerents.

In mid-2007, after gaining control of the East, the Sri Lankan government of increasingly hardline President Mahinda Rajapaksa focused its offensive on the LTTE's northern stronghold, the Vanni. January 2008 marked the official abrogation of the ceasefire, already no more than a paper truce.

In September 2008 the Sri Lankan government ordered UN agencies and NGOs to leave the Vanni region, saying it could no longer guarantee their safety. This may have been true, but their withdrawal denied a beleaguered population of an estimated 230,000 ethnic Tamils access to humanitarian support and the security of a human-rights watchdog. Since the departure of the NGOs, and with independent journalists barred from the conflict region, verifying the claims of either side has been impossible, in particular the plight of the local populations that have apparently retreated (voluntarily? forcibly?) with the LTTE, some think as a defensive human shield. International reporters brought in by the government to bear witness to captured lands have reported little more than ruined 'ghost towns'.

Government and LTTE forces remained dug in around Kilinochchi (the Tigers' capital) until the SLA declared victory there in January 2009. This was followed rapidly by claims of control throughout the Vanni, including at Elephant Pass and the LTTE's former stronghold of Mullaittivu.

From January to April 2009, the LTTE and a large number of Tamil civilians were forced into an increasingly small wedge of land at the northeast corner of the Vanni. While military operations continued, escape routes were opened for those fleeing the fighting to move to no-fire zones from which there was further transport to welfare centres. Perhaps in response to growing international clamour for a ceasefire, in mid-April the government declared a pause in offensive manoeuvres during which trapped war refugees were implored to move to safe areas.

VAVUNIYA
☎ 024

When the A9 was open through to Jaffna virtually all ground transport to and from the North funnelled through energetically bustling Vavuniya (*vow*-nya). If you were using public transport, an overnight stay here allowed for an early start to the cross-Vanni trip to Jaffna. It may still be a convenient stopping point before onward travel to points throughout the Vanni, depending on what opens to civilian access. Although there are no real sights, an afternoon here isn't unpleasant and the local people are charmingly hospitable.

Information

Reasonably fast internet access is available at **SeeNet** (☎ 222 1222; 395/1 Horowapatana Rd; per hr Rs 50; ❧ 7.30am-9pm; ✄) and **Vastec** (☎ 222 2869; 2nd fl, 65 Station Rd; per 15 min/hr Rs 15/40; ❧ 8am-9pm). In town, west of the clock tower on Station Rd, **Sanpath Bank**, **People's Bank**, **Bank of Ceylon** and **Commercial Bank** all have ATMs.

Sights

The town arcs around a quietly attractive **tank** that's best observed from **Sothida Niliyam Kovil**, a tiled, shedlike Ganesh temple. More photogenic is the **Kandasamy Kovil** (Kandasamy Kovil Rd), a Murugan (Skanda) temple with a very ornate, if faded, *gopuram* (gateway tower) and a gold-clad image in its sanctum. The **Grand Jummah Mosque** (Horowapatana Rd) might really be pretty grand one day when the building work is finally complete.

Vavuniya's **Archaeological Museum** (☎ 222 4805; 2 Horowapatana Rd; admission free; ❧ 8am-5pm Wed-Mon) is unlikely to impress if you're arriving from the ancient cities, but some of the pinched-faced terracotta figures from Kilinochchi (4th to 5th century) are delightfully primitive, while the central hexagonal chamber has some fine 5th-to-8th-century Buddha statues in Mannar limestone.

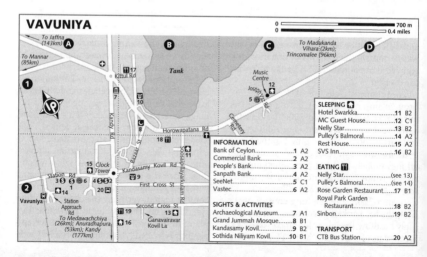

The quietly charming **Madukanda Vihara** (Horowapatana Rd) is a Rs 100 three-wheeler ride from central Vavuniya, beyond the 3km post on the A29. It was reputedly the fourth resting point in the journey of the sacred Buddha tooth relic from Mullaittivu to Anuradhapura during the 4th-century reign of King Mahsen. Near the white dagoba (stupa) and a 150-year-old bodhi tree, appealing ancient ruins include fine guard stones and lion-and-elephant-decorated banisters.

Sleeping

Few Vavuniya hotels have mosquito nets – annoying in the wet season.

SVS Inn (☎ 222 2978; Kandy Rd; s/tw with fan from Rs 400/650, tw with air-con Rs 1500; ☒) Of the cheap, almost-clean rooms, those costing over Rs 500 have attached toilet. Air-con twins are small, functional and slightly messy.

Rest House (☎ 222 2299; Station Rd; s/d Rs 600/750, with air-con Rs 750/800; ☒) This place has plain, decent-value rooms with bare, thick walls behind a beer garden that attracts local ex-office alkies. Not ideal for single women.

Pulley's Balmoral (☎ 222 2364; Station Approach Rd; s/d without bathroom Rs 600/900, tw with bathroom & fan/air-con Rs 1375/1650; ☒) Entered through a snack-stall alley opposite the train station, this old villa sits in a big palm garden. Air-con rooms are big and well equipped, but lack real windows.

Hotel Swarkka (☎ 222 1291; Soosaipillayarkulam Rd; tr with fan/air-con Rs 1200/1800; ☒) The recent renovations and very good-humoured staff make this the best of many ordinary boxroom guest houses.

Nelly Star (☎ 222 4477; 84 Second Cross St; r with fan/air-con Rs 1700/2200, VIP Rs 3000; ☒) Striking modernistic architecture with brightly coloured paintwork makes Nelly Star Vavuniya's place of the moment. Standard rooms don't quite live up to expectations but persist as the best in town. The VIP rooms are much more spacious and have a minibar, TV and bathtub.

MC Guest House (☎ 222 0445, 077 662 5292; 411 Horowapatana Rd; apt Rs 3300; ☒) Families might consider renting this fairly lovable house with two twin bedrooms (one with air-con, both with bathrooms), basic kitchen and big, if somewhat sparse, sitting room. Keys are available from the nearby Music Centre.

Eating

Sinbon (Kandy Rd; ◷ 6.30am-8pm; ☒) Unusually, local women feel confident enough to come to this modern cafe unchaperoned for coffee (Nescafé Rs 40), cakes or ice-cream sundaes (Rs 80). It's ideal for passing the time when you're waiting for a bus. Next door is an air-conditioned supermarket.

Rose Garden Restaurant (☎ 222 4473; 8 Kittul Rd; meals Rs 60-380) This is a big, excellent-value, party-hall restaurant. Food of widely varying styles includes a spicy *tom yam goong* (Thai shrimp soup) that lacks lemon grass but is generously full of shrimps for a mere Rs 80.

Royal Park Garden Restaurant (☎ 222 4026; 200 Horowapatana Rd; meals Rs 110-550; ◷ 11.30am-10pm) The cosy garden here is a great place for dinner when the weather's not unbearably hot: attractive twinkling lights and little pavilions nestle amid ornamental trees. The Rs 180 mushroom *paneer* masala (mushroom and unfermented cheese curry) is richly delicious, and there's tasty soup for Rs 60. No prices on menus.

Food at **Pulley's Balmoral** (☎ 222 2364; Station Approach Rd; meals Rs 80-350) and **Nelly Star** (☎ 222 4477; 84 Second Cross St; mains from Rs 180) is good value. At the former, diners bring their own booze (until the place gets licensed).

Getting There & Away

If travelling by private vehicle be aware that, at the time of writing, all vehicles required a permit from the Ministry of Defence/Vanni Security Forces Head Quarters to pass through the Medawachchiya checkpoint (in or out).

BUS

At the time of writing, the only way to Vavuniya was through a checkpoint set up north of Medawachchiya, 26km to the south. Once at the Medawachchiya bus stand, a bus (Rs 10) or three-wheeler (Rs 100) saw you to the checkpoint, from which there was regular service to Vavuniya (1½ hours, Rs 40). The Vavuniya CTB bus station is close to the clock tower. From Vavuniya, there were no buses headed further north, although irregular service could be had west to Mannar and east to Trincomalee.

TRAIN

Vavuniya is the northern railhead for the line from Colombo. One confirmed departure sets out to Colombo daily at 1.15pm ('semiexpress'; 9½ hours, Rs 600/330/185 in 1st/2nd/3rd class). Other departures – one in the morning and one late in the evening – should be confirmed locally; they may only run from the checkpoint town of Medawachchiya.

VAVUNIYA TO MANNAR

For the first time in a long time, the road to Mannar is no longer contested and could logically open for regular travel.

Murunkan (at the 60km post) is the only village between Vavuniya and Mannar with shops, a basic guest house and three-wheelers for hire.

Thirukketeeswaram Kovil

Between the 76km and 77km markers are a large military camp and a big, colourful gateway. ID checks are still required here to pass through the latter on a side road that leads 5km north to **Thirukketeeswaram Kovil**. Like Naguleswaram Kovil (p283), Thirukketeeswaram is one of the *pancha vishwaram*, the five historical Sri Lankan Hindu temples dedicated to Shiva and established to protect the island from natural disaster. It's an imposing site, with a towering, colourful *gopuram* that leads to relatively new structures. *Pujas* (offerings or prayers) occur at 5.30am, 8.05am, 12.30pm and 5.30pm, and are busiest on Fridays. Ranged around the temple are open-fronted pavilions containing five gigantic floats – called juggernauts – waiting to be wheeled out each February for the impressive Maha Sivarathiri festival.

Our Lady of Madhu Church

This **church** (5.30am-8.30pm) is Sri Lanka's most hallowed Christian shrine. Its walls shelter Our Lady of Madhu, a diminutive but revered Madonna-and-child statue brought here in 1670 by Catholics fleeing Protestant Dutch persecution in Mannar. The statue rapidly developed a reputation for miracles, notably as a protector against snakebites. Madhu has been a place of pilgrimage – and, in modern times, refuge – ever since. During the last round of fighting, the statue was removed from the church and taken further into LTTE territory, apparently to protect it from damage. It was reinstated in August 2008.

The present church dates from 1872 and has soaring, if unembellished, central columns apparently fashioned from hugely long tree trunks. Outside, the most striking feature is the elongated portico painted cream and duck-egg blue. The church's spacious grounds attract huge crowds of pilgrims (and superstitious non-Christians) to its 10 annual festivals, especially around 15 August.

VAVUNIYA TO JAFFNA ON THE A9

For a brief period during the ceasefire the A9 was the only permitted land route for tourists to cross **Tamil Eelam**, the LTTE-controlled Vanni region. This flat, savannah-like area was effectively another country, sometimes nicknamed Tigerland. Travellers stutter-stepped through a series of SLA and LTTE entry and exit checkpoints, complete with customs and 'immigration' for LTTE-controlled territory.

One highlight of the crossing was a stop at Murukandy's old and tiny **Ankaran Temple**. Locals considered a prayer here imperative to ensure a safe journey, so virtually all road transport stopped, including buses. The atmosphere was lively, with plenty of food stalls and truck drivers slapping holy ash on their vehicles as well as their brows.

Buses then passed without stopping through **Kilinochchi**, the only sizeable town en route and, at the time, the administrative capital of Tigerland. In 2007 and 2008, however, Tamil Eelam's capital suffered heavy damage and may not again be a liveable town for many years. It was recaptured by government forces in early 2009.

The final stretch of the journey followed the A9 north between saltpans and across the **Elephant Pass**, a 1km-long causeway that anchors the Jaffna peninsula to the rest of Sri Lanka. Its capture from the SLA in 2000 was considered the LTTE's most audacious and profound military victory. At the time of writing, control of the causeway had recently been regained by the SLA.

In early 2009 control of the causeway was regained by the SLA. Despite the government's best intentions (see p282), it will take time before the A9 is reopened and buses ply Vanni roads. At present there are few reliable independent reports of how badly the road and land (and, for that matter, Ankaran Temple) may have been pummelled. Whatever the case, when traffic does flow, it will be a whole new trip through once fiercely contested territory.

The church is 12km north of the Vavuniya–Mannar road. Turn at the 47km post, a lonely spot nicknamed Madhu Road. Until July 2008 this was 'LTTE country'. It's now under government control but, at the time of writing, not yet open to the public.

If the road has opened, ask in Medawachchiya or Mannar for direct public buses (two hours) or buses to and from Vavuniya that would allow you to get off at Murunkan or the Madhu Road junction, and then take a three-wheeler (Rs 800 return from Murunkan).

MANNAR
☎ 023

Mannar Island thrusts out into the Palk Strait as a narrow, dry, barren near-peninsula, home to a population of wild donkeys, lots of gulls and terns, and a now-disused international ferry port. Off the island's western end, Adam's Bridge is a chain of reefs, sandbanks and islets that nearly connects Sri Lanka to Rameswaram, India. In the Ramayana these were the stepping stones that the monkey king Hanuman used in his bid to help rescue Rama's wife Sita from Rawana, the demon king of Lanka.

Mannar Island has been hard hit by the hostilities of the last 25 years. Because of its location, it was a major exit and entry point to and from India, and became a key host of refugees. The island's large Muslim population was driven out by the LTTE in 1990, and some of the land is still mined. The rapid advances of the SLA against the LTTE in late 2008, including the former's control of all mainland areas abutting Mannar, is bound to begin a new chapter in Mannar's history.

The town of Mannar, the island's only large population centre, is also its gateway. Located at the southeastern extremity of the island, Mannar is at the end of a 3km-long causeway from the mainland. A Japan-sponsored project to widen the causeway and build a new railway bridge may sadly soften the Biblical quality of the crossing when the road is low in the water. SLA gains in the Vanni have not yet relaxed security in the area, but SLA checkpoints, including within residential areas of Mannar, should present no real problems.

There's not much here for tourists. The town welcomes you with a glimpse of its Portuguese–Dutch **star fortress** but, as a military camp, it's out of bounds. The one

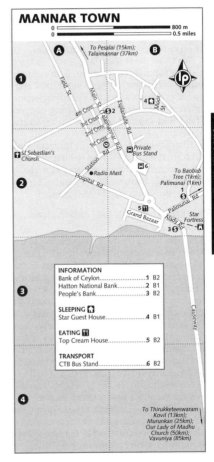

MANNAR TOWN

INFORMATION		
Bank of Ceylon	1	B2
Hatton National Bank	2	B1
People's Bank	3	B2
SLEEPING 🏠		
Star Guest House	4	B1
EATING 🍴		
Top Cream House	5	B2
TRANSPORT		
CTB Bus Stand	6	B2

offbeat attraction is a **baobab tree** (Palimunai Rd), 1.2km northeast of the Bank of Ceylon. Believed to have been planted in 1477 by Arab traders, it's shaped like a giant ball with a 19m circumference.

Mannar's **Bank of Ceylon** (Palimunai Rd) has an ATM that currently accepts only Sri Lankan bank cards, but **Hatton National Bank** (21 Main St) is good with international cards. The **People's Bank** (3 Alady Rd) is located at the causeway entrance to town (no ATM).

At present there is only one functioning lodge in Mannar. Others may reopen once the hostilities have ended, security controls are relaxed and traffic picks up. **Star Guest House** (☎ 222 2177; Moor St; s/tw with fan Rs 900/1100, with air-con Rs 1750/2000; ❄) has clean, if virtually windowless, air-con rooms that are the best option for sweaty Mannar. Some travellers have complained about conditions in the cheaper rooms, which share bathrooms.

Top Cream House (Grand Bazaar; meals from Rs 50), right at the main roundabout, is an ordinary eatery (watch out for flies), but it has a relatively extensive and high-quality selection of curries with fresh *rotti* or string hoppers (tangles of steamed noodles). Shrimp curry, shells and all, costs Rs 50.

The only bus operating from Mannar town's CTB bus stand at the time of writing was to the Medawachchiya checkpoint (Rs 100, irregular departures), 26km south of Vavuniya, for onward travel south (Rs 250 to Colombo).

JAFFNA
☎ 021 / pop 120,000

Low-rise Jaffna can be a welcome jolt to the senses after time spent elsewhere in Sri Lanka. More complex than the 'low-impact India' some have called it, it's a sprawling patchwork of easygoing, palm-shaded, colonial-era suburbs, wrapped around an animated compact commercial centre; both areas are at odds with the adjacent eerie emptiness of bombed-out former civic offices. More importantly, it's an intriguing, unimposing, friendly and utterly untouristed place that rewards time taken to find and adapt to the local rhythm. You'll appreciate Jaffna more for its insights into the people, the place and yourself than for any specific points of interest, especially in light of any routine restrictions on movement or all-too-common curfews, like the 9pm to 4am shutdowns in effect at the time of writing.

History
For centuries Jaffna (or Yarl) has been Sri Lanka's Hindu–Tamil cultural and religious centre, although the 17th-century Portuguese tried hard to change that. In 1620 they captured Jaffna's King Sangli (whose horseback statue stands on Point Pedro Rd), and then set about systematically demolishing the city's Hindu temples. A substantial wave of mass Christian conversions followed – hence all the beautiful churches. Many Hindu temples were not rebuilt until the mid-19th century.

Jaffna surrendered to the Dutch after a bitter three-month siege in 1658. Various Portuguese and Dutch fortifications from the time that followed remain dotted around the peninsula, but most are either ruined or still in military use (and thus inaccessible to tourists).

In 1795 the British took over, sowing the seeds of future interethnic unrest by 'favouring' the Jaffna Tamils (see p268).

Escalating tensions overwhelmed Jaffna in the early 1980s, and for two decades the city became a no-go war zone. Variously besieged by Tamil guerrillas, SLA troops and a so-called peacekeeping force, the city lost almost half of its population to emigration. In 1990 the LTTE ordered Jaffna's few remaining Sinhalese and all Muslim residents to leave, though around 3000 Muslims returned during the ceasefire years after 2002.

Resilient Jaffna nevertheless survived the endless bombings and a crippling blockade (kerosene once retailed here for 20 times the market price). In 1996 the SLA recaptured Jaffna and imposed military rule. Then in

JAFFNA

the sudden peace created by the 2002 accords, the sense of occupation was relaxed and Jaffna sprang back to life. A six-year ban on domestic flights was lifted, mobile-phone use proliferated, expatriated Sri Lankans returned, new businesses opened and building projects commenced.

All that came to a grinding halt in August 2006, when hostilities recommenced. Conditions have deteriorated since then, made no easier in December 2008 by Cyclone Nisha–prompted flooding, the worst in a generation.

Today Jaffna again feels 'occupied' – soldiers far outnumber civilians – but surprisingly calm and relaxed. Although the town has officially been held by the government since 1995, the LTTE has wielded considerable power (see boxed text, opposite), though this is likely to be eliminated in light of the events of early 2009.

Orientation

Commercial activity is crammed into the colourful hurly-burly of Hospital, Kasturiya and Kankesanturai (KKS) Rds. Their fascinating but functional ugliness – a riot of crumbling concrete architecture – is enhanced by humidity stains and occasional shell holes. Southeast of the fort is an area of war-torn building cadavers: shattered, empty and sorrowfully photogenic. Most guest houses are a world away in the delightfully leafy Nallur and Chundukuli residential areas, notably around Kandy Rd. If you can get your hands on wheels, Jaffna makes for fascinating bicycle rides, especially since distances and temperatures are often too great for long walks.

Jaffna's addresses have 'old' or 'new' street numbers that can create an apparently nonconsecutive jumble. This guide uses the most visible numbers – those used by local proprietors.

Information

INTERNET ACCESS

At the time of research there was no reliable public internet access in Jaffna. If conditions improve, only two places are likely to provide trustworthy connections:

Jaffna Public Library (☎ 222 7835; Esplanade Rd; per hr Rs 30; ☽ 9am-7pm) Head up the library's stairs, then turn right to the back beyond the reference and self-study sections.

Theresa Communications (☎ 222 2597; 72A Racca Rd) This guest house's communications hut has a connection from time to time.

MONEY

All of the following banks have ATMs:
Bank of Ceylon (52 Stanley Rd)
Commercial Bank (Hospital Rd)
HNB (Hospital Rd)
Seylan Bank (Hospital Rd)

POST

Post office (Postal Complex, KKS Rd; ☽ 7am-6pm Mon-Fri, 7am-1pm Sat)

Sights

NALLUR KANDASWAMY KOVIL

Approximately 2km northeast of the centre, the **Nallur Kandaswamy Kovil** (Temple Rd; donation appropriate; ☽ 4.30am-6pm) is the most impressive religious building in Jaffna and one of the most significant Hindu temple complexes in Sri Lanka. Its sacred deity, Murugan (or Skanda), is central to temple activity, especially during the punctual, cacophonic *pujas* (5am, 10am, noon, 4pm and 5pm), when offerings are made to his brass-framed image and other Hindu deities like Ganesh, Murugan's elephant-headed brother, in shrines surrounding the inner sanctum.

The *kovil's* 15th-century structure fell victim to Portuguese destructive ruthlessness in the 17th century; the current one dates from 1734. Its beautifully maintained large and airy space shelters decorative brasswork, larger-than-life murals, pillared halls and a colonnaded, stepped holy pool, all dominated by the golden-ochre, god-encrusted *gopuram* peering down one length of Point Pedro Rd. Visitors must remove their shoes; men need to remove their shirts as well.

The temple is the focus of an enormous and spectacular Hindu festival over 25 days in July/August, which climaxes on day 24 with parades of juggernaut floats and gruesome displays of self-mutilation by entranced devotees.

OTHER PLACES OF WORSHIP

Jaffna's countless other **Hindu temples** range from tiny shrines to sprawling complexes featuring *mandapaya* (raised platforms with decorated pillars), ornate ponds and towering *gopuram*. Most are easily identified by vertical red-and-white-striped walls.

The city's abundance of **churches** isn't a reflection of its legions of Christian parishioners, now somewhat reduced from their 12% of the prewar population. Touring the many fine Catholic and Protestant structures is nevertheless an interesting excuse for discovering lush backstreets and quietly comfortable colonial-era homes. The grandest church is **St James'** (Main St), a classical Italianate edifice. From Hospital Rd, **Our Lady of Refuge Church** looks like a whitewashed version of a Gloucestershire village church. Built along classical lines, **St Mary's Cathedral** (Cathedral Rd) is astonishingly large, but it's curious to see corrugated-iron roofing held up by such a masterpiece of wooden vaulting.

For Buddhists there's the solitary **Sri Nagavihara International Buddhist Centre** (Stanley Rd), quickly rebuilt after government forces retook Jaffna in 1995. The **Jummah Mosque** (Jummah Mosque Lane) is quirkily colourful.

JAFFNA FORT
On a map the polygonal Dutch fort is a powerful presence. In reality, however, its walls are virtually invisible, hidden beneath overgrown slopes and covered with signs warning about mines. The original structure was built in 1680 over an earlier Portuguese original, though the defensive triangles were added in 1792 to produce the classic Vaubanesque star form. It is perhaps the best Dutch fort in Asia.

The fort has withstood much fighting. In 1990 the LTTE – at the time in control of the rest of Jaffna – finally forced out government forces after a grisly 107-day siege. It remains a military garrison, now back in the hands of the SLA. Civilian access to the fort is prohibited.

WAR RUINS
East of the fort sprawls the heartbreaking wreckage of Jaffna's former government district. Bankshall St, western Main St and the numbered Cross streets between them are particularly moving. Ruined structures, like the **former kachcheri** (administrative office), are pockmarked by bullets and shrapnel, moss-encrusted and slowly folding in on themselves.

Some of Jaffna's best hotels once boasted unobstructed lagoon views. These have now succumbed to bombs, military occupation or both, and the lagoon is off-limits. To reach their boats, fishermen have for years routinely filed through a security-checked access point on Beach Rd, west of Third Cross St.

The owner of the Yarl Beach Inn (p280), though caught behind army lines at the time of research, has a fascinating photo album and plenty of stories to tell about the last few decades in Jaffna.

WHO CONTROLS JAFFNA? *Mark Elliott*

A week before the November 2005 presidential election, I interviewed dozens of local Tamils. All told me excitedly that they planned to vote for the opposition 'peace' candidate, Ranil Wickremasinghe. One strong LTTE sympathiser had travelled from Colombo to Jaffna specifically to vote. An almost 100% vote for Wickremasinghe seemed assured among Jaffna district's 400,000-plus electorate.

Then came the bombshell.

The LTTE had originally been noncommittal about the 'irrelevant' election. But a few days before polling day, its line hardened. A boycott was announced. Ominous little fliers announced 'unfortunate repercussions' for Tamils who dared to vote. Suddenly my pro-Wickremasinghe Tamil friends claimed they had 'no interest' in the election!

On polling day an army of international observers sat around to check that voting was free and fair. But Jaffna was utterly silent. Voter turnout was a record-low 0.014%; virtually everyone stayed home praying for Wickremasinghe's victory rather than making it happen. He lost by around 180,000 – entirely because of the boycott.

Why would the LTTE want to hand victory to its most vociferous opponent? Many suspected it was because the election's victor, Mahinda Rajapaksa, would provide the LTTE with an excuse to restart the war, something that did occur soon after he took power. The string of military victories claimed by the SLA in early 2009, however, does make one wonder if this was the best tactic.

Whatever the reality, the election showed all too graphically just who at the time held the real power in Jaffna.

WHO'S WHO IN THE TAMIL STRUGGLE

■ **Vellupillai Prabhakaran** Unquestioned LTTE leader known for his extraordinary ruthlessness and single-minded strength of purpose. *Inside an Elusive Mind*, by MR Narayan Swamy, is an insightful and very readable unofficial biography. His death was reported during the final days of the civil war.

■ **Anton Balasingham** The LTTE's eloquent British-Tamil spokesperson and ideologist passed away in 2006. His various books are available through www.eelamstore.com.

■ **Vinayagamoorthi Muralitharan Karuna** Former LTTE East Coast commander who split from the Tigers in March 2004, setting off a bloody internal rift. In October 2008, over many objections, he was appointed a member of parliament with support from the majority party. In March 2009, he was appointed as Minister of National Integration and Reconciliation.

■ **Rasaiah Parthipan Thileepan** Hallowed LTTE icon, usually depicted wearing glasses and slouched on a chair during his fatal high-profile public hunger strike (see below).

■ **Douglas Devananda** Leader of the Tamil Eelam People's Democratic Party. As a cabinet minister he's considered a 'collaborator' by the LTTE, who have reportedly made more than 10 attempts to assassinate him, the latest one on 28 November 2007 by a female Tamil Tiger suicide bomber, who blew herself up in his office. He escaped unhurt, but his personal secretary died.

JAFFNA ARCHAEOLOGICAL MUSEUM

This unkempt but interesting **museum** (Nawalar Rd; admission by donation; ☯ 8.30am-5pm Wed-Mon) is hidden away at the end of a messy garden behind a cubic concrete events hall that looks rather like a masonic lodge. Asking for directions may elicit odd responses since most locals don't think of or refer to it as a museum. At the door are a rusty pair of Dutch cannons from the fort and a set of whale bones. Inside, the most interesting items are 11th-century Buddha torsos found at Kantarodai (p282), a poorly conserved life-sized portrait of Queen Victoria and the 1845 palanquin of Point Pedro's *mudiyalar* (district governor). He must have been very small.

LTTE SITES

LTTE martyrs are recognised in numerous Jaffna-area memorials, one common motif of which is a helmet on an upturned gun. Most were damaged, desecrated or destroyed in 1995, when Jaffna was retaken by the SLA, but after 2002 many were patched up or rebuilt.

Perhaps the most sobering is the **Mavira Thuyilim Illam** (Martyrs' Sleeping House) at Kopay, just beyond the city's northeastern limits. Around 2000 grave markers in neat rows commemorate Tiger cadres killed in action; the majority (the smaller memorials) are for Tigers whose bodies have not been retrieved. The movingly understated box of older tombstone shards commemorates the 1995 SLA bulldozing of the original graveyard.

The monolithic **Thileepan Memorial**, which was reportedly partly destroyed in 2006, celebrates the LTTE's former political officer, Rasaiah Parthipan Thileepan. Seeking concessions from the IPKF in 1987, Thileepan went on a very public hunger strike and died on a plinth facing the Nallur Kandaswamy Kovil (p276). The original memorial's design (hands with broken chains grasping a flame) is repeated in other parts of town, including the **Martyr's Monolith** (Beach Rd), which remembers 31 locals killed by the military in 1986. The nearby **statue** of a grinning Ray Charles looka-like represents MGR (MG Ramachandran), a famous Indian–Tamil actor-turned-politician who became an important backer of Tamil rebels between 1983 and 1987. His two-finger V sign symbolises his offer of two crore (200 million) Indian rupees (around US$4 million) to the LTTE. At the time, the Tiger leaders thought he'd meant two lakhs (US$40,000). They sure got a happy surprise.

JAFFNA PUBLIC LIBRARY & AROUND

Symbolically, one of the first major public buildings to be rebuilt after the 2002 ceasefire was the **Jaffna Public Library** (Esplanade Rd; ☯ 9am-7pm). Architects kept true to the original neo-Mughal design and books were donated from around the world. The earlier library (inaugurated 1841) had been lost in a fiery blaze set by pro-government mobs after the violent Jaffna District Council elections of July 1981. Few acts were more significant in the build-up to full-scale civil war. The world-renowned collection had included more than 90,000 volumes, including irreplaceable Tamil documents such as the one surviving copy of *Yalpanam Vaipavama*, a history of Jaffna.

The strange, top-heavy pillar erected nearby is the **SJV Chelvanayakum Monument** (KKS Rd), celebrating the founder of the Tamil Federal Party. His somewhat Gandhi-esque statue stands beside the monument.

Another nearby architectural curiosity is the spindly **clock tower** (Vembadi St), whose Moorish domed top makes it look like it belongs somewhere in North Africa.

Sleeping

The closure of the A9 highway and renewed hostilities hit Jaffna's small guest houses hard. Some shut permanently, while others, still operational, receive no drop-in visitors. Calling ahead is essential so that preparations can be made and long-idle rooms readied. At the time of research, most visitors (principally NGO workers and non-Jaffna-based Sri Lankans) stuck to just a few choice lodges. The most popular were the Bastian Hotel, Thinakkural

Rest and NGO favourite GTZ Guesthouse. The greatest concentrations of guest houses, all desperate for guests, are in the leafy Chundukuli and Nallur districts. Most guest houses are adapted from local homes rather than being purpose-built buildings.

BUDGET

YMCA (☎ 222 2499; 109 Kandy Rd; s/tw Rs 250/400) The rooms are plain but share indoor and frequently mopped toilets and showers. Some rooms have private facilities for Rs 100 extra. It's often full.

Holiday Resort (☎ 222 5643; St John's Lane; tw with fan/air-con Rs 500/1750; 🔀) This four-room getaway is in a quiet garden of chirruping caged birds. The basic rooms share bathrooms and are cheap but well looked after. High ceilings in the two air-con rooms make the extra expense seem wasted. Food is available by advance order.

Bastian Hotel (☎ 222 2605; 37 Kandy Rd; d/q/ste Rs 825/1650/6000) The basic, presently clean fan rooms share slightly grubby bathrooms. There are no mosquito nets. Much better rooms are available in the associated New Bastian Hotel (p280).

'BURNING MEMORIES'

The following is an extract from http://guruchetra.blogspot.com, written anonymously by a young blogger from Jaffna:

'I was born four years after the library was burnt in 1981 and I very well remember the blackened library that stood in front of the Jaffna Central College until efforts to refurbish it started taking place after CBK [then-president Chandrika Bandaranaike Kumaratunga] came.

I was back home in Jaffna last June and I went to the Public Library twice when I was there. I like the spacious library a lot… It now does not have a lot of books. A few thousand possibly…

The significance of the Jaffna Public Library burning is to be understood by the weight that the Jaffna people attach to education. As has been widely commented on, education was one of the key areas that the peninsula's economic base rested on. I use the word 'was'… Jaffna no more enjoys a pride of place as an educationally advanced district… The decline of standards in education in Jaffna is a direct resultant of the war and the burning of the library symbolically kick-started the decline.

There is a statue of Goddess Saraswathi that is still found at the entrance to the library. She is regarded as the Goddess of Education in Hindu religious belief. Users of the library have to remove footwear before entering the library. This might be possibly to keep the floor, which is white tiled, clean. But I can't help thinking that it is also in a sense a show of respect to the place.

I also remember the politics behind the effort to refurbish and restore the Public Library. I identify with those who stood for the burnt library to stand as a memory of a part of history that should not be forgotten. That never happened. They could have constructed a new one if they wanted. CBK was adamant and wanted to force this act of benevolence down the Tamil people's throat while she was waging a war for peace. I also recall the debates about the act of opening the refurbished library. I agree with those who felt that there should be no opening ceremony as such. I couldn't appreciate any extravagance associated with opening the library to public use again… The library was later opened for public use without anybody opening it.'

Yarl Beach Inn (☎ 222 5490; 8 Old Park Rd; s/tw/tr with fan Rs 500/900/1200, with air-con Rs 1250/2000/3000; 🔁) The Yarl bravely struggles on, despite losing its key assets – the nearby beach (under military occupation) and a Dutch-era mansion (to 1990 bombings). In fact, at the time of research the whole inn was caught behind an impassable checkpoint, so specific updates were impossible. At our last visit, rooms had attached bathrooms and were shipshape, if ageing. Great seafood dinners may still be available if preordered. Fan rooms were great value last time we checked for single travellers, and the owner can spin many a heart-rending yarn.

New Rest House (☎ 222 7839; 19 Somasutharam Rd; tw & tr Rs 1000) Tidy, good-value rooms with slightly tatty attached bathrooms in a house-restaurant with great food (breakfast Rs 150, meals Rs 200 to 300).

Cosy Hotel (☎ 222 5899; 15 Sirampiyadi Lane; r with fan/air-con Rs 1000/1500) The restaurant (opposite) is better than the hotel, which has functional, albeit musty rooms.

Thinakkural Rest (☎ 222 6476; 45 Chetty Street Lane; tw with fan/air-con Rs 1100/2200; 🔁) The big, well-kept rooms have OK private bathrooms; a desk and wardrobe are the only adornments. The fan rooms are a little musty but otherwise decent value. The attached bar is totally without character; you'd do better to retreat to the hotel's pleasant upstairs terrace.

Theresa Inn (Do Drop Inn; ☎ 071 856 5375; calistus joseph89@gmail.com; 72A Racca Rd; s/tr incl breakfast Rs 750/1250; 🔁 🔲) If you want a homestay experience, Theresa Inn's three rooms offer a great opportunity to lodge with a local family. The two singles share a bathroom. All have optional air-con for Rs 750 extra if used. Joseph speaks English, two free bicycles are available and the communications hut out front means that, if service is operational, you can get internet access on the spot. Meals can be arranged.

MIDRANGE

GTZ Guesthouse (☎ 222 2203; 114A Temple Rd; tw Rs 2000) The neat twin rooms here share big, bright bathrooms, set between pairs of rooms. There's a pleasant lounge, a library of books in German and an eye-opening map of the Jaffna district's many minefields.

Sarras Guest House (☎ 222 3627, 077 717 2039; 20 Somasutharam Rd; s Rs 1250-1750, tw/tr Rs 2000/2500; 🔁) This thick-walled old colonial mansion has been tastefully developed as a comfortable and sensibly priced guest house. Each of the four rooms is unique. The top-floor suite is fabulous, as is the upstairs single, which has three sides of windows, polished old floorboards and art-deco furniture. All have private bathrooms with hot water, and towels are provided. Booking ahead is advised, either directly or through Theresa Inn (left).

Old Park Restaurant (☎ 222 3790; 40 Kandy Rd; tw Rs 2500; 🔁) The at-home ambience of the restaurant (opposite) extends to Old Park's comfortable air-con guestrooms.

Pillaiyar Inn (☎ 222 2829; pIyarinn@sltnet.lk; 31 Manipay Rd; s/d/ste from Rs 1700/2500/5000; 🔲) With better upkeep this breezy three-storey place could be a top choice. Some slightly older rooms in the annexe are downright uninviting. On the plus side, the central location on a quiet garden is great. The food, too, is excellent if you live long enough for it to be served. Unreliable internet access is available.

Jaffna City Hotel (☎ 222 5969; tilkoholidays@yahoo .com; 70/6 KKS Rd; s/tw Rs 2000/2500; 🔁) The city centre's best option is set in a lovely large garden, complete with a silly dolphin fountain. The eight rooms are appealingly smart, except for the discordantly tatty desks. All have hot water. Construction of a 26-room new wing has been stalled since fighting began anew. Breakfast/lunch/dinner packages are available for Rs 250/400/350.

New Bastian Hotel (☎ 222 7374; 11 Kandy Rd; s Rs 2200, d Rs 2750-3300, tr Rs 3850; 🔁) Entered from beneath a vine trellis, this appealing pad has leather sofas in the communal sitting room. Rooms are outwardly modern with TV, though not all of the bathrooms have hot water and some walls show signs of premature ageing.

Morgan's Guest House (Maria's, UN Guesthouse; ☎ 222 3666; 103 Temple Rd; tw Rs 3000; 🔁) Art, chests, stylish mirrors and real lampshades give this four-room place far more character than any standard guest house. The best room has hot water and a lovely mosquito-shaded sitting area/veranda. The building is totally unmarked except for '103' (old number) on the red postbox.

Eating

Jaffna is a good place to try South Indian–style cuisine. Red-hued *pittu* (a mixture of rice flour and coconut, steamed in bamboo moulds), *idiyappam* (string hoppers, or steamed rice noodles curled into a pancake of flat spirals) and *vadai* (a tasty fried snack made of ground lentils and spices) are local favourites. Many guest houses will provide food if you ask in advance. The Pillaiyar Inn and New Rest House are particularly good, and keep some food in stock.

Thanj Hotel (Main St; �),5am-9.30pm) Basic, friendly place for fresh hoppers (bowl-shaped pancakes) in the evening.

Hotel Rolex (☎ 222 2808; 340 Hospital Rd; meals from Rs 100) This is a bustling local eatery with a good range of food choices.

Malayan Café (36-38 Grand Bazaar; meals from Rs 90) This downmarket but popular and wonderfully olde-worlde eatery has marble-topped tables, long glass-and-wood cabinets and occasional blasts of incense to bless the in-house shrine. The cheap vegetarian fare is served on banana leaves and eaten by hand. When you're finished, fold up the leaf and post it through the letterbox-shaped waste chute in the hand-washing area.

Old Park Restaurant (☎ 222 3790; 40 Kandy Rd; meals Rs 160-600) Although it's a bit like eating in someone's front room, the Old Park offers some of Jaffna's tastiest cuisine and is paradise for garlic lovers. Its small garden is pleasant for a cold beer.

Sri Palm Beach (☎ 077 132 8432; 205 Kasturiya Rd; mains Rs 180-350; �),11.30am-10pm; 🛜) The menu of this comfortably air-conditioned upstairs place is wide and reliable. It serves very good fried chicken '65', as well as masala dosas (paper-thin rice- and lentil-flour pancakes) after 6.30pm.

Cosy Restaurant (☎ 222 5899; Cosy Hotel, 15 Sirampiyadi Lane; mains Rs 300-1900; 🛜) Along with its attractively lantern-lit dining terrace, sheltered by *cadjan* (coconut-frond matting), the great attraction here is the tandoori oven, with which the chef produces excellent fresh naan (flat breads), as well as succulent chicken tikka (chicken marinated in spices and dry roasted); arrive early, as supplies are limited. There's a long menu of alternatives.

For a typical Jaffna treat, head to the trio of popular ice-cream parlours behind the Nallur Kandaswamy Kovil. **Rio Ice Cream** (448A Point Pedro Rd; sundaes Rs 150; �),9am-10pm) is the biggest and brightest.

Food City (175 KKS Rd; �),8.30am-8.30pm) is central Jaffna's most Western-style supermarket; **TCT Supermarket** (☎ 222 8025; 527 Nawalar Rd; �),7am-10pm) is a perfectly reasonable food-shopping option.

Drinking

Morgan's Guest House (☎ 222 3666; 103 Temple Rd; drinks Rs 200; �),6-11pm) The garden bar of this unsigned but characterful guest house is the unchallenged meeting place for NGO types.

Pleasant alternatives include Old Park Restaurant (left) and the garden of the Jaffna City Hotel (opposite).

Shopping

Rosarian Convent (☎ 222 3388; 333 Main St; �),8am-1pm & 2-5.30pm) The convent makes Rosetto 'wine' (Rs 250 per bottle, takeaway only). Sweet and laced with cinnamon and cloves, it tastes like German *gluhwein*. There's startlingly coloured grape 'juice' (Rs 125) and 'nelli crush' (Rs 175), both nonalcoholic, flavourful fruit cordials supposedly with laxative properties. Add water.

Getting There & Away

AIR

After a temporary halt due to security concerns, in September 2006 Expo Aviation and AeroLanka resumed Jaffna air service to and from Colombo's Ratmalana Air Force Base (one way/return Rs 11,000/21,000, 75 minutes). At the time of writing, however, AeroLanka service was again suspended and unlikely to recommence. Flights depart from Jaffna daily in the morning, though schedules are very likely to change as conditions evolve.

Jaffna's Palali Airport is 17km north of town, deep within a high-security military zone. Until new conditions prevail, airfare includes an obligatory shuttle bus (the only way into the zone) that departs from an unlikely looking tin-roofed **shelter** (Hospital Rd) at the Sinhala Maha Vidyalaya next to Our Lady of Refuge Church. You need to be present three hours before flight departure time for identity and security checks. Bring your own refreshments. Coming from Palali, the shuttle drops arriving passengers on Clock Tower Rd.

AeroLanka and Expo Aviation offices:

AeroLanka (www.aerolanka.aero) Jaffna (☎ 222 6242; 243 Nawalar Rd); Colombo (Map p88; ☎ 011-250 5632; 500 Galle Rd)

Expo Aviation (www.expoavi.com) Jaffna (☎ 222 3891; 1E Stanley Rd); Colombo (Map pp84-5; ☎ 011-236 0290/1; 296A/1 Galle Rd)

Several agencies in Jaffna sell air tickets. Try **Manoj Express** (☎ 222 3916, 077 780 1038; 32 Clock Tower Rd; �),8am-6.30pm) and **Thampi Travels** (☎ 222 2040; Kandappasegaram Lane; �),8.30am-6pm).

BUS

An extensive CTB network covers the Jaffna peninsula, all routes duplicated by numbered private minibuses that leave from a stand behind the bus station. Around the peninsula, no bus trip should cost more than Rs 30. CTB services run on a schedule from about 6.30am to 7pm; private buses depart when there are enough passengers. Some services are infrequent; check return times before you head out.

Useful, frequent services include bus 750 to Point Pedro via Nelliady, bus 751 to Point Pedro via Valvettiturai (VVT) and the northbound bus 769 to Thurkhai Amman Kovil via Chunnakam (for the Kantarodai Ruins).

Prior to the closure of the A9 highway in 2006, local buses and direct air-con transport trundled south across the LTTE-controlled Vanni region to Colombo (12 hours). Direct services left Jaffna early in the morning, with returns from Colombo at around 10pm.

At the time of writing, with the A9 under government control for the first time in 23 years, the Transport Ministry had announced plans for five return intercity bus journeys per day between Colombo and Jaffna. They're slated to begin as soon as reconstruction work on the A9 is completed, although no timeline has been given. In the meantime, Vavuniya will serve as the hub for bus services throughout the North.

Whatever happens, with the North in government hands, the trip across the Vanni should no longer require multiple local bus connections or the security checks once enforced by both the SLA and the LTTE (see boxed text, p272).

Until 2006, agencies handling direct air-con bus tickets to Colombo included **SNJ Travels** (☎ 222 2837; Hotel Rolex, 340 Hospital Rd). When government bus traffic on the A9 has recommenced, parallel private service shouldn't be far behind. Ask again at SNJ Travels on Hospital Rd. In Colombo inquire at travel agencies on Galle Rd in Wellawatta about bus tickets to Jaffna.

TAXI

A convenient and relatively good-value way to visit the Jaffna peninsula is to rent a van or taxi. Capable drivers with reliable vehicles cost about the same whether you go through a guest house or hire one off the street. Relying on a guest-house owner's inside contacts means you could even get a driver who speaks a modicum of English. Costs range between Rs 3000 and 4500 per day for up to 100km. Add Rs 30 to 40 per kilometre for extra mileage. Around 130km covers virtually every 'sight' on the peninsula except the offshore islands.

Getting Around

From the guest-house clusters in the Chundukuli and Nallur districts, all buses (Rs 5) and minibuses (Rs 7) bound west and southwest on Kandy Rd and Point Pedro Rd, respectively, terminate at the central bus station. To head out of town, take the frequent eastbound bus 769 for Chundukuli or bus 750 for Nallur via Point Pedro Rd.

You never have to seek long for a three-wheeler or wonderfully antiquated taxis, especially around Hospital Rd. Three-wheelers cost Rs 60 for short trips, Rs 120 to Nallur or Rs 330 per hour to putt-putt around town. A bicycle is more pleasant, and several guest houses will lend or help you find one.

JAFFNA PENINSULA

The visual and olfactory impact is astonishing. Once you get beyond Jaffna's already rustic outer boroughs, you're plunged into a green labyrinth of bananas, palmyra palms, cassava plantations and even little plots of grapevines. Despite decades of instability, most of the dry-land parts of the Jaffna peninsula have been intensively cultivated. And what hasn't been subject to the buffalo-pulled plough is probably a Hindu holy spot, sacred well, LTTE memorial or SLA security zone. Add to the mix a healthy amount of lagoon or wetland and you've got the ingredients for an interesting day trip or two, especially if you hire your own transport. However, few of the sights are individually especially memorable and, for the time being, almost all decent beaches remain out of reach behind High Security Zone fences.

Towards Kankesanturai (KKS)

The port of KKS and its once-famous Palm Beach are presently totally out of bounds to all but military personnel. There are, however, a few places to see en route. At the Chunnakam bus stand grab a three-wheeler for the 3km squiggle of lanes leading west to the puzzling **Kantarodai Ruins** (Purana Rajamaha Vihara). Discovered in 1916 in a palmyra patch the

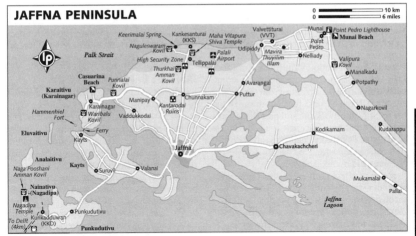

JAFFNA PENINSULA

size of a modest garden, some two-dozen pudding-shaped little dagobas, 1m to 2m in height, grow like mushrooms. The ruined foundations of many more are easy to make out. It's hardly a mind-blowing vista, and the dagobas are somewhat crudely patched up, but they're probably 2000 years old and nobody really knows why they were built.

Beside the KKS road at the 13km marker, in the 'new' village of Tellippalai, the vast **Thurkhai Amman Kovil** is set behind a fairly deep, stepped pool. The temple celebrates the goddess Durga and draws relatively large crowds of women on Tuesdays. *Puja* occurs at 7am, 11am, 4pm and 6pm.

At the time of research, Tellippalai was as far as public transport went (northbound bus 769, Rs 20 from Jaffna). A kilometre further north lies the **Palali KKS Military Camp**, one of Sri Lanka's largest and perhaps most controversial High Security Zones. Between 1983 and 1993, the entire population (more than 25,000 families) was evicted from 58.5 sq km of prime agricultural land. Everything within the zone was either destroyed or converted for military use. However, unexpectedly, as of early 2009, moves were underway to prepare the zone for resettlement, including the 'old' village of Tellippalai.

Perhaps changes afoot will also mean that access is eased to the sacred **Keerimalai spring**. Alas, despite waves crashing melodramatically over razor wire behind, the site is about as photogenic as a neglected swimming pool. Nonetheless, the trip to get there is one of Sri Lanka's more surreal experiences. Although the rules are now likely to change, previously, if you had your own transportation, you could make the trip in after a security search, surrender of all phones, cameras and passports to the duty officer, and space made for a soldier-escort to the springs. He stopped you from exploring the wreckage en route, but you got a good view of abandoned **Tellippalai** just by driving through. Bored military patrols shuffled about the otherwise deserted roads; it felt like a very real war-movie set.

The turn-off for the Keerimalai spring from the KKS road is next to the greying *gopuram* of the **Maha Vitapura Shiva Temple**. Just before the spring is the **Naguleswaram Kovil**, one of the *pancha vishwaram* (see p272). Only traces of the original 6th-century-BC buildings have survived. This temple was bombed by the army in 1990 and has reportedly been undergoing repairs.

Towards Point Pedro

About 26km northeast of Jaffna, in front of the school in Nelliady, is a gilded **statue of 'Captain Miller'** (MMV Rd), nom de guerre of the first Black Tiger (LTTE suicide bomber). On 5 July 1987 he drove an explosives-laden truck into the school, which was then being used as an army camp. Hero or villain, he died taking at least 200 SLA soldiers with him. The statue and some overgrown shattered ruins are 450m north of the Point Pedro road junction, where bus 750 stops.

Ramshackle **Point Pedro** is the Jaffna peninsula's second town, and has a few very faint hints of colonial style. The harbour is off-limits within a military zone, but 1km east, more attractive **Munai** remains accessible. From Point Pedro bus station walk 100m south and then east, crossing through a curious stone **tollgate** that locals claim dates from the Dutch era. Some 250m beyond, turn left towards the sea up St Anthony's Lane and past the town's two finest **churches**. The coast road continues 1km east to **Point Pedro Lighthouse** (officially no photos), beyond which the fishermen's beach becomes wider and sandier.

Military checkpoints around here have shifted with the tides, but if you can get through, the nicest area of sandbar is nearly 2km further on, as are some attractive views southeast towards a lagoon area. However, the army presence hardly makes this a relaxing place to unroll your bathing towel.

Even further southeast is the much-revered **Valipura Kovil**, 5km from central Point Pedro. It's famous for the boisterous water-cutting festival (devotees are sprayed in holy water) it revived in October 2004, attracting around 75,000 pilgrims.

Valvettiturai

On the peninsula's north coast, unassuming Valvettiturai (VVT), once a rich smuggling town, is now most famous as the birthplace of the LTTE supreme leader Vellupillai Prabhakaran. The green-walled **Prabhakaran family house** (Vampady Lane) was damaged by security forces in 1985, in an attack that also killed 70 VVT citizens and reportedly instigated the infamous Anuradhapura killings as reprisal. The house has long since been abandoned. Nonetheless, somewhat in the style of Jim Morrison's grave, the ruins continue to attract a trickle of curious gawkers. There's graffiti in Tamil, Sinhalese and English, and, from time to time, a painted sign describing Prabhakaran as the 'President of Tamil Eelam'.

From the bus stop in central VVT, walk west for about 400m, passing the sizeable **Amman Kovil** with its fine *gopuram*. Continue 200m to the first asphalted lane on the left. There's a seat around a tree in the middle. Prabhakaran's house is the first on the left up this lane.

Around 8km southeast of VVT, halfway to Nelliady by a circuitous back lane, is the Samurabahe **Mavira Thuyilim Illam**, another graveyard for LTTE cadres. Similar to the more accessible version at Kopay (p278), it feels somewhat less stark given the attractive backing of palmyra palms and manicured gardens.

JAFFNA'S OFFSHORE ISLANDS

Southwest of the Jaffna peninsula is a clutch of low-lying islands, some attached to one another and the mainland by causeways. The main pleasure in exploring here is not any specific sight, but the hypnotic quality of the waterscapes and the escapist feeling of boat rides to end-of-earth removes.

Realistically, during stable times, there have been two day-trip possibilities. One is to loop around through Karaitivu (Karainagar), ferry-hop to Kayts and return via the causeway. The second and generally more agreeable option is an out-and-back excursion to windswept Delft (Nadantivu) or sacred Nainativu (Nagadipa) via the causeways to Kurikadduwan (KKD) and then a ferry.

The LTTE was once active on these waters and unpopulated islands. As a consequence, the Sri Lankan navy presence has been strong, and ferry service and causeway access are not always guaranteed. At the time of research, island outings were restricted and no one could reliably say when boats were sailing or even how much they cost. It's very likely that many services are now already returning to 'normal'.

Karaitivu & Kayts

The principal reason for visiting Karaitivu (Karainagar) is the approach across the long, water-skimming **causeway**, with its views of the fascinating maze of fish traps. Look right at the start of the causeway to spy the towering *gopuram* of **Punnalai Kovil** through the palms. Karaitivu's popular-with-locals Casuarina Beach, 3km off the main road, is litter-strewn and a disappointment to many, but still the only easy-to-reach beach in the 'hood.

The roughly three buses per hour (bus 782 and bus 785) from Jaffna to **Karainagar town** (Rs 25, one hour) do not service the ferry to Kayts. For that, once across the causeway, hop off the bus as soon as you see a three-wheeler and charter it for the 6km ride to the tiny jetty. It's within a small naval zone, where you're at the mercy of their rules. In good times, there's a security check before boarding the wire-pulled ferry (Rs 5, seven minutes, eight daily).

You'll need to wade through knee-deep water on sharp stones, so waterproof sandals would be useful. Ferry access is currently limited to pedestrians and bicycles.

The traverse terminates at eerie, semideserted **Kayts town** between a dozen scuttled fishing boats. Two somewhat noteworthy churches are visible by walking straight up Sunuvil Rd from the jetty. A little beyond the second one, the first asphalt lane to the right leads 600m to a waterfront cemetery with views of offshore **Hammenhiel Fort**, built by the Dutch and now a navy camp.

Minibuses leave for Jaffna from Kayts town, with the last departure around 5.30pm.

Nainativu & Delft

A long, delightful **causeway** links Kayts to the island of Punkudutivu. Observe lagoon fishermen who use wade-out traps and sail little wind-powered canoes. **Punkudutivu village**, the scene of minor riots in December 2005, has one of Jaffna's most screechingly colourful Hindu temples. Many old houses lie in various stages of decay. A smaller causeway links the island to the curiously isolated little ferry port at **Kurikadduwan (KKD)**, where there's a pair of desultory drink stands but no village. From here you've a choice of destinations. The boat to Delft leaves at 10am, returning at 3pm (Rs 50, one hour), but is prone to cancellations. Boats to Nainativu (Rs 15, 17 minutes) are vastly more frequent, with sailings every half-hour from 8am to noon and hourly from 12.30pm to 5.30pm. Often unmarked, Jaffna–KKD minibuses (Rs 35, 1½ hours) depart approximately hourly; the last return is around 5pm.

NAINATIVU (NAGADIPA)

Known as Nainativu in Tamil and Nagadipa in Sinhalese, this 6km-long lozenge of palmyra groves is holy to both Buddhist and Hindu pilgrims.

Right in front of you as you step off the jetty is the **Naga Pooshani Amman Kovil** complex, an airy Hindu temple set amid mature neem trees. The main temple deity is the *naga* goddess Meenakshi, a consort of Shiva. (The term *naga* refers variously to serpent deity figures and to the ancient inhabitants of the island.) Women wishing to conceive come here seeking blessings, delivered during the trance-inducing midday *puja*. Male devotees must remove shirts and shoes before entering. An impressive 18-day festival is usually held in early June.

Walk 10 minutes south along the coast road (ID check en route) to find the **Nagadipa temple**, the North's only major Buddhist pilgrimage site. The Buddha is said to have come here to prevent war between a *naga* king and his nephew over ownership of a gem-studded throne. The solution: give it to the temple instead. The precious chair and original temple disappeared long ago, but today there is an attractive silver-painted dagoba. Just behind, three happy-looking Buddhas sit in a domed temple.

DELFT

The intriguing, windswept island of Delft (Nadantivu) is 10km across the water southwest of KKD. A small, very ruined **Dutch fort** is a short walk from the ferry dock. Behind it is a beach with many exquisite shells. Like Mannar, Delft has a rare, ancient **baobab tree** shaped like an immensely overgrown bamboo shoot.

The hundreds of field-dividing walls are hewn from chunks of brain and fan corals. Local Delft ponies descended from Dutch mounts roam the island.

Directory

CONTENTS

ACCOMMODATION

Sri Lanka has accommodation ranging from rooms in family homes to five-star resorts. Unlike India, not many places in Sri Lanka have dormitory-style rooms. The main option for solo travellers is single rooms: sometimes in tiny boxes, or costing the same as double rooms. For groups of travellers, some guest houses will have a 'family' room with three or four beds for only 20% to 50% more than a double room.

Prices are very seasonal, particularly at beach resorts. The prices quoted in this guide

---

LIVING THE HERITAGE HIGH LIFE

Sri Lanka is one of the travel world's best-value destinations if you're looking to splurge in a restored coastal villa or a refurbished colonial hotel. See **Boutique Sri Lanka** (www.boutiquesrilanka.com) or **Sri Lanka In Style** (www.srilankainstyle.com) for comprehensive listings of many heritage Sri Lankan properties that are now open as accommodation.

---

are high-season rates; look forward to good discounts in the low season. The high season begins around 15 December on the west and south coasts, and 1 April on the east coast. The monsoon may have ended before the season starts. High season ends around March in the south and west, and around September on the east coast. It's always worth negotiating a discount year-round.

Guest houses and hotels are in demand during April in Nuwara Eliya for the Sinhalese/Tamil New Year, and in Kandy during the Kandy Esala Perahera (July/August). Book ahead for both occasions. Many places have different rooms at different prices; it's always worth asking if there are any cheaper rooms.

In this guide, doubles (or equivalent) costing less than Rs 1500 a night are in the budget category, Rs 1500 to 8000 in the midrange category and over Rs 8000 in top end. Some midrange and top-end hotels quote room prices in US dollars or euros, but will accept the rupee equivalent. Note that a service charge of 10% will be added to the rate you're usually quoted. At top-end hotels an additional Value Added Tax (VAT) of 15% is added. Reviews in this book include the addition of both service charge and VAT.

Unless stated otherwise, all rooms have a private bathroom, fan and mosquito net or electric insecticide 'mat'. Air-conditioning is available in most midrange and top-end accommodation, especially in the south and west of the country; the availability of air-con is noted in specific reviews. In the Hill Country's cooler climate, air-con is not usually needed. Many places have their own restaurant or can provide meals on request.

An increasing number of environmentally friendly accommodation is opening in Sri Lanka (see p21).

Guest houses

Sri Lankan guest houses cater to travellers on a variety of budgets. Some guest houses rent a couple of rooms, like B&B establishments, while other guests are like small hotels.

Apart from lower rates, the 'meeting local people' aspect is a benefit of guest houses. Expect to pay up to Rs 1500 for a simple, double room in a family guest house. Good negotiation skills might see you secure a 10% to 15% discount. Many guest houses are small, so it can pay to phone ahead.

At the time of writing, the economic situation in Sri Lanka had seen a few lower-end guesthouses offering rooms on an hourly basis for sexual assignations. It's worth paying a little extra for a better place.

Hotels

The line between lower-priced hotels and upper-range guest houses is blurred as places that call themselves 'hotels' are really guest houses, while other small hotels are called inns, lodges or villas. Whatever the name, doubles in hotels start at around Rs 2200 and escalate up to high-priced luxury places.

Larger hotels are either modern resort hotels or colonial-style places in heritage buildings. Many of these heritage places are decked out with modern conveniences, including wi-fi internet and air-con. It's worth splurging on them occasionally to break up the guest house routine and really capture the languid essence – think rattan furniture and slowly spinning ceiling fans – of colonial Sri Lanka.

More contemporary hotels offer facilities such as tennis courts, windsurfing instruction, nightclubs, as well as prime beach, riverside or hill-top locations. Most are geared to package tourists. Expect comfortable rooms, but an occasional lack of ambience and personality.

National Parks

The **Department of Wildlife Conservation** (☎ 011-256 0380; www.dwlc.lk 7) has bungalows, each accommodating up to 10 adults and two children, in national parks, including Uda Walawe and Horton Plains. Many national parks also have camp sites available.

Adventure Sports Lanka (☎ 01-279 1584; www.actionlanka.com; 366/3 Rendapola Horagahakanda Lane, Talagama, Koswatta) also arranges trips to parks.

Rest houses

Originally created for travelling government officials by the Dutch and then developed into a network of wayside inns by the British, rest houses now mostly function as small midrange hotels. Standards and rates vary widely – those run by the **Ceylon Hotels Corporation** (www.ceylonhotels.lk) are well maintained – but most rest houses are old-fashioned with big rooms featuring wooden floors and high ceilings.

Rest houses usually have locations on the highest hills, near the most spectacular beaches or beside the prettiest rivers. Doubles cost US$45 (Rs 5000) up to US$80 (Rs 9000).

Tea-estate Bungalows

In the Hill Country, a number of bungalows once the homes of British tea-estate managers have been converted into guest houses or hotels. Despite the 'bungalow' appellation, they're often rambling villas with beautiful gardens and antique-stuffed living rooms.

These bungalows fall into the midrange category, with a few luxury properties. Tea Trails (p177) offers accommodation in four beautifully renovated bungalows near Dikoya.

ACTIVITIES

Sri Lanka offers more than just stunning scenery, beaches and temples.

Ayurveda

Ayurveda (eye-your-veda) is an ancient system of medicine using herbs, oils, metals and animal products to heal and rejuvenate. Influenced by the system of the same name in India, Ayurveda is widely used in Sri Lanka for a range of ailments.

BOOK YOUR STAY ONLINE

For more accommodation reviews and recommendations by Lonely Planet authors, check out the online booking service at www.lonelyplanet.com/hotels. You'll find the true, insider low-down on the best places to stay. Reviews are thorough and independent. Best of all, you can book online.

DIRECTORY

PRACTICALITIES

- The *Daily News* (www.dailynews.lk), *Daily Mirror* (www.dailymirror.lk), *Morning Leader* (www .morningleader.lk) and *Island* (www.island.lk) newspapers are published in English daily, while the *Sunday Times* (www.sundaytimes.lk), *Sunday Observer* (www.sundayobserver.lk) and the *Sunday Leader* (www.thesundayleader.lk) are available on weekends. Your best bet for an independent point of view is the *Morning Leader* and the *Sunday Leader*. The monthly magazine *Travel Sri Lanka* (www.travelsrilanka.com) is an excellent source of information on Sri Lanka.

- Sri Lanka Broadcasting dominates the national AM/FM radio networks with English-, Sinhala- and Tamil-language programming; Colombo has a few private FM stations that broadcast a variety of music, news and talk. Short-wave radios can pick up the BBC.

- Eight TV channels broadcast in English, including the state-run Sri Lanka Rupavahini Corporation (SLRC) and Independent TV Network (ITN), and the privately owned Sisara, MTV (no relation), Swarnawahini and TNL. Dialog is offered by most midrange and top-end accommodation, and features international news channels, including BBC World, Al Jazeera and CNN.

- The electric current is 230V, 50 cycles. Plugs come in two varieties: three round pins, or one flat pin and two round. Adaptors are readily available at electrical shops for around Rs 90.

- Sri Lanka uses the international metric system, though some Sri Lankans still express distance in yards and miles. The term *lakh* is often used in place of '100,000'.

Ayurveda postulates that the five elements (earth, air, ether, water and light) are linked to the five senses, which in turn shape the nature of an individual's constitution – their *dosha* (life force). Disease and illness occurs when *dosha*s are out of balance. The purpose of Ayurvedic treatment is to restore the balance.

For therapeutic treatments, patients must be prepared to make a commitment of weeks or months. More commonly, tourists treat themselves at Ayurvedic massage centres attached to major hotels and in popular tourist centres.

Full treatments take up three hours and include the following relaxing regimens.

Herbal saunas (Sweda Karma) are based on a 2500-year-old design. The plaster walls are infused with herbal ingredients, including honey and sandalwood powder. The floor of the sauna is covered with herbs. Like a European sauna, a steady mist of medicinal steam is maintained with water sprinkled onto hot coals.

The steam bath (Vashpa Swedanam) looks like a cross between a coffin and a torture chamber. Patients lie stretched out on a wooden platform, and a giant hinged door covers the body with only the head exposed. From the base of the wooden steam bath, up to 50 different herbs and spices infuse the body.

The highlight for many patients is the so-called Third Eye of the Lord Shiva treatment (Shiro Dhara). For up to 45 minutes, a delicate flow of warm oil is poured slowly onto the forehead and then smoothed gently into the temples by the masseuse.

The standards at some Ayurvedic centres are low. The massage oils may be simple coconut oil and the practitioners may be unqualified, except in some instances where they may even be sex workers. As several poisoning cases have resulted from herbal treatments being misadministered, it pays to enquire precisely what the medicine contains and then consult with a conventional physician.

For massage, enquire whether there are both male and female therapists available; we've received complaints from female readers about sexual advances from some male Ayurvedic practitioners. In general it's not acceptable Ayurvedic practice for males to massage females and vice versa.

In this book we've included only clinics where the staff are qualified with relevant university degrees and all treatments are above board and professionally administered.

Birdwatching

Among 'twitchers' Sri Lanka is a highly regarded birdwatching destination. For more detailed information, see p67.

Recommended operators running wildlife-watching trips include **Jetwing Eco Holidays** (www.jetwingeco.com) and **Sri Lanka Expeditions** (www. srilankaexpeditions.com). In Kitulgala, Channa Perera at Rafter's Retreat (p178) is an excellent guide.

Cycling

Cycling is a great way to get around in Sri Lanka, and mountain biking is also becoming more popular. See p307 for places to hire bicycles and companies organising mountain-biking trips.

Diving & Snorkelling

There are interesting shipwrecks at Unawatuna, and the reef at Kirinda is in fine shape; however rough seas make it inaccessible for all but a couple of weeks in April and May. There are also reefs at the Basses in the southeast and along the east coast. Pigeon Island off Nilaveli is a fine place to go snorkelling. You can also snorkel at Hikkaduwa, Unawatuna, Mirissa and at Polhena, near Matara.

Diving shops can be found in Colombo and in the major west-coast resorts. They hire and sell gear, including snorkelling equipment. PADI courses are also available.

Along the west coast, the best time to dive and snorkel is generally from November to April. On the east coast, the seas are calmest from April to September.

Coral bleaching (where coral loses its algae due to higher-than-average ocean temperatures and regional influences) in 1998 struck about half of the island's reefs. The affected reefs were recovering when the 2004 tsunami struck. However, it's estimated that not more than 5% of the reef systems were affected by the tsunami, and some divers reported that visibility actually improved. For tips on responsible diving and snorkelling, see boxed text, p290.

Golf

There are three excellent golf courses in Sri Lanka. Green fees and club hire are around US$50 a day. Near Kandy, the scenic Victoria Golf & Country Resort (p163) overlooks the Victoria Reservoir. The historic Nuwara Eliya Golf Club (p183) and the Royal Colombo Golf Club (p90) have long-established courses.

Golfing tours of Sri Lanka are run by a variety of companies, including **Dream Vacations** (www.tourlanka.com) and **Red Dot Tours** (www.reddot tours.com).

Meditation

Many visitors to Sri Lanka participate in Buddhist meditation retreats. You'll find monasteries around the island, but Kandy is the main area. For retreats in Kandy, see p173, and for meditation centres throughout Sri Lanka where practitioners speak English, check **Vipassanā Fellowship** (www.vipassana.com /resources/ meditation_in_sri_lanka.php).

Surfing

Sri Lanka has consistent surf year-round, but the quality of waves is far lower than the nearby Maldives and Indonesia. You visit Sri Lanka more for the culture, climate, ease of travelling and cost of living than for the chance to get barreled. Despite this Sri Lanka is a superb place to learn how to surf or for intermediate surfers to get their first reef-break experiences. Sri Lanka's best-known wave is Arugam Bay on the east

---

SAFETY GUIDELINES FOR DIVING

Before embarking on a scuba diving, skin diving or snorkelling trip, carefully consider the following points to ensure a safe and enjoyable experience:

- Possess a current diving certification card from a recognised scuba-diving instructional agency (if scuba diving).

- Be sure you are healthy and feel comfortable diving.

- Obtain reliable information about physical and environmental conditions at the dive site (eg from a reputable local dive operation).

- Be aware of local laws, regulations and etiquette about marine life and the environment.

- Dive only at sites within your realm of experience; if available, engage the services of a competent, professionally trained dive instructor or dive master.

- Be aware that underwater conditions vary significantly from one region, or even site, to another. Seasonal changes can significantly alter any site and dive conditions. These differences influence the way divers dress for a dive and what diving techniques they use.

- Ask about the environmental characteristics that can affect your diving and how local trained divers deal with these considerations.

> ## RESPONSIBLE DIVING
>
> Please consider the following tips when diving and help preserve the ecology and beauty of reefs:
>
> - Never use anchors on the reef, and take care not to ground boats on coral.
> - Avoid touching or standing on living marine organisms or dragging equipment across the reef. Polyps can be damaged by even the gentlest contact. If you must hold on to the reef, only touch exposed rock or dead coral.
> - Be conscious of your fins. Even without contact, the surge from fin strokes near the reef can damage delicate organisms. Take care not to kick up clouds of sand, which can smother organisms.
> - Practise and maintain proper buoyancy control. Major damage can be done by divers descending too fast and colliding with the reef.
> - Take great care in underwater caves. Spend as little time within them as possible as your air bubbles may be caught within the roof and thereby leave organisms high and dry. Take turns to inspect the interior of a small cave.
> - Resist the temptation to collect or buy corals or shells or to loot marine archaeological sites (mainly shipwrecks).
> - Ensure that you take home all your rubbish and any litter you may find as well. Plastics in particular are a serious threat to marine life.
> - Do not feed fish.
> - Minimise your disturbance of marine animals.

coast. Surf's up at this long right point from April to October.

On the west and south coasts, the best surfing is from November to April, with the start and end of this season more consistent than January and February (when, bizarrely, most surfers choose to visit). The reefs of Hikkaduwa are a long-time favourite, although more for the ease of living than for the quality of the waves. The Midigama area is the best spot along the south coast, with a mellow left point, a nearby consistent beach break and a short and sharp right reef, which offers about the only frequently hollow wave in Sri Lanka.

Boards can be hired and lessons are available at most beach towns. **Low Pressure Stormrider Guides** (www.lowpressure.co.uk) offers good advice on surfing Sri Lanka.

Walking

Walking and hiking are growing in popularity in Sri Lanka. Compared withIndia, there isn't as much of an organised hiking industry, so it's more a matter of striking out on your own. A few guest houses in the Hill Country, such as White Monkey/Dias Rest (p192) in Haputale and Single Tree Hotel (p184) in Nuwara Eliya, arrange guided hikes.

Adam's Peak (Sri Pada), Sri Lanka's most sacred mountain, is a solid hike with stunning views as a reward.

Some of Sri Lanka's most spectacular mountain scenery is in the Knuckles Ranges. Based in Kandy, **Sri Lanka Trekking** (☎ 602 996 070; www.sri lankatrekking.com) runs multiday expeditions to the area (see p163). Rainforest fans can explore the Sinharaja Forest Reserve with the Rathnayaka brothers at Sinharaja Rest (p205).

Other companies to arrange hiking include **Adventure Sports Lanka** (☎ 011-279 1584; www .actionlanka.com) and **Eco Team** (☎ 011-583 5893; www .srilankaecotourism.com).

An online hub for local walking and nature fans in Sri Lanka is **Lakdasun** (www.lakdasun.com), which includes downloadable trail guides.

Wildlife Watching

It's definitely not Africa, but Sri Lanka's national parks do provide good opportunities for sighting animals, including elephants and the occasional leopard. For when and where to visit, see boxed text, p71. Recommended operators running wildlife-watching trips include **Jetwing Eco Holidays** (☎ 011-238 1201; www .jetwingeco.com) and **Sri Lanka Expeditions** (☎ 011-281 9457; www.srilankanexpeditions.com).

Whale Watching

From January to April, whale watching is possible at locations along the south coast, including Hikkaduwa, Unawatuna and Weligama.

White-water Rafting, Canoeing & Boating

White-water rafting can be done near Kitulgala in the Hill Country. **Adventure Sports Lanka** (☎ 011-279 1584; www.actionlanka.com) arranges trips. Also in Kitulgala, Rafter's Retreat (p178) can arrange rafting and canoeing trips.

You can organise boat or catamaran trips for sightseeing, birdwatching or fishing around Negombo, Bentota and Weligama.

Windsurfing

Top-end hotels on the west coast are the only places that hire sailboards. Bentota is the best spot to windsurf, and several outfits there hire out equipment and provide lessons.

BUSINESS HOURS

The working week in offices, including post offices, is from 8.30am to 4.30pm Monday to Friday. Some businesses also open until 1pm on Saturday. Shops normally open from 10am to 7pm weekdays, and until 3pm on Saturday.

Businesses run by Muslims may take an extended lunch break on Friday. Banks are open from 9am to 3pm on weekdays.

Restaurants usually open between 7am and 10pm. Traveller-friendly bars and pubs usually open from 5pm to midnight.

All exceptions to these opening hours are noted in reviews.

CHILDREN

Sri Lankans adore children, and hotels and restaurants will happily cater for them. Lonely Planet's *Travel with Children* has lots of road-tested advice.

Practicalities

Sri Lankan hotels and guest houses invariably have triple rooms, and extra beds are supplied on demand. Most restaurants don't supply highchairs.

For very young children, a dilemma is to bring either a backpack carrier or a pram/stroller. If you can, bring both. Backpacks can be sweaty in the tropical heat, but prams are tough going on uneven or nonexistent footpaths. A pram is worthwhile around Colombo, Kandy Lake and the Peradeniya Botanical Gardens. Strollers should definitely be the

---

SAFE SWIMMING

Every year drownings occur off Sri Lanka's beaches. If you aren't an experienced swimmer or surfer, it's easy to underestimate the dangers – or even to be totally unaware of them. There are few full-time lifesaving patrols, so there's usually no one to jump in and rescue you. A few common-sense rules should be observed:

- Don't swim out of your depth. If you are a poor swimmer, always stay in the shallows.
- Don't stay in the water when you feel tired.
- Never go swimming under the influence of alcohol or drugs.
- Supervise children at *all* times.
- Watch out for rips. Water brought onto the beach by waves is sucked back to sea and this current can be strong enough to drag you out with it; the bigger the surf, the stronger the rip. Rips in rough surf can sometimes be seen as calm patches in the disturbed water. It's best to check with someone reliable before venturing into the water. If you do get caught in a rip, swim *across* the current if you can – not *against* it. If it's too strong for you to do this, keep afloat and raise a hand so that someone on shore can see that you are in distress. A rip eventually weakens; the important thing is not to panic.
- Exercise caution when there is surf.
- Beware of coral; coming into contact with coral can be painful for the swimmer and fatal for the coral. Always check with someone reliable if you suspect the area you're about to swim in may have coral.
- Never dive into the water. Hazards may be lurking under the surface or the water may not be as deep as it looks. It pays to be cautious.

DIRECTORY

robust-wheeled 'Mountain Buggy' type. Car-hire companies usually have childrens' car seats.

Buy pharmaceutical supplies, imported baby food and disposable nappies at Cargills Food City supermarkets throughout the country. Hotel staff can arrange laundry for cloth nappies.

For meals, less spicy options include egg and string hoppers and egg and vegetable *rotti* (a doughy pancake). Spicy meat in curries can be washed in milk to reduce the heat.

Breastfeeding in public is accepted, but parents will struggle with finding dedicated baby-changing rooms. It's not a major problem as it's acceptable for toddlers to be naked in public. Just use a flat, clear surface, like under a tree in a park. Rabies and animal-borne parasites are present in Sri Lanka, so keep children away from stray animals, including cats, dogs and monkeys.

Sights & Activities

There aren't many attractions dedicated solely to children. For elephant fans there is the Pinnewala Elephant Orphanage (p157), the Millennium Elephant Foundation (p157) and the Elephant Transit Home (p203). The turtle hatcheries on the west coast (see boxed text, p116) are popular, and a national park safari will also appeal. Sri Lanka is famous for its beaches. In particular the beach at Polhena near Matara (p139) is safe and shallow for little ones.

Sri Lanka's diversity in transport from rattling three-wheelers to backwater boat trips will also keep kids amused.

CLIMATE CHARTS

Sri Lanka is tropical with distinct dry and wet seasons. The seasons are slightly complicated by having two monsoons. From May to August the Yala monsoon brings rain to the island's southwestern half, while the dry season here lasts from December to March. The southwest has the highest rainfall – up to 4000mm a year. The Maha monsoon blows from October to January, bringing rain to the North and East, while the dry season is from May to September. The North and East are comparatively dry, with around 1000mm of rain annually. There is also an intermonsoonal period in October and November when rain can occur in many parts of the island.

Colombo and the low-lying coastal regions have an average temperature of 27°C. At Kandy (altitude 500m), the average tempera-

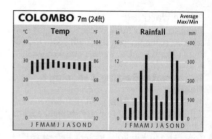

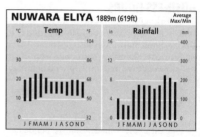

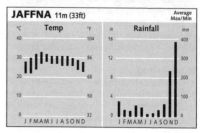

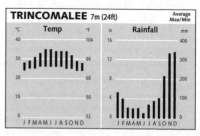

ture is 20°C, while Nuwara Eliya (at 1889m) has a temperate 16°C average. The sea stays at around 27°C all year.

COURSES

The nonprofit, grass-roots organisation **Woodlands Network** (☎ 057-222 3213; www.visit woodlandsnetwork.org; 18 UCT, Dharmapla Mawath) in Bandarawela offers cooking and meditation courses; see p194. Other cookery classes are listed in the boxed text, p60. Visitors to Galle can also study lacemaking at the **Power of Hands Foundation** (www.powerofhandsfoundation.com); see p131). For opportunities to study meditation in Sri Lanka, see p289.

The **University of Peradeniya** (☎ 081-238 8301; www.arts.pdn.ac.lk/pali/) in Kandy has a comprehensive program of Pali and Buddhist studies.

CUSTOMS REGULATIONS

You may bring 1.5L of spirits, 1.5L of wine, 200 cigarettes or 200g of tobacco, 250mL of perfume, and travel souvenirs (not exceeding US$125 in value for stays of less than 90 days, or up to US$500 for stays between 90 days and a year) into the country. Up to 3kg of tea may be exported duty free. For more details, check **Sri Lanka Customs** (www.customs.gov.lk).

To export an antique (any article older than 50 years), you need an exemption permit from the Commissioner of Archaeology. Huge amounts of red tape make it difficult to get the permit. You'll need to go to the **Department of Archaeology** (Map pp84-5; ☎ 011-266 7155; www.archaeology.gov.lk; National Museum, 106 Ananda Coomaraswamy Mawatha, Col 7). Phone ahead to make an appointment.

DANGERS & ANNOYANCES

See also the Dangers & Annoyances sections in all destination chapters, especially p82 and p103 and the boxed text, p268.

Ethnic Tension

From 1985 to 2009 the Sri Lankan civil war scared away many potential visitors to the country. At the time of writing the traditionally fought conflict between the Sri Lankan government and the LTTE had recently ended. However the future remained uncertain and travellers should be cognisant of the current situation.

During the life of this book, expect many changes in the ease and openness of travelling in the North and East of the country. Undoubtedly there will be still be roadblocks and significant security to negotiate, but key thoroughfares, such as the A9 north to Jaffna, should be open. Check the security situation carefully before you leave home (see boxed text, right), and while travelling in Sri Lanka remain mindful of unexploded ordnance and minefields. Do not stray from well-marked roads and paths.

During the most recent ceasefire in 2005, travellers were warmly welcomed in the North,

---

> ### GOVERNMENT TRAVEL ADVICE
>
> The following government websites offer travel advisories and information on current hot spots:
>
> **Australia** (☎ 1300 139 281; www.smarttraveller.gov.au)
>
> **Canada** (☎ 800-267 6788; www.dfait-maeci.gc.ca)
>
> **New Zealand** (☎ 04-439 8000; www.safetravel.govt.nz)
>
> **UK** (☎ 0845-850-2829; www.fco.gov.uk/country advice)
>
> **USA** (☎ 888-407 4747; http://travel.state.gov)

---

and following the end of the war this situation will no doubt be replicated. The key safety issue around the long-standing ethnic tension between the Sinhalese and Tamil population will depend on what happens following the end of the war. Will former LTTE cadres be offered an amnesty by the Sri Lankan government and will they be successfully reintegrated into society? Or will a hard core of LTTE fighters disappear into the trail of refugees from northern Sri Lanka and continue the struggle by instigating more suicide bombings and guerrilla activity in Colombo for years to come? And on the political front, will another organisation emerge to take the place of the LTTE, a group that never received wholesale support among all Tamils anyway.

For travellers using this guidebook, chances are that a greater part of the country will be open for exploring than in recent years. However, the quickly changing nature of Sri Lankan war (and peace) means it's imperative to seek out the latest information before you depart and arrive in Sri Lanka.

Theft

With the usual precautions, most people's visit to Sri Lanka is trouble free. However, pickpockets can be active on crowded city buses, notably in Colombo along Galle Rd. They often work together – one to jostle you and the other to pick your pocket or slit your bag, often as you board a bus. Keep space around you and hold tight to your personal items.

Don't sleep with your windows open, especially if you're on the ground floor. Thieves sometimes use long poles with hooks. Monkeys are genetically gifted pilferers and can steal food from your room.

If you're robbed, it's important to file a report with the police. You probably won't get your money or personal items back, but a police report will expedite travel insurance claims when you get back home.

Touts

Sri Lanka's tourism industry provides income to many, from hotel owners to three-wheeler drivers. Those at the top do well, but further down commissions are the name of the game. Touts (AKA 'friends' or 'guides') lurk around bus and train stations, trying to lure you to a particular hotel or guest house. They'll often tell you stories – 'It's closed' or 'It burnt down last month' – about competing places. It's almost always a lie. If you stay at their suggested hotel, the tout gains a commission. This is sometimes subsidised by extra charges to you, but often the hotelier attempts to make up the difference by providing you with food and tours.

Saying you have a reservation, whether true or not, is a good ploy to fend off touts. Many travellers still like going with a tout, as you don't have the headache of tramping the streets. Use our recommendations as a starting point.

The airport is a prime breeding ground for touts (and scams). As the gateway to the Hill Country, Kandy train station is also a favourite haunt.

Most restaurants, gem shops, handicraft stalls and spice gardens also play the commission game. Just remember: this is how many make a living. You can help out, or you can spend your money elsewhere. Either way, don't get hung up on beating the commission racket. At the time of writing, travel to Sri Lanka was at a particularly low ebb and the ability to secure commissions was making a major difference in many people's lives.

Traffic

The fundamental rule of Sri Lankan traffic is 'size does matter'. It's dangerously acceptable for a bus, car or truck to overtake in the face of oncoming smaller road users. Three-wheelers, cyclists, or smaller cars and vans simply have to move over or risk getting hit. To announce they are overtaking, or want to overtake, drivers sound a shrill melody on their horns. If you're walking or cycling along any kind of main road, be alert.

DISCOUNT CARDS

An International Student ID Card is not widely recognised in Sri Lanka. You can't get a discount on the pricey Cultural Triangle round ticket, but you can sometimes get half-price individual site tickets after friendly banter with the ticket seller. It's the same story for seniors.

EMBASSIES & CONSULATES

It's important to realise the limits to what your embassy can do if you're in trouble. Generally speaking, their hands are tied if you've broken Sri Lankan law. In real emergencies you might get some assistance, but only if all other channels have been exhausted. Embassies can recommend hospitals and dentists, but you'll need insurance to pay for it all.

Unless indicated, the following embassies are in Colombo:

Australia (Map pp84-5; ☎ 011-246 3200; www.srilanka .embassy.gov.au; 21 Gregory's Rd, Col 7)

Canada (Map pp84-5; ☎ 011-522 6296; clmbo@interna tional.gc.ca; 6 Gregory's Rd, Col 7)

France (Map pp84-5; ☎ 011-269 8815; ambfrclb@dree .org; 89 Rosmead Pl, Col 7)

Germany (Map pp84-5; ☎ 011-258 0431; www .colombo.diplo.de; 40 Alfred House Ave, Col 3)

India Colombo (Map pp84-5; ☎ 011-242 1605; info .colombo@mea.gov.in; 36-38 Galle Rd, Col 3); Kandy (Map pp160-1; ☎ 081-222 4563; 31 Rajapihilla Mawatha; ⓧ visa applications 9-11.30am Mon-Fri) The Kandy outpost is OK for three-month Indian visas, but for six months you'll do better in Colombo. See p301.

Italy (Map pp84-5; ☎ 011-258 8388; http://sedi.esteri .it/colombo; 55 Jawatta Rd, Col 5)

Japan (Map pp84-5; ☎ 011-269 3831; www.lk.emb -japan.go.jp; 20 Gregory's Rd, Col 7)

Maldives (Map p88; ☎ 011-551 6302; www.maldives high com.lk; 23 Kaviratne Pl, Col 8)

Netherlands (Map pp84-5; ☎ 011-259 6914; nethemb@ sri.lanka.net; 25 Torrington Ave, Col 7) Despite the address, the Dutch embassy is on the street next to Torrington Ave.

Sweden (Map pp84-5; ☎ 011-479 5400; ambassaden .colombo@sida.se; 49 Bullers Lane, Col 7)

UK (Map pp84-5; ☎ 011-539 0639; www.britishhighcom mission.gov.uk/srilanka; 389 Bauddhaloka Mw, Col 7)

USA (Map pp84-5; ☎ 011-249 8500; http://colombo .usembassy.gov; 210 Galle Rd, Col 3)

FESTIVALS & EVENTS

Sri Lanka has many Buddhist, Hindu, Christian and Muslim festivals. Many of the festivals, particularly those on the *poya* (full moon) days, are based on the lunar calendar so dates vary from year to year according to the Gregorian calendar; for upcoming *poya* dates, see boxed text, p297.

Hindu festivals often depend on complicated astrological calculations, and the exact dates are often only decreed around a month in advance.

Muslim festivals are timed according to local sightings of various phases of the moon and vary from year to year. During the lunar month of Ramadan, normal business patterns may be interrupted.

The **Sri Lanka Tourist Board** (SLTB; www.srilanka tourism.org) publishes information on festivals and events on its website.

JANUARY
Duruthu Perahera Held on the *poya* day in January at the Kelaniya Raja Maha Vihara in Colombo and second in importance only to the huge Kandy *perahera* (procession), this festival celebrates a visit by the Buddha to Sri Lanka.
Thai Pongal Held in mid-January, this Hindu harvest festival honours the Sun God.

FEBRUARY
Galle Literary Festival (www.galleliteraryfestival.com) Past attending authors have included travel writers Colin Thubron and Pico Iyer.
Navam Perahera First celebrated in 1979, Navam Perahera is one of Sri Lanka's biggest *peraheras*. Held on the February *poya*, it starts from the Gangaramaya Temple and travels around Viharamahadevi Park and Beira Lake in Colombo.

FEBRUARY/MARCH
Maha Sivarathri In late February or early March the Hindu festival of Maha Sivarathri commemorates the marriage of Shiva to Parvati.

MARCH/APRIL
Easter The Christian Good Friday holiday usually falls in April, but can fall in late March.
Aurudu (New Year) Both New Year's Eve on 13 April and New Year's Day on 14 April are holidays in Sri Lanka, coinciding with the end of the harvest season and the start of the southwest monsoon; see also the boxed text, below.

CELEBRATING THE NEW YEAR SRI LANKAN STYLE
In mid-April Buddhist and Hindu Sri Lankans celebrate their new year – Aurudu. Significant tasks, including the lighting of the hearth to cook *kiri bath* (coconut-milk rice), bathing, the first business transaction and first meal of the new year, are performed at astrologically determined auspicious moments. There are also auspicious colours to be worn and directions to face, all to ensure good fortune for the year ahead.

Aurudu occurs when the harvest ends and the fruit trees produce bounteous crops. The festival brings the country to a standstill for almost a week. Public transport is packed as everyone returns to their parental homes. Businesses close down to allow staff to travel home for a few days.

The rituals begin with cleaning the house and lighting the oil lamp. The pounding of the *raban* (a one-sided traditional drum type played with the hands) sounds the dawning of the new year. The lighting of the hearth is the first ceremonial act for the new year, and even women who are not especially devoted to astrology ensure they light the fire to heat the new pot filled with milk. Families constantly watch the clock, assisted by countdowns on state TV, until it's time to take the first meal for the new year. A booming salvo of firecrackers reinforces the moment.

After the other rituals are performed, the family visits friends or joins in on village games, and children ride swings hanging from nearby mango or jackfruit trees.

Special Aurudu food is enjoyed during the following days. The ubiquitous plantains (bananas) are a staple, and treats at this time are *kaung* (oil cake) and *kokis* (a light, crisp sweetmeat of Dutch origin).

Family members exchange gifts after eating, usually clothes, and give sweetmeats or fruit to neighbours. Aurudu sales and markets provide all sorts of bargains.

Aurudu is deeply embedded in Sinhalese Buddhist and Tamil Hindu culture. It's not celebrated by Buddhists or Hindus anywhere else, and many expat Sri Lankans return to share the holiday season with their family and friends. In the cooler climes of Nuwara Eliya, wealthier folk spend the days playing golf and tennis, riding horses, or motor racing in the annual hill climb. Accommodation prices escalate wildly – that's if you can find anywhere to stay at all.

MAY

Vesak Poya This two-day holiday – *poya* day and the day after – commemorates the birth, enlightenment and death of the Buddha. Puppet shows and open-air theatre performances take place; the high point is the lighting of paper lanterns and oil lamps. The Adam's Peak pilgrimage season ends at Vesak.

JUNE

Poson Poya The Poson *poya* day celebrates the bringing of Buddhism to Sri Lanka by Mahinda. In Anuradhapura and Mihintale, thousands of white-clad pilgrims ascend Mihintale.

JULY/AUGUST

Kandy Esala Perahera The Kandy Esala Perahera, Sri Lanka's most important and spectacular festival, is the climax of 10 days and nights of celebrations during the month of Esala. This great procession honours the sacred tooth relic of Kandy; see boxed text, p159. Smaller *peraheras* are held at other locations around the island.
Vel This festival is held in Colombo and Jaffna. In Colombo the gilded chariot of Murugan (Skanda), the god of war, is ceremonially hauled from Pettah to Bambalapitiya. In Jaffna the Nallur Kandaswamy Kovil has a 25-day festival.
Kataragama Another important Hindu festival is held at Kataragama, where devotees put themselves through the whole gamut of ritual masochism; see boxed text, p152.

OCTOBER/NOVEMBER

Deepavali The Hindu festival of lights takes place in late October or early November. Thousands of flickering oil lamps celebrate the triumph of good over evil and the return of Rama after his period of exile.

DECEMBER

Adam's Peak The pilgrimage season, when pilgrims (and the odd tourist) climb Adam's Peak, starts in December.
Unduvap Poya This full-moon day commemorates Sangamitta, who brought a cutting from the sacred bodhi tree, still standing in Anuradhapura.

FOOD

Sri Lankan cuisine has clear links with Indian food, but also many unique traditions. The staple meal is 'rice and curry', a misleadingly simple descriptor for what can be a miniban-quet of up to eight or nine dishes.

Colombo has the widest range of international food options, and west- and south-coast restaurants offer backpacker and traveller standards.

Rice and curry can take up to 1½ hours to prepare. Get into the habit of preordering your meal. Peruse the menu during the day, order and turn up at the allocated time.

Some Eating sections of this book are divided into budget, midrange and top-end categories. We define eating price breakdowns according to the following prices per person: budget up to Rs 200; midrange Rs 200 to 600; and top end over Rs 600.

For more information on Sri Lankan cuisine, see p56.

GAY & LESBIAN TRAVELLERS

Male homosexual activity is illegal in Sri Lanka (there is no law against female homosexuality), and the subject is not discussed publicly. No one has been convicted for over 60 years, but it pays to be discreet.

The situation is changing, and Colombo has a low-key scene. **Gay Sri Lanka** (www.gayslanka.com) is a comprehensive online resource. **Sri Lankan Gay Friends** (www.geocities.com/srilankangay) has listings of events. A specific site for lesbians is **Women's Support Group Sri Lanka** (www.wsglanka.com).

In 2005 Colombo held it first annual Gay Pride celebration, courtesy of **Equal Ground** (www.equal-ground.org), a Colombo-based organisation supporting gay and lesbian rights.

HOLIDAYS

New Years Day 1 January
Independence Day 4 February
Labour Day 1 May
Good Friday March-April
Christmas Day 25 December
Note also that all *poya* days are public holidays (see boxed text, opposite).

INSURANCE

A travel insurance policy to cover theft, loss and medical problems is highly recommended. Different policies have different conditions and benefits, so check the small print. Policies with higher medical expense options are chiefly for countries like the USA, which have extremely high medical costs.

Some policies specifically exclude 'dangerous activities', including scuba diving, motorcycling and even trekking. A locally acquired motorcycle licence is not valid under some policies; check the fine print.

You may prefer a policy that pays doctors or hospitals directly, rather than having to pay on the spot and claim later. Check that your policy covers ambulances and emergency flights home.

Worldwide travel insurance is available online at www.lonelyplanet.com/travel_services.

POYA

Every *poya* or full-moon day is a holiday. *Poya* causes buses, trains and accommodation to fill up, especially if it falls on a Friday or Monday. No alcohol is supposed to be sold on *poya* days, and some establishments close. Some hotels and guest houses discreetly provide their thirsty guests with a cold beer 'under the table'.

The *poya* days in the second half of 2009 are 5 August, 4 September, 3 October, 2 November and 1 December. In 2010 *poya* days fall on 30 January, 28 February, 30 March, 28 April, 27 May, 26 June, 26 July, 24 August, 23 September, 23 October, 21 November and 21 December. In 2011 the dates are 19 January, 18 February, 19 March, 18 April, 17 May, 15 June, 15 July, 13 August, 12 September, 12 October, 10 November and 10 December. For the first half of 2012 *poya* days fall on 9 January, 7 February, 8 March, 6 April, 6 May, 4 June and 3 August.

INTERNET ACCESS

Internet facilities are available across Sri Lanka. In the smallest of towns, look around the bus stand.

Access in Colombo and provincial towns and cities is cheap (around Rs 60 per hour), but in tourist areas and on the coast costs can increase to around Rs 150 per hour.

Some larger hotels offer internet in-room access at higher prices. Wi-fi is increasingly available in some of the larger hotels, but at the time of writing was not common in lower-priced guest houses or at internet cafes. Wi-fi access is also available through **Dialog** (www.dialog.lk) and **Suntel** (www.suntel.lk) with a prepaid card system (around Rs 250 per hour). Hot spots are focused on Colombo's Bandaranaike International Airport and higher-end accommodation. See their websites for specific locations.

For websites with information on Sri Lanka, see p20.

LEGAL MATTERS

Sri Lanka's legal system is a complex, almost arcane mix of British, Roman–Dutch and national law. The legal system tends to move slowly, and even a visit to a police station to report a small theft can involve a whole lot of time-consuming filling out of forms. The tourist police in major towns and tourist hotspots should be your first point of contact in the case of minor matters such as theft.

Drug use, mainly locally grown marijuana, but also imported heroin and methamphetamine, is common in tourist centres such as Hikkaduwa, Negombo and Unawatuna. Dabbling is perilous; you can expect to end up in jail if you're caught using anything illegal.

MAPS

One of the best foreign-produced maps is the Nelles Verlag 1:450,000 (1cm = 4.5km) *Sri Lanka,* which also includes maps of Colombo, Anuradhapura, Kandy and Galle. Berndston & Berndston's *Sri Lanka Road Map* is excellent for extra detail on routes and sites. Globetrotter's 1:600,000 (1cm = 6km) *Sri Lanka* has a decent colour country map and a handful of simplified town maps. Most bookshops sell the excellent *A to Z Colombo* (Rs 400).

The Sri Lankan Survey Department's 1:500,000 (1cm = 5km) *Road Map of Sri Lanka* is an excellent overall map. It also produces a *Road Atlas of Sri Lanka* at the same scale, but with 17 town maps at the back.

A very different map is *LOCALternative Sri Lanka – a responsible travel map* (www .localternative.com) listing 170 opportunities to practise responsible tourism in Sri Lanka, ranging from village homestays to wildlife refuges. In Colombo it's available from Vijitha Yapa bookshop (p76) and Lake House Bookshop (p76), and in Kandy from Vijitha Yapa bookshop (p158).

For the widest selection of maps, take your passport to the **Surveyor General's Office** (Map p88; ☎ 011-258 5111; Kirula Rd, Narahenpita; ☺ 9am-4pm Mon-Fri) in Colombo. It's closed on government holidays.

MONEY

The Sri Lankan currency is the rupee (Rs), divided into 100 cents. Coins come in denominations of 25 and 50 cents and one, two, five and 10 rupees. Notes come in denominations of 10, 20, 50, 100, 200, 500, 1000 and 2000 rupees. ATMs often issue Rs 500 and 1000 notes. Try and break them as soon as possible as small vendors may not accept large notes.

DIRECTORY

Dirty or torn notes might not be accepted, except at a bank. For exchange rates, see the Quick Reference inside this book's front cover and for information on costs, see p17.

ATMs

Commercial Bank has ATMs accepting international Visa, MasterCard and Cirrus/Maestro cards. Other options include Bank of Ceylon, NationsTrust Bank, People's Bank, Hatton National Bank, Seylan Bank, Sampath Bank and HSBC. You will find ATMs in all cities and most provincial towns.

Black Market

Unlicensed moneychangers trade currency at slightly better rates than officially licensed moneychangers. They're not worth the very real risk in getting ripped off. ATMs are safer and more reliable.

Cash

Any bank or exchange bureau will change major currencies in cash, including US dollars, euros and British pounds. Change rupees back into hard currency at the airport before you leave the country.

Credit Cards

MasterCard and Visa are the most commonly accepted credit cards. Amex and Diners Club are also accepted.

Moneychangers

Moneychangers can be found in Colombo and major tourist centres. They generally don't charge commission and their rates are competitive.

Tipping

Although a 10% service charge is added to food and accommodation bills, this usually goes straight to the owner rather than the worker. Drivers expect a tip, as do people who 'guide' you through a site. A rule of thumb is to tip 10% of the total amount due. Also appropriate is Rs 15 for the person who minds your shoes at temples, and Rs 30 for a hotel porter.

Travellers Cheques

Thomas Cook, Visa and Amex are the most widely accepted. Expect a smallish transaction fee of around Rs 150.

PHOTOGRAPHY & VIDEO
Film & Equipment

Memory cards are available from computer shops, internet cafes and photographic shops. Most internet cafes and computer shops can transfer digital images onto CD.

In Colombo **Millers** (Map p80; ☎ 232 9151, York St, Col 1) is a reliable place to have your film developed. Film and slide film is becoming more difficult to buy in Sri Lanka, so bring all that you'll need.

The following places sell photographic supplies and do repairs: **Photoflex** (Map pp84-5; ☎ 258 7824; 1st fl, 451/2 Galle Rd, Col 3); **Photo Technica** Kollupitiya (Map pp84-5; ☎ 257 6271; 288 Galle Rd, Col 3); Liberty Plaza (Map pp84-5; RA de Mel Mawatha, Col 3); Majestic City (Map p88; Galle Rd, Col 4).

Photography Etiquette

In general Sri Lankans love getting their picture taken, but it's common courtesy to ask permission. A few business-oriented folk like the stilt fishermen at Koggala or the mahouts at the Pinnewala Elephant Orphanage will ask for payment. It's sometimes less hassle to just buy a postcard.

Restrictions

It's forbidden to film or photograph dams, airports, road blocks or anything associated with the military. In Colombo, the port and the Fort district are especially sensitive. Take particular care in the North and East, where there are many High Security Zones.

Never pose beside or in front of a statue of the Buddha (ie with your back to it) as this is considered extremely disrespectful. Flash photography can damage ages-old frescoes and murals, so respect the restrictions at places like Dambulla and Sigiriya.

POST

Airmail letters less than 10g sent to the UK, continental Europe or Australia cost Rs 40. The fee rises by Rs 15 for every extra 10g. Airmail letters to North America up to 10g cost Rs 45, plus Rs 20 for every additional 10g. Postcards to these destinations cost Rs 20.

If you have something valuable to send home, either use a courier service (for reliable couriers, see p77) or use the international courier services offered at post offices.

Post offices in larger centres have poste restante, and will generally keep your mail for two months in Colombo and one month in other towns.

SHOPPING

Sri Lanka has a wide variety of attractive handicrafts on sale. Laksala, a government-run store found in most cities and tourist towns, has items of reasonable quality. All are moderately priced with fixed-price tags. There are other handicraft outlets in Colombo; see p97 for details. Street stalls can be found in touristy areas, but you'll need to bargain.

Bargaining

Unless you are shopping at a fixed-price shop, you should bargain. Before you hit the open markets, peruse the prices in a fixed-price shop for an idea of what to pay. Generally, if someone quotes you a price, halve it. The seller will come down about halfway to your price, and the last price will be a little higher than half the original price. Try and keep a sense of perspective. Chances are you're arguing over less than US$1.

Batik

Originally introduced by the Dutch in colonial times, the Indonesian art of batik is very popular in Sri Lanka. Some of the best and most original batik is made in the west-coast towns of Marawila, Mahawewa and Ambalangoda, and there are also several worthwhile outlets in Kandy. Batik pictures cost Rs 250 to Rs 1500.

Batik is also used for a variety of clothing items, although most designs are slightly naff examples of ethno-tourist kitsch.

Gems

You'll find showrooms and private dealers all across Sri Lanka. In Ratnapura, the centre of the gem trade, it seems that everybody is a part-time gem dealer. Your challenge is to make sure what you're being offered is not worthless glass.

There is a government-run gem-testing laboratory in the **Sri Lanka Gem & Jewellery Exchange** (Map p80; ☎ 239 1132; www.slgemexchange.com; 4th & 5th fl, East Low Block, World Trade Centre, Bank of Ceylon Mw, Col 1) where tourists can get any stone tested for free. The only snag with the testing service is that it's not always easy, or practical, to 'borrow' a stone to take in for testing before you buy it. Reputable dealers, in Colombo at least, will normally accompany you to the lab for testing.

We continue to get emails from travellers who have had Sri Lankans try to sell them gems with the promise that they can be resold for a big profit in other countries. It's a scam, and unless you happen to be a world-class gem expert you're sure to lose money. If a deal looks too good to be true, you know what? It definitely is.

Guidebooks from 100 years ago make exactly the same warning. When will people learn?

For more information on the gems found in Sri Lanka, see boxed text, p209.

Leather

Cheap, good-quality leatherwork includes bags and cases. In Colombo look in the leatherwork and shoe shops around Fort. The bazaar on Olcott Mawatha, beside Colombo Fort train station, is cheaper than Laksala for similar-quality goods. Hikkaduwa is also a good place for leather bags.

Masks

Sri Lankan masks are a popular collector's item. They're carved at a number of places, principally along the southwest coast. Ambalangoda is Sri Lanka's mask-carving centre, with several showroom-workshops.

Touristy or not, the masks are good value and remarkably well made. They're available from key-ring size for a few rupees to high-quality masks for over Rs 2500. For more information, see boxed text, p46.

Spices & Tea

Spices are integral to Sri Lanka's cuisine and Ayurvedic traditions. A visit to a spice garden is an excellent way to discover the alternative uses of familiar spices. The usual procedure is to be shown around the gardens to view spice plants as diverse as cinnamon, cloves, nutmeg, vanilla beans, cardamom and black pepper. After this spicy show-and-tell, you'll be given an Ayurvedic reading to establish your body type and what spices you should incorporate into your diet for the ultimate health benefits.

You can buy the pure products, oils or Ayurvedic potions, but prices (and freshness) are better at local markets. For a spicy experience without an overbearing salesman, check out the spice garden at the Peradeniya Botanical Gardens in Kandy. Note that some countries may restrict the import of fresh spices, so check with your own country's powers-that-be before you leave home.

Tea is another popular purchase and tea factories in the Hill Country have a bewildering array of options on offer. To learn more about tea, see boxed text, p180.

DIRECTORY

Other Souvenirs

The ubiquitous coconut shell is transformed into tacky souvenirs – think cheeky monkeys and rampant elephants – and useful household items. Coir (rope fibre from coconut husks) is made into baskets, bags and mats.

Sri Lankans also make delicate lacquerware bowls with layers of lacquer built up carefully on a light framework, made of gossamer-thin bamboo strips.

Kandy is a centre for jewellery and brassware, both antique and modern, although the busy designs are not to everyone's taste. Weligama on the south coast turns out some attractive lacework.

SMOKING

Compared with other countries, smoking is not overly prevalent in Sri Lanka. From January 2007 smoking was outlawed on buses, trains and public places. Bars and restaurants are legally required to have separate smoking and nonsmoking sections. Since the legislation was passed, the Sri Lankan government has reported a 90% decline in smoking in public places. At the time of writing the law was largely being upheld, although we did notice smoking still taking place in Sri Lanka's few pubs and bars.

The legal age for purchasing tobacco products is 21.

SOLO TRAVELLERS

Travelling alone isn't a major issue in Sri Lanka, although women should take extra care (see p302 for more information). It's not wise to hike alone in the Hill Country or to walk alone on deserted beaches late at night, as such situations are prime targets for potential thieves.

TELEPHONE

Local calls are timed and cost about Rs 40 for two minutes, depending on the distance. To call Sri Lanka from abroad, dial your international access code, the country code (☎ 94), the area code (minus '0', which is used when dialling domestically) and the number.

International calls can be made from thousands of communications bureaus and booths; many offices also provide internet access. Look out for signs saying IDD. You'll normally phone from inside a private booth with an LED panel indicating how long you've talked for and how much the call is costing.

Some more rudimentary places use a manual stopwatch, so keep your own eye on the time to make sure you're not being duped.

There are no national emergency phone numbers.

Mobile Phones

There are five network operators, and coverage across Sri Lanka is excellent and cheap. GSM phones from Europe, the Middle East and Australasia can be used in Sri Lanka. Local SIM cards cost about Rs 300 to 500, and competition keeps prices low. Shop around for the best deal and plan. Prepaid plans are around Rs 3 to 5 per minute.

Sri Lanka's mobile-phone companies are **Mobitel** (www.mobitel.lk), **Dialog** (www.dialog.lk), **Tigo** (www.tigo.lk), **Hutch** (www.hutch.lk) and **Airtel** (www.airtel.lk).

Phone Codes

All regions have a three-digit area code followed by a six- or seven-digit number. In addition, companies operating wireless loop systems also have three- or four-digit prefixes. Calls to these phones cost about the same as to a standard telephone. Mobile phone companies also have separate prefix codes.

Company	Access code
Airtel	☎ 075
Dialog	☎ 077
Hutch	☎ 078
Mobitel	☎ 071
Sri Lanka Telecom	☎ 070
Suntel	☎ 074
Tigo	☎ 072

TIME

Sri Lanka is 5½ hours ahead of GMT (the same as India), 4½ hours behind Australian EST and 10½ hours ahead of American EST.

TOILETS

All top-end and midrange accommodation will have sit-down flush toilets, but if you're staying in budget digs, you may have squat toilets and will need to bring your own toilet paper. Public toilets are scarce, so dive into restaurants and hotels.

TOURIST INFORMATION

The Colombo main office of the **Sri Lanka Tourist Board** (SLTB; Map pp84-5; ☎ 011-243 7059; www .srilankatourism.org; 80 Galle Rd, Col 3; ☼ 9am-4.45pm Mon-

Fri, 9am-12.30pm Sat) is near the Taj Samudra. The board also runs a **Tourist Information Centre** (Map pp160-1; ☎ 081-222 2661; Palace Sq; ☺ 9am-1pm & 1.30-4.45pm Mon-Fri) in Kandy, and a 24-hour **booth** (☎ 011-225 7055) at Bandaranaike International Airport. Staff can help with hotel bookings and have maps and brochures. In Colombo **JF Tours & Travels** (Map pp84-5; ☎ 258 7996; www.jftours .com; 189 Bauddhaloka Mawatha, Col 4) at Colombo Fort train station is very helpful.

Among publications provided by the SLTB is an *Accommodation Guide*, updated every six months, and *Explore Sri Lanka*, a magazine with feature articles and information on things to see and places to stay, shop and eat. The SLTB has offices in the following countries:

Australia (☎ 02-6230 6002; kohinoorcentre@yahoo .com; 29 Lonsdale St, Braddon, Canberra, ACT 2612)

France (☎ 01 42 60 49 99; www.srilanka.fr) At the time of writing this office was being relocated. Check the website for the latest details.

Germany (☎ 069-28 77 34; ctbfra@t-online.de; Aller-heiligentor 2-4, D-60311 Frankfurt am Main)

India (☎ 011-373 0477; ctbindia@tracrep.com; 6th fl, Himalaya House, Kasturba Gandhi Marg, New Delhi 110 001)

Ireland (☎ 03 149 69621; fax 03 149 65345; 59 Ranleagh Rd, Dublin 6)

Japan (☎ 03-3289 0771; ctb-toky@zaf.att.ne.jp; Sabo Kai-kan, 5F, 2-7-5, Hirakawa-Cho, Chiyoda-ku, Tokyo 102-1-93)

UK (☎ 0845 880 6333 Ext 201; info@srilankantourism .org.uk; 3rd fl, Devonshire Sq, London EC2M 4WD)

TRAVELLERS WITH DISABILITIES

Sri Lanka is a challenge for travellers with disabilities, but the ever-obliging Sri Lankans are always ready to assist. If you have restricted mobility, you may find it difficult, if not impossible, to get around on public transport. Buses and trains don't have facilities for wheelchairs. Moving around towns and cities can also be difficult for those in a wheelchair and for the visually impaired because of the continual roadworks and very ordinary roads; don't expect many smooth footpaths. The chaotic nature of Sri Lankan traffic is also a potentially dangerous challenge. A car and driver is your best transport option. If possible, travel with a strong, able-bodied person.

Apart from top-end places, accommodation is generally not geared for wheelchairs. However, many places can provide disabled travellers with rooms and bathrooms that are accessible without stairs. It might take a bit of time to find places with the right facilities, but it is possible.

VISAS

Dozens of nationalities, including Australians, New Zealanders, North Americans and virtually all Europeans, receive a tourist visa upon entry, valid for 30 days. It is sometimes possible to obtain a visa for longer than 30 days in your home country; this is more often the case at Sri Lanka's bigger overseas missions (eg London and Washington). For the latest regulations, check **Department of Immigration & Emigration Sri Lanka** (www.immigrat ion.gov.lk).

Extensions can be made at the **Department of Immigration & Emigration Sri Lanka** (Map pp84-5; ☎ 011-532 9000; www.immigration.gov.lk; 41 Ananda Rajakaruna Mawatha; ☺ 9am-3pm Mon-Fri). Catch bus No 103, 144 or 171 from Fort and get off at the first stop after Kularatne Mawatha.

The last payments are received at 3.30pm. The department sets the cost in US dollars, but you pay in rupees. A visa extension gives you a full three months in the country, and you can apply for your extension almost as soon as you arrive (the 30-day visa given upon entry is included in the three months). A further three-month extension is possible, but you must again pay the extension fee plus another Rs 10,000. Extensions beyond this are at the discretion of the department, and incur a Rs 15,000 fee plus the extension fee. For fees for the first 90-day extension, see boxed table, below. You will need your passport, an onward ticket and either a credit card or foreign-exchange receipts.

Tourist visas for India can be obtained at the **Indian Visa Office** (Map pp84-5; ☎ 011-450 5588; www .vfs-in-lk.com; 433 Galle Rd, Col 3; ☺ 8am-1pm & 2-4pm Mon-Fri). The cost of a six-month visa depends on your nationality; most countries cost around Rs 5000. You'll need to supply two photos and you must pay in Sri Lankan rupees. It takes at

VISA EXTENSION FEES	
Country of origin	Cost (US$)
Australia	30
Canada	50
France	26
Germany	26.80
Ireland	16
Italy	35
Netherlands	49
New Zealand	34.50
Switzerland	27.20
UK	54
USA	100

least five days to process a tourist visa. Queues are usually shorter in Kandy.

You can also obtain an Indian visa in Kandy at the **Assistant High Commission of India** (Map pp160-1; ☎ 081-222 4563; 31 Rajapihilla Mawatha; ☷ visa applications 9-11.30am Mon-Fri). Kandy makes a good alternative to Colombo because it's not as busy. It's OK for three-month visas, but if you're after six months, apply in Colombo.

VOLUNTEERING

Following the tsunami in 2004, Sri Lanka became a focus for many volunteer efforts and organisations. The focus on post-tsunami relief has now decreased, but several local organisations still accept volunteers. Many NGOs are also active in Sri Lanka. Check out **Working Abroad** (www.workingabroad. com) for opportunities.

Local Sri Lankan organisations include **Millennium Elephant Foundation** (☎ 035-226 5377; www.millenniumelephantfoundation.org), **Turtle Conservation Project** (www.tcpsrilanka.org), **Responsible Tourism Partnership Sri Lanka** (www.responsibletourism.srilanka.org) and **Rainforest Rescue International** (www.rainforestrescueinternational.org).

The **Sewalanka Foundation** (www.sewalanka.org) also seeks volunteers for one- to three-month placements; contact amanda@sewalanka.org.

WOMEN TRAVELLERS

Few Sri Lankan women travel unchaperoned, so women travelling alone may experience uncomfortable levels of male attention. The relative isolation caused by the Sri Lankan civil war and exposure to more open and provocative Western media have created a small group of Sri Lankan men lacking the fundamentals in how to deal with Western women. On the whole women travellers are treated with respect, but we've also received reports of sleazebag behaviour on buses, inappropriate propositioning and sexually explicit name-calling.

Covering your legs and shoulders helps you blend in more effectively, though you'll be stared at no matter what you wear. In Colombo you can relax the dress code a little and get away with wearing sleeveless shirts. 'Are you married?' could be the snappy conversation starter you hear most often, so consider wearing a fake wedding ring and carrying a few pics of your imaginary loved one back home.

Women travelling alone may be hassled while walking around at night, or while exploring isolated places. We've had specific feedback about women being physically harassed on the Kandy lakeside at dusk (see p158). On some Sri Lankan beaches we've also heard reports of women being followed, so try and stay in touch with larger groups of people.

However, don't imagine travelling in Sri Lanka is one long hassle. Such unpleasant incidents are the exception, not the rule. Women travellers have the opportunity to enter the society of Sri Lankan women,

---

VOLUNTEERING – BEFORE YOU SIGN UP

Many volunteer and gap-year organisations offer programs in Sri Lanka. **Ethical Volunteering** (www.ethicalvolunteering.org) has compiled a handy guide outlining the questions to ask before you sign up for your volunteer experience. These questions will ensure that the work you're planning on undertaking will really make a difference. Download the full guide at www.ethicalvolunteering. org/downloads/ethicalvolunteering.pdf.

- Exactly what work will you be doing?

- Does the organisation work with a local partner organisation?

- What financial contribution does the organisation make to its volunteer program?

- What are the organisation's policies on eco and ethical tourism?

- What is the amount of time a volunteer is expected to commit to the program?

- Can the organisation give precise contact details for the programme you've chosen?

- What support and training will you receive?

For more information on volunteering see Lonely Planet's *Volunteer: A Traveller's Guide* and www.lonelyplanet.com/volunteer.

something that is largely out of bounds for male travellers. On the other hand, there are many social environments that are almost exclusively male in character – local bars, for example. If you feel uncomfortable in local eateries or hotels, try to find one where women are working or staying.

Stock up on tampons as they can be hard to find outside Colombo.

Bus & Train Travel

Women travelling solo may find buses and trains trying at times. In Colombo ordinary buses are so packed that sometimes it's impossible to avoid bodily contact with other passengers. Stray hands on crowded buses and trains are something else to watch out for. According to feedback from women travellers this is something that local women are also subjected to; their response is often the 'accidental' but well-targeted use of a sharp sari pin. If another passenger is making a concerted effort to invade your space or physically touching you, put your bag up as a shield, move to another part of the bus if you can, or get off and catch another bus. Colombo buses are frequent, so you shouldn't have to wait long for one that's less crowded. The most important thing in situations like this is to trust your gut instinct. If you feel the need to get off a bus, get off.

We strongly suggest not travelling on trains alone, as we've received warnings from women who have been sexually assaulted on such trips. Consider finding a travelling companion. Always try and sit next to another woman on a train or a bus, and on buses stand at the front near the driver if you can't get a seat.

Transport

TRANSPORT

GETTING THERE & AWAY

Flights, tours and rail tickets can be booked online at www.lonelyplanet .com/travel_services.

ENTERING THE COUNTRY

Immigration at Bandaranaike International Airport is straightforward. An official will check your visa and stamp your passport with an exit date.

Passport

You must have your passport with you at all times in Sri Lanka. Before leaving home, check that it will be valid for the entire period you intend to remain overseas. For information on visas, see p301.

AIR
Airports & Airlines

Sri Lanka's only international airport is **Bandaranaike International Airport** (airport code CMB; ☎ 011-225 2861) at Katunayake, 30km north of Colombo. There are 24-hour money-changing facilities in the arrivals and departures halls. The travel desks in the arrivals hall often have discounts for midrange and top-end hotels in Negombo and Colombo. There's also a decent range of travel information in English and German available. Look out for the *Explore Sri Lanka* maga-

zine. Wi-fi access is available with Dialog's prepay system (p297).

AIRLINES FLYING TO & FROM SRI LANKA

All the phone numbers listed below are for the airlines' Colombo offices; only add the ☎ 011 if calling from elsewhere. These are the key airlines flying into Sri Lanka; other secondary airlines are listed in the Colombo chapter.

Cathay Pacific (code CX; Map pp84-5; ☎ 011-233 4145; www .cathaypacific.com; hub Hong Kong)

Emirates (code EK; Map pp84-5; ☎ 011-230 0200; www.emir ates.com; hub Dubai)

Indian Airlines (code IC; Map p80; ☎ 011-232 3136; www .indian-airlines.nic.in; hub New Delhi)

Kuwait Airways (code KU; Map p80; ☎ 011-244 5531; www.kuwait-airways.com; hub Kuwait City)

Malaysia Airlines (code MH; Map p80; ☎ 011-234 2291; www.malaysia-airlines.com; hub Kuala Lumpur)

Qatar Airways (code QR; Map pp84-5; ☎ 011-577 0000; www .qatarairways.com; hub Doha)

Royal Jordanian (code RJ; Map pp84-5; ☎ 011-230 1621; www.rja.com.jo; hub Amman)

Singapore Airlines (code SQ; Map pp84-5; ☎ 011-230 0750; www.singaporeair.com; hub Singapore)

Sri Lankan Airlines (code UL; Map p80; ☎ 011-733 5500; www.srilankan.aero; hub Colombo)

United Airlines (code UA; Map p80; ☎ 011-234 6024; www .united.com)

Thai Airways (code TG; Map pp84-5; ☎ 011-230 7100; www.thaiairways.com.lk; hub Bangkok)

Tickets

Some of the cheapest flight tickets have to be bought months in advance and popular flights sell out quickly. Booking online is

---

THINGS CHANGE...

The information in this chapter is particularly vulnerable to change. Check directly with the airline or a travel agent to make sure you understand how a fare (and ticket you may buy) works and be aware of the security requirements for international travel. Shop carefully. The details given in this chapter should be regarded as pointers and are not a substitute for your own careful, up-to-date research.

CLIMATE CHANGE & TRAVEL

Climate change is a serious threat to the ecosystems that humans rely upon, and air travel is the fastest-growing contributor to the problem. Lonely Planet regards travel, overall, as a global benefit, but believes we all have a responsibility to limit our personal impact on global warming.

Flying & Climate Change

Pretty much every form of motor travel generates CO_2 (the main cause of human-induced climate change), but planes are far and away the worst offenders: not just because of the sheer distances they allow us to travel, but because they release greenhouse gases high into the atmosphere. The statistics are frightening: two people taking a return flight between Europe and the US will contribute as much to climate change as an average household's gas and electricity consumption over a whole year.

Carbon Offset Schemes

Climatecare.org and other websites use 'carbon calculators' that allow jetsetters to offset the greenhouse gases they are responsible for with contributions to energy-saving projects and other climate-friendly initiatives in the developing world – including projects in India, Honduras, Kazakhstan and Uganda.

Lonely Planet, together with Rough Guides and other concerned partners in the travel industry, supports the carbon offset scheme run by climatecare.org. Lonely Planet offsets all of its staff and author travel.

For more information check out our website: lonelyplanet.com.

---

becoming increasingly important to secure the best deals.

Colombo is not as good as some other Asian centres for cheap flights, so you're probably better off booking your onward tickets before you leave home. For details of travel agencies in Colombo, see p81.

Departure tax will be included in your ticket.

Asia
INDIA

Sri Lankan Airlines links Colombo with Bangalore, Chennai, Delhi, Goa, Tiruchirappalli (Trichy) and Trivandrum. One-way fares start at around US$150. Indian Airlines flies from Chennai to Colombo for a similar price.

Indian low-cost airlines flying to Colombo include **Jet Airways** (www.jetairways.com) from Chennai, **JetLite** (www.jetlite.com) from Chennai, **Kingfisher** (www.flykingfisher.com) from Bangalore and Chennai, and **Air-India Express** (www.airindia

---

AVOIDING COLOMBO

Although we think Colombo has its good points, some travellers opt to bypass it altogether and take a taxi straight from the airport to Negombo (Rs 1200) or to Kandy (Rs 4600).

---

express.com) from Chennai. One-way fares to Colombo on the ultracompetitive Chennai–Colombo route start at around US$70.

India is a convenient hub for travel from the UK to Sri Lanka, with Kingfisher flying from London to Bangalore, and Jet Airways linking London with Mumbai, Delhi and Amritsar.

For an Indian travel agent, **STIC Travels** (www.stictravel.com; Chennai ☎ 044-2433 0211; Delhi ☎ 011-2373 7135; Mumbai ☎ 022-2218 1431) is recommended.

MALDIVES

Many visitors combine a visit to Sri Lanka with the Maldives. One-way/return fares on Sri Lankan Airlines between Colombo and Malé cost US$194/281. Malaysia Airlines and Emirates also fly between Colombo and Malé.

SINGAPORE

Apart from Singapore Airlines and Sri Lankan Airlines, Emirates, Malaysian Airlines and Cathay Pacific also fly between Colombo and Singapore. One-way/return fares start at around US$240/405.

THAILAND

One-way/return fares for Bangkok to Colombo cost around US$250/425 on Thai Airways, Sri Lankan Airlines, Cathay Pacific and Malaysia Airlines.

Australia

The best flight deals from Australia to Sri Lanka are with Singapore Airlines, Malaysian Airlines or Thai Airways. Return fares between Sydney and Colombo begin at around A$1500. Perth to Colombo fares are slightly cheaper.

STA Travel (☎ 1300 733 035; www.statravel.com.au) and **Flight Centre** (☎ 133 133; www.flightcentre.com.au) have offices throughout Australia. For online bookings, try www.travel.com.au.

Canada

Return fares for flights between Vancouver and Colombo start at around C$2400 with Cathay Pacific, Thai Airways and Singapore Airlines. From eastern Canada, you're looking at around C$2600.

Travel Cuts (☎ 800-667-2887; www.travelcuts.com) is Canada's national student travel agency. For online bookings try www.expedia.ca or www.travelocity.ca.

Continental Europe

Sri Lankan Airlines links Colombo with Paris, Rome and Frankfurt. Middle Eastern airlines Emirates, Kuwait Airways, **Etihad** (www.etihadairways.com), Royal Jordanian and Qatar Airways fly from major European hubs, such as London, Paris, Rome and Frankfurt. Check online for specific departure airports for specific airlines. Kuwait Airways and Royal Jordanian are usually the cheapest with return flights to Colombo from Europe for around €900.

FRANCE

Sri Lankan Airlines has direct flights between Paris and Colombo. Return flights start at around €1000. Middle Eastern airlines (see above) also link to Colombo from Paris.

Recommended agencies are:

Anyway (☎ 0892 893 892; www.anyway.fr)
Lastminute (☎ 0892 705 000; www.lastminute.fr)
Nouvelles Frontières (☎ 0825 000 747; www.nouvelles-frontieres.fr)
OTU Voyages (www.otu.fr) This agency specialises in student and youth travellers.
Voyageurs du Monde (☎ 01 40 15 11 15; www.vdm.com)

GERMANY

Sri Lankan Airlines has direct flights between Frankfurt and Colombo. Return flights start at around €900. Middle Eastern airlines (see left) also link to Colombo from Frankfurt. **Condor** (www.condor.com) operates seasonal charter flights (November to April) between Frankfurt and Colombo. Prices start at €618.

Recommended agencies are:

Expedia (www.expedia.de)
Just Travel (☎ 089 747 3330; www.justtravel.de)
Lastminute (☎ 01805 284 366; www.lastminute.de)
STA Travel (☎ 01805 456 422; www.statravel.de) For travellers under the age of 26.

New Zealand

The best flight deals from New Zealand to Sri Lanka are with Singapore Airlines, Malaysian Airlines or Thai Airways. Return fares between Auckland and Colombo begin at around NZ$2100.

Flight Centre (☎ 0800 243 544; www.flightcentre.co.nz), **STA Travel** (☎ 0800 474 400; www.statravel.co.nz) and the **House of Travel** (☎ 0800 838 747; www.houseoftravel.co.nz) have branches throughout New Zealand.

UK & Ireland

Sri Lankan Airlines has direct flights between Colombo and London. Return flights start at around UK£350. Middle Eastern airlines (left) also link to Colombo from London. Another popular route is to fly via India (see p305). **Thomson** (www.thomson.co.uk) operates weekly flights between London and Colombo from November to March.

Recommended travel agencies are:

Bridge the World (☎ 0870 444 7474; www.b-t-w.co.uk)
Flightbookers (☎ 0870 814 4001; www.ebookers.com)
Flight Centre (☎ 0870 890 8099; flightcentre.co.uk)
North-South Travel (☎ 01245 608 291; www.northsouthtravel.co.uk) North-South Travel donates part of its profit to projects in the developing world.
Quest Travel (☎ 0870 442 3542; www.questtravel.com)
STA Travel (☎ 0870 160 0599; www.statravel.co.uk) For travellers under the age of 26.
Trailfinders (www.trailfinders.co.uk)
Travel Bag (☎ 0870 890 1456; www.travelbag.co.uk)

USA

Return fares for flights between Los Angeles and Colombo start at around US$1600 with Cathay Pacific, Thai Airways and Singapore Airlines. From the east coast, you're looking at around US$2000. Another option is on United Airlines code-share flights with Etihad via Doha, with fares from around US$2600.

The following agencies are recommended for online bookings:

- www.cheaptickets.com
- www.expedia.com
- www.itn.net
- www.lowestfare.com
- www.orbitz.com
- www.sta.com
- www.travelocity.com

SEA

Plans to resume ferry services between Mannar in northwest Sri Lanka and India have been rumoured for many years, but the civil war precluded all developments. Any schemes to relaunch the route will need to wait until the ports are repaired, so check with the **Sri Lanka Ports Authority** (www.slpa.lk) for the latest information.

A projected passenger-ferry service between Tuticorin (Tamil Nadu) and Colombo hasn't materialised for the same reasons. There has also been talk of ferry services between Chennai and Colombo, and Kochi and Colombo. The recent expansion of Indian low-cost airlines into Sri Lanka will probably make these developments more far-fetched.

GETTING AROUND

In Sri Lanka the only regular domestic flights are between Jaffna and Colombo. At the time of writing, flights from Colombo to Trincomalee had been suspended, but they will probably be reinstated following the cessation of the civil war.

Travelling on public transport is therefore mostly a choice between buses and trains, both are cheap. Trains can be crowded, but it's nothing compared with the seemingly endless numbers of passengers that squash into ordinary buses. Trains are a bit slower than buses, but a seat on a train is preferable to standing on a bus. Even standing on a train is better than standing on a bus.

On the main roads from Colombo to Kandy, Negombo and Galle, buses cover around 40km to 50km per hour. On highways across the plains, it can be 60km or 70km an hour. In the Hill Country, it can slow to just 20km an hour.

All public transport gets crowded around *poya* (full moon) holidays and their nearest weekends, so try to avoid travelling then.

AIR

Regular flights between Colombo and Jaffna are available with **Expo Aviation** (Map pp84–5; ☎ 011-257 6941; info@expoavi.com) 3). Another option is **AeroLanka** (Map p88; ☎ 011-250 5632; www.aerolanka.com). Flights were on hold at the time of writing but should be operating by this book's publication.

For addresses of airline offices in Colombo and Jaffna, see p98 and p281. Checking in takes at least 2½ hours due to security measures.

BICYCLE

Keen cyclists will find Sri Lanka a joy, apart from the steeper areas of the Hill Country and the busy roads exiting Colombo. When heading out of Colombo in any direction, take a train to the edge of the city before you start cycling.

Start early in the day to avoid the heat, and pack water and sunscreen. Your daily distances will be limited by the roads; be prepared for lots of prudent 'eyes down' cycling as you negotiate a flurry of obstacles from potholes to chickens. Remember, too, that size really does matter on Sri Lankan roads, and to most drivers of 4WDs, avoiding the median strip is a recommendation, not a mandate.

If you bring your own bicycle, also pack a supply of spare tyres and tubes. These suffer from the poor road surfaces, and replacement parts can be hard to obtain. The normal bicycle tyre size in Sri Lanka is 28in by 1.5in. Some imported 27in tyres for 10-speed bikes are available but only in Colombo and at high prices. Keep an eye on your bicycle at all times and use a good lock.

When taking a bicycle on a train, every part has to be described on the travel documents, so deliver the bicycle at least half an hour before departure. At Colombo Fort train station you may want to allow up to two hours. It costs about twice the 2nd-class fare to take a bicycle on a train.

Hire

In terms of hired bicycles, those with gears are the exception rather than the rule. You'll find that most range from merely adequate to desperately uncomfortable with dodgy brakes. Bikes imported from China and India are the norm. You should seriously consider bringing your own gear.

The **National Mountain Biking Association** (☎ 011-269 1505) in Colombo acts as a clearing house for information on mountain biking in Sri Lanka, and also arranges guides for individual or custom tours. **Adventure Asia** (☎ 011-536 8468; www.ad-asia.com), **Adventure Sports Lanka** (☎ 011-279 1584; www.actionlanka.com) and **Eco Team** (☎ 011-583 5893; www.srilankaecotourism.com) all arrange mountain-biking excursions in the Hill Country.

Purchase

Expect to pay US$125 to US$300 for a new bike, depending on the quality. Most are made in India or China; the Chinese bikes are sturdier and more reliable than the Indian bikes. Recommended bike shops are:

City Cycle Stores (Map p80; ☎ 011-250 4632; alamul@ slt.lk; 117-119 Dam Str, Col 12)

Cycle Bazaar (Map pp84-5; ☎ 011-268 6255; 82 Danister De Silva Mawatha, Col 8)

BUS

Bus routes cover about 80% of the nation's 90,000km of roads. There are two kinds of bus in Sri Lanka – Ceylon Transport Board (CTB) buses and private buses. CTB buses are usually painted red and ply most long-distance and local routes. You'll also see red buses with a Sri Lanka Transport Board (SLTB) logo. They're exactly the same as the CTB buses – the same red colour and the same propensity to belch diesel fumes while going very slowly.

Private bus companies have vehicles ranging from late-model Japanese coaches used on intercity-express runs to decrepit old minibuses that sputter and limp along city streets or short runs between towns and villages. Private air-con intercity buses cover all the major routes. For long-distance travel they are far more comfortable and faster than other bus services.

Bus travel in Sri Lanka is both interesting and entertaining. Most locals speak at least some English, so you're guaranteed interesting conversations. Vendors board to sell snacks, books and gifts on long-distance routes. Blind singers sometimes get on and work their way down the aisle, warbling away melancholy Sri Lankan folk songs and collecting coins. Beggars may approach passengers with a litany of misfortunes – which they may also sing. Buses sometimes stop at temples so that the driver and passengers can donate a few coins.

The first two seats on CTB buses are reserved for 'clergy' (Buddhist monks) and this is never ignored. If you want to guarantee a seat, you'll need to board the bus at the beginning of its journey; Sri Lankans seem to know when to sprint after the right bus as it pulls in, and throw a bag or a handkerchief through the window to reserve a seat.

Finding the right bus at the chaotic bus stations in Colombo and Kandy can be challenging. Many of the destination signs are in Sinhala script only, although this is changing for private buses heading for tourist-friendly destinations. There is usually no central ticket office, so you must locate the right parking area and buy your bus ticket either from a small booth or on board the bus. Usually the best strategy is to walk through the station saying the name of your destination until someone leads you to the right bus. There's a pretty good chance a tout from the correct bus will find you first if you're travelling on a route that's popular with travellers. A few provincial bus stations are becoming slightly more orderly, but most likely the atmosphere will still be bustling and chaotic.

When you arrive somewhere it's a good idea to spend five minutes at the bus station confirming departure details for the next stage of your journey.

In smaller towns it's much easier, as there are usually separate bus stops for each destination or direction, and your hotel or guest house can tell you where these stops are. If in doubt, ask a local three-wheeler jockey to steer you (literally…) in the right direction. These switched-on guys usually know everything.

Costs

In most cases, private bus companies run services parallel to CTB services. Intercity expresses charge about twice as much as CTB buses, but are more than twice as comfortable and usually faster. Fares for CTB buses and ordinary private buses are very cheap. The journey between Kandy and Colombo costs Rs 124 on a CTB bus and Rs 250 on an air-con intercity express. A bus trip from Colombo to Anuradhapura costs Rs 224 on an ordinary private bus and Rs 350 by intercity express.

Most buses have unbelievably small luggage compartments and they rarely have storage on the roof. For your own sake, travel light. If you have a large pack, you can buy an extra ticket for your bag.

Reservations

Private buses cannot be booked before the day of travel; to book CTB buses you can call ☎ 011-258 1120.

CAR & MOTORCYCLE

Self-drive car hire is possible in Sri Lanka, though it is far more common to hire a car and driver for a day or more. If you're on a relatively short visit to Sri Lanka on a mid-range budget, the costs of hiring a car and driver can be quite reasonable.

When planning your itinerary, you can count on covering about 35km/h in the Hill Country and 55km/h in most of the rest of the country.

Motorcycling is an alternative for intrepid travellers. Distances are relatively short and some of the roads are a motorcyclist's delight; the trick is to stay off the main highways. The quieter Hill Country roads offer some glorious views, and secondary roads along the coast and the plains are reasonably quick. There are motorcycle-hire agencies in Hikkaduwa and Kandy. In addition to a cash deposit you must provide your passport number and leave your airline ticket as security. The official size limit on imported motorbikes is 350cc.

Driving Licence

An International Driving Permit can be used to roam Sri Lanka's roads, but it's valid for only three months. To extend the permit, turn up at the **Department of Motor Traffic** (Map pp84-5; ☎ 011-269 4331; www.motortraffic.gov.lk; Elvitigala Mawatha, Narahenpita) in Colombo. You'll need to bring your driving licence and two photos.

Hire

HIRING A CAR & DRIVER

You can find taxi drivers who will happily become your chauffeur for a day or more in all the main tourist centres. Guest-house owners can put you in touch with a driver, or you can ask at travel agencies or big hotels.

Various formulas exist for setting costs, such as rates per kilometre plus a lunch and dinner allowance. The simplest way is to agree on a flat fee with no extras. Expect to pay Rs 5500 to 6600 per day, excluding fuel, or more for a newer, air-con vehicle. At the time of writing, petrol cost Rs 120 per L and diesel cost Rs 80, but fuel prices were fluctuating wildly.

Most drivers will expect a tip of about 10%, but of course it's up to you. It pays to meet the driver before you set off as there may be a difference between who the travel agent has led you to expect and who turns up. Some travellers find themselves being almost bullied by their driver: the driver chooses where they go, where they stay and what time they leave. Hiring a driver for only two or three days at first can avoid these problems.

Some travel agencies may suggest you take a guide along as well. Unless you speak absolutely no English or Sinhala, this is unnecessary.

Be aware that drivers make a fair part of their income from commissions. Most hotels and many guest houses pay drivers a flat fee or a percentage, although others refuse to. This can lead to disputes between you and the driver over where you're staying the night – they'd prefer to go where the money is. Some hotels have appalling accommodation for drivers – sometimes just a dirty mattress under the stairs. Some of the worst conditions are in the big hotels; drivers share a dormitory and prison-style meals, people come and go all night, and no one gets a good night's rest. The smarter hotels and guest houses know that keeping drivers happy is good for their business, and provide decent food and lodgings.

A local driver with an excellent knowledge of Sri Lanka is **Nilam Sahabdeen** (http://srilankatour .wordpress.com/). Also recommended is **Mr Dimuthu** (☎ 077 630 2070; dimuthu81@hotmail.com).

SELF-DRIVE HIRE

Colombo-based company **Quickshaws Tours** (Map p88; ☎ 011-258 3133; www.quickshaws.com; 3 Kalinga Pl, Col 5) offers self-drive car hire. A Nissan Sunny costs Rs 23,385 per week, while a larger, more comfortable Nissan Bluebird sedan will set you back Rs 28,050 per week. Both have air-con and include 700km per week. Generally you're not allowed to take the car into national parks, wildlife sanctuaries or jungle, or along unsealed roads.

Road Conditions

Although you may see a number of accidents during your time on the road, driving seems fairly safe provided you take care and watch out for other road users. Country roads are often narrow and potholed, with constant pedestrian, bicycle and animal traffic to navigate.

Punctures are a part of life here, so every little village has a repair expert.

TRANSPORT

Road Rules

The speed limit for vehicles is 56km/h in built-up areas and 72km/h in rural areas. Driving is on the left-hand side of the road, as in the UK and Australia. The **Automobile Association of Ceylon** (Map pp84-5; ☎ 011-242 1528; www.aaceylon.lk; 40 Sir Mohamed Macan Markar Mawatha, Col 3; ☺ 8am-4.30pm Mon-Fri) can supply maps and touring information.

HITCHING

Hitching is never entirely safe in any country in the world, and we don't recommend it. In any case, Sri Lanka's cheap fares make it an unnecessary option. Travellers who do decide to hitch should understand that they are taking a small but potentially serious risk. They can attempt to minimise this risk by travelling in pairs and letting someone know where they are planning to go.

LOCAL TRANSPORT

Many Sri Lankan towns are small enough to walk around. In larger towns, you can get around by bus, taxi or three-wheeler.

Bus

Local buses go to most places, including villages outside main towns, for fares from Rs 10 to 40. Their signboards are usually in Sinhala or Tamil, so you'll have to ask which is the right bus.

Taxi

Sri Lankan taxis are often reconditioned Japanese vans. They're common in all sizable towns, and even some villages will be able to dig up a taxi. Only a few are metered, but over longer distances their prices are comparable to those of three-wheelers, and they provide more comfort and security. Radio taxis are available in Kandy and Colombo. You can count on most taxi rides costing around Rs 60 to 80 per kilometre.

Three-wheeler

Three-wheelers, known in other parts of Asia as *túk-túks*, *bajajs* or autorickshaws, are literally waiting on every corner. Use your best bargaining skills and agree on the fare before you get in. Some keen drivers will offer to take you around Mars and back, and we've even heard of travellers who have gone from Kandy to Nuwara Eliya in the back of a three-wheeler, which would be a slow, but very in-teresting, five hours or so. After an hour, the thrill may dissipate, but you'll have loads of fun with the wind (and often the Hill Country rain) swirling around. You'll also be closer to the locals than in a car or van. Note the average three-wheeler jockey tends to regard road rules as optional recommendations rather than official mandates.

As a rule of thumb, a three-wheeler should cost no more than Rs 80 per kilometre, but this ebbs and flows with the changing cost of fuel. Other travellers and guest-house owners are a good source of up-to-date costs.

Three-wheelers and taxis waiting outside hotels and tourist sights expect higher-than-usual fares. Walk a few hundred metres to get a much better deal.

TOURS

Sri Lanka has many inbound travel companies providing tours. Many of the tours are focused on a particular interest or activity.

A Baur & Co Ltd (www.baurs.com) Specialises in bird-watching tours.

Adventure Asia (www.ad-asia.com) A Western-run outfit specialising in white-water rafting, kayaking, hot-air ballooning and bicycling tours.

Adventure Sports Lanka (www.actionlanka.com) White-water rafting, hiking, mountain biking, canoeing and diving.

Aitken Spence Travels (www.aitkenspencetravels.com) One of the biggest tour operators; organises tour packages, hires out cars and drivers, and books hotels.

Blue Haven Tours (www.bluehaventours.com) Island-wide tours and accommodation in Kandy and the Knuckles Range.

Boutique Sri Lanka (www.boutiquesrilanka.com) Specialises in interesting accommodation, Ayurvedic retreats, and luxury resorts, guest houses and small, heritage hotels.

Carolanka (www.carolanka.co.uk) A good contact for renting private villas.

Eco Team (www.srilankaecotourism.com) Wide range of wilderness-based active adventures, including white-water rafting, hiking and wildlife safaris.

Jetwing Eco (www.jetwingeco.com) Specialises in wildlife- and birdwatching tours.

Jetwing Travels (www.jetwing.net) A big operator, with upmarket hotels and resorts, and organises tours within Sri Lanka and to the Maldives.

JF Tours & Travels (www.jftours.com) Specialises in steam-train tours (groups only), and booking train tickets in general.

Kulu Safaris (www.kulusfaris.com) Offers tented camp safaris in Sri Lankan national parks.

Quickshaws Tours (www.quickshaws.com) Organises standard tours, but specialises in personalised tours with a car and driver. Also hires out self-drive cars.

Red Dot Tours (www.reddottours.com) Sri Lankan specialists, offering everything from golf and cricket to wildlife and wellness.

Sri Lanka Expeditions (www.srilankaexpeditions.com) Activity-based tours, including rock climbing, trekking, mountain biking and white-water rafting.

Sri Lanka In Style (www.srilankainstyle.com) Excellent selection of splurge-worthy and unique accommodation.

Major global companies also offer tours of Sri Lanka, many using local transport and sharing a responsible travel ethos with Lonely Planet. We recommend the following:

Explore Worldwide (www.explore.co.uk)

Intrepid Travel (www.intrepidtravel.com)

Peregrine Adventures (www.pergerineadventure.com)

The Imaginative Traveller (www.imaginative-traveller.com)

TRAIN

Sri Lanka's rickety railways are a great way to cross the country. Although they are slow, trains travel short distances so there are few overnight or all-day ordeals to contend with. A train ride is almost always more relaxed than a bus ride. Just be prepared for the odd journey, crammed cheek by jowl with a fair smattering of Sri Lanka's population.

There are three main lines. The coast line runs south from Colombo, past Aluthgama and Hikkaduwa to Galle and Matara. The main line pushes east from Colombo into the Hill Country, through Kandy, Nanu Oya (for Nuwara Eliya) and Ella to Badulla. The northern line launches from Colombo through Anuradhapura to Vavuniya (it once ran beyond Jaffna to the northern tip of Sri Lanka). One branch of the northern line reaches Trincomalee on the east coast, while another branch heads south to Polonnaruwa and Batticaloa.

The Puttalam line runs along the coast north from Colombo, although rail buses run between Chilaw and Puttalam. The Kelani Valley line winds 60km from Colombo to Avissawella.

Trains are often late. For long-distance trains, Sri Lankans sometimes measure the lateness in periods of the day: quarter of a day late, half a day late and so on.

There's a helpful information desk (No 10) at Colombo Fort train station, and also an **information office** (☎ 011-244 0048; ☺ 9am-5pm Mon-Fri, 9am-1pm Sat) to the right of the main entrance, run by JF Tours. The staff can provide information on timetables and routes. For details of the main trains leaving Colombo and Kandy, see the boxed tables, p100 and p169, respectively.

The **Sri Lankan Railways** (www.railway.gov.lk) website has a surprisingly helpful online trip planner.

Classes

There are three classes on Sri Lankan trains. Third class is dirt cheap and invariably crowded, but with a little luck you'll get a seat on a bench. Second class has padded seats and fans that sometimes work, and it's generally less crowded. There are no 2nd-class sleeping berths, only 'sleeperettes' (fold-down beds in a shared compartment). First class comes in three varieties, all with air-con – coaches, sleeping berths and observation saloons (with large windows) – but is available on relatively few lines.

Costs

As a sample, the intercity express from Kandy to Colombo costs Rs 400/250 in 1st/2nd class. From Colombo to Anuradhapura, the intercity express costs Rs 600/400 in 1st/2nd class.

Reservations

You can reserve places in 1st class and on intercity expresses. On four of the daily intercity services between Colombo and Kandy, you can also book on 2nd-class sleeperettes.

On weekends and public holidays it pays to make a booking for 24-seat observation saloons, which only run on the main line, as these carriages often fill up. The best seats to book are Nos 11, 12, 23 and 24, all with full window views. The observation saloon is at the rear of the train and is quite bumpy. If you're prone to motion sickness, note that from Kandy to Colombo the observation saloon travels backwards.

Reservations can be made at train stations up to 10 days before departure. You can book a return ticket up to 14 days before departure.

If travelling more than 80km, you can break your journey at any intermediate station for 24 hours without penalty. You'll need to make fresh reservations for seats on the next leg.

Health

CONTENTS

While the potential dangers of Sri Lankan travel may seem ominous, most travellers experience nothing more serious than an upset stomach. Hygiene is generally poor throughout the country, so food- and water-borne illnesses are common. Travellers tend to worry about contracting infectious diseases, but infections rarely cause *serious* illness or death in travellers. Pre-existing medical conditions, such as heart disease, and accidental injury (especially traffic accidents) account for most life-threatening problems.

Most travellers' illnesses can either be prevented by common-sense behaviour or be treated easily with a well-stocked traveller's medical kit. The following advice is a general guide only and does not replace the advice of a doctor trained in travel medicine.

BEFORE YOU GO

Pack medications in their original, clearly labelled containers. A signed and dated letter from your physician describing your medical conditions and medications, including generic names, is very useful. If carrying syringes or needles, have a physician's letter documenting their medical necessity. If you have a heart condition, bring a copy of your ECG taken just before travelling.

If you take any regular medication, bring double your needs in case of loss or theft. You can buy many medications over the counter in Sri Lanka without a doctor's prescription, but it can be difficult to find newer drugs, particularly the latest antidepressant drugs, blood pressure medications and contraceptive pills.

INSURANCE

Even if you're fit and healthy don't travel without health insurance; accidents do happen. Declare any existing medical conditions; the insurance company will check if your problem is pre-existing and will not cover you if it is undeclared. You may require extra cover for adventure activities, such scuba diving. If your health insurance doesn't cover you for medical expenses abroad, consider getting extra insurance. If you're uninsured, emergency evacuation is expensive, and bills of more than US$100,000 are not uncommon.

Find out in advance if your insurance company will make payments directly to providers or reimburse you later for overseas expenditures. (In many countries, doctors expect payment in cash.) Some policies offer a range of medical-expense options; the higher ones for countries that have high medical costs, such as the USA. You may prefer a policy that pays doctors or hospitals directly rather than you having to pay on the spot and claim later. If you have to claim later, keep all documentation. Some policies ask you to phone (reverse charges) a centre in your home country where an immediate assessment of your problem is made.

VACCINATIONS

Specialised travel-medicine clinics stock all available vaccines and can give specific recommendations for your trip. The doctors will consider factors including past vaccination history, your trip's duration, activities you may be undertaking and underlying medical conditions, such as pregnancy.

Most vaccines don't give immunity until at least two weeks after they're given, so visit a doctor four to eight weeks before departure. Ask your doctor for an International Certificate of Vaccination (aka the 'yellow booklet') to list all your vaccinations.

Recommended Vaccinations

The World Health Organization (WHO) recommends the following vaccinations for travellers to Sri Lanka (as well as being up to date with measles, mumps and rubella vaccinations).

Adult diphtheria and tetanus Single booster recommended if none in the previous 10 years. Side effects include sore arm and fever.

Hepatitis A Provides almost 100% protection for up to a year; a booster after 12 months provides at least another 20 years' protection. Mild side effects, such as headache and sore arm, occur in 5% to 10% of people.

Hepatitis B Now considered routine for most travellers. Given as three shots over six months. A rapid schedule is also available, as is a combined vaccination with Hepatitis A. Side effects are mild and uncommon, usually headache and sore arm. In 95% of people, lifetime protection results.

Polio Incidence has been unreported in Sri Lanka for several years but must be assumed to be present. Only one booster is required as an adult for lifetime protection. Inactivated polio vaccine is safe during pregnancy.

Rabies Three injections in all. A booster after one year will then provide 10 years' protection. Side effects are rare – occasionally headache and sore arm.

Typhoid Recommended for all travellers to Sri Lanka, even if you only visit urban areas. The vaccine offers around 70% protection, lasts for two to three years and comes as a single shot. Tablets are also available; however, the injection is usually recommended as it has fewer side effects. Sore arm and fever may occur.

Varicella If you haven't had chickenpox, discuss this vaccination with your doctor.

Immunisations recommended for long-term travellers (more than one month) or those at special risk:

Japanese B Encephalitis Three injections in all. Booster recommended after two years. Sore arm and headache are the most common side effects. Rarely, an allergic reaction of hives and swelling can occur up to 10 days after any of the three doses.

Meningitis Single injection. There are two types of vaccination: the quadravalent vaccine gives two to three years' protection; meningitis group C vaccine gives around 10 years' protection. Recommended for long-term backpackers aged under 25.

Tuberculosis (TB) A complex issue. Adult long-term travellers are usually recommended to have a TB skin test before and after travel, rather than vaccination. Only one vaccine is given in a lifetime.

Required Vaccinations

The only vaccine required by international regulations is yellow fever. Proof of vaccination will only be required if you have visited a country in the yellow-fever zone within the six days before entering Sri Lanka.

MEDICAL CHECKLIST

Recommended items for a personal medical kit:

- antibacterial cream, eg Muciprocin
- antibiotic for skin infections, eg Amoxicillin/Clavulanate or Cephalexin
- antifungal cream, eg Clotrimazole
- antihistamine: there are many options, eg Cetrizine for day and promethazine for night
- anti-inflammatory, eg ibuprofen
- antiseptic, eg Betadine
- antispasmodic for stomach cramps, eg Buscopan
- contraceptive
- decongestant, eg pseudoephedrine
- DEET-based insect repellent
- diarrhoea medication: consider an oral rehydration solution (eg Gastrolyte), diarrhoea 'stopper' (eg Loperamide) and antinausea medication (eg Prochlorperazine); antibiotics for diarrhoea include Norfloxacin or ciprofloxacin, for bacterial diarrhoea Azithromycin, for giardia or amoebic dysentery Tinidazole
- first-aid items, eg scissors, sticking plasters, bandages, gauze, thermometer (but not mercury), sterile needles and syringes, safety pins and tweezers
- indigestion tablets or liquid, eg Quick Eze or Mylanta
- insect repellent to impregnate clothing and mosquito nets, eg permethrin
- iodine tablets (unless you're pregnant or have a thyroid problem) to purify water
- laxative, eg Coloxyl
- migraine medication if you are a sufferer
- painkiller tablets, eg paracetamol
- steroid cream for allergic or itchy rashes, eg 1% to 2% hydrocortisone
- sunscreen and hat
- throat lozenges
- thrush (vaginal yeast infection) treatment, eg Clotrimazole pessaries or Diflucan tablet
- urinary tract infection treatment, such as Ural or equivalent, if you're prone to urinary infections

HEALTH

INTERNET RESOURCES

There is a wealth of travel health advice on the internet. **Lonely Planet** (www.lonelyplanet.com) is a good place to start. Other suggestions:
Centers for Disease Control & Prevention (CDC; www.cdc.gov) Good general information.
MD Travel Health (www.mdtravelhealth.com) Provides complete travel health recommendations for every country, updated daily.
World Health Organization (WHO; www.who.int/ith/) Its book *International Travel & Health* is revised annually and available online.

FURTHER READING

Lonely Planet's handy pocket-sized *Healthy Travel: Asia & India* is packed with useful information. Other recommended references include *Traveller's Health* by Dr Richard Dawood and *Travelling Well* by Dr Deborah Mills – check out the website of **Travelling Well** (www.travellingwell.com.au).

IN TRANSIT

DEEP VEIN THROMBOSIS (DVT)

DVT occurs when blood clots form in the legs during plane flights, chiefly due to prolonged immobility. The longer the flight the greater the risk. Although most blood clots are reabsorbed uneventfully, some may break off and travel through the blood vessels to the lungs where they could cause life-threatening complications.

The chief symptom of DVT is swelling or pain in the foot, ankle or calf, usually but not always on just one side. When a blood clot travels to the lungs it may cause chest pain and difficulty in breathing. Travellers with any of these symptoms should seek medical attention immediately.

To prevent the onset of DVT on long flights you should walk about, perform isometric compressions of the leg muscles (ie contract the leg muscles while sitting), drink plenty of fluids and avoid alcohol and tobacco.

JET LAG & MOTION SICKNESS

Jet lag is common when crossing more than five time zones; it results in insomnia, fatigue, malaise or nausea. To avoid jet lag drink plenty of (nonalcoholic) fluids and eat light meals. On arrival, seek exposure to natural sunlight and readjust your schedule (for meals, sleep etc) as soon as possible.

Antihistamines, such as dimenhydrinate (Dramamine), promethazine (Phenergan) and meclizine (Antivert, Bonine), are usually the first choice for treating motion sickness. Their main side effect is drowsiness. A herbal alternative is ginger, which works like a charm for some people.

IN SRI LANKA

AVAILABILITY OF HEALTH CARE

Medical care is hugely variable in Sri Lanka. Colombo has some good clinics; they may be more expensive than local medical facilities, but they're worth using because a superior standard of care is offered.

Self-treatment may be appropriate if your problem is minor (eg traveller's diarrhoea), if you are carrying the relevant medication and if you cannot attend a recommended clinic. If you think you may have a serious disease, especially malaria, do not waste time: travel to the nearest quality facility to receive attention. It is always better to be assessed by a doctor than to rely on self-treatment.

Before buying medication over the counter, always check the use-by date and ensure the packet is sealed. Don't accept items that have been poorly stored (eg lying in a glass cabinet exposed to the sun).

INFECTIOUS DISEASES
Dengue

This mosquito-borne disease is becomingly increasingly problematic in the tropical world, especially in the cities. As there is no vaccine it can only be prevented by avoiding mosquito bites. The dengue-carrying mosquito bites both day and night, so use insect avoidance measures at all times. Symptoms include high fever, severe headache and body ache (dengue was previously known as 'breakbone fever'). Some people develop a rash and experience diarrhoea. There is no specific treatment – just rest and paracetamol; do not take aspirin because it increases the likelihood of haemorrhaging. See a doctor for diagnosis and monitoring.

Hepatitis A

This food- and water-borne virus infects the liver, causing jaundice (yellow skin and eyes), nausea and lethargy. There is no specific treatment for hepatitis A, as you just need to allow time for the liver to heal. All travellers to Sri Lanka should be vaccinated against hepatitis A.

Hepatitis B

The only sexually transmitted disease that can be prevented by vaccination, hepatitis B is spread by body fluids. The long-term consequences can include liver cancer and cirrhosis.

Hepatitis E

Hepatitis E is transmitted through contaminated food and water. It has similar symptoms to hepatitis A, but is far less common. It's a severe problem in pregnant women, and can result in the death of both mother and baby. There is currently no vaccine, and prevention is by following safe eating and drinking guidelines.

HIV

HIV is spread via contaminated body fluids. Avoid unsafe sex, unsterile needles (including in medical facilities) and procedures such as tattooing.

Japanese B Encephalitis

This viral disease is transmitted by mosquitoes and is rare in travellers. Like most mosquito-borne diseases, it is becoming a more common problem in many countries affected by mosquitoes. Most cases occur in rural areas, and vaccination is recommended for travellers spending more than one month outside of cities. There is no treatment, and a third of infected people will die, while another third will suffer permanent brain damage.

Malaria

In recent years Sri Lanka has been successful in limiting malaria, and at the time of writing it was restricted to isolated areas of the north and east.

Malaria is caused by a parasite transmitted by the bite of an infected mosquito. The most important symptom of malaria is fever, but general symptoms such as headache, diarrhoea, cough or chills may also occur. Diagnosis can only be made by taking a blood sample.

Two strategies should be combined to prevent malaria – mosquito avoidance and antimalarial medications. Most people who catch malaria are taking inadequate or no antimalarial medication. Travellers are advised to prevent mosquito bites by taking these steps:

- using a DEET-containing insect repellent on exposed skin – wash this off at night, as long as you are sleeping under a mosquito net; natural repellents such as citronella can be effective but must be applied more frequently than products containing DEET;
- sleeping under a mosquito net impregnated with permethrin;
- choosing accommodation with screens and fans (if not air-conditioned);
- impregnating clothing with permethrin in high-risk areas;
- wearing long sleeves and trousers in light colours;
- using mosquito coils;
- spraying your room with insect repellent before going out for your evening meal.

There are a variety of medications available. The effectiveness of the chloroquine and Paludrine combination is limited in many parts of South Asia. Common side effects include nausea (40% of people) and mouth ulcers.

The daily tablet doxycycline is a broad-spectrum antibiotic that has the added benefit of helping to prevent a variety of diseases, including leptospirosis, tick-borne disease and typhus. Potential side effects include photosensitivity (a tendency to sunburn), thrush (in women), indigestion, heartburn, nausea and interference with the contraceptive pill. More-serious side effects include ulceration of the oesophagus; you can help prevent this by taking your tablet with a meal and a large glass of water, and never lying down within half an hour of taking it. It must be taken for four weeks after leaving the risk area.

Lariam (Mefloquine) has received much bad press, some of it justified, some not. This weekly tablet suits many people. Serious side effects are rare but include depression, anxiety, psychosis and fits. Anyone with a history of depression, anxiety, other psychological disorders or epilepsy should not take Lariam. If you are pregnant, you should consult your doctor before taking it. Tablets must be taken for four weeks after leaving the risk area.

Malarone is a combination of Atovaquone and Proguanil. Side effects are uncommon and mild, most commonly nausea and headache. It is the best tablet for scuba divers and for those on short trips to high-risk areas. It must be taken for one week after leaving the risk area.

Rabies

This uniformly fatal disease is spread by the bite or lick of an infected animal, most commonly a dog or monkey. You should seek medical advice immediately after any animal bite and begin postexposure treatment. Having a pretravel vaccination means that the postbite treatment is very much simplified. If an animal bites you, gently wash the wound with soap and water and apply iodine-based antiseptic. If you are not prevaccinated, you will need to receive rabies immunoglobulin as soon as possible, and this is almost impossible to obtain in much of Sri Lanka.

Tuberculosis

While TB is rare in travellers, those who have significant contact with the local population (such as medical and aid workers and long-term travellers) should take precautions. Vaccination is usually only given to children under the age of five, but adults at risk are recommended to have pre- and post-travel TB testing. The main symptoms are fever, a cough, weight loss, night sweats and tiredness.

Typhoid

This serious bacterial infection is spread via food and water. It gives a high and slowly progressive fever and a headache, and it may be accompanied by a dry cough and stomach pain. It is diagnosed by blood tests and treated with antibiotics. Vaccination is recommended for all travellers spending more than a week in Sri Lanka. Be aware that vaccination is not 100% effective, so be careful with what you eat and drink.

TRAVELLER'S DIARRHOEA

Traveller's diarrhoea is usually caused by a bacteria (there are numerous potential culprits), and therefore responds promptly to antibiotic treatment. Treatment with antibiotics will depend on your situation – how sick you are, how quickly you need to get better, where you are and so on.

Traveller's diarrhoea is defined as the passage of more than three watery bowel actions within 24 hours, plus at least one other symptom, such as fever, cramps, nausea, vomiting or feeling generally unwell.

Treatment consists of staying well hydrated; rehydration solutions like Gastrolyte are the best for this. Antibiotics, such as Norfloxacin, Ciprofloxacin or Azithromycin, will kill the bacteria quickly.

Loperamide is just a 'stopper' and doesn't get to the cause of the problem, though it can be helpful (eg if you have to go on a long bus ride). Don't take Loperamide if you have a fever or blood in your stools. Seek medical attention quickly if you do not respond to an appropriate antibiotic.

ENVIRONMENTAL HAZARDS

Diving & Surfing

Divers and surfers should seek specialised advice before travelling to ensure their medical kit contains treatment for coral cuts and tropical ear infections, as well as the standard problems. Divers should make sure their insurance covers decompression illness; consider getting specialised dive insurance through an organisation such as **Divers Alert Network** (DAN; www.danseap.org).

Food

Eating in restaurants is the biggest risk for contracting traveller's diarrhoea. Ways to avoid it include eating only freshly cooked food, and avoiding shellfish and food that has been sitting in buffets. Peel all fruit, cook vegetables, and soak salads in iodine water for at least 20 minutes. Eat in busy restaurants that have a high turnover of customers.

Heat

Much of Sri Lanka is hot year-round. Avoid dehydration and excessive activity in the heat. Take it easy when you first arrive. Don't eat salt tablets (they aggravate the gut); drinking rehydration solution or eating salty food helps.

Dehydration is the main contributor to heat exhaustion. Symptoms include weakness, headache, irritability, nausea, sweaty skin, a fast, weak pulse, and a normal or slightly elevated body temperature. Treatment involves getting out of the heat and sun, fanning the sufferer and applying cool wet cloths to the skin, laying the sufferer flat with their legs raised and rehydrating with water containing a ¼-teaspoon of salt per litre. Recovery is usually rapid, but it is common to feel weak for some days afterwards.

Heatstroke is a serious medical emergency. Symptoms come on suddenly and include weakness, nausea, a hot dry body with a body temperature of over 41°C, dizziness, confusion, loss of coordination, fits, and eventually collapse and loss of consciousness. Seek medical help and start cooling by getting the person out of the heat, removing their clothes, fanning them and applying cool wet cloths or ice to their body, especially to the groin and armpits.

Prickly heat is a common skin rash in the tropics, caused by sweat being trapped under the skin. The result is an itchy rash of tiny lumps. Treat it by moving out of the heat and into an air-conditioned area for a few hours and by having cool showers. Creams and ointments clog the skin, so they should be avoided. Locally bought prickly heat powder can be helpful.

Insect Bites & Stings

Bedbugs don't carry disease, but their bites are very itchy. They live in the cracks of furniture and walls, and then migrate to the bed at night to feed on you. You can treat the itch with an antihistamine.

Lice inhabit various parts of your body but most commonly your head and pubic area.

Ticks are contracted after walking in rural areas and are commonly found behind the ears, on the belly and in armpits. If you have had a tick bite and experience symptoms, such as a rash at the site of the bite or elsewhere, fever or muscle aches, you should see a doctor. The antimalarial drug doxycycline prevents tick-borne diseases.

Leeches are found in humid rainforest areas. They do not transmit any disease, but their bites are often intensely itchy for weeks afterwards and can easily become infected. Apply an iodine-based antiseptic to any leech bite to help prevent infection.

Bee and wasp stings mainly cause problems for people who are allergic to them. Anyone with a serious bee or wasp allergy should carry an adrenaline injection (such as an Epipen) for emergency treatment.

Skin Problems

Fungal rashes are common in humid climates. There are two fungal rashes that affect travellers. The first occurs in moist areas of the body that get less air, such as the groin, armpits and between the toes. It starts as a red patch that slowly spreads and is usually itchy. Treatment involves keeping the skin dry, avoiding chafing and using an antifungal cream, such as Clotrimazole or Lamisil.

Cuts and scratches become easily infected in humid climates. Take meticulous care of any cuts and scratches to prevent complications, such as abscesses. Immediately wash all wounds in clean water and apply antiseptic.

Snakes

There are five species of venomous snakes in Sri Lanka, and it is relatively common to spot them, especially in the dry zone area around Anuradhapura and Polonnaruwa. Be careful when wandering around the ancient ruins. Snake bites do not cause instantaneous death, and antivenins are usually available. Wrap the bitten limb tightly, as you would for a sprained ankle, and then attach a splint to immobilise it. Keep the victim still and seek medical help, if possible with the dead snake for identification.

Sunburn

Even on a cloudy day, sunburn can occur rapidly. Always use a strong sunscreen (at least factor 30), making sure to reapply after a swim, and always wear a wide-brimmed hat and sunglasses outdoors. Avoid lying in the sun during the hottest part of the day (10am to 2pm).

WOMEN'S HEALTH

Pregnant women should receive specialised advice before travelling. The ideal time to travel is in the second trimester (between 16 and 28 weeks), when the risk of pregnancy-related problems is at its lowest. Always carry a list of quality medical facilities available at your destination and ensure you continue your standard antenatal care at these facilities. Avoid rural travel in areas with poor transport and medical facilities. Most of all, ensure travel insurance covers all pregnancy-related issues, including premature labour.

Malaria is a high-risk disease during pregnancy. WHO recommends that pregnant women do *not* travel to areas with malaria that is chloroquine resistant. None of the more effective antimalarial drugs are completely safe in pregnancy.

Traveller's diarrhoea can quickly lead to dehydration and result in inadequate blood flow to the placenta. Many of the drugs used to treat various diarrhoea bugs are not recommended in pregnancy. Azithromycin is considered safe.

HEALTH

Language

CONTENTS

Sinhala and Tamil are both national languages, with English commonly described as a linking language. It's easy to get by in Sri Lanka with English, and the Sri Lankan variety has its own unique characteristics – 'You are having a problem, isn't it, no?' While English may be widely spoken in the main centres, off the beaten track its spread thins. In any case, even a few words of Sinhala or Tamil will win you smiles. People really appreciate the effort when they meet foreigners willing to greet them in their own language.

SRI LANKAN ENGLISH

Like every other country where English is spoken, Sri Lanka has its own peculiar versions of some words and phrases. Life can be a bit confusing if you don't have a grasp of some of the essentials of Sri Lankan English, so we've included a few examples here.

Greetings & Questions
Go and come – farewell greeting, similar to 'see you later'; not taken literally
How? – How are you?
Nothing to do – Can't do anything

What to do? – What can be done about it?; more of a rhetorical question
What country? – Where are you from?

People
baby/bubba – term used for any child up to about adolescence
batchmate – university classmate
paining – hurting
peon – office helper
to gift – to give a gift
uncle/auntie – term of respect for elder

Getting Around
backside – part of the building away from the street
bajaj – three-wheeler
bus halt – bus stop
coloured lights – traffic lights
down south – the areas south of Colombo, especially coastal areas
dropping – being dropped off at a place by a car
get down (from bus/train/three-wheeler) – to alight
normal bus – not a private bus
outstation – place beyond a person's home area
petrol shed – petrol/gas station
pick-up (noun) – 4WD utility vehicle
seaside/landside – indicates locations, usually in relation to Galle Rd
two-wheeler – motorcycle
up and down – return trip
up country/Hill Country – Kandy and beyond, tea plantation areas
vehicle – car

Food
bite – snack usually eaten with alcoholic drinks
boutique – a little, hole-in-the-wall shop, usually selling small, inexpensive items
cool spot – traditional, small shop that sells cool drinks and snacks
hotel – a small, cheap restaurant that doesn't offer accommodation
lunch packet/rice packet – portion of rice and curry wrapped in plastic and newspaper and taken to office or school for lunch
short eats – snack food

Money
buck – rupee
last price – final price when bargaining
purse – wallet

SINHALA

Sinhala is somewhat simplified by the use of many *eka* words. Eka is used more or less similarly to the English definite article 'the' and *ekak* is used like 'a' or 'any'. English words for which there is no Sinhala equivalent have often been incorporated into Sinhala with the simple addition of *eka* or *ekak*. So, if you're in search of a telephone, it's simply *telifon ekak,* but if it is a specific telephone, then you should say *telifon eka*. Similarly, English definitions of people have been included in Sinhala simply by adding *kenek* – if you hire a car, the driver is the *draiwar kenek*.

Two useful little Sinhala words are *da* and *ge. Da* turns a statement into a question – thus if *nohna* means a lady then *nohna-da* means 'This lady?' or 'Is this the lady?' The suffix *ge* is the Sinhala equivalent of an apostrophe indicating possession; thus 'Tony's book' in Sinhala is *Tony-ge potha. Ta* is like the English preposition 'to' – if you want to go 'to the beach', it's *valla-ta*.

As in many other Asian countries, Sri Lankans do not use the multitude of greetings that you find in English ('Hello', 'Good morning', 'How are you?', 'Goodbye'). Saying *aayu-bowan* more or less covers them all. Similarly, there isn't really a Sinhala word for 'Thank you'. You could try *istuhtee* but it's a bit stiff and formal – a simple smile will often suffice. Appreciation of a meal can be expressed by *bohoma rahay,* which is both a compliment and an expression of appreciation. *Hari sho-ke* translates as 'wonderful', 'terrific' or even 'fine'. A side-to-side wiggle of the head often means 'yes' or 'OK'.

For a more comprehensive guide to the language, pick up a copy of Lonely Planet's *Sinhala Phrasebook*.

FORMS OF ADDRESS

In Sinhala there are more than 20 ways to say 'you' depending on the person's age, social status, sex, position and even how well you know them. The best solution is to simply avoid saying 'you'. The word for Mr is *mahaththeya* – 'Mr Jayewardene' is *Jayewardene mahaththeya*. The word for 'Mrs' is *nohna* and it also comes after the person's name. Any non-Eastern foreigner is defined as white *(sudha),* so a male foreigner is a *sudha mahaththeya*.

Sinhala is officially written using a cursive script and there are about 50 letters in the alphabet.

PRONUNCIATION

The transliteration system used in this guide to represent the sounds of Sinhala uses the closest English equivalents – they are approximations only. Listening to Sri Lankans is the best way to learn Sinhala pronunciation.

When consonants are doubled they should be pronounced very distinctly, almost as two separate sounds belonging to two separate words. The letters **t** and **d** are pronounced less forcefully than in English, and **g** is pronounced as in 'go', not as in 'rage'. The letter **r** is more like a flap of the tongue against the roof of the mouth – it's not pronounced as an American 'r'.

Vowels

a	as the 'u' in 'cup'; aa is pronounced more like the 'a' in 'father'
e	as in 'met'
i	as in 'bit'
o	as in 'hot'
u	as in 'put', not as in 'hut'

Vowel Combinations

ai	as the word 'eye'
au	as the 'ow' in 'how'

Consonants

dh	one sound, as the 'th' in 'then' (not as in 'thin')
g	as in 'go'
r	a flap of the tongue against the roof of the mouth – not pronounced as an American 'r'
th	one sound, as in 'thin'

ACCOMMODATION

Do you have any rooms available?	kaamara thiyanawada?
for one person	ek-kenek pamanai
for two people	den-nek pamanai
for one night	ek rayak pamanai
for two nights	raya dekak pamanai
How much is it per night?	ek ra-yakata kiyada
How much is it per person?	ek kenek-kuta kiyada

LANGUAGE

Is breakfast included?	*udeh keh-emath ekkada?*
hotel	*hotel eka*
guesthouse	*gesthaus eka*
youth hostel	*yut-hostel eka*
camping ground	*kamping ground eka*

CONVERSATION & ESSENTIALS

Hello.	*aayu-bowan/hello*
Goodbye.	*aayu-bowan*
Yes.	*owu*
No.	*naha*
Please.	*karuna kara*
Thank you.	*istuh-tee*
Excuse me.	*samah venna*
Sorry/Pardon.	*kana gaatui*
Do you speak English?	*oyaa in-ghirisih kata karenawa da?*
How much is it?	*ehekka keeyada?*
What's your name?	*oyaaghe nama mokka'da?*
My name is ...	*maaghe nama ...*

EMERGENCIES – SINHALA

Help!	*aaney!/aaeeyoh!/ammoh!*
Call a doctor!	*dostara gen-nanna!*
Call the police!	*polisiyata kiyanna!*
Leave me alone!	*mata maghe paduweh inna arinna!*
Go away!	*methanin yanna!*
I'm lost.	*maa-meh nativelaa*

NUMBERS

0	*binduwa*
1	*eka*
2	*deka*
3	*thuna*
4	*hathara*
5	*paha*
6	*haya*
7	*hatha*
8	*atta*
9	*navaya*
10	*dahaya*
100	*seeya*
200	*deh seeya*
1000	*daaha*
2000	*deh daaha*
100,000	*lakshaya*
1,000,000	*daseh lakshaya*
10,000,000	*kotiya*

SHOPPING & SERVICES

bank	*bankuwa*
chemist/pharmacy	*faahmisiya*

SIGNS – SINHALA

Entrance	*etul veema*	ඇතුල්වීම
Exit	*pita veema*	පිටවීම
Information	*toraturu*	තොරතුරු දැන්වුම
Open	*virutai etta*	විවෘතව ඇත.
Closed	*vasaa etta*	වසා ඇත.
Prohibited	*tahanam*	තහනම් මව.
Police Station	*polis staaneya*	පොලිස් ස්ථානය
Rooms Available	*kamara etta*	කාමර ඇත.
No Vacancies	*ida netu*	කාමර නැත.
Toilets	*vasikili*	වැසිකිළි
Men	*purusha*	පුරුෂ
Women	*isthree*	ස්ත්‍රී

... embassy	*... embasiya*
market	*maakat eka*
my hotel	*mang inna hotalaya*
newsagency	*pattara ejensiya*
post office	*tepal kantohruwa*
public telephone	*podu dura katanayak*
stationers	*lipi dravya velendoh*
tourist office	*sanchaaraka toraturu karyaalayak*
big	*loku*
small	*podi, punchi*
medicine	*behe-yat*

What time does it open/close?
ehika kiyatada arinneh/vahanneh?

TIME & DAYS

What time is it?	*velaave keeyada?*
day	*davasa*
night	*raah*
week	*sumaanayak*
month	*maasayak*
year	*avuurudeh*
today	*ada (uther)*
tomorrow	*heta*
yesterday	*ee-yeh*
morning	*udai*
afternoon	*havasa*

Monday	sandu-da
Tuesday	angaharuwaa-da
Wednesday	badaa-da
Thursday	braha-spetin-da
Friday	sikuraa-da
Saturday	senasuraa-da
Sunday	iri-da

TRANSPORT

When does does the next ... leave/arrive?
meelanga ... pitaht venne/paminenne?

boat	bohtuwa
bus (city)	bus eka
bus (intercity)	bus eka (nagaraantara)
train	koh-chiya
plane	plane eka

I want to get off.
   mama methana bahinawa
I'd like a one-way ticket.
   mata tani gaman tikat ekak ganna ohna
I'd like a return ticket.
   mata yaam-eem tikat ekak ganna ohna

1st class	palamu veni paantiya
2nd class	deveni paantiya
3rd class	tunveni paantiya
timetable	kaala satahana
bus stop	bus nevathuma/bus hohlt eka
train station	dumriya pala
ferry terminal	totu pala

I'd like to hire ...
mata ... ekak bad-dhata ganna ohna

| a car | kar (eka) |
| a bicycle | baisikeleya |

Directions

Where is (a/the) ...?	... koheda?
Go straight ahead.	kelinma issarahata yaanna
Turn left.	wamata harenna
Turn right.	dakunata harenna
near	lan-ghai
far	durai

TAMIL

The vocabulary of Sri Lankan Tamil is much the same as that of South India – the written form is identical, using the traditional cursive script – but there are marked differences in pronunciation between speakers from the two regions. The transliteration system used in this guide is intended to represent the sounds of Sri Lankan Tamil

using the Roman alphabet – as with all such systems it is an approximate guide only. The best way to improve your pronunciation is to listen to the way Sri Lankans themselves speak the language. You can also check out the Tamil chapter in Lonely Planet's *India Phrasebook*.

PRONUNCIATION
Vowels

a	as the 'u' in 'cup'; aa is pronounced as the 'a' in 'father'
e	as in 'met'
i	as in 'bit'
o	as in 'hot'
u	as in 'put'

Vowel Combinations

| ai | as in 'eye' |
| au | as in 'how' |

Consonants

Most consonants are fairly similar to their English counterparts. The following are a few that may cause confusion:

dh	one sound, as the 'th' in 'then' (not as in 'thin')
g	as in 'go'
r	a flap of the tongue against the roof of the mouth – not pronounced as an American 'r'
s	as in 'sit'
th	one sound, as in 'thin'

ACCOMMODATION

Do you have any rooms available?
   ingu room kideikkumaa?
for one/two people
   oruvarukku/iruvarukku
for one/two nights
   oru/irandu iravukku
How much is it per night/per person?
   oru iravukku/oru aalukku evvalavur?
Is breakfast included?
   kaalei unavum sehrtha?

hotel	hotehl
guesthouse	virun-dhinar vidhudheh
youth hostel	ilainar vidhudheh
camping ground	mukhaamidum idahm

CONVERSATION & ESSENTIALS

Hello.	vanakkam
Goodbye.	poytu varukirehn
Yes.	aam

No.	il-lay
Please.	tayavu saydhu
Thank you.	nandri
You're welcome.	nalladu varukha
Excuse me.	mannikavum
Sorry/Pardon.	mannikavum
Do you speak English?	nin-gal aangilam paysu-virhalaa?
How much is it?	adhu evvalavu?
What's your name?	ungal peyr en-na?
My name is ...	en peyr ...

EMERGENCIES – TAMIL

Help!	udavi!
Call a doctor!	daktarai kuppidunga!
Call the police!	polisai kuppidunga!
Leave me alone!	enna taniyaahu irukkavidunga!
Go away!	pohn-goh!/poi-vidu!
I'm lost.	naan vali tavari-vittehn

NUMBERS

0	saifer
1	ondru
2	iranduh
3	muundruh
4	naan-guh
5	ainduh
6	aaruh
7	ealluh
8	ettu
9	onbaduh
10	pat-tuh
100	nooruh
1000	aayirem
2000	irandaayirem
100,000	oru latcham
1,000,000	pattuh lat-chem
10,000,000	kohdee

SHOPPING & SERVICES

bank	vanghee
chemist/pharmacy	marunduh kadhai/pharmacy
... embassy	... tudharalayem
market	maarket
my hotel	enadu hotehl
newsagency	niyuz paper vitku-midam
post office	tafaal nilayem
public telephone	podhu tolai-pessee
stationers	eludhuporul vitku-midam
tourist office	toorist nilayem
big	periyeh
small	siriyeh
medicine	marunduh

SIGNS – TAMIL

Entrance
  vahli ullay — வழி உள்ளே
Exit
  vahli veliyeh — வழி வெளியே
Information
  tahavwel — தகவல்
Open
  thirandul-ladhu — திறந்துள்ளது
Closed
  adek-kappattulladhu
  அடைக்கப்பட்டுள்ளது
Prohibited
  anumadee-illay — அனுமதி இல்லை
Police Station
  kaav'l nilayem — காவல் நிலையம்
Rooms Available
  arekahl undu — அறைகள் உண்டு
Full, No Vacancies
  illay, kaali illay
  நிரம்பியுள்ளது, காலி இல்லை
Toilets
  kahlippadem — மலசலகூடம்
Men
  aan — ஆண்
Women
  pen — பெண்

What time does it open/close?
  et-thana manikka tirakhum/mudhum?

TIME & DAYS

What time is it?	mani eth-tanai?
day	pahel
night	iravu
week	vaarem
month	maadhem
year	varudem
today	indru
tomorrow	naalay
yesterday	neh-truh
morning	kaalai
afternoon	pit-pahel

Monday	tin-gal
Tuesday	sevvaay
Wednesday	budahn
Thursday	viyaalin
Friday	vellee
Saturday	san-nee
Sunday	naayiru

TRANSPORT
What time does the next ... leave/arrive?
eththanai manikku aduththa ... sellum/varum?

boat	*padakhu/boat*
bus (city)	*baas (naharam/ul-loor)*
bus (intercity)	*baas (veliyoor)*
train	*rayill*

I want to get off.
naan iranga vendum
I'd like a one-way ticket.
enakku oru vahly tikket veynum
I'd like a return ticket.
enakku iru vahlay tikket veynum

1st class	*mudalahaam vahuppu*
2nd class	*irandaam vahuppu*
luggage lockers	*porul vaikku-midam*

timetable	*haala attavanay*
bus/trolley stop	*baas nilayem*
train station	*rayill nilayem*

I'd like to hire ...
enakku ... vaadakhaikku vaynum

a car	*car*
a bicycle	*sai-kul*

Directions

Where is it?	*adhu en-ghe irukkaradhu?*
Where is a/the ...?	*... en-ghe?*
Go straight ahead.	*neraha sellavum*
Turn left.	*valadhur pakkam tirumbavum*
Turn right.	*itadhu pakkam thirumbavum*
near	*aruhil*
far	*tu-rahm*

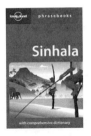

Also available from Lonely Planet:
Sinhala Phrasebook & *India Phrasebook*

Glossary

ambalama – wayside shelter for pilgrims
Aurudu – Sinhalese and Tamil New Year, celebrated on 14 April
Avalokitesvara – the *Bodhisattva* of compassion
Ayurveda – traditional system of medicine that uses herbs and oils to heal and rejuvenate

bailas – folk tunes based on Portuguese, African and local music styles
baobab – water-storing tree *(Adansonia digitata)*, probably introduced to Mannar Island and the Vanni in northern Sri Lanka by Arab traders
bodhi tree – large spreading tree *(Ficus religiosa);* the tree under which the Buddha sat when he attained enlightment, and the many descendants grown from cuttings of this tree
Bodhisattva – divine being who, although capable of attaining *nirvana*, chooses to reside on the human plane to help ordinary people attain salvation
Brahmi – early Indian script used from the 5th century BC
bund – built-up bank or dyke surrounding a *tank*
Burgher – Sri Lankan Eurasian, generally descended from Portuguese-Sinhalese or Dutch-Sinhalese intermarriage

cadjan – coconut fronds woven into mats and used as building material
Ceylon – British-colonial name for Sri Lanka
chetiya – Buddhist shrine
Chola – powerful ancient South Indian kingdom that invaded Sri Lanka on several occasions
coir – mat or rope made from coconut fibres
copra – dried coconut kernel used to make cooking oil; also exported for the manufacture of confectionery
CTB – Central Transport Board, the state bus network

dagoba – Buddhist monument composed of a solid hemisphere containing relics of the Buddha or a Buddhist saint; a *stupa*
devale – complex designed for worshipping a Hindu or Sri Lankan deity
dharma – the word used by both Hindus and Buddhists to refer to their respective moral codes of behaviour

eelam – Tamil word for precious land

gala – rock
ganga – river
gedige – hollow temple with thick walls and a corbelled roof
geta bera – Kandyan double-ended drum

guardstones – carved stones that flank doorways or entrances to temples
gurulu – legendary bird that preys on snakes, used as an image in carved *raksha* masks

Hanuman – the monkey king from the *Ramayana*

illama – a gravel-bearing stratum likely to hold gem-stones

Jataka tales – stories of the previous lives of the Buddha
juggernaut – decorated temple cart dragged through the streets during Hindu festivals (sometimes called a 'car')

kachcheri – administrative office
Karava – fisherfolk of Indian descent
karma – Hindu-Buddhist principle of retributive justice for past deeds
Kataragama – see *Murugan*
kiri bath – dessert of rice cooked in coconut milk
kolam – meaning costume or guise, it refers to masked dance-drama; also the rice-flour designs that adorn buildings in Tamil areas
kovil – Hindu temple dedicated to the worship of Shiva
kulam – Tamil word for *tank*

lakh – 100,000; unit of measurement in Sri Lanka and India
lingam – phallic symbol; symbol of Shiva
LTTE – Liberation Tigers of Tamil Eelam, also known as the Tamil Tigers; separatist group fighting for an independent Tamil Eelam in the North and the East

Maha – northeast monsoon season
Mahaweli Ganga – Sri Lanka's longest river, starting near Adam's Peak and reaching the sea near Trincomalee
Mahayana – later form of Buddhism prevalent in Korea, Japan and China, which literally means 'greater vehicle'
Mahinda – son of the Indian Buddhist emperor Ashoka, credited with introducing Buddhism to Sri Lanka
mahout – elephant master
Maitreya – future Buddha
makara – mythical beast combining a lion, a pig and an elephant, often carved into temple staircases
makara torana – ornamental archway
mandapaya – a raised platform with decorative pillars
masala – mix (often spices)
moonstone – semiprecious stone; also a carved 'door-step' at temple entrances

mudra – symbolic hand position of a Buddha image
Murugan – Hindu god of war; also known as *Skanda* and *Kataragama*

naga – snake; also applies to snake deities and spirits
naga raksha – *raksha* mask featuring a 'coiffure' of writhing cobras
nirvana – ultimate aim of Buddhists, final release from the cycle of existence
nuwara – city

ola – leaves of the talipot palm; used in manuscripts and traditional books
oruva – outrigger canoe
oya – stream or small river

Pali – the language in which the Buddhist scriptures were originally recorded
palmyra – tall palm tree found in the dry northern region
perahera – procession, usually with dancers, drummers and elephants
pirivena – centre of learning attached to monastery
poya – full-moon day; always a holiday
puja – 'respect', offering or prayers

rajakariya – 'workers for the king', the tradition of feudal service
raksha – type of mask used in parades and festivals
Rakshasas – legendary rulers of Sri Lanka, who could also assume the form of demons; led by *Rawana*
Ramayana – ancient story of Rama and Sita and their conflict with *Rawana*
Rawana – 'demon king of Lanka' who abducts Rama's beautiful wife Sita in the Hindu epic the *Ramayana*
relic chamber – chamber in a *dagoba* housing a relic of the Buddha or a saint and representing the Buddhist concept of the cosmos
Ruhunu – ancient southern centre of Sinhalese power near Tissamaharama that survived even when Anuradhapura and Polonnaruwa fell to Indian invaders

samudra – large *tank* or inland sea
Sangamitta – sister of *Mahinda;* she brought the sacred *bodhi tree* sapling from Bodhgaya in India
sanni – devil-dance mask
sangha – the community of Buddhist monks and nuns; in Sri Lanka, an influential group divided into several nikayas (orders)

Sanskrit – ancient Indian language, the oldest known member of the family of Indo-European languages
sari – traditional garment worn by women
school pen – ballpoint pen, often requested (or demanded!) from tourists by Sri Lankan children
sikhara – dome- or pyramid-shaped structure rising above the shrine room of a Hindu *kovil*
sinha – lion
Sinhala – language of the Sinhalese people
Sinhalese – majority population of Sri Lanka; principally Sinhala-speaking Buddhists
Skanda – see *Murugan*
stupa – see *dagoba*

Tamils – a people of South Indian origin, comprising the largest minority population in Sri Lanka; principally Tamil-speaking Hindus
tank – artificial water-storage lake or reservoir; many of the tanks in Sri Lanka are very large and ancient
Theravada – orthodox form of Buddhism practised in Sri Lanka and Southeast Asia, which is characterised by its adherence to the *Pali* canon

unavakam – Tamil name for a streetside hut; called *kadé* or boutiques by the Sinhalese

vahalkada – solid panel of sculpture
vatadage – circular relic house consisting of a small central *dagoba* flanked by Buddha images and encircled by columns
Vedas – Hindu sacred books; a collection of sacred hymns composed in preclassical Sanskrit during the 2nd millennium BC and divided into four books: Rig-Veda, Yajur-Veda, Sama-Veda and Atharva-Veda
Veddahs – original inhabitants of Sri Lanka prior to the arrival of the Sinhalese from India; also called the *Wanniyala-aetto*
vel – trident; the god *Murugan* is often depicted carrying a *vel*
vihara, viharaya – Buddhist complex, including a shrine containing a statue of the Buddha, a congregational hall and a monks' house

Wanniyala-aetto – see *Veddahs*
wewa – see *tank*

yak bera – double-ended drum used in the South
Yala – southwest monsoon season

The Authors

BRETT ATKINSON
Coordinating Author, The Hill Country

Brett Atkinson first travelled to Sri Lanka in 2001 and returned with tales of gloriously arcing beaches, improbable rock temples and statues, and the poignant remnants of the British colonial heritage. He's written about the teardrop-shaped island nation for magazines in New Zealand and Australia, and is very happy that he lives so close to New Zealand's only Sri Lankan restaurant in his hometown of Auckland. Guess what's for dinner? Brett's travelled to more than 60 countries and has contributed to 15 Lonely Planet guidebooks. He's forever on the lookout for great street food and Sri Lanka didn't disappoint.

STUART BUTLER
West Coast, The South, The East

English-born Stuart Butler first hit Sri Lanka during a long trans-Asia surf trip many years ago. One wave and one curry and he was hooked. Since then the food, beaches, wildlife, waves, people and hills have called him back a number of times and after each visit he returns home a little more infatuated. He now calls the beaches of southwest France home, and in addition to Sri Lanka his travels have taken him across South Asia and beyond, from the desert beaches of Pakistan to the coastal jungles of Colombia. He still waxes lyrical over Sri Lankan curries.

ETHAN GELBER
Jaffna & the North

In September 2004, accompanying his fiancée on her year-long work contract, Ethan landed in Sri Lanka with plans only for travel and personal writing projects. Three months later the tsunami changed everything. Among other things, he journeyed with friends to Jaffna to deliver aid. Shortly after he trawled the East and returned to the North for Lonely Planet for a post-tsunami update. He cemented lifelong friendships throughout the island and avowed a commitment to it that has brought him back several times, most recently with his wife and new son, sadly watching the war in the North unfold. An unapologetic native New Yorker, Ethan is nevertheless currently based out of Australia.

LONELY PLANET AUTHORS

Why is our travel information the best in the world? It's simple: our authors are passionate, dedicated travellers. They don't take freebies in exchange for positive coverage so you can be sure the advice you're given is impartial. They travel widely to all the popular spots, and off the beaten track. They don't research using just the internet or phone. They discover new places not included in any other guidebook. They personally visit thousands of hotels, restaurants, palaces, trails, galleries, temples and more. They speak with dozens of locals every day to make sure you get the kind of insider knowledge only a local could tell you. They take pride in getting all the details right, and in telling it how it is. Think you can do it? Find out how at **lonelyplanet.com**.

MICHAEL KOHN   Colombo, The Ancient Cities

Michael caught the travel bug from a young age and by the time he reached 21 he had already set foot on six continents. For the past 10 years he has worked as a foreign correspondent in Asia, writing dispatches from far-flung outposts like Mongolia, Nepal, Gujarat and Myanmar. His work has appeared in the *New York Times*, the *San Francisco Chronicle* and over the BBC airwaves. Michael hooked up with Lonely Planet in 2003 and has since written or updated 15 guidebooks. For this book he scoured the back alleys of Colombo, rocked out at Barefoot, scaled the Sigiriya rock and fought off angry monkeys at Mihintale. More of his work is available online at www.michaelkohn.us.

Behind the Scenes

THIS BOOK

This 11th edition of *Sri Lanka* was updated by Brett Atkinson (coordinating author), Stuart Butler, Ethan Gelber and Michael Kohn. Tony Wheeler wrote and researched the first three editions of *Sri Lanka*, John Noble tackled the 4th edition and, together with Susan Forsyth, updated the 5th edition. Christine Niven updated the 6th and 7th editions, the 8th edition was updated by Verity Campbell, and Richard Plunkett and Brigitte Ellemor updated the 9th edition. Joe Cummings, Mark Elliott, Ryan Ver Berkmoes and Teresa Cannon updated the 10th edition. This guidebook was commissioned in Lonely Planet's Melbourne office, and produced by the following:

Commissioning Editors William Gourlay, Maryanne Netto, Suzannah Shwer, Sam Trafford
Coordinating Editors Rosie Nicholson, Kristin Odijk
Coordinating Cartographer Marc Milinkovic
Coordinating Layout Designer Nicholas Colicchia
Managing Editors Brigitte Ellemor, Bruce Evans, Katie Lynch
Managing Cartographer Adrian Persoglia
Managing Layout Designer Sally Darmody
Assisting Editors Jocelyn Hargrave, Victoria Harrison, Amy Karafin, Katie O'Connell, Stephanie Pearson
Cover Designer Peter Morris
Project Manager Fabrice Rocher

Language Content Coordinator Branislava Vladisavljevic
Thanks to Lucy Birchley, Diana Duggan, Martin Heng, Corey Hutchison, Brice Gosnell, Amanda Sierp, Lyahna Spencer, Marg Toohey, Kate Whitfield

THANKS
BRETT ATKINSON

Thanks to all of the crew in Kandy, especially my careful and insightful drivers. Special thanks to Malik for his assistance. In Nuwara Eliya thanks to the barman at the Grand Hotel who went easy on me on the snooker table. Thanks to Maryanne Netto, Will Gourlay, Brigitte Ellemor and Adrian Persoglia at Lonely Planet, and to my talented and tireless author team of Michael, Ethan and Stuart. On the road, thanks to the fellow travellers whose brains I picked, especially Emmanuelle and Miriam. Back home in Auckland, thanks to Carol and to my parents for their love and support.

MICHAEL KOHN

Foremost thanks to the wonderful people of Sri Lanka for making this a great research trip. Special thanks to Linton at Blue Haven Tours and driver extraordinaire Tony de Silva. Cheers also to the fearless three-wheeler drivers of Colombo who showed me the ins and outs of the city. Thanks also to my cowriters and editors at Lonely Planet:

THE LONELY PLANET STORY

Fresh from an epic journey across Europe, Asia and Australia in 1972, Tony and Maureen Wheeler sat at their kitchen table stapling together notes. The first Lonely Planet guidebook, *Across Asia on the Cheap*, was born.

Travellers snapped up the guides. Inspired by their success, the Wheelers began publishing books to Southeast Asia, India and beyond. Demand was prodigious, and the Wheelers expanded the business rapidly to keep up. Over the years, Lonely Planet extended its coverage to every country and into the virtual world via lonelyplanet.com and the Thorn Tree message board.

As Lonely Planet became a globally loved brand, Tony and Maureen received several offers for the company. But it wasn't until 2007 that they found a partner whom they trusted to remain true to the company's principles of travelling widely, treading lightly and giving sustainably. In October of that year, BBC Worldwide acquired a 75% share in the company, pledging to uphold Lonely Planet's commitment to independent travel, trustworthy advice and editorial independence.

Today, Lonely Planet has offices in Melbourne, London and Oakland, with over 500 staff members and 300 authors. Tony and Maureen are still actively involved with Lonely Planet. They're travelling more often than ever, and they're devoting their spare time to charitable projects. And the company is still driven by the philosophy of *Across Asia on the Cheap*: 'All you've got to do is decide to go and the hardest part is over. So go!'

Maryanne, Will, Adrian, Brett, Stuart and Ethan. During the write-up stage I received generous support from my wife Gail and daughter Molly.

ETHAN GELBER
Surrogate eyes and ears made my work possible. With hostilities in the North too hot for safe passage, S Pathmanath, Seran Sivananthamoorthy and Pathman Soundarrajan did what I couldn't, guided by Gurupuran Kumaravadivel, a wise scholar and friend. Other important sources of wisdom include Renton de Alwis, Andrew Kittle, Richard Boyle, Sarojinie Ellawela, TG Navindran, the Sewalanka Foundation team and, of course, all the Gelbers and Higgins. Rydah and Sanjeewa, our home is always yours. Thanks, too, to fellow scribes Brett, Stuart and Michael, and the intuitions of Lonely Planet's Sam, Maryanne and Will. My beloved Jane, it was your able pen, too, between Rohan's needs.

STUART BUTLER
Thank you to the many Sri Lankans who knowingly and unknowingly helped me. In particular thanks to Mr Dimuthu for being both driver/guide/translator/bank and friend – good luck with everything. Thank you also to Mr Linton of Blue Haven Tours, Jai and Ram in Midigama, Juliet Coombe for help in Galle and beyond, Mr Stephens for the absolute pleasure of meeting you and also to Sanjeewa Senanake. Finally, and as always, huge thanks and more to Heather for being a perfect travel companion and also for her patience on this project.

OUR READERS

Many thanks to the travellers who used the last edition and wrote to us with helpful hints, useful advice and interesting anecdotes:

A Diana Aczel, Carol Adams, William Anderson, Helen Atkinson **B** Lisa Barlow, Donna Bartlett, Louise Bell, Mike Berry, Gretchen Biery, Wendy Blake, Bernadette Bond, Inge Bouwman, Andrew Bruce, R Burgess, Nig Burke, Peter Burke-Murphy **C** Sara Caillere, Aaron Cashman, Ramilla Chaminda, Kimberley Coole **D** Andrew Darler, Anil De Silva, Helga Desilva, Martin Dixon, Geoffrey Dixon, Michelle Dooley, Charles Dourville, Tom Dyson **E** Wendy Earl, Albrecht W Eberts, Agneta Ehn, Scott Elliott, Beth Ericson **F** Norman Family, Emanuela Farris, Melody Fennell, Megan Ferguson, Felician Fernandopulle, Terry Friel **G** Jennifer Gadney, Shaun Galliver, James Geake, Anne Goddard, Caroline Gowan, Louise Gray, Marilyn Griffin, John Hall, Roslyn Hall, Georgette Harrison, Patrick Hass, Johanna Gerstein **H** Tom Haythornthwaite, Sam Henderson, Luitgard Heusel, Sherrin Hibbard, Helen Highmoor, Katy Hinton, Lerena Holloway, Ernest Howe, David Hughes **I** Alex Itty **J** Taylor Janis **K** Margriet Katoen, Alan Keenan, Tom Kingsley, Irene Koerber, Mieke Kort, Ursula Kuermayr **L** Kate Lamacraft, Jeremy Lazell, Melanie Lewis, Frank Lieber, Angelika Lorek, Alan Lowe, Pat Lowe **M** Linda Mackenzie, Eran Madar, Lou Mair, David Marsden, John Mcvey, Amber Mezbourian, Madhu Mihiraj, Moixa Moixa, Guy Monson, Edward Moore, Harris Moore, Anthony Moore, Selene Moore, Anita Morgan, Helen Morgan Edwards, Torsten Mueller, Chris Myatt **N** Serhat Narsap, Stephanie Neubauer, Mark Noble, Kristoffer Nyrop, Angela **O** O'Connor, Louise Obermayer, Malcolm Obrien, Else Olesen, Valentina Otmacic **P** Ian Pace, Nina Pantic, Ellie Parker, Farida Parkyn, Damir Pavlovic, P Phillips, Geoff Piggott, Ian Pilbeam **R** Michael Richardson, Peter Richter, Gav Riggs, Lombardo Rodolfo, Untuly Rose, Matthew Ross, Karen Rumble **S** Joan Schrecker, Ekkehard Schwehn, Richard Seeebohm, Meagan Shand, Anura Shantha, Mia Sharp, RP Shine, Brijinder Singh, Jarmila Souckova, Louise Spencer, SJ Srinivas, John Stifler, Victoria Stoneman, Ann Stoughton, Bill Stoughton **T** Mark Thamel, Nguyen Quy Thanh, Jamie Tomilson, David Trattnig, Ian Trim **U** Mahendra Udumullage, Nithila Unamboowe **V** David Van Damme, Peter Van Luyn, SS Vasan, Trish Veitch, Adelina Velikova, Conny Von Soehnen **W** Kelly Webb, Jeppe Westerhof, ND Wijenayake, Bob Williams, Veronica Williams, Elizabeth Woolley, Rachel Wright **Y** Keiji Yoshimura, Wendy Young **Z** Irena Zahon-Colling, Willy Zelen, Andreas Zimdars

ACKNOWLEDGMENTS

Many thanks to the following for the use of their content:

Globe on title page ©Mountain High Maps 1993, Digital Wisdom, Inc.

BEHIND THE SCENES

Index

000 Map pages
000 Photograph pages

INDEX

000 Map pages
000 Photograph pages

INDEX

000 Map pages
000 Photograph pages

GREENDEX

The following attractions, accommodation and restaurants have been selected because they demonstrate a commitment to sustainability through supporting local communities, recycling or conserving energy.

For more tips about travelling sustainably in Sri Lanka, turn to the Getting Started chapter (p16). We want to keep developing our sustainable-travel content. If you think we've omitted someone who should be listed here, email us at www.lonelyplanet.com/contact. For more information about sustainable tourism and Lonely Planet, see www.lonelyplanet.com/responsibletravel.

INDEX

accommodation
    Amaya Lake (Dambulla) 216
    Arugam Bay Hilton Guest House (Arugam Bay) 251
    Bambarakanda Holiday Resort (Belihul Oya) 190
    Boulder Garden (Kudawa) 206
    Ella Adventure Park (Ella) 198
    Hunas Falls Hotel (Knuckles Range) 175
    Kandalama Hotel (Dambulla) 216
    Kandy Samadhicentre (Kandy region) 174
    Kudawa Homestays (Kudawa) 206
    Mangrove Cabanas (Marakolliya Beach) 145
    Mangrove Chalets (Marakolliya Beach) 145

Maussawa Estate Eco Lanka Villa (Pundaluoya region) 179
Mederapitiya Homestays (Deniyaya) 206
Rafter's Retreat (Kitulgala) 178
Rainforest Edge (Kudawa) 206
Rangala House (Knuckles Range) 175
Ranweli Holiday Village (Waikkal) 110
River Garden Resort (Belihul Oya) 190
St Andrew's Hotel (Nuwara Eliya) 185
Selara River Eco Resort (Uda Walawe National Park region) 204
Sigiriya Village (Sigiriya) 220

Yala Village Hotel (Yala National Park region) 152

activities
    Mangrove tours (Pottuvil) 250

attractions
    Kosgoda Turtle Conservation Project (Kosgoda) 144
    Kosgoda Turtle Hatcheries (Kosgoda) 116
    Muthurajawela Visitor Centre (Muthurajawela Marsh) 110
    Shoba Display Gallery (Galle) 131
    Turtle Research Project (Induruwa) 112

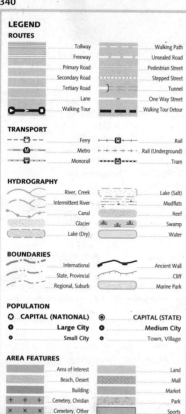

LEGEND

ROUTES

Tollway
Freeway
Primary Road
Secondary Road
Tertiary Road
Lane
Walking Tour
Walking Path
Unsealed Road
Pedestrian Street
Stepped Street
Tunnel
One Way Street
Walking Tour Detour

TRANSPORT

Ferry
Metro
Monorail
Rail
Rail (Underground)
Tram

HYDROGRAPHY

River, Creek
Intermittent River
Canal
Glacier
Lake (Dry)
Lake (Salt)
Mudflats
Reef
Swamp
Water

BOUNDARIES

International
State, Provincial
Regional, Suburb
Ancient Wall
Cliff
Marine Park

POPULATION

☉ CAPITAL (NATIONAL)   ◉ CAPITAL (STATE)
● Large City   ● Medium City
● Small City   ○ Town, Village

AREA FEATURES

Area of Interest
Beach, Desert
Building
Cemetery, Christian
Cemetery, Other
Forest
Land
Mall
Market
Park
Sports
Urban

SYMBOLS

SIGHTS/ACTIVITIES
Beach
Buddhist
Castle, Fortress
Christian
Confucian
Diving, Snorkeling
Hindu
Islamic
Jain
Jewish
Monument
Museum, Gallery
Picnic Area
Point of Interest
Ruin
Shinto
Sikh
Skiing
Taoist
Winery, Vineyard
Zoo, Bird Sanctuary

INFORMATION
Bank, ATM
Embassy/Consulate
Hospital, Medical
Information
Internet Facilities
Parking Area
Petrol Station
Police Station
Post Office, GPO
Telephone
Toilets

SLEEPING
Sleeping
Camping

EATING
Eating

DRINKING
Drinking
Café

ENTERTAINMENT
Entertainment

SHOPPING
Shopping

TRANSPORT
Airport, Airfield
Border Crossing
Bus Station
Cycling, Bicycle Path
General Transport
Taxi Rank
Trail Head

GEOGRAPHIC
Hazard
Lighthouse
Lookout
Mountain, Volcano
National Park
Oasis
Pass, Canyon
River Flow
Shelter, Hut
Spot Height
Waterfall

NOTE: Not all symbols displayed above appear in this guide.

LONELY PLANET OFFICES

Australia
Head Office
Locked Bag 1, Footscray, Victoria 3011
☎ 03 8379 8000, fax 03 8379 8111
talk2us@lonelyplanet.com.au

USA
150 Linden St, Oakland, CA 94607
☎ 510 250 6400, toll free 800 275 8555
fax 510 893 8572
info@lonelyplanet.com

UK
2nd fl, 186 City Rd,
London EC1V 2NT
☎ 020 7106 2100, fax 020 7106 2101
go@lonelyplanet.co.uk

Published by Lonely Planet Publications Pty Ltd
ABN 36 005 607 983

© Lonely Planet Publications Pty Ltd 2009

© photographers as indicated 2009

Cover photograph: Fishermen from Weligama make their daily catch using traditional stilts, Weligama, Sri Lanka, Dallas Stribley/Lonely Planet Images. Many of the images in this guide are available for licensing from Lonely Planet Images: www.lonelyplanetimages.com.

Printed by SNP Security Printing Pte Ltd, Singapore.

Mixed Sources
Product group from well-managed forests and other controlled sources
www.fsc.org Cert no. SGS-COC-005002
© 1996 Forest Stewardship Council